The Sources of Economic Growth in India
1950–1 to 1999–2000

The Sources of Economic Growth in India
1950–1 to 1999–2000

S. Sivasubramonian

OXFORD
UNIVERSITY PRESS

OXFORD
UNIVERSITY PRESS

YMCA Library Building, Jai Singh Road, New Delhi 110 001

Oxford University Press is a department of the University of Oxford.
It furthers the University's objective of excellence in research, scholarship,
and education by publishing worldwide in

Oxford New York
Auckland   Cape Town   Dar es Salaam   Hong Kong   Karachi
Kuala Lumpur   Madrid   Melbourne   Mexico City   Nairobi
New Delhi   Shanghai   Taipei   Toronto

With offices in
Argentina   Austria   Brazil   Chile   Czech Republic   France   Greece
Guatemala   Hungary   Italy   Japan Poland   Portugal   Singapore
South Korea   Switzerland   Thailand   Turkey   Ukraine   Vietnam

Oxford is a registered trade mark of Oxford University Press
in the UK and in certain other countries

Published in India
By Oxford University Press, New Delhi

© Oxford University Press 2004
First published 2004
Second Impression 2005

ISBN-13: 978-0-19-566601-4
ISBN-10: 0-19-566601-1

Typeset in Garamond 10 on 12 by Ino Soft Systems, NOIDA, UP
Printed in India at Mahalaxmi Printers, New Delhi 110020
Published by Manzar Khan, Oxford University Press
YMCA Library Building, Jai Singh Road, New Delhi 110 001

Foreword

Indian research in national accounts started in the 1860s with the work of Dadabhai Naoroji. Siva Sivasubramonian (1929–2002) was one of the most distinguished scholars in this long tradition. He first made his mark in 1965 with a significant study of Indian national income for the years 1900–46. This was quickly recognized as authoritative and was widely cited by analysts of Indian economic development and economic history. After completing it, he spent nearly thirty years as an advisor to the United Nations advisor, establishing and improving official national accounts in the Middle East and Africa. In 1995, he returned to India, revised his earlier work, and expanded its temporal coverage. The result was *National Income of India in the Twentieth Century*, Oxford University Press, Delhi, 2000.

From 2000 to his death in August 2002, Siva undertook this major interpretative work on the causes of India's accelerated growth in the half century since Independence. India is now the world's fourth largest economy and there are very few countries which can match its income growth in real terms per head of population over the past decade. Hence, this book is of major interest to readers outside as well as inside India. It provides a coherent statistical framework of impeccable scholarship, which will be of fundamental importance to economists and economic historians who want to put Indian performance into historical perspective.

Siva uses the growth accounting approach first developed by Edward Denison for the US in 1962. I have used the same method in analysing European performance in several publications since 1972. There was a previous application of the method to India in an excellent study of Bakul Dholakia, published by Good Companions Press, Vadodra, 1974. Similar studies were made by Denison and Chung for Japan in 1976, and by Kim and Park for Korea in 1985.

Siva's book is the fruit of great dedication and required immense and meticulous research, underpinned by a lifetime of experience in this field. The presentation is very professional and fully transparent. It will remain a basic reference work for further studies in this field for many years.

He uses the same measure of output as in his previous book. What is new is the presentation of detailed evidence on and causal analysis of factors affecting growth of output. He estimates the growth of employment by age and sex, and by level of education in different sectors of the economy. He presents new estimates of the main components of gross and net fixed capital stock and inventories, and shows how they differ from the official estimates. He shows changes in the cultivated area. He provides weights to add together the different inputs in order to derive his measure of total factor productivity, which gives a measure of the rate of technical progress. His growth accounts also show the impact of foreign trade, structural change in output and inputs, changing energy inputs, and the effect of weather fluctuations on agricultural performance. The macroeconomic analysis broken down by economic sector compares the differing rates of change in urban and rural areas, and distinguishes between developments in the 'organized' and 'unorganized' sectors. He gives a full explanation of the relation of his work to previous scholarly endeavour, e.g., the work of Bina Roy, Mukherjee and others on capital stock and the weights used in Dholakia's growth accounts.

It is a magnificent effort by a scholar of great integrity and dedication. It is unlikely that such a work could have been replicated by a large team of researchers. It is a masterpiece in its field.

30 June 2003   Angus Maddison
                                                    Chevincourt, France.

Contents

Tables

Appendix Tables

Figures

Abbreviations

AIDIS	All India Debt and Investment Survey
ASI	Annual Survey of Industries
..	Nil or Negligible
CE	Compensation of Employees
CFC	Consumption of Fixed Capital
CMIE	Centre for Monitoring Indian Economy
Crore	Hundred Lakhs
CSO	Central Statistical Organization
EPW	Economic and Political Weekly
FCS	Fixed Capital Stock
FISIM	Financial Intermediary Services Indirectly Measured
GCS	Gross Capital Stock
GDP	Gross Domestic Product
GFCF	Gross Fixed Capital Formation
GFCS	Gross Fixed Capital Stock
GVA	Gross Value Added
HIV	High Yielding Variety
IBC	Imputed Bank Charges
ILO	International Labour Organization
Lakh	100,000
M&E	Machinery and Equipment
Million	Ten Lakhs
MTOE	Million Tonnes of Oil Equivalent
n.e.c.	not elsewhere covered
NA	Not Applicable
NAS	National Accounts Statistics
NDP	Net Domestic Product
NFCS	Net Fixed Capital Stock
NNP	Net National Product
NSS	National Sample Survey
NSSO	National Sample Survey Organisation
NVA	Net Value Added
OECD	Organisation for Economic Cooperation and Development
OS	Operating Surplus

PAD   Public Administration and Defence
PIM   Perpetual Inventory Method
ps   principal status worker
RBI   Reserve Bank of India
ss   subsidiary status worker
TFI   Total Factor Input
TFP   Total Factor Productivity
WPI   Wholesale Price Index
WPR   Worker–Population Ratio

Rate of Growth of Gross Domestic Product

The transformation of the Indian economy from a state of near stagnation under colonial rule during the first half of the twentieth century to one of moderate to rapid growth in the second half following the attainment of independence in 1947 and the launching of an era of planned economic development from 1951-2 has evoked much interest and attention.[1] This study attempts to trace the pace and pattern of economic growth and its determinants during the time span 1950-1 to 1999-2000. The publication by the Central Statistical Organisation (CSO) of the back-series of the recently revised national accounts (1993-4 series) at current and constant prices for the period 1950-1 to 1992-3[2] in October 2001 along with the latest issue of the annual *National Accounts Statistics 2001*[3] provided the comparable series for the whole period covered by this study.

GROWTH OF GDP: AGGREGATE AND PER CAPITA

Real gross domestic product (GDP) at factor cost, the most commonly adopted indicator of economic growth, is used as the measure of output in this study. GDP at 1993-4 prices—aggregate, per capita, and per worker—population, and workforce data and the corresponding indices for the time span 1950-1 to 1999-2000 are shown in Appendix Table 1(a).

Figure 1.1 shows the index of GDP at constant 1993-4 prices. Aggregate real GDP doubled in the 19 years starting from 1950-1, doubled again in the next 18 years from 1969-70, and doubled further in 12 years from 1987-8. At the end of the century it was 8.2 times the level in 1950-1, with the compound annual growth rate being 4.39 per cent for the whole period. In the meanwhile, the population growth rate surged from 1.7 per cent in 1951-2 to 2.3 per cent in the 1970s; hence it took 39 years for GDP per capita to double. The first

---

[1] S. Sivasubramonian, *The National Income of India in the Twentieth Century*, Oxford University Press, New Delhi, 2000, pp. 438-511, 550-646.

[2] CSO, *National Accounts Statistics, Back Series, 1950-51 to 1992-93*, Department of Statistics, Ministry of Planning, New Delhi, 2001, p. 389.

[3] CSO, *National Accounts Statistics, 2001*, Department of Statistics, Ministry of Planning, New Delhi, p. 229.

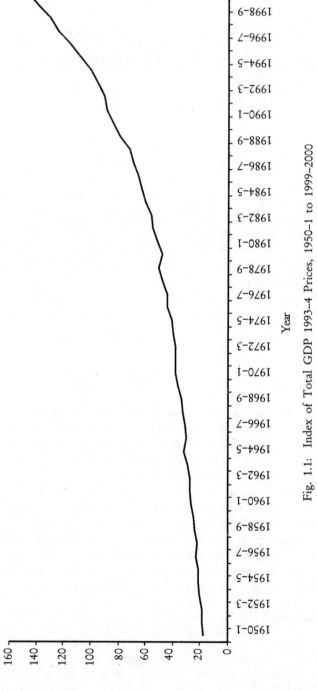

Fig. 1.1: Index of Total GDP 1993–4 Prices, 1950–1 to 1999–2000

Year

Source: Appendix Table 1(a), Col. (6).

2

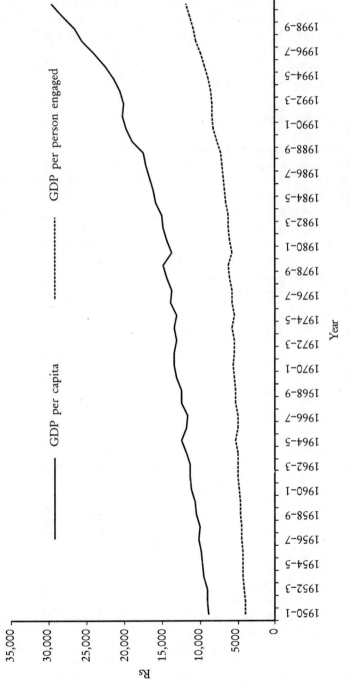

Fig. 1.2: GDP Per Capita and Per Worker at 1993–4 Prices, 1950–1 to 1999–2000

Source: Appendix Table 1(a), Cols (4) and (5).

3

Five Year Plan aimed at doubling the national income by 1971-2 (in about 21 years) and per capita income by 1977-8 (in 27 years).[4] While the first goal was achieved in 19 years, achievement of the second goal was delayed by 12 years. Per capita GDP increased threefold during the whole period. Gross domestic product per worker, i.e. per person engaged, also followed more or less the same pace of growth as that of GDP per capita—it increased 3.35 times during the same time span. Figure 1.2 shows the course of GDP per capita and GDP per worker, at 1993-4 prices.

GROWTH RATES FOR SELECTED PERIODS

Along with annual data, growth rates for selected periods are also presented in this study. For long-term analysis, growth rates are presented in Table 1.1 for the entire period 1950-1 to 1999-2000 and also for the periods 1950-1 to 1964-5, 1964-5 to 1980-1, and 1980-1 to 1999-2000. The choice of the sub-periods was dictated by considerations of the pattern of growth, viz. moderate growth during the first sub-period, deceleration during the second, and acceleration of growth during the third, and certain distinctive influences during the periods. For short-term analysis, growth rates are presented by decades.

Following E. F. Denison[5] and Angus Maddison,[6] growth rates presented in this study are compound growth rates based on terminal years. As such, they

Table 1.1: Growth Rates of Aggregate and Per Capita GDP at 1993-4 Prices, 1950-1 to 1999-2000

(in per cent)

Period	Total GDP	GDP per capita	GDP per worker	Population	Workforce
	(1)	(2)	(3)	(4)	(5)
Long Periods					
1950-1 to 1999-2000	4.39	2.25	2.50	2.09	1.85
1950-1 to 1964-5	4.06	2.02	2.39	2.00	1.63
1964-5 to 1980-1	3.12	0.83	1.60	2.27	2.16
1980-1 to 1999-2000	5.71	3.63	3.90	2.01	1.74
Shorter periods					
1950-1 to 1960-1	3.91	1.96	2.30	1.92	1.57
1960-1 to 1970-1	3.70	1.43	1.87	2.23	1.79
1970-1 to 1980-1	3.08	0.76	0.69	2.30	2.37
1980-1 to 1990-1	5.62	3.41	3.53	2.14	2.02
1990-1 to 1999-2000	5.81	3.87	4.32	1.87	1.43

Source: Appendix Table 1(a).

[4] Planning Commission, Ministry of Planning, Government of India, *Second Five Year Plan, Summary*, Delhi, 1956, p. 3.

[5] Edward F. Denison, *Accounting for United States Economic Growth 1929-1969*, The Brookings Institution, Washington, D.C. 1974, p. 12, 21-3.

[6] Angus Maddison, *Explaining the Economic Performance of Nations: Essays in Time and Space*, Edward Elgan Publication Limited, Cheltenham, 1995, pp. 36-85.

do not reflect the fluctuations in the data during the intervening years and differ from the trend growth rates shown in an earlier study by the author.[7]

Aggregate GDP grew at an impressive annual rate of 4.39 per cent between 1950–1 and 1999–2000. The growth was rather uneven over the years, as it was influenced by a number of unfavourable factors such as the border conflict with China in 1962, the severe droughts[8] of 1965, 1966, 1972, 1974, 1979, 1982, 1985, and 1987 and a number of moderate droughts in between, the Indo-Pakistan conflicts of 1965 and 1972, and the oil price shocks of 1973 and 1979. The policy of import-substitution adopted by the government stimulated the growth of industries initially but inhibited their growth subsequently. Among the favourable factors may be mentioned the launching of the Five Year Plans which led to massive public investment, the Green Revolution consequent to the introduction of HYV (high yielding variety) seeds and extension of irrigation facilities and use of chemical fertilizer which gave a boost to agricultural production, the limited liberalization of controls in the 1980s, and the radical economic reforms in the post-1991 period which stimulated industrial growth. Accordingly, after a good start in the initial sub-period and opening decade, the growth rates slumped to lower levels in the second sub-period. The decade 1970–1 to 1980–1 recorded the lowest growth rate during the time span covered, with GDP per capita and GDP per worker growing at less than one per cent. The acceleration of population growth in the 1970s also contributed to the deceleration in per capita growth. During 1980–1 to 1990–1, there was acceleration in growth and eventually supported by the economic reforms of the 1990s, India became one of the fastest growing economies of the world.

Over the whole period 1950–1 to 1999–2000, average annual growth rates were 4.39 per cent for aggregate GDP, 2.09 per cent for population, 1.85 per cent for workforce, 2.25 per cent for GDP per capita, and 2.5 per cent for GDP per worker engaged. Table 1.1 provides similar rates for all the sub-periods and decades. It is clear from the table that the rates of growth of GDP, GDP per capita and GDP per worker engaged varied widely in the sub-periods. This study attempts to provide a breakdown of the sources of growth of GDP in each of the sub-periods and the period as a whole.

GDP BY SECTOR

Both labour and capital are used to produce output in most sectors of the economy. Two sectors, however, are different in this respect. In the case of services of dwellings, output is equivalent to the property income received while in the case of public administration and defence (PAD) and non-profit institutions it is based on labour income, that is compensation of employees

[7] Sivasubramonian, *The National Income of India in the Twentieth Century*, pp. 562, 564–5.
[8] Centre for Monitoring Indian Economy (CMIE), *Basic Statistics Relating to Indian Economy*, Mumbai, August 1994, Table 6.16: Droughts in India: 1867 to 1993.

only. For the study of economic growth and its determinants both these sectors are often excluded and the study confined to the rest of the domestic product. This is what has been done by Denison in his studies relating to USA,[9] terming it as non-residential business sector. He, however, adopted the national income at factor cost as the output measure. Maddison used total GDP as the measure of output in his study on growth and slowdown in advanced capitalist economies.[10] Data limitations, especially on the characteristics of labour, viz. age–sex composition, educational achievements, and salary differentials for employees in PAD and non-profit institutions, do not facilitate their exclusion as far as India is concerned. In this study, only the services of dwellings are kept out and the remainder of the GDP is designated as non-residential GDP or GDP excluding the services of dwellings. Dholakia also adopted a similar sectoring in his study,[11] for which he adopted national income as the output measure. The sources of economic growth are analysed separately for non-residential GDP as well as GDP from Sector A and Sector non-A. Since non-residential GDP forms about 95 to 96 per cent of total GDP, the determinants of growth of the latter are not separately investigated.

GDP ORIGINATING FROM DWELLINGS

The disaggregated statements provided in the *National Accounts Statistics* (NAS) present GDP from the sub-sector real estate, ownership of dwellings, and business services. Gross Domestic Product from dwellings is shown as part of this sub-sector. While GDP arising from the sub-sector is shown inclusive as well as exclusive of financial intermediary services indirectly measured (FISIM), that for dwellings is available only inclusive of FISIM. The GDP from dwellings excluding FISIM is estimated using the same proportional relationship found for GDP from the whole sub-sector for GDP including and excluding FISIM. The results are shown in Col. (5) of Appendix Tables 1(b) and 1(c) at current and constant (1993–4) prices respectively.

For the derivation of factor incomes it is necessary to have an estimate of Net Domestic Product (NDP) originating from ownership of dwellings. The NAS presents NDP for the whole sub-sector only and not separately for the three constituents, viz. real estate, ownership of dwellings, and business services. The GDP, on the other hand, is available separately for each of these constituents. Since consumption of fixed capital (CFC) is available for the whole sub-sector only, an attempt is made to estimate CFC in respect of dwellings alone on the basis of the ratio of GDP from dwellings to total GDP of the sub-sector. The CFC so estimated is shown in Col. (8) of Appendix Tables 1(b) and 1(c) at current and constant prices and the corresponding estimates of NDP from dwellings in Col. (9) of the respective tables.

---

[9] Denison, *Accounting for Economic Growth*, p. 17.

[10] Maddison, *Explaining the Economic Performance of Nations*, p. 42.

[11] Bakul H. Dholakia, *The Sources of Economic Growth in India*, Good Companions, Baroda, 1974, p. 40.

GDP FROM NON-RESIDENTIAL SECTOR: SECTOR A AND
SECTOR NON-A

Appendix Tables 1(d) and 1(e) show GDP from the non-residential sector, that
is, total GDP minus GDP from dwellings for the entire period 1950–1 to 1999–
2000, at current and constant (1993–4) prices respectively. Non-residential
GDP is further subdivided into GDP from Sector A, i.e. agriculture, forestry,
and fishing, and from Sector non-A, i.e. non-agriculture excluding dwellings.
At current prices, GDP from dwellings constitutes about 9 to 10 per cent of
total GDP in the beginning of the period and drops to 4 per cent by the end
of the period. Consequently, GDP from the non-residential sector increases
from 91 per cent to 96 per cent over the period. At constant prices, however,
the share of GDP from dwellings varies within a much narrower range of 4
to 5 per cent only. Correspondingly, GDP from the non-residential sector is
around 95 to 96 per cent of total GDP at 1993–4 prices during the period.
The share of Sector A in non-residential GDP declined from 60.8 per cent in
1950–1 to 26.4 per cent in 1999–2000 and that of Sector non-A moved up from
39.2 per cent to 73.6 per cent during the same period. The relative importance
of sectors A and non-A has undergone significant change over the period.

Indexes of total GDP, GDP from dwellings, and GDP from non-residential
sector are shown in Table 1.2. The movement of non-residential GDP, which
is the measure of output adopted in this study for the detailed analysis of the
sources of growth, is given in Col. (3) of this table. The overall growth of GDP
for the economy as a whole and non-residential GDP seems to be more or less
the same, being 720.2 per cent and 725.9 per cent respectively. GDP from
dwellings moved up by 616.55 per cent but, in view of its low share in GDP,
has not had much effect on overall growth. On the other hand, there is wide
difference in the growth of GDP from Sector A and Sector non-A, the former
being 258.2 per cent and the latter 1451.5 per cent during the period.

Table 1.2: Indexes of GDP at Constant (1993–4) Prices 1950–1 to 1999–2000

Year	Total GDP	Services of dwellings	Non-residential sector		
			GDP	Sector A	Sector non-A
	(1)	(2)	(3)	(4)	(5)
1950–1	17.98	16.50	18.06	33.50	10.53
1951–2	18.40	16.86	18.49	34.00	10.92
1952–3	18.92	17.24	19.02	35.08	11.19
1953–4	20.07	17.62	20.21	37.78	11.65
1954–5	20.92	18.02	21.09	38.89	12.41
1955–6	21.46	18.42	21.64	38.55	13.39
1956-57	22.68	18.84	22.91	40.65	14.25
1957–8	22.41	19.26	22.59	38.82	14.67
1958–9	24.11	19.68	24.37	42.73	15.41
1959–60	24.63	20.11	24.90	42.30	16.41
1960–1	26.38	20.57	26.72	45.15	17.73

(Contd.)

Table 1.2 Contd.

	(1)	(2)	(3)	(4)	(5)
1961–2	27.20	21.03	27.56	45.19	18.96
1962–3	27.77	21.58	28.13	44.29	20.25
1963–4	29.18	22.16	29.59	45.33	21.91
1964–5	31.39	22.74	31.90	49.51	23.31
1965–6	30.24	2.33	31.88	44.04	25.95
1966–7	30.55	23.96	30.94	43.42	24.85
1967–8	33.04	24.61	33.53	49.87	25.56
1968–9	33.90	25.26	34.41	49.79	26.90
1969–70	36.11	25.93	36.71	52.99	28.76
1970–1	37.92	26.63	38.58	56.75	29.72
1971–2	38.30	27.90	38.91	55.69	30.73
1972–3	38.18	28.27	38.76	52.89	31.87
1973–4	39.92	29.10	40.55	56.70	32.68
1974–5	40.38	29.97	40.99	55.84	33.75
1975–6	44.02	30.85	44.79	63.03	35.89
1976–7	44.57	31.80	45.32	59.39	38.45
1977–8	47.90	32.70	48.79	65.35	40.71
1978–9	50.53	33.68	51.52	66.86	44.04
1979–80	47.90	34.69	48.68	58.32	43.98
1980–1	51.34	35.65	52.26	65.83	45.64
1981–2	54.40	38.77	55.32	69.32	48.49
1982–3	56.07	41.80	56.90	68.84	51.08
1983–4	60.38	45.11	61.27	75.42	54.37
1984–5	62.98	48.35	63.84	76.53	57.64
1985–6	65.78	52.04	66.59	77.11	61.46
1986–7	68.63	56.51	69.34	76.61	65.80
1987–8	71.26	61.89	71.81	75.59	69.96
1988–9	78.72	67.86	79.36	87.28	75.50
1989–90	84.00	72.50	84.67	88.57	82.77
1990–1	88.68	78.53	89.27	92.21	87.84
1991–2	89.83	85.15	90.10	90.78	89.77
1992–3	94.43	91.41	94.60	96.04	93.90
1993–4	100.00	100.00	100.00	100.00	100.00
1994–5	107.25	101.74	107.58	105.01	108.83
1995–6	115.13	105.55	115.69	104.10	121.34
1996–7	124.16	108.47	125.08	114.10	130.43
1997–8	130.07	111.48	131.16	111.33	140.83
1998–9	138.61	114.95	140.00	119.19	150.15
1999–2000	147.44	118.23	149.15	119.99	163.37

Source: Appendix Table 1(e) Cols (1) to (5).

CONTRIBUTIONS OF THE SECTORS TO GROWTH

Table 1.3 shows the terminal growth rates of the GDP arising from different sectors and the economy as a whole during the nine time periods selected.

Growth rates of GDP from non-residential sector are generally higher than those for the economy as a whole in all time periods except for 1980–1 to 1999–2000 and for the decade 1980–1 to 1990–1. This variation can be traced to the sudden spurt of growth exhibited by services of dwellings in the new (1993–4) series. In attempting to reconstruct the GDP series for the back years 1950–1 to 1992–3 according to the 1993–4 revision, the CSO has used the splicing method

Table 1.3: Growth Rates of GDP at 1993–4 Prices by Sector and Contribution of Sectors to the Growth Rate of Total GDP, 1950–1 to 1999–2000

Period	Whole economy	Services of dwellings	Non-residential sector		
			Sector A	Sector non-A	Total
	(1)	(2)	(3)	(4)	(5)
Growth rate of GDP					
Long periods					
1950–1 to 1999–2000	4.39	4.10	2.64	5.75	4.40
1950–1 to 1964–5	4.06	2.32	2.83	5.84	4.15
1964–5 to 1980–81	3.12	2.85	1.80	4.29	3.13
1980–1 to 1999–2000	5.71	6.51	3.20	6.94	5.67
Shorter periods					
1950–1 to 1960–1	3.91	2.23	3.03	5.34	3.99
1960–1 to 1970–1	3.70	2.62	2.31	5.30	3.74
1970–1 to 1980–1	3.08	2.96	1.50	4.38	3.08
1980–1 to 1990–1	5.62	8.22	3.43	6.77	5.50
1990-1 to 1999–2000	5.81	4.65	2.97	7.14	5.87
Weights for calculation of contributions					
Long periods					
1950–1 to 1999–2000	1.0000	0.0439	0.4243	0.5318	0.9561
1950–1 to 1964–5	1.0000	0.0460	0.5413	0.4127	0.9540
1964–5 to 1980–1	1.0000	0.0379	0.4370	0.5251	0.9621
1980–1 to 1999–2000	1.0000	0.0469	0.3276	0.6255	0.9531
Shorter periods					
1950–1 to 1960–1	1.0000	0.0475	0.5583	0.3942	0.9525
1960–1 to 1970–1	1.0000	0.0382	0.4763	0.4855	0.9618
1970–1 to 1980–1	1.0000	0.0396	0.4249	0.5355	0.9604
1980–1 to 1990–1	1.0000	0.0441	0.3604	0.5955	0.9559
1990–1 to 1999–2000	1.0000	0.0500	0.2911	0.6589	0.9500
Contribution to growth rate of whole economy (percentage points)					
Long periods					
1950–1 to 1999–2000	4.39	0.18	1.12	3.06	4.21
1950–1 to 1964–5	4.06	0.11	1.53	2.41	3.95
1964–5 to 1980–1	3.12	0.11	0.79	2.25	3.01
1980–1 to 1999–2000	5.71	0.31	1.05	4.34	5.40
Shorter periods					
1950–1 to 1960–1	3.91	0.11	1.69	2.11	3.80
1960–1 to 1970–1	3.70	0.10	1.10	2.57	3.60
1970–1 to 1980–1	3.08	0.12	0.64	2.35	2.96
1980–1 to 1990–1	5.62	0.36	1.24	4.03	5.26
1990–1 to 1999–2000	5.81	0.23	0.86	4.70	5.58
Percentage contribution to growth rate					
Long periods					
1950–1 to 1999–2000	100.00	4.10	25.53	69.71	95.90
1950–1 to 1964–5	100.00	2.63	37.76	59.41	97.37
1964–5 to 1980–1	100.00	3.46	25.22	72.22	96.54
1980–1 to 1999–2000	100.00	5.35	18.36	76.03	94.65
Shorter periods					
1950–1 to 1960–1	100.00	2.71	43.30	53.89	97.29
1960–1 to 1970–1	100.00	2.71	29.76	69.60	97.29
1970–1 to 1980–1	100.00	3.81	20.73	76.27	96.19
1980–1 to 1990–1	100.00	6.45	22.00	71.74	93.55
1990–1 to 1999–2000	100.00	4.00	14.88	80.99	96.00

Source: Appendix Table 1(e).

generally. But a different procedure has been followed for ownership of dwellings for which the benchmark estimates used for the current series are found to differ significantly from those used in the earlier ones. 'The method of double deflation has been used in the estimates of gross value added generated from ownership of dwellings for the period 1980–1 to 1992–3. The estimates of gross rental in rural and urban areas are obtained by applying the compound growth rate observed between the base year estimates for 1980–1 and 1993–4 series. For the earlier years 1950–1 to 1979–80 the estimates of gross rental are obtained by the splicing method applying the growth rate of current price estimates of the earlier series separately for rural and urban areas. For estimates of repair and maintenance, a similar method of splicing has been used for the period 1950–1 to 1992–3'.[12] This difference in approach has resulted in the GDP estimates for the whole sub-sector real estate, ownership of dwellings, and business services for 1950–1 to 1979–80 being around 9 per cent higher compared to the earlier (1980–1) series and 13 to 96 per cent higher for the years 1981–2 to 1996–7 [see Appendix Table 1(e)]. For the years 1993–4 to 1996–7 for which estimates are obtained by revised calculation based on recent data, the current price series for dwelling services are more than twice that of the estimates according to the 1980–1 series. This revision of GDP from dwellings since 1980–1 has resulted in its registering a growth rate of 8.22 per cent during the decade 1980–1 to 1990–1 compared to a growth rate of 5.62 per cent for total GDP. The growth rates of dwelling services during all other periods are lower than that of GDP for the whole economy and that of GDP for the non-residential sector. The growth rate of Sector A was 2.64 per cent per annum while that of the Sector non-A was 5.75 per cent during the period covered. After an impressive start during the first period and the first decade the growth rates slumped for both the sectors, the lowest recorded being during 1970–1 to 1980–1 when the growth of total GDP was just 3.08 per cent per year. Since 1980–1 there has been acceleration of growth with overall growth rates recording 5.62 per cent and 5.81 per cent per annum during the decades 1980–1 to 1990–1 and 1990–1 to 1999–2000. The growth rate of Sector A during 1990–1 to 1999–2000 was slightly lower than that during the previous decade.

The contribution made by each sector to the overall growth rate is obtained as the product of its growth rate and its weight in the total GDP. The latter measured by the sector's share in total GDP is shown in the second panel in Table 1.3. The contribution of each sector to overall growth in absolute terms (in percentage points) and in relative terms (as per cent) are shown in the two lower panels of the table. Non-residential sector, which is studied in detail, accounts for 94 to 97 per cent of the growth while services of dwellings explain 3 to 6 per cent during the different periods. The influence of Sector A has dropped from 43.3 per cent in the decade 1950–1 to 1960–1 to 14.9 per cent during the closing decade while that for Sector non-A went up from 53.9 per cent to 81.1 per cent. For the period as a whole, Sector A accounted for 25.5 per cent of the growth and Sector non-A for 69.7 per cent, the rest being accounted for by dwelling services.

---

[12] CSO *National Accounts Statistics, Back Series, 1950–1 to 1992–3*, p. xxxiv.

APPENDIX: 1

Appendix Table 1(a): GDP Total, GDP Per Capita, and GDP Per Person Engaged, Whole Economy at 1993–4 Prices, 1950–1 to 1999–2000

Year	GDP at factor cost (Rs crore)	Population (million)	Workforce ('000)	GDP per capita (Rs)	GDP per person engaged (Rs)	Indexes 1993–4 = 100				
						GDP total	GDP per capita	GDP per person engaged	Population	Workforce
	(1)	(2)	(3)	(4)	(5)	(6)	(7)	(8)	(9)	(10)
1950–1	140,466	359	160,139	3913	8772	17.98	44.62	41.62	40.29	43.19
1951–2	143,745	365	162,661	3938	8837	18.40	44.91	41.93	40.97	43.87
1952–3	147,824	372	165,223	3974	8947	18.92	45.31	42.45	41.75	44.56
1953–4	156,822	379	167,825	4138	9344	20.07	47.18	44.34	42.54	45.27
1954–5	163,479	386	170,468	4235	9590	20.92	48.30	45.51	43.32	45.98
1955–6	167,667	393	173,153	4266	9683	21.46	48.65	45.95	44.11	46.70
1956–7	177,211	401	175,880	4419	10,076	22.68	50.39	47.81	45.01	47.44
1957–8	175,068	409	178,651	4280	9,799	22.41	48.81	46.50	45.90	48.19
1958–9	188,354	418	181,464	4506	10,380	24.11	51.38	49.25	46.91	48.94
1959–60	192,476	426	184,322	4518	10,442	24.63	51.52	49.55	47.81	49.71
1960–1	206,103	434	187,225	4749	11,008	26.38	54.15	52.24	48.71	50.50
1961–2	212,499	444	190,389	4786	11,161	27.20	54.58	52.96	49.83	51.35
1962–3	216,994	454	193,822	4780	11,196	27.77	54.50	53.12	50.95	52.28
1963–4	227,980	464	197,317	4913	11,554	29.18	56.03	54.83	52.08	53.22
1964–5	245,270	474	200,874	5174	12,210	31.39	59.01	57.94	53.20	54.18
1965–6	236,306	485	204,496	4872	11,556	30.24	55.56	54.83	54.43	55.16
1966–7	238,710	495	208,183	4822	11,466	30.55	54.99	54.41	55.56	56.15
1967–8	258,137	506	211,937	5102	12,180	33.04	58.17	57.80	56.79	57.16
1968–9	264,873	518	215,758	5113	12,276	33.90	58.31	58.25	58.14	58.19
1969–70	282,134	529	219,648	5333	12,845	36.11	60.82	60.95	59.37	59.24
1970–1	296,278	541	223,608	5476	13,250	37.92	62.45	62.87	60.72	60.31
1971–2	299,269	554	227,640	5402	13,147	38.30	61.60	62.38	62.18	61.40
1972–3	298,316	567	231,744	5261	12,873	38.18	60.00	61.08	63.64	62.51

(Contd.)

11

Appendix Table 1(a) Contd.

	(1)	(2)	(3)	(4)	(5)	(6)	(7)	(8)	(9)	(10)
1973–4	311,894	560	237,021	5570	13,159	39.92	63.51	62.44	62.85	63.93
1974–5	315,514	593	243,520	5321	12,956	40.38	60.67	61.48	66.55	65.68
1975–6	343,924	607	250,198	5666	13,746	44.02	64.61	65.23	68.13	67.48
1976–7	348,223	620	257,059	5617	13,546	44.57	64.05	64.28	69.58	69.33
1977–8	374,235	634	263,614	5903	14,196	47.90	67.31	67.36	71.16	71.10
1978–9	394,828	648	269,845	6093	14,632	50.53	69.48	69.43	72.73	72.78
1979–80	374,291	664	276,222	5637	13,550	47.90	64.28	64.30	74.52	74.50
1980–1	401,128	679	282,751	5908	14,187	51.34	67.37	67.32	76.21	76.26
1981–2	425,073	692	289,434	6143	14,686	54.40	70.05	69.69	77.67	78.07
1982–3	438,079	708	296,688	6188	14,766	56.07	70.56	70.07	79.46	80.02
1983–4	471,742	723	302,957	6525	15,571	60.38	74.40	73.89	81.14	81.71
1984–5	492,077	739	307,784	6659	15,988	62.98	75.93	75.86	82.94	83.01
1985–6	513,990	755	312,688	6808	16,438	65.78	77.63	78.00	84.74	84.34
1986–7	536,257	771	317,671	6955	16,881	68.63	79.31	80.10	86.53	85.68
1987–8	556,778	788	322,732	7066	17,252	71.26	80.57	81.86	88.44	87.05
1988–9	615,098	805	329,197	7641	18,685	78.72	87.13	88.66	90.35	88.79
1989–90	656,331	822	337,119	7985	19,469	84.00	91.05	92.38	92.26	90.93
1990–1	692,871	839	345,231	8258	20,070	88.68	94.17	95.23	94.16	93.11
1991–2	701,863	856	353,539	8199	19,852	89.83	93.50	94.20	96.07	95.36
1992–3	737,792	872	362,047	8461	20,378	94.43	96.48	96.70	97.87	97.65
1993–4	781,345	891	370,759	8769	21,074	100.00	100.00	100.00	100.00	100.00
1994–5	838,031	908	376,705	9229	22,246	107.25	105.25	105.56	101.91	101.60
1995–6	899,563	927	379,793	9704	23,686	115.13	110.66	112.39	104.04	102.44
1996–7	970,083	943	382,907	10,287	25,335	124.16	117.31	120.22	105.84	103.28
1997–8	1,016,266	959	386,047	10,597	26,325	130.07	120.84	124.92	107.63	104.12
1998–9	1,083,047	975	389,212	11,108	27,827	138.61	126.67	132.04	109.43	104.98
1999–2000	1,151,991	991	392,403	11,625	29,357	147.44	132.56	139.30	111.22	105.84

Sources: Cols (1) and (2) from *NAS, Back Series, 1950–1 to 1992–3*, pp. 25–7 and *NAS 2001*, p. 15; Col. (3) from Appendix Table 3(b); Col. (4) = Col. (1)/Col. (2); Col. (5) = Col. (1)/Col. (3); Cols (6) to (10) derived.

12

Appendix Table 1(b): GDP and NDP from Dwellings at Current Prices, 1950-1 to 1999-2000

Year	GDP from real estate, ownership of dwellings and business services (Rs crore)		Col. (2)/ Col. (1) (Rs crore)	GDP from dwellings (Rs crore)		Col. (5) as % of Col. (2)	CFC for real estate and business services (Rs crore)	CFC for dwellings only (Rs crore)	NDP from dwellings (Rs crore)
	incl. FISIM*	excl. FISIM*		incl. FISIM	excl. FISIM				
	(1)	(2)	(3)	(4)	(5)	(6)	(7)	(8)	(9)
1950-1	889	889	1.000	848	848	95.39	129	123	725
1951-2	952	952	1.000	908	908	95.38	137	131	777
1952-3	1021	1021	1.000	974	974	95.40	140	134	840
1953-4	1097	1097	1.000	1046	1046	95.35	140	133	913
1954-5	1181	1181	1.000	1126	1126	95.34	143	136	913
1955-6	1263	1263	1.000	1204	1204	95.33	147	140	1064
1956-7	1356	1356	1.000	1292	1292	95.28	159	151	1141
1957-8	1451	1451	1.000	1383	1383	95.31	169	161	1222
1958-9	1555	1554	0.999	1482	1481	95.31	177	169	1312
1959-60	1667	1666	0.999	1589	1588	95.32	187	178	1410
1960-1	1787	1786	0.999	1703	1702	95.30	202	193	1510
1961-2	1803	1802	0.999	1718	1717	95.29	216	206	1511
1962-3	2053	2052	1.000	1959	1958	95.42	227	217	1741
1963-4	2215	2214	1.000	2112	2111	95.35	233	222	1889
1964-5	2383	2382	1.000	2272	2271	95.34	241	230	2041
1965-6	2544	2543	1.000	2429	2428	95.48	260	248	2180
1966-7	2715	2713	0.999	2591	2589	95.43	295	282	2308
1967-8	2957	2955	0.999	2823	2821	95.47	318	304	2518
1968-9	3152	3150	0.999	3012	3010	95.56	344	329	2681
1969-70	3354	3352	0.999	3206	3204	95.59	380	363	2841
1970-1	3589	3587	0.999	3429	3427	95.54	395	377	3050
1971-2	3882	3879	0.999	3706	3703	95.47	429	410	3294
1972-3	4202	4199	0.999	4008	4005	95.38	470	448	3557
1973-4	4564	4560	0.999	4346	4342	95.22	560	533	3809

(Contd.)

13

Appendix Table 1(b) Contd.

	(1)	(2)	(3)	(4)	(5)	(6)	(7)	(8)	(9)
1974–5	4977	4972	0.999	4724	4719	94.92	701	665	4054
1975–6	5411	5404	0.999	5132	5125	94.84	776	736	4389
1976–7	5881	5873	0.999	5574	5566	94.78	852	808	4758
1977–8	6382	6373	0.999	6036	6027	94.58	917	867	5160
1978–9	6865	6855	0.999	6488	6479	94.51	1022	966	5513
1979–80	7435	7424	0.999	7008	6998	94.26	1224	1154	5844
1980–1	7973	7957	0.998	7481	7466	93.83	1454	1364	6102
1981–2	9118	9096	0.998	8547	8526	93.74	1814	1700	6826
1982–3	10,431	10,405	0.998	9772	9748	93.68	2201	2062	7686
1983–4	12,169	12,138	0.997	11,178	11,150	91.86	2566	2357	8792
1984–5	13,879	13,843	0.997	12,696	12,663	91.48	2964	2711	9952
1985–6	15,968	15,925	0.997	14,564	14,525	91.21	3367	3071	11,454
1986–7	18,341	18,292	0.997	16,645	16,601	90.75	3913	3551	13,049
1987–8	20,904	20,846	0.997	19,104	19,051	91.39	4301	3931	15,120
1988–9	24,025	23,956	0.997	21,952	21,889	91.37	4711	4305	17,584
1989–90	27,552	27,458	0.997	25,158	25,072	91.31	5097	4654	20,418
1990–1	31,802	31,667	0.996	28,691	28,569	90.22	5550	5007	23,562
1991–2	36,616	36,429	0.995	32,952	32,784	89.99	6475	5827	26,957
1992–3	42,177	41,990	0.996	37,835	37,667	89.71	7114	6382	31,286
1993–4	48,684	48,419	0.995	43,507	43,270	89.37	7988	7139	36,132
1994–5	53,759	52,918	0.984	47,206	46,468	87.81	8245	7240	39,228
1995–6	59,432	58,995	0.993	50,899	50,525	85.64	8527	7303	43,222
1996–7	66,021	65,543	0.993	55,380	54,979	83.88	8858	7430	47,549
1997–8	73,386	72,844	0.993	59,716	59,275	81.37	9258	7533	51,741
1998–9	86,145	85,763	0.996	67,766	67,465	78.67	9847	7746	59,719
1999–2000	102,275	101,852	0.996	77,827	77,505	76.10	10,553	8030	69,475

Note: * FISIM = Financial intermediary services indirectly measured

Sources: Cols (1), (2), (4) and (7) for 1950–1 to 1992–3 from *NAS, Back Series, 1950–1 to 1992–3*, Table 62, pp. 374–7, and for 1993–4 to 1999–2000 from NAS 2001, Table 70, p. 174; Col. (3) = Col. (2)/Col. (1); Col. (5) = Col. (4) × Col. (3); Col. (6) = [Col. (5)/ Col. (2)] × 100; Col. (8) = Col. (7) × Col. (6); Col. (9) = Col. (5) – Col. (8).

14

Appendix Table 1(c): GDP and NDP from Dwellings at Constant (1993–4) Prices, 1950–1 to 1999–2000

Year	GDP from real estate, ownership of dwellings and business services (Rs crore) incl. FISIM	excl. FISIM	Col. (2)/ Col. (1) (Rs crore)	GDP from dwellings (Rs crore) incl. FISIM	excl. FISIM	Col. (5) as % of Col. (2)	CFC for real estate and business services (Rs crore)	CFC for dwellings only (Rs crore)	NDP from dwellings (Rs crore)
	(1)	(2)	(3)	(4)	(5)	(6)	(7)	(8)	(9)
1950–1	7752	7752	1.000	7138	7138	92.08	3445	3172	3966
1951–2	7922	7922	1.000	7297	7297	92.11	3461	3188	4109
1952–3	8106	8106	1.000	7460	7460	92.03	3488	3210	4250
1953–4	8287	8287	1.000	7626	7626	92.02	3507	3227	4399
1954–5	8468	8468	1.000	7796	7796	92.06	3558	3276	4520
1955–6	8656	8656	1.000	7972	7972	92.10	3577	3294	4678
1956–7	8846	8846	1.000	8151	8151	92.14	3624	3339	4812
1957–8	9041	9041	1.000	8334	8334	92.18	3636	3352	4982
1958–9	9241	9233	0.999	8521	8514	92.21	3702	3414	5100
1959–60	9445	9435	0.999	8712	8703	92.24	3718	3429	5273
1960–1	9665	9655	0.999	8910	8901	92.19	3776	3481	5420
1961–2	9888	9878	0.999	9108	9099	92.11	3795	3496	5603
1962–3	10,143	10,134	0.999	9347	9339	92.15	3831	3530	5808
1963–4	10,414	10,403	0.999	9597	9587	92.15	3846	3544	6043
1964–5	10,669	10,658	0.999	9851	9841	92.33	3846	3551	6290
1965–6	10,951	10,941	0.999	10111	10,102	92.33	3877	3580	6522
1966–7	11,236	11,224	0.999	10,378	10,367	92.36	4095	3782	6585
1967–8	11,543	11,532	0.999	10,658	10,648	92.33	4138	3821	6827
1968–9	11,839	11,826	0.999	10,940	10,928	92.41	4181	3864	7064
1969–70	12,153	12,139	0.999	11,235	11,222	92.45	4231	3911	7311
1970–1	12,476	12,460	0.999	11,538	11,523	92.48	4379	4050	7473
1971–2	12,682	12,865	1.014	11,902	12,074	93.85	4449	4175	7898
1972–3	13,267	13,248	0.999	12,251	12,233	92.34	4523	4177	8057

(Contd.)

15

Appendix Table 1(c) Contd.

	(1)	(2)	(3)	(4)	(5)	(6)	(7)	(8)	(9)
1973–4	13,680	13,660	0.999	12,610	12,592	92.18	4617	4256	8336
1974–5	14,091	14,075	0.999	12,984	12,969	92.14	4710	4340	8629
1975–6	14,531	14,512	0.999	13,367	13,350	91.99	4808	4423	8927
1976–7	14,961	14,958	1.000	13,763	13,760	91.99	5088	4681	9080
1977–8	15,465	15,439	0.998	14,172	14,148	91.64	5236	4798	9350
1978–9	15,949	15,919	0.998	14,600	14,573	91.54	5384	4929	9644
1979–80	16,463	16,434	0.998	15,035	15,009	91.33	5539	5059	9950
1980–1	16,938	16,904	0.998	15,455	15,424	91.24	5695	5196	10,228
1981–2	18,447	18,409	0.998	16,809	16,774	91.12	5878	5356	11,418
1982–3	19,889	19,843	0.998	18,131	18,089	91.16	6061	5525	12,564
1983–4	21,947	21,893	0.998	19,569	19,521	89.16	6221	5547	13,974
1984–5	23,607	23,547	0.997	20,975	20,922	88.85	6400	5686	15,235
1985–6	25,480	25,408	0.997	22,581	22,517	88.62	6587	5838	16,680
1986–7	27,774	27,689	0.997	24,525	24,450	88.30	6785	5991	18,459
1987–8	30,044	29,948	0.997	26,867	26,781	89.43	6902	6172	20,609
1988–9	32,829	32,721	0.997	29,458	29,361	89.73	7026	6305	23,057
1989–90	35,136	34,998	0.996	31,495	31,371	89.64	7151	6410	24,961
1990–1	38,340	38,160	0.995	34,142	33,982	89.05	7346	6542	27,440
1991–2	41,409	41,205	0.995	37,027	36,845	89.42	7540	6742	30,102
1992–3	44,447	44,236	0.995	39,740	39,551	89.41	7762	6940	32,611
1993–4	48,684	48,419	0.995	43,507	43,270	89.37	7988	7139	36,132
1994–5	50,668	49,894	0.985	44,706	44,023	88.23	8245	7275	36,748
1995–6	53,065	52,732	0.994	45,958	45,670	86.61	8527	7385	38,285
1996–7	55,372	55,001	0.993	47,252	46,935	85.34	8858	7559	39,376
1997–8	58,385	57,966	0.993	48,585	48,236	83.21	9258	7704	40,532
1998–9	61,776	61,495	0.995	49,968	49,741	80.89	9847	7965	41,776
1999–2000	66,421	66,119	0.995	51,391	51,157	77.37	10,553	8165	42,992

Sources: Cols (1), (2), (4) and (7) for 1950–1 to 1992–3 from NAS, *Back Series*, Table 63, pp. 378–81, and for 1993–4 to 1999–2000 from NAS 2001, Table 70, p. 175; rest of the columns same as in Appendix Table 1(b).

16

Appendix Table 1(d): Non-residential GDP at Current Prices, 1950-1 to 1999-2000

Year	Total GDP (Rs crore)	GDP from dwellings (Rs crore)	Non-residential GDP (Rs crore)			% distribution of non-residential GDP		% to total GDP	
			Total	Sector A	Sector non-A	Sector A	Sector non-A	Dwellings	Non-residential GDP
	(1)	(2)	(3)	(4)	(5)	(6)	(7)	(8)	(9)
1950–1	9547	848	8699	5432	3267	62.44	37.56	8.88	91.12
1951–2	10,080	908	9172	5609	3563	61.15	38.85	9.01	90.99
1952–3	9941	974	8967	5464	3503	60.93	39.07	9.80	90.20
1953–4	10,824	1046	9778	6020	3758	61.57	38.43	9.66	90.34
1954–5	10,168	1126	9042	5121	3921	56.64	43.36	11.07	88.93
1955–6	10,332	1204	9128	4966	4162	54.40	45.60	11.65	88.35
1956–7	12,334	1292	11,042	6309	4733	57.14	42.86	10.48	89.52
1957–8	12,610	1383	11,227	6178	5049	55.03	44.97	10.97	89.03
1958–9	14,106	1481	12,625	7168	5457	56.78	43.22	10.50	89.50
1959–60	14,816	1588	13,228	7201	6027	54.44	45.56	10.72	89.28
1960–1	16,220	1702	14,518	7581	6937	52.22	47.78	10.49	89.51
1961–2	17,116	1717	15,399	7852	7547	50.99	49.01	10.03	89.97
1962–3	18,302	1958	16,344	8017	8327	49.05	50.95	10.70	89.30
1963–4	20,916	2111	18,805	9435	9370	50.17	49.83	10.09	89.91
1964–5	24,436	2271	22,165	11,528	10,637	52.01	47.99	9.29	90.71
1965–6	25,586	2428	23,158	11,496	11,662	49.64	50.36	9.49	90.51
1966–7	29,123	2589	26,534	13,373	13,161	50.40	49.60	8.89	91.11
1967–8	34,225	2821	31,404	16,735	14,669	53.29	46.71	8.24	91.76
1968–9	36,092	3010	33,082	17,250	15,832	52.14	47.86	8.34	91.66
1969–70	39,691	3204	36,487	18,867	17,620	51.71	48.29	8.07	91.93
1970–1	42,222	3427	38,795	19,453	19,342	50.14	49.86	8.12	91.88
1971–2	44,923	3703	41,220	19,872	21,348	48.21	51.79	8.24	91.76
1972–3	49,415	4005	45,410	21,857	23,553	48.13	51.87	8.11	91.89
1973–4	60,560	4342	56,218	28,803	27,415	51.23	48.77	7.17	92.83
1974–5	71,283	4719	66,564	31,555	35,009	47.41	52.59	6.62	93.38

(Contd.)

17

Appendix Table 1(d) Contd.

	(1)	(2)	(3)	(4)	(5)	(6)	(7)	(8)	(9)
1975–6	75,709	5125	70,584	31,276	39,308	44.31	55.69	6.77	93.23
1976–7	81,381	5566	75,815	31,953	43,862	42.15	57.85	6.84	93.16
1977–8	92,881	6027	86,854	37,832	49,022	43.56	56.44	6.49	93.51
1978–9	99,823	6479	93,344	38,881	54,463	41.65	58.35	6.49	93.51
1979–80	108,927	6998	101,929	40,223	61,706	39.46	60.54	6.42	93.58
1980–1	130,178	7466	122,712	50,592	72,120	41.23	58.77	5.74	94.26
1981–2	152,056	8526	143,530	56,883	86,647	39.63	60.37	5.61	94.39
1982–3	169,525	9748	159,777	60,881	98,896	38.10	61.90	5.75	94.25
1983–4	198,630	11,150	187,480	72,729	114,751	38.79	61.21	5.61	94.39
1984–5	222,706	12,663	210,043	78,288	131,755	37.27	62.73	5.69	94.31
1985–6	249,547	14,525	235,022	84,152	150,870	35.81	64.19	5.82	94.18
1986–7	278,258	16,601	261,657	90,541	171,116	34.60	65.40	5.97	94.03
1987–8	315,993	19,051	296,942	100,759	196,183	33.93	66.07	6.03	93.97
1988–9	378,491	21,889	356,602	123,901	232,701	34.74	65.26	5.78	94.22
1989–90	438,020	25,072	412,948	136,891	276,057	33.15	66.85	5.72	94.28
1990–1	510,954	28,569	482,385	159,760	322,625	33.12	66.88	5.59	94.41
1991–2	589,086	32,784	556,302	185,712	370,590	33.38	66.62	5.57	94.43
1992–3	673,221	37,667	635,554	208,265	427,289	32.77	67.23	5.60	94.40
1993–4	781,345	43,270	738,075	241,967	496,108	32.78	67.22	5.54	94.46
1994–5	917,058	46,468	870,590	278,773	591,817	32.02	67.98	5.07	94.93
1995–6	1,073,271	50,525	1,022,746	303,102	719,644	29.64	70.36	4.71	95.29
1996–7	1,243,546	54,979	1,188,567	362,605	825,962	30.51	69.49	4.42	95.58
1997–8	1,390,042	59,275	1,330,767	387,008	943,759	29.08	70.92	4.26	95.74
1998–9	1,616,033	67,465	1,548,568	459,900	1,088,668	29.70	70.30	4.17	95.83
1999–2000	1,786,459	77,505	1,708,954	484,221	1,224,733	28.33	71.67	4.34	95.66

Sources: Cols (1) and (4) for 1950–1 to 1992–3 from *NAS, Back Series, 1950–1 to 1992–3,* pp. 20–3, and for 1993–4 to 1999–2000 from *NAS 2001,* p. 14; Col. (2) from Appendix Table 1(b), Col. (4); Col. (3) = Col. (1) – Col. (2); Col. (5) = Col. (3) – Col. (4); Cols (6) to (9) derived.

18

Appendix Table 1(e): Non-residential GDP at Constant (1993-4) Prices, 1950-1 to 1999-2000

Year	Total GDP (Rs crore)	GDP from dwellings (Rs crore)	Non-residential GDP (Rs crore)			% distribution of non-residential GDP		% to total GDP	
			Total	Sector A	Sector non-A	Sector A	Sector non-A	Dwellings	Non-residential GDP
	(1)	(2)	(3)	(4)	(5)	(6)	(7)	(8)	(9)
1950-1	140,466	7138	133,328	81,069	52,259	60.80	39.20	5.08	94.92
1951-2	143,745	7297	136,448	82,278	54,170	60.30	39.70	5.08	94.92
1952-3	147,824	7460	140,364	84,873	55,491	60.47	39.53	5.05	94.95
1953-4	156,822	7626	149,196	91,409	57,787	61.27	38.73	4.86	95.14
1954-5	163,479	7796	155,683	94,096	61,587	60.44	39.56	4.77	95.23
1955-6	167,667	7972	159,695	93,283	66,412	58.41	41.59	4.75	95.25
1956-7	177,211	8151	169,060	98,354	70,706	58.18	41.82	4.60	95.40
1957-8	175,068	8334	166,734	93,936	72,798	56.34	43.66	4.76	95.24
1958-9	188,354	8514	179,840	103,401	76,439	57.50	42.50	4.52	95.48
1959-60	192,476	8703	183,773	102,360	81,413	55.70	44.30	4.52	95.48
1960-1	206,103	8901	197,202	109,254	87,948	55.40	44.60	4.32	95.68
1961-2	212,499	9099	203,400	109,346	94,054	53.76	46.24	4.28	95.72
1962-3	216,994	9339	207,655	107,171	100,484	51.61	48.39	4.30	95.70
1963-4	227,980	9587	218,393	109,678	108,715	50.22	49.78	4.21	95.79
1964-5	245,270	9841	235,429	119,795	115,634	50.88	49.12	4.01	95.99
1965-6	236,306	10,102	226,204	106,567	119,637	47.11	52.89	4.27	95.73
1966-7	238,710	10,367	228,343	105,051	123,292	46.01	53.99	4.34	95.66
1967-8	258,137	10,648	247,489	120,673	126,816	48.76	51.24	4.12	95.88
1968-9	264,873	10,928	253,945	120,482	133,463	47.44	52.56	4.13	95.87
1969-70	282,134	11,222	270,912	128,226	142,686	47.33	52.67	3.98	96.02
1970-1	296,278	11,523	284,755	137,320	147,435	48.22	51.78	3.89	96.11
1971-2	299,269	12,074	287,195	134,742	152,453	46.92	53.08	4.03	95.97
1972-3	298,316	12,233	286,083	127,980	158,103	44.74	55.26	4.10	95.90
1973-4	311,894	12,592	299,302	137,197	162,105	45.84	54.16	4.04	95.96

(Contd.)

19

Appendix Table 1(e) Contd.

	(1)	(2)	(3)	(4)	(5)	(6)	(7)	(8)	(9)
1974-5	315,514	12,969	302,545	135,107	167,438	44.66	55.34	4.11	95.89
1975-6	343,924	13,350	330,574	152,522	178,052	46.14	53.86	3.88	96.12
1976-7	348,223	13,760	334,463	143,709	190,754	42.97	57.03	3.95	96.05
1977-8	374,235	14,148	360,087	158,132	201,955	43.91	56.09	3.78	96.22
1978-9	394,828	14,573	380,255	161,773	218,482	42.54	57.46	3.69	96.31
1979-80	374,291	15,009	359,282	141,107	218,175	39.27	60.73	4.01	95.99
1980-1	401,128	15,424	385,704	159,293	226,411	41.30	58.70	3.85	96.15
1981-2	425,073	16,774	408,299	167,723	240,576	41.08	58.92	3.95	96.05
1982-3	438,079	18,089	419,990	166,577	253,413	39.66	60.34	4.13	95.87
1983-4	471,742	19,521	452,221	182,498	269,723	40.36	59.64	4.14	95.86
1984-5	492,077	20,922	471,155	185,186	285,969	39.30	60.70	4.25	95.75
1985-6	513,990	22,517	491,473	186,570	304,903	37.96	62.04	4.38	95.62
1986-7	536,257	24,450	511,807	185,363	326,444	36.22	63.78	4.56	95.44
1987-8	556,778	26,781	529,997	182,899	347,098	34.51	65.49	4.81	95.19
1988-9	615,098	29,361	585,737	211,184	374,553	36.05	63.95	4.77	95.23
1989-90	656,331	31,371	624,960	214,315	410,645	34.29	65.71	4.78	95.22
1990-1	692,871	33,982	658,889	223,114	435,775	33.86	66.14	4.90	95.10
1991-2	701,863	36,845	665,018	219,660	445,358	33.03	66.97	5.25	94.75
1992-3	737,792	39,551	698,241	232,386	465,855	33.28	66.72	5.36	94.64
1993-4	781,345	43,270	738,075	241,967	496,108	32.78	67.22	5.54	94.46
1994-5	838,031	44,023	794,008	254,090	539,918	32.00	68.00	5.25	94.75
1995-6	899,563	45,670	853,893	251,892	602,001	29.50	70.50	5.08	94.92
1996-7	970,083	46,935	923,148	276,091	647,057	29.91	70.09	4.84	95.16
1997-8	1,016,266	48,236	968,030	269,383	698,647	27.83	72.17	4.75	95.25
1998-9	1,083,047	49,741	1,033,306	288,401	744,905	27.91	72.09	4.59	95.41
1999-2000	1,151,991	51,157	1,100,834	290,334	810,500	26.37	73.63	4.44	95.56

Sources: Cols (1) and (4) from *NAS, Back Series, 1950–1 to 1992–3*, pp. 24–7 and *NAS 2001*, p. 15 for 1993–4 to 1999–2000; Col. (2) from Appendix Table 1(c), Col. (5); Col. (3) = Col. (1) – Col. (2); Col. (5) = Col. (3) – Col. (4); Cols (6) to (9) derived.

Distribution of NDP and GDP by Factor Incomes

The distribution by factor incomes is required to determine the relative shares of the factors of production, viz., land, labour, and capital, in the domestic product. The estimates of Net Domestic Product (NDP) by factor incomes at current prices were first introduced by the Central Statistical Organisation (CSO) in 1976 for the period beginning from 1960–1. For the years prior to 1960–1,while there are no official estimates of factor incomes, estimates by individual scholars are available.[1]

The CSO has revised the national accounts series periodically; with every revision since 1976 the corresponding distribution of NDP at current prices by factor income has also been provided. The position can be summarized as follows:

Source	Period for which available
1960–1 series National Accounts Statistics 1960–1 to 1974–5, October 1976, and subsequent issues	Provides the distribution of NDP by factor incomes for the years 1960–1 to 1974–5, at current prices
1970–1 series National Accounts Statistics February 1980, February 1982, and February 1985	For the years 1970–1 to 1982–3
1980–1 series National Accounts Statistics (New Series), Factor Incomes (1980–1 to 1989–90), 1994 and NAS subsequent issues up to 1998	For the years 1980–1 to 1995–6
1993–4 series National Accounts Statistics 1999 and subsequent issues up to 2001	For the years 1993–4 to 1998–9

The distribution by factor incomes is presented for the following institutional and industrial categories in the 1960–1 and 1970–1 series:

a. Factor Incomes by broad sectors in primary, secondary, and service sectors;

---

[1] Bakul H. Dholakia, *The Sources of Economic Growth in India*, Baroda, 1974, contains a review of past estimates and estimates made by him, pp. 43–63.

b. Factor Incomes by organized and unorganized sectors;
c. Factor incomes by public and private organized sectors;
d. Factor incomes by industry of origin.

For the 1980–1 and 1993–4 series, details are given as follows:

a. Factor incomes by kind of economic activity and by organized/ unorganized sectors;
b. Factor incomes of public sector by type of economic activity and by type of institution.

In the 1980–1 and 1993–4 series, factor incomes of private enterprises, that is, private organized sector, are not separately presented but can be derived. These are, however, available for the years 1980–1 to1995–6 in the publication *National Accounts Statistics of India, 1950–1 to 1996–7* issued by the *EPW* Research Foundation.[2]

For the organized sector factor incomes are distributed according to compensation of employees and operating surplus. Further, property incomes in the form of rent and interest and imputed bank charges (IBC) are shown separately in the *EPW* Research Foundation issues of *National Accounts Statistics of India, 1950–1 to 1996–7*. For the unorganized sector, in addition to compensation of employees, rent, and interest, a new category known as 'mixed income of the self-employed' is also introduced. This is to allow for the fact that income from labour and operating surplus cannot be distinguished in the case of the self-employed. The category 'mixed income of the self-employed' includes income of own-account workers and profits and dividends of unincorporated enterprises.[3]

FACTOR SHARES FOR THE PERIOD 1960–1 TO 1999–2000

The estimates of NDP at current prices according to the different series are not comparable in view of the changes in the methodology and source data used. Moreover, NDP by factor incomes as per the recent (1993–4) revision are available only for the years 1993–4 to 1998–9. It, therefore, becomes necessary to derive a comparable series for factor shares for the period 1960–1 to 1992–3 by the splicing method. The available figures for total NDP, NDP from the organized sector, and the corresponding spliced values are given in Appendix Table 2(a). NDP from the unorganized sector is derived as a residual and shown in Col. (9). It may be noted that the spliced values of NDP for 1960–1 to 1992–3 differ only slightly from the estimates for back years provided by the CSO for the same period.[4] Since the distribution by

[2] *Economic and Political Weekly (EPW)* Research Foundation, National Accounts Statistics of India, 1950–1 to 1996–7, Mumbai, October 1998, p. 76.
[3] CSO, *National Accounts Statistics, October 1976*, Department of Statistics, Ministry of Planning, New Delhi, p. 141.
[4] CSO, *National Accounts Statistics, Back Series, 1950–1 to 1992–3*, April 2001, Department of Statistics, Ministry of Planning, New Delhi, pp. 28–31.

factor incomes is not available for the earlier years according to the revised official estimates of NDP, it has been decided to work with the spliced values of NDP initially and relate them to the official estimates of NDP at a later stage.

The available data on factor incomes of the organized sector for 1960–1 to 1999–2000 are presented in Appendix Table 2(b). Figures for 1999–2000 are obtained on the basis of the 'Quick Estimates' for the year as reported by the CSO.[5] The spliced values for compensation of employees for 1960–1 to 1992–3 and the actual estimates by the CSO for 1993–4 to 1999–2000 are shown in Col. (5) of Appendix Table 2(b) as the 1993–4 series. Operating surplus, the other component, is obtained as a residual. For the unorganized sector, estimates are made by splicing for compensation of employees, interest and rent and are presented in Appendix Table 2(c).

The treatment of net output of dwellings, that is, net rent, varies over the different series. In the 1960–1 and 1970–1 series the whole of net value added by ownership of dwellings in the unorganized sector was treated as rent,[6] while in the 1980–1 series and 1993–4 series it was considered as factor income as part of mixed income of the self-employed.[7] Public sector net value added (NVA) by ownership of dwellings has been treated as compensation of employees;[8] the absolute values in this category are, however, negligible being only Rs 4 crore for the period 1992–3 to 1994–5. In view of the differences in the treatment of net output of dwellings, significant changes are noticed in the percentage shares of rent for the years 1980–1 to 1982–3 according to the 1970–1 series and 1980–1 series. For instance, the percentage share of rent in NDP of the unorganized sector is 5.1 for 1980–1 according to the 1970–1 series while it is 2.1 according to 1980–1 series. This drop in the share of rent seems to have been made up partly by the increase in the share of mixed income. The more noticeable drop in compensation of employees in 1980–1 from 26 per cent in the 1970–1 series to 20.8 per cent in the 1980–1 series is somewhat puzzling. Compared to this the changes seem to be in the reverse direction between the 1980–1 series and the 1993–4 series for the common year 1993–4. The percentage share of mixed income for 1993–4 shows a drop from 71.1 in the 1980–1 series to 65.4 in the 1993–4 series. Further, the share of rent for 1993–4 shows an upward jump from 2.4 per cent in 1980–1 series to 11.7 per cent in the 1993–4 series. This also needs explanation, especially so when net output of dwellings which has doubled in the new series is treated as part of mixed income. The treatment of net

[5] CSO, *National Accounts Statistics, 2001,* New Delhi, July 2001, p. 210.

[6] CSO, *National Accounts Statistics Sources and Methods,* New Delhi, April 1980, p. 74.

[7] CSO, *National Accounts Statistics Factor Income (New Series), 1980–1 to 1989–90,* New Delhi, March 1994, p. 26. CSO, *National Accounts Statistics, 2000,* New Delhi, 2000, p. 216.

[8] CSO, *National Accounts Statistics Factor Income (New Series), 1980–1 to 1989–90,* New Delhi, March 1994, p. 21.

output of dwellings either as rent or as part of mixed income is not of much relevance to this study as the study of treatment of net output of dwellings is concerned only with non-residential NDP and Gross Domestic Product (GDP).

Mixed income of the self-employed taken as the residual after deducting compensation of employees interest and rent from NDP of the unorganized sector is shown in Col. (14) of Appendix Table 2(c). It includes the labour share of the self-employed and family workers, their investment income, and profits of unincorporated enterprises. Mixed income accounts for 58 to 70 per cent of the NDP of the unorganized sector and 47 to 50 per cent of the NDP for the whole economy up to 1981–2 and declines thereafter to 38 per cent by the end of the period. In view of this, the allocation of mixed income to labour and capital on the basis of assumptions will have a definite influence on the share of compensation of employees. Dholakia has estimated that the share of labour income will be about 52.9, 60.84, and 64.81 per cent of national income respectively under alternative assumptions of one-half, two-thirds, and three-fourths as the proportion of pure labour income in the income of the self-employed[9] for the period 1950–62 for India.

To estimate the labour share of proprietor's income, Denison[10] assumed that the percentage of national income that is allocable to labour in USA is the same for proprietorships and partnerships as for non-financial corporations. On this basis 63 per cent of proprietor's income was allocated to labour in the 1950s for USA. In his 1974 and 1979 studies, he used the average compensation of employees in the business sector to estimate the imputed earnings of the non-farm proprietors and unpaid family workers.[11] A similar approach was adopted by Dirk Pilat for Japan. He assumed that for non-agricultural income, labour compensation of self-employed and family workers is the same as that of employees. For agricultural income, Pilot assumed that 60 per cent of the operating surplus consists of labour income.[12] For this study, I have assumed that the labour share of mixed income will be the same as the share of compensation of employees in the NDP from the private organized sector. The distribution of factor income for the private organized sector is readily available for the years 1960–1 to 1974–5 according to the 1960–1 series and for 1970–1 to 1982–3 according to the 1970–1 series. But the 1980–1 series and 1993–4 series do not explicitly present the factor income distribution for the private organized sector. The same can, however, be

---

[9] Dholakia, *The Sources of Economic Growth in India*, p. 46.

[10] E. F. Denison, *Why Growth Rates Differ*, Brookings Institution, Washington, D.C., 1967, p. 37.

[11] E. F. Denison, *Accounting for United States Economic Growth, 1929–1969*, Washington, D.C. 1974, p. 26; E. F. Denison, *Accounting for Slower Economic Growth in the 1970s*, Washington, D.C., 1979, p. 171.

[12] Dirk Pilat, 'Explaining Japan's Post-war Economic Growth' in A. Szirmai, B. Van Ark, and D. Pilat (eds), *Explaining Economic Growth: Essays in Honour of Angus Maddison*, Amsterdam, 1993, p. 177.

derived by deducting the components of factor incomes of the public sector from those of the organized sector as a whole. Using this approach, the *EPW* Research Foundation[13] has already presented the factor incomes of the private organized sector for the years 1980–1 to 1995–6. Following the same procedure, the factor incomes of the private organized sector has been estimated for the period 1993–4 to 1998–9 according to the 1993–4 series. These are presented in Appendix Table 2(d). Compensation of employees of the private organized sector is found to vary between 50 and 55 per cent during 1960–1 to 1992–3. Thereafter it shows a steady decline to 36 per cent by 1999–2000. This may be due to the accelerated growth of capital stock in the 1990s and hence of capital income.

The relative shares of compensation of employees in the private organized sector are applied to the 'mixed income' of the unorganized sector to derive its labour component. The labour income thus estimated is added to the compensation of employees already shown as part of factor incomes in the unorganized sector to obtain the total compensation of employees. The residual obtained by deducting the estimated total compensation of employees from the NDP of the unorganized sector is treated as operating surplus. The calculations are shown in Cols (16)–(19) of Appendix Table 2(c). Factor incomes of the public sector are presented in Appendix Table 2(e).

The distribution of factor incomes for the whole economy obtained by adding the respective components in the organized and unorganized sectors on the basis of estimated values of NDP is shown in Appendix Table 2(f). Compensation of employees is found to vary between 50 per cent and 61 per cent of the NDP for the whole economy, while for the public sector, which includes public administration, the component is found to vary between 75 and 97 per cent.

The spliced values of NDP used for deriving factor incomes for the years 1960–1 to 1992–3 differ slightly from the official estimates of NDP provided by the CSO. The two series and the extent of variation are shown in Appendix Table 2(g). For the years 1993–4 to 1998–9, both the estimates of NDP are from the CSO's *National Accounts Statistics 2001*. The estimates in Col. (1) correspond to NDP by factor incomes[14] and those in Col. (2) refer to NDP by industrial origin.[15] The variations between them, though minor, are not explained in the *National Accounts Statistics*.

FACTOR SHARES FOR THE PERIOD 1950–1 TO 1959–60

Official estimates of factor incomes are not available for this period. The estimates presented here are based on Dholakia's calculations for the years

---

[13] *EPW* Research Foundation, *National Accounts Statistics of India, 1950–1 to 1996–7*, March 1994, p. 76, Table 24.

[14] CSO, *National Accounts Statistics, 2001*, pp. 86–7.

[15] Ibid., p. 21.

1948–9 to 1968–9.[16] His estimates of the share of labour income for 1960–1 to 1965–6 are found to be higher by 10 to 15 per cent than those obtained by me from official sources. To a large extent this difference may be due to the assumption made for the allocation of mixed income. Instead of using Dholakia's figures as they are, the estimate of the share of labour income for 1960–1 based on official sources has been carried backward to 1950–1 using the index numbers of the percentage share of labour income derived from his estimates. This implies that the trend indicated by Dholakia's figures has been accepted. The percentage shares of labour income and property income thus derived are shown in Cols (20) and (21) of Appendix Table 2(h).

CSO ESTIMATES OF NDP AND CORRESPONDING FACTOR INCOMES

For the years 1950–1 to 1959–60, the relative factor shares have been estimated. For 1960–1 to 1999–2000, the factor shares based on spliced values of NDP have also been obtained. These are shown in Cols (2) and (3) of Table 2.1. Applying these percentages to the CSO estimates of NDP at current prices shown in Col. (1), the corresponding labour and non-labour income (hitherto referred as compensation of employees and operating surplus) are estimated. The derivation of factor incomes of NDP excluding dwellings or non-residential NDP are shown in Cols (8) and (9). Labour income is found to vary between 57 and 62 per cent of non-residential NDP during the period 1950–1 to 1992–3. From 1993–4 onwards, the share of labour income has steadily declined to 52 per cent. On the other hand, labour income in non-residential business in USA is reported to have risen from 79.2 per cent in 1967 to 85.5 per cent in 1982.[17] Not only is the share of labour earnings considerably higher in USA as compared to India, it also shows a rising trend over the years. The share of labour earnings in West European countries during 1950–62 are also nearly as high as in USA.[18] Compared to this, the lower shares of labour income in India is characteristic of a developing economy and the declining trend over the years is indicative of the increasing importance of capital in the production process.

FACTOR SHARES OF NDP FROM SECTOR A AND SECTOR NON-A

The National Accounts Statistics provides factor income for Sector A (agriculture, forestry, and fishing) as part of the table on distribution of factor incomes by economic activity. Sector A accounts for a large portion of the

---

[16] Dholakia, *The Sources of Economic Growth in India*, pp. 49–54.

[17] Edward F. Denison, *Trends in American Economic Growth, 1929–82*, Brookings Institution, Washington, D.C., 1985, p. 121.

[18] Denison, *Why Growth Rates Differ*, p. 38.

Table 2.1: Distribution of NDP (Whole Economy) by Factor Incomes at Current Prices, 1950–1 to 1999–2000

Year	NDP CSO estimates (Rs crore)	% factor shares		Factor incomes (Rs crore)		NDP from dwellings (Rs crore)	NDP excluding dwellings (Rs crore)			% share in NDP excluding dwellings	
		Labour income	Non-labour income	Labour income	Non-labour income		NDP	Labour income	Non-labour income	Labour income	Non-labour income
	(1)	(2)	(3)	(4)	(5)	(6)	(7)	(8)	(9)	(10)	(11)
1950–1	9183	54.06	45.85	4964	4210	725	8458	4964	3494	58.69	41.31
1951–2	9669	53.65	46.36	5187	4483	777	8892	5187	3705	58.33	41.67
1952–3	9499	54.05	45.86	5134	4357	840	8659	5134	3525	59.29	40.71
1953–4	10,360	52.21	48.14	5409	4987	913	9447	5409	4038	57.26	42.74
1954–5	9,657	53.20	46.92	5137	4531	990	8667	5137	3530	59.27	40.73
1955–6	9,786	53.55	46.47	5241	4548	1064	8722	5241	3481	60.09	39.91
1956–7	11,723	52.35	47.96	6137	5623	1141	10,582	6137	4445	58.00	42.00
1957–8	11,948	55.84	43.64	6672	5214	1222	10,726	6672	4054	62.20	37.80
1958–9	13,334	53.71	46.29	7161	6172	1312	12,022	7161	4861	59.57	40.43
1959–60	13,973	55.00	44.68	7686	6243	1410	12,563	7686	4877	61.18	38.82
1960–1	15,276	53.67	46.33	8199	7077	1510	13,766	8199	5567	59.56	40.44
1961–2	16,058	52.97	47.03	8506	7552	1511	14,547	8506	6041	58.47	41.53
1962–3	17,137	53.71	46.29	9205	7932	1741	15,396	9205	6191	59.79	40.21
1963–4	19,603	53.02	46.98	10,394	9209	1889	17,714	10,394	7320	58.68	41.32
1964–5	22,959	53.39	46.61	12,257	10,702	2041	20,918	12,257	8661	58.59	41.41
1965–6	23,916	54.75	45.25	13,094	10,822	2180	21,736	13,094	8642	60.24	39.76
1966–7	27,148	56.14	43.86	15,242	11,906	2308	24,840	15,242	9598	61.36	38.64
1967–8	32,003	59.13	40.87	18,924	13,079	2518	29,485	18,924	10,561	64.18	35.82
1968–9	33,676	59.73	40.27	20,113	13,563	2681	30,995	20,113	10,882	64.89	35.11
1969–70	37,013	57.97	42.03	21,456	15,557	2841	34,172	21,456	12,716	62.79	37.21
1970–1	39,252	58.22	41.78	22,851	16,401	3050	36,202	22,851	13,351	63.12	36.88
1971–2	41,631	58.11	41.89	24,191	17,440	3294	38,337	24,191	14,146	63.10	36.90
1972–3	45,694	59.03	40.97	26,974	18,720	3557	42,137	26,974	15,163	64.01	35.99
1973–4	56,221	57.06	42.94	32,081	24,140	3809	52,412	32,081	20,331	61.21	38.79

(Contd.)

27

Table 2.1 Contd.

	(1)	(2)	(3)	(4)	(5)	(6)	(7)	(8)	(9)	(10)	(11)
1974-5	65,723	56.07	43.93	36,853	28,870	4054	61,669	36,853	24,816	59.76	40.24
1975-6	69,260	58.35	41.65	40,411	28,849	4389	64,871	40,411	24,460	62.29	37.71
1976-7	74,475	56.61	43.39	42,161	32,314	4759	69,716	42,161	27,555	60.47	39.53
1977-8	85,384	58.26	41.74	49,745	35,639	5160	80,224	49,745	30,479	62.01	37.99
1978-9	91,250	58.24	41.76	53,142	38,108	5513	85,737	53,142	32,595	61.98	38.02
1979-80	98,478	57.67	42.33	56,789	41,689	5844	92,634	56,789	35,845	61.31	38.69
1980-1	117,891	58.72	41.28	69,223	48,668	6102	111,789	69,223	42,566	61.92	38.08
1981-2	137,348	56.83	43.17	78,057	59,291	6826	130,522	78,057	52,465	59.80	40.20
1982-3	152,350	57.29	42.71	87,285	65,065	7686	144,664	87,285	57,379	60.34	39.66
1983-4	179,065	57.26	42.74	102,534	76,531	8792	170,273	102,534	67,739	60.22	39.78
1984-5	200,218	58.70	41.30	117,528	82,690	9952	190,266	117,528	72,738	61.77	38.23
1985-6	222,830	57.70	42.30	128,581	94,249	11,454	211,376	128,581	82,795	60.83	39.17
1986-7	247,869	60.40	39.60	149,713	98,156	13,049	234,820	149,713	85,107	63.76	36.24
1987-8	282,019	61.21	38.79	172,622	109,397	15,120	266,899	172,622	94,277	64.68	35.32
1988-9	338,798	58.30	41.70	197,533	141,265	17,584	321,214	197,533	123,681	61.50	38.50
1989-90	391,460	55.92	44.08	218,909	172,551	20,418	371,042	218,909	152,133	59.00	41.00
1990-1	457,690	56.53	43.47	258,716	198,974	23,562	434,128	258,716	175,412	59.59	40.41
1991-2	524,684	57.07	42.93	299,456	225,228	26,957	497,727	299,456	198,271	60.16	39.84
1992-3	598,709	58.38	41.62	349,510	249,199	31,286	567,423	349,510	217,913	61.60	38.40
1993-4	697,992	51.90	48.10	362,277	335,715	36,132	661,860	362,277	299,583	54.74	45.26
1994-5	819,064	49.67	50.33	406,794	412,270	39,228	779,836	406,794	373,042	52.16	47.84
1995-6	955,345	52.27	47.73	499,339	456,006	43,222	912,123	499,339	412,784	54.74	45.26
1996-7	1,107,043	47.96	52.04	530,921	576,122	47,549	1,059,494	530,921	528,573	50.11	49.89
1997-8	1,237,992	50.74	49.26	628,211	609,781	51,741	1,186,251	628,211	558,040	52.96	47.04
1998-9	1,449,424	49.54	50.46	718,103	731,321	59,719	1,389,705	718,103	671,602	51.67	48.33
1999-2000	1,605,732	49.54	50.46	795,498	810,234	69,475	1,536,257	795,498	740,759	51.78	48.22

Sources: Col. (1) from NAS 1950–1 to 1992–3 and NAS 2001; Cols (2) and (3) from 1950–1 to 1959–60 from Appendix Table 2(h), Cols (20) and (21) and from 1960–1 to 1999–2000 from Table Appendix 2(f), Cols (10) and (11); Col. (4) = Col. (1) × Col. (2)/100; Col. (5) = Col. (1) × Col. (3)/100; Col. (6) from Appendix Table 1(b), Col. (9); Col. (7) = Col. (1) – Col. (6); Col. (8) = Col (4); Col (9) = Col. (7)–(8); Cols (10) and (11) derived.

28

unorganized sector; hence the allocation of mixed income according to labour income and non-labour income assumes importance. From the data available on factor incomes of Sector A according to the different series, viz. 1960–1, 1970–1, 1980–1, and 1993–4 series, comparable estimates of NDP from Sector A and its distribution by factor incomes, especially the components compensation of employees in the case of both organized and unorganized agriculture and operating surplus in the case of organized sector have been obtained by splicing for the years 1960–1 to 1992–3. For the years 1993–4 to 1998–9, actual values reported in the National Accounts Statistics have been used and for 1999–2000 the relevant figures have been estimated. Mixed income has been obtained as a residual. The allocation of mixed income into compensation of employees and operating surplus has been done on the same assumption as adopted earlier. By adding the allocated components to those already reported, the distribution of NDP from Sector A by factor incomes is obtained for 1960–1 to 1999–2000. The percentage shares of labour and non-labour income are shown in Cols (20) and (21) of Appendix Table 2(i). For the preceding years 1950–1 to 1959–60, the percentage shares of labour and non-labour income in Sector A have been taken from Dholakia's calculations,[19] shown in Appendix Table 2(h).

Estimates of compensation of employees in the unorganized Sector A for hired labour and family labour separately are provided in *National Accounts Statistics, Factor Incomes (New Series) 1980–1 to 1989–90* by the CSO.[20] The percentage share of compensation of employees to NDP from Sector A including the organized sector as estimated by the CSO and as calculated by me are shown below:

Compensation of Employees as Percentage of NDP
for Sector A, 1980–1 to 1989–90

Year	CSO estimates	My estimates
	(1)	(2)
1980–1	60.26	60.38
1981–2	60.41	58.90
1982–3	59.95	59.91
1983–4	55.27	59.55
1984–5	59.38	61.59
1985–6	60.56	60.14
1986–7	61.98	64.18
1987–8	61.44	64.33
1988–9	55.43	60.38
1989–90	54.51	57.01

Sources: Col. 1 from CSO, NAS, Factor Incomes, 1980–1 to 1989–90, p. 65; Col. (2) from Appendix Table 2(j).

[19] Dholakia, *The Sources of Economic Growth in India*, p. 75.
[20] CSO *National Accounts Statistics, Factor Incomes (New Series), 1980–1 to 1989–90*, New Delhi, March 1994, Statement 13, p. 65.

The relative shares of compensation of employees for the years 1980–1 to 1985–6 are close to each other while those for the remaining years differ considerably.

The percentage shares of labour income from Sector A obtained by our calculations are applied to the CSO estimates of NDP from Sector A. Non-labour income is taken as a residual. The factor incomes for Sector non-A derived as residuals using the distribution by factor income of total NDP and NDP from Sector A are shown in Appendix Table 2(j).

DISTRIBUTION OF GDP BY FACTOR INCOMES

The output indicator adopted in this study is the GDP, especially non-residential GDP. Hence it is necessary to derive the distribution of GDP by factor incomes. This is done by deducting labour income estimates derived above [Appendix Table 2(j), Cols (3), (7), and (10)] from the corresponding estimates of total GDP, non-residential GDP, GDP for Sector A, and GDP for Sector non-A (non-residential). These are presented in Table 2.2.

Labour income as share of non-residential sector GDP declined from 62.6 per cent in 1950–1 to 47 per cent in 1999–2000. The share of non-labour income has risen from 37 per cent to 53 per cent in the same period. This latter share needs to be further distributed between non-residential structures and construction, machinery and equipment, inventories, and land to derive the weighting structures for inputs. This is considered in Chapter 4.

Table 2.2: Distribution of GDP at Current Prices by Factor Incomes, 1950-1 to 1999-2000

Year	Whole economy					Non-residential sector				
	GDP CSO estimates (Rs crore)	Labour income (Rs crore)	Non-labour income (Rs crore)	% to GDP		GDP (Rs crore)	Labour income (Rs crore)	Non-labour income (Rs crore)	% to GDP	
				Labour income	Non-labour income				Labour income (Rs crore)	Non-labour income (Rs crore)
	(1)	(2)	(3)	(4)	(5)	(6)	(7)	(8)	(9)	(10)
1950–1	9547	4964	4583	52.00	48.00	8699	4964	3735	57.07	42.93
1951–2	10,080	5187	4893	51.46	48.54	9172	5187	3985	56.55	43.45
1952–3	9941	5134	4807	51.64	48.36	8967	5134	3833	57.25	42.75
1953–4	10,824	5409	5415	49.97	50.03	9778	5409	4369	55.32	44.68
1954–5	10,168	5137	5031	50.52	49.48	9042	5137	3905	56.82	43.18
1955–6	10,332	5241	5091	50.72	49.28	9128	5241	3887	57.42	42.58
1956–7	12,334	6137	6197	49.76	50.24	11,042	6137	4905	55.58	44.42
1957–8	12,610	6672	5938	52.91	47.09	11,227	6672	4555	59.43	40.57
1958–9	14,106	7161	6945	50.77	49.23	12,625	7161	5464	56.72	43.28
1959–60	14,816	7686	7130	51.87	48.13	13,228	7686	5542	58.10	41.90
1960–1	16,220	8199	8021	50.55	49.45	14,518	8199	6319	56.48	43.52
1961–2	17,116	8506	8610	49.70	50.30	15,399	8506	6893	55.24	44.76
1962–3	18,302	9205	9097	50.30	49.70	16,344	9205	7139	56.32	43.68
1963–4	20,916	10,394	10,522	49.69	50.31	18,805	10,394	8411	55.27	44.73
1964–5	24,436	12,257	12,179	50.16	49.84	22,165	12,257	9908	55.30	44.70
1965–6	25,586	13,094	12,492	51.18	48.82	23,158	13,094	10,064	56.54	43.46
1966–7	29,123	15,242	13,881	52.34	47.66	26,534	15,242	11,292	57.44	42.56
1967–8	34,225	18,924	15,301	55.29	44.71	31,404	18,924	12,480	60.26	39.74
1968–9	36,092	20,113	15,979	55.73	44.27	33,082	20,113	12,969	60.80	39.20
1969–70	39,691	21,456	18,235	54.06	45.94	36,487	21,456	15,031	58.80	41.20
1970–1	42,222	22,851	19,371	54.12	45.88	38,795	22,851	15,944	58.90	41.10
1971–2	44,923	24,191	20,732	53.85	46.15	41,220	24,191	17,029	58.69	41.31
1972–3	49,415	26,974	22,441	54.59	45.41	45,410	26,974	18,436	59.40	40.60

(Contd.)

31

Table 2.2 Contd.

	(1)	(2)	(3)	(4)	(5)	(6)	(7)	(8)	(9)	(10)
1973-4	60,560	32,081	28,479	52.97	47.03	56,218	32,081	24,137	57.06	42.94
1974-5	71,283	36,853	34,430	51.70	48.30	66,564	36,853	29,711	55.36	44.64
1975-6	75,709	40,411	35,298	53.38	46.62	70,584	40,411	30,173	57.25	42.75
1976-7	81,381	42,161	39,220	51.81	48.19	75,815	42,161	33,654	55.61	44.39
1977-8	92,881	49,745	43,136	53.56	46.44	86,854	49,745	37,109	57.27	42.73
1978-9	99,823	53,142	46,681	53.24	46.76	93,344	53,142	40,202	56.93	43.07
1979-80	108,927	56,789	52,138	52.14	47.86	101,929	56,789	45,140	55.71	44.29
1980-1	130,178	69,223	60,955	53.18	46.82	122,712	69,223	53,489	56.41	43.59
1981-2	152,056	78,057	73,999	51.33	48.67	143,530	78,057	65,473	54.38	45.62
1982-3	169,525	87,285	82,240	51.49	48.51	159,777	87,285	72,492	54.63	45.37
1983-4	198,630	102,534	96,096	51.62	48.38	187,480	102,534	84,946	54.69	45.31
1984-5	222,706	117,528	105,178	52.77	47.23	210,043	117,528	92,515	55.95	44.05
1985-6	249,547	128,581	120,966	51.53	48.47	235,022	128,581	106,441	54.71	45.29
1986-7	278,258	149,713	128,545	53.80	46.20	261,657	149,713	111,944	57.22	42.78
1987-8	315,993	172,622	143,371	54.63	45.37	296,942	172,622	124,320	58.13	41.87
1988-9	378,491	197,533	180,958	52.19	47.81	356,602	197,533	159,069	55.39	44.61
1989-90	438,020	218,909	219,111	49.98	50.02	412,948	218,909	194,039	53.01	46.99
1990-1	510,954	258,716	252,238	50.63	49.37	482,385	258,716	223,669	53.63	46.37
1991-2	589,086	299,456	289,630	50.83	49.17	556,302	299,456	256,846	53.83	46.17
1992-3	673,221	349,510	323,711	51.92	48.08	635,554	349,510	286,044	54.99	45.01
1993-4	781,345	362,277	419,068	46.37	53.63	738,075	362,277	375,798	49.08	50.92
1994-5	917,058	406,794	510,264	44.36	55.64	870,590	406,794	463,796	46.73	53.27
1995-6	1,073,271	499,339	573,932	46.52	53.48	1,022,746	499,339	523,407	48.82	51.18
1996-7	1,243,546	530,921	712,625	42.69	57.31	1,188,567	530,921	657,646	44.67	55.33
1997-8	1,390,042	628,211	761,831	45.19	54.81	1,330,767	628,211	702,556	47.21	52.79
1998-9	1,616,033	718,103	897,930	44.44	55.56	1,548,568	718,103	830,465	46.37	53.63
1999-2000	1,786,459	795,498	990,961	44.53	55.47	1,708,954	795,498	913,456	46.55	53.45

(Cols Contd.)

32

Table 2.2 Contd.: Distribution of GDP at Current Prices by Factor Incomes, 1950–1 to 1999–2000

Year	Sector A					Non-residential non-agricultural sector				
	GDP (Rs crore)	Labour income (Rs crore)	Non-labour income (Rs crore)	% to GDP Labour income	Non-labour income	GDP (Rs crore)	Labour income (Rs crore)	Non-labour income (Rs crore)	% to GDP Labour income (Rs crore)	Non-labour income (Rs crore)
	(11)	(12)	(13)	(14)	(15)	(16)	(17)	(18)	(19)	(20)
1950–1	5432	2919	2513	53.74	46.26	3267	2045	1222	62.60	37.40
1951–2	5609	2993	2616	53.35	46.65	3563	2195	1368	61.59	38.41
1952–3	5464	2870	2594	52.52	47.48	3503	2264	1239	64.63	35.37
1953–4	6020	2979	3041	49.49	50.51	3758	2430	1328	64.65	35.35
1954–5	5121	2556	2565	49.92	50.08	3921	2581	1340	65.82	34.18
1955–6	4966	2543	2423	51.20	48.80	4162	2698	1464	64.82	35.18
1956–7	6309	3148	3161	49.90	50.10	4733	2989	1744	63.16	36.84
1957–8	6178	3464	2714	56.08	43.92	5049	3208	1841	63.53	36.47
1958–9	7168	3739	3429	52.16	47.84	5457	3422	2035	62.71	37.29
1959–60	7201	3951	3250	54.86	45.14	6027	3735	2292	61.97	38.03
1960–1	7581	4385	3196	57.84	42.16	6937	3814	3123	54.98	45.02
1961–2	7852	4460	3392	56.80	43.20	7547	4046	3501	53.62	46.38
1962–3	8017	4686	3331	58.45	41.55	8327	4519	3808	54.27	45.73
1963–4	9435	4818	4617	51.06	48.94	9370	5576	3794	59.51	40.49
1964–5	11,528	6588	4940	57.15	42.85	10,637	5669	4968	53.29	46.71
1965–6	11,496	6728	4768	58.53	41.47	11,662	6365	5297	54.58	45.42
1966–7	13,373	7893	5480	59.02	40.98	13,161	7349	5812	55.84	44.16
1967–8	16,735	10,301	6434	61.55	38.45	14,669	8623	6046	58.78	41.22
1968–9	17,250	10,764	6486	62.40	37.60	15,832	9349	6483	59.05	40.95
1969–70	18,867	11,332	7535	60.06	39.94	17,620	10,123	7497	57.45	42.55
1970–1	19,453	11,608	7845	59.67	40.33	19,342	11,243	8099	58.13	41.87
1971–2	19,872	11,833	8039	59.55	40.45	21,348	12,358	8990	57.89	42.11
1972–3	21,857	13,235	8622	60.55	39.45	23,553	13,739	9814	58.33	41.67
1973–4	28,803	16,354	12,449	56.78	43.22	27,415	15,727	11,688	57.37	42.63

(Contd.)

33

Table 2.2 Contd.

	(11)	(12)	(13)	(14)	(15)	(16)	(17)	(18)	(19)	(20)
1974–5	31,555	17,195	14,360	54.49	45.51	35,009	19,657	15,352	56.15	43.85
1975–6	31,276	18,114	13,162	57.92	42.08	39,308	22,296	17,012	56.72	43.28
1976–7	31,953	18,215	13,738	57.01	42.99	43,862	23,945	19,917	54.59	45.41
1977–8	37,832	21,868	15,964	57.80	42.20	49,022	27,877	21,145	56.87	43.13
1978–9	38,881	23,169	15,712	59.59	40.41	54,463	29,973	24,490	55.03	44.97
1979–80	40,223	23,660	16,563	58.82	41.18	61,706	33,129	28,577	53.69	46.31
1980–1	50,592	29,137	21,455	57.59	42.41	72,120	40,086	32,034	55.58	44.42
1981–2	56,883	31,916	24,967	56.11	43.89	86,647	46,141	40,506	53.25	46.75
1982–3	60,881	34,623	26,258	56.87	43.13	98,896	52,661	46,235	53.25	46.75
1983–4	72,729	41,256	31,473	56.73	43.27	114,751	61,278	53,473	53.40	46.60
1984–5	78,288	45,829	32,459	58.54	41.46	131,755	71,699	60,056	54.42	45.58
1985–6	84,152	47,890	36,262	56.91	43.09	150,870	80,690	70,180	53.48	46.52
1986–7	90,541	54,946	35,595	60.69	39.31	171,116	94,768	76,348	55.38	44.62
1987–8	100,759	61,317	39,442	60.85	39.15	196,183	111,306	84,877	56.74	43.26
1988–9	123,901	71,081	52,820	57.37	42.63	232,701	126,452	106,249	54.34	45.66
1989–90	136,891	73,976	62,915	54.04	45.96	276,057	144,933	131,124	52.50	47.50
1990–1	159,760	88,259	71,501	55.24	44.76	322,625	170,456	152,169	52.83	47.17
1991–2	185,712	105,104	80,608	56.60	43.40	370,590	194,352	176,238	52.44	47.56
1992–3	208,265	121,963	86,302	58.56	41.44	427,289	227,548	199,741	53.25	46.75
1993–4	241,967	122,037	119,930	50.44	49.56	496,108	240,240	255,868	48.42	51.58
1994–5	278,773	134,551	144,222	48.27	51.73	591,817	272,243	319,574	46.00	54.00
1995–6	303,102	160,471	142,631	52.94	47.06	719,644	338,868	380,776	47.09	52.91
1996–7	362,605	163,421	199,184	45.07	54.93	825,962	367,500	458,462	44.49	55.51
1997–8	387,008	185,880	201,128	48.03	51.97	943,759	442,330	501,429	46.87	53.13
1998–9	459,900	208,768	251,132	45.39	54.61	1,088,668	509,335	579,333	46.79	53.21
1999–2000	484,221	219,458	264,763	45.32	54.68	1,224,733	576,040	648,693	47.03	52.97

Sources: Col. (1) from NAS 1950–1 to 1992–3 and NAS 2001; Col. (2) from Table 2.1, Col. (4); Col. (3) = Col. (1)–Col. (2); Cols (4) and (5) derived; Col. (6) from Appendix Table 1(d), Col. (3); Col. (7) = Col. (2); Col. (8) = Col. (6)–Col. (7); Cols (9) and (10) derived; Col. (11) from Appendix Table 1(d), Col (4); Col (12) from Appendix Table 2(i), Col. (7); Col. (13) = Col. 11–Col. (12); Cols. (14) and (15) derived; Col. (16) from Appendix Table 1(d), Col. (5); Col. (17) from Appendix Table 2(i), Col. (10); Col. (18) = Col (16)–Col. (17); Cols (19) and (20) derived.

APPENDIX: 2

Appendix Table 2(a): NDP from Organized and Unorganized Sectors at Current Prices, 1960-1 to 1999-2000

| Year | Total NDP (Rs crore) | | | | NDP from organized sector (Rs crore) | | | | NDP from unorganized sector 1993-4 prices (Rs crore) | % share in NDP | |
| | 1960-1 series | 1970-1 series | 1980-1 series | 1993-4 series by splicing* | 1960-1 series | 1970-1 series | 1980-1 series | 1993-4 series | | Organized sector | Unorganized sector |
	(1)	(2)	(3)	(4)	(5)	(6)	(7)	(8)	(9)	(10)	(11)
1960-1	13,335			15,151	3409			3319	11,832	21.91	78.09
1961-2	14,085			16,003	3748			3649	12,354	22.80	77.20
1962-3	14,903			16,933	4201			4091	12,842	24.16	75.84
1963-4	17,089			19,417	4870			4742	14,675	24.42	75.58
1964-5	20,148			22,892	5432			5289	17,603	23.10	76.90
1965-6	20,801			23,634	6070			5910	17,724	25.01	74.99
1966-7	24,078			27,357	6584			6411	20,947	23.43	76.57
1967-8	28,312			32,168	7096			6909	25,259	21.48	78.52
1968-9	28,862			32,793	7811			7606	25,187	23.19	76.81
1969-70	31,877			36,219	8828			8596	27,623	23.73	76.27
1970-1	34,746	34,519		38,996	9832	9483		9460	29,536	24.26	75.74
1971-2	36,623	36,864		41,645	10,917	10,641		10,615	31,030	25.49	74.51
1972-3	39,945	40,572		45,834	11,880	11,724		11,696	34,138	25.52	74.48
1973-4	49,720	50,749		57,331	13,578	13,387		13,355	43,976	23.29	76.71
1974-5	58,485	59,737		67,485	16,853	16,881		16,840	50,644	24.95	75.05
1975-6		62,324		70,407		19,084		19,038	51,369	27.04	72.96
1976-7		67,157		75,867		22,201		22,148	53,720	29.19	70.81
1977-8		75,907		85,752		24,256		24,198	61,554	28.22	71.78
1978-9		81,588		92,170		27,243		27,178	64,992	29.49	70.51
1979-80		88,774		100,288		30,875		30,801	69,487	30.71	69.29
1980-1		105,877	110,339	117,544		35,493	33,073	34,489	83,056	29.34	70.66
1981-2		120,813	128,756	137,164		42,134	40,628	42,367	94,797	30.89	69.11

(Contd.)

Appendix Table 2(a) Contd.

	(1)	(2)	(3)	(4)	(5)	(6)	(7)	(8)	(9)	(10)	(11)
1982–3		133,151	142,510	151,816		49,230	47,660	49,700	102,116	32.74	67.26
1983–4			167,494	178,431			55,943	58,337	120,094	32.69	67.31
1984–5			186,442	198,617			64,164	66,910	131,706	33.69	66.31
1985–6			207,562	221,116			72,376	75,474	145,642	34.13	65.87
1986–7			230,207	245,240			83,972	87,566	157,674	35.71	64.29
1987–8			261,510	278,587			95,317	99,397	179,190	35.68	64.32
1988–9			314,596	335,139			113,275	118,123	217,016	35.25	64.75
1989–90			363,016	386,721			131,656	137,291	249,430	35.50	64.50
1990–1			425,619	453,412			153,947	160,536	292,876	35.41	64.59
1991–2			489,689	521,666			179,604	187,291	334,375	35.90	64.10
1992–3			557,826	594,252			203,831	212,555	381,697	35.77	64.23
1993–4			651,322	697,385			245,795	256,849	440,536	36.83	63.17
1994–5			772,680	818,322			295,644	306,425	511,897	37.45	62.55
1995–6			894,700	954,519			360,976	377,768	576,751	39.58	60.42
1996–7				1,106,044				426,911	679,133	38.60	61.40
1997–8				1,236,994				485,946	751,048	39.28	60.72
1998–9				1,448,321				564,889	883,432	39.00	61.00
1999–2000				1,605,732				625,754	979,978	38.97	61.03

Note: * up to 1992–3.

Sources: Cols (1) and (5) from *NAS October 1976*, pp. 22–3; Cols (2) and (6) from *NAS February 1980*, pp. 20–1, *NAS February 1982*, pp. 30–1, and *NAS February 1985*, pp. 32–3; Cols (3) and (7) from *NAS Factor Incomes, 1980–1 to 1989–90, 1994*, p. 65 and *NAS (Annual Issues)* from 1992 to 1998; Cols (4) and (8) for 1950–1 to 1992–3 estimated by splicing values in (1), (2), and (3) and (5), (6) and (7) respectively with the average value for 1993–4 to 1995–6; for 1993–4 to 1999–2000 from *NAS 2001*; Col. (9) = Col. (4) – Col. (8); Cols (10) and (11) derived.

Appendix Table 2(b): Factor Incomes of Organized Sector at Current Prices, 1960–1 to 1999–2000

Year	NDP (Rs crore)	Compensation of Employees (Rs crore)				Operating surplus (Rs crore)	% distribution of NDP	
		1960–1 series	1970–1 series	1980–1 series	1993–4 series		Compensation of employees	Operating surplus
	(1)	(2)	(3)	(4)	(5)	(6)	(7)	(8)
1960–1	3319	2273			2286	1033	68.87	31.13
1961–2	3649	2470			2484	1165	68.07	31.93
1962–3	4091	2784			2800	1291	68.45	31.55
1963–4	4742	3189			3207	1535	67.63	32.37
1964–5	5289	3616			3637	1653	68.76	31.24
1965–6	5910	4086			4109	1801	69.53	30.47
1966–7	6411	4530			4556	1855	71.06	28.94
1967–8	6909	5096			5125	1784	74.18	25.82
1968–9	7606	5613			5645	1961	74.22	25.78
1969–70	8596	6201			6236	2359	72.55	27.45
1970–1	9460	6935	6840		6867	2594	72.58	27.42
1971–2	10,615	7677	7679		7709	2907	72.62	27.38
1972–3	11,696	8496	8631		8665	3031	74.08	25.92
1973–4	13,355	9785	9735		9773	3582	73.18	26.82
1974–5	16,840	11,924	12,038		12,085	4756	71.76	28.24
1975–6	19,038		13,781		13,835	5203	72.67	27.33
1976–7	22,148		15,138		15,197	6951	68.62	31.38
1977–8	24,198		16,767		16,832	7365	69.56	30.44
1978–9	27,178		18,870		18,944	8234	69.70	30.30
1979–80	30,801		21,223		21,306	9495	69.17	30.83
1980–1	34,489		24,809	24,550	24,577	9912	71.26	28.74
1981–2	42,367		28,156	28,499	28,530	13,837	67.34	32.66

(Contd.)

37

Appendix Table 2(b) Contd.

	(1)	(2)	(3)	(4)	(5)	(6)	(7)	(8)
1982–3	49,700		33,008	33,169	33,205	16,494	66.81	33.19
1983–4	58,337			39,110	39,153	19,184	67.11	32.89
1984–5	66,910			45,673	45,723	21,187	68.34	31.66
1985–6	75,474			50,981	51,037	24,437	67.62	32.38
1986–7	87,566			59,763	59,829	27,737	68.32	31.68
1987–8	99,397			69,451	69,527	29,869	69.95	30.05
1988–9	118,123			79,593	79,681	38,443	67.46	32.54
1989–90	137,291			90,578	90,678	46,613	66.05	33.95
1990–1	160,536			105,198	105,314	55,222	65.60	34.40
1991–2	187,291			120,587	120,720	66,571	64.46	35.54
1992–3	212,555			137,785	137,937	74,618	64.89	35.11
1993–4	256,849			153,140	153,983	102,866	59.95	40.05
1994–5	306,425			177,424	175,255	131,170	57.19	42.81
1995–6	377,768			216,049	217,960	159,808	57.70	42.30
1996–7	426,911				242,123	184,788	56.72	43.28
1997–8	485,946				287,356	198,590	59.13	40.87
1998–9	564,889				335,252	229,637	59.35	40.65
1999–2000	625,754				371,385	254,369	59.35	40.65

Sources: Col. (1) from Appendix Table 2(a), Col. (8); Col. (2) from *NAS October 1976*; Col. (3) from *NAS February 1980, NAS February 1982*, and *NAS February 1985*; Col. (4) from *NAS Factor Incomes, 1980–1 to 1989–90*, p. 65 and *NAS (Annual Issues)*, 1992 to 1998; Col. (5) from 1993–4 to 1999–2000 from *NAS 2001*, pp. 84–7 and for 1950–1 to 1992–3 spliced using values in Cols (2), (3) and (4); Col. (6) = Col. (1) ÷ Col. (5); Cols (7) and (8) derived.

38

Appendix Table 2(c): Factor Incomes of Unorganized Sector at Current Prices, 1960–1 to 1999–2000

Year	NDP (Rs crore)	Compensation of Employees (Rs crore)				Interest (Rs crore)				Rent (Rs crore)	
		1960–1 series	1970–1 series	1980–1 series	1993–4 series	1960–1 series	1970–1 series	1980–1 series	1993–4 series	1960–1 series	1970–1 series
	(1)	(2)	(3)	(4)	(5)	(6)	(7)	(8)	(9)	(10)	(11)
1960–1	11,832	2224			2258	228			242	646	
1961–2	12,354	2288			2323	262			278	683	
1962–3	12,842	2533			2571	315			335	746	
1963–4	14,675	2678			2718	355			377	850	
1964–5	17,603	2999			3044	389			413	913	
1965–6	17,724	3288			3338	455			484	937	
1966–7	20,947	3808			3866	459			488	984	
1967–8	25,259	4596			4665	540			574	995	
1968–9	25,187	4685			4756	582			619	1067	
1969–70	27,623	5078			5155	665			707	1150	
1970–1	29,536	5299	6523		5681	713	794		656	1222	1607
1971–2	31,030	5486	6778		5903	766	931		769	1379	1774
1972–3	34,138	5747	7173		6247	862	1284		1061	1586	1896
1973–4	43,976	6645	8083		7039	972	1304		1077	1707	1934
1974–5	50,644	7353	9312		8110	1103	1696		1401	1657	2053
1975–6	51,369		10,560		9197		1906		1574		2371
1976–7	53,720		11,433		9957		2302		1901		2685
1977–8	61,554		13,935		12,136		2491		2058		2831
1978–9	64,992		14,902		12,978		2847		2352		3160
1979–80	69,487		16,297		14,193		2997		2476		3505
1980–1	83,056		18,302	16,047	16,078		3408	3230	2703		3600
1981–2	94,797		20,705	18,065	18,100		4118	4041	3382		4031
1982–3	102,116		22,757	19,574	19,612		4472	4577	3830		4252
1983–4	120,094			22,915	22,959			5353	4479		

(Contd.)

39

Appendix Table 2(c) Contd.

	(1)	(2)	(3)	(4)	(5)	(6)	(7)	(8)	(9)	(10)	(11)
1984–5	131,706			26,015	26,065			6414	5367		
1985–6	145,642			28,856	28,911			7819	6543		
1986–7	157,674			31,421	31,481			8596	7193		
1987–8	179,190			35,732	35,801			9850	8242		
1988–9	217,016			42,755	42,837			11,496	9620		
1989–90	249,430			49,774	49,870			13,736	11,494		
1990–1	292,876			58,253	58,365			15,192	12,713		
1991–2	334,375			65,637	65,763			17,536	14,674		
1992–3	381,697			73,992	74,134			19,246	16,105		
1993–4	440,536			84,917	81,847			22,435	19,163		
1994–5	511,897			99,370	101,110			25,313	20,839		
1995–6	576,751			113,101	115,001			29,211	24,397		
1996–7	679,133				132,297				27,277		
1997–8	751,048				152,747				31,065		
1998–9	883,432				178,266				32,423		
1999–2000	979,978				197,750				35,965		

(Cols Contd.)

Appendix Table 2(c) Contd.: Factor Incomes of Unorganized Sector at Current Prices, 1960–1 to 1999–2000

Year	Rent (Rs crore)		Mixed income self-employed (Rs crore)	% of CE to NDP of private sector	Distribution of mixed income of self-employed (Rs crore)		Distribution of NDP from unorganized sector (Rs crore)		% distribution of NDP from unorganized sector		Mixed income as % of NDP of unorganized sector
	1980-1 series	1993-4 series			CE	OS	CE	OS	Total CE	OS	
	(12)	(13)	(14)	(15)	(16)	(17)	(18)	(19)	(20)	(21)	(22)
1960-1		2139	7193	49.89	3589	3604	5846	5986	49.41	50.59	60.79
1961-2		2262	7491	49.00	3670	3821	5993	6361	48.51	51.49	60.64
1962-3		2470	7466	49.89	3724	3741	6296	6547	49.02	50.98	58.13
1963-4		2815	8764	49.86	4370	4394	7088	7587	48.30	51.70	59.72
1964-5		3023	11,122	49.81	5540	5582	8584	9019	48.77	51.23	63.18
1965-6		3103	10,800	50.86	5493	5307	8830	8894	49.82	50.18	60.93
1966-7		3259	13,335	52.03	6938	6397	10,803	10,143	51.58	48.42	63.66
1967-8		3295	16,724	55.19	9231	7494	13,896	11,363	55.02	44.98	66.21
1968-9		3533	16,280	56.42	9185	7095	13,941	11,247	55.35	44.65	64.63
1969-70		3808	17,953	53.50	9604	8349	14,759	12,864	53.43	46.57	64.99
1970-1		4222	18,977	53.51	10,154	8823	15,835	13,701	53.61	46.39	64.25
1971-2		4663	19,695	53.76	10,588	9108	16,490	14,539	53.14	46.86	63.47
1972-3		4983	21,847	55.59	12,145	9702	18,392	15,746	53.88	46.12	64.00
1973-4		5083	30,776	51.67	15,902	14,875	22,941	21,035	52.17	47.83	69.98
1974-5		5396	35,738	49.38	17,646	18,092	25,756	24,889	50.86	49.14	70.57
1975-6		6232	34,366	52.52	18,049	16,317	27,245	24,124	53.04	46.96	66.90
1976-7		7057	34,804	51.13	17,795	17,009	27,752	25,968	51.66	48.34	64.79
1977-8		7441	39,920	52.58	20,991	18,929	33,127	28,427	53.82	46.18	64.85
1978-9		8306	41,357	52.61	21,756	19,600	34,734	30,258	53.44	46.56	63.63
1979-80		9213	43,606	51.22	22,334	21,272	36,527	32,960	52.57	47.43	62.75
1980-1	1654	8987	55,288	51.30	28,365	26,923	44,443	38,613	53.51	46.49	66.57
1981-2	1921	10,438	62,878	49.81	31,322	31,555	49,422	45,375	52.13	47.87	66.33

(Contd.)

41

Appendix Table 2(c) Contd.

	(12)	(13)	(14)	(15)	(16)	(17)	(18)	(19)	(20)	(21)	(22)
1982–3	2171	11,797	66,878	51.08	34,162	32,716	53,773	48,343	52.66	47.34	65.49
1983–4	2560	13,910	78,745	50.87	40,059	38,686	63,018	57,076	52.47	47.53	65.57
1984–5	2881	15,654	84,620	52.94	44,800	39,820	70,865	60,842	53.81	46.19	64.25
1985–6	3094	16,812	93,376	51.02	47,643	45,733	76,554	69,088	52.56	47.44	64.11
1986–7	3351	18,208	100,791	56.37	56,815	43,976	88,296	69,377	56.00	44.00	63.92
1987–8	3734	20,289	114,858	56.76	65,193	49,664	100,994	78,196	56.36	43.64	64.10
1988–9	4490	24,397	140,162	52.00	72,882	67,280	115,719	101,297	53.32	46.68	64.59
1989–90	5371	29,184	158,882	47.65	75,711	83,171	125,581	123,849	50.35	49.65	63.70
1990–1	6,246	33,939	187,860	49.30	92,619	95,241	150,984	141,892	51.55	48.45	64.14
1991–2	7,151	38,856	215,081	51.72	111,250	103,831	177,013	157,361	52.94	47.06	64.32
1992–3	8,251	44,833	246,624	54.67	134,838	111,787	208,972	172,725	54.75	45.25	64.61
1993–4	9711	51,648	287,878	43.81	126,132	161,746	207,979	232,557	47.21	52.79	65.35
1994–5	11,446	61,862	328,086	39.64	130,060	198,026	231,170	280,727	45.16	54.84	64.09
1995–6	13,145	72,877	364,476	45.53	165,946	198,530	280,947	295,804	48.71	51.29	63.19
1996–7		81,048	438,511	35.58	156,021	282,490	288,318	390,815	42.45	57.55	64.57
1997–8		89,252	477,984	39.25	187,601	290,383	340,348	410,700	45.32	54.68	63.64
1998–9		106,456	566,287	36.03	204,039	362,248	382,305	501,127	43.27	56.73	64.10
1999–2000		118,087	628,176	36.03	226,363	401,813	424,113	555,865	43.28	56.72	64.10

Note: CE = Compensation of employees
OS = Operating surplus

Sources: Col. (1) from Appendix Table 2(a), Col. (9); Cols (2), (6), (10): *National Accounts Statistics*, October 1976; Cols (3), (7), (11): *National Accounts Statistics*, February 1980, 1982, 1985; Cols (4), (8), (12): *National Accounts Statistics*, 'Factor Incomes', 1980–1 to 1989–90, p. 65 and *National Accounts Statistics*, Annual issues, 1992 to 1998; Cols (5), (9), and (13) derived as in Appendix Table 2(b). Col. (14) = Col. (1) – Col. (5) – Col. (9) – Col. (13); Col. (15) from Appendix Table 2(d), Col. (10); Col. (16) = Col. (14) × Col. (15); Col. (17) = Col. (14) – Col. (16); Col. (18) = Col. (5) + Col. (16); Col. (19) = Col. (1) – Col. (18); Cols (20) and (21) derived; Col. (22) = Col. (14)/Col. (1) × 100.

Appendix Table 2(d): Factor Incomes in Private Organized Sector, 1960–1 to 1999–2000

Year	NDP (Rs crore)				Compensation of employees (Rs crore)				Operating surplus (Rs crore)	% distribution of NDP	
	1960–1 series	1970–1 Series	1980–1 series	1993–4 series	1960–1 series	1970–1 series	1980–1 series	1993–4 series		CE	OS
	(1)	(2)	(3)	(4)	(5)	(6)	(7)	(8)	(9)	(10)	(11)
1960–1	1987			2178	1105			1087	1091	49.89	50.11
1961–2	2146			2352	1172			1153	1199	49.00	51.00
1962–3	2365			2593	1315			1293	1300	49.89	50.11
1963–4	2737			3000	1521			1496	1504	49.86	50.14
1964–5	3051			3345	1694			1666	1679	49.81	50.19
1965–6	3327			3647	1886			1855	1792	50.86	49.14
1966–7	3516			3854	2039			2005	1849	52.03	47.97
1967–8	3633			3983	2235			2198	1784	55.19	44.81
1968–9	3872			4245	2435			2395	1850	56.42	43.58
1969–70	4357			4776	2598			2555	2221	53.50	46.50
1970–1	4784	4476		5108	2883	2793		2733	2375	53.51	46.49
1971–2	5229	5020		5729	3146	3147		3080	2649	53.76	46.24
1972–3	5608	5510		6288	3437	3572		3496	2792	55.59	44.41
1973–4	6361	6159		7029	3858	3711		3632	3397	51.67	48.33
1974–5	7790	7355		8394	4494	4235		4144	4249	49.38	50.62
1975–6		7710		8799		4722		4621	4178	52.52	47.48
1976–7		8822		10,068		5260		5147	4920	51.13	48.87
1977–8		9726		11,099		5964		5836	5263	52.58	47.42
1978–9		11,104		12,672		6812		6666	6006	52.61	47.39
1979–80		12,386		14,135		7398		7240	6895	51.22	48.78
1980–1		13,950	13797	15,135		8268	7785	7765	7370	51.30	48.70
1981–2		15,802	16,628	18,240		8945	9110	9086	9154	49.81	50.19
1982–3		17,181	18,400	20,184		10,419	10,337	10,310	9874	51.08	48.92
1983–4			21,757	23,867			12,173	12,141	11,725	50.87	49.13

(Contd.)

43

Appendix Table 2(d) Contd.

	(1)	(2)	(3)	(4)	(5)	(6)	(7)	(8)	(9)	(10)	(11)
1984–5			24,425	26,793			14,222	14,185	12,608	52.94	47.06
1985–6			25,483	27,954			14,300	14,263	13,691	51.02	48.98
1986–7			28,034	30,752			17,380	17,335	13,417	56.37	43.63
1987–8			30,766	33,749			19,206	19,156	14,593	56.76	43.24
1988–9			36,717	40,277			20,998	20,943	19,334	52.00	48.00
1989–90			43,250	47,444			22,667	22,608	24,835	47.65	52.35
1990–1			52,007	57,050			28,200	28,127	28,923	49.30	50.70
1991–2			57,796	63,400			32,879	32,794	30,606	51.72	48.28
1992–3			64,847	71,135			38,993	38,892	32,243	54.67	45.33
1993–4			81,748	91,721			42,155	40,187	51,534	43.81	56.19
1994–5			105,829	115,463			50,926	45,772	69,691	39.64	60.36
1995–6			144,943	157,577			65,029	71,745	85,832	45.53	54.47
1996–7				186,038				66,192	119,846	35.58	64.42
1997–8				195,162				76,598	118,564	39.25	60.75
1998–9				226,905				81,756	145,149	36.03	63.97
1999–2000				251,353				90,575	160,778	36.03	63.97

Sources: Cols (1) to (3) and Cols (5) to (7) from *NAS, October 1976*, pp. 22–3; *NAS, February 1980*, pp. 20–1; *NAS February 1982*, pp. 30–1, *NAS, February 1985*, pp. 32–3; *NAS Factor Incomes, 1980–1 to 1989–90*, p. 65; and *NAS (annual issues)* from 1992 to 1998; Cols (4) and (8) for 1993–4 to 1999–2000 from *NAS 2001*, pp. 184–7, 66–7; for 1950–1 to 1992–3 obtained by splicing; and for 1999–2000 estimated pro-rata on the basis of 1998–9 values, Col. (9) = Col. (4) – Col. (8); Cols (10) and (11) derived.

44

Appendix Table 2(e): Factor Incomes in Public Sector at Current Prices 1960–1 to 1999–2000

Year	NDP (Rs crore)				Compensation of employees (Rs crore)				Operating surplus (Rs crore)	% distribution of NDP	
	1960–1 series	1970–1 Series	1980–1 series	1993–4 series	1960–1 series	1970–1 series	1980–1 series	1993–4 series		CE	OS
	(1)	(2)	(3)	(4)	(5)	(6)	(7)	(8)	(9)	(10)	(11)
1960–1	645			935	391			797	138	85.21	14.79
1961–2	741			1075	437			891	184	82.90	17.10
1962–3	866			1256	499			1017	239	81.00	19.00
1963–4	1016			1473	551			1123	350	76.23	23.77
1964–5	1110			1610	651			1327	283	82.44	17.56
1965–6	1326			1923	783			1596	327	83.00	17.00
1966–7	1483			2151	906			1847	304	85.88	14.12
1967–8	1673			2426	1069			2179	247	89.82	10.18
1968–9	1962			2845	1201			2448	397	86.05	13.95
1969–70	2286			3315	1418			2891	425	87.19	12.81
1970–1	2647	2606		3797	1646	1646		3355	442	88.36	11.64
1971–2	2930	2930		4269	1841	1841		3753	517	87.90	12.10
1972–3	3272	3272		4768	2117	2117		4315	453	90.51	9.49
1973–4	3923	3923		5716	2719	2719		5542	174	96.95	3.05
1974–5	5171	5393		7858	3301	3670		7481	378	95.20	4.80
1975–6		6654		9696		4340		8846	849	91.24	8.76
1976–7		8206		11,957		4705		9590	2367	80.21	19.79
1977–8		8943		13,031		5216		10,632	2399	81.59	18.41
1978–9		9,945		14,491		5,864		11,953	2538	82.48	17.52
1979–80		11,517		16,781		6863		13,989	2793	83.36	16.64
1980–1		13,194	19,276	19,492		8192	16,765	17,239	2252	88.44	11.56
1981–2		16,668	24,000	24,269		9547	19,389	19,938	4331	82.15	17.85
1982–3		20,478	29,260	29,588		11,018	22,832	23,478	6110	79.35	20.65
1983–4			34,186	34,569			26,937	27,699	6870	80.13	19.87

(Contd.)

45

Appendix Table 2(e) Contd.

(1)	(2)	(3)	(4)	(5)	(6)	(7)	(8)	(9)	(10)	(11)
1984–5		39,739	40,184			31,451	32,341	7843	80.48	19.52
1985–6		46,938	47,464			36,681	37,719	9745	79.47	20.53
1986–7		55,938	56,565			42,383	43,582	12,982	77.05	22.95
1987–8		64,551	65,274			50,245	51,667	13,607	79.15	20.85
1988–9		76,558	77,415			58,595	60,253	17,162	77.83	22.17
1989–90		88,406	89,396			67,911	69,833	19,563	78.12	21.88
1990–1		101,940	103,082			76,998	79,177	23,905	76.81	23.19
1991–2		121,808	123,172			87,708	90,190	32,982	73.22	26.78
1992–3		138,984	140,541			100,852	103,706	36,835	73.79	26.21
1993–4		164,047	165,128			110,985	113,796	51,332	68.91	31.09
1994–5		189,815	190,962			126,498	129,483	61,479	67.81	32.19
1995–6		216,033	220,191			151,020	156,215	63,976	70.95	29.05
1996–7			240,873				175,931	64,942	73.04	26.96
1997–8			290,784				210,758	80,026	72.48	27.52
1998–9			337,984				253,496	84,488	75.00	25.00
1999–2000			374,401				279,153	95,248	74.56	25.44

Sources: Cols (1) to (3) and Cols (5) to (7) from *NAS October 1976*, pp. 22–3; *NAS February 1980*, pp. 20–1; *NAS February 1982*, pp. 30–1; *NAS February 1985*, pp. 32–3; *NAS Factor Incomes, 1980–1 to 1989–90*, p. 65, and *NAS Annual Issues* from 1992 to 1998; Cols (4) and (8) for 1993–4 to 1999–2000 from *NAS 2001*, pp. 184–7; for 1950–1 to 1992–3 obtained by splicing and for 1999–2000 estimated pro-rata on the basis of 1998–9 values; Col. (9) = Col. (4) – Col. (8); Cols (10) and (11) derived.

46

Appendix Table 2(f): Distribution of Factor Incomes for Whole Economy at Current Prices, 1960–1 to 1999–2000
(On the basis of estimated values of NDP)

Year	Net domestic product (Rs crore)			Compensation of employees (Rs crore)			Operating surplus (Rs crore)			% to total NDP of	
	Organized sector	Unorganised sector	Total	Organised sector	Unorganised sector	Total	Organized sector	Unorganized sector	Total	Compensation of employees	Operating surplus
	(1)	(2)	(3)	(4)	(5)	(6)	(7)	(8)	(9)	(10)	(11)
1960–1	3319	11,832	15,151	2286	5846	8132	1033	5986	7019	53.67	46.33
1961–2	3649	12,354	16,003	2484	5993	8477	1165	6361	7526	52.97	47.03
1962–3	4091	12,842	16,933	2800	6296	9095	1291	6547	7837	53.71	46.29
1963–4	4742	14,675	19,417	3207	7088	10,295	1535	7587	9121	53.02	46.98
1964–5	5289	17,603	22,892	3637	8584	12,221	1653	9019	10,671	53.39	46.61
1965–6	5910	17,724	23,634	4109	8830	12,939	1801	8894	10,695	54.75	45.25
1966–7	6411	20,947	27,357	4556	10,803	15,359	1855	10,143	11,998	56.14	43.86
1967–8	6909	25,259	32,168	5125	13,896	19,021	1784	11,363	13,147	59.13	40.87
1968–9	7606	25,187	32,793	5645	13,941	19,586	1961	11,247	13,207	59.73	40.27
1969–70	8596	27,623	36,219	6236	14,759	20,995	2359	12,864	15,223	57.97	42.03
1970–1	9460	29,536	38,996	6867	15,835	22,702	2594	13,701	16,294	58.22	41.78
1971–2	10,615	31,030	41,645	7709	16,490	24,199	2907	14,539	17,446	58.11	41.89
1972–3	11,696	34,138	45,834	8665	18,392	27,057	3031	15,746	18,777	59.03	40.97
1973–4	13,355	43,976	57,331	9773	22,941	32,714	3582	21,035	24,617	57.06	42.94
1974–5	16,840	50,644	67,485	12,085	25,756	37,840	4756	24,889	29,644	56.07	43.93
1975–6	19,038	51,369	70,407	13,835	27,245	41,080	5203	24,124	29,327	58.35	41.65
1976–7	22,148	53,720	75,867	15,197	27,752	42,949	6951	25,968	32,919	56.61	43.39
1977–8	24,198	61,554	85,752	16,832	33,127	49,959	7365	28,427	35,793	58.26	41.74
1978–9	27,178	64,992	92,170	18,944	34,734	53,678	8234	30,258	38,492	58.24	41.76
1979–80	30,801	69,487	100,288	21,306	36,527	57,833	9495	32,960	42,455	57.67	42.33
1980–1	34,489	83,056	117,544	24,577	44,443	69,020	9912	38,613	48,524	58.72	41.28
1981–2	42,367	94,797	137,164	28,530	49,422	77,952	13,837	45,375	59,212	56.83	43.17

(Contd.)

47

Appendix Table 2(f) Contd.

	(1)	(2)	(3)	(4)	(5)	(6)	7	(8)	(9)	(10)	(11)
1982–3	49,700	102,116	151,816	33,205	53,773	86,979	16,494	48,343	64,837	57.29	42.71
1983–4	58,337	120,094	178,431	39,153	63,018	102,171	19,184	57,076	76,260	57.26	42.74
1984–5	66,910	131,706	198,617	45,723	70,865	116,588	21,187	60,842	82,029	58.70	41.30
1985–6	75,474	145,642	221,116	51,037	76,554	127,591	24,437	69,088	93,524	57.70	42.30
1986–7	87,566	157,674	245,240	59,829	88,296	148,125	27,737	69,377	97,114	60.40	39.60
1987–8	99,397	179,190	278,587	69,527	100,994	170,521	29,869	78,196	108,065	61.21	38.79
1988–9	118,123	217,016	335,139	79,681	115,719	195,399	38,443	101,297	139,740	58.30	41.70
1989–90	137,291	249,430	386,721	90,678	125,581	216,259	46,613	123,849	170,462	55.92	44.08
1990–1	160,536	292,876	453,412	105,314	150,984	256,297	55,222	141,892	197,115	56.53	43.47
1991–2	187,291	334,375	521,666	120,720	177,013	297,733	66,571	157,361	223,933	57.07	42.93
1992–3	212,555	381,697	594,252	137,937	208,972	346,908	74,618	172,725	247,344	58.38	41.62
1993–4	256,849	440,536	697,385	153,983	207,979	361,962	102,866	232,557	335,423	51.90	48.10
1994–5	306,425	511,897	818,322	175,255	231,170	406,425	131,170	280,727	411,897	49.67	50.33
1995–6	377,768	576,751	954,519	217,960	280,947	498,907	159,808	295,804	455,612	52.27	47.73
1996–7	426,911	679,133	1,106,044	242,123	288,318	530,441	184,788	390,815	575,603	47.96	52.04
1997–8	485,946	751,048	1,236,994	287,356	340,348	627,704	198,590	410,700	609,290	50.74	49.26
1998–9	564,889	883,432	1,448,321	335,252	382,305	717,557	229,637	501,127	730,764	49.54	50.46
1999–2000	625,754	979,978	1,605,732	371,385	424,113	795,498	254,369	555,865	810,234	49.54	50.46

Note: This table is for calculations only for deriving the percentage shares of compensation of employees and operating surplus in estimated NDP.

Sources: Cols (1), (2), and (3) from Appendix Table 2(a), Cols (8), (9), and (4); Col. (4) from Table 2(b), Col. (5); Col. (5) from Appendix Table 2(c), Col. (18); Col. (6) = Col. (4) + Col. (5); Col. (7) from Appendix Table 2(b), Col. (6); Col. (8) from Table 2(c), Col. (19); Col. (9) = Col. (7) + Col. (8); Cols (10) and (11) derived.

48

Appendix Table 2(g): Comparison of Spliced Values of NDP with CSO Estimates
of NDP at Current Prices, 1960-1 to 1999-2000

Year	Estimates of NDP (Rs crore)		Col. (2)/ Col. (1)
	Spliced values	CSO estimates	
	(1)	(2)	(3)
1960-1	15,151	15,276	1.0082
1961-2	16,003	16,058	1.0034
1962-3	16,933	17,137	1.0121
1963-4	19,417	19,603	1.0096
1964-5	22,892	22,959	1.0029
1965-6	23,634	23,916	1.0119
1966-7	27,357	27,148	0.9923
1967-8	32,168	32,003	0.9949
1968-9	32,793	33,676	1.0269
1969-70	36,219	37,013	1.0219
1970-1	38,996	39,252	1.0066
1971-2	41,645	41,631	0.9997
1972-3	45,834	45,694	0.9969
1973-4	57,331	56,221	0.9806
1974-5	67,485	65,723	0.9739
1975-6	70,407	69,260	0.9837
1976-7	75,867	74,475	0.9816
1977-8	85,752	85,384	0.9957
1978-9	92,170	91,250	0.9900
1979-80	100,288	98,478	0.9820
1980-1	117,544	117,891	1.0030
1981-2	137,164	137,348	1.0013
1982-3	151,816	152,350	1.0035
1983-4	178,431	179,065	1.0036
1984-5	198,617	200,218	1.0081
1985-6	221,116	222,830	1.0078
1986-7	245,240	247,869	1.0107
1987-8	278,587	282,019	1.0123
1988-9	335,139	338,798	1.0109
1989-90	386,721	391,460	1.0123
1990-1	453,412	457,690	1.0094
1991-2	521,666	524,684	1.0058
1992-3	594,252	598,709	1.0075
1993-4	697,385	697,992	1.0009
1994-5	818,322	819,064	1.0009
1995-6	954,519	955,345	1.0009
1996-7	1,106,044	1,107,043	1.0009
1997-8	1,236,994	1,237,992	1.0008
1998-9	1,448,321	1,449,424	1.0008
1999-2000	1,605,732	1,605,732	1.0000

Sources: Col. (1) from Appendix Table 2(a), Col. (4); Col. (2): up to 1992-3 from *NAS Back Series*, pp. 28-361; for 1993-4 to 1999-2000 from *NAS 2001*, p. 20; Col. (3) = Col. (2)/ Col. (1).

Appendix Table 2(h): Dholakia's Data on Factor Incomes at Current Prices, 1948-9 to 1968-9

Year	Sector A (Rs crore)			Sector non-A (Rs crore)			Whole economy excl. dwellings (Rs crore)			% of labour income to NDP	% property income to NDP	Net income from dwellings (Rs crore)
	Net product	Labour income	Property income	Net product excl. dwellings	Labour income	Property income	Net product excl. dwellings	Labour income	Property income			
	(1)	(2)	(3)	(4)	(5)	(6)	(7)	(8)	(9)	(10)	(11)	(12)
1948-9	4406	2326	2080	3385	2352	1033	7791	4678	3113	60.04	39.96	255
1949-50	4633	2415	2218	3511	2487	1024	8144	4902	3242	60.19	39.81	259
1950-1	4878	2668	2210	3607	2536	1071	8485	5204	3281	61.33	38.67	277
1951-2	5001	2722	2279	3897	2694	1203	8898	5416	3482	60.87	39.13	291
1952-3	4768	2561	2207	3907	2763	1144	8675	5324	3351	61.37	38.63	291
1953-4	5282	2671	2611	4006	2828	1178	9288	5499	3789	59.21	40.79	298
1954-5	4322	2223	2099	4080	2866	1214	8402	5089	3313	60.57	39.43	305
1955-6	4502	2381	2121	4371	3024	1347	8873	5405	3468	60.92	39.08	313
1956-7	5518	2830	2688	4704	3236	1468	10,222	6066	4156	59.34	40.66	324
1957-8	5259	3035	2224	4984	3456	1528	10,243	6491	3752	63.37	36.63	337
1958-9	6215	3341	2874	5263	3640	1623	11,478	6981	4497	60.82	39.18	353
1959-60	6182	3504	2678	5652	3871	1781	11,834	7375	4459	62.32	37.68	370
1960-1	6749	3612	3137	6164	4227	1937	12,913	7839	5074	60.71	39.29	381
1961-2	6982	3829	3153	6695	4558	2137	13,677	8387	5290	61.32	38.68	398
1962-3	7123	4128	2995	7342	5027	2315	14,465	9155	5310	63.29	36.71	442
1963-4	8285	4810	3475	8330	5634	2696	16,615	10,444	6171	62.86	37.14	521
1964-5	10,145	5455	4690	9441	6434	3007	19,586	11,889	7697	60.70	39.30	554
1965-6	9854	6291	3563	10,253	7028	3225	20,107	13,319	6788	66.24	33.76	588
1966-7	11,909	7775	4134	11,495	7892	3603	23,404	15,667	7737	66.94	33.06	630
1967-8	15,039	8522	6517	12,842	8860	3982	27,881	17,382	10,499	62.34	37.66	651
1968-9	14,404	8361	6043	13,744	9477	4267	28,148	17,838	10,310	63.37	36.63	690

(Cols Contd.)

Appendix Table 2(h) Contd.: Dholakia's Data on Factor Incomes at Current Prices, 1948-9 to 1968-9

Year	Including dwellings (Rs crore)			% share in NDP including dwellings		Index of % shares with 1960-1 = 100		Revised % shares in NDP incl. dwellings		% shares of factor incomes in NDP from sector-A	
	NDP	Labour income	Property income	Labour income	Property income	Labour income	Property income	Labour income	Property income	Labour income	Property income
	(13)	(14)	(15)	(16)	(17)	(18)	(19)	(20)	(21)	(22)	(23)
1948-9	8046	4678	3368	58.14	41.86	98.60	102.01	52.92	47.26	52.79	47.21
1949-50	8403	4902	3501	58.34	41.66	98.93	101.54	53.10	47.04	52.13	47.87
1950-1	8762	5204	3558	59.39	40.61	100.72	98.96	54.06	45.85	54.69	45.31
1951-2	9189	5416	3773	58.94	41.06	99.96	100.06	53.65	46.36	54.43	45.57
1952-3	8966	5324	3642	59.38	40.62	100.70	98.99	54.05	45.86	53.71	46.29
1953-4	9586	5499	4087	57.36	42.64	97.28	103.90	52.21	48.14	50.57	49.43
1954-5	8707	5089	3618	58.45	41.55	99.12	101.27	53.20	46.92	51.43	48.57
1955-6	9186	5405	3781	58.84	41.16	99.78	100.31	53.55	46.47	52.89	47.11
1956-7	10,546	6066	4480	57.52	42.48	97.55	103.53	52.35	47.96	51.29	48.71
1957-8	10,580	6491	4089	61.35	38.65	104.04	94.19	55.84	43.64	57.71	42.29
1958-9	11,831	6981	4850	59.01	40.99	100.07	99.90	53.71	46.29	53.76	46.24
1959-60	12,204	7375	4829	60.43	39.57	102.48	96.43	55.00	44.68	56.68	43.32
1960-1	13,294	7839	5455	58.97	41.03	100.00	100.00	53.67	46.33	53.52	46.48
1961-2	14,075	8387	5688	59.59	40.41	101.05	98.49	54.24	45.63	54.84	45.16
1962-3	14,907	9155	5752	61.41	38.59	104.15	94.04	55.90	43.57	57.95	42.05
1963-4	17,136	10,444	6692	60.95	39.05	103.36	95.17	55.47	44.09	58.06	41.94
1964-5	20,140	11,889	8251	59.03	40.97	100.11	99.84	53.73	46.26	53.77	46.23
1965-6	20,695	13,319	7376	64.36	35.64	109.14	86.86	58.58	40.24	63.84	36.16
1966-7	24,034	15,667	8367	65.19	34.81	110.55	84.84	59.33	39.31	65.29	34.71
1967-8	28,532	17,382	11,150	60.92	39.08	103.31	95.24	55.45	44.12	56.67	43.33
1968-9	28,838	17,838	11,000	61.86	38.14	104.90	92.96	56.30	43.07	58.05	41.95

Sources: Cols (1) to (6) from B.H. Dholakia, *The Sources of Economic Growth in India*, Appendix Table II. B-8, p. 74; Col. (7) = Col. (1) + Col. (4); Col. (8) = Col. (2) + Col. (5); Col. (9) = Col. (3) + Col. (6); Cols (10) and (11) derived; Col. (12) from Dholakia, *The Sources of Economic Growth in India*, p. 73. Col. (13) = Col. (7) + Col. (12); Col. (14) = Col. (8); Col. (15) = Col. (9); Col. (16) to (19) derived; Cols (20) and (21) derived by taking 1960-1 values as equal to values obtained on the basis of CSO estimates. Col. (22) = Col. (2)/Col. (1) × 100; Col. (23) = Col. (3)/Col. (1) × 100.

51

Appendix Table 2(i): Estimation of Factor Incomes at Current Prices for Sector A as per 1993–4 Series, 1960–1 to 1999–2000

Year	NDP (Rs crore)				Compensation of employees (Rs crore)				Operating surplus (Rs crore)			
	1960–1 series	1970–1 series	1980–1 series	1993–4 series	1960–1 series	1970–1 series	1980–1 series	1993–4 series	1960–1 series	1970–1 series	1980–1 series	1993–4 series
	(1)	(2)	(3)	(4)	(5)	(6)	(7)	(8)	(9)	(10)	(11)	(12)
1960–1	6831			7942	1680			1744	572			183
1961–2	7060			8208	1710			1775	640			204
1962–3	7199			8370	1950			2025	729			233
1963–4	8360			9719	1104			1146	1831			584
1964–5	10,218			11,879	2345			2435	896			286
1965–6	9,973			11,595	2514			2610	999			319
1966–7	11,901			13,836	2815			2923	1007			321
1967–8	14,732			17,127	3392			3522	1072			342
1968–9	14,338			16,669	3372			3501	1167			373
1969–70	15,719			18,275	3659			3799	1275			407
1970–1	16,958	16,980		19,715	3816	3736		3962	1366	1213		436
1971–2	17,449	17,595		20,430	4037	3851		4084	1549	1374		494
1972–3	19,052	19,385		22,508	4281	4077		4324	1750	1501		540
1973–4	25,553	26,162		30,377	5217	4661		4943	1932	1542		555
1974–5	28,504	28,281		32,837	5408	4909		5206	2028	1809		651
1975–6		26,968		31,313		5627		5968		2138		769
1976–7		27,616		32,065		6060		6427		2502		900
1977–8		31,692		36,798		7706		8173		2528		909
1978–9		32,531		37,772		8259		8759		2715		976
1979–80		33,348		38,720		9053		9602		3022		1087
1980–1		41,463	44,091	48,143		9641	9727	10,225		3293	1170	1184
1981–2		44,941	49,735	54,306		10,530	10,667	11,213		4023	1372	1389

(Contd.)

52

Appendix Table 2(i) Contd.

(1)	(2)	(3)	(4)	(5)	(6)	(7)	(8)	(9)	(10)	(11)	(12)
1982-3	47,227	52,780	57,630		11,288	11,312	11,891		4256	1414	1431
1983-4		63,725	69,581			13,205	13,881			1512	1530
1984-5		67,719	73,942			14,589	15,336			1539	1,558
1985-6		72,288	78,931			15,650	16,451			1667	1687
1986-7		77,032	84,111			16,716	17,572			1922	1945
1987-8		86,438	94,382			17,962	18,882			1772	1793
1988-9		107,339	117,203			21,534	22,637			1984	2008
1989-90		119,283	130,245			24,069	25,301			2198	2225
1990-1		139,298	152,099			27,511	28,920			2409	2438
1991-2		162,358	177,279			30,635	32,204			2812	2846
1992-3		181,038	197,675			33,102	34,797			2936	2972
1993-4		210,476	229,829			38,979	40,974			3794	3840
1994-5		243,840	264,970			45,197	51,622			4208	4154
1995-6		259,088	287,221			48,691	58,692			4862	4986
1996-7			344,496				66,211				5069
1997-8			366,965				72,591				5727
1998-9			437,686				82,867				5393
1999-2000			460,084				87,094				5668

(Cols Contd.)

53

Appendix Table 2(i) Contd.: Estimation of Factor Incomes at Current Prices for Sector A as per 1993-4 Series, 1960-1 to 1999-2000

Year	Mixed income 1993-4 series (Rs crore)	% of CE to NDP of private sector	Distribution of mixed income of agriculture (Rs crore)		Distribution of NDP from agriculture, forestry, and fishing (Rs crore)			% distribution of NDP	
			CE	OS	NDP	CE	OS	Labour income	Non-labour income
	(13)	(14)	(15)	(16)	(17)	(18)	(19)	(20)	(21)
1960-1	6015	49.89	3001	3014	7942	4745	3196	59.75	40.25
1961-2	6228	49.00	3052	3177	8208	4827	3381	58.81	41.19
1962-3	6112	49.89	3049	3063	8370	5074	3296	60.62	39.38
1963-4	7989	49.86	3983	4006	9719	5129	4590	52.77	47.23
1964-5	9159	49.81	4562	4596	11,879	6997	4882	58.90	41.10
1965-6	8665	50.86	4407	4258	11,595	7017	4577	60.52	39.48
1966-7	10,592	52.03	5511	5081	13,836	8434	5402	60.95	39.05
1967-8	13,263	55.19	7321	5943	17,127	10,842	6285	63.30	36.70
1968-9	12,796	56.42	7219	5576	16,669	10,721	5949	64.31	35.69
1969-70	14,069	53.50	7526	6542	18,275	11,325	6949	61.97	38.03
1970-1	15,317	53.51	8196	7121	19,715	12,158	7557	61.67	38.33
1971-2	15,851	53.76	8521	7330	20,430	12,605	7824	61.70	38.30
1972-3	17,644	55.59	9809	7836	22,508	14,133	8375	62.79	37.21
1973-4	24,879	51.67	12,854	12,024	30,377	17,798	12,579	58.59	41.41
1974-5	26,980	49.38	13,322	13,658	32,837	18,528	14,309	56.42	43.58
1975-6	24,576	52.52	12,907	11,669	31,313	18,875	12,438	60.28	39.72
1976-7	24,738	51.13	12,648	12,090	32,065	19,075	12,990	59.49	40.51
1977-8	27,716	52.58	14,574	13,142	36,798	22,747	14,051	61.82	38.18
1978-9	28,036	52.61	14,749	13,287	37,772	23,508	14,264	62.24	37.76
1979-80	28,032	51.22	14,358	13,674	38,720	23,959	14,761	61.88	38.12
1980-1	36,734	51.30	18,846	17,888	48,143	29,071	19,072	60.38	39.62
1981-2	41,704	49.81	20,775	20,929	54,306	31,988	22,318	58.90	41.10

(Contd.)

54

Appendix Table 2(i) Contd.

	(13)	(14)	(15)	(16)	(17)	(18)	(19)	(20)	(21)
1982–3	44,308	51.08	22,633	21,675	57,630	34,524	23,106	59.91	40.09
1983–4	54,170	50.87	27,557	26,613	69,581	41,438	28,143	59.55	40.45
1984–5	57,049	52.94	30,203	26,846	73,942	45,539	28,403	61.59	38.41
1985–6	60,793	51.02	31,018	29,775	78,931	47,469	31,462	60.14	39.86
1986–7	64,594	56.37	36,411	28,183	84,111	53,983	30,128	64.18	35.82
1987–8	73,707	56.76	41,836	31,871	94,382	60,718	33,664	64.33	35.67
1988–9	92,559	52.00	48,129	44,430	117,203	70,766	46,438	60.38	39.62
1989–90	102,719	47.65	48,948	53,771	130,245	74,250	55,995	57.01	42.99
1990–1	120,742	49.30	59,528	61,213	152,099	88,448	63,652	58.15	41.85
1991–2	142,229	51.72	73,568	68,661	177,279	105,771	71,507	59.66	40.34
1992–3	159,907	54.67	87,426	72,481	197,675	122,223	75,452	61.83	38.17
1993–4	185,015	43.81	81,063	103,952	229,829	122,037	107,792	53.10	46.90
1994–5	209,194	39.64	82,929	126,265	264,970	134,551	130,419	50.78	49.22
1995–6	223,543	45.53	101,779	121,764	287,221	160,471	126,750	55.87	44.13
1996–7	273,216	35.58	97,210	176,006	344,496	163,421	181,075	47.44	52.56
1997–8	288,647	39.25	113,289	175,358	366,965	185,880	181,085	50.65	49.35
1998–9	349,426	36.03	125,901	223,525	437,686	208,768	228,918	47.70	52.30
1999–2000	367,322	36.03	132,364	234,958	460,084	219,458	240,626	47.70	52.30

Sources: Cols (1), (5) and (9) from *NAS October 1976*, pp. 120–1; Cols (2), (6), and (10) from *NAS February 1980*, pp. 118–19; *NAS February 1982*, pp. 136–7; *NAS 1985*, pp. 140–1; Cols (3), (7) and (11) from *NAS Factor Incomes, 1980–1 to 1989–90*, p. 32 and Annual Issues of *NAS 1992 to 1998*; Cols (4), (8) and (12) spliced from 1960–1 to 1992–3 and from *NAS 2001* for 1993–4 to 1998–9; for 1999–2000 estimated. Col. (13) = Col. (4) – Col. (8) – Col. (12); Col. (14) from Appendix Table 2(d), Col. (10); Col. (15) = [Col. (13)/Col. (14) × 100; Col. (16) = Col. (13) – Col. (15) – Col. (17) = Col. (4); Col. (18) = Col. (8) + Col. (15); Col. (19) = Col. (17) – Col. (18); Cols (20) and (21) derived.

55

Appendix Table 2(j): Factor Incomes in Relation to CSO Estimates of NDP at Current Prices, 1950–1 to 1999–2000

Year	Distribution of total NDP (Rs crore)				Distribution of NDP from agriculture (Rs crore)				Distribution of NDP from sector Non-A (Rs crore)		
	Total NDP	% share of CE	Labour income	Non-labour income	NDP from agriculture	% share of CE	Labour income	Non-labour income	NDP	Labour income	Non-labour income
	(1)	(2)	(3)	(4)	(5)	(6)	(7)	(8)	(9)	(10)	(11)
1950–1	9183	54.06	4964	4219	5337	54.69	2919	2418	3846	2045	1801
1951–2	9669	53.65	5187	4482	5498	54.43	2993	2505	4171	2195	1976
1952–3	9499	54.05	5134	4365	5343	53.71	2870	2473	4156	2264	1892
1953–4	10,360	52.21	5409	4951	5892	50.57	2979	2913	4468	2430	2038
1954–5	9657	53.20	5137	4520	4970	51.43	2556	2414	4687	2581	2106
1955–6	9786	53.55	5241	4545	4808	52.89	2543	2265	4978	2698	2280
1956–7	11,723	52.35	6137	5586	6138	51.29	3148	2990	5585	2989	2596
1957–8	11,948	55.84	6672	5276	6003	57.71	3464	2539	5945	3208	2737
1958–9	13,334	53.71	7161	6173	6955	53.76	3739	3216	6379	3422	2957
1959–60	13,973	55.00	7686	6287	6970	56.68	3951	3019	7003	3735	3268
1960–1	15,276	53.67	8199	7077	7339	59.75	4385	2954	7937	3814	4123
1961–2	16,058	52.97	8506	7552	7583	58.81	4460	3123	8475	4046	4429
1962–3	17,137	53.71	9205	7932	7730	60.62	4686	3044	9407	4519	4888
1963–4	19,603	53.02	10,394	9209	9129	52.77	4818	4311	10,474	5576	4898
1964–5	22,959	53.39	12,257	10,702	11,185	58.90	6588	4597	11,774	5669	6105
1965–6	23,916	54.75	13,094	10,822	11,117	60.52	6728	4389	12,799	6365	6434
1966–7	27,148	56.14	15,242	11,906	12,949	60.95	7893	5056	14,199	7349	6850
1967–8	32,003	59.13	18,924	13,079	16,272	63.30	10,301	5971	15,731	8623	7108
1968–9	33,676	59.73	20,113	13,563	16,737	64.31	10,764	5973	16,939	9349	7590
1969–70	37,013	57.97	21,456	15,557	18,286	61.97	11,332	6954	18,727	10,123	8604
1970–1	39,252	58.22	22,851	16,401	18,823	61.67	11,608	7215	20,429	11,243	9186
1971–2	41,631	58.11	24,191	17,440	19,178	61.70	11,833	7345	22,453	12,358	10,095
1972–3	45,694	59.03	26,974	18,720	21,079	62.79	13,235	7844	24,615	13,739	10,876
1973–4	56,221	57.06	32,081	24,140	27,912	58.59	16,354	11,558	28,309	15,727	12,582

(Contd.)

56

Appendix Table 2(j) Contd.

	(1)	(2)	(3)	(4)	(5)	(6)	(7)	(8)	(9)	(10)	(11)
1974-5	65,723	56.07	36,853	28,870	30,475	56.42	17,195	13,280	35,248	19,657	15,591
1975-6	69,260	58.35	40,411	28,849	30,051	60.28	18,114	11,937	39,209	22,296	16,913
1976-7	74,475	56.61	42,161	32,314	30,619	59.49	18,215	12,404	43,856	23,945	19,911
1977-8	85,384	58.26	49,745	35,639	35,376	61.82	21,868	13,508	50,008	27,877	22,131
1978-9	91,250	58.24	53,142	38,108	37,227	62.24	23,169	14,058	54,023	29,973	24,050
1979-80	98,478	57.67	56,789	41,689	38,237	61.88	23,660	14,577	60,241	33,129	27,112
1980-1	117,891	58.72	69,223	48,668	48,253	60.38	29,137	19,116	69,638	40,086	29,552
1981-2	137,348	56.83	78,057	59,291	54,184	58.90	31,916	22,268	83,164	46,141	37,023
1982-3	152,350	57.29	87,285	65,065	57,796	59.91	34,623	23,173	94,554	52,661	41,893
1983-4	179,065	57.26	102,534	76,531	69,276	59.55	41,256	28,020	109,789	61,278	48,511
1984-5	200,218	58.70	117,528	82,690	74,414	61.59	45,829	28,585	125,804	71,699	54,105
1985-6	222,830	57.70	128,581	94,249	79,631	60.14	47,890	31,741	143,199	80,690	62,509
1986-7	247,869	60.40	149,713	98,156	85,611	64.18	54,946	30,665	162,258	94,768	67,490
1987-8	282,019	61.21	172,622	109,397	95,313	64.33	61,317	33,996	186,706	111,306	75,400
1988-9	338,798	58.30	197,533	141,265	117,725	60.38	71,081	46,644	221,073	126,452	94,621
1989-90	391,460	55.92	218,909	172,551	129,765	57.01	73,976	55,789	261,695	144,933	116,762
1990-1	457,690	56.53	258,716	198,974	151,775	58.15	88,259	63,516	305,915	170,456	135,459
1991-2	524,684	57.07	299,456	225,228	176,160	59.66	105,104	71,056	348,524	194,352	154,172
1992-3	598,709	58.38	349,510	249,199	197,254	61.83	121,963	75,291	401,455	227,548	173,907
1993-4	697,992	51.90	362,277	335,715	229,829	53.10	122,037	107,792	468,163	240,240	227,923
1994-5	819,064	49.67	406,794	412,270	264,970	50.78	134,551	130,419	554,094	272,243	281,851
1995-6	955,345	52.27	499,339	456,006	287,221	55.87	160,471	126,750	668,124	338,868	329,256
1996-7	1,107,043	47.96	530,921	576,122	344,496	47.44	163,421	181,075	762,547	367,500	395,047
1997-8	1,237,992	50.74	628,211	609,781	366,965	50.65	185,880	181,085	871,027	442,330	428,697
1998-9	1,449,424	49.54	718,103	731,321	437,686	47.70	208,768	228,918	1,011,738	509,335	502,403
1999-2000	1,605,732	49.54	795,498	810,234	460,084	47.70	219,458	240,626	1,145,648	576,040	569,608

Sources: Cols (1) and (2) from Table 2.1; Col. (3) = Col. (1) × Col. (2); Col. (4) = Col. (1) − Col. (3); Col. (5) for 1950-1 to 1992-3 from *NAS Back Series, 1950–51 to 1992–93*, July 2001, pp. 28–31, and for 1993–4 to 1999–2000 from *NAS 2001*, p. 20; Col. (6) for 1950–1 to 1959–60 from Appendix Table 2(h), Col. (22); from 1960–1 to 1991–2000 Appendix Table 2(i), Col. (20); Col. (7) = Col. (5) × Col. (7); Col. (8) = Col. (5) − Col. (7); Col. (9) = Col. (1) − Col. (5); Col. (10) = Col. (2) − Col. (7); Col. (11) = Col. (7) − Col. (10).

3

Labour Input

The sources of growth are divided into two broad groups: changes in input and changes in output per unit of input. The study of the former requires quantities of inputs, *viz.* labour, capital, and land, and their relative marginal products for use as weights. 'Estimates of relative products are ordinarily based on the general proposition that earnings of different inputs are proportional to marginal products because of efforts by producing enterprises to minimize costs'.[1] This chapter, based on this principle, is concerned with labour input.

Labour input is the same for the non-residential sector as it is for the whole economy because the sub-sector 'ownership of dwellings' does not use any labour. Labour input takes into account not only the numbers employed but also their personal characteristics such as age–sex composition and levels of education that affect the quality of their work. In his studies on growth in developed countries, Denison[2] has used total weekly hours worked as a measure of the quantity of labour input, calculated from annual data on employment and average number of hours worked per week. Actual employment figures on an annual basis covering all sectors of the economy and number of hours or even days worked are not available for India. Annual employment figures are published only for the organized sector; number of man-days worked are available only for manufacturing industries[3] and that too from 1980–1 only from the *Annual Survey of Industries*. Limited data on the average number of days worked during the year by usually occupied workers in rural labour households are available for survey years on the basis of employment data collected through the daily status approach as part of the quinquennial employment and unemployment surveys by the National Sample Survey Organisation (NSSO).[4] But these are not adequate to develop an

[1] Edward F. Denison, 'Classification of Sources of Growth', *The Review of Income and Wealth,* Income and Wealth Series 18, No. 1, Blackwell Publishers, Oxford, March 1972, p. 6.

[2] Edward F. Denison, *Why Growth Rates Differ*, Washington, D.C., 1967, pp. 45–69; *Accounting for United States Economic Growth*, Washington, D.C., 1974, p. 132.

[3] Government of India, *Annual Survey of Industries, 1992–3, Summary Results for Factory Sector*, CSO, pp. 100–1.

[4] National Sample Survey Organization, *Rural Labour Economy, Report on Employment and Unemployment of Rural Labour Households, 38th Round, NSS, 1983, Main Report*, NSSO, New Delhi, pp. 109–10.

annual series of labour input in terms of number of man-days worked, especially because of the dominance of the self-employed and unpaid family workers. In view of these limitations, the estimated number in the workforce is used as the measure of the quantity of labour input. Even the possible variations in the number of holidays from year to year have not been taken into account. Age–sex composition and educational qualifications and their effect on labour input are separately considered. The labour input measure developed for use in this study is presented in Table 3.1. The derivation of each of the columns is outlined below.

Table 3.1: Indexes of Labour Input in the Non-residential Sector, 1950–1 to 1999–2000 (1993–4 = 100)

Year	Employment	Age–sex composition	Effect of education	Labour input
	(1)	(2)	(3)	(4)
1950–1	43.19	98.46	89.65	38.12
1951–2	43.87	98.52	89.91	38.86
1952–3	44.56	98.58	90.16	39.60
1953–4	45.27	98.64	90.42	40.37
1954–5	45.98	98.69	90.68	41.15
1955–6	46.70	98.76	90.94	41.94
1956–7	47.44	98.82	91.20	42.75
1957–8	48.19	98.88	91.46	43.58
1958–9	48.94	98.94	91.72	44.41
1959–60	49.71	99.00	91.98	45.27
1960–1	50.50	99.02	92.24	46.12
1961–2	51.35	98.99	92.36	46.95
1962–3	52.28	98.96	92.49	47.85
1963–4	53.22	98.93	92.61	48.76
1964–5	54.18	98.90	92.74	49.69
1965–6	55.16	98.88	92.86	50.65
1966–7	56.15	98.85	92.99	51.61
1967–8	57.16	98.82	93.11	52.60
1968–9	58.19	98.80	93.24	53.60
1969–70	59.24	98.77	93.36	54.63
1970–1	60.31	98.74	93.49	55.67
1971–2	61.40	98.72	93.61	56.74
1972–3	62.51	98.69	93.74	57.83
1973–4	63.93	98.67	94.00	59.30
1974–5	65.68	98.64	94.27	61.07
1975–6	67.48	98.62	94.53	62.91
1976–7	69.33	98.60	94.79	64.80
1977–8	71.10	98.57	95.06	66.62
1978–9	72.78	98.55	95.37	68.41
1979–80	74.50	98.53	95.68	70.23
1980–1	76.26	98.51	95.99	72.11
1981–2	78.07	98.49	96.31	74.05
1982–3	80.02	98.47	96.62	76.13
1983–4	81.71	98.44	96.91	77.95
1984–5	83.01	98.65	97.19	79.59
1985–6	84.34	98.93	97.48	81.33
1986–7	85.68	99.26	97.77	83.15

(Contd.)

Table 3.1 Contd.

	(1)	(2)	(3)	(4)
1987–8	87.05	99.64	98.06	85.06
1988–9	88.79	99.69	98.38	87.08
1989–90	90.93	99.74	98.70	89.51
1990–1	93.11	99.80	99.03	92.01
1991–2	95.36	99.86	99.35	94.60
1992–3	97.65	99.93	99.67	97.26
1993–4	100.00	100.00	100.00	100.00
1994–5	101.6	100.13	100.39	102.13
1995–6	102.44	100.26	100.79	103.52
1996–7	103.28	100.41	101.18	104.93
1997–8	104.12	100.56	101.58	106.35
1998–9	104.98	100.72	101.98	107.83
1999–2000	105.84	100.88	102.38	109.32

Sources: Col. (1) from Table 3.4, Col. (1); Col. 2 from Table 3.13, Col. (4); Col. (3) from Table 3.21, Col. (2); Col. (4) = Col. (1) × Col. (2) × Col. (3).

EMPLOYMENT

There are two basic sources of data for employment: the decennial population censuses which provide estimates of the number in the workforce and the quinquennial employment and unemployment surveys conducted by the NSSO which give the worker-population ratio (WPR), that is the ratio of number of persons employed to thousand persons in the sample. The WPRs calculated from the census data and those available from the employment surveys show wide variation.

Beginning with 1951, India has conducted six population censuses including the 2001 census. The economic data collected through the censuses are strictly not comparable due to changes in definitions and classification. In the 1951 census, income was adopted as a criteria to classify persons into 'self-supporting', 'earning dependent', and 'non-earning dependent'. A 'self-supporting person' was one who was in receipt of an income sufficient at least for his own maintenance. A person who earned income which was not sufficient for his maintenance was classified as an 'earning dependent'. All others who had no incomes whatsoever were designated as 'non-earning dependents'. In the 1961 census, the population was divided into two classes: 'workers' and 'non-workers' on the basis of the work done. In the case of regular employment in any trade, profession, services, business, or commerce, a person was classified as a 'worker' if he had been employed during any of the 15 days preceding the date of enumeration. In the case of seasonal work like cultivation, livestock dairying, or household industry, if a person had some regular work for more than one hour a day throughout the greater part of the working season he was regarded as a 'worker'. Persons who were not engaged in any economic activity were classified as 'non-workers'. In the 1971 census, a 'worker' was defined as a person whose main activity was participation in economically productive work. For regular work in trade, industry, or services the reference period was the week prior to the enumeration date (it was a fortnight in 1961) and in the case of seasonal work it was the preceding one year. Secondary work by main workers and marginal contribution by non-workers were also taken into account. In the 1981 and 1991 censuses, the whole population was divided into three categories, viz. 'main workers', 'marginal workers', and 'non-workers'. The 'main worker' was defined as one who participated in any economically productive work for 183 days or more. Anyone who participated in productive activity for less than 183 days was defined as a 'marginal worker'. The reference period was one year preceding the date of enumeration. A 'non-worker' was defined as a person who had not done any work at any time. The definitions adopted to classify persons into main workers, marginal workers, and non-workers were the same in the 1981 and 1991 Censuses. But to net the workers more effectively, particularly those working on farm or in family enterprises, the words 'including unpaid work on farm or in family enterprise' were added in the 1991 census questionnaire, to ensure that they are not excluded from 'workers'. Apart from such changes of definitions and criteria, the geographical coverage of the censuses was not uniform. The 1951 census did not cover Jammu and Kashmir, Daman and Diu, Goa, Dadra and Nagar Haveli, and Pondicherry. The region of NEFA was not fully covered in the 1961 census. Assam was not included in the 1981 census while Jammu and Kashmir was not covered in the 1991 census.

Since 1972–3, the NSSO has conducted six large quinquennial surveys on employment and unemployment. The survey results are available for the years 1972–3, 1977–8, 1983, 1987–8, 1993–4, and 1999–2000. The NSS data included simultaneous canvassing of alternative approaches to the measurement of employment and unemployment in terms of the 'usual status' (or activities of the previous year), the current status (or the week preceding the date of survey) and the activities on different days of the reference week.[5] The data collected through the 'usual status' approach are considered comparable to the population census estimates. A person's principal usual status was considered 'working' or 'employed' if he/she was engaged relatively for a longer time during the reference period of 365 days in any one or more work activities. A person categorized as a worker on the basis of his principal status is referred to as a 'principal status worker'. A 'non-worker' who pursued some gainful activity in a subsidiary capacity is referred to as a 'subsidiary status worker'. These two groups, viz. the principal status worker (ps) and subsidiary status worker (ss) together constituted 'all workers' according to the 'usual status' classification. The same concept has been used from the 32nd round onwards conducted in 1977–8. In the 27th (1972–3) round, however, a person was considered working if he pursued gainful activity over a long period of time in the past (say one year or so) which was also likely to continue in future. Persons (excepting full-time regular students) who were pursuing gainful activities in the subsidiary status were also considered as 'workers'. The

[5] National Sample Survey, *Key Results of Employment and Unemployment Survey— All India, Part I, Special Report, 43rd Round*, NSS, 1987–8, pp. 12–3.

estimates of 'usual status workers' based on the 27th round data included both principal and subsidiary status workers and hence would be comparable to the estimates of workers in the 32nd, 38th, 43rd, 50th, and 55th rounds.

Table 3.2 and Fig. 3.1 present the crude worker-population ratios (percentage of workers to total population) calculated from the different censuses and surveys. The census estimates cover both main and secondary or marginal workers and the NSS estimates based on usual status concept include the principal status and subsidiary status workers. It is seen that the estimates of WPRs based on the 1971, 1981, and the 1991 censuses are markedly lower than those obtained from the 1961 census and the six quinquennial surveys of the NSS from 1972–3 to 1999–2000. The NSS estimates of overall WPRs show a reasonable amount of stability around 41–2 per cent between 1972–3 and 1993–4. Pravin Visaria has pointed out that 'it hardly needs any persuasion to accept that the estimates of WPRs could not be fluctuating downwards in the Census years 1971,1981, and 1991 and returning to the former level, comparable to the 1961 Census, whenever NSS conducted its five quinquennial surveys. There is little doubt that the NSS investigators have done better than more than million

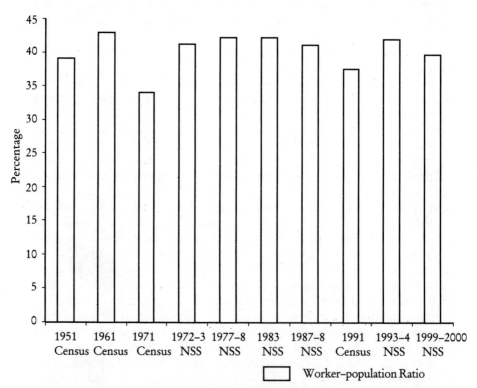

Fig. 3.1: Worker–population ratio according to censuses and national sample surveys, 1951 to 1999–2000

Sources: 1951 to 1993–4 from Pravin Visaria, 'Workforce and Employment in India, 1961–1994', Table 1, 1998; For 1999–2000 from *NSS Report No. 458, Employment and Unemployment Situation in India, (July1999–June 2000)*, New Delhi, May 2001, p. 67.

Table 3.2: Worker–Population Ratios by Sex and Rural–Urban Residence, 1951 to 1999–2000

Year	Source	All-India			Rural India			Urban India		
		Persons	Males	Females	Persons	Males	Females	Persons	Males	Females
	(1)	(2)	(3)	(4)	(5)	(6)	(7)	(8)	(9)	(10)
1951	Census	39.10	53.90	23.40	39.50	53.50	25.00	37.10	56.40	14.70
1961	Census	43.00	57.10	28.00	45.10	58.20	31.40	33.50	52.40	11.10
1971	Census	34.00	52.70	13.90	36.10	53.60	15.50	29.60	48.90	7.10
1972–3	NSS 27th Round	41.30	53.50	28.20	43.50	54.50	31.80	33.10	5.10	13.40
1977–8	NSS 32rd Round	42.20	54.20	29.30	44.40	55.20	33.10	34.40	50.80	15.60
1983	NSS 38th Round	42.20	53.80	29.60	44.60	54.70	34.00	34.30	51.20	15.10
1987–8	NSS 43rd Round	41.10	53.10	28.10	43.40	53.90	32.30	33.90	50.60	15.20
1991	Census	37.50	51.60	22.30	40.00	52.50	26.70	30.20	48.90	9.20
1993–4	NSS 50nd Round	42.00	54.50	28.60	44.40	55.30	32.80	34.70	52.00	15.40
1999–2000	NSS 55th Round	39.70	52.70	25.90	41.70	53.10	29.90	33.70	51.80	13.90

Sources: 1951 to 1993–4 from Pravin Visaria, 'Workforce and Employment in India, 1961–1994', Table 1, 1998; For 1999–2000 from NSS Report No. 458, *Employment and Unemployment Situation in India*, (July1999–June 2000), New Delhi, May 2001, p. 67.

Census enumerators who are asked to enumerate the population of our continental country'.[6] While the WPRs for males according to the censuses and NSS show some consistency, those for females are found to be widely fluctuating. The WPRs for females obtained from the 1971, 1981, and 1991 censuses are too low compared to those obtained from the 1961 census. The broad comparability of the survey based estimates of female WPRs with that of the 1961 census confirms that the declines in these ratios suggested by the subsequent censuses are not real.[7] In view of this, it is proposed to use the 1961 census-based WPRs along with those of the quinquennial surveys of 1972–3 to 1999–2000 in this study. The lower values for WPR for 1987–8 compared to 1983 and 1993–4 are attributed to the influence of the severe drought that prevailed during the year.[8] The WPRs based on the 1999–2000 survey are the lowest recorded in quinquennial surveys, the overall WPR being 39.7 compared to 41–42 for the previous years. According to K. Sundaram this reduction in the worker-population ratio reflects a beneficial rise in the student-population ratio not only in the 5–9 and the 10–14 age groups but also in the 15–19 and 20–4 age groups indicating a rising participation in secondary and higher level education.[9]

The overall WPR derived from the 1951 census is far below that obtained from the 1961 census. This is partly due to the use of 'income earned' as a criterion to identify workers in the 1951 census instead of 'time spent on economic activity' in the 1961 census, which is believed to have led to some underestimation of the number of workers. Apart from this, Sinha has identified gross underreporting of female workers in the 1951 census due largely to 'misinterpretation and faulty implementation of Census instructions in some restricted regions' especially in the three states of Andhra Pradesh, Madras, and Mysore.[10] In his study *The Sources of Economic Growth in India*, B. H. Dholakia has not only attempted meticulous corrections for the underestimation of workers in the 1951 census data, but has also made adjustments for making the territorial coverage comparable to the 1961 census.[11] Dholakia's revised estimates[12] for 1951 and the census estimates as

---

[6] 'Pravin Visaria, 'Workforce and Employment in India, 1961–1994', Paper submitted to the International Conference on Income and Wealth, jointly organized by the Indian Association for Income and Wealth, the International Association for Research in Income and Wealth, and the Government of India, New Delhi, November 1998, p. 4 (mimeo).

[7] Pravin Visaria, 'Structure of Indian Workforce, 1961–1994', *The Indian Journal of Labour Economics*, Vol. 39, No. 4, 1996, Indian Society of Labour Economics, p. 726.

[8] Ibid., p. 727.

[9] K. Sundaram, 'Employment-Unemployment Situation in the Nineties, Some Results of the NSS 55th Round Survey', *Economic and Political Weekly*, 17 March 2001, Vol. XXXVI, No. 9, EPW Research Foundation, Mumbai, p. 932.

[10] J. N. Sinha, 'Comparability of the 1961 and 1951 Census Economic Data', in *Artha Vignana*, Vol. 14, No. 4, December 1964, Gokhale Institute of Politics and Economics, Pune.

[11] The territories not covered in the 1951 census are Jammu and Kashmir, Diu, Daman and Goa, Dadra and Nagar Haveli, and Pondicherry.

[12] Bakul H. Dholakia, *The Sources of Economic Growth in India*, Baroda, 1974, p. 84.

reported for 1961[13] have been adopted as benchmark values for the respective years in this study. For the survey years 1972–3 to 1993–4 the estimates of the number of workers made by Visaria[14] by applying the segment-specific (rural/urban; male/female) WPRs to the respective populations have been accepted as they are. Similar estimates made by Sundaram[15] as on 1 January 2000 from the results of the NSS 55th round have also been used. The benchmark estimates of the number of workers as on specific dates obtained from the above-mentioned sources are presented in Table 3.3. The preliminary results of the 2001 census have not been used here in order to be consistent with the estimates of workforce adopted by the CSO in the compilation of national accounts.

Based on these periodic estimates, using inter-period rates of growth, annual estimates of the number in the workforce as on 1 April have been obtained. These are presented in Appendix Table 3(a). The employment series have been worked out as on 1 October, the mid-point of the fiscal year April to March, to be consistent with the measure of output, viz. gross domestic product (GDP). These are shown in Appendix Table 3(b). Table 3.4 shows the employment series in index form. Column (1) of Table 3.4 corresponds to Col. (1) of Table 3.1.

The annual growth rate of the number in the workforce (employment) for inter-census/survey dates and for long and shorter periods are shown in Table 3.5. The number in the workforce increased 2.45 times during the period while population multiplied 2.76 times. The annual growth rate of employment was generally lower than that of population except during the long period 1964–5 to 1980–1 and during the decade 1970–1 to 1980–1. It was lowest at 1.43 per cent during the closing decade covered by the economic reforms. Employment of females almost kept pace with that of males, the former being 1.73 per cent per year and latter 1.9 per cent over the entire period. The share of females in total employment remained more or less the same. Employment in Sector non-A grew at more than twice the rate recorded in Sector A between 1950–1 to 1999–2000. Still, the share of Sector A declined only by 16 percentage points from 76.2 per cent in 1950–1 to 60.4 per cent in 1999–2000 [see Appendix Table 3(b)]. In the meanwhile, the share of Sector non-A moved up from 23.8 per cent to 39.6 per cent. An interesting feature, however, is that employment in Sector A declined in absolute terms between January 1994 and January 2000; that is, it recorded negative growth for the first time. Overall employment increased by less than one per cent per year during the same period.

The indexes of employment presented in Table 3.4 give only a measure of the quantity of labour input. The effect of changes in the age–sex composition of workers on labour input will be taken up next.

[13] *Census of India 1961, Vol. I, Part II-B(i) General Economic Tables*, 1961, New Delhi, p. 86.
[14] Visaria, 'Workforce and Employment in India, 1961–1994', Table 8 (mimeo), International Association of Income and Wealth, Government of India, November, 1998.
[15] Sundaram, 'Employment-Unemployment Situation in India in the Nineties', pp. 931–2.

Table 3.3: Number of Workers (in Terms of Usual Status) by Sex and Rural–Urban Residence, 1951 to 1999–2000

(in millions)

Reference Date/Source	All-India			Rural			Urban		
	Persons	Males	Females	Persons	Males	Females	Persons	Males	Females
(1)	(2)	(3)	(4)	(5)	(6)	(7)	(8)	(9)	(10)
1 April 1951, Census 1951	161.39	108.55	52.84	–	–	–	–	–	–
1 April 1961, Census 1961	188.68	129.17	59.51	162.25	106.75	55.49	26.43	22.42	4.01
1 April 1973, NSS 27th Round (1972–3)	233.81	156.90	76.51	194.8	125.20	69.20	39.01	31.70	7.31
1 January 1973, NSS 32nd Round (1977–8)	265.87	176.79	89.08	217.21	138.41	78.80	48.66	38.38	10.28
1 July 1983, NSS 38th Round (1983)	302.32	200.13	102.19	243.94	153.49	90.45	58.38	46.64	11.74
1 January 1988, NSS 43rd Round (1987–8)	324.61	217.50	107.11	257.67	164.67	93.00	66.94	52.83	14.11
1 January 1994, NSS 50th Round (1993–4)	374.39	252.76	121.63	291.95	187.66	104.29	82.44	65.10	17.34
1 January 2000, NSS 55th Round (1999–2000)	393.19	271.37	121.82	298.05	195.00	103.05	95.14	76.37	18.77

Sources: Row (1) from B. H. Dholakia, *The Sources of Economic Growth in India*, Baroda, 1974, p. 92; Rows (2) to (7) from Pravin Visaria, 'Workforce and Employment in India, 1961–1994', (mimeo), Table 8; Row (8) from K. Sundaram, 'Employment–Unemployment Situation in the Nineties', *Economic and Political Weekly*, Table 1, 17 March 2001, Vol. XXXVI, No. 9, p. 932.

Table 3.4: Indexes of Employment, 1950–1 to 1999–2000 (1993–4 = 100)

Year	All-India		
	Total	Male	Female
	(1)	(2)	(3)
1950–1	43.19	42.93	43.75
1951–2	43.87	43.68	44.28
1952–3	44.56	44.44	44.81
1953–4	45.27	45.22	45.35
1954–5	45.98	46.02	45.90
1955–6	46.70	46.82	46.45
1956–7	47.44	47.65	47.01
1957–8	48.19	48.48	47.57
1958–9	48.94	49.33	48.14
1959–60	49.71	50.20	48.71
1960–1	50.50	51.08	49.29
1961–2	51.35	51.94	50.12
1962–3	52.28	52.79	51.20
1963–4	53.22	53.65	52.31
1964–5	54.18	54.53	53.45
1965–6	55.16	55.42	54.60
1966–7	56.15	56.33	55.78
1967–8	57.16	57.25	56.99
1968–9	58.19	58.18	58.22
1969–70	59.24	59.13	59.47
1970–1	60.31	60.10	60.75
1971–2	61.40	61.08	62.06
1972–3	62.51	62.08	63.40
1973–4	63.93	63.38	65.08
1974–5	65.68	64.99	67.12
1975–6	67.48	66.65	69.23
1976–7	69.33	68.34	71.40
1977–8	71.10	70.08	73.23
1978–9	72.78	71.77	74.89
1979–80	74.50	73.41	76.79
1980–1	76.26	75.08	78.73
1981–2	78.07	76.79	80.72
1982–3	80.02	78.54	83.11
1983–4	81.71	80.17	84.93
1984–5	83.01	81.67	85.83
1985–6	84.34	83.19	86.73
1986–7	85.68	84.75	87.64
1987–8	87.05	86.33	88.55
1988–9	88.79	88.23	89.96
1989–90	90.93	90.47	91.88
1990–1	93.11	92.76	93.85
1991–2	95.36	95.11	95.86
1992–3	97.65	97.53	97.91
1993–4	100.00	100.00	100.00
1994–5	101.60	101.86	101.08
1995–6	102.44	103.07	101.12
1996–7	103.28	104.30	101.15
1997–8	104.12	105.54	101.17
1998–9	104.98	106.79	101.18
1999–2000	105.84	108.07	101.18

Source: Cols (1) to (3) derived from Appendix Table 3(b), Cols (1) to (3).

Table 3.5: Annual Rate of Growth of Employment, 1950–1 to 1999–2000

(in per cent)

Period	Employment			Employment in	
	Total	Males	Females	Sector A	Sector non-A
	(1)	(2)	(3)	(4)	(5)
Inter-census/Survey dates					
April 1951 to April 1961	1.57	1.75	1.20	1.49	1.83
April 1961 to April 1973	1.80	1.63	2.12	1.61	2.38
April 1973 to January 1978	2.74	2.54	3.25	1.88	5.05
January 1978 to July 1983	2.36	2.28	2.53	1.72	3.85
July 1983 to January 1988	1.59	1.87	1.05	0.38	4.07
January 1988 to January 1994	2.41	2.54	2.14	2.33	2.55
January 1994 to January 2000	0.82	1.19	0.03	–0.49	2.98
Long periods					
1950–1 to 1999–2000	1.85	1.90	1.73	1.36	2.91
1950–1 to 1964–5	1.63	1.72	1.44	1.53	1.97
1964–5 to 1980–1	2.16	2.02	2.45	1.71	3.36
1980–1 to 1999–2000	1.74	1.94	1.33	0.95	3.23
Shorter periods					
1950–1 to 1960–1	1.58	1.75	1.20	1.50	1.82
1960–1 to 1970–1	1.79	1.64	2.11	1.60	2.35
1970–1 to 1980–1	2.37	2.25	2.63	1.77	3.95
1980–1 to 1990–1	2.02	2.14	1.77	1.15	3.82
1990–1 to 1999–2000	1.43	1.71	0.84	0.74	2.59

Sources: Tables 3.3 and 3.4.

AGE–SEX COMPOSITION OF WORKERS

The age–sex composition of the workers vary over time. The average wages/salaries paid to those in each age–sex group also differ. It is necessary to develop an index to measure the effect of these changes on labour input. As stated by Denison, the calculation of such an index rests on the assumption that average earnings in the different age–sex groups are proportional to the marginal products of labour of these groups. Following this, the work done by a group whose average earnings are twice as high as those of another group will be taken to represent twice as much labour input.[16]

The presentation of data on age–sex distribution of workers began only from the 1961 census. The quinquennial employment and unemployment surveys also present percentage age–sex distribution of the employed from the 1983 survey onwards. The classification scheme, though same for all the surveys, differs from that of the census and between censuses too, as can be seen from Appendix Table 3(d). In view of these variations, the broad common age-groupings applicable for the period 1961 to 2000 are: 5–14, 15–59, and 60 plus years. A more detailed grouping will provide better understanding of the age–sex structure of the employed over time especially in relation to their earnings, but it is limited in this study to the three groups mentioned

[16] Denison, *Accounting for Economic Growth*, p. 32.

above, not only because of the limitations in age–sex composition adopted in the surveys and censuses but also because the average earnings data are restricted to these groups only in the quinquennial surveys.

Age–Sex Distribution of Workers, 1960–1 to 1999–2000

The percentage distribution of workers according to age–sex groups available from Censuses and surveys is given in Table 3.6.

Table 3.6 Percentage Distribution of Workers by Sex and Age, 1961 to 1999–2000

Age/Sex groups	Censuses				NSS			
	1961	1971	1981	1991	1983	1987–8	1993–4	1999–2000
	(1)	(2)	(3)	(4)	(5)	(6)	(7)	(8)
Males								
5–14	4.61	4.37	3.32	1.97	4.03	2.02	1.94	1.40
15–59	58.83	71.37	64.85	63.77	57.42	59.84	60.54	62.54
60+	5.62	6.90	5.86	5.67	4.92	5.20	5.14	5.10
Total males	68.46	82.64	74.03	71.41	66.37	67.06	67.62	69.01
Females								
5–14	3.06	1.58	2.26	1.63	3.10	2.35	1.58	1.20
15–59	27.01	14.85	22.50	25.55	28.94	29.09	29.16	28.14
60+	1.47	0.92	1.21	1.41	1.59	1.50	1.64	1.62
Total females	31.54	17.35	25.97	28.59	33.63	32.94	32.38	30.96
Grand total	100.00	100.00	100.00	100.00	100.00	100.00	100.00	100.00

Sources: Col. (1) from *Census of India 1961, Vol. I, Part II-B(i), General Economic Tables,* pp. 86–7; Col. (2) from *Census of India 1971, Paper No. 3 of 1972,* p. 2; Col. 3 from *Census of India 1981, Part III A(i), General Economic Tables,* Table B-1, pp. 134–5; Col. 4 from *Census of India 1991, Series I, India, Part III B Series Table B-1 (s),* p. 78; Col. 5 from *Key Results of Employment and Unemployment Survey—All India, Part I, Special Report 1983,* 43rd round, p. 82; Col. 6 and 7 from *Employment and Unemployment in India, 1993–4, Report 409,* NSSO, p. 69; Col. 8 from *NSS Report No. 458, Employment and Unemployment Situation in India, 1999–2000,* May 2001, p. 70.

It is seen from this table that the survey results taken along with those of the 1961 census exhibit a definite pattern. The percentage of workers in the age-group 5–14 years gradually declined over the period in the case of both males and females. Correspondingly, those in the age-group 15–59 years increased for both males and females (except for 1999–2000). The percentage of women workers shows a slight decline. In absolute terms the number of women workers is stagnant since 1995 [see Table 3.3, Col. (3) and Appendix Table 3(b), Col. 3]. On the other hand, the age–sex distribution of workers according to the 1971 census shows a rather erratic pattern. The percentage of male workers in the age group 15–59 years is found to be abnormally high at 71.4 compared to 58.8 according to the 1961 census and 64.8 as per the 1981 census. This deviation is also reflected in the drastic decline in the percentage of female workers in the same age-group in 1971 compared to the 1961, 1981, and 1991 censuses. In view of this, further analysis of the age–sex distribution for the benchmark years 1961, 1983, 1987–8, 1993–4, and 1999–2000 is based on the 1961 census and the quinquennial surveys of the respective years. Annual percentage age–sex distributions for the years 1960–1 to 1999–2000 worked out on the basis of the observed growth rates between the benchmark years (see Table 3.6) are given in Table 3.7, Col. (1)–(9).

Age–Sex Distribution of Workers, 1950–1 to 1959–60

Age–sex distribution of workers is not available from the official sources for years prior to 1961. Dholakia has attempted estimates for the benchmark year 1950–1 using a simple algebraic relationship between 1950–1 and 1960–1 proportions.[17] He, however, distinguished only three broad categories of total working force, viz. children (aged below 15 years), women and men (of age both 15 years and above) to represent the changes in the age–sex distribution between these years. The percentages worked out by him for 1950–1[18] and the corresponding values according to the 1961 census are as follows:

Percentage Distribution of Workers, 1950–1 and 1961

	Children	Men	Women
1950–1 (Dholakia)	8.14	62.5	29.36
1961 (Census)	7.67	63.85	28.48

The annual percentage age–sex distribution for the years 1950–1 to 1960–1 are shown in Table 3.8 Col. (1)–(4).

DERIVATION OF DAILY EARNINGS WEIGHTS

The percentage distribution of workers classified by sex and age-groups have been obtained for the years 1960–1 to 1999–2000 and for 1950–1 to 1960–1 according to men, women, and children. The next step is to develop labour input indexes based on the relative earnings of workers in the different demographic groups.

Data relating to wage differentials of workers by sex and age are extremely limited. The quinquennial employment and unemployment surveys of 1993–4 and 1999–2000 provide average daily earnings of casual labourers classified by age-sex and rural/urban residence. Only three age-groups are distinguished, viz. 5–14, 15–59, and 60 plus years. For rural areas, a simple average of the

---

[17] Dholakia, *The Sources of Economic Growth in India*, pp. 125, 132–3. The algebraic formula used is: $Y_{1950-1} = \dfrac{Y_{1960-1} \times \text{Index of WPR'} \times \text{Index of K}}{\text{Index of WPR}}$, where WPR stands for the overall worker–population ratio, WPR' the worker rate for a given age-group, K is the proportion of population in that age-group for the year 1950–1 with 1961 = 1.0000, Y_{1950-1} is the proportion of working force in the given age-group in 1950–1, and Y_{1960-1} is the proportion of working force in the same age-group in 1960–1.

[18] Ibid., p. 134.

Table 3.7: Labour Input Index for Changes in Age-Sex Composition, 1960–1 to 1999–2000

Year	Males by age-group				Females by age-group				Grand Total
	5–14	15–59	60+	Total	5–14	15–59	60+	Total	
	(1)	(2)	(3)	(4)	(5)	(6)	(7)	(8)	(9)
1960–1	4.61	58.83	5.02	68.46	3.06	27.01	1.47	31.54	100.00
1961–2	4.58	58.77	5.02	68.36	3.06	27.09	1.48	31.63	99.99
1962–3	4.56	58.70	5.01	68.27	3.06	27.18	1.48	31.72	99.99
1963–4	4.53	58.64	5.01	68.17	3.07	27.26	1.49	31.81	99.99
1964–5	4.50	58.57	5.00	68.08	3.07	27.35	1.49	31.91	99.98
1965–6	4.47	58.51	5.00	67.98	3.07	27.43	1.50	32.00	99.98
1966–7	4.45	58.45	4.99	67.89	3.07	27.52	1.50	32.09	99.98
1967–8	4.42	58.38	4.99	67.79	3.07	27.60	1.51	32.18	99.98
1968–9	4.40	58.32	4.98	67.70	3.07	27.69	1.51	32.28	99.97
1969–70	4.37	58.26	4.98	67.60	3.08	27.77	1.52	32.37	99.97
1970–1	4.34	58.19	4.97	67.51	3.08	27.86	1.52	32.46	99.97
1971–2	4.32	58.13	4.97	67.42	3.08	27.95	1.53	32.56	99.97
1972–3	4.29	58.07	4.97	67.32	3.08	28.03	1.53	32.65	99.97
1973–4	4.27	58.00	4.96	67.23	3.08	28.12	1.54	32.74	99.97
1974–5	4.24	57.94	4.96	67.14	3.09	28.21	1.54	32.84	99.98
1975–6	4.22	57.88	4.95	67.04	3.09	28.30	1.55	32.93	99.98
1976–7	4.19	57.81	4.95	66.95	3.09	28.38	1.56	33.03	99.98
1977–8	4.17	57.75	4.94	66.86	3.09	28.47	1.56	33.12	99.98
1978–9	4.14	57.69	4.94	66.77	3.09	28.56	1.57	33.22	99.99
1979–80	4.12	57.62	4.93	66.68	3.09	28.65	1.57	33.32	99.99
1980–1	4.09	57.56	4.93	66.58	3.10	28.74	1.58	33.41	100.00
1981–2	4.07	57.50	4.93	66.49	3.10	28.83	1.58	33.51	100.00
1982–3	4.04	57.44	4.92	66.40	3.10	28.92	1.59	33.61	100.01
1983–4	4.02	57.37	4.92	66.31	3.10	29.01	1.59	33.70	100.01

Percentage age-sex composition

(Contd.)

71

Table 3.7 Contd.

	(1)	(2)	(3)	(4)	(5)	(6)	(7)	(8)	(9)
1984–5	3.45	57.90	4.98	66.33	2.92	29.04	1.57	33.53	99.86
1985–6	2.96	58.44	5.04	66.43	2.74	29.07	1.55	33.37	99.80
1986–7	2.54	58.97	5.10	66.61	2.58	29.11	1.53	33.22	99.83
1987–8	2.18	59.52	5.17	66.86	2.42	29.14	1.51	33.08	99.94
1988–9	2.16	59.63	5.16	66.95	2.27	29.15	1.54	32.96	99.91
1989–90	2.15	59.75	5.15	67.04	2.12	29.16	1.56	32.85	99.89
1990–1	2.13	59.87	5.14	67.13	1.99	29.18	1.58	32.75	99.88
1991–2	2.12	59.98	5.13	67.22	1.86	29.19	1.61	32.66	99.88
1992–3	2.10	60.10	5.12	67.32	1.74	29.20	1.63	32.57	99.89
1993–4	2.09	60.21	5.11	67.41	1.63	29.21	1.66	32.50	99.91
1994–5	1.98	60.54	5.10	67.62	1.56	29.04	1.65	32.25	99.87
1995–6	1.87	60.87	5.09	67.84	1.49	28.87	1.65	32.00	99.84
1996–7	1.78	61.20	5.09	68.06	1.42	28.70	1.64	31.76	99.82
1997–8	1.68	61.53	5.08	68.29	1.36	28.53	1.64	31.52	99.82
1998–9	1.59	61.87	5.07	68.53	1.30	28.36	1.64	31.29	99.82
1999–2000	1.51	62.20	5.07	68.78	1.24	28.19	1.63	31.06	99.84

(Cols Contd.)

72

Table 3.7 Contd.: Labour Input Index for Changes in Age-Sex Composition, 1960-1 to 1999-2000

Year	Wage wts.	Average of 1993-4 and 1999-2000 weights × percentage age-sex composition						Age-sex effect on labour input
		Males by age-group			Females by age-group			
		5-14 55.28	15-59 100	60+ 85.54	5-14 51.47	15-59 64.48	60+ 53.15	
		(10)	(11)	(12)	(13)	(14)	(15)	(16)
1960-1		254.84	5883.00	429.41	157.50	1741.60	78.13	85.44
1961-2		253.33	5876.59	429.02	157.59	1747.02	78.41	85.42
1962-3		251.83	5870.18	428.63	157.68	1752.44	78.68	85.39
1963-4		250.34	5863.78	428.25	157.77	1757.89	78.96	85.37
1964-5		248.85	5857.39	427.86	157.87	1763.35	79.24	85.35
1965-6		247.38	5851.01	427.47	157.96	1768.83	79.52	85.32
1966-7		245.91	5844.63	427.09	158.05	1774.33	79.80	85.30
1967-8		244.45	5838.26	426.70	158.14	1779.84	80.08	85.27
1968-9		243.00	5831.90	426.32	158.24	1785.37	80.37	85.25
1969-70		241.56	5825.54	425.93	158.33	1790.91	80.65	85.23
1970-1		240.13	5819.19	425.54	158.42	1796.48	80.94	85.21
1971-2		238.71	5812.85	425.16	158.51	1802.06	81.22	85.19
1972-3		237.29	5806.51	424.78	158.61	1807.66	81.51	85.16
1973-4		235.89	5800.18	424.39	158.70	1813.28	81.80	85.14
1974-5		234.49	5793.86	424.01	158.79	1818.91	82.09	85.12
1975-6		233.10	5787.54	423.62	158.88	1824.56	82.38	85.10
1976-7		231.72	5781.23	423.24	158.98	1830.23	82.67	85.08
1977-8		230.34	5774.93	422.86	159.07	1835.92	82.96	85.06
1978-9		228.98	5768.64	422.48	159.16	1841.62	83.25	85.04
1979-80		227.62	5762.35	422.09	159.26	1847.34	83.55	85.02
1980-1		226.27	5756.07	421.71	159.35	1853.08	83.84	85.00
1981-2		224.93	5749.80	421.33	159.44	1858.84	84.14	84.98
1982-3		223.59	5743.53	420.95	159.53	1864.62	84.43	84.97

(Contd.)

Table 3.7 Contd.

	(10)	(11)	(12)	(13)	(14)	(15)	(16)
1983–4	222.27	5737.27	420.57	159.63	1870.41	84.73	84.95
1984–5	190.64	5790.17	425.78	150.10	1872.56	83.64	85.13
1985–6	163.52	5843.55	431.06	141.14	1874.71	82.57	85.37
1986–7	140.25	5897.43	436.41	132.71	1876.86	81.50	85.65
1987–8	120.30	5951.80	441.82	124.79	1879.02	80.46	85.98
1988–9	119.49	5963.35	440.96	116.80	1879.77	81.66	86.02
1989–90	118.69	5974.92	440.11	109.32	1880.52	82.88	86.06
1990–1	117.89	5986.51	439.26	102.32	1881.28	84.13	86.11
1991–2	117.10	5998.12	438.41	95.77	1882.03	85.39	86.17
1992–3	116.32	6009.76	437.57	89.64	1882.78	86.67	86.23
1993–4	115.54	6021.42	436.72	83.90	1883.53	87.96	86.29
1994–5	109.42	6054.13	436.16	80.14	1872.39	87.78	86.40
1995–6	103.63	6087.01	435.59	76.55	1861.31	87.61	86.52
1996–7	98.15	6120.08	435.02	73.12	1850.30	87.43	86.64
1997–8	92.95	6153.32	434.46	69.84	1839.35	87.25	86.77
1998–9	88.04	6186.75	433.89	66.71	1828.47	87.07	86.91
1999–2000	83.38	6220.35	433.33	63.72	1817.65	86.89	87.05

Sources: Table 3.6; for weights, refer to Table 3.12, Col. (3). Col. (10) to (12) = Col. (1) to (3). Col. (13) to (15) = Col. (5) to (7) × respective weights; Col. (16) = sum of Col. (10) to (15)/100.

74

Table 3.8: Labour Input Index for Changes in Age–Sex Composition, 1950–1 to 1960–1

Year	Percentage age–sex composition				Average of 1993–4 and 1999–2000 weights × % distribution			Age–sex effect on labour input
	Men	Women	Children	Total	wt. 100 Men	wt. 64.35 Women	wt. 53.96 Children	
	(1)	(2)	(3)	(4)	(5)	(6)	(7)	(8)
1950–1	62.50	29.36	8.14	100.00	6250.00	1889.32	439.23	85.79
1951–2	62.63	29.27	8.09	100.00	6263.37	1883.58	436.63	85.84
1952–3	62.77	29.18	8.04	99.99	6276.77	1877.85	434.04	85.89
1953–4	62.90	29.09	8.00	99.99	6290.19	1872.15	431.47	85.94
1954–5	63.04	29.00	7.95	99.99	6303.65	1866.46	428.91	85.99
1955–6	63.17	28.92	7.90	99.99	6317.13	1860.79	426.36	86.04
1956–7	63.31	28.83	7.85	99.99	6330.64	1855.14	423.84	86.10
1957–8	63.44	28.74	7.81	99.99	6344.18	1849.50	421.32	86.15
1958–9	63.58	28.65	7.76	99.99	6357.75	1843.88	418.82	86.20
1959–60	63.71	28.57	7.72	100.00	6371.35	1838.28	416.34	86.26
1960–1	63.85	28.48	7.67	100.00	6384.98	1832.70	413.87	86.32

Source: Refer to the text.

average daily earnings of those engaged in 'public works' and 'other works' is taken. For urban areas, the average daily earnings of workers in all industrial divisions is accepted. The earnings data are not comprehensive enough as they exclude regular employees who receive salaries and self-employed and family workers who do not get any regular payment. The adoption of average daily wages of casual labourers as the guideline for differentials implies the assumption that they will be indicative of the overall variations among age–sex groups and persons of different employment status. The available data leading to the calculation of index numbers of wage differentials are given in Table 3.9.

Panel A of Table 3.9 shows the average daily wages of casual labourers in rural and urban areas for the different age–sex groups for the years 1993–4 and 1999–2000. The proportions of workers in each age–sex group classified according to rural–urban residence are given in Panel B. These are derived from the percentage distributions of the employed taken from the quinquennial surveys. The number of workers in each group is worked out by applying the relevant percentage to the estimated total number of workers in each category—rural male, rural female, urban male, and urban female. The detailed worksheets for 1993–4 and 1999–2000 are shown in Appendix Table 3(e).

Weighted average daily wages of male and female workers in each age-bracket computed as the sum of the products of the average daily wages shown in Panel A and the proportion of workers shown in rural and urban areas given in Panel B are presented in Panel C. It is seen that in both 1993–4 and 1999–2000 male workers in the age-group 15–59 years receive the highest wage followed by the males in the 60+ years group. Wage levels of female workers are generally lower than those of males in the respective age-groups. The differentials in the wage-structure are expressed in index form in

Table 3.9: Weighted Average Daily Wage Earnings of Casual Labourers by Sex and Age, 1993–4 and 1999–2000

	1993–4 Age-groups			1999–2000 Age-groups		
	5–14	15–59	60+	5–14	15–59	60+
	(1)	(2)	(3)	(4)	(5)	(6)
Panel A	Average daily wages (Rs)					
Males						
Rural	13.70	23.18	20.84	29.87	47.26	40.13
Urban	13.69	32.38	30.75	28.80	63.25	57.67
Females						
Rural	12.60	15.33	14.41	28.02	34.43	24.70
Urban	11.71	18.49	15.94	30.99	38.22	33.29
Panel B	Weights for rural/urban workers					
Males						
Rural	0.8565	0.7313	0.8412	0.8488	0.7083	0.8294
Urban	0.1435	0.2687	0.1588	0.1512	0.2917	0.1706
Total	1.0000	1.0000	1.0000	1.0000	1.0000	1.0000
Females						
Rural	0.8953	0.8555	0.8651	0.8677	0.8444	0.8588
Urban	0.1047	0.1445	0.1349	0.1232	0.1556	0.1412
Total	1.0000	1.0000	1.0000	1.0000	1.0000	1.0000
Panel C	Weighted average daily wages (Rs)					
Males	13.69	25.65	22.58	29.70	51.92	43.12
Females	12.51	15.78	14.61	28.13	35.02	25.61
Panel D	Index numbers of wages with 15–59 males wage = 100					
Males	53.37	100.00	88.03	57.20	100.00	83.05
Females	48.77	61.52	56.96	54.18	67.45	49.33

Sources: For 1993–4, *NSS Report No. 409, Employment and Unemployment in India, 1993–4*, New Delhi, March 1997, pp. 69, 315–35. For 1999–2000, *NSS Report No. 458, Employment and Unemployment Situation in India, 1999–2000*, New Delhi, May 2001, pp. 70, 292–309. For calculations, see the text.

Panel D, taking the wage level of male workers in the age-group 15–59 years as equal to 100. These index numbers for 1993–4 and 1999–2000 are used later to derive a weighting system based on daily earnings applicable for the period 1960–1 to 1999–2000.

Due to the non-availability of the distribution of workers by age and sex in the 1951 census, it has been possible to classify them only into three broad groups—children (below 15 years), men, and women (both 15 years and above) instead of the six demographic groups for the subsequent census and survey years. The derivation of the weighted average daily wages of the three groups of workers—children, men, and women are shown in Panels A, B, and C of Table 3.10. The numbers in each group are obtained from Appendix Tables 3(e) and 3(h) for 1993–4 and 1999–2000 respectively. The weighted average wages of male and female children and men and women workers are taken from Panel C of Table 3.9. The combined weighted average wage for children (male and female taken together) is obtained as equal to the sum of the products of average daily wage of male children and their proportion to

Table 3.10: Weighted Average Daily Earnings for Casual Labourers (Men, Women, and Children), 1993–4 and 1999–2000

	1993–4			1999–2000		
	(1)	(2)	(3)	(4)	(5)	(6)
Panel A for children						
	Male	Female	Total	Male	Female	Total
(a) Number ('000)	7179	5867	13046	5516	4690	10206
(b) Proportion	0.5503	0.4497	1.0000	0.5405	0.4595	1.0000
(c) Average wage in Rs	13.69	12.51	13.16	29.70	28.13	28.98
Panel B for men		Age-group			Age-group	
	15–59	60+	Total	15–59	60+	Total
(a) Number ('000)	224,475	19,050	243,525	245,415	19,996	265,411
(b) Proportion	0.9218	0.0782	1.0000	0.9247	0.0753	1.0000
(c) Average wage in Rs	25.65	22.58	25.41	51.92	43.12	51.26
Panel C for women		Age-group			Age-group	
	15–59	60+	Total	15–59	60+	Total
(a) Number ('000)	108,116	6072	114,188	110,439	6345	116,784
(b) Proportion	0.9468	0.0532	1.0000	0.9457	0.0543	1.0000
(c) Average wage in Rs	15.78	14.61	15.72	35.02	25.61	34.51

Sources: (a) and (b) in all panels from Appendix Table 3(g), Cols (9) and (10); (c) Cols (1) and (2) in all panels from Table 3.9, Panel C, and Col. (3) calculated as weighted average of wages in Cols (1) and (2) with weights in line (b).

total and average daily wage of female children and the corresponding proportion to total. They are shown as Rs 13.16 for 1993–4 and Rs 28.98 for 1999–2000. In a similar manner, the combined weighted average wages of men workers in the age-groups 15–59 and 60 plus years and similar figure for women workers are also calculated and shown as Rs 25.41 and Rs 51.26 for men in 1993–4 and 1999–2000 and Rs 15.72 and Rs 34.51 for women in the same years. The index numbers of wage differentials among men, women, and children with the weighted average wage of men workers as equal to 100 are shown in Table 3.11. The two sets of indexes of wage differentials have thus been derived, one set applicable for the years 1950–1 to 1960–1 and the other for 1960–1 to 1999–2000.

Table 3.11: Index of Wage Differentials of Casual Labourers Classified as Men (15 years and above), Women (15 years and above), and Children (below 15 years) with Average Weights for Men = 100 for 1993–4 and 1999–2000

Category of labour	1993–4	1999–2000	Average
	(1)	(2)	(3)
Children (below 15 years)	51.79	56.13	53.96
Men (15 years and above)	100.00	100.00	100.00
Women (15 years and above)	61.87	66.84	64.36

Source: Col. (1) calculated from Table 3.10, Col. (3); Col. (2) calculated from Table 3.10, Col (6); Col. (3) = [Col. (1) + Col. (2)]/2.

CALCULATION OF THE LABOUR INPUT INDEX FOR CHANGES IN THE AGE–SEX COMPOSITION

The indexes of wage differentials shown in Table 3.9 and Table 3.11 are used as weights to derive the labour input index. The simple averages of the indexes of wage differentials for the two years 1993–4 and 1999–2000 are taken as our final weights.

The *Report* of the 1983 employment-unemployment survey also presents data on average daily earnings of regular wage/salaried earners. But the results could not be accepted because (a) of abnormal values for certain categories and the presence of some unclear corrections in the mimeographed report, (b) much wider variation in average daily earnings between groups than what was observed in the case of casual labourers, and (c) the lack of data on salaried employees at least for another year to support the wider variations in wage rates. It, therefore, became necessary to rely on the wage data relating to casual labourers only for the two years 1993–4 and 1999–2000.

Table 3.12: Indexes of Wage Differentials Used as Weights for 1960–1 to 1999–2000

| Age–sex group | Wage for males in the age-group 15–59 = 100 | | |
| | 1993–4 | 1999–2000 | Average |
	(1)	(2)	(3)
Males			
5–14	53.37	57.20	55.28
15–59	100.00	100.00	100.00
60+	88.03	83.05	85.54
Females			
5–14	48.77	54.18	51.47
15–59	61.52	67.45	64.48
60+	56.90	49.33	53.15

Sources: Cols (1) and (2) from Table 3.9 Panel D; Col. (3) = [Col. (1) + Col. (2)]/2.

The values given in Col. 3 are used as weights applicable for the period 1960–1 to 1999–2000. Similar weights shown in Col. 3, Table 3.11 are accepted for the period 1950–1 to 1960–1.

The reliance on just two years data on wage differentials, and that too for casual labourers only, as valid for the whole period and entire workforce may raise some doubts about their representative character. Regular wage/salary earners, self-employed, and family workers are left out. It would have been desirable to have a much wider database in terms of time series and coverage of different categories of the employed. The problem relating to inadequate wage data is not peculiar to India. It has been faced by growth accountants in the case of developed countries too. In his study *Accounting for United States Economic Growth, 1929–1969*, Denison[19] used 1966 wage data for the entire period. Further wage data were limited to male employees only. For

[19] Denison, *Accounting for Growth*, p. 34, 189–90.

his next work on *Accounting for Slower Growth in the 1970s*,[20] annual wage data for 1967 through 1974 became available and weights were based on averages of several years. Due to non-availability of wage data for the 1913–50 period, Maddison in his study on 'Growth and Slowdown in Advanced Capitalist Economies' did not make any adjustment for changes in the age-composition but applied 0.6 weight for female employment.[21] Andre Hofman also did not attempt any adjustment for changes in the quality of labour input due to changes in the age–sex composition but confined himself only to education in his study on the economic development of Latin American countries.[22] E. F. Denison and Willam K. Chung consider the main limitation of the wage data used in their study on *How Japan's Economy Grew So Fast* as the omission of self-employed and unpaid family workers. According to them, the limitation would be difficult to remedy because there is no suitable method by which to allocate the earnings of unincorporated enterprises among individual proprietors and unpaid family workers.[23] In the light of the experience in the case of other countries, especially the developed ones, our acceptance of available wage data of casual labourers for two years as valid for the whole period and indicative of differentials among the entire workforce seem justified.

Table 3.13: Labour Input Index for Changes in Age–Sex Composition, 1950–1 to 1999–2000

Year	On the basis of average of 1993–4 and 1999–2000 weights			
	Labour input index	Labour input index	Linked Labour input index	Linked index with 1993–4 = 100
	(1)	(2)	(3)	(4)
1950–1	85.79		84.96	98.46
1951–2	85.84		85.01	98.52
1952–3	85.89		85.06	98.58
1953–4	85.94		85.11	98.64
1954–5	85.99		85.16	98.69
1955–6	86.04		85.22	98.76
1956–7	86.10		85.27	98.82
1957–8	86.15		85.32	98.88
1958–9	86.20		85.38	98.94
1959–60	86.26		85.43	99.00

(Contd.)

[20] Denison, *Accounting for Slower Economic Growth in the United States in the 1970s*, Washington, D.C., 1979, p. 157.

[21] Maddison, 'Growth and Slowdown in Advanced Capitalist Economies'— 'Techniques of Quantitative Assessment' in *Idem, Explaining the Economic Performance of Nations—Essays in Time and Space*, Cheltenham, 1995, p. 481.

[22] Andre Hofman, 'Economic Development in Latin America in the 20th Century—A Comparative Perspective', in *Explaining Economic Growth: Essays in Honour of Angus Maddison*, A. Szirmai, B. Van Ark, and D. Pilat (eds), Amsterdam, 1993, p. 252.

[23] E. F. Denison and William K. Chung, *How Japan's Economy Grew So Fast: The Sources of Post-war Expansion*, Brookings Institution, Washington, D.C., 1976, p. 188.

Table 3.13 Contd.

	(1)	(2)	(3)	(4)
1960–1	86.32	85.44	85.44	99.02
1961–2		85.42	85.42	98.99
1962–3		85.39	85.39	98.96
1963–4		85.37	85.37	98.93
1964–5		85.35	85.35	98.90
1965–6		85.32	85.32	98.88
1966–7		85.30	85.30	98.85
1967–8		85.27	85.27	98.82
1968–9		85.25	85.25	98.80
1969–70		85.23	85.23	98.77
1970–1		85.21	85.21	98.74
1971–2		85.19	85.19	98.72
1972–3		85.16	85.16	98.69
1973–4		85.14	85.14	98.67
1974–5		85.12	85.12	98.64
1975–6		85.10	85.10	98.62
1976–7		85.08	85.08	98.60
1977–8		85.06	85.06	98.57
1978–9		85.04	85.04	98.55
1979–80		85.02	85.02	98.53
1980–1		85.00	85.00	98.51
1981–2		84.98	84.98	98.49
1982–3		84.97	84.97	98.47
1983–4		84.95	84.95	98.44
1984–5		85.13	85.13	98.65
1985–6		85.37	85.37	98.93
1986–7		85.65	85.65	99.26
1987–8		85.98	85.98	99.64
1988–9		86.02	86.02	99.69
1989–90		86.06	86.06	99.74
1990–1		86.11	86.11	99.80
1991–2		86.17	86.17	99.86
1992–3		86.23	86.23	99.93
1993–4		86.29	86.29	100.00
1994–5		86.40	86.40	100.13
1995–6		86.52	86.52	100.26
1996–7		86.64	86.64	100.41
1997–8		86.77	86.77	100.56
1998–9		86.91	86.91	100.72
1999–2000		87.05	87.05	100.88

Sources: Col. (1) from Table 3.8, Col. (8); Col. (2) Table 3.7, Col. (16); for Col. (3) and (4), see the text.

The labour input indexes (Table 3.1, Col. (2)) are computed separately for the years 1960–1 to 1999–2000 and 1950–1 to 1960–1 as the weighting system and demographic groups are not same. For the former, the percentage age-sex composition of the employed given in Cols (1)–(3) and (5)–(7) of Table 3.7 were multiplied by the weights shown in Table 3.12, Col. (3) and Table 3.7 Cols (10)–(15). The products for each year were then added and divided by the sum of the percentages shown in Col. (9) of Table 3.7, which do not always add up to 100 due to rounding. The resulting series are shown in Col. (16) of Table 3.7 and also in Col. (2) of Table 3.13. Similarly, for 1950–1 to

1960-1 the percentage composition in the three groups—adult males, adult females, and children—given in Col (1)-(3) of Table 3.8 were multiplied by the weights shown in Col. (3) of Table 3.11. The products shown in Cols (5)-(7) of Table 3.8 were then divided by the sum of the percentages given in Col. (4) of the same table. The resulting series for 1950-1 to 1960-1 are presented in Col. (8) of Table 3.8 and also in Col. (2) of Table 3.13. The two series in Cols (1) and (2) of Table 3.13 were then linked [Col. (3)] and converted to index form with 1993-4 = 100. These indexes reflect the effect of the changes in age-sex composition on labour input and are shown in Col. (4) of Table 3.13 and also in Col. (2) of Table 3.1. The index shows a gradual increase from 98.46 in 1950-1 to 99.02 in 1960-1, a decline thereafter till 1983-4 and again a slow upward movement up to to 100.85 in 1999-2000. There are no violent fluctuations. To what extent it reflects the actual situation is hard to guess. The limitations of the index arising from the procedure adopted for deriving the annual percentage age-sex distributions and the use of constant weights based on just two years' data for casual labourers only need to be kept in mind. But the census and survey results on which the estimates are based also do not show any appreciable change as far as male-female distribution of the workers as shown in Table 3.14. Regarding the variations in age composition, the adoption of the three broad groups 5-14, 15-59 and 60+years do conceal some trends. The more detailed age distribution presented in Table 3.15 shows a clear declining trend in the percentage workers in the age-groups 5-14 and 15-29 years. These show a gradual decrease in the share of child labour and the effect of increasing enrolment in educational institutions.[24]

[24] The increasing enrolment in educational institutions can be seen from the following:

Percentage of Youth (15-24 years) Currently Attending School or College According to the NSS Surveys of 1987-8 and 1993-4 and the 1991 Census

Sector/Age	Year	Male	Female	Both series
	(1)	(2)	(3)	(4)
Rural India				
15-19	1987-8 (NSS)	36.6	13.2	25.7
	1991* (Census)	40.6	18.0	30.2
	1993-4 (NSS)	41.2	20.8	32.0
20-24	1987-8	8.3	1.7	4.8
	1991*	12.5	3.0	7.7
	1993-4	10.8	2.9	6.8
Urban India				
15-19	1987-8	52.9	39.5	46.7
	1991*	56.8	46.1	51.8
	1993-4	56.9	49.7	53.7
20-9	1987-8	19.5	9.0	14.4
	1991*	22.3	11.6	17.2
	1993-4	22.5	13.4	18.1

* Data excludes Jammu and Kashmir.
Source: Pravin Visaria, *Unemployment among Youth in India: Level, Nature and Policy Implications*, Employment and Training Papers 36, International Labour Office, Geneva, 1998, p. 18.

Table 3.14: Average Age of Workers in Years and Percentage of Male and
Female Workers, 1961 to 1999–2000

Year/Source	Average age in years		Percentage of workers	
	Male	Female	Male	Female
	(1)	(2)	(3)	(4)
1961 Census	34.49	32.52	68.45	31.55
1983 NSS	34.31	32.75	66.40	33.60
1987–8 NSS	35.49	33.23	67.06	32.94
1993–4 NSS	35.57	34.36	67.62	32.38
1999–2000 NSS	36.02	34.93	69.05	30.95

Source: Calculated from *Census of India, 1961*, Vol. I, Part II-B(i), p. 86 and;
Appendix Table 3(e).

Table 3.15: Percentage Distribution of Workers by Age, 1961 to 1999–2000

Age-group	NSS				
	1961 Census	1983	1987–8	1993–4	1999–2000
	(1)	(2)	(3)	(4)	(5)
Males					
5–14	6.73	6.07	3.01	2.86	2.03
15–29	..	37.05	36.13	35.74	34.48
30–44	..	30.55	33.44	33.99	35.75
45–59	..	18.92	19.67	19.81	20.35
15–59	85.94	86.52	89.24	89.54	90.58
60+	7.33	7.41	7.75	7.60	7.39
Total	100.00	100.00	100.00	100.00	100.00
Females					
5–14	9.73	9.22	7.12	4.89	3.86
15–29	..	37.07	37.45	35.77	34.02
30–44	..	30.78	32.48	34.90	37.56
45–59	..	18.20	18.39	19.38	19.32
15–59	85.62	86.05	88.33	90.05	90.91
60+	4.65	4.73	4.55	5.06	5.22
Total	100.00	100.00	100.00	100.00	100.00

Source: Table 3.14.

The two middle groups 30–44 and 45–59 years exhibit increasing shares. These
groups may also claim higher weights due to their earnings being higher due
to work experience and qualifications. The share of age-group 60+ years for
males and females is more or less same over the period. This reduction in the
shares of the two lower age-groups has had an impact on the average age of
workers which increased from 34.5 to 36.0 in the case of males and from 32.5
to 34.9 in the case of females. The effect of age–sex composition on labour
input, perhaps, might be more visible if more detailed age-distributions could
be used for deriving the percentage share of workers and the earnings weights.

EDUCATION OF WORKERS

Tremendous progress has been made in the field of education in India since 1950–1. The number of recognized educational institutions and the number of pupils enrolled has increased manifold, rapidly in the first two decades and at a slower pace in the subsequent decades. The number of illiterates in the population came down from 83 per cent in 1951 to 38 per cent in 1997. The total enrolment in the primary stage during the period 1950–1 to 1996–7 increased 5.75 times while for girls the increase was more than nine times. At the upper primary stage of education the increase was more than 13 times while that for girls it was more than 32 times. At the secondary and higher secondary stage the corresponding increases were 18 times for total enrolment and 49 times for girls. The number of primary schools increased threefold, while upper primary schools and higher secondary schools and junior colleges multiplied 14 times.[25] In the field of higher education, the number of universities increased from 27 to 1950–1 to 229 in 1997–8 and the colleges of general education from 370 to 7199 during the same period. The number of colleges for professional education increased from 208 to 2075 over the same period. Total enrolment in colleges increased 37 times between 1950–1 and 1995–6, that is at a phenomenal rate of 8.4 per cent per year.[26] In addition to this, a number of highly specialized institutions such as the Indian Institutes of Technology, Indian Institutes of Management, institutes or organizations in the field of basic sciences and social sciences, and centres for advanced studies and research in various disciplines were set up in different parts of the country over the years. All these have thrown up a large reservoir of educated and technically trained manpower. This would have naturally brought about a qualitative change in the composition of the workforce and hence in labour input. The effect of these changes in labour input is measured by an index which combines the percentage of workers with different levels of education using weights to reflect the wage differentials between them. This approach developed by Denison[27] in his 1967 study *Why Growth Rates Differ* and followed by Dholakia in his work *The Sources of Economic Growth in India*[28] has also been used in this study.

DERIVATION OF EDUCATION WEIGHTS

The basic data required to evolve a weighting system to distinguish workers with different educational attainments are their distribution according to

[25] Department of Statistics, Government of India, 'Educational Statistics' from the website of the Department of Statistics.

[26] Association of Indian Universities, *Higher Education in India: Retrospect and Prospect*, by Monis Raza (ed.), New Delhi, 1991, pp. 39–40; Central Statistical Organization, *Statistical Abstract of India, 1997*, Vol. II, New Delhi, pp. 509–607.

[27] Denison, *Why Growth Rates Differ*, pp. 82–4.

[28] Dholakia, *The Sources of Economic Growth in India*, p. 121.

educational levels and earnings. The quinquennial surveys of employment and unemployment, especially for the years 1993–4 and 1999–2000 provide information on average wage/salary earnings per day received by regular wage/salaried employees of age 15–59 years by sector (industry) of work and broad education category. The employees are further classified by sex and rural–urban residence. Four levels of education are distinguished, viz. not literate, literate up to middle, secondary, and graduate and above. Thus, along with sex distinction and rural/urban residence, wage/salary data classified into sixteen groups for the years 1993–4 and 1999–2000 are shown in Table 3.16. There is considerable variation between the wage levels in different groups but there is stability in the wage differentials between years. The salary of the urban male graduate, the highest among the groups, was found to be 2.7 times that of an urban male with primary (literate up to middle) education both in 1993–4 and 1999–2000. The ratio of wages of females to that of males in the same categories was found to be more or less stable in both years as shown in Table 3.17.

For purposes of comparison the average wages of different groups of workers are expressed as indexes, taking the level of wage of the urban male 'graduate and above' as equal to 100. These indexes are shown in Cols (2) and (4) of Table 3.16. The weights based on simple average of the indexes for the two survey years are assumed to be applicable for the whole period in view of the stability exhibited by them. But the averages so derived cannot be considered to represent wage differentials due to the differences in education only. There are other characteristics influencing the wages, viz. age, family background, aptitude, etc. To allow for these factors, Denison assumed that 'three-fifths of the reported income differentials between each of the other group and the group with 8 years of education represented differences on earnings due to differences in education as distinguished from other associated characteristics'.[29] Dholakia adopted a similar procedure but varied the assumption to two-thirds based on the observations of Blaug and others 'that the two major factors which affect the earnings differentials, viz. family background and native ability are when taken together likely to be of equal importance in India and the United States' and their choice of 65 per cent out of the three alternatives 50 per cent, 65 per cent, and 100 per cent as the best estimate for their calculation.[30] This assumption that two-thirds of the wage differentials can be attributed to differences in educational levels is also followed in this study. The system of weights evolved on this basis is shown in Col. (6) of Table 3.16. The procedure is subject to certain limitations. The weights are based on the data available for two years only. In defence of this it may be stated that the wage differentials in 1993–4 and 1999–2000 showed a certain amount of consistency which can be verified only if we have data for other time points. The other limitation is that the wage differentials are based only on the wage data of regular wage/salaried employees and do not

[29] Denison, *Why Growth Rates Differ*, pp. 83–4.
[30] Dholakia, *The Sources of Economic Growth in India*, p. 121.

Table 3.16: Wage Differentials by Levels of Education, Sex, and Rural–Urban Residence, 1993–4 and 1999–2000

Classification of workers	1993–4		1999–2000		Average of indexes	Used for education weights
	Salary/wage in Rs per day	Index with salary of urban male graduate = 100	Salary/wage in Rs per day	Index with salary of urban male graduate = 100		
	(1)	(2)	(3)	(4)	(5)	(6)
Rural male						
Not literate	31.27	21.49	71.23	25.30	23.40	49.6791
Literate up to middle	45.87	35.92	91.63	32.54	34.23	55.9367
Secondary and higher secondary	72.31	56.63	148.23	52.65	54.64	69.6078
Graduate and above	97.71	76.52	220.93	78.47	77.50	84.9218
Rural female						
Not literate	17.98	14.08	40.32	14.32	14.20	42.5146
Literate up to middle	23.92	18.73	51.85	18.42	18.57	45.4448
Secondary and higher secondary	57.61	45.12	126.09	44.78	44.95	63.1169
Graduate and above	72.16	56.51	159.92	56.80	56.66	70.9594
Urban male						
Not literate	46.28	36.24	87.63	31.12	33.68	55.5683
Literate up to middle	53.02	41.52	105.08	37.32	39.42	59.4129
Secondary and higher secondary	80.33	62.91	168.16	59.73	61.32	74.0833
Graduate and above	127.69	100.00	281.55	100.00	100.00	100.0000
Urban female						
Not literate	26.75	20.95	51.83	18.41	19.68	46.1849
Literate up to middle	30.11	23.58	64.41	22.88	23.23	48.5633
Secondary and higher secondary	70.93	55.55	145.73	51.76	53.65	68.9484
Graduate and above	98.59	77.21	234.74	83.37	80.29	86.7958

Sources: Col. (1) from *NSS Report No. 409, Employment and Unemployment in India, 1993–4*, pp. A306–10; Col. (2) derived from Col. (1); Col. (3) from *NSS Report No. 458, Employment and Unemployment Situation in India, 1999–2000*, pp. A280–6; Col. (4) derived from Col. (3); Col. (5) = [Col. (2) + Col. (4)]/2: Col. (6) derived from Col. (5).

Table 3.17: Ratio of Wages of Female Employees to that of
Male Employees in each Educational Category

	1993–4	1999–2000
	(1)	(2)
Urban		
Not literate	0.58	0.59
Literate up to middle	0.57	0.61
Secondary and higher secondary	0.88	0.87
Graduate and above	0.78	0.83
Rural		
Not literate	0.57	0.57
Literate up to middle	0.52	0.57
Secondary and higher secondary	0.80	0.85
Graduate and above	0.72	0.72

Source: Table 3.16.

take into account casual labourers, self-employed, and unpaid family workers. Similar problems were faced in other growth accounting studies also. Denison used the 1959 earnings data for males for the whole period 1929–69 and used the weights developed for males for female employees also.[31] Similarly, to provide a rough correction for the remuneration attracted by the different levels of education, Maddison assigned a weight of 1 for primary education, 1.4 for secondary education, and 2 for higher education.[32] He further weighted the increments by 0.6 for compression of the education weights for the influence of other characteristics.[33] On the basis of the weighting system developed, taking the labour of an urban male graduate as 1 unit, the labour of an urban male 'not literate' works out to 0.56, that of an urban 'literate up to middle' to 0.59, and that of an urban male with 'secondary' education to 0.74 units and so on. [Table 3.16, Col (6)]

DISTRIBUTION OF WORKERS BY LEVELS OF EDUCATION

The decennial population censuses and the quinquennial surveys of employment and unemployment provide the distribution of workers classified by sex, rural–urban residence, and educational levels. The censuses give absolute numbers while the surveys present percentage composition of workers by educational level. The classification schemes followed in censuses and surveys also vary as shown below:

[31] Denison, *Accounting for Growth*, p. 44.

[32] Angus Maddison, *Monitoring the World Economy 1820–1992*, OECD, Paris, 1995, p. 37, 77.

[33] Angus Maddison, 'Growth and Slowdown in Advanced Capitalist Economies', p. 65.

Classification of Workers by Educational Level

1961 Census	1971 to 1991 Censuses	Quinquennial surveys	Quinquennial survey (educational level and earnings)
(1)	(2)	(3)	(4)
Illiterate	Illiterate	Not literate	Not literate
Literate without educational level	Literate below primary	Literate up to primary	Literate up to middle
Primary/Junior basic	Primary Middle	Middle	
Matriculation/ higher secondary	Matriculation/ Secondary	Secondary and higher secondary	Secondary and higher secondary
Technical diploma not up to degree	Higher secondary Diploma certificate Non-technical level		
Non-technical diploma not up to degree	Diploma certificate Technical level	Graduate and above	Graduate and above
University degree and technical degree	Graduate and above		

It is obvious from the above that the classification by educational level of workers has to be limited to the broad groups followed in Col. (4) for the earnings data. The percentage distribution of workers by levels of education derived from the various sources are given in Tables 3.18 and 3.19. The results from the quinquennial surveys show a consistent trend. The percentage of illiterate workers declined from 66.12 in 1972–3 to 44.07 in 1999–2000. Workers with secondary education increased from 3.90 per cent to 13.52 per cent between 1972–3 and 1999–2000. The share of graduates in the meanwhile moved up from 1.14 per cent to 5.75 per cent.

Table 3.18: Percentage Distribution of Workers by Levels of Education as Reported in Quinquennial Surveys, 1972–3 to 1999–2000

Category	1972–3	1977–8	1983	1987–8	1993–4	1999–2000
	(1)	(2)	(3)	(4)	(5)	(6)
Not literate	66.12	61.50	57.18	53.84	49.05	44.07
Literate up to primary	23.30	24.34	23.82	24.63	24.01	22.76
Middle	5.54	7.17	9.39	9.65	11.53	13.90
Secondary and higher secondary	3.90	5.15	7.00	8.55	11.17	13.52
Graduate and above	1.14	1.84	2.58	3.33	4.44	5.75
Total	100.00	100.00	100.00	100.00	100.00	100.00

Source: Appendix Table 3(h).

Table 3.19: Percentage Distribution of Workers by Levels of Education
Based on Decennial Censuses, 1961 to 1991

Category	1961	1971	1981	1991
	(1)	(2)	(3)	(4)
Illiterate	72.86	62.85	57.49	51.02
Literate up to primary		23.56	22.98	21.72
Middle	24.40	6.90	7.90	10.91
Matriculation and higher secondary	2.29	5.43	11.36	11.91
Graduate and above	0.44	1.26	2.68	4.43
Total	100.00	100.00	100.00	100.00

Sources: Col. (1) *Census of India, 1961, Vol. I, Part II–B(i), General Economic Tables*, pp. 86–7; also Appendix Table 3(g); Col. (2) *Census of India, 1971, Paper 3 of 1972*, Tables B-III, Parts A&B, pp. 188–253; Col. (3) *Census of India, 1981 Part III–A(i), General Economic Tables, Tables B.1 to B.5*, 1985, pp. 404–661; Col. (4) *Census of India, 1991 Series 1, India, Part–III-B Series Tables B-1(s) to B-4(s)*, pp. 369–513.

The percentage shares worked out from census data show a broadly similar pattern but do not merge with the survey results consistently. While the percentage of illiterates indicated by the 1971 census is 62.85, that from the 1972–3 survey is 66.12, a reversal of the trend. Similar rather inconsistent trends are observed in the case of 'literate up to primary' between the 1971 census and the 1972–3 survey and also for 'secondary and higher secondary' between the 1991 census and the 1993–4 survey. For this reason as well as those mentioned while studying age–sex distributions, the census results except that of 1961 are not used. The latter along with the subsequent survey figures seem to give a consistent picture.

As noted earlier, the census reports show absolute numbers of workers in each category while the survey results present only percentage shares. The absolute numbers corresponding to the latter for each of the survey years are worked out by applying the respective percentages to the totals of the group as shown in Appendix Table 3(c). The results are shown in Appendix Table 3(h) as well as in Table 3.20 in the columns showing total number of workers in each of the sixteen groups.

CONSTRUCTION OF THE EDUCATION INDEX FOR 1950–1 TO 1999–2000

The numbers of workers at four different educational levels classified by rural, urban residence and sex have been obtained, giving in all sixteen groups. The ratios of workers in each one of the sixteen groups to the respective total for 1961, 1972–3, 1977–8, 1983, 1987–8, 1993–4, and 1999–2000 are multiplied by the corresponding earnings weights [Table 3.16 Col. (6)] and added to derive a measure of the education effect. This measure, shown in Table 3.20, is found to increase from 50.17 in 1961 to 55.68 in 1999–2000. These values are then expressed in index form with the 1993–4 value of 54.39 = 100. The index of education is found to vary from 92.24 in 1961 to 102.38 in 1999–2000 (Table 3.20).

Table 3.20: Measurement of Education Effect, 1961 to 1999–2000

Educational level/ Rural/Urban /Male/Female	Employment 1999–2000		Education weights	Education effect 1999–2000 Col. (2) × Col. (3)	Employment 1993–4		Education effect 1993–4 Col. (6) × Col. (3)	Employment 1987–8		Education effect 1987–8 Col. (9) × Col. (3)
	No. ('000)	Ratio to total			No. ('000)	Ratio to total		No. ('000)	Ratio to total	
	(1)	(2)	(3)	(4)	(5)	(6)	(7)	(8)	(9)	(10)
Rural male										
Not literate	75,407	0.1973	49.6791	9.80	78,918	0.2206	10.96	77,549	0.2513	12.48
Literate up to middle	83,024	0.2172	55.9367	12.15	77,116	0.2156	12.06	65,338	0.2117	11.84
Secondary and higher secondary	25,707	0.0673	69.6079	4.68	19,459	0.0544	3.79	12,687	0.0411	2.86
Graduate and above	6284	0.0164	84.9218	1.40	4685	0.0131	1.11	3013	0.0098	0.83
Rural female										
Not literate	72,944	0.1909	42.5146	8.11	76,824	0.2148	9.13	70,968	0.2299	9.78
Literate up to middle	21,510	0.0563	45.4448	2.56	18,082	0.0505	2.30	13,007	0.0421	1.92
Secondary and higher secondary	3652	0.0096	63.1169	0.60	2443	0.0068	0.43	1370	0.0044	0.28
Graduate and above	582	0.0015	70.9594	0.11	391	0.0011	0.08	257	0.0008	0.06
Urban Male:										
Not literate	12,148	0.0318	55.5683	1.77	11,656	0.0326	1.81	10,419	0.0338	1.88
Literate up to middle	30,521	0.0799	59.4129	4.74	27,303	0.0763	4.53	24,072	0.0780	4.63
Secondary and higher secondary	19,722	0.0516	74.0833	3.82	15,330	0.0429	3.17	10,932	0.0354	2.62
Graduate and above	12,598	0.0330	100.0000	3.30	9059	0.0253	2.53	5902	0.0191	1.91
Urban Female										
Not literate	7937	0.0208	46.1849	0.96	8059	0.0225	1.04	7235	0.0234	1.08
Literate up to middle	5044	0.0132	48.5633	0.64	4622	0.0129	0.63	3374	0.0109	0.53
Secondary and higher secondary	2585	0.0068	68.9483	0.47	2023	0.0057	0.39	1405	0.0046	0.31
Graduate and above	2513	0.0066	86.7958	0.57	1743	0.0049	0.42	1116	0.0036	0.31
Total	382,178	1.0000		55.68	357,713	1.0000	54.39	308,644	1.0000	53.33
Total of education effect with 1993–4 = 100				102.38			100.00			98.06

(Cols Contd.)

89

Table 3.20 Contd.: Measurement of Education Effect, 1961 to 1999–2000

Educational level/ Rural/Urban / Male/Female	Employment 1983		Education effect 1983	Employment 1977–8		Education effect 1977–8	Employment 1972–3		Education effect 1972–3	Employment 1961		Education effect 1961
	No. ('000)	Ratio to total	Col. (12) × Col. (3)	No. ('000)	Ratio to total	Col. (15) × Col. (3)	No. ('000)	Ratio to total	Col. (18) × Col. (3)	No. ('000)	Ratio to total	Col. (21) × Col. (3)
	(11)	(12)	(13)	(14)	(15)	(16)	(17)	(18)	(19)	(20)	(21)	(22)
Rural Male												
Not literate	73,375	0.2663	13.23	76,972	0.2920	14.51	76,845	0.3316	16.47	73,244	0.3882	19.29
Literate up to middle	56,615	0.2055	11.49	53,976	0.2048	11.45	43,912	0.1895	10.60	31,917	0.1692	9.46
Secondary and higher secondary	8873	0.0322	2.24	5645	0.0214	1.49	3493	0.0151	1.05	1591	0.0084	0.59
Graduate and above	1972	0.0072	0.61	1102	0.0042	0.36	499	0.0022	0.18	0	0.0000	0.00
Rural Female												
Not literate	68,238	0.2477	10.53	69,818	0.2648	11.26	63,561	0.2743	11.66	53,078	0.2813	11.96
Literate up to middle	10,998	0.0399	1.81	7645	0.0290	1.32	5470	0.0236	1.07	2351	0.0125	0.57
Secondary and higher secondary	883	0.0032	0.20	468	0.0018	0.11	208	0.0009	0.06	65	0.0003	0.02
Graduate and above	161	0.0006	0.04	78	0.0003	0.02	0	0.0000	0.00	0	0.0000	0.00
Urban Male												
Not literate	9837	0.0357	1.98	8728	0.0331	1.84	7828	0.0338	1.88	7896	0.0418	2.33
Literate up to middle	21,307	0.0773	4.59	19194	0.0728	4.33	16,054	0.0693	4.12	11,243	0.0596	3.54
Secondary and higher secondary	8602	0.0312	2.31	6688	0.0254	1.88	4912	0.0212	1.57	2508	0.0133	0.98
Graduate and above	4367	0.0158	1.58	3174	0.0120	1.20	1903	0.0082	0.82	774	0.0041	0.41
Urban Female												
Not literate	6109	0.0222	1.02	6603	0.0250	1.16	5000	0.0216	1.00	3254	0.0172	0.80
Literate up to middle	2669	0.0097	0.47	2248	0.0085	0.41	1398	0.0060	0.29	531	0.0028	0.14
Secondary and higher secondary	927	0.0034	0.23	770	0.0029	0.20	424	0.0018	0.13	162	0.0009	0.06
Graduate and above	598	0.0022	0.19	506	0.0019	0.17	240	0.0010	0.09	64	0.0003	0.03
Total	275,531	1.0000	52.55	263,615	1.0000	51.70	231,747	1.0000	50.98	188,678	1.0000	50.17
Total of education effect with 1993–4 = 100			96.62			95.06			93.74			92.24

Sources: Col. (1), (5), (8), (11), (14) and (17) from Appendix Table 3(h); Col. (20) from Appendix Table 3(f); Col. (2), (6), (9), (12), (15), (18) and (21) derived; Col. (3) from Table 3.16 Col. 6; Col. (4), (7), (10), (13), (16), (19), and (22) as explained in the column headings.

Distribution of workers by level of education is not available for the benchmark year 1950–1. Dholakia has made estimates for 1950–1 by applying the 'education-specific worker rates' (obtained from the 1960–1 census) to the estimated stock of educated males and females in the broad educational categories. It also involves the assumption that the percentage increase in the educated working force is the same as the percentage in the educated population (in each category) between 1950–1 and 1960–1.[34] He based his earnings data largely for males for 1960–1. He used the same set of weights for females also.[35] As a rough approximation, I have taken Dholakia's quality index for education of 100 for 1960–1 as corresponding to the 92.24 obtained in Table 3.20 as per our calculations. For 1950–1, Dholakia's estimate of 97.21[36] when spliced will give a figure of 89.65 to correspond to my figures. On this basis the quality indexes have been obtained for the benchmark years and the interpolated annual values are shown in Cols (1) and (2) of Table 3.21.

Table 3.21: Quality Index Showing the Effect of Increased Education on the Average Quality of Labour in India, 1950–1 to 1999–2000 (1993–4 = 100)

Year	Quality index (1)	Quality index (2)
1950–1	89.65	89.65
1951–2		89.91
1952–3		90.16
1953–4		90.42
1954–5		90.68
1955–6		90.94
1956–7		91.20
1957–8		91.46
1958–9		91.72
1959–60		91.98
1960–1	92.24	92.24
1961–2		92.36
1962–3		92.49
1963–4		92.61
1964–5		92.74
1965–6		92.86
1966–7		92.99
1967–8		93.11
1968–9		93.24
1969–70		93.36
1970–1		93.49
1971–2		93.61
1972–3	93.74	93.74
1973–4		94.00
1974–5		94.27
1975–6		94.53
1976–7		94.79

(Contd.)

[34] Dholakia, *The Sources of Economic Growth in India*, p. 117.
[35] Ibid., p. 121.
[36] Ibid., p. 123.

Table 3.21 Contd.

	(1)	(2)
1977–8	95.06	95.06
1978–9		95.37
1979–80		95.68
1980–1		95.99
1981–2		96.31
1982–3	96.62	96.62
1983–4		96.91
1984–5		97.19
1985–6		97.48
1986–7		97.77
1987–8	98.06	98.06
1988–9		98.38
1989–90		98.70
1990–1		99.03
1991–2		99.35
1992–3		99.67
1993–4	100.00	100.00
1994–5		100.39
1995–6		100.79
1996–7		101.18
1997–8		101.58
1998–9		101.98
1999–2000	102.38	102.38

Source: Col. (1) from Table 3.20, last line; Col. (2) derived from Col. (1).

MOVEMENT IN THE EDUCATION INDEX

As the weighting system has been kept constant, the movements in the education index can be attributed to the changes in the composition of workers according to levels of education. Table 3.18 shows impressive changes in the distribution of workers by educational level. The share of illiterate workers declined drastically from 73 per cent in 1961 to 44 per cent in 1999–2000. Those with secondary education increased from 2 per cent to 14 per cent in the same period. The share of workers with educational level 'graduates and above' moved up from less than half per cent in 1961 to 6 per cent in 1999–2000. This group is a very broad one, including in its scope postgraduates in different disciplines, engineers, doctors, management specialists, software engineers, etc. A more detailed distribution at these levels along with the relevant earnings data may have made the changes in labour input more impressive. The changes in the education level had only modest influence on the education index which grew by 14.2 per cent over the period, i.e., at an annual average rate of 0.27 per cent. The pace of growth varied from period to period as shown below, the highest growth 0.37 per cent per annum recorded being during the 1990s. Compared to this, the annual growth rate of the education index for USA was 0.61 per cent for 1929–69[37]

---

[37] Denison, *Accounting for United States Economic Growth*, p. 46.

and 0.74 per cent for 1973–9.[38] For Japan, the growth rate of the index was 0.54 in 1952–60 and 0.53 in 1960–71.[39] The growth rate of educational attainment was even more impressive in the case of Taiwan and Korea at 0.8 per cent and 0.9 per cent respectively between 1960 and 1996.[40]

Annual Percentage Change in Education Index

Periods	Per cent
Long periods	
1950–1 to 1999–2000	0.27
1950–1 to 1964–5	0.24
1964–5 to 1980–1	0.22
1980–1 to 1999–2000	0.34
Shorter period	
1950–1 to 1960–1	0.29
1960–1 to 1970–1	0.13
1970–1 to 1980–1	0.26
1980–1 to 1990–1	0.31
1990–1 to 1999–2000	0.37

Source: Table 3.21.

The education index, it may be noted, takes into account only the quantitative aspects of formal education. Education outside the formal sphere, such as nursery and kindergarten and commercial institutes are not taken into account. The changes, if any, in the quality of education due to the changes in the content of education, i.e. curriculum revision and updating, improved attendance, length of school year over the period, and inter-state differences in the classification of educational levels are also not considered. As Denison has observed: 'the index is intended only as a component of labour input, not as an indication of all the economic effects of education'.[41]

LABOUR INPUT

The index of labour input shown in Col. (4) of Table 3.1 is constructed by multiplication of the separate indexes already derived. The index of labour input increased by 186.8 per cent during the period 1950–1 to 1999–2000 while the index of employment moved up by only 145 per cent, the difference being accounted for by changes in age–sex composition and educational levels. The annual growth rate of labour input was 2.17 per cent while that of employment was 1.85 per cent (see Table 3.22). The movements in the employment index

[38] Edward F. Denison, *Trends in American Economic Growth 1929–1982*, Washington, D.C. 1985, p. 15

[39] Denison and Chung, *How Japan's Economy Grew So Fast*, p. 216

[40] Bart Van Ark and Marcel P. Timmer, 'Realising Growth Potential: South Korea and Taiwan, 1960 to 1998', in Angus Maddison, D. S. Prasada Rao, and William F. Shepherd (eds), *The Asian Economies in the Twentieth Century*, Edward Elgan Publication Ltd, Cheltenham, 2002, p. 234.

[41] Denison, *Accounting for United States Growth*, p. 46.

Table 3.22: Compound Annual Growth Rates of Indexes of
Employment and Labour Input, 1950-1 to 1999-2000

(in per cent)

Period	Index of employment	Index of Age–Sex	Index of education	Index of labour input
	(1)	(2)	(3)	(4)
Long periods				
1950–1 to 1999–2000	1.85	0.05	0.27	2.17
1950–1 to 1964–5	1.63	0.03	0.24	1.91
1964–5 to 1980–1	2.16	–0.02	0.22	2.35
1980–1 to 1999–2000	1.74	0.13	0.34	2.22
Shorter periods				
1950–1 to 1960–1	1.58	0.06	0.29	1.92
1960–1 to 1970–1	1.79	–0.03	0.12	1.90
1970–1 to 1980–1	2.37	–0.02	0.26	2.62
1980–1 to 1990–1	2.02	0.13	0.31	2.47
1990–1 to 1999–2000	1.43	0.12	0.37	1.93

Source: Table 3.1.

and labour index are shown in Fig. 3.2. The movements of the two indexes are more or less parallel with the level of labour input index higher than that of employment index throughout. The growth rates of the two indexes varied over the different sub-periods, the highest recorded during the decade 1970–1 to 1980–1. The variations between the growth rates of the indexes of labour input and employment are explained by the changes in the indexes of age–sex composition and education as shown in Cols 2 and 3.

LABOUR INPUT IN SECTOR A AND SECTOR NON-A

Estimates of the number of workers engaged in Sector A and Sector non-A are presented in Appendix Table 3(b). To derive the corresponding estimates of labour input adjusted for quality change, further cross classification by age–sex and educational characteristics is necessary. In the absence of such formation, an attempt has been made to use the percentage distribution of rural workforce by age–sex and educational levels as proxy for similar distribution of those employed in Sector A. That it seems justifiable can be seen from the following:

Distribution of Workforce by Rural/Urban Sector A and
Sector Non-A, 1950-1 and 1999-2000

	1950–1		1999–2000	
	No. ('000)	% to total	No. ('000)	% to total
Rural/Urb.an				
Rural	141,081	88.10	297,923	75.92
Urban	19,058	11.90	94,480	24.08
Total	160,139	100.00	392,403	100.00
Sector A/Sector Non-A				
Sector A	122,024	76.2	237,112	60.43
Sector Non-A	38,115	23.80	155,291	39.57
Total	160,139	100.00	392,403	100.00

Sources: Appendix Tables 3(b) and 3(c).

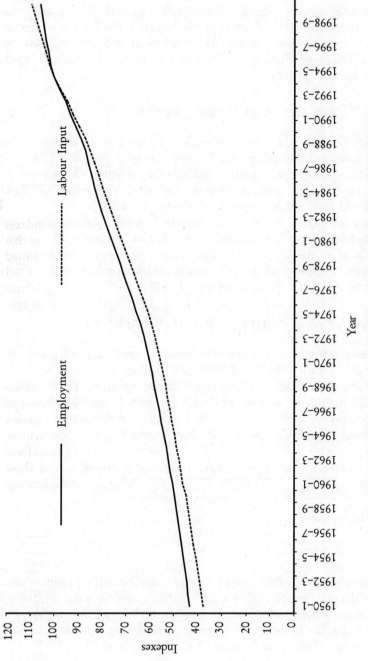

Fig. 3.2: Indexes of Employment and Labour Input, 1950–1 to 1999–2000

Source: Table 3.1.

95

Since most of the agricultural activities are carried on in rural areas, the age–sex educational characteristics of rural workforce can be assumed to be applicable to the workers in Sector A. Based on this assumption, the indexes of changes in the age–sex composition and of changes in the educational levels of rural workers worked out from available data are applied to the workforce in Sector A to obtain the augumented labour input in Sector A, shown in Table 3.23. The procedures, similar to those followed for total labour input, are briefly indicated below.

AGE–SEX COMPOSITION OF RURAL WORKFORCE

The percentage composition of rural workers by sex and age available from the 1961 census and the quinquennial surveys are given in Table 3.24.

On the basis of inter-period growth rates of the percentages in each group, the annual age–sex distribution has been worked out for the period 1960–1 and 1999–2000 and is shown in Appendix Table 3(i), Cols (1)–(9).

For the years 1950–1 to 1960–1, I have relied on the distribution worked out by Dholakia for adult males, adult females, and children.[42] The growth rates calculated on the basis of these figures have been applied to the 1960–1 figures shown in Appendix Table 3(i) and worked backwards to 1950–1. These are shown in Appendix Table 3(j), Cols (1) to (4).

DAILY EARNINGS WEIGHTS OF RURAL WORKFORCE

Average daily wages of casual labourers in rural areas by age–sex groups are given in Table 3.9 for 1993–4 and 1999–2000. Taking the average wage of a male labourer (urban and rural combined) in the age-group 15–59 years as equal to 100, the relative earnings of the age-groups 5–14 and 60+ years were worked out for both these years. The average of these relatives used as earnings weights for 1960–1 to 1999–2000 are shown below:

Index of Daily Earnings Weights for Rural Workforce

Age-group	Males	Females
5–14	55.47	51.54
15–59	90.69	63.04
60+	79.28	51.86

Source: Table 3.9.

These are shown in the top row of the Appendix Table 3(i). From the same basic wage data relating to 1993–4 and 1999–2000, earnings weights obtained for adult males, adult females, and children for the years 1950–1 to 1960–1 to match with the classification of workers as men, women, and child workers are: adult males: 89.69; adult females: 62.42, and children: 53.65.

---

[42] Dholakia, *The Sources of Economic Growth in India*, p. 125.

Table 3.23: Labour Input in Sector A Adjusted for Changes in Age-Sex Composition and Education, 1950–1 to 1999–2000

Year	Workforce in Sector A ('000)	Age-sex composition	Effect of education	Labour input in Sector A ('000)	Index of workforce in Sector A	Index of labour input in Sector A	Index of labour input in Sector A 1993-4 = 100
	(1)	(2)	(3)	(4)	(5)	(6)	(7)
1950–1	122,024	77.89	47.35	45,004	51.48	18.99	46.82
1951–2	123,895	77.95	47.48	45,858	52.27	19.35	47.71
1952–3	125,747	77.99	47.62	46,700	53.05	19.70	48.58
1953–4	127,627	78.04	47.75	47,563	53.85	20.07	49.48
1954–5	129,535	78.09	47.89	48,442	54.65	20.44	50.39
1955–6	131,472	78.14	48.03	49,337	55.47	20.82	51.32
1956–7	133,437	78.19	48.16	50,249	56.30	21.20	52.27
1957–8	135,432	78.24	48.30	51,177	57.14	21.59	53.24
1958–9	137,457	78.30	48.43	52,130	57.99	21.99	54.23
1959–60	139,512	78.35	48.57	53,093	58.86	22.40	55.23
1960–1	141,598	78.32	48.71	54,019	59.74	22.79	56.19
1961–2	143,797	78.28	48.74	54,866	60.67	23.15	57.08
1962–3	146,112	78.25	48.77	55,764	61.65	23.53	58.01
1963–4	148,464	78.22	48.80	56,676	62.64	23.91	58.96
1964–5	150,855	78.19	48.84	57,604	63.65	24.30	59.92
1965–6	153,283	78.16	48.87	58,547	64.67	24.70	60.90
1966–7	155,751	78.13	48.90	59,505	65.71	25.11	61.90
1967–8	158,259	78.11	48.93	60,487	66.77	25.52	62.92
1968–9	160,807	78.08	48.96	61,477	67.85	25.94	63.95
1969–70	163,396	78.05	48.99	62,483	68.94	26.36	65.00
1970–1	166,026	78.02	49.03	63,506	70.05	26.79	66.06
1971–2	168,699	78.00	49.06	64,553	71.18	27.24	67.15
1972–3	171,415	77.97	49.09	65,610	72.32	27.68	68.25
1973–4	174,408	77.95	49.17	66,852	73.58	28.21	69.54

(Contd.)

97

Table 3.23 Contd.

	(1)	(2)	(3)	(4)	(5)	(6)	(7)
1974–5	177,686	77.92	49.26	68,199	74.97	28.77	70.95
1975–6	181,026	77.90	49.34	69,581	76.38	29.36	72.38
1976–7	184,429	77.88	49.43	70,992	77.81	29.95	73.85
1977–8	187,895	77.85	49.51	72,421	79.28	30.56	75.34
1978–9	191,280	77.83	49.60	73,838	80.70	31.15	76.81
1979–80	194,580	77.81	49.69	75,226	82.10	31.74	78.26
1980–1	197,937	77.79	49.77	76,640	83.51	32.34	79.73
1981–2	201,351	77.77	49.86	78,080	84.95	32.94	81.23
1982–3	204,825	77.75	49.95	79,548	86.42	33.56	82.75
1983–4	206,973	77.67	50.04	80,442	87.32	33.94	83.68
1984–5	207,769	78.46	50.18	81,804	87.66	34.51	85.10
1985–6	208,567	78.63	50.32	82,530	88.00	34.82	85.85
1986–7	209,368	78.89	50.47	83,356	88.33	35.17	86.71
1987–8	210,173	79.20	50.61	84,244	88.67	35.54	87.64
1988–9	212,792	79.16	50.72	85,443	89.78	36.05	88.88
1989–90	217,272	79.13	50.84	87,406	91.67	36.88	90.93
1990–1	221,846	79.11	50.95	89,425	93.60	37.73	93.03
1991–2	226,517	79.09	51.07	91,491	95.57	38.60	95.18
1992–3	231,286	79.07	51.18	93,605	97.58	39.49	97.37
1993–4	237,016	79.06	51.30	96,128	100.00	40.56	100.00
1994–5	240,043	79.13	51.43	97,694	101.28	41.22	101.63
1995–6	239,454	79.22	51.57	97,817	101.03	41.27	101.76
1996–7	238,866	79.30	51.70	97,928	100.78	41.32	101.87
1997–8	238,280	79.40	51.83	98,063	100.53	41.37	102.01
1998–9	237,695	79.50	51.97	98,199	100.29	41.43	102.15
1999–2000	237,112	79.60	52.10	98,334	100.04	41.49	102.29

Sources: Col. 1 from Appendix Table 3(b), Col. 4; Col. (2) from Table 3.25, Col. (3); Col. (3) from Table 3.26, Col. (2); Col. (4) = Col. (1) × Col. (2) × Col. (3); Col (5) from Col. (1); from Col. (6) = Col. (1) × Col. (2); Col. (5) × Col. (3); Col. (7) derived from Col. (6).

98

Table 3.24: Age–Sex Distribution of Rural Workforce, 1961 to 1999–2000

Age/Sex	1961 Census	1983	1987–8	1993–4	1999–2000
	(1)	(2)	(3)	(4)	(5)
Males					
5–14	5.01	4.41	2.11	2.12	1.57
15–59	55.62	53.51	56.34	56.74	58.35
60+	5.17	.5.11	5.50	5.54	5.57
Total	65.80	63.03	63.95	64.40	65.49
Females					
5–14	3.42	3.55	2.66	1.82	1.38
15–59	29.21	31.71	31.75	31.96	31.30
60+	1.57	1.71	1.64	1.82	1.83
Total	34.20	36.97	36.05	35.60	34.51
Grand total	100.00	100.00	100.00	100.00	100.00

Sources: Col. (1) from *Census of India 1961, Vol. I, Part II-B, General Economic Tables*, pp. 86–7; Col. (2) from *Key Results of Employment and Unemployment Surveys—All India, Part I*, Special Report 1983, 43rd Round, p. 82; Col. (3) from *Employment and Unemployment in India, 1993–4, Report 409*, NSSO, p. 69; Cols (4) and (5) from *NSS Report No. 458, Employment and Unemployment Situation in India, 1999–2000*, May 2001, p. 70.

INDEX OF RURAL LABOUR INPUT FOR CHANGES IN THE AGE–SEX COMPOSITION OF RURAL WORKFORCE

Based on the percentage distribution of rural workers by age–sex and index of wage differentials, labour input indexes have been worked out. The indexes are shown in Col. (16) of Appendix Table 3(i) for 1960–1 to 1999–2000 and in Col. (8) of Appendix Table 3(j) for 1950–1 to 1960–1. Using the overlapping values for 1960–1, the two series are then linked to give a continuous series for the whole period. The linked index is then expressed with base 1993–4 = 100 to give the input index of rural labour input showing the effect of changes in age–sex composition and shown in Col. (4) Table 3.25. This index is later applied to the workforce in Sector A to obtain the labour input in the sector adjusted for age–sex composition.

EFFECT OF EDUCATION ON RURAL LABOUR INPUT

Based on the calculations shown in Table 3.20, using only the data relating to rural male and rural female workers, the weighted indexes of education have been derived for the benchmark years 1961, 1972–3, 1977–8, 1983, 1987–8, 1993–4, and 1999–2000 and shown in Appendix Table 3(k) and Table 3.26. For 1950–1 the relevant value has been obtained by splicing our estimates for 1960–1 with Dholakia's estimates for 1960–1 and 1950–1. The annual series of the index for education effect are then obtained by interpolation of the following benchmark figures:

Table 3.25: Index of Input Showing the Effect of Changes in Age–Sex
Composition of Rural Labour, 1950–1 to 1999–2000

Year	Labour input index	Labour input index	Linked labour input index	Linked index 1993–4 = 100
	(1)	(2)	(3)	(4)
1950–1	81.90		77.89	98.52
1951–2	81.96		77.95	98.59
1952–3	82.01		77.99	98.65
1953–4	82.06		78.04	98.71
1954–5	82.11		78.09	98.77
1955–6	82.16		78.14	98.83
1956–7	82.22		78.19	98.91
1957–8	82.27		78.24	98.97
1958–9	82.33		78.30	99.04
1959–60	82.38		78.35	99.10
1960–1	82.43	78.32	78.32	99.06
1961–2		78.28	78.28	99.02
1962–3		78.25	78.25	98.98
1963–4		78.22	78.22	98.94
1964–5		78.19	78.19	98.90
1965–6		78.16	78.16	98.87
1966–7		78.13	78.13	98.83
1967–8		78.11	78.11	98.79
1968–9		78.08	78.08	98.76
1969–70		78.05	78.05	98.73
1970–1		78.02	78.02	98.69
1971–2		78.00	78.00	98.66
1972–3		77.97	77.97	98.63
1973–4		77.95	77.95	98.59
1974–5		77.92	77.92	98.56
1975–6		77.90	77.90	98.53
1976–7		77.88	77.88	98.50
1977–8		77.85	77.85	98.47
1978–9		77.83	77.83	98.45
1979–80		77.81	77.81	98.42
1980–1		77.79	77.79	98.39
1981–2		77.77	77.77	98.36
1982–3		77.75	77.75	98.34
1983–4		77.67	77.67	98.24
1984–5		78.46	78.46	99.24
1985–6		78.63	78.63	99.46
1986–7		78.89	78.89	99.78
1987–8		79.20	79.20	100.18
1988–9		79.16	79.16	100.13
1989–90		79.13	79.13	100.09
1990–1		79.11	79.11	100.06
1991–2		79.09	79.09	100.03
1992–3		79.07	79.07	100.01
1993–4		79.06	79.06	100.00
1994–5		79.18	79.18	100.15
1995–6		79.30	79.30	100.31
1996–7		79.43	79.43	100.47
1997–8		79.56	79.56	100.63
1998–9		79.69	79.69	100.80
1999–2000		79.83	79.83	100.98

Sources: Col. 1 from Appendix Table 3(j), Col. (8); Col. (2) from Appendix Table 3(i), Col. (16); Cols 3 from Cols (1) and (2) linked; Col. (4) derived from Col. (3) with 1993–4 = 100.

Indexes of Education Effect on Rural Labour for Benchmark Years

Year	Index	Indexes (1993–4 = 100)
1951	47.35	92.30
1961	48.71	94.95
1972–3	49.09	95.69
1977–8	49.51	96.51
1983	50.04	97.54
1987–8	50.61	98.65
1993–4	51.30	100.00
1999–2000	52.10	101.56

The annual series are shown in Table 3.26.

Table 3.26: Index Showing the Effect of Education on Rural
Labour Input, 1950–1 to 1999–2000

Year	Quality index	Quality index	Quality index 1993–4 = 100
	(1)	(2)	(3)
1950–1	47.35	47.35	92.30
1951–2		47.48	92.56
1952–3		47.62	92.82
1953–4		47.75	93.09
1954–5		47.89	93.35
1955–6		48.03	93.62
1956–7		48.16	93.88
1957–8		48.30	94.15
1958–9		48.43	94.42
1959–60		48.57	94.68
1960–1	48.71	48.71	94.95
1961–2		48.74	95.01
1962–3		48.77	95.07
1963–4		48.80	95.14
1964–5		48.84	95.20
1965–6		48.87	95.26
1966–7		48.90	95.32
1967–8		48.93	95.38
1968–9		48.96	95.44
1969–70		48.99	95.51
1970–1		49.03	95.57
1971–2		49.06	95.63
1972–3	49.09	49.09	95.69
1973–4		49.17	95.86
1974–5		49.26	96.02
1975–6		49.34	96.18
1976–7		49.43	96.35
1977–8	49.51	49.51	96.51
1978–9		49.60	96.68
1979–80		49.69	96.85
1980–1		49.77	97.03
1981–2		49.86	97.20
1982–3		49.95	97.37
1983–4	50.04	50.04	97.54

(Contd.)

Table 3.26 Contd.

	(1)	(2)	(3)
1984–5		50.18	97.82
1985–6		50.32	98.10
1986–7		50.47	98.38
1987–8	50.61	50.61	98.65
1988–9		50.72	98.88
1989–90		50.84	99.10
1990–1		50.95	99.33
1991–2		51.07	99.55
1992–3		51.18	99.77
1993–4	51.30	51.30	100.00
1994–5		51.43	100.26
1995–6		51.57	100.52
1996–7		51.70	100.78
1997–8		51.83	101.04
1998–9		51.97	101.30
1999–2000	52.10	52.10	101.56

Sources: Col. (1) from Appendix Table 3(k), last row; Col. 2 derived from Col. (1); Col. (3) derived from Col. 2 with 1993–4 = 100.

LABOUR INPUT IN SECTOR A ADJUSTED FOR QUALITY CHANGE

As mentioned earlier, the indexes showing the changes in the age–sex composition and educational levels of rural workforce are assumed to be applicable to the workers in Sector A. Applying these indexes to the index of employment in Sector A with base 1993–4 = 100, the index of labour input in Sector A, adjusted for quality change, is shown in Col. 7 of Table 3.23.

LABOUR INPUT IN SECTOR NON-A ADJUSTED FOR QUALITY CHANGE

The indicators of changes in age–sex composition and educational levels of urban workforce cannot be considered relevant for Sector non-A because the latter accounts for a far higher share of the workforce (almost twice in 1950–1 and 60 per cent more in 1999–2000) than the former. To estimate the effect of quality change in labour input of Sector non-A a slightly different procedure is adopted. The augmented labour input in the non-residential sector and in Sector A are expressed in terms of equivalent numbers by multiplying the respective workforce by the corresponding indexes of age–sex composition and educational levels. The labour input thus calculated for the non-residential sector of the economy in terms of numbers is given in Col. (4) of Appendix Table 3(l). Similarly, the labour input in Sector A adjusted for quality change expressed in number of persons is given in Col. (4) of Table 3.23. From these the labour input adjusted for quality in Sector non-A is derived as a residual and shown in Col. (3) of Table 3.27. The indexes of augmented labour input in Sector A and Sector non-A and the percentage distribution of labour input are shown in Cols (4) to (7) of Table 3.27.

Table 3.27: Labour Input Total, Sector A and Sector Non-A, 1950–1 to 1999–2000

Year	Total labour input ('000)	Labour input ('000)		% distribution of labour input		Index of labour input		% to total workforce	
		Sector A	Sector non-A	Sector A	Sector non-A	Sector A	Sector non-A	Sector A	Sector non-A
	(1)	(2)	(3)	(4)	(5)	(6)	(7)	(8)	(9)
1950–1	62,967	45,004	17,964	71.47	28.53	46.82	23.07	76.20	23.80
1951–2	64,515	45,858	18,656	71.08	28.92	47.71	23.96	76.17	23.83
1952–3	66,101	46,700	19,401	70.65	29.35	48.58	24.91	76.11	23.89
1953–4	67,727	47,563	20,164	70.23	29.77	49.48	25.89	76.05	23.95
1954–5	69,393	48,442	20,951	69.81	30.19	50.39	26.90	75.99	24.01
1955–6	71,101	49,337	21,763	69.39	30.61	51.32	27.94	75.93	24.07
1956–7	72,851	50,249	22,602	68.98	31.02	52.27	29.02	75.87	24.13
1957–8	74,645	51,177	23,467	68.56	31.44	53.24	30.13	75.81	24.19
1958–9	76,483	52,130	24,353	68.16	31.84	54.23	31.27	75.75	24.25
1959–60	78,367	53,093	25,274	67.75	32.25	55.23	32.45	75.69	24.31
1960–1	80,259	54,019	26,240	67.31	32.69	56.19	33.69	75.63	24.37
1961–2	81,700	54,866	26,834	67.16	32.84	57.08	34.46	75.53	24.47
1962–3	83,260	55,764	27,496	66.98	33.02	58.01	35.31	75.38	24.62
1963–4	84,850	56,676	28,174	66.80	33.20	58.96	36.17	75.24	24.76
1964–5	86,470	57,604	28,866	66.62	33.38	59.92	37.06	75.10	24.90
1965–6	88,122	58,547	29,575	66.44	33.56	60.90	37.97	74.96	25.04
1966–7	89,806	59,505	30,301	66.26	33.74	61.90	38.91	74.81	25.19
1967–8	91,522	60,487	31,035	66.09	33.91	62.92	39.85	74.67	25.33
1968–9	93,272	61,477	31,795	65.91	34.09	63.95	40.82	74.53	25.47
1969–70	95,055	62,483	32,572	65.73	34.27	65.00	41.82	74.39	25.61
1970–1	96,873	63,506	33,367	65.56	34.44	66.06	42.84	74.25	25.75
1971–2	98,726	64,553	34,172	65.39	34.61	67.15	43.88	74.11	25.89
1972–3	100,614	65,610	35,004	65.21	34.79	68.25	44.95	73.97	26.03
1973–4	103,169	66,852	36,317	64.80	35.20	69.54	46.63	73.58	26.42

(Contd.)

103

Table 3.27 Contd.

	(1)	(2)	(3)	(4)	(5)	(6)	(7)	(8)	(9)
1974-5	106,269	68,199	38,071	64.18	35.82	70.95	48.88	72.97	27.03
1975-6	109,464	69,581	39,883	63.57	36.43	72.38	51.21	72.35	27.65
1976-7	112,755	70,992	41,763	62.96	37.04	73.85	53.62	71.75	28.25
1977-8	115,928	72,421	43,506	62.47	37.53	75.34	55.86	71.28	28.72
1978-9	119,028	73,838	45,190	62.03	37.97	76.81	58.02	70.89	29.11
1979-80	122,211	75,226	46,985	61.55	38.45	78.26	60.33	70.44	29.56
1980-1	125,481	76,640	48,841	61.08	38.92	79.73	62.71	70.00	30.00
1981-2	128,838	78,080	50,758	60.60	39.40	81.23	65.17	69.57	30.43
1982-3	132,470	79,548	52,922	60.05	39.95	82.75	67.95	69.04	30.96
1983-4	135,640	80,442	55,198	59.31	40.69	83.68	70.87	68.32	31.68
1984-5	138,501	81,804	56,697	59.06	40.94	85.10	72.80	67.50	32.50
1985-6	141,515	82,530	58,986	58.32	41.68	85.85	75.74	66.70	33.30
1986-7	144,678	83,356	61,322	57.61	42.39	86.71	78.74	65.91	34.09
1987-8	147,985	84,244	63,741	56.93	43.07	87.64	81.84	65.12	34.88
1988-9	151,514	85,443	66,070	56.39	43.61	88.88	84.83	64.64	35.36
1989-90	155,749	87,406	68,343	56.12	43.88	90.93	87.75	64.45	35.55
1990-1	160,113	89,425	70,688	55.85	44.15	93.03	90.76	64.26	35.74
1991-2	164,609	91,491	73,118	55.58	44.42	95.18	93.88	64.07	35.93
1992-3	169,240	93,605	75,635	55.31	44.69	97.37	97.12	63.88	36.12
1993-4	174,010	96,128	77,881	55.24	44.76	100.00	100.00	63.93	36.07
1994-5	177,718	97,694	80,024	54.97	45.03	101.63	102.75	63.72	36.28
1995-6	180,119	97,817	82,302	54.31	45.69	101.76	105.68	63.05	36.95
1996-7	182,568	97,928	84,640	53.64	46.36	101.87	108.68	62.38	37.62
1997-8	185,064	98,063	87,001	52.99	47.01	102.01	111.71	61.72	38.28
1998-9	187,609	98,199	89,410	52.34	47.66	102.15	114.80	61.07	38.93
1999-2000	190,202	98,334	91,868	51.70	48.30	102.29	117.96	60.43	39.57

Sources: Col. (1) from Appendix Table 3(l), Col (4); Col. (2) from Table 3.23, Col. (4); Col. (3) = Col. (1) − Col. (2); Cols (4) to (7) derived; Cols (8) and (9) from Appendix Table 3(b), Cols (10) and (11).

104

MOVEMENTS IN LABOUR INPUT INDEX AND
EMPLOYMENT INDEX

The labour input index in Sector A increased by 118.5 per cent during the whole period, i.e. at the rate of 1.61 per cent per annum, while employment increased by 94.3 per cent, i.e., at a slightly lower rate of 1.36 per cent. Compared to this, the rates of growth of labour input and employment in Sector non-A are much higher throughout, as can be seen from Table 3.28.

Table 3.28: Rates of Growth of Labour Input and Employment, 1950–1 to 1999–2000

Period	Sector A		Sector non-A		Total	
	Employment	Labour input	Employment	Labour input	Employment	Labour input
	(1)	(2)	(3)	(4)	(5)	(6)
Long periods						
1950–1 to 1999–2000	1.36	1.61	2.91	3.39	1.85	2.28
1950–1 to 1964–5	1.53	1.68	1.96	3.44	1.63	2.29
1964–5 to 1980–1	1.71	1.80	3.36	3.34	2.16	2.36
1980–1 to 1999–2000	0.95	1.32	3.23	3.38	1.74	2.21
Shorter periods						
1950–1 to 1960–1	1.50	1.84	1.82	3.86	1.57	2.46
1960–1 to 1970–1	1.60	1.63	2.35	2.43	1.79	1.90
1970–1 to 1980–1	1.77	1.90	3.95	3.88	2.37	2.62
1980–1 to 1990–1	1.13	1.55	3.82	3.77	2.02	2.47
1990–1 to 1999–2000	0.74	1.06	2.59	2.96	1.43	1.93

Sources: Col. (1) and (2) from Appendix Table 3(b), Col. (1) and 4; Col. (3), from Appendix Table 3(b), Col. (7); Col. (4) from Table 3.27, Col. (3); Col. (5) from Appendix Table 3(c), Col. (1); Col. (6) from Table 3.27, Col. (1).

Appendix Table 3(a): Estimated Number of Workers by Sex and in Sector A and Sector Non-A, 1950 to 2000 (as on 1 April)

(in thousands)

Year	All-India			Sector A			Sector Non-A		
	Total	Males	Females	Total	Males	Females	Total	Males	Females
	(1)	(2)	(3)	(4)	(5)	(6)	(7)	(8)	(9)
1950	158,887	106,683	52,204	121,072	77,571	43,501	37,815	29,112	8703
1951	161,390	108,550	52,840	122,976	78,791	44,185	38,414	29,759	8655
1952	163,932	110,454	53,478	124,814	80,009	44,806	39,117	30,445	8672
1953	166,514	112,391	54,122	126,680	81,245	45,435	39,833	31,146	8687
1954	169,136	114,363	54,774	128,574	82,501	46,073	40,562	31,862	8700
1955	171,800	116,369	55,432	130,497	83,776	46,721	41,304	32,593	8711
1956	174,506	118,410	56,096	132,447	85,071	47,377	42,059	33,339	8720
1957	177,255	120,487	56,768	134,428	86,385	48,042	42,827	34,101	8726
1958	180,046	122,600	57,446	136,437	87,721	48,717	43,609	34,879	8730
1959	182,882	124,750	58,132	138,477	89,076	49,401	44,405	35,674	8731
1960	185,763	126,938	58,824	140,547	90,453	50,094	45,215	36,486	8730
1961	188,688	129,165	59,523	142,648	91,851	50,797	46,040	37,314	8726
1962	192,090	131,276	60,815	144,945	93,096	51,849	47,145	38,179	8966
1963	195,554	133,421	62,133	147,279	94,358	52,920	48,275	39,062	9213
1964	199,080	135,601	63,479	149,650	95,637	54,012	49,430	39,963	9467
1965	202,669	137,816	64,853	152,059	96,934	55,125	50,610	40,882	9727
1966	206,323	140,068	66,255	154,507	98,248	56,259	51,816	41,820	9996
1967	210,043	142,357	67,686	156,995	99,580	57,415	53,048	42,777	10,271
1968	213,830	144,683	69,147	159,523	100,930	58,592	54,308	43,753	10,555
1969	217,686	147,047	70,638	162,091	102,298	59,792	55,595	44,749	10,846
1970	221,610	149,450	72,160	164,700	103,685	61,015	56,910	45,765	11,145
1971	225,606	151,892	73,714	167,352	105,091	62,261	58,254	46,801	11,453
1972	229,674	154,374	75,300	170,047	106,516	63,531	59,627	47,858	11,769
1973	233,815	156,896	76,918	172,784	107,960	64,825	61,030	48,937	12,094

(Contd.)

106

Appendix Table 3(a) Contd.

	(1)	(2)	(3)	(4)	(5)	(6)	(7)	(8)	(9)
1974	240,226	160,889	79,337	176,032	109,599	66,433	64,194	51,291	12,904
1975	246,814	164,984	81,830	179,341	111,263	68,078	67,473	53,721	13,752
1976	253,582	169,183	84,399	182,712	112,952	69,760	70,870	56,231	14,639
1977	260,535	173,489	87,047	186,146	114,667	71,479	74,390	58,822	15,568
1978	266,693	177,904	88,789	189,645	116,408	73,237	77,048	61,496	15,552
1979	272,996	181,960	91,036	192,916	118,053	74,863	80,080	63,907	16,174
1980	279,449	186,109	93,340	196,244	119,723	76,522	83,204	66,386	16,818
1981	286,053	190,352	95,701	199,630	121,415	78,214	86,424	68,937	17,487
1982	292,814	194,692	98,122	203,073	123,132	79,941	89,741	71,560	18,181
1983	300,562	199,131	101,431	206,577	124,873	81,704	93,986	74,258	19,728
1984	305,351	202,849	102,503	207,370	125,398	81,972	97,981	77,450	20,531
1985	310,217	206,636	103,581	208,167	125,926	82,241	102,050	80,710	21,340
1986	315,160	210,494	104,666	208,967	126,456	82,511	106,193	84,038	22,155
1987	320,182	214,424	105,758	209,770	126,988	82,781	110,412	87,436	22,976
1988	325,283	218,427	106,856	210,576	127,808	82,768	114,708	90,620	24,088
1989	333,111	223,966	109,145	215,009	130,535	84,474	118,102	93,431	24,671
1990	341,127	229,646	111,481	219,535	133,321	86,215	121,592	96,325	25,266
1991	349,336	235,470	113,866	224,157	136,166	87,991	125,179	99,304	25,875
1992	357,742	241,442	116,301	228,876	139,072	89,804	128,866	102,370	26,496
1993	366,351	247,565	118,786	233,695	142,040	91,655	132,656	105,525	27,131
1994	375,167	253,843	121,324	240,338	145,071	95,267	134,829	108,772	26,057
1995	378,243	256,866	121,377	239,748	144,963	94,785	138,495	111,903	26,592
1996	381,344	259,925	121,419	239,160	144,856	94,304	142,184	115,070	27,115
1997	384,471	263,021	121,450	238,573	144,748	93,825	145,898	118,273	27,625
1998	387,623	266,154	121,469	237,987	144,640	93,347	149,636	121,513	28,123
1999	390,801	269,323	121,478	237,403	144,533	92,870	153,398	124,790	28,607
2000	394,005	272,531	121,474	236,821	144,426	92,395	157,185	128,106	29,079

Sources: Cols (1), (2), and (3) based on Table 3.3, Cols (1) to (3); for Cols (4) to (9), sources same as in Table 3.3.

107

Appendix Table 3(b): Estimated Number of Workers by Sex and in Sector A and Sector Non-A, 1950–1 to 1999–2000 (Mid-year Values)

Year	All-India ('000)			Sector A ('000)			Sector non-A ('000)			% to total workforce	
	Total	Males	Females	Total	Males	Females	Total	Males	Females	Sector A	Sector non-A
	(1)	(2)	(3)	(4)	(5)	(6)	(7)	(8)	(9)	(10)	(11)
1950–1	160,139	107,616	52,522	122,024	78,181	43,843	38,115	29,435	8679	76.20	23.80
1951–2	162,661	109,502	53,159	123,895	79,400	44,495	38,766	30,102	8664	76.17	23.83
1952–3	165,223	111,423	53,800	125,747	80,627	45,120	39,475	30,796	8680	76.11	23.89
1953–4	167,825	113,377	54,448	127,627	81,873	45,754	40,198	31,504	8694	76.05	23.95
1954–5	170,468	115,366	55,103	129,535	83,138	46,397	40,933	32,227	8706	75.99	24.01
1955–6	173,153	117,389	55,764	131,472	84,423	47,049	41,681	32,966	8715	75.93	24.07
1956–7	175,880	119,448	56,432	133,437	85,728	47,709	42,443	33,720	8723	75.87	24.13
1957–8	178,651	121,543	57,107	135,432	87,053	48,379	43,218	34,490	8728	75.81	24.19
1958–9	181,464	123,675	57,789	137,457	88,398	49,059	44,007	35,277	8730	75.75	24.25
1959–60	184,322	125,844	58,478	139,512	89,765	49,747	44,810	36,080	8730	75.69	24.31
1960–1	187,225	128,052	59,174	141,598	91,152	50,446	45,628	36,900	8728	75.63	24.37
1961–2	190,389	130,220	60,169	143,797	92,474	51,323	46,593	37,747	8846	75.53	24.47
1962–3	193,822	132,348	61,474	146,112	93,727	52,385	47,710	38,621	9089	75.38	24.62
1963–4	197,317	134,511	62,806	148,464	94,998	53,466	48,852	39,513	9340	75.24	24.76
1964–5	200,874	136,709	64,166	150,855	96,286	54,569	50,020	40,423	9597	75.10	24.90
1965–6	204,496	138,942	65,554	153,283	97,591	55,692	51,213	41,351	9862	74.96	25.04
1966–7	208,183	141,213	66,970	155,751	98,914	56,837	52,432	42,299	10,133	74.81	25.19
1967–8	211,937	143,520	68,417	158,259	100,255	58,004	53,678	43,265	10,413	74.67	25.33
1968–9	215,758	145,865	69,893	160,807	101,614	59,192	54,951	44,251	10,700	74.53	25.47
1969–70	219,648	148,249	71,399	163,396	102,992	60,404	56,252	45,257	10,996	74.39	25.61
1970–1	223,608	150,671	72,937	166,026	104,388	61,638	57,582	46,283	11,299	74.25	25.75
1971–2	227,640	153,133	74,507	168,699	105,803	62,896	58,941	47,330	11,611	74.11	25.89
1972–3	231,744	155,635	76,109	171,415	107,238	64,178	60,329	48,397	11,931	73.97	26.03

(Contd.)

108

Appendix Table 3(b) Contd.

	(1)	(2)	(3)	(4)	(5)	(6)	(7)	(8)	(9)	(10)	(11)
1973–4	237,021	158,893	78,128	174,408	108,779	65,629	62,612	50,114	12,499	73.58	26.42
1974–5	243,520	162,937	80,583	177,686	110,431	67,256	65,834	52,506	13,328	72.97	27.03
1975–6	250,198	167,083	83,114	181,026	112,107	68,919	69,172	54,976	14,195	72.35	27.65
1976–7	257,059	171,336	85,723	184,429	113,809	70,619	72,630	57,526	15,103	71.75	28.25
1977–8	263,614	175,696	87,918	187,895	115,537	72,358	75,719	60,159	15,560	71.28	28.72
1978–9	269,845	179,932	89,913	191,280	117,230	74,050	78,564	62,701	15,863	70.89	29.11
1979–80	276,222	184,034	92,188	194,580	118,888	75,692	81,642	65,146	16,496	70.44	29.56
1980–1	282,751	188,230	94,521	197,937	120,569	77,368	84,814	67,661	17,153	70.00	30.00
1981–2	289,434	192,522	96,912	201,351	122,274	79,078	88,082	70,248	17,834	69.57	30.43
1982–3	296,688	196,912	99,777	204,825	124,003	80,822	91,863	72,909	18,954	69.04	30.96
1983–4	302,957	200,990	101,967	206,973	125,136	81,838	95,983	75,854	20,129	68.32	31.68
1984–5	307,784	204,742	103,042	207,769	125,662	82,106	100,015	79,080	20,935	67.50	32.50
1985–6	312,688	208,565	104,123	208,567	126,191	82,376	104,121	82,374	21,748	66.70	33.30
1986–7	317,671	212,459	105,212	209,368	126,722	82,646	108,303	85,737	22,566	65.91	34.09
1987–8	322,732	216,425	106,307	210,173	127,398	82,775	112,560	89,028	23,532	65.12	34.88
1988–9	329,197	221,197	108,000	212,792	129,171	83,621	116,405	92,025	24,380	64.64	35.36
1989–90	337,119	226,806	110,313	217,272	131,928	85,344	119,847	94,878	24,969	64.45	35.55
1990–1	345,231	232,558	112,673	221,846	134,743	87,103	123,385	97,815	25,570	64.26	35.74
1991–2	353,539	238,456	115,083	226,517	137,619	88,898	127,022	100,837	26,185	64.07	35.93
1992–3	362,047	244,503	117,544	231,286	140,556	90,730	130,761	103,947	26,814	63.88	36.12
1993–4	370,759	250,704	120,055	237,016	143,556	93,461	133,743	107,148	26,594	63.93	36.07
1994–5	376,705	255,354	121,350	240,043	145,017	95,026	136,662	110,337	26,325	63.72	36.28
1995–6	379,793	258,396	121,398	239,454	144,910	94,544	140,340	113,486	26,854	63.05	36.95
1996–7	382,907	261,473	121,434	238,866	144,802	94,064	144,041	116,671	27,370	62.38	37.62
1997–8	386,047	264,587	121,459	238,280	144,694	93,586	147,767	119,893	27,874	61.72	38.28
1998–9	389,212	267,739	121,473	237,695	144,587	93,108	151,517	123,152	28,365	61.07	38.93
1999–2000	392,403	270,927	121,476	237,112	144,479	92,633	155,291	126,448	28,843	60.43	39.57

Sources: Cols (1) to (9) calculated from Cols (1) to (9) of Appendix Table 3(a) as simple averages of two consecutive values; Cols (10) and (11) derived from Cols (1), (4), and (7).

109

Appendix Table 3(c): Estimated Number of Workers by Sex and Rural–Urban Residence, 1950–1 to 1999–2000 (Mid-year Values)

(in thousands)

Year	Rural India			Urban India		
	Total	Males	Females	Total	Males	Females
	(1)	(2)	(3)	(4)	(5)	(6)
1950–1	141,081	92,467	48,613	19,058	15,149	3909
1951–2	142,972	93,741	49,231	19,689	15,761	3928
1952–3	144,890	95,033	49,857	20,333	16,390	3943
1953–4	146,832	96,342	50,491	20,993	17,035	3957
1954–5	148,801	97,669	51,132	21,667	17,697	3970
1955–6	150,797	99,015	51,782	22,356	18,375	3982
1956–7	152,819	100,379	52,441	23,061	19,070	3992
1957–8	154,868	101,761	53,107	23,782	19,782	4000
1958–9	156,945	103,163	53,782	24,519	20,512	4007
1959–60	159,050	104,584	54,465	25,272	21,260	4012
1960–1	161,183	106,025	55,158	26,043	22,027	4016
1961–2	163,502	107,464	56,037	26,888	22,756	4132
1962–3	166,011	108,902	57,110	27,811	23,447	4364
1963–4	168,560	110,358	58,202	28,757	24,153	4604
1964–5	171,147	111,834	59,313	29,727	24,875	4853
1965–6	173,774	113,330	60,445	30,722	25,613	5109
1966–7	176,441	114,845	61,596	31,742	26,367	5374
1967–8	179,150	116,381	62,769	32,787	27,139	5648
1968–9	181,900	117,938	63,962	33,858	27,928	5930
1969–70	184,692	119,515	65,177	34,956	28,734	6222
1970–1	187,527	121,113	66,414	36,081	29,558	6523
1971–2	190,406	122,733	67,673	37,234	30,400	6834
1972–3	193,328	124,374	68,954	38,416	31,261	7155
1973–4	197,059	126,536	70,523	39,961	32,356	7605
1974–5	201,629	129,237	72,393	41,891	33,700	8191
1975–6	206,305	131,995	74,310	43,893	35,089	8804
1976–7	211,089	134,811	76,278	45,969	36,524	9445
1977–8	215,984	137,688	78,296	47,630	38,008	9622
1978–9	220,790	140,462	80,328	49,055	39,470	9585
1979–80	225,499	143,128	82,371	50,723	40,906	9817
1980–1	230,309	145,845	84,464	52,442	42,385	10,056
1981–2	235,222	148,613	86,609	54,212	43,909	10,303
1982–3	240,239	151,434	88,805	56,449	45,478	10,971
1983–4	244,260	154,061	90,199	58,697	46,929	11,768
1984–5	247,250	156,488	90,762	60,534	48,255	12,280
1985–6	250,276	158,952	91,324	62,412	49,613	12,800
1986–7	253,339	161,456	91,884	64,331	51,003	13,328
1987–8	256,440	163,999	92,442	66,292	52,427	13,865
1988–9	260,714	167,100	93,615	68,483	54,097	14,386
1989–90	266,200	170,779	95,420	70,919	56,027	14,892
1990–1	271,801	174,540	97,261	73,431	58,018	15,413
1991–2	277,519	178,383	99,136	76,020	60,073	15,947
1992–3	283,358	182,311	101,047	78,688	62,192	16,497
1993–4	289,320	186,326	102,994	81,439	64,378	17,061
1994–5	292,836	188,959	103,877	83,868	66,395	17,473
1995–6	293,847	190,173	103,674	85,947	68,223	17,724
1996–7	294,860	191,394	103,467	88,047	70,080	17,967
1997–8	295,878	192,622	103,255	90,169	71,965	18,204
1998–9	296,898	193,859	103,040	92,314	73,880	18,434
1999–2000	297,923	195,103	102,819	94,480	75,824	18,657

Sources: Same as in Appendix Table 3(a).

Appendix Table 3(d): Age Classification of Workers Adopted in
Various Censuses and Surveys

Census 1961	Census 1971	Census 1981	Census 1991	NSS Surveys 1983, 1987–8, 1993–4 and 1999–2000
(1)	(2)	(3)	(4)	(5)
0–14	0–14	0–14	5–14	5–9
15–34	15–19	15–19	15–19	10–14
35–59	20–24	20–24	20–24	15–29
60+	25–29	25–29	25–29	30–44
	30–39	30–34	30–34	30–44
	40–49	35–39	35–39	45–59
	50–59	40–49	40–49	60+
	60+	50–59	50–59	
		60+	60+	

Sources: *Census of India* 1961, 1971, 1981, and 1991, and *NSS Reports on Quinquennial Surveys of Employment and Unemployment.*

Appendix Table 3(e): Age-Sex Distribution of Usually Employed (ps and ss) 1983 to 1999–2000

Age-group	Rural male		Rural female		Urban male		Urban female		Total		Total workforce ('000)
	%	No. ('000)	%	No. ('000)	%	No. ('000)	%	No. ('000)	Male ('000)	Female ('000)	
	(1)	(2)	(3)	(4)	(5)	(6)	(7)	(8)	(9)	(10)	(11)
					1983						
5–9	0.7	1060	1.0	888	0.2	91	0.5	55	1151	943	2094
10–14	6.3	9540	8.6	7637	2.8	1273	5.6	614	10,814	8252	19,065
15–29	36.7	55,576	37.2	33,035	38.2	17,373	36.0	3950	72,949	36,985	109,934
30–44	29.3	44,370	30.5	27,086	34.7	15,781	33.1	3631	60,151	30,717	90,868
45–59	18.9	28,621	18.1	16,074	19.0	8641	19.0	2084	37,262	18,158	55,420
60+	8.1	12,266	4.6	4085	5.1	2319	5.8	636	14,586	4721	19,307
Total	100.0	151,434	100.0	88,805	100.0	45,478	100.0	10,971	196,912	99,776	296,688
15 and above		140,834		80,280		44,114		10,302	184,957	90,581	275,528
					1987–8						
5–9	0.6	492	0.9	832	0.1	52	0.3	42	544	874	1418
10–14	4.5	4920	6.5	6009	2.0	1049	5.0	693	5969	6702	12,670
15–29	36.9	59,204	37.8	34,943	36.2	18,979	35.1	4867	78,182	39,810	117,992
30–44	30.5	53,136	32.0	29,581	36.7	19,241	35.7	4950	72,376	34,531	106,908
45–59	19.5	32,144	18.3	16,917	19.9	10,433	19.0	2634	42,577	19,551	62,128
60+	8.0	14,104	4.5	4160	5.1	2674	4.9	679	16,778	4839	21,617
Total	100.0	163,999	100.0	92,442	100.0	52,427	100.0	13,865	216,426	106,307	322,733
15 and above		158,587		85,601		51,326		13,130	209,913	98,732	308,645

(Contd.)

112

Appendix Table 3(e) Contd.

	(1)	(2)	(3)	(4)	(5)	(6)	(7)	(8)	(9)	(10)	(11)
					1993-4						
5-9	0.3	559	0.5	515	0.1	64	0.3	51	623	566	1190
10-14	3.0	5590	4.6	4738	1.5	966	3.3	563	6555	5301	11,856
15-29	36.1	67,264	36.3	37,387	34.7	22,339	32.6	5562	89,603	42,949	132,552
30-44	32.4	60,370	34.2	35,224	38.6	24,850	39.1	6671	85,220	41,895	127,114
45-59	19.6	36,520	19.3	19,878	20.4	13,133	19.9	3395	49,653	23,273	72,926
60+	8.6	16,024	5.1	5253	4.7	3026	4.8	819	19,050	6072	25,121
Total	100.0	186,326	100.0	102,994	100.0	64,378	100.0	17,061	250,704	120,055	370,759
15 and above		180,177		97,741		63,348		16,447	243,526	114,187	327,713
					1999-2000						
5-9	0.20	390	0.30	308	0.10	76	0.20	37	466	346	812
10-14	2.20	4292	3.70	3804	1.00	758	2.90	541	5051	4345	9396
15-29	34.90	68,091	34.60	35,575	33.40	25,325	30.90	5765	93,416	41,340	134,757
30-44	34.10	66,530	36.90	37,940	40.00	30,330	41.20	7687	96,860	45,627	142,487
45-59	20.10	39,216	19.20	19,741	21.00	15,923	20.00	3731	55,139	23,473	78,611
60+	8.50	16,584	5.30	5449	4.50	3412	4.80	896	19,996	6345	26,341
Total	100.00	195,103	100.00	102,819	100.00	75,824	100.00	18,657	270,927	121,476	392,403
15 and above		190,421		98,707		74,990		18,079	265,411	116,786	382,197

Sources: 1983: Cols (1), (3), (5), and (7) *Key Results of Employment and Unemployment Survey–All India Part I, Special Report*, 43rd Round, p. 82; Totals in Cols (2), (4), (6) and (8) from Appendix Table 3(b). Cols (9) and (10) obtained by adding Cols (2) and (6), Col. (4) and (8) respectively; Cols (11) = Col. (9) + Col. (10).
1987–8: Cols (1), (3), (5) and (7) from *Employment and Unemployment in India, 1993-4*, Report No. 409, NSSO, p. 69. Cols (2), (4), (6), and (8)–totals only from Appendix Table 3(b); Cols (9) to (11) as above.
1993–4: Cols (1), (3), (5), and (7) from *Employment and Unemployment in India, 1993-4*, Report No. 409, NSSO, p. 69. Cols (2), (4), (6), and (8)–totals only from Appendix Table 3(b); Cols (9) to (11) as above.
1999–2000: Cols (1), (3), (5) and (7) from *NSS Report No. 458, Employment and Unemployment Situation in India, 1999–2000*, May 2001. Cols (2), (4), (6), and (8)–totals only from Appendix Table 3(b); Cols (9) to (11) as above.

113

Appendix Table 3(f): Workers Classified by Age and Sex, 1961 Census

Age-group	Workers ('000)			Percentage distribution		
	Males	Females	Total	Males	Females	Total
	(1)	(2)	(3)	(4)	(5)	(6)
			Total			
0–14	8691	5779	14,470	6.73	9.71	7.67
15–34	62,803	30,256	93,059	48.62	50.85	49.32
35–59	48,182	20,695	68,877	37.30	34.78	36.51
60+	9467	2765	12,232	7.33	4.65	6.48
Age not stated	28	10	38	0.02	0.02	0.02
Total	129,171	59,505	188,676	100.00	100.00	100.00
			Rural			
0–14	8125	5547	13,672	7.61	10.00	8.43
15–34	50,965	28,279	79,244	47.74	50.96	48.84
35–59	39,275	19,106	58,381	36.79	34.43	35.98
60+	8361	2554	10,915	7.83	4.60	6.73
Age not stated	25	10	35	0.02	0.02	0.02
Total	106,751	55,496	162,247	100.00	100.00	100.00
			Urban			
0–14	566	233	799	2.52	5.81	3.02
15–34	11,838	1977	13,815	52.80	49.30	52.27
35–59	8908	1589	10,497	39.73	39.63	39.72
60+	1105	211	1316	4.93	5.26	4.98
Age not stated	3			0.01		
Total	22,420	4010	26,430	100.00	100.00	100.00

Note: Excludes NEFA—Total population 297,853; Males = 147,100; Females = 150,753.
Source: Census of India, 1961.

114

Appendix Table 3(g): Distribution of Workers by Sex and Educational Level, 1961 Census

Educational level	Workers–Urban ('000)			Workers–Rural ('000)			Total workers ('000)			Percentage distribution of total workers by educational level		
	Males	Females	Total	Males	Females	Total	Males	Females	Total	Males	Females	Total
	(1)	(2)	(3)	(4)	(5)	(6)	(7)	(8)	(9)	(10)	(11)	(12)
Illiterate	7896	3254	11,150	73,244	53,078	126322	81,140	56,332	137,472	62.81	94.67	72.86
Literate without educational level	6793	322	7115	23,404	1772	25,176	30,197	2094	32,291	23.38	3.52	17.11
Primary/junior basic	4450	209	4659	8513	579	9092	12,963	788	13,751	10.04	1.32	7.29
Matriculation or higher secondary	2331	143	2474	1591	65	1656	3922	208	4130	3.04	0.35	2.19
Technical diploma not equal to degree	67	7	74				67	7	74	0.05	0.01	0.04
Non-technical diploma not equal to degree	110	12	122				110	12	122	0.09	0.02	0.06
Matriculation and above but not degree												
University degree + technical degree	774	64	838				774	64	838	0.60	0.11	0.44
Total	22,421	4011	26,432	106,752	55,494	162,246	129,173	59,505	188,678	100.00	100.00	100.00

Sources: Census of India, 1961, Vol. I, Part II–B(i), General Economic Tables, pp. 86–7.

115

Appendix Table 3(h): Distribution of Usually Employed 15 years and above by Educational Category, 1972–3 to 1999–2000

Category	Rural				Urban			
	Male		Female		Male		Female	
	%	No. ('000)	%	No. ('000)	%	No. ('000)	%	No. ('000)
	(1)	(2)	(3)	(4)	(5)	(6)	(7)	(8)
1972–3								
Not Literate	61.60	76,845	91.80	63,561	25.50	7828	70.80	5000
Literate up to								
Primary	29.10	36,302	7.10	4916	37.80	11,603	16.60	1172
Middle	6.10	7610	0.80	554	14.50	4451	3.20	226
Secondary	2.80	3493	0.30	208	16.00	4912	6.00	424
Higher Secondary								
Graduate and above	0.40	499	0.00	0	6.20	1903	3.40	240
Total	100.00	124,748	100.00	69,239	100.00	30,697	100.00	7062
1977–8								
Not Literate	55.90	76,972	89.50	69,818	23.10	8728	65.20	6603
Literate up to								
Primary	31.00	42,685	8.70	6787	34.20	12,922	17.50	1772
Middle	8.20	11,291	1.10	858	16.60	6272	4.70	476
Secondary	4.10	5645	0.60	468	17.70	6688	7.60	770
Higher Secondary								
Graduate and above	0.80	1102	0.10	78	8.40	3174	5.00	506
Total	100.00	137,695	100.00	78,009	100.00	37,783	100.00	10,127
1983								
Not Literate	52.10	73,375	85.00	68,238	22.30	9837	59.30	6109
Literate up to								
Primary	29.30	41,264	11.20	8991	30.50	13,455	19.40	1999
Middle	10.90	15,351	2.50	2007	17.80	7852	6.50	670
Secondary	6.30	8873	1.10	883	19.50	8602	9.00	927
Higher Secondary								

(Contd.)

116

Appendix Table 3(h) Contd.

	(1)	(2)	(3)	(4)	(5)	(6)	(7)	(8)
Graduate and above	1.40	1972	0.20	161	9.90	4367	5.80	598
Total	100.00	140,834	100.00	80,280	100.00	44,114	100.00	10,302
1987–8								
Not Literate	48.90	77,549	82.90	70,963	20.30	10,419	55.10	7235
Literate up to Primary	29.80	47,259	12.10	10,358	30.90	15,860	19.30	2534
Middle	11.40	18,079	3.10	2654	16.00	8212	6.40	840
Secondary	8.00	12,687	1.60	1370	21.30	10,932	10.70	1405
Higher Secondary		..						
Graduate and above	1.90	3013	0.30	257	11.50	5902	8.50	1116
Total	100.00	158,587	100.00	85,601	100.00	51,326	100.00	13,130
1993–4								
Not Literate	43.80	78,918	78.60	76824	18.40	11,656	49.00	8059
Literate up to Primary	29.10	52,432	14.20	13,879	25.80	16,344	19.70	3240
Middle	13.70	24,684	4.30	4203	17.30	10,959	8.40	1382
Secondary	7.50	13,513	1.90	1857	15.50	9819	7.60	1250
Higher Secondary	3.30	5946	0.60	586	8.70	5511	4.70	773
Graduate and above	2.60	4685	0.40	391	14.30	9059	10.60	1743
Total	100.00	180,177	100.00	97,741	100.00	63,348	100.00	16,447
1999–2000								
Not Literate	39.60	75,407	73.90	72,944	16.2	12,148	43.90	7937
Literate up to Primary	27.30	51,985	15.60	15,398	21.9	16,423	17.60	3182
Middle	16.30	31,039	6.20	6120	18.8	14,098	10.30	1862
Secondary	9.30	17,709	2.80	2764	16.9	12,673	8.80	1591
Higher Secondary	4.20	7998	0.90	888	9.4	7049	5.50	994
Graduate and above	3.30	6284	0.60	592	16.8	12,598	13.90	2513
Total	100.00	190,421	100.00	98,707	100.00	74,990	100.00	18,079

(Cols Contd.)

117

Appendix Table 3(h) Contd.: Distribution of Usually Employed 15 years and above by Educational Category, 1972-3 to 1999-2000

Category	Total			Percentage distribution		
	Male ('000)	Female ('000)	Total ('000)	Male	Female	Total
	(9)	(10)	(11)	(12)	(13)	(14)
			1972-3			
Not Literate	84,673	68,561	153,234	54.47	89.86	66.12
Literate up to						
Primary	47,905	6088	53,993	30.82	7.98	23.30
Middle	12,061	780	12,841	7.76	1.02	5.54
Secondary	8404	631	9036	5.41	0.83	3.90
Higher Secondary						
Graduate and above	2402	240	2642	1.55	0.31	1.14
Total	155,445	76,301	231,746	100.00	100.00	100.00
			1977-8			
Not Literate	85,699	76,421	162,120	48.84	86.71	61.50
Literate up to						
Primary	55,607	8559	64,166	31.69	9.71	24.34
Middle	17,563	1334	18,897	10.01	1.51	7.17
Secondary	12,333	1238	13,571	7.03	1.40	5.15
Higher Secondary						
Graduate and above	4275	584	4860	2.44	0.66	1.84
Total	175,478	88,136	263,614	100.00	100.00	100.00
			1983			
Not Literate	83,212	74,347	157,559	44.99	82.08	57.18
Literate up to						
Primary	54,719	10,990	65,709	29.59	12.13	23.85
Middle	23,203	2677	25,880	12.55	2.95	9.39
Secondary	17,475	1810	19,285	9.45	2.00	7.00
Higher Secondary						
Graduate and above	6339	758	7097	3.43	0.84	2.58
Total	184,948	90,582	275,530	100.00	100.00	100.00

(Contd.)

Appendix Table 3(h) Contd.

	(9)	(10)	(11)	(12)	(13)	(14)
1987–8						
Not Literate	87,968	78,198	166,166	41.91	79.20	53.84
Literate up to						
Primary	63,119	12,892	76,010	30.07	13.06	24.63
Middle	26,291	3494	29,785	12.52	3.54	9.65
Secondary						
Higher Secondary	23,619	2775	26,394	11.25	2.81	8.55
Graduate and above	8916	1373	10,288	4.25	1.39	3.33
Total	209,913	98,731	308,644	100.00	100.00	100.00
1993–4						
Not Literate	90,574	84,883	175,457	37.19	74.34	49.05
Literate up to						
Primary	68,775	17,119	85,895	28.24	14.99	24.01
Middle	35,643	5584	41,228	14.64	4.89	11.53
Secondary	23,332	3107	26,439	9.58	2.72	7.39
Higher Secondary	11,457	1359	12,817	4.70	1.19	3.58
Graduate and above	13,743	2134	15,878	5.64	1.87	4.44
Total	243,525	114,188	357,713	100.00	100.00	100.00
1999–2000						
Not Literate	87,555	80,881	168,436	32.99	69.26	44.07
Literate up to						
Primary	68,408	18,580	86,988	25.77	15.91	22.76
Middle	45,137	7982	53,119	17.01	6.83	13.90
Secondary	30,382	4355	34,737	11.45	3.73	9.09
Higher Secondary	15,047	1883	16,929	5.67	1.61	4.43
Graduate and above	18,882	3105	21,987	7.11	2.66	5.75
Total	265,411	116,786	382,197	100.00	100.00	100.00

Sources: Cols (1), (3), (5) and (7) for 1972–3 and 1977–8 from *Manpower Profile India Yearbook 2000*, Institute of Applied Manpower Research, New Delhi, Table, 3.2.1, p. 292; for 1983 from NSS, *Key Results of Survey of Employment and Unemployment, Part I, Special Report*, 43rd Round, Statement 31, p. 92; for 1987–8 and 1993–4 from *NSS Report 409*, Table 6.5, p. 71; for 1999–2000, *NSS Report No. 458*, Table 6.5, p. 72; Cols (2), (4), (6), and (8), totals only from Appendix Table 3(c), Cols (2), (3), (5) and (6); Col. (9) = Col. (2) + Col. (6); Col. (10) = Col. (4) + Col. (8); Col. (11) = Col. (9) + Col. (10); Cols (12), (13) and (14) derived.

119

Appendix Table 3(i): Rural Labour Input Index for Changes in Age–Sex Composition, 1960–1 to 1999–2000

Year	Percentage age–sex composition								
	Males by age-group				Females by age-group				Grand total
	5–14	15–59	60+	Total	5–14	15–59	60+	Total	
	(1)	(2)	(3)	(4)	(5)	(6)	(7)	(8)	(9)
1960–1	5.01	55.62	5.17	65.80	3.42	29.21	1.58	34.21	100.01
1961–2	4.98	55.52	5.17	65.67	3.43	29.32	1.59	34.33	100.00
1962–3	4.95	55.43	5.16	65.54	3.43	29.43	1.59	34.45	99.99
1963–4	4.92	55.33	5.16	65.42	3.44	29.54	1.60	34.57	99.99
1964–5	4.90	55.23	5.16	65.29	3.44	29.65	1.60	34.69	99.98
1965–6	4.87	55.14	5.16	65.16	3.45	29.76	1.61	34.81	99.98
1966–7	4.84	55.04	5.15	65.04	3.45	29.87	1.61	34.94	99.97
1967–8	4.81	54.95	5.15	64.91	3.46	29.98	1.62	35.06	99.97
1968–9	4.79	54.85	5.15	64.78	3.47	30.09	1.62	35.18	99.97
1969–70	4.76	54.76	5.15	64.66	3.47	30.21	1.63	35.31	99.97
1970–1	4.73	54.66	5.14	64.53	3.48	30.32	1.63	35.43	99.96
1971–2	4.70	54.56	5.14	64.41	3.48	30.43	1.64	35.56	99.96
1972–3	4.68	54.47	5.14	64.28	3.49	30.55	1.64	35.68	99.96
1973–4	4.65	54.37	5.13	64.16	3.50	30.66	1.65	35.81	99.97
1974–5	4.62	54.28	5.13	64.04	3.50	30.78	1.65	35.93	99.97
1975–6	4.60	54.19	5.13	63.91	3.51	30.89	1.66	36.06	99.97
1976–7	4.57	54.09	5.13	63.79	3.51	31.01	1.67	36.19	99.97
1977–8	4.54	54.00	5.12	63.67	3.52	31.12	1.67	36.31	99.98
1978–9	4.52	53.90	5.12	63.54	3.52	31.24	1.68	36.44	99.98
1979–80	4.49	53.81	5.12	63.42	3.53	31.36	1.68	36.57	99.99
1980–1	4.47	53.72	5.12	63.30	3.54	31.47	1.69	36.70	100.00
1981–2	4.44	53.62	5.11	63.18	3.54	31.59	1.69	36.83	100.00
1982–3	4.42	53.53	5.11	63.06	3.55	31.71	1.70	36.96	100.01
1983–4	4.41	53.44	5.11	62.95	3.55	31.72	1.70	36.98	99.93

(Contd.)

120

Appendix Table 3(i) Contd.

	(1)	(2)	(3)	(4)	(5)	(6)	(7)	(8)	(9)
1984–5	3.67	54.77	5.26	63.70	3.32	31.73	1.68	36.73	100.42
1985–6	3.05	55.40	5.35	63.80	3.09	31.74	1.66	36.49	100.29
1986–7	2.54	56.04	5.44	64.01	2.88	31.74	1.64	36.27	100.28
1987–8	2.11	56.68	5.53	64.32	2.69	31.75	1.62	36.07	100.38
1988–9	2.11	56.69	5.53	64.33	2.52	31.79	1.66	35.96	100.30
1989–90	2.11	56.70	5.53	64.34	2.36	31.82	1.69	35.87	100.22
1990–1	2.11	56.71	5.53	64.36	2.21	31.86	1.72	35.79	100.15
1991–2	2.12	56.72	5.54	64.37	2.07	31.89	1.76	35.72	100.09
1992–3	2.12	56.73	5.54	64.39	1.94	31.93	1.79	35.66	100.05
1993–4	2.12	56.74	5.54	64.40	1.82	31.96	1.82	35.61	100.01
1994–5	2.02	57.00	5.54	64.57	1.74	31.85	1.83	35.42	99.98
1995–6	1.92	57.27	5.55	64.74	1.66	31.74	1.83	35.23	99.97
1996–7	1.82	57.54	5.55	64.92	1.58	31.63	1.83	35.05	99.96
1997–8	1.74	57.81	5.56	65.10	1.51	31.52	1.83	34.87	99.97
1998–9	1.65	58.08	5.56	65.29	1.45	31.41	1.83	34.69	99.98
1999–2000	1.57	58.35	5.57	65.49	1.38	31.30	1.83	34.52	100.01

(Cols Contd.)

121

Appendix Table 3(i) Contd.: Rural Labour Input Index for Changes in Age-Sex Composition, 1960-1 to 1999-2000

Year	Wage weights * Percentage Males by age-group			Age-sex composition of females by age-group			Age-Sex composition of labour
Weights	5-14 55.47	15-59 90.69	60+ 79.27	5-14 51.54	15-59 63.04	60+ 51.86	
	(10)	(11)	(12)	(13)	(14)	(15)	(16)
1960-1	277.90	5044.18	409.83	176.27	1841.40	81.94	78.32
1961-2	276.32	5035.40	409.61	176.56	1848.21	82.21	78.2
1962-3	274.74	5026.64	409.40	176.86	1855.12	82.48	78.25
1963-4	273.17	5017.89	409.18	177.16	1862.06	82.75	78.22
1964-5	271.61	5009.16	408.97	177.45	1869.03	83.03	78.19
1965-6	270.05	5000.45	408.75	177.75	1876.02	83.30	78.16
1966-7	268.51	4991.75	408.54	178.05	1883.03	83.57	78.13
1967-8	266.97	4983.06	408.32	178.35	1890.08	83.85	78.11
1968-9	265.44	4974.39	408.11	178.65	1897.14	84.13	78.08
1969-70	263.93	4965.73	407.89	178.95	1904.24	84.40	78.05
1970-1	262.42	4957.09	407.68	179.25	1911.36	84.68	78.02
1971-2	260.92	4948.47	407.47	179.55	1918.51	84.96	78.00
1972-3	259.42	4939.86	407.25	179.85	1925.68	85.24	77.97
1973-4	257.94	4931.26	407.04	180.16	1932.89	85.52	77.95
1974-5	256.46	4922.68	406.82	180.46	1940.12	85.81	77.92
1975-6	255.00	4914.12	406.61	180.76	1947.37	86.09	77.90
1976-7	253.54	4905.57	406.40	181.07	1954.66	86.37	77.88
1977-8	252.09	4897.03	406.18	181.37	1961.97	86.66	77.85
1978-9	250.65	4888.51	405.97	181.67	1969.30	86.94	77.83
1979-80	249.21	4880.00	405.76	181.98	1976.67	87.23	77.81
1980-1	247.79	4871.51	405.54	182.28	1984.06	87.52	77.79
1981-2	246.37	4863.04	405.33	182.59	1991.48	87.81	77.77
1982-3	244.96	4854.57	405.12	182.90	1998.93	88.10	77.75

(Contd.)

122

Appendix Table 3(i) Contd.

	(10)	(11)	(12)	(13)	(14)	(15)	(16)
1983-4	244.61	4846.13	404.91	183.21	1999.49	88.39	77.67
1984-5	203.44	4966.81	417.02	170.87	2000.05	87.33	78.46
1985-6	169.20	5024.03	423.90	159.37	2000.61	86.28	78.63
1986-7	140.72	5081.90	430.88	148.65	2001.17	85.25	78.89
1987-8	117.04	5140.45	437.98	138.64	2001.73	84.23	79.20
1988-9	117.13	5141.33	438.18	129.90	2003.93	85.88	79.16
1989-90	117.22	5142.21	438.37	121.71	2006.14	87.56	79.13
1990-1	117.31	5143.10	438.57	114.04	2008.34	89.28	79.11
1991-2	117.41	5143.98	438.76	106.85	2010.55	91.03	79.09
1992-3	117.50	5144.87	438.96	100.12	2012.76	92.81	79.07
1993-4	117.59	5145.75	439.16	93.80	2014.98	94.63	79.06
1994-5	111.85	5169.78	439.55	89.58	2007.99	94.71	79.13
1995-6	106.39	5193.93	439.95	85.54	2001.02	94.80	79.22
1996-7	101.20	5218.18	440.34	81.68	1994.07	94.89	79.30
1997-8	96.26	5242.55	440.74	78.00	1987.16	94.97	79.40
1998-9	91.56	5267.03	441.14	74.48	1980.26	95.06	79.50
1999-2000	87.09	5291.63	441.53	71.13	1973.39	95.15	79.60

Sources: Cols (1) to (9) from Table 3.24. Weights based on Table 3.9; for Cols (10) to (16), refer to the text.

Appendix Table 3(j): Rural Labour Input for Changes in Age-Sex Composition, 1950-1 to 1960-1

Year	Percentage age-sex composition				Weights * % distribution			
	Adult male	Adult female	Children	Total	wt. 89.69 Men	wt. 62.42 Women	wt. 53.65 Children	Weighted index
	(1)	(2)	(3)	(4)	(5)	(6)	(7)	(8)
1960-1	75.75	16.92	7.33	100.00	6794.02	1056.15	393.25	82.43
1959-60	75.59	16.97	7.44	100.00	6779.55	1059.37	399.16	82.38
1958-9	75.43	17.02	7.55	100.00	6765.11	1062.60	405.06	82.33
1957-8	75.27	17.08	7.66	100.00	6750.70	1065.84	410.96	82.27
1956-7	75.11	17.13	7.77	100.00	6736.32	1069.09	416.86	82.22
1955-6	74.95	17.18	7.86	99.99	6721.97	1072.35	421.69	82.16
1954-5	74.79	17.23	7.98	100.00	6707.65	1075.62	428.13	82.11
1953-4	74.63	17.28	8.09	100.00	6693.36	1078.90	434.03	82.06
1952-3	74.47	17.34	8.19	100.00	6679.11	1082.19	439.39	82.01
1951-2	74.31	17.39	8.30	100.00	6664.88	1085.49	445.30	81.96
1950-1	74.15	17.44	8.40	100.00	6650.68	1088.80	450.66	81.90

Source: See the text.

124

Appendix Table 3(k): Weighted Index Showing the Effect of Education of Rural Labour Input, 1961 to 1999–2000

Educational level/ Rural/Urban/Male/Female	Employment 1999–2000		Education weights	Education effect Col. (2) × Col. (3) 1999–2000	Employment 1993–4		Education effect Col. (6) × Col. (3) 1993–4
	No. ('000)	Ratio to total			No. ('000)	Ratio to total	
	(1)	(2)	(3)	(4)	(5)	(6)	(7)
Rural male							
Not literate	75,407	0.2608	49.6791	12.96	78,918	0.2840	14.11
Literate up to middle	83,024	0.2872	55.9367	16.06	77,116	0.2775	15.52
Secondary and higher secondary	25,707	0.0889	69.6079	6.19	19,459	0.0700	4.87
Graduate and above	6284	0.0217	84.9218	1.85	4685	0.0169	1.43
Rural female							
Not literate	72,944	0.2523	42.5146	10.73	76,824	0.2764	11.75
Literate up to middle	21,510	0.0744	45.4448	3.38	18,082	0.0651	2.96
Secondary and higher secondary	3652	0.0126	63.1169	0.80	2443	0.0088	0.55
Graduate and above	582	0.0020	70.9594	0.14	391	0.0014	0.10
Total	28,9110	1.0000		52.10	277,918	1.0000	51.30

(Cols Contd.)

Appendix Table 3(k) Contd.: Weighted Index Showing the Effect of Education of Rural Labour Input, 1961 to 1999–2000

Educational level/ Rural/Urban/Male/Female	Employment 1987-8		Education effect 1987-8 Col. (9) × Col. (3)	Employment 1983		Education effect 1983 Col. (12) × Col. (3)	Employment 1977-8	
	No. ('000)	Ratio to total		No. ('000)	Ratio to total		No. ('000)	Ratio to total
	(8)	(9)	(10)	(11)	(12)	(13)	(14)	(15)
Rural male								
Not literate	77,549	0.3176	15.78	73,375	0.3318	16.49	76,972	0.3568
Literate up to middle	65,338	0.2676	14.97	56,615	0.2560	14.32	53,976	0.2502
Secondary and higher secondary	12,687	0.0520	3.62	8873	0.0401	2.79	5645	0.0262
Graduate and above	3013	0.0123	1.05	1972	0.0089	0.76	1102	0.0051
Rural female								
Not literate	70,968	0.2906	12.36	68,238	0.3086	13.12	69,818	0.3237
Literate up to middle	13,007	0.0533	2.42	10,998	0.0497	2.26	7645	0.0354
Secondary and higher secondary	1370	0.0056	0.35	883	0.0040	0.25	468	0.0022
Graduate and above	257	0.0011	0.07	161	0.0007	0.05	78	0.0004
Total	244,189	1.0000	50.61	221,115	1.0000	50.04	215,704	1.0000

(Cols Contd.)

126

Appendix Table 3(k) Contd.: Weighted Index Showing the Effect of Education of Rural Labour Input, 1961 to 1999–2000

Educational level/ Rural/Urban/Male/Female	Education effect 1977-8 Col. (15) × Col. (3)	Employment 1972-3 No. ('000)	Ratio to total	Education effect 1972-3 Col. (18) × Col. (3)	Employment 1961 No. ('000)	Ratio to total	Education effect 1972-3 Col. (21) × Col. (3)
	(16)	(17)	(18)	(19)	(20)	(21)	(22)
Rural male							
Not literate	17.73	76,845	0.3961	19.68	73,244	0.4514	22.43
Literate up to middle	14.00	43,912	0.2264	12.66	31,917	0.1967	11.00
Secondary and higher secondary	1.82	3493	0.0180	1.25	1591	0.0098	0.68
Graduate and above	0.43	499	0.0026	0.22	0	0.0000	0.00
Rural female							
Not literate	13.76	63,561	0.3277	13.93	53,078	0.3271	13.91
Literate up to middle	1.61	5470	0.0282	1.28	2351	0.0145	0.66
Secondary and higher secondary	0.14	208	0.0011	0.07	65	0.0004	0.03
Graduate and above	0.03	0	0.0000	0.00	0	0.0000	0.00
Total	49.51	193,988	1.0000	49.09	162,246	1.0000	48.71

Sources: Cols (1), (5), (8), (11), (14), (17) and (20) from corresponding Cols of Table 3.20; Cols (2), (6), (9), (12), (15), (18) and (21) derived; Col. (3) from Table 3.20, Col. (3); Cols (4), (7), (10), (13), (16), (19) and (22) derived.

128 ❖ *The Sources of Economic Growth in India*

Appendix Table 3(l): Total Labour Input Adjusted for Changes in Age–Sex Composition of Education for the Non-residential sector, 1950–1 to 1999–2000

Year	Employment ('000)	Age–Sex composition index	Effect of education	Labour input ('000)
	(1)	(2)	(3)	(4)
1950–1	160,139	84.96	46.28	62,967
1951–2	162,661	85.01	46.66	64,515
1952–3	165,223	85.06	47.03	66,101
1953–4	167,825	85.11	47.41	67,727
1954–5	170,468	85.16	47.80	69,393
1955–6	173,153	85.22	48.19	71,101
1956–7	175,880	85.27	48.58	72,851
1957–8	178,651	85.32	48.97	74,645
1958–9	181,464	85.38	49.37	76,483
1959–60	184,322	85.43	49.77	78,367
1960–1	187,225	85.44	50.17	80,259
1961–2	190,389	85.42	50.24	81,700
1962–3	193,822	85.39	50.30	83,260
1963–4	197,317	85.37	50.37	84,850
1964–5	200,874	85.35	50.44	86,470
1965–6	204,496	85.32	50.51	88,122
1966–7	208,183	85.30	50.57	89,806
1967–8	211,937	85.27	50.64	91,522
1968–9	215,758	85.25	50.71	93,272
1969–70	219,648	85.23	50.78	95,055
1970–1	223,608	85.21	50.84	96,873
1971–2	227,640	85.19	50.91	98,726
1972–3	231,744	85.16	50.98	100,614
1973–4	237,021	85.14	51.12	103,169
1974–5	243,520	85.12	51.27	106,269
1975–6	250,198	85.10	51.41	109,464
1976–7	257,059	85.08	51.55	112,755
1977–8	263,614	85.06	51.70	115,928
1978–9	269,845	85.04	51.87	119,028
1979–80	276,222	85.02	52.04	122,211
1980–1	282,751	85.00	52.21	125,481
1981–2	289,434	84.98	52.38	128,838
1982–3	296,688	84.97	52.55	132,470
1983–4	302,957	84.95	52.70	135,640
1984–5	307,784	85.13	52.86	138,501
1985–6	312,688	85.37	53.02	141,515
1986–7	317,671	85.65	53.17	144,678
1987–8	322,732	85.98	53.33	147,985
1988–9	329,197	86.02	53.51	151,514
1989–90	337,119	86.06	53.68	155,749
1990–1	345,231	86.11	53.86	160,113
1991–2	353,539	86.17	54.03	164,609
1992–3	362,047	86.23	54.21	169,240
1993–4	370,759	86.29	54.39	174,010
1994–5	376,705	86.40	54.60	177,718
1995–6	379,793	86.52	54.82	180,119
1996–7	382,907	86.64	55.03	182,568
1997–8	386,047	86.77	55.25	185,064
1998–9	389,212	86.91	55.46	187,609
1999–2000	392,403	87.05	55.68	190,202

Sources: Col. (1) from Appendix Table 3(b), Col. (1); Col. (2) from Table 3.13, Col. 3; Col. (3) from Table 3.20; Col. (4) = Col. (1) × Col. (2) × Col. (3)/100 × 100.

4

Capital, Land, and Total Input in the Non-residential Sector

A combined index of labour, capital, and land inputs is developed in this chapter. The procedures followed for the derivation of the index of labour input adjusted for the effects of changes in age–sex composition and educational attainment have been dealt with already. Attention is now devoted to the construction of indexes of other components: capital and land inputs and the procedure for combining them with the index of labour input to arrive at the index of total factor input.

Capital is divided into two types: (i) fixed capital stock and (ii) inventories. In October 2001 the CSO released the official estimates of net fixed capital stock (NFCS) at current and constant (1993–4) prices for the period 1951 to 1993.[1] This, combined with the estimates available in *National Accounts Statistics 2001* for the years 1994 to 2000[2], provide the series of capital stock at current and constant prices for the time span 1951 to 2000. These form the basis of this study. The estimates relate to 31 March of each year. The official estimates do not provide a breakdown of NFCS by type of assets, that is, structures and construction (hereafter referred to as structures) and machinery and equipment (hereafter referred to as equipment). Estimates of gross fixed capital stock (GFCS) are also not provided. An attempt is made as part of this study to derive estimates of GFCS and the breakdown of GFCS and NFCS into structures and equipment.

OFFICIAL ESTIMATES OF NET FIXED CAPITAL STOCK

The estimates of NFCS issued by the CSO at current and constant prices are presented in Table 4.1. The method of compilation of the estimates as explained in the *NAS* is as follows: 'Estimates of NFCS from 1980–81 are based on the expected life of each type of asset and have been generated using the perpetual inventory method (PIM). For the years prior to 1980–81, estimates of NFCS industry-wise at constant prices for total economy have

---

[1] CSO, *National Accounts Statistics, Back Series, 1950–51 to 1992–93*, New Delhi, 2001, pp. 146–67.
[2] CSO, *National Accounts Statistics, 2001*, New Delhi, 2001, pp. 50–9.

Table 4.1: Net Fixed Capital Stock at Current and Constant (1993–4)
Prices, 1951 to 2000 (as on 31 March)

As on 31 March	Net fixed capital stock (Rs crore)		Implicit deflator	Indexes of NFCS	
	At current prices	1993–4 prices		At current prices	At 1993–4 prices
	(1)	(2)	(3)	(4)	(5)
1951	16,359	377,924	4.33	100.00	100.00
1952	17,830	389,082	4.58	108.99	102.95
1953	18,355	398,306	4.61	112.20	105.39
1954	18,673	409,054	4.56	114.15	108.24
1955	19,133	421,445	4.54	116.96	111.52
1956	20,419	437,337	4.67	124.82	115.72
1957	22,651	455,972	4.97	138.46	120.65
1958	25,056	475,763	5.27	153.16	125.89
1959	26,514	492,967	5.38	162.08	130.44
1960	28,500	510,330	5.58	174.22	135.04
1961	31,201	531,928	5.87	190.73	140.75
1962	33,832	552,029	6.13	206.81	146.07
1963	36,609	576,356	6.35	223.79	152.51
1964	39,194	602,986	6.50	239.59	159.55
1965	43,499	630,773	6.90	265.90	166.90
966	49,416	660,449	7.48	302.07	174.76
1967	55,571	687,194	8.09	339.70	181.83
1968	61,423	713,176	8.61	375.47	188.71
1969	66,894	736,025	9.09	408.91	194.75
1970	74,540	760,725	9.80	455.65	201.29
1971	82,737	785,429	10.53	505.76	207.83
1972	92,098	811,261	11.35	562.98	214.66
1973	103,084	842,408	12.24	630.14	222.90
1974	123,110	870,632	14.14	752.55	230.37
1975	152,685	896,281	17.04	933.34	237.16
1976	172,747	929,024	18.59	1055.98	245.82
1977	185,540	962,718	19.27	1134.18	254.74
1978	200,230	998,557	20.05	1223.97	264.22
1979	225,822	1,040,403	21.71	1380.41	275.29
1980	270,436	1,078,594	25.07	1653.13	285.40
1981	310,669	1,121,610	27.70	1899.07	296.78
1982	381,653	1,188,209	32.12	2332.98	314.40
1983	452,612	1,244,576	36.37	2766.75	329.32
1984	520,828	1,295,600	40.20	3183.74	342.82
1985	597,918	1,347,822	44.36	3654.98	356.64
1986	693,136	1,402,628	49.42	4237.03	371.14
1987	791,770	1,462,759	54.13	4839.97	387.05
1988	890,329	1,517,223	58.68	5442.44	401.46
1989	1,005,150	1,575,554	63.80	6144.32	416.90
1990	1,144,039	1,634,309	70.00	6993.33	432.44
1991	1,296,299	1,704,760	76.04	7924.07	451.09
1992	1,534,234	1,781,854	86.10	9378.53	471.48
1993	1,737,747	1,853,469	93.76	10622.57	490.43
1994	1,921,762	1,921,762	100.00	11747.43	508.50
1995	2,222,611	2,048,289	108.51	13586.47	541.98
1996	2,696,837	2,212,699	121.88	16485.34	585.49
1997	3,086,238	2,365,943	130.44	18865.69	626.04
1998	3,424,020	2,499,312	137.00	20930.50	661.33
1999	3,738,780	2,620,206	142.69	22854.58	693.32
2000	4,041,414	2,739,223	147.54	24704.53	724.81

Sources: Col. (1) for 1950–1 to 1992–3 from *NAS Back Series*, pp. 147–56, and for 1993–4 to 1999–2000, *NAS 2001*, pp. 108, 110, 112, and 114; from Col. (2) for 1950–1 to 1992–3, *NAS Back Series*, pp. 157–67 and for 1993–4 to 1999–2000 from *NAS 2001*, pp. 109, 111, 113, and 115; Col. (3) = Col. (1)/Col. (2) × 100; Cols (4) and (5) derived.

been obtained by the splicing method. The current price estimates have been prepared using the implicit price indexes of gross fixed capital formation (GFCF) for various industry groups'.[3] Since no further details are available, reference is made to the earlier official series issued by the CSO.

The official estimates for net capital stock were published for the first time in 1988[4] for the period beginning from 1980-1. Net fixed capital stock was distinguished from inventories; but separate estimates were not provided for NFCS by type of assets, that is structures and equipment. Estimates were given separately for the public sector, private corporate sector, and households. Industry-wise breakdown of capital was also available. The procedures of estimation as outlined in *National Accounts Statistics: Sources and Methods, 1989*[5] are as follows: 'For the public sector, the estimates of NFCS as on 31st March 1981 were compiled separately for the assets created before and after 1949-50. The assets prior to 1949-50 accumulated over the past years were assumed to have completed half their lives. For applying PIM, half of the assumed life was taken for such assets and the annual consumption of fixed capital (CFC) was kept constant until the assets were retired. For the assets created from 1950-1, the estimates of GFCF at constant (1980-1) prices were accumulated to derive the GFCS at the end of each year. The CFC was estimated using the straight line formula and assumed life-table for different types of assets. For the private corporate sector, the estimates of the book value of fixed assets for the year ended 1949-50 were based on the sample survey of company balance sheets by the Reserve Bank of India. To arrive at the estimates of fixed assets at the replacement value, the book values for 1949-50 were extended backwards to 1900-1, using an index of industrial production and an index number of wholesale prices. The series of fixed capital formation so derived were accumulated over the years to obtain the estimates of fixed capital stock as on 31 March 1950 at replacement cost. With the help of estimates of GFCF in the private corporate sector from 1950-1 onwards, the estimates of NFCS and CFC were derived using PIM.[6] The estimates of NFCS of household enterprises and ownership of dwellings were based on the *All India Debt and Investment Survey (AIDIS) 1981-2*. In the case of livestock, AIDIS provides data on capital stock inclusive of poultry and young stock, which form part of inventories. The latter was separated using data available in the Livestock Census. In the case of agriculture, the stock of fixed assets as at the end of 1949-50 was not taken into account as the same would have retired by 1980-1. For ownership of dwellings and non-profit

[3] CSO, *National Accounts Statistics, Back Series 1950-51 to 1992-93*, p. xxxvi.

[4] CSO, *Estimates of Capital Stock of Indian Economy*, New Delhi, December 1988.

[5] CSO, *National Accounts Statistics: Sources and Methods, 1989*, Delhi, October 1989, pp. 250-88.

[6] A. C. Kulshreshtha and V. K. Malhotra, 'Estimation of Capital Stock and Consumption of Fixed Capital in Indian National Acounts', (downloaded) Document submitted to the second meeting of the Canberra Group on Capital Stock Statistics convened by OECD, Paris, 1998.

institutions the NFCS as at the end of 1949–50 was taken from Mukherjee and Sastry (1959)[7] and marked up, using data on fixed capital formation.

One of the major shortcomings of the official estimates is the absence of firm data on life-table of fixed assets. The average life for different types of assets has been assumed on the basis of discussions with various agencies and opinions of experts. The assets have been assumed to have served their estimated life and retired at the end of it. No survival function for assets is used to estimate the spread of their useful lives. Capital losses are also not taken into account due to lack of data. The estimates by the CSO are comprehensive in scope and database but do not provide the breakdown of assets into structures and equipment. This is attempted here on the basis of the available data on gross fixed capital formation.

ESTIMATES OF GROSS FIXED CAPITAL FORMATION

Official estimates of GFCF at current and constant (1993–4) prices by type of assets available in *National Accounts Statistics* for the period 1950–1 to 1999–2000 are presented in Appendix Tables 4(a) and 4(b). At current prices, the share of GFCF in gross domestic product (GDP) at market prices increased from 8.9 per cent in 1950–1 to 21.3 per cent in 1999–2000. Between 1950–1 and 1965–6, the share of GFCF moved up from 8.9 per cent to 15.1 per cent but remained stagnant for the next ten years. From 1976–7, it rose steadily to 24.4 per cent in 1995–6 but declined thereafter to reach 21.3 per cent during the last three years. The GFCF at constant prices followed the same pattern in its relationship to real GDP. It increased from 15.4 per cent in 1950–1 to 23.8 per cent in 1999–2000. Real gross fixed capital formation increased at the rate of 5.4 per cent per annum while real GDP at market prices grew by 4.5 per cent.

As expected, the composition of GFCF changed over the years both at current and constant prices with the share of construction declining and that of machinery and equipment rising. Construction accounted for 72.3 per cent of GFCF in current prices in 1950–1 but declined to 48.9 per cent by 1999–2000. In the meanwhile, the share of machinery and equipment went up from 27.7 per cent to 51.1 per cent. At constant prices, machinery and equipment claimed a higher share of the GFCF than at current prices and moved up from 30.3 per cent in 1950–1 to 56.5 per cent in 1999–2000. The share of real GFCF in construction declined from 69.7 per cent to 43.5 per cent over the same period.

Residential construction forms an important part of total construction but estimates of residential construction are not separately available according to the new series. A rough attempt has been made to estimate the share of residential construction by assuming that it will be reflected by and large in the investment in the sector real estate, ownership of dwellings, and business services which is separately shown in *NAS*. Since ownership of dwellings

[7] M. Mukherjee and NSR Sastry, *An Estimate of Tangible Wealth of India* in R. Goldsmith and C. Saunders (eds), *Income and Wealth Series, VIII*, London, 1959, pp. 365–87.

accounted for 95 per cent of the GDP originating in the sector, it is further assumed that 95 per cent of the investment in this sector will be devoted to residential buildings. Based on this assumption, the share of dwellings in construction has been worked out both at current and constant prices and shown in Col. (7) of Appendix Tables 4(c) and 4(d). The totals of GFCF by type of assets and by industry of use differ, the former higher than the latter due to the adjustment for errors and omission in the former. The GFCF in real estate, ownership of dwellings, and business services is available only in respect of unadjusted total GFCF. An attempt has been made to mark up this unadjusted figure on a pro rata basis using the ratio between adjusted and unadjusted GFCF. The adjusted figures of real estate, ownership of dwellings, and business services and the corresponding estimates for dwellings are shown in Cols (4) and (5) of Appendix Tables 4(c) and 4(d). At current prices, the share of dwellings in construction declined progressively from 27.5 per cent in 1950–1 to 12.6 per cent in 1970–1. It increased in the subsequent years to reach 23.4 per cent by 1999–2000. At constant prices, the trend was the same with the shares in 1950–1, 1970–1, and 1999–2000 at 32.8 per cent, 15.1 per cent, and 23.8 per cent respectively. This method of derivation of the component residential construction can be justified because the CSO includes ownership of dwellings in public sector, real estate companies and household sector in their estimates.[8] Estimates of the share of residential construction in the net domestic capital formation worked out by M. Mukherjee also reveal the same declining trend between 1950–1 and 1959–60. According to him, it declined from 18.7 per cent to 14.5 per cent during the period. This, according to Mukherjee, 'is of course quite expected, because some of the other sectors are expected to make greater strides than residential construction'.[9] While investment in residential construction increased at 3.7 per cent per annum, real investment in non-residential construction moved up at 4.7 per cent per year.

Bina Roy has made estimates of gross fixed capital formation at 1980–1 prices for the period 1850–1 to 1950–1.[10] Starting with the official estimates of GFCF (1980–1 series) for 1950–1 as base, she projected backwards the two components of GFCF, using specially constructed indicators for construction and machinery and equipment. She dealt with construction in three parts: public construction, urban construction, and rural construction. The expenditure approach was used to estimate public construction. Urban construction was based on an index of value of building materials, viz. portion of iron and steel used in construction, cement, bricks and tiles, wood and wood products, other building materials, and wages and salaries of construction workers. A weighted

[8] CSO, *National Accounts Statistics, Sources and Methods, 1989*, para 21.37, p. 239.

[9] M. Mukherjee, *National Income of India, Trends and Structure*, Calcutta, 1969, p. 346.

[10] Bina Roy, *An Analysis of Long-term Growth of National Income and Capital Formation in India (1850–1 to 1950–1)*, Firma KLM (P) Ltd, Kolkata, 1996, pp. 302–5.

index of cultivated area, irrigated area, and number of rural houses, with weights based on *Capital Formation in Indian Agriculture* by Tara Shukla was used for rural construction.[11] The indicator for machinery and equipment was based on imports and domestic production of relevant items. To derive a series for domestic output, she used employment in the concerned industries as an indicator and for imports, the current value figures adjusted for trade and transport margins and customs duties by a price index.[12]

The series developed by Bina Roy for GFCF and GDP at 1980–1 prices for the years 1900–1 to 1949–50 are given in Appendix Table 4(e). Gross fixed capital formation averaged around 6.6 per cent of GDP for the whole period. For the first half of the period it was around 5 per cent and for the second half it was 7.7 per cent of GDP. For the period as a whole, construction accounted for 58.5 per cent of GDP and machinery and equipment for 41.5 per cent. For the first half of the period the share of construction was 51.3 per cent and for the second half it was 62.1 per cent of GFCF. Correspondingly, the share of machinery and equipment registered a decline from 48.7 per cent to 37.9 per cent. The shares of construction and machinery and equipment in GFCF mentioned above are at variance from the ratios indicated by Goldsmith on the basis of an earlier set of estimates at current prices by Bina Roy but the declining trend in the share of machinery and equipment was corroborated by him. According to him, for the period 1914–46 'construction accounted for nearly two-thirds of gross capital formation and machinery and equipment for less than one-third, the share actually declining from 31 per cent in the first half of the period to 29 per cent in the second half, contrary to what one would expect in an industrialising country'.[13]

ESTIMATES OF FIXED CAPITAL STOCK BY TYPE OF ASSETS

To estimate the components of GFCS, an attempt has been made to apply PIM to the series on GFCF obtained by combining Bina Roy's estimates for 1850–1 to 1950–1[14] with the official estimates for 1950–1 to 1999–2000.[15] Bina Roy's estimates on GFCF.in construction and machinery and equipment at 1980–1 prices are reproduced in Cols (1) and (2) of Appendix Table 4(f). Index numbers of the above series with 1950–1 as base are shown in Cols (3) and (4). These index numbers are then applied to the official estimates for 1950–1 of capital formation in construction and machinery and equipment to extend the series backwards at 1993–4 prices. The series so obtained for 1900–1 to

[11] Ibid., p. 77.

[12] Ibid., p. 81.

[13] R. W. Goldsmith, *The Financial Development of India, 1860–1977*, York University Press, New Haven, 1983, p. 79.

[14] Roy, *An Analysis of Long-term Growth*, pp. 302–5.

[15] CSO, *National Accounts Statistics, Back Series, 1950–1 to 1992–3*, New Delhi, pp. 54–7 and; CSO, *National Accounts Statistics, 2001*, New Delhi, July 2001, pp. 37–49.

1949–50 are shown in Cols (5) and (6). Splicing the 1980–1 series with the 1993–4 series would have yielded the same results. The official estimates at 1993–4 prices for 1950–1 to 1999–2000 are also shown in the same columns. The PIM is applied to these series of gross capital formation in construction and machinery and equipment.

Information on the average service lives of assets is essential for the application of the PIM. The CSO's official series distinguishes nine different types of construction and thirteen different categories of machinery and equipment with varying service lives. In the exercise attempted here, only two groups are distinguished, that is, structures and equipment. The term 'structure' here includes all categories of construction with varying service lives, viz. residential and non-residential pucca buildings (average life 80 years), residential kutcha buildings (20 years), bridges and irrigation works such as dams, canals etc. (100 years), railway track (55 years), electricity transmission works (45 years), improvement of lands (30 years), and other construction work (35 years). Similarly, for equipment the assumed life varies between 9 to 33 years with most of them in the range of 10 to 20 years.[16] It is necessary in this exercise to make an assumption of average service life for all construction taken together and all machinery and equipment as a single category. In his study on 'Standardised Estimates of Fixed Capital Stock: A Six Country Comparison', Angus Maddison has drawn attention to the varying assumptions regarding service lives in different countries, viz., 'In Germany . . . the average life assumed for non-residential structures is 57 years (Schmidt 1986) whereas it is about 39 years in USA and O'Mahony (1993) estimates it to be 66 years in the U.K. For machinery and equipment, the German and the US official estimates of life are similar at 14 years, but O'Mahony suggests that the average UK life is 25 years. These differing assumptions have a significant effect on the levels and rates of growth exhibited by the stocks.'[17] To obtain standardized estimates of capital stock, Maddison used 39 years for non-residential buildings and 14 years for machinery and equipment. Hofman, in his study on 'Economic Development in Latin America', has adopted service lives of 15, 40, and 50 years for machinery and equipment, structures, and dwellings respectively.[18] Since assets are classified into only two broad categories in this exercise, the average service life has been assumed to be 50 years for structures and 15 years for equipment for the application of the PIM.

The estimates of GFCS in structures at 1993–4 prices for the years 1949–50 to 1999–2000 are obtained by cumulating the GFCF in construction

[16] CSO, *National Accounts Statistics, Sources and Methods, 1989*, Delhi, p. 280.

[17] Angus Maddison, 'Standardised Estimates of Fixed Capital Stock: A Six Country Comparison', in *Explaining the Economic Performance of Nations: Essays in Time and Space*, Cheltenham, 1995, p. 138.

[18] Andre Hofman, 'Economic Development in Latin America in the 20th Century—A Comparative Perspective' in A. Szirmai, B. Van Ark, and D. Pilat (eds), *Explaining Economic Growth, Essays in Honour of Angus Maddison*, Amsterdam, 1993, p. 251.

for 50 years from 1900–1. Similarly, the estimates of GFCS in equipment for the period 1949–50 to 1999–2000 are based on fifteen-year cumulative totals of GFCF from 1935–6. This naturally implies the assumption that the assets are retired completely at the expiry of their assumed lives. In practice, it need not be so; assets may continue to render service even after the assumed life or may get discarded prematurely.

The consumption of fixed capital (CFC) has been estimated using the straight line formula. For structures, CFC has been calculated at the rate of 2.0 per cent per annum and for machinery and equipment at 6.7 per cent. The accumulated CFC is obtained as the sum of the yearly CFC figures over the past service life of the assets.

The estimates of NFCS at 1993–4 prices for structures and equipment are derived separately from the corresponding figures of GFCS and the cumulative CFC. The total NFCS estimates so derived for the period 1950–1 to 1999–2000 (hereafter referred to as preliminary estimates) are found to be considerably lower than the official estimates. This may be partly due to the underestimation of the level and growth of gross fixed capital formation reflected by the indicators used by Bina Roy to project backwards the official estimates of GFCF for 1950–1. Mukherjee had a similar experience while using Bina Roy's estimates for his study on tangible wealth of India during the pre-independence period.[19] The difference may also be partly due to the possible variations in the assumed life of the assets used by me and those in the official estimates. In view of this discrepancy, the preliminary estimates of GFCS obtained by me using the PIM have not been used as such. Instead, only the percentage distribution of assets into structures and equipment derived from the preliminary estimates of NFCS has been used to split the official estimates of NFCS into the two types, on the assumption that while the absolute values may have been subject to underestimation, the relative shares of structures and equipment may not be affected to the same extent. The official estimates of net fixed capital stock at 1993–4 prices along with the breakdown into structures and equipment for the whole economy as on 31 March for the years 1950 to 2000 are presented in Appendix Table 4(f), Cols (24) to (26). It may be mentioned that while the total NFCS estimates used here are from official sources, only their distribution into type of assets are estimated by me and hence may have some deficiencies.

ESTIMATES OF GFCS AT 1993–4 PRICES BY TYPE OF ASSETS

To estimate the GFCS corresponding to the official figures of NFCS, the gross/net ratio derived from the preliminary estimates of GFCS and NFCS obtained on the basis of the historical series of GFCF by Bina Roy and the CSO are used. The gross/net ratios of total fixed capital stock are found to vary between 1.89 and 2.00 for all years except the initial years 1949–50 to 1956–7 when it ranged from 2.10 to 2.58. These ratios have been used to

---

[19] M. Mukherjee, 'An Exercise on the Growth of Tangible Wealth in India Since 1900', *The Indian Economic Journal*, Vol. XIX, No. 2, October–December 1971, Indian Economic Association, Bangalore, p. 241.

multiply the NFCS to derive the corresponding GFCS. A slight modification has, however, been made to the estimates for 1949–50 and 1950–1 which are considered on the high side. Instead of 2.585 for 1950–1 and 2.434 for 1951–2, the observed value of 2.355 for 1952–3 has been used. The actual ratios used, referred to as corrected ratios (only for these two years), and the corresponding GFCS estimates at 1993–4 prices are shown in Cols (36) and (37) of Appendix Table 4(f). The further distribution of GFCS by type of assets is made on the basis of their relative shares in the preliminary estimates of GFCS obtained by the PIM. The GFCS at 1993–4 prices by type of assets is shown in Cols (37) to (39) of Appendix Table 4(f).

CAPITAL STOCK OF DWELLINGS

Capital stock of dwellings is not separately shown in the official estimates. The distribution of NFCS by industry, however, provides figures for the sub-group real estate, ownership of dwellings, and business services. Real estate includes real estate agents and brokers. From the disaggregated tables on domestic product, gross value added (GVA) by dwellings is seen to vary between 85 and 95 per cent of the GVA of the sub-group.[20] On the basis of this relationship, the capital stock in dwellings has been assumed to be equal to 95 per cent of the NFCS of the sub-group real estate, ownership of dwellings, and business services for the purpose of the present study. The values of the net stock of dwellings at current and constant prices as on 31 March are shown in Appendix Table 4(g). The corresponding GFCS in dwellings has been obtained by applying the gross/net ratios of construction to the NFCS series in dwellings. Table 4.2 gives the mid-year values of gross and net fixed capital stock of dwellings at current and constant prices. The

Table 4.2: NFCS of Dwellings at Constant (1993–4) Prices and Current Prices, 1950–1 to 1999–2000 (Mid-year Values)

Year	At 1993–4 Prices			At current prices		
	NFCS value (Rs crore)	Dwellings index	GFCS value (Rs crore)	Dwellings index	Dwellings NFCS (Rs crore)	Dwellings GFCS (Rs crore)
	(1)	(2)	(3)	(4)	(5)	(6)
1950–1	211,837	53.35	525,779	78.90	9167	23,523
1951–2	213,512	53.77	515,970	77.42	9250	23,197
1952–3	214,889	54.11	496,965	74.57	9529	22,804
1953–4	216,425	54.50	484,665	72.73	9610	21,896
1954–5	218,092	54.92	473,223	71.01	9604	20,567
1955–6	219,875	55.37	461,831	69.30	9731	20,021
1956–7	221,829	55.86	449,943	67.52	10,165	20,839
1957–8	223,858	56.37	439,610	65.97	10,816	22,108

(Contd.)

[20] Refer to statement 70 in *National Accounts Statistics, 2000*, p. 163 and *National Accounts Statistics, 1998*, p. 179.

Table 4.2 Contd.

	(1)	(2)	(3)	(4)	(5)	(6)
1958–9	226,006	56.91	432,850	64.95	11,390	22,099
1959–60	228,436	57.53	427,796	64.19	11,876	21,832
1960–1	231,030	58.18	423,869	63.60	12,540	22,736
1961–2	233,682	58.85	421,260	63.21	13,401	23,685
1962–3	236,399	59.53	419,778	62.99	14,207	24,658
1963–4	239,220	60.24	418,598	62.81	14,767	25,099
1964–5	242,265	61.01	417,097	62.59	15,330	25,798
1965–6	245,333	61.78	415,832	62.40	16,299	27,747
1966–7	248,197	62.50	414,676	62.22	17,596	29,412
1967–8	251,138	63.24	413,643	62.07	18,912	30,852
1968–9	254,298	64.04	414,011	62.13	20,316	33,061
1969–70	257,588	64.87	415,262	62.31	22,138	35,911
1970–1	260,663	65.64	416,644	62.52	23,869	39,170
1971–2	263,596	66.38	418,812	62.85	25,491	42,818
1972–3	266,840	67.20	422,204	63.35	27,742	46,806
1973–4	270,365	68.08	427,669	64.17	31,619	53,254
1974–5	274,065	69.02	434,943	65.27	38,933	63,852
1975–6	278,178	70.05	442,668	66.43	45,916	73,686
1976–7	282,739	71.20	450,062	67.53	49,024	79,694
1977–8	287,522	72.41	457,120	68.59	51,189	84,637
1978–9	292,619	73.69	464,911	69.76	55,770	91,784
1979–80	298,141	75.08	474,719	71.23	65,055	104,928
1980–1	304,329	76.64	486,210	72.96	76,837	121,445
1981–2	310,620	78.22	497,411	74.64	92,188	141,380
1982–3	315,930	79.56	507,386	76.14	111,103	166,251
1983–4	320,558	80.72	517,031	77.58	130,210	190,650
1984–5	325,373	81.94	527,298	79.12	149,813	216,161
1985–6	330,725	83.28	538,548	80.81	169,435	246,444
1986–7	335,590	84.51	549,235	82.42	192,006	278,759
1987–8	340,433	85.73	560,121	84.05	216,256	312,519
1988–9	346,719	87.31	573,101	86.00	237,968	348,207
1989–90	354,944	89.38	588,913	88.37	259,466	389,902
1990–1	365,431	92.02	608,030	91.24	283,091	439,612
1991–2	376,614	94.84	628,166	94.26	320,632	503,661
1992–3	388,055	97.72	648,879	97.37	362,944	575,920
1993–4	397,101	100.00	666,414	100.00	400,658	641,622
1994–5	408,325	102.83	688,478	103.31	444,752	718,676
1995–6	421,146	106.06	713,022	106.99	521,232	831,373
1996–7	432,795	108.99	735,760	110.41	602,909	951,070
1997–8	447,171	112.61	762,333	114.39	658,642	1,052,595
1998–9	462,095	116.37	788,632	118.34	715,643	1,151,224
1999–2000	477,482	120.24	814,912	122.28	775,491	1,247,463

Source: Appendix Table 4(g).

real NFCS of dwellings increased at the rate of 1.87 per cent while GFCS in dwellings went up at the rate of 0.9 per cent.

NET FIXED CAPITAL STOCK FOR THE WHOLE ECONOMY AND FOR THE NON-RESIDENTIAL SECTOR AT 1993–4 PRICES

The estimates of NFCS by type of assets for the whole economy and for the non-residential sector derived by subtracting the NFCS in dwellings from the structures component of the former at 1993–4 prices as on 31 March of each year are shown in Appendix Table 4(h). Mid-year values corresponding to the fiscal years derived from this table by averaging the values of the two consecutive years are shown in Table 4.3.

In absolute terms, the NFCS in dwellings more than doubled during the period, that is, it increased at a rate of 1.67 per cent per annum—far below the average annual growth of population at 2.09 per cent—thus explaining the acute shortage in housing. The share of dwellings in the structures component of NFCS declined from two-thirds in 1950–1 to one-fourth in 1999–2000, indicating the growing importance of non-residential construction—industrial buildings, roads, dams, irrigation facilities, etc.—as the economy developed. Net Fixed Capital Stock in the non-residential sector increased nearly 14 times, that is at the rate of 5.49 per cent during the period which led to nearly doubling of its share in total NFCS from 43.4 per cent in 1950–1 to 82.2 per cent in 1999–2000.

As regards the composition of NFCS in the whole economy, the share of structures fluctuated, declining from 86.9 per cent in 1950–1 to 81.9 per cent in 1959–60, rising again to 90.6 per cent of NFCS by 1980–1. It declined thereafter to 71.4 per cent by the end of the period. The share of equipment followed a complementary pattern, rising in the earlier years, declining between 1960–1 and 1990–1, and rising again to 28.6 per cent by 1999–2000. For the non-residential sector of the economy also, the structure of NFCS varied over the period. The share of structures declined from 69.6 per cent to 66.7 per cent between 1950–1 and 1959–60. It increased after 1960–1, peaking at 87.0 per cent in 1980–1. From 1981–2 it declined gradually to reach 65.2 per cent in 1999–2000. The share of machinery and equipment also fluctuated and did not exhibit any overall trend during the period. There appears to be more or less equal importance to the development of structures and acquisition of equipment in the non-residential sector as they grew at 5.4 per cent and 5.8 per cent respectively, the latter having a slight edge over the former.

GROSS FIXED CAPITAL STOCK FOR THE WHOLE ECONOMY AND FOR THE NON-RESIDENTIAL SECTOR AT 1993–4 PRICES

The estimates of GFCS at 1993–4 prices by type of assets for the whole economy and for the non-residential sector as on 31 March of each year are shown in Appendix Table 4(i). Mid-year values corresponding to the fiscal years derived from this table are shown in Table 4.4.

GFCS for the non-residential sector registered a higher growth rate of 4.75 per cent per annum compared to 3.46 per cent for GFCS of the whole economy. The component structures of the non-residential sector increased at 4.51 per cent per year while that of the whole economy grew at 2.89 per cent. The stock of equipment increased at the rate of 5.11 per cent.

As regards the composition of GFCS, the share of structures in the non-residential sector showed a declining trend from 83.2 per cent in 1950–1 to 63.6

Table 4.3: Net Fixed Capital Stock at 1993–4 Prices, Whole Economy and Non-residential Sector 1950-1 to 1999–2000 (Mid-year Values)

Year	NFCS whole economy						NFCS non-residential sector					
	Structures (Rs crore)	Equipment (Rs crore)	Total (Rs crore)	Index 1993–4=100			Structures (Rs crore)	Equipment (Rs crore)	Total (Rs crore)	Index 1993–4=100		
				Structures	Equipment	Total				Structures	Equipment	Total
	(1)	(2)	(3)	(4)	(5)	(6)	(7)	(8)	(9)	(10)	(11)	(12)
1950-1	323,227	48,752	371,979	22.00	11.66	19.71	111,389	48,752	160,142	10.39	11.66	10.74
1951-2	329,883	53,620	383,503	22.45	12.82	20.32	116,371	53,620	169,991	10.85	12.82	11.40
1952-3	336,004	57,690	393,694	22.87	13.79	20.86	121,115	57,690	178,805	11.30	13.79	12.00
1953-4	344,625	59,055	403,680	23.45	14.12	21.39	128,201	59,055	187,255	11.96	14.12	12.56
1954-5	355,792	59,457	415,250	24.21	14.22	22.00	137,700	59,457	197,157	12.84	14.22	13.23
1955-6	366,476	62,915	429,391	24.94	15.04	22.75	146,601	62,915	209,516	13.67	15.04	14.06
1956-7	376,274	70,381	446,655	25.61	16.83	23.66	154,445	70,381	224,826	14.40	16.83	15.08
1957-8	384,164	81,704	465,868	26.14	19.54	24.68	160,306	81,704	242,010	14.95	19.54	16.24
1958-9	394,639	89,726	484,365	26.86	21.45	25.66	168,632	89,726	258,359	15.73	21.45	17.33
1959-60	410,694	90,954	501,649	27.95	21.75	26.58	182,258	90,954	273,212	17.00	21.75	18.33
1960-1	429,070	92,059	521,129	29.20	22.01	27.61	198,041	92,059	290,099	18.47	22.01	19.46
1961-2	448,632	93,346	541,979	30.53	22.32	28.71	214,950	93,346	308,297	20.05	22.32	20.68
1962-3	468,241	95,951	564,193	31.87	22.94	29.89	231,842	95,951	327,793	21.62	22.94	21.99
1963-4	490,100	99,571	589,671	33.35	23.81	31.24	250,881	99,571	350,452	23.40	23.81	23.51
1964-5	513,116	103,764	616,880	34.92	24.81	32.68	270,851	103,764	374,615	25.26	24.81	25.13
1965-6	537,279	108,332	645,611	36.57	25.90	34.20	291,946	108,332	400,278	27.23	25.90	26.86
1966-7	565,086	108,735	673,822	38.46	26.00	35.70	316,889	108,735	425,625	29.55	26.00	28.56
1967-8	594,634	105,551	700,185	40.47	25.24	37.09	343,496	105,551	449,047	32.03	25.24	30.13
1968-9	621,649	102,952	724,601	42.31	24.62	38.39	367,351	102,952	470,303	34.26	24.62	31.55
1969-70	647,138	101,237	748,375	44.04	24.21	39.65	389,550	101,237	490,787	36.33	24.21	32.93
1970-1	675,140	97,937	773,077	45.95	23.42	40.96	414,477	97,937	512,414	38.65	23.42	34.38
1971-2	705,426	92,919	798,345	48.01	22.22	42.29	441,830	92,919	534,749	41.20	22.22	35.88
1972-3	739,399	87,435	826,835	50.32	20.91	43.80	472,559	87,435	559,994	44.07	20.91	37.57
1973-4	769,676	86,844	856,520	52.38	20.76	45.38	499,311	86,844	586,155	46.57	20.76	39.33

(Contd.)

140

Table 4.3 Contd.

	(1)	(2)	(3)	(4)	(5)	(6)	(7)	(8)	(9)	(10)	(11)	(12)
1974–5	793,105	90,351	883,457	53.98	21.60	46.80	519,040	90,351	609,391	48.41	21.60	40.88
1975–6	820,801	91,852	912,653	55.86	21.96	48.35	542,623	91,852	634,474	50.60	21.96	42.57
1976–7	852,528	93,343	945,871	58.02	22.32	50.11	569,789	93,343	663,132	53.14	22.32	44.49
1977–8	885,596	95,041	980,638	60.27	22.72	51.95	598,075	95,041	693,116	55.78	22.72	46.50
1978–9	922,289	97,191	1,019,480	62.77	23.24	54.01	629,670	97,191	726,861	58.72	23.24	48.77
1979–80	959,853	99,646	1,059,499	65.32	23.82	56.13	661,711	99,646	761,357	61.71	23.82	51.08
1980–1	996,960	103,142	1,100,102	67.85	24.66	58.28	692,632	103,142	795,773	64.59	24.66	53.39
1981–2	1,042,007	112,903	1,154,910	70.91	26.99	61.18	731,387	112,903	844,289	68.21	26.99	56.64
1982–3	1,087,210	129,183	1,216,393	73.99	30.89	64.44	771,280	129,183	900,462	71.93	30.89	60.41
1983–4	1,122,268	147,820	1,270,088	76.38	35.34	67.29	801,710	147,820	949,530	74.77	35.34	63.70
1984–5	1,153,383	168,328	1,321,711	78.49	40.25	70.02	828,010	168,328	996,338	77.22	40.25	66.85
1985–6	1,184,315	190,910	1,375,225	80.60	45.65	72.86	853,590	190,061	1,044,500	79.61	45.65	70.08
1986–7	1,217,632	215,061	1,432,694	82.87	51.42	75.90	882,042	215,061	1,097,103	82.26	51.42	73.61
1987–8	1,247,907	242,084	1,489,991	84.93	57.88	78.94	907,474	242,084	1,149,558	84.63	57.88	77.12
1988–9	1,275,528	270,860	1,546,389	86.81	64.76	81.92	928,809	270,860	1,199,669	86.62	64.76	80.49
1989–90	1,303,406	301,526	1,604,932	88.70	72.09	85.02	948,462	301,526	1,249,987	88.45	72.09	83.86
1990–1	1,333,886	335,649	1,669,535	90.78	80.25	88.45	968,455	335,649	1,304,104	90.32	80.25	87.49
1991–2	1,377,543	365,764	1,743,307	93.75	87.45	92.35	1,000,929	365,764	1,366,693	93.35	87.45	91.69
1992–3	1,426,670	390,992	1,817,662	97.09	93.48	96.29	1,038,615	390,992	1,429,606	96.86	93.48	95.91
1993–4	1,469,375	418,241	1,887,616	100.00	100.00	100.00	1,072,273	418,241	1,490,514	100.00	100.00	100.00
1994–5	1,526,693	458,333	1,985,026	103.90	109.59	105.16	1,118,368	458,333	1,576,701	104.30	109.59	105.78
1995–6	1,604,905	525,589	2,130,494	109.22	125.67	112.87	1,183,759	525,589	1,709,348	110.40	125.67	114.68
1996–7	1,685,077	604,244	2,289,321	114.68	144.47	121.28	1,252,282	604,244	1,856,526	116.79	144.47	124.56
1997–8	1,766,291	666,337	2,432,628	120.21	159.32	128.87	1,319,120	666,337	1,985,457	123.02	159.32	133.21
1998–9	1,843,533	716,226	2,559,759	125.46	171.25	135.61	1,381,438	716,226	2,097,664	128.83	171.25	140.73
1999–2000	1,914,118	765,597	2,679,715	130.27	183.05	141.96	1,436,635	765,597	2,202,232	133.98	183.05	147.75

(Cols Contd.)

141

Table 4.3 Contd.: Net Fixed Capital Stock at 1993–4 Prices, Whole Economy and Non-Residential Sector 1950–1 to 1999–2000 (Mid-year Values)

	Percentage distribution						NFCS dwellings (Rs crore)	Dwellings as Non-residential NFCS	
	NFCS non-residential sector			NFCS whole economy				% of NFCS structures	as % of NFCS for the whole economy
Year	Structures	Equipment	Total	Structures	Equipment	Total			
	(13)	(14)	(15)	(16)	(17)	(18)	(19)	(20)	(21)
1950–1	69.56	30.44	100.00	86.89	13.11	100.00	211,837	65.54	43.05
1951–2	68.46	31.54	100.00	86.02	13.98	100.00	213,512	64.72	44.33
1952–3	67.74	32.26	100.00	85.35	14.65	100.00	214,889	63.95	45.42
1953–4	68.46	31.54	100.00	85.37	14.63	100.00	216,425	62.80	46.39
1954–5	69.84	30.16	100.00	85.68	14.32	100.00	218,092	61.30	47.48
1955–6	69.97	30.03	100.00	85.35	14.65	100.00	219,875	60.00	48.79
1956–7	68.70	31.30	100.00	84.24	15.76	100.00	221,829	58.95	50.34
1957–8	66.24	33.76	100.00	82.46	17.54	100.00	223,858	58.27	51.95
1958–9	65.27	34.73	100.00	81.48	18.52	100.00	226,006	57.27	53.34
1959–60	66.71	33.29	100.00	81.87	18.13	100.00	228,436	55.62	54.46
1960–1	68.27	31.73	100.00	82.33	17.67	100.00	231,030	53.84	55.67
1961–2	69.72	30.28	100.00	82.78	17.22	100.00	233,682	52.09	56.88
1962–3	70.73	29.27	100.00	82.99	17.01	100.00	236,399	50.49	58.10
1963–4	71.59	28.41	100.00	83.11	16.89	100.00	239,220	48.81	59.43
1964–5	72.30	27.70	100.00	83.18	16.82	100.00	242,265	47.21	60.73
1965–6	72.94	27.06	100.00	83.22	16.78	100.00	245,333	45.66	62.00
1966–7	74.45	25.55	100.00	83.86	16.14	100.00	248,197	43.92	63.17
1967–8	76.49	23.51	100.00	84.93	15.07	100.00	251,138	42.23	64.13
1968–9	78.11	21.89	100.00	85.79	14.21	100.00	254,298	40.91	64.91
1969–70	79.37	20.63	100.00	86.47	13.53	100.00	257,588	39.80	65.58
1970–1	80.89	19.11	100.00	87.33	12.67	100.00	260,663	38.61	66.28
1971–2	82.62	17.38	100.00	88.36	11.64	100.00	263,596	37.37	66.98
1972–3	84.39	15.61	100.00	89.43	10.57	100.00	266,840	36.09	67.73
1973–4	85.18	14.82	100.00	89.86	10.14	100.00	270,365	35.13	68.43

(Contd.)

142

Table 4.3 Contd.

	(13)	(14)	(15)	(16)	(17)	(18)	(19)	(20)	(21)
1974–5	85.17	14.83	100.00	89.77	10.23	100.00	274,065	34.56	68.98
1975–6	85.52	14.48	100.00	89.94	10.06	100.00	278,178	33.89	69.52
1976–7	85.92	14.08	100.00	90.13	9.87	100.00	282,739	33.16	70.11
1977–8	86.29	13.71	100.00	90.31	9.69	100.00	287,522	32.47	70.68
1978–9	86.63	13.37	100.00	90.47	9.53	100.00	292,619	31.73	71.30
1979–80	86.91	13.09	100.00	90.60	9.40	100.00	298,141	31.06	71.86
1980–1	87.04	12.96	100.00	90.62	9.38	100.00	304,329	30.53	72.34
1981–2	86.63	13.37	100.00	90.22	9.78	100.00	310,620	29.81	73.10
1982–3	85.65	14.35	100.00	89.38	10.62	100.00	315,930	29.06	74.03
1983–4	84.43	15.57	100.00	88.36	11.64	100.00	320,558	28.56	74.76
1984–5	83.11	16.89	100.00	87.26	12.74	100.00	325,373	28.21	75.38
1985–6	81.72	18.28	100.00	86.12	13.88	100.00	330,725	27.93	75.95
1986–7	80.40	19.60	100.00	84.99	15.01	100.00	335,590	27.56	76.58
1987–8	78.94	21.06	100.00	83.75	16.25	100.00	340,433	27.28	77.15
1988–9	77.42	22.58	100.00	82.48	17.52	100.00	346,719	27.18	77.58
1989–90	75.88	24.12	100.00	81.21	18.79	100.00	354,944	27.23	77.88
1990–1	74.26	25.74	100.00	79.90	20.10	100.00	365,431	27.40	78.11
1991–2	73.24	26.76	100.00	79.02	20.98	100.00	376,614	27.34	78.40
1992–3	72.65	27.35	100.00	78.49	21.51	100.00	388,055	27.20	78.65
1993–4	71.94	28.06	100.00	77.84	22.16	100.00	397,101	27.03	78.96
1994–5	70.93	29.07	100.00	76.91	23.09	100.00	408,325	26.75	79.43
1995–6	69.25	30.75	100.00	75.33	24.67	100.00	421,146	26.24	80.23
1996–7	67.45	32.55	100.00	73.61	26.39	100.00	432,795	25.68	81.10
1997–8	66.44	33.56	100.00	72.61	27.39	100.00	447,171	25.32	81.62
1998–9	65.86	34.14	100.00	72.02	27.98	100.00	462,095	25.07	81.95
1999–2000	65.24	34.76	100.00	71.43	28.57	100.00	477,482	24.95	82.18

Sources: Cols (1) to (3) obtained from Cols (1), (2) and (3) of Appendix Table 4(h); Cols (4) to (6) derived; Cols (7) to (9) obtained by averaging Cols (5) to (7) of Appendix Table 4(h); Cols (10) to (12) derived. Cols (13) to (21) derived.

143

Table 4.4: Gross Fixed Capital Stock, Whole Economy and Non-Residential Sector (at 1993-4) Prices, 1950-1 to 1999-2000

Year	GFCS whole economy						GFCS non-residential sector					
	Mid-year values (Rs crore)			Index 1993-4=100			Mid-year values (Rs crore)			Index 1993-4=100		
	Structures	Equipment	Total	Structures	Equipment	Total	Structures	Equipment	Total	Structures	Equipment	Total
	(1)	(2)	(3)	(4)	(5)	(6)	(7)	(8)	(9)	(10)	(11)	(12)
1950-1	807,890	163,131	971,021	32.76	15.28	27.48	282,111	163,131	445,242	15.68	15.28	15.53
1951-2	797,085	164,824	961,909	32.32	15.44	27.22	281,115	164,824	445,939	15.62	15.44	15.55
1952-3	776,971	165,477	942,448	31.51	15.50	26.67	280,006	165,477	445,483	15.56	15.50	15.54
1953-4	771,627	166,560	938,187	31.29	15.60	26.55	286,962	166,560	453,522	15.95	15.60	15.82
1954-5	771,845	167,608	939,453	31.30	15.70	26.59	298,622	167,608	466,230	16.59	15.70	16.26
1955-6	769,650	171,576	941,226	31.21	16.07	26.64	307,819	171,576	479,395	17.11	16.07	16.72
1956-7	763,080	179,169	942,249	30.94	16.79	26.67	313,137	179,169	492,306	17.40	16.79	17.17
1957-8	754,390	191,414	945,804	30.59	17.93	26.77	314,780	191,414	506,195	17.49	17.93	17.66
1958-9	755,692	203,258	958,950	30.65	19.04	27.14	322,842	203,258	526,100	17.94	19.04	18.35
1959-60	768,989	210,409	979,398	31.18	19.71	27.72	341,193	210,409	551,603	18.96	19.71	19.24
1960-1	787,082	218,402	1,005,484	31.92	20.46	28.46	363,213	218,402	581,614	20.18	20.46	20.29
1961-2	808,652	227,383	1,036,034	32.79	21.30	29.32	387,391	227,383	614,774	21.53	21.30	21.44
1962-3	831,373	238,151	1,069,523	33.71	22.31	30.27	411,594	238,151	649,745	22.87	22.31	22.66
1963-4	857,483	250,488	1,107,971	34.77	23.47	31.36	438,885	250,488	689,373	24.39	23.47	24.05
1964-5	883,295	262,908	1,146,204	35.82	24.63	32.44	466,198	262,908	729,106	25.91	24.63	25.43
1965-6	910,555	275,942	1,186,497	36.93	25.85	33.58	494,723	275,942	770,665	27.49	25.85	26.88
1966-7	943,977	285,645	1,229,622	38.28	26.76	34.80	529,301	285,645	814,946	29.41	26.76	28.43
1967-8	979,279	291,348	1,270,627	39.71	27.30	35.96	565,636	291,348	856,984	31.43	27.30	29.89
1968-9	1,012,016	297,330	1,309,346	41.04	27.86	37.06	598,005	297,330	895,335	33.23	27.86	31.23
1969-70	1,043,189	303,942	1,347,132	42.30	28.47	38.13	627,927	303,942	931,869	34.89	28.47	32.50
1970-1	1,079,086	309,557	1,388,642	43.76	29.00	39.30	662,441	309,557	971,998	36.81	29.00	33.90
1971-2	1,120,761	314,331	1,435,092	45.45	29.45	40.62	701,949	314,331	1,016,280	39.01	29.45	35.45
1972-3	1,169,870	319,360	1,489,230	47.44	29.92	42.15	747,666	319,360	1,067,027	41.55	29.92	37.22
1973-4	1,217,504	329,702	1,547,206	49.37	30.89	43.79	789,835	329,702	1,119,537	43.89	30.89	39.05

(Contd.)

144

Table 4.4 Contd.

	(1)	(2)	(3)	(4)	(5)	(6)	(7)	(8)	(9)	(10)	(11)	(12)
1974–5	1,258,685	344,262	1,602,947	51.04	32.25	45.37	823,741	344,262	1,168,004	45.78	32.25	40.74
1975–6	1,306,161	357,643	1,663,803	52.97	33.51	47.09	863,493	357,643	1,221,135	47.98	33.51	42.59
1976–7	1,357,040	370,315	1,727,355	55.03	34.69	48.89	906,978	370,315	1,277,293	50.40	34.69	44.55
1977–8	1,407,965	382,030	1,789,995	57.10	35.79	50.66	950,845	382,030	1,332,874	52.84	35.79	46.49
1978–9	1,465,328	395,202	1,860,529	59.42	37.02	52.66	1,000,417	395,202	1,395,618	55.59	37.02	48.68
1979–80	1,528,365	410,680	1,939,046	61.98	38.47	54.88	1,053,646	410,680	1,464,327	58.55	38.47	51.08
1980–1	1,592,809	427,581	2,020,389	64.59	40.06	57.18	1,106,599	427,581	1,534,180	61.49	40.06	53.51
1981–2	1,668,641	452,567	2,121,209	67.67	42.40	60.03	1,171,230	452,567	1,623,798	65.09	42.40	56.64
1982–3	1,746,100	485,498	2,231,598	70.81	45.48	63.16	1,238,714	485,498	1,724,212	68.84	45.48	60.14
1983–4	1,810,147	519,927	2,330,074	73.41	48.71	65.95	1,293,116	519,927	1,813,043	71.86	48.71	63.24
1984–5	1,869,192	556,743	2,425,935	75.80	52.16	68.66	1,341,894	556,743	1,898,637	74.57	52.16	66.23
1985–6	1,928,544	597,357	2,525,901	78.21	55.96	71.49	1,389,996	597,357	1,987,353	77.24	55.96	69.32
1986–7	1,992,849	642,793	2,635,643	80.82	60.22	74.59	1,443,615	642,793	2,086,408	80.22	60.22	72.78
1987–8	2,053,216	692,945	2,746,161	83.26	64.92	77.72	1,493,095	692,945	2,186,040	82.97	64.92	76.25
1988–9	2,108,360	745,791	2,854,151	85.50	69.87	80.78	1,535,259	745,791	2,281,050	85.31	69.87	79.56
1989–90	2,162,559	802,150	2,964,709	87.70	75.15	83.91	1,573,646	802,150	2,375,797	87.45	75.15	82.87
1990–1	2,219,409	864,808	3,084,217	90.00	81.02	87.29	1,611,379	864,808	2,476,187	89.54	81.02	86.37
1991–2	2,297,663	930,969	3,228,632	93.18	87.22	91.38	1,669,497	930,969	2,600,465	92.77	87.22	90.71
1992–3	2,385,581	997,117	3,382,698	96.74	93.42	95.74	1,736,702	997,117	2,733,819	96.51	93.42	95.36
1993–4	2,465,933	1,067,402	3,533,335	100.00	100.00	100.00	1,799,519	1,067,402	2,866,921	100.00	100.00	100.00
1994–5	2,574,190	1,163,166	3,737,356	104.39	108.97	105.77	1,885,712	1,163,166	3,048,878	104.79	108.97	106.35
1995–6	2,717,258	1,301,507	4,018,766	110.19	121.93	113.74	2,004,237	1,301,507	3,305,744	111.38	121.93	115.31
1996–7	2,864,710	1,460,184	4,324,894	116.17	136.80	122.40	2,128,950	1,460,184	3,589,134	118.31	136.80	125.19
1997–8	3,011,172	1,606,806	4,617,978	122.11	150.53	130.70	2,248,839	1,606,806	3,855,645	124.97	150.53	134.49
1998–9	3,146,261	1,740,645	4,886,907	127.59	163.07	138.31	2,357,630	1,740,645	4,098,275	131.01	163.07	142.95
1999–2000	3,266,796	1,872,521	5,139,317	132.48	175.43	145.45	2,451,883	1,872,521	4,324,404	136.25	175.43	150.84

(Cols Contd.)

145

Table 4.4 Contd.: Gross Fixed Capital, Stock, Whole Economy and Non-Residential Sector (at 1993–4) Prices, 1950–1 to 1999–2000

| Year | GFCS non-residential sector Mid-year values (% distribution) | | | GFCS whole economy Mid-year values (% distribution) | | | Mid-year values dwellings (Rs crore) | Dwellings as % of structures (Rs crore) | Non-residential GFCS as % of total GFCS (Rs crore) |
| | Structures | Equipment | Total | Structures | Equipment | Total | | | |
	(13)	(14)	(15)	(16)	(17)	(18)	(19)	(20)	(21)
1950–1	63.36	36.64	100.00	83.20	16.80	100.00	525,779	65.08	45.85
1951–2	63.04	36.96	100.00	82.86	17.14	100.00	515,970	64.73	46.36
1952–3	62.85	37.15	100.00	82.44	17.56	100.00	496,965	63.96	47.27
1953–4	63.27	36.73	100.00	82.25	17.75	100.00	484,665	62.81	48.34
1954–5	64.05	35.95	100.00	82.16	17.84	100.00	473,223	61.31	49.63
1955–6	64.21	35.79	100.00	81.77	18.23	100.00	461,831	60.01	50.93
1956–7	63.61	36.39	100.00	80.98	19.02	100.00	449,943	58.96	52.25
1957–8	62.19	37.81	100.00	79.76	20.24	100.00	439,610	58.27	53.52
1958–9	61.37	38.63	100.00	78.80	21.20	100.00	432,850	57.28	54.86
1959–60	61.85	38.15	100.00	78.52	21.48	100.00	427,796	55.63	56.32
1960–1	62.45	37.55	100.00	78.28	21.72	100.00	423,869	53.85	57.84
1961–2	63.01	36.99	100.00	78.05	21.95	100.00	421,260	52.09	59.34
1962–3	63.35	36.65	100.00	77.73	22.27	100.00	419,778	50.49	60.75
1963–4	63.66	36.34	100.00	77.39	22.61	100.00	418,598	48.82	62.22
1964–5	63.94	36.06	100.00	77.06	22.94	100.00	417,097	47.22	63.61
1965–6	64.19	35.81	100.00	76.74	23.26	100.00	415,832	45.67	64.95
1966–7	64.95	35.05	100.00	76.77	23.23	100.00	414,676	43.93	66.28
1967–8	66.00	34.00	100.00	77.07	22.93	100.00	413,643	42.24	67.45
1968–9	66.79	33.21	100.00	77.29	22.71	100.00	414,011	40.91	68.38
1969–70	67.38	32.62	100.00	77.44	22.56	100.00	415,262	39.81	69.17
1970–1	68.15	31.85	100.00	77.71	22.29	100.00	416,644	38.61	70.00
1971–2	69.07	30.93	100.00	78.10	21.90	100.00	418,812	37.37	70.82
1972–3	70.07	29.93	100.00	78.56	21.44	100.00	422,204	36.09	71.65
1973–4	70.55	29.45	100.00	78.69	21.31	100.00	427,669	35.13	72.36

(Contd.)

Table 4.4 Contd.

	(13)	(14)	(15)	(16)	(17)	(18)	(19)	(20)	(21)
1974–5	70.53	29.47	100.00	78.52	21.48	100.00	434,943	34.56	72.87
1975–6	70.71	29.29	100.00	78.50	21.50	100.00	442,668	33.89	73.39
1976–7	71.01	28.99	100.00	78.56	21.44	100.00	450,062	33.16	73.95
1977–8	71.34	28.66	100.00	78.66	21.34	100.00	457,120	32.47	74.46
1978–9	71.68	28.32	100.00	78.76	21.24	100.00	464,911	31.73	75.01
1979–80	71.95	28.05	100.00	78.82	21.18	100.00	474,719	31.06	75.52
1980–1	72.13	27.87	100.00	78.84	21.16	100.00	486,210	30.53	75.93
1981–2	72.13	27.87	100.00	78.66	21.34	100.00	497,411	29.81	76.55
1982–3	71.84	28.16	100.00	78.24	21.76	100.00	507,386	29.06	77.26
1983–4	71.32	28.68	100.00	77.69	22.31	100.00	517,031	28.56	77.81
1984–5	70.68	29.32	100.00	77.05	22.95	100.00	527,298	28.21	78.26
1985–6	69.94	30.06	100.00	76.35	23.65	100.00	538,548	27.93	78.68
1986–7	69.19	30.81	100.00	75.61	24.39	100.00	549,235	27.56	79.16
1987–8	68.30	31.70	100.00	74.77	25.23	100.00	560,121	27.28	79.60
1988–9	67.30	32.70	100.00	73.87	26.13	100.00	573,101	27.18	79.92
1989–90	66.24	33.76	100.00	72.94	27.06	100.00	588,913	27.23	80.14
1990–1	65.08	34.92	100.00	71.96	28.04	100.00	608,030	27.40	80.29
1991–2	64.20	35.80	100.00	71.17	28.83	100.00	628,166	27.34	80.54
1992–3	63.53	36.47	100.00	70.52	29.48	100.00	648,879	27.20	80.82
1993–4	62.77	37.23	100.00	69.79	30.21	100.00	666,414	27.02	81.14
1994–5	61.85	38.15	100.00	68.88	31.12	100.00	688,478	26.75	81.58
1995–6	60.63	39.37	100.00	67.61	32.39	100.00	713,022	26.24	82.26
1996–7	59.32	40.68	100.00	66.24	33.76	100.00	735,760	25.68	82.99
1997–8	58.33	41.67	100.00	65.21	34.79	100.00	762,333	25.32	83.49
1998–9	57.53	42.47	100.00	64.38	35.62	100.00	788,632	25.07	83.86
1999–2000	56.70	43.30	100.00	63.56	36.44	100.00	814,912	24.95	84.14

Sources: Cols (1) to (3) and Cols (7) to (9) derived from Appendix Table 4(i), Cols (1) to (3) and (5) to (7); rest of the columns derived.

147

per cent in 1999–2000. The share of machinery and equipment in the GFCS of the non-residential sector increased from 16.8 per cent to 36.4 per cent during the period. During the intervening years from the mid 1960s to the late 1970s, its share either declined or remained stagnant, reflecting the structural retrogression experienced by the economy. This long period trend in the ratio of gross stock of machinery and equipment to total non-residential gross stock appears similar to the experience of other countries for which Maddison has provided estimates. These are: between 1950 and 1991 the ratio moved up from 0.13 to 0.33 in France, 0.13 to 0.34 in the Netherlands, 0.26 to 0.35 in the USA, and 0.22 to 0.31 in Germany. For UK and Japan it declined from 0.38 to 0.36 and from 0.42 to 0.35 respectively.[21]

GROWTH RATES OF NON-RESIDENTIAL FIXED CAPITAL STOCK

The growth rates of non-residential fixed capital stock based on the index of gross and net stocks by type of assets shown in Tables 4.3 and 4.4 are presented in Table 4.5.

The growth rates of GFCS and NFCS show a rather uneven pattern over the period. Taking the period as a whole, NFCS grew slightly faster than GFCS the respective growth rates being 5.5 per cent and 4.74 per cent. Net Fixed Capital Stock recorded the highest growth rate, exceeding 6 per cent per annum during the period 1950–1 to 1964–5 which included the decade 1950–1 to 1960–1. It is noteworthy that gross domestic investment recorded the highest growth of 7.03 per cent per year during this period, compared to the overall average of 5.73 per cent.

The growth rate of GFCS during the first period was much lower than that of NFCS, almost half. As gross fixed capital formation slowed down in the next time span, the rates of growth of GFCS and NFCS became more or less equal, with the former exceeding the latter slightly. The general pattern experienced in other countries of the net stock growing faster than gross stock when capital formation is accelerating and the reverse being the case when capital growth slows down is confirmed by the data presented here.[22] Higher growth rate in structures contributed to the high growth rate of NFCS in between 1950–1 and 1964–5 while equipment accounted for the faster growth of GFCS in the last decade. The negative growth rate recorded by NFCS in equipments during the middle period is supported by the drastic decline in the pace of capital formation in machinery and equipment from 7.21 per cent to 3.88 per cent per annum (see Table 4.6). The investment in machinery and equipment declined even in absolute terms at constant prices during the period (see Table 4.3).

---

[21] Maddison, *Explaining the Economic Performance of Nations*, p. 144.
[22] Ibid., p. 43.

Table 4.5: Growth Rates of Non-residential Fixed Capital Stock, Gross and Net at 1993–4 Prices, 1950–1 to 1999–2000

(in per cent)

Period	Gross fixed capital stock			Net fixed capital stock			Average ratio GFCF/GDP	Capital stock per worker	
	Structures	Equipment	Total	Structures	Equipment	Total		Gross	Net
	(1)	(2)	(3)	(4)	(5)	(6)	(7)	(8)	(9)
Long periods									
1950–1 to 1999–2000	4.51	5.11	4.74	5.36	5.78	5.50	19.55	2.85	3.58
1950–1 to 1964–5	3.65	3.47	3.59	6.55	5.54	6.26	16.38	1.92	4.55
1964–5 to 1980–1	5.55	3.08	4.76	6.04	-0.04	4.82	19.74	2.76	2.61
1980–1 to 1999–2000	4.28	8.08	5.61	3.91	11.11	5.50	21.81	3.78	3.70
Shorter periods									
1950–1 to 1960–1	2.56	2.96	2.71	5.92	6.56	6.12	15.66	1.11	4.47
1960–1 to 1970–1	6.20	3.55	5.27	7.66	0.62	5.86	19.16	3.42	3.99
1970–1 to 1980–1	5.26	3.28	4.67	5.27	0.52	4.50	19.49	2.24	2.08
1980–1 to 1990–1	3.83	7.30	4.90	3.41	12.52	5.06	21.01	2.83	2.99
1990–1 to 1999–2000	4.78	8.96	6.39	4.48	9.59	6.00	22.73	4.89	4.50

Sources: Tables 4.3 and 4.4.

Table 4.6: Growth Rates of Gross Fixed Capital Formation in
Non-residential Sector at 1993–4 Prices, 1950–1 to 1999–2000

(in per cent)

Period	Construction	M & E	Total
	(1)	(2)	(3)
Long periods			
1950–1 to 1999–2000	4.66	6.75	5.73
1950–1 to 1964–5	6.91	7.21	7.03
1964–5 to 1980–1	3.43	3.88	3.61
1980–1 to 1999–2000	4.07	8.89	6.58
Shorter periods			
1950–1 to 1960–1	6.67	5.27	6.14
1960–1 to 1970–1	6.32	3.40	5.35
1970–1 to 1980–1	2.19	7.64	4.11
1980–1 to 1990–1	3.33	9.90	6.54
1990–1 to 1999–2000	4.90	7.78	6.62

Note: M & E — Machinery and equipment.
Sources: Tables 4.3 and 4.4.

FIXED CAPITAL STOCK PER PERSON EMPLOYED

Fixed capital stock per person employed, gross and net, at 1993–4 prices and the corresponding indexes are shown in Appendix Table 4(j). Gross fixed capital stock per person engaged nearly quadrupled and NFCS per person employed increased nearly 5.6 times.

Growth rates of the stock of non-residential structures and equipment per person employed are shown in Cols (8) and (9) of Table 4.5. For the period as a whole, GFCS per person engaged grew at 2.85 per cent per annum while net stock increased at 3.58 per cent. While gross stock per person employed increased over the different periods from 1.92 per cent to 3.78 per cent, net stock registered a higher growth rate of 4.5 per cent during the first period, declined to 2.61 per cent in the next, and rose again to 3.70 per cent in the last period. The growth rates of net stock per person employed was almost same at 4.5 per cent during the first and last decades and was lowest during 1970–1 to 1980–1 at 2.08 per cent. Gross fixed stock per person employed recorded the highest growth during the last decade.

The ratios of GFCF to GDP at market prices are shown in the Col. (7) of Table 4.5. The growth rates of fixed capital stock do not seem to have any correspondence to these ratios. While the rates of gross domestic fixed investment to GDP have been gradually increasing, the growth rates of fixed capital stock, both net and gross, have been fluctuating. It has been pointed out by Denison that the gross investment ratio is a very poor substitute for the growth rate of the capital stock.[23]

The contributions to the growth rate of non-residential GDP by gross and net fixed capital stock are shown in Table 4.7.

[23] Edword F. Denison, *Why Growth Rates Differ*, Washington, D.C., 1967, p. 138.

Table 4.7: Contribution to Growth Rates of Non-residential GDP by
Fixed Capital Stock, 1950–1 to 1999–2000

(in per cent)

Period	Gross stock	Net stock	Average	Percentage contribution
	(1)	(2)	(3)	(4)
Long periods				
1950–1 to 1999–2000	1.50	1.74	1.62	36.82
1950–1 to 1964–5	0.85	1.49	1.17	28.19
1964–5 to 1980–1	1.38	1.40	1.39	44.41
1980–1 to 1999–2000	2.22	2.17	2.19	38.62
Shorter periods				
1950–1 to 1960–1	0.61	1.39	1.00	25.06
1960–1 to 1970–1	1.39	1.54	1.46	39.04
1970–1 to 1980–1	1.43	1.37	1.40	45.45
1980–1 to 1990–1	1.77	1.82	1.79	32.55
1990–1 to 1999–2000	2.77	2.60	2.68	45.66

Sources: Tables 4.5 and 1.3.

In Table 4.7, a simple average of the contribution to growth rates of gross stock and net stock is used to work out the overall contribution. The choice of an appropriate combination of capital stock measure for the study of its contribution to the growth rate of GDP is dealt with in the next section.

MEASUREMENT OF FIXED CAPITAL INPUT

In the previous section, a simple average of the gross and net fixed stock growth rates was used to represent the overall contribution to GDP growth. Use of net stock with depreciation calculated on the basis of straight line method would indicate a gradually declining ability of the capital stock as the stock grows older. On the other hand, use of gross stock would imply that its ability to contribute to production remains constant. This is an extreme possibility because as the capital stock grows older it is subject to wear and tear and requires increasing maintenance and repair costs. Angus Maddison adopted gross capital stock as the appropriate measure for capital input while some others have adopted net stock.[24] But Denison has pointed out that a correct index of capital services would fall somewhere between the indexes of the gross and net stocks and it would be much closer to gross stock than net stock. He used the simple average of gross and net stock indexes in his study *Why Growth Rates Differ*[25] and a weighted average of the indexes of gross stock and net stock based on a straight line depreciation, with the gross stock weighted three and net stock one in his study *Accounting for United States Economic Growth 1929–69*.[26] A weighted average of gross and net stock

---

[24] Maddison, *Explaining the Economic Performance of Nations*, p. 43.
[25] Denison, *Why Growth Rates Differ*, p. 141.
[26] Edward Denison, *Accounting for United States Economic Growth, 1929–69*, The Brookings Institution, Washington, D.C., 1974, p. 55.

indexes with weights three and one respectively is used in this study. The resulting index is shown in Table 4.8.

The net–gross ratio of total fixed capital stock for the non-residential sector rose steadily from 0.36 in 1950–1 to 0.527 in 1970–1, indicating that fixed capital was becoming newer. From 1970–1 to 1980–1, the net-gross ratio fell steadily from 0.527 to 0.519, implying that capital stock was becoming older. During the decade 1980–1 to 1990–1 it increased again from 0.519 to 0.527, but declined to 0.509 by the end of the period. In the case of structures, the net-gross ratio rose steadily from 0.395 in 1950–1 to 0.632 in 1973–4 but declined gradually thereafter to reach 0.586 in 1999–2000. In the first two decades, considerable investment was made for the creation of non-residential structures but it tapered of gradually in the remaining years. The net-gross ratio of equipment fluctuated during the period but at much lower levels. It rose from 0.299 in 1950–1 to 0.441 in 1958–9, but declined steadily to 0.241 by 1980–1. During the rest of the period it moved up to reach 0.411 by 1998–9.

STOCK OF INVENTORIES

Official estimates of the stock of inventories at current and 1993–4 prices are available from 1980–1 onwards.[27] The CSO has made estimates of the stock of inventories by type of institution that is, the public sector, private corporate sector, and household sector, within each industry group, using the available source material. In the case of administrative departments of the government, the stocks held are in the nature of policy stocks like food, fertilizers etc., and work stores. For the former, the net purchases during the year are taken as changes in stocks. For the latter, that is, work stores, based on the common practice to maintain the stock of commodities for at least one month, changes in stocks have been assumed to be one-tenth of the capital formation during the year. For departmental commercial undertakings like railways and communication the stock of inventories as on 31 March available in their annual reports as well as budget documents are used. The annual balance sheets provide the necessary information for non-departmental commercial undertakings. The sample studies of private and public limited companies carried out annually by the Reserve Bank of India (RBI) provide estimates of the stock of inventories as on 31 March each year. For the household sector, inventories in agriculture pertain to livestock only. For registered manufacturing, the *Annual Survey of Industries* (*ASI*) provide relevant data while for unregistered manufacturing the estimates are based on the results of the National Sample Survey and Survey of Small Scale Industries in the unorganized sector. The ratio of inventories to GVA observed in road and water transport in the public sector has been applied to obtain the inventories of the household sector for transport by other means. The consumption of food grains has been subtracted from the net availability with

[27] CSO, *National Accounts Statistics, Back Series, 1952–3 to 1992–3*, pp. 144–5. CSO, *National Accounts Statistics, 2001*, pp. 50–1.

Table 4.8: Fixed Capital Stock Values for the Non-residential Sector at 1993–4 Prices, 1950–1 to 1999–2000

Year	Gross fixed capital stock (Rs crore)			Net fixed capital stock (Rs crore)			Net/Gross ratios (Rs crore)		
	Structures	Equipment	Total	Structures	Equipment	Total	Structures	Equipment	Total
	(1)	(2)	(3)	(4)	(5)	(6)	(7)	(8)	(9)
1950–1	282,111	163,131	445,242	111,389	48,752	160,141	0.395	0.299	0.360
1951–2	281,115	164,824	445,939	116,371	53,620	169,991	0.414	0.325	0.381
1952–3	280,006	165,477	445,483	121,115	57,690	178,805	0.433	0.349	0.401
1953–4	286,962	166,560	453,522	128,201	59,055	187,255	0.447	0.355	0.413
1954–5	298,622	167,608	466,230	137,700	59,457	197,157	0.461	0.355	0.423
1955–6	307,819	171,576	479,395	146,601	62,915	209,516	0.476	0.367	0.437
1956–7	313,137	179,169	492,306	154,445	70,381	224,826	0.493	0.393	0.457
1957–8	314,780	191,414	506,195	160,306	81,704	242,010	0.509	0.427	0.478
1958–9	322,842	203,258	526,100	168,632	89,726	258,359	0.522	0.441	0.491
1959–60	341,193	210,409	551,603	182,258	90,954	273,212	0.534	0.432	0.495
1960–1	363,213	218,402	581,614	198,041	92,059	290,099	0.545	0.422	0.499
1961–2	387,391	227,383	614,774	214,950	93,346	308,297	0.555	0.411	0.501
1962–3	411,594	238,151	649,745	231,842	95,951	327,793	0.563	0.403	0.504
1963–4	438,885	250,488	689,373	250,881	99,571	350,452	0.572	0.398	0.508
1964–5	466,198	262,908	729,106	270,851	103,764	374,615	0.581	0.395	0.514
1965–6	494,723	275,942	770,665	291,946	108,332	400,278	0.590	0.393	0.519
1966–7	529,301	285,645	814,946	316,889	108,735	425,625	0.599	0.381	0.522
1967–8	565,636	291,348	856,984	343,496	105,551	449,047	0.607	0.362	0.524
1968–9	598,005	297,330	895,335	367,351	102,952	470,303	0.614	0.346	0.525
1969–70	627,927	303,942	931,869	389,550	101,237	490,787	0.620	0.333	0.527
1970–1	662,441	309,557	971,998	414,477	97,937	512,414	0.626	0.316	0.527
1971–2	701,949	314,331	1,016,280	441,830	92,919	534,749	0.629	0.296	0.526
1972–3	747,666	319,360	1,067,027	472,559	87,435	559,994	0.632	0.274	0.525
1973–4	789,835	329,702	1,119,537	499,311	86,844	586,155	0.632	0.263	0.524
1974–5	823,741	344,262	1,168,004	519,040	90,351	609,391	0.630	0.262	0.522
1975–6	863,493	357,643	1,221,135	542,623	91,852	634,474	0.628	0.257	0.520

(Contd.)

153

Table 4.8 Contd.

	(1)	(2)	(3)	(4)	(5)	(6)	(7)	(8)	(9)
1976–7	906,978	370,315	1,277,293	569,789	93,343	663,132	0.628	0.252	0.519
1977–8	950,845	382,030	1,332,874	598,075	95,041	693,116	0.629	0.249	0.520
1978–9	1,000,417	395,202	1,395,618	629,670	97,191	726,861	0.629	0.246	0.521
1979–80	1,053,646	410,680	1,464,327	661,711	99,646	761,357	0.628	0.243	0.520
1980–1	1,106,599	427,581	1,534,180	692,632	103,142	795,773	0.626	0.241	0.519
1981–2	1,171,230	452,567	1,623,798	731,387	112,903	844,289	0.624	0.249	0.520
1982–3	1,238,714	485,498	1,724,212	771,280	129,183	900,462	0.623	0.266	0.522
1983–4	1,293,116	519,927	1,813,043	801,710	147,820	949,530	0.620	0.284	0.524
1984–5	1,341,894	556,743	1,898,637	828,010	168,328	996,338	0.617	0.302	0.525
1985–6	1,389,996	597,357	1,987,353	853,590	190,910	1,044,500	0.614	0.320	0.526
1986–7	1,443,615	642,793	2,086,408	882,042	215,061	1,097,103	0.611	0.335	0.526
1987–8	1,493,095	692,945	2,186,040	907,474	242,084	1,149,558	0.608	0.349	0.526
1988–9	1,535,259	745,791	2,281,050	928,809	270,860	1,199,669	0.605	0.363	0.526
1989–90	1,573,646	802,150	2,375,797	948,462	301,526	1,249,987	0.603	0.376	0.526
1990–1	1,611,379	864,808	2,476,187	968,455	335,649	1,304,104	0.601	0.388	0.527
1991–2	1,669,497	930,969	2,600,465	1,000,929	365,764	1,366,693	0.600	0.393	0.526
1992–3	1,736,702	997,117	2,733,819	1,038,615	390,992	1,429,606	0.598	0.392	0.523
1993–4	1,799,519	1,067,402	2,866,921	1,072,273	418,241	1,490,514	0.596	0.392	0.520
1994–5	1,885,712	1,163,166	3,048,878	1,118,368	458,333	1,576,701	0.593	0.394	0.517
1995–6	2,004,237	1,301,507	3,305,744	1,183,759	525,589	1,709,348	0.591	0.404	0.517
1996–7	2,128,950	1,460,184	3,589,134	1,252,282	604,244	1,856,526	0.588	0.414	0.517
1997–8	2,248,839	1,606,806	3,855,645	1,319,120	666,337	1,985,457	0.587	0.415	0.515
1998–9	2,357,630	1,740,645	4,098,275	1,381,438	716,226	2,097,664	0.586	0.411	0.512
1999–2000	2,451,883	1,872,521	4,324,404	1,436,635	765,597	2,202,232	0.586	0.409	0.509

(Cols Contd.)

154

Table 4.8 Contd.: Fixed Capital Stock Values for the Non-residential Sector at 1993-4 Prices, 1950-1 to 1999-2000

Year	Indexes with 1993-4 = 100 Gross fixed capital stock			Indexes with 1993-4 = 100 Net fixed capital stock			Weighted average at 3:1 of GFCS and NFCS indexes		
	Structures	Equipment	Total	Structures	Equipment	Total	Structures	Equipment	Total
	(10)	(11)	(12)	(13)	(14)	(15)	(16)	(17)	(18)
1950-1	15.68	15.28	15.53	10.39	11.66	10.74	14.36	14.38	14.33
1951-2	15.62	15.44	15.55	10.85	12.82	11.40	14.43	14.79	14.52
1952-3	15.56	15.50	15.54	11.30	13.79	12.00	14.49	15.08	14.65
1953-4	15.95	15.60	15.82	11.96	14.12	12.56	14.95	15.23	15.01
1954-5	16.59	15.70	16.26	12.84	14.22	13.23	15.66	15.33	15.50
1955-6	17.11	16.07	16.72	13.67	15.04	14.06	16.25	15.82	16.06
1956-7	17.40	16.79	17.17	14.40	16.83	15.08	16.65	16.80	16.65
1957-8	17.49	17.93	17.66	14.95	19.54	16.24	16.86	18.33	17.30
1958-9	17.94	19.04	18.35	15.73	21.45	17.33	17.39	19.65	18.10
1959-60	18.96	19.71	19.24	17.00	21.75	18.33	18.47	20.22	19.01
1960-1	20.18	20.46	20.29	18.47	22.01	19.46	19.76	20.85	20.08
1961-2	21.53	21.30	21.44	20.05	22.32	20.68	21.16	21.56	21.25
1962-3	22.87	22.31	22.66	21.62	22.94	21.99	22.56	22.47	22.50
1963-4	24.39	23.47	24.05	23.40	23.81	23.51	24.14	23.55	23.91
1964-5	25.91	24.63	25.43	25.26	24.81	25.13	25.74	24.68	25.36
1965-6	27.49	25.85	26.88	27.23	25.90	26.86	27.43	25.86	26.87
1966-7	29.41	26.76	28.43	29.55	26.00	28.56	29.45	26.57	28.46
1967-8	31.43	27.30	29.89	32.03	25.24	30.13	31.58	26.78	29.95
1968-9	33.23	27.86	31.23	34.26	24.62	31.55	33.49	27.05	31.31
1969-70	34.89	28.47	32.50	36.33	24.21	32.93	35.25	27.41	32.61
1970-1	36.81	29.00	33.90	38.65	23.42	34.38	37.27	27.60	34.02
1971-2	39.01	29.45	35.45	41.20	22.22	35.88	39.56	27.64	35.56
1972-3	41.55	29.92	37.22	44.07	20.91	37.57	42.18	27.67	37.31
1973-4	43.89	30.89	39.05	46.57	20.76	39.33	44.56	28.36	39.12
1974-5	45.78	32.25	40.74	48.41	21.60	40.88	46.43	29.59	40.78

(Contd.)

Table 4.8 Contd.

	(10)	(11)	(12)	(13)	(14)	(15)	(16)	(17)	(18)
1975-6	47.98	33.51	42.59	50.60	21.96	42.57	48.64	30.62	42.59
1976-7	50.40	34.69	44.55	53.14	22.32	44.49	51.09	31.60	44.54
1977-8	52.84	35.79	46.49	55.78	22.72	46.50	53.57	32.52	46.49
1978-9	55.59	37.02	48.68	58.72	23.24	48.77	56.38	33.58	48.70
1979-80	58.55	38.47	51.08	61.71	23.82	51.08	59.34	34.81	51.08
1980-1	61.49	40.06	53.51	64.59	24.66	53.39	62.27	36.21	53.48
1981-2	65.09	42.40	56.64	68.21	26.99	56.64	65.87	38.55	56.64
1982-3	68.84	45.48	60.14	71.93	30.89	60.41	69.61	41.83	60.21
1983-4	71.86	48.71	63.24	74.77	35.34	63.70	72.59	45.37	63.36
1984-5	74.57	52.16	66.23	77.22	40.25	66.85	75.23	49.18	66.38
1985-6	77.24	55.96	69.32	79.61	45.65	70.08	77.83	53.38	69.51
1986-7	80.22	60.22	72.78	82.26	51.42	73.61	80.73	58.02	72.98
1987-8	82.97	64.92	76.25	84.63	57.88	77.12	83.39	63.16	76.47
1988-9	85.31	69.87	79.56	86.62	64.76	80.49	85.64	68.59	79.80
1989-90	87.45	75.15	82.87	88.45	72.09	83.86	87.70	74.39	83.12
1990-1	89.54	81.02	86.37	90.32	80.25	87.49	89.74	80.83	86.65
1991-2	92.77	87.22	90.71	93.35	87.45	91.69	92.92	87.28	90.95
1992-3	96.51	93.42	95.36	96.86	93.48	95.91	96.60	93.43	95.50
1993-4	100.00	100.00	100.00	100.00	100.00	100.00	100.00	100.00	100.00
1994-5	104.79	108.97	106.35	104.30	109.59	105.78	104.67	109.13	106.21
1995-6	111.38	121.93	115.31	110.40	125.67	114.68	111.13	122.87	115.15
1996-7	118.31	136.80	125.19	116.79	144.47	124.56	117.93	138.72	125.03
1997-8	124.97	150.53	134.49	123.02	159.32	133.21	124.48	152.73	134.17
1998-9	131.01	163.07	142.95	128.83	171.25	140.73	130.47	165.12	142.40
1999-2000	136.25	175.43	150.84	133.98	183.05	147.75	135.68	177.33	150.07

Sources: Cols (1) to (3), Table 4.4, Cols (7) to (9); Cols (4) to (6) from Table 4.3, Cols (7) to (9); Cols (7) to (9) derived. Cols (10) to (18) derived.

156

the public to arrive at the estimate of stock of food grains with private traders, producers, and consumers. The inventories of commodities other than food grains in household trade have been worked out on the basis of bank advances to traders against the stocks held by them.[28]

An attempt made by me to derive the stock figures for 1950–1 to 1979–80 by combining the benchmark estimate for 1980–1 with the annual changes in inventories[29] resulted in very low or even negative figures for the initial years. This may be due to the deficiencies in the estimate of changes in inventories. Hence, this approach could not be used. Instead the stock of inventories has been taken as a fixed per cent of the NFCS. From the available data for the period 1980–1 to 1984–5 the stock of inventories was found to be around 10 per cent of the NFCS at 1993–4 prices and 12 to 13 per cent at current prices. Backward projection of the 1980–1 figure using the change in inventories in 1980–1 resulted in an estimate for 1979–80 which was found to be 10 per cent and 13 per cent of the corresponding NFCS at constant and current prices. In view of this, the stocks of inventories at current and constant prices have been assumed to be 10 per cent of NFCS for the years 1949–50 to 1979–80 for constant prices and 13 per cent at current prices. The estimates of inventories at current and constant prices are given in Appendix Table 4(k).

FIXED CAPITAL STOCK ESTIMATES AT CURRENT PRICES

Capital stock estimates at current prices by type of assets are required to calculate the share of each category of asset in total non-labour income. Official estimates of total NFCS are available at current prices but not their breakdown into structures and equipment. Implicit price deflators derived from gross capital formation estimates at current and constant prices are shown separately for construction and machinery and equipment in Appendix Table 4(l). Implicit price deflators on the basis of total NFCS at current and constant prices are also obtained and shown in the same appendix table. An attempt has been made to estimate NFCS in structures and equipment at current prices from the corresponding NFCS estimates at 1993–4 prices by applying the implicit price deflators derived from GFCF at current and constant prices. The total NFCS at current prices so obtained is found to differ from the official estimates at current prices. The ratio between the two has been used as an adjustment factor to mark up the calculated values of structures and equipment at current prices so that their total matches the official estimates. The adjusted estimates of NFCS in structures and equipment are shown in Cols (11) and (12) of Appendix Table 4(m) with the corresponding total in Col. (13). The implicit deflators after adjustment are given in Cols (16) to (18).

---

[28] CSO, *National Accounts Statistics, Sources and Methods, 1989*, Delhi, October 1989, pp. 263–6.
[29] EPW Research Foundation, *National Accounts Statistics, 1996–7*, Mumbai, 1998, pp. 33, 35.

Appendix Table 4(n) shows the derivation of NFCS at current prices by type of assets for the non-residential sector.

In a similar manner, estimates of GFCS have also been obtained and shown in Appendix Table 4(o).

The mid-year values of NFCS and GFCS at current prices are shown in Table 4.9.

LAND UTILIZATION STATISTICS

The actual land area of the country has not undergone any change; however, the geographical coverage of land utilization statistics has been gradually increasing. Land utilization statistics are based on the returns prepared by the village staff for revenue purposes. The reporting area increased from 284 million hectares in 1950–1 to 305 million hectares in 1962–3;[30] thereafter it remained more or less at the same level. According to the data for 1996–7, land use statistics are available for 93 per cent of the geographical area. Nearly 73 per cent of the non-reporting area is in occupied Jammu & Kashmir and the rest is covered by forests, barren mountains, and the hilly tracts of Himachal Pradesh.[31] The statistics relate to the agricultural year July to June.

In this study, interest centres around land used for agricultural and non-agricultural purposes. According to one approach, the former is defined to include net area sown and fallow lands. Fallow lands include all lands which are temporarily out of cultivation for a period of not less than one year but not more than five years. Following this definition adopted by Tara Shukla, Dholakia has adopted the same for land in agricultural use.[32] In addition, land use statistics also provide the gross area sown (net area sown plus area sown more than once) or total cropped area. In view of this, the total cropped area may be more relevant to the study of output in relation to land. While net area sown increased over the period by 20.3 per cent, the increase in total cropped area was more than double at 43.7 per cent. The area under double cropping moved up from 11.1 per cent of net area sown in 1950–1 to one-third by the end of the period. Over the years there has been a massive increase in the area under irrigation from 22.6 million hectares in 1950–1 to 68.4 million hectares in 1993–4.[33]

To arrive at the estimates of land input, two definitions have been adopted for the land in agricultural use. According to the first definition, it is taken as equal to net area sown and fallow lands, while as per the second definition it is considered to be equal to total cropped area and fallow lands. The latter

[30] Ministry of Agriculture, Government of India, *Indian Agricultural Statistics, Vol. I, 1985–6 to 1992–3*, Delhi, 1991, pp. 2–3.

[31] CSO, *Guide to Official Statistics, 1999*, New Delhi, p. 117.

[32] Bakul H. Dholakia, *The Sources of Economic Growth in India*, Baroda, 1974, p. 176.

[33] Government of India, *Agricultural Situation in India, March 1992*, p. 965 and CSO, *Statistical Abstract of India, 2000*, CSO, New Delhi, pp. 106–12.

Table 4.9: Fixed Capital Stock at Current Prices for the Whole Economy and Non-residential Sector, 1950–1 to 1999–2000

As on 31 March	NFCS whole economy (Rs crore)			Mid-year values NFCS for non-residential sector (Rs crore)			% distribution of non-residential NFCS	
	Structures	Equipment	Total	Structures	Equipment	Total	Structures	Equipment
	(1)	(2)	(3)	(4)	(5)	(6)	(7)	(8)
1950–1	13,837	1809	15,646	5128	1809	6937	73.92	26.08
1951–2	14,842	2253	17,095	6055	2253	8307	72.88	27.12
1952–3	15,418	2675	18,093	6365	2675	9040	70.41	29.59
1953–4	15,564	2950	18,514	6434	2950	9385	68.56	31.44
1954–5	15,452	3451	18,903	6329	3451	9780	64.71	35.29
1955–6	15,897	3879	19,776	6653	3879	10,532	63.17	36.83
1956–7	17,447	4088	21,535	7791	4088	11,879	65.59	34.41
1957–8	19,332	4521	23,854	9057	4521	13,578	66.70	33.30
1958–9	20,135	5650	25,785	9315	5650	14,965	62.25	37.75
1959–60	20,973	6534	27,507	9691	6534	16,225	59.73	40.27
1960–1	23,031	6820	29,851	11,118	6820	17,938	61.98	38.02
1961–2	25,238	7279	32,517	12,507	7279	19,786	63.21	36.79
1962–3	27,518	7702	35,221	14,021	7702	21,724	64.54	35.46
1963–4	29,386	8516	37,902	15,358	8516	23,873	64.33	35.67
1964–5	31,761	9586	41,347	17,197	9586	26,783	64.21	35.79
1965–6	35,890	10,567	46,458	20,406	10,567	30,973	65.88	34.12
1966–7	40,100	12,394	52,494	23,384	12,394	35,777	65.36	34.64
1967–8	44,387	14,110	58,497	26,421	14,110	40,531	65.19	34.81
1968–9	49,674	14,484	64,159	30,375	14,484	44,859	67.71	32.29
1969–70	56,008	14,709	70,717	34,977	14,709	49,686	70.40	29.60
1970–1	63,523	15,116	78,639	40,848	15,116	55,963	72.99	27.01
1971–2	72,179	15,239	87,418	47,963	15,239	63,202	75.89	24.11
1972–3	82,033	15,558	97,591	55,678	15,558	71,236	78.16	21.84

(Contd.)

Table 4.9 Contd.

	(1)	(2)	(3)	(4)	(5)	(6)	(7)	(8)
1973–4	95,894	17,203	113,097	65,856	17,203	83,059	79.29	20.71
1974–5	116,493	21,405	137,898	79,506	21,405	100,911	78.79	21.21
1975–6	136,690	26,026	162,716	93,071	26,026	119,096	78.15	21.85
1976–7	150,994	28,150	179,144	104,421	28,150	132,571	78.77	21.23
1977–8	164,015	28,870	192,885	115,385	28,870	144,255	79.99	20.01
1978–9	182,166	30,860	213,026	129,185	30,860	160,045	80.72	19.28
1979–80	212,267	35,862	248,129	150,465	35,862	186,327	80.75	19.25
1980–1	249,108	41,445	290,553	176,113	41,445	217,558	80.95	19.05
1981–2	296,491	49,670	346,161	208,913	49,670	258,583	80.79	19.21
1982–3	356,437	60,696	417,133	250,889	60,696	311,585	80.52	19.48
1983–4	413,926	72,794	486,720	290,227	72,794	363,021	79.95	20.05
1984–5	472,896	86,477	559,373	330,574	86,477	417,051	79.26	20.74
1985–6	542,023	103,504	645,527	381,061	103,504	484,564	78.64	21.36
1986–7	618,169	124,284	742,453	435,763	124,284	560,047	77.81	22.19
1987–8	696,248	144,802	841,050	490,804	144,802	635,606	77.22	22.78
1988–9	774,980	172,760	947,740	548,910	172,760	721,670	76.06	23.94
1989–90	862,742	211,853	1,074,595	616,250	211,853	828,102	74.42	25.58
1990–1	964,264	255,905	1,220,169	695,329	255,905	951,233	73.10	26.90
1991–2	1,104,716	310,550	1,415,267	800,116	310,550	1,110,666	72.04	27.96
1992–3	1,266,230	369,761	1,635,991	921,433	369,761	1,291,194	71.36	28.64
1993–4	1,414,893	414,862	1,829,755	1,034,268	414,862	1,449,130	71.37	28.63
1994–5	1,593,812	478,375	2,072,187	1,171,297	478,375	1,649,672	71.00	29.00
1995–6	1,872,865	586,859	2,459,724	1,377,695	586,859	1,964,554	70.13	29.87
1996–7	2,178,602	712,936	2,891,538	1,605,838	712,936	2,318,774	69.25	30.75
1997–8	2,439,276	815,853	3,255,129	1,813,567	815,853	2,629,420	68.97	31.03
1998–9	2,691,319	890,081	3,581,400	2,011,459	890,081	2,901,539	69.32	30.68
1999–2000	2,930,262	959,835	3,890,097	2,193,545	959,835	3,153,381	69.56	30.44

(Cols Contd.)

Table 4.9 Contd.: Fixed Capital Stock at Current Prices for the Whole Economy and Non-residential Sector, 1950–1 to 1999–2000

As on 31 March	% distribution of NFCS whole economy (Rs crore)		GFCS at current prices whole economy: mid-year value (Rs crore)			GFCS at current prices non-residential sector: mid-year values (Rs crore)		
	Structures	Equipment	Structures	Equipment	Total	Structures	Equipment	Total
	(9)	(10)	(11)	(12)	(13)	(14)	(15)	(16)
1950–1	88.44	11.56	34,578	6044	40,621	11,054	6044	17,098
1951–2	86.82	13.18	35,840	6898	42,738	12,642	6898	19,540
1952–3	85.22	14.78	35,653	7669	43,321	12,848	7669	20,517
1953–4	84.07	15.93	34,855	8320	43,176	12,959	8320	21,279
1954–5	81.74	18.26	33,535	9728	43,263	12,968	9728	22,696
1955–6	80.38	19.62	33,373	10,591	43,964	13,351	10,591	23,942
1956–7	81.02	18.98	35,355	10,415	45,771	14,516	10,415	24,932
1957–8	81.05	18.95	37,943	10,603	48,546	15,835	10,603	26,437
1958–9	78.09	21.91	38,568	12,814	51,381	16,469	12,814	29,282
1959–60	76.24	23.76	39,259	15,117	54,376	17,427	15,117	32,544
1960–1	77.15	22.85	42,238	16,184	58,422	19,502	16,184	35,686
1961–2	77.61	22.39	45,482	17,737	63,219	21,797	17,737	39,534
1962–3	78.13	21.87	48,851	19,118	67,969	24,194	19,118	43,312
1963–4	77.53	22.47	51,414	21,433	72,847	26,315	21,433	47,747
1964–5	76.82	23.18	54,659	24,288	78,947	28,861	24,288	53,149
1965–6	77.25	22.75	60,806	26,922	87,728	33,059	26,922	59,981
1966–7	76.39	23.61	66,978	32,654	99,632	37,567	32,654	70,221
1967–8	75.88	24.12	73,083	38,991	112,074	42,231	38,991	81,222
1968–9	77.42	22.58	80,854	41,836	122,690	47,793	41,836	89,630
1969–70	79.20	20.80	90,266	44,180	134,446	54,355	44,180	98,535
1970–1	80.78	19.22	101,516	47,833	149,349	62,346	47,833	110,179
1971–2	82.57	17.43	114,663	51,596	166,258	71,845	51,596	123,440

(Contd.)

161

Table 4.9 Contd.

	(9)	(10)	(11)	(12)	(13)	(14)	(15)	(16)
1972–3	84.06	15.94	129,784	56,961	186,745	82,979	56,961	139,939
1973–4	84.79	15.21	151,703	65,297	217,001	98,449	65,297	163,746
1974–5	84.48	15.52	184,911	81,634	266,545	121,058	81,634	202,692
1975–6	84.01	15.99	217,525	101,424	318,949	143,839	101,424	245,263
1976–7	84.29	15.71	240,347	111,680	352,027	160,653	111,680	272,333
1977–8	85.03	14.97	260,754	116,051	376,806	176,117	116,051	292,169
1978–9	85.51	14.49	289,426	125,499	414,925	197,643	125,499	323,142
1979–80	85.55	14.45	338,040	147,926	485,965	233,111	147,926	381,037
1980–1	85.74	14.26	398,019	171,792	569,812	276,574	171,792	448,367
1981–2	85.65	14.35	474,827	198,779	673,606	333,448	198,779	532,226
1982–3	85.45	14.55	572,526	228,005	800,531	406,275	228,005	634,280
1983–4	85.04	14.96	667,716	255,782	923,498	477,066	255,782	732,847
1984–5	84.54	15.46	766,484	285,922	1,052,405	550,322	285,922	836,244
1985–6	83.97	16.03	882,751	323,536	1,206,287	636,307	323,536	959,843
1986–7	83.26	16.74	1,011,862	371,278	1,383,139	733,103	371,278	1,104,381
1987–8	82.78	17.22	1,145,695	414,388	1,560,083	833,175	414,388	1,247,563
1988–9	81.77	18.23	1,281,088	475,277	1,756,365	932,881	475,277	1,408,158
1989–90	80.29	19.71	1,431,544	563,136	1,994,680	1,041,642	563,136	1,604,778
1990–1	79.03	20.97	1,604,479	658,998	2,263,477	1,164,867	658,998	1,823,865
1991–2	78.06	21.94	1,842,757	790,523	2,633,280	1,339,096	790,523	2,129,619
1992–3	77.40	22.60	2,117,406	942,987	3,060,393	1,541,486	942,987	2,484,473
1993–4	77.33	22.67	2,374,731	1,058,781	3,433,512	1,733,109	1,058,781	2,791,890
1994–5	76.91	23.09	2,687,603	1,213,755	3,901,358	1,968,928	1,213,755	3,182,683
1995–6	76.14	23.86	3,171,357	1,452,504	4,623,861	2,339,984	1,452,504	3,792,48
1996–7	75.34	24.66	3,704,019	1,722,495	5,426,514	2,752,950	1,722,495	4,475,445
1997–8	74.94	25.06	4,158,560	1,967,450	6,126,009	3,105,965	1,967,450	5,073,415
1998–9	75.15	24.85	4,593,184	2,163,194	6,756,379	3,441,961	2,163,194	5,605,155
1999–2000	75.33	24.67	5,000,992	2,347,630	7,348,622	3,753,529	2,347,630	6,101,159

Source: Appendix Table 4(n) and Appendix Table 4(o).

takes into consideration the increase in area sown more than once during the period and is used in this study.

The area reported under non-agricultural uses includes land under buildings (residential and non-residential), roads, railways, water, and others. The area under residential use and general government land has to be excluded. In the absence of detailed information, this has been, following the assumption made by Dholakia, estimated as equal to half of the area under non-agricultural uses.

Land as capital stock is, therefore, considered to be the following:

Definition I: Net area sown + fallow lands + ½ of land under non-agricultural use.

Definition II: Total cropped area + fallow lands + ½ of land under non-agricultural use.

The relevant figures are shown in Table 4.10.

According to definition I, the index of land input increased from 85.4 in 1950–1 to 99.7 in 1999–2000, that is, by 16.7 per cent, while as per definition II adopted in this study, the increase was by 35.8 per cent, that is at the rate of 0.32 per annum according to definition I and 0.63 per cent as per definition II. The latter has been adopted in this study. Land input per person employed in the non-residential sector declined to almost half, that is, from 0.95 hectares in 1950–1 to 0.45 hectares 1999–2000 according to definition I and from 1.03 hectares to 0.57 hectares as per definition II. It may be mentioned that Denison used a constant index of 100 to measure the quantity of land available for use other than residence or by general government as there was no change in the land area of the USA.[34] As against his measure of the total land available, I have used the total land utilized as the land brought under cultivation and under double cropping and land used for non-agricultural purposes which increased considerably over the years. The increase has, of course, tapered off as time passed, due to the physical limits of expansion.

ESTIMATION OF LAND VALUE

The value of land at current prices is required to estimate the share of land in property income. For this purpose, only net area sown and fallow lands are considered under agricultural use under definition I and cropped area and fallow lands under definition II.

Dholakia's estimate[35] of land value in 1960–1 at 1960–1 prices, which was found to be quite close to the RBI, estimate has been used as a benchmark. For lands under agricultural use, the benchmark figure is found to be Rs 21,554 crore. This has been carried backward to 1950–1 and forward to 1999–2000 by the index of net area sown plus fallow lands for definition I. For definition II, the benchmark figure which refers to net area sown plus fallow lands has been marked up by 12.5 per cent to allow for the area sown more than once. The

[34] Denison, *Why Growth Rates Differ*, pp. 180–1.
[35] Dholakia, *The Sources of Economic Growth in India*, p. 178.

Table 4.10: Distribution of Land Area According to Agricultural and Non-agricultural Uses, 1950-1 to 1999-2000

Year	Reporting area for land utilization ('000 hectares)	Not available for cultivation ('000 hectares)			Total fallow lands ('000 hectares)	Net area sown ('000 hectares)	Total cropped area ('000 hectares)
		Area under non-agricultural use	Barren and unculturable waste	Total			
	(1)	(2)	(3)	(4)	(5)	(6)	(7)
1950-1	284,315	9357	38,160	47,517	28,124	118,746	131,893
1951-2	287,827	12,690	37,484	50,174	28,962	119,400	133,234
1952-3	290,787	12,321	37,420	49,741	26,379	123,442	137,675
1953-4	291,901	13,283	37,379	50,662	24,775	126,806	142,480
1954-5	291,378	13,784	34,517	48,301	25,008	127,845	144,087
1955-6	291,917	13,921	34,475	48,396	24,127	129,516	147,311
1956-7	292,179	13,981	33,387	47,368	23,326	130,848	149,492
1957-8	293,435	14,105	33,232	47,337	25,320	129,080	145,832
1958-9	293,667	14,300	33,155	47,455	23,707	131,828	151,629
1959-60	297,254	14,899	33,434	48,333	23,001	132,939	152,824
1960-1	298,458	14,840	35,911	50,751	22,819	133,199	152,772
1961-2	299,151	14,795	35,921	50,716	21,613	135,399	156,209
1962-3	304,977	15,111	35,164	50,275	21,253	136,341	156,760
1963-4	305,169	15,270	34,811	50,081	21,288	136,483	156,963
1964-5	305,252	15,442	34,795	50,237	20,322	138,120	159,229
1965-6	305,535	15,170	34,327	49,497	22,446	136,198	155,276
1966-7	305,487	15,357	32,159	47,516	22,575	137,232	157,355
1967-8	306,120	15,474	31,830	47,304	20,724	139,876	163,736
1968-9	305,885	15,648	31,591	47,239	23,285	137,313	159,529
1969-70	303,896	15,868	30,331	46,199	21,806	138,772	162,265
1970-1	303,758	16,478	28,161	44,639	19,875	140,267	165,791
1971-2	304,141	16,972	27,996	44,968	20,981	139,721	165,186

(Contd.)

164

Table 4.10 Contd.

	(1)	(2)	(3)	(4)	(5)	(6)	(7)
1972–3	303,992	16,658	25,821	42,479	24,369	137,144	162,150
1973–4	304,093	16,799	25,217	42,016	19,947	142,416	169,872
1974–5	304,141	18,377	23,160	41,537	25,276	137,791	164,191
1975–6	304,329	18,660	21,578	40,238	21,775	141,652	171,296
1976–7	304,680	19,834	21,522	41,356	23,955	139,476	167,334
1977–8	304,179	19,047	20,219	39,266	22,595	141,953	172,232
1978–9	304,681	19,201	30,143	49,344	21,836	142,981	174,802
1979–80	304,130	19,543	20,156	39,699	25,724	138,903	169,589
1980–1	304,159	19,656	19,962	39,618	24,748	140,002	172,630
1981–2	304,272	19,686	20,010	39,696	23,035	141,928	176,750
1982–3	304,084	19,914	20,030	39,944	24,627	140,220	172,748
1983–4	304,180	20,340	20,246	40,586	22,837	142,841	179,560
1984–5	304,338	20,551	20,214	40,765	24,914	140,892	176,330
1985–6	304,698	20,631	20,090	40,721	24,945	140,901	178,464
1986–7	305,009	20,879	20,164	41,043	26,495	139,578	176,405
1987–8	304,837	21,168	20,112	41,280	31,774	134,085	170,738
1988–9	304,826	21,229	19,916	41,145	24,570	141,891	182,277
1989–90	304,878	21,258	19,699	40,957	23,967	142,339	182,269
1990–1	304,862	21,087	19,389	40,476	23,365	142,999	185,742
1991–2	304,900	21,465	19,270	40,735	24,613	141,632	182,242
1992–3	304,845	21,771	19,141	40,912	23,830	142,717	185,700
1993–4	304,881	21,771	..	40,904	24,212	142,419	186,595
1994–5	304,829	21,771	..	41,019	23,219	142,960	188,053
1995–6	304,875	21,771	..	41,371	23,847	142,197	187,471
1996–7	304,877	21,771	..	41,542	23,215	142,819	189,543
1997–8	304,877	21,771	..	41,542	23,215	142,819	189,543
1998–9	304,877	21,771	..	41,542	23,215	142,819	189,543
1999–2000	304,877	21,771	..	41,542	23,215	142,819	189,543

(Cols Contd.)

Table 4.10 Contd.: Distribution of Land Area According to Agricultural and Non-agricultural Uses, 1950–1 to 1999–2000

Year	Land as capital stock ('000 hectares)		Index of land as capital stock, 1993–4 = 100		Land input per person engaged ('000 hectares)		Index of land input per person engaged (1993–4 = 100)	
	Definition I	Definition II	Definition I	Definition II	Definition I	Definition II	Definition I	Definition II
	(8)	(9)	(10)	(11)	(12)	(13)	(14)	(15)
1950-1	151,549	164,696	85.37	74.29	0.95	1.03	197.65	172.00
1951-2	154,707	168,541	87.15	76.02	0.95	1.04	198.65	173.29
1952-3	155,982	170,215	87.87	76.78	0.94	1.03	197.18	172.29
1953-4	158,223	173,897	89.13	78.44	0.94	1.04	196.91	173.29
1954-5	159,745	175,987	89.99	79.38	0.94	1.03	195.72	172.65
1955-6	160,604	178,399	90.47	80.47	0.93	1.03	193.72	172.31
1956-7	161,165	179,809	90.79	81.11	0.92	1.02	191.38	170.98
1957-8	161,453	178,205	90.95	80.38	0.90	1.00	188.75	166.82
1958-9	162,685	182,486	91.65	82.31	0.90	1.01	187.24	168.18
1959-60	163,390	183,275	92.04	82.67	0.89	0.99	185.14	166.29
1960-1	163,438	183,011	92.07	82.55	0.87	0.98	182.32	163.48
1961-2	164,410	185,220	92.62	83.55	0.86	0.97	180.36	162.70
1962-3	165,150	185,569	93.03	83.71	0.85	0.96	177.96	160.12
1963-4	165,406	185,886	93.18	83.85	0.84	0.94	175.08	157.55
1964-5	166,163	187,272	93.60	84.47	0.83	0.93	172.77	155.92
1965-6	166,229	185,307	93.64	83.59	0.81	0.91	169.78	151.55
1966-7	167,486	187,609	94.35	84.63	0.80	0.90	168.03	150.71
1967-8	168,337	192,197	94.83	86.70	0.79	0.91	165.89	151.66
1968-9	168,422	190,638	94.88	85.99	0.78	0.88	163.04	147.77
1969-70	168,512	192,005	94.93	86.61	0.77	0.87	160.23	146.19
1970-1	168,381	193,905	94.85	87.47	0.75	0.87	157.27	145.02
1971-2	169,188	194,653	95.31	87.80	0.74	0.86	155.23	143.01
1972-3	169,842	194,848	95.68	87.89	0.73	0.84	153.07	140.61
1973-4	170,763	198,219	96.20	89.41	0.72	0.84	150.47	139.86

(Contd.)

Table 4.10 Contd.

	(8)	(9)	(10)	(11)	(12)	(13)	(14)	(15)
1974-5	172,256	198,656	97.04	89.61	0.71	0.82	147.74	136.43
1975-6	172,757	202,401	97.32	91.30	0.69	0.81	144.21	135.29
1976-7	173,348	201,206	97.65	90.76	0.67	0.78	140.84	130.90
1977-8	174,072	204,351	98.06	92.18	0.66	0.78	137.92	129.64
1978-9	174,418	206,239	98.25	93.03	0.65	0.76	135.00	127.82
1979-80	174,399	205,085	98.24	92.51	0.63	0.74	131.87	124.17
1980-1	174,578	207,206	98.34	93.47	0.62	0.73	128.96	122.56
1981-2	174,806	209,628	98.47	94.56	0.60	0.72	126.14	121.13
1982-3	174,804	207,332	98.47	93.52	0.59	0.70	123.06	116.87
1983-4	175,848	212,567	99.06	95.88	0.58	0.70	121.23	117.34
1984-5	176,082	211,520	99.19	95.41	0.57	0.69	119.49	114.93
1985-6	176,162	213,725	99.24	96.41	0.56	0.68	117.67	114.31
1986-7	176,513	213,340	99.43	96.23	0.56	0.67	116.05	112.31
1987-8	176,443	213,096	99.40	96.12	0.55	0.66	114.19	110.43
1988-9	177,076	217,462	99.75	98.09	0.54	0.66	112.35	110.48
1989-90	176,935	216,865	99.67	97.82	0.52	0.64	109.62	107.58
1990-1	176,908	219,651	99.66	99.08	0.51	0.64	107.03	106.41
1991-2	176,978	217,588	99.70	98.15	0.50	0.62	104.55	102.93
1992-3	177,433	220,416	99.95	99.42	0.49	0.61	102.36	101.82
1993-4	177,517	221,693	100.00	100.00	0.48	0.60	100.00	100.00
1994-5	177,065	222,158	99.75	100.21	0.47	0.59	98.17	98.63
1995-6	176,930	222,204	99.67	100.23	0.47	0.59	97.30	97.85
1996-7	176,920	223,644	99.66	100.88	0.46	0.58	96.50	97.68
1997-8	176,920	223,644	99.66	100.88	0.46	0.58	95.72	96.89
1998-9	176,920	223,644	99.66	100.88	0.45	0.57	94.94	96.10
1999-2000	176,920	223,644	99.66	100.88	0.45	0.57	94.17	95.32

Sources: Cols (1) to (7) from *Indian Agricultural Statistics, 1985-6 to 1992-3*, Vol. I, p. 2 and *Statistical Abstract 2000*, pp. 54-60; Col. 8 = Col. (6) + Col. (5) + Col. (2)/2; Col. (9) = Col. (7) + Col. (5) + Col. (2)/2; Cols (10) and (11) derived. Table 4.10 and Appendix Table 3(b), Col. (1).

167

benchmark figure for definition II accordingly is Rs 24,258 crore which has been carried forward and backward by the index of cropped area plus fallow lands. The resulting series provide land value at 1960–1 prices. These have been converted to current prices, using the index number of wholesale prices for agricultural commodities. The figures are shown in Appendix Table 4(p).

For land under non-agricultural use, the benchmark value figure from Dholakia is Rs 880 crore. To this, the index of land under non-agricultural uses have been applied to estimate the value figure at 1960–1 prices for 1950–1 to 1959–60 and 1961–2 to 1999–2000. This constant price series has been expressed in current prices, using the index number of wholesale prices for non-agricultural commodities, and is shown in Appendix Table 4(q).

The total value of land at current prices according to the two definitions is shown in Table 4.11. The value of land according to definition II is used for further calculations. The wholesale price indexes used are shown in Appendix Tables 4(r), 4(s), and 4(t).

Table 4.11: Value of Land for Agricultural and Non-agricultural Use at Current Prices, 1950–1 to 1999–2000

(Rs crore)

| Year | Value of land | | | | | |
| | Definition I | | | Definition II | | |
	Agricultural use	Non-agricultural use	Total	Agricultural use	Non-agricultural use	Total
	(1)	(2)	(3)	(4)	(5)	(6)
1950–1	19,300	435	19,735	21,028	435	21,462
1951–2	20,095	652	20,747	21,968	652	22,621
1952–3	16,720	581	17,301	18,308	581	18,889
1953–4	17,896	649	18,545	19,747	649	20,395
1954–5	16,085	650	16,735	17,794	650	18,444
1955–6	15,087	632	15,719	16,835	632	17,467
1956–7	17,979	699	18,677	20,153	699	20,851
1957–8	18,504	727	19,231	20,512	727	21,238
1958–9	19,785	755	20,540	22,304	755	23,059
1959–60	20,272	826	21,098	22,857	826	23,683
1960–1	21,554	880	22,434	24,258	880	25,138
1961–2	21,533	886	22,419	24,387	886	25,273
1962–3	22,111	945	23,057	24,976	945	25,922
1963–4	23,455	1016	24,470	26,499	1016	27,515
1964–5	28,445	1091	29,535	32,234	1091	33,325
1965–6	30,830	1144	31,975	34,538	1144	35,682
1966–7	36,514	1302	37,816	41,112	1302	42,413
1967–8	41,452	1453	42,905	47,610	1453	49,064
1968–9	39,515	1484	40,998	44,981	1484	46,464
1969–70	40,699	1521	42,219	46,653	1521	48,174
1970–1	44,234	1687	45,921	51,284	1687	52,971
1971–2	44,566	1895	46,462	51,628	1895	53,524
1972–3	49,209	2050	51,259	56,828	2050	58,878
1973–4	58,584	2407	60,991	72,986	2407	75,393

(Contd.)

Table 4.11 Contd.

	(1)	(2)	(3)	(4)	(5)	(6)
1974–5	76,529	3354	79,883	88,919	3354	92,273
1975–6	71,009	3509	74,517	83,889	3509	87,398
1976–7	71,552	3835	75,387	83,749	3835	87,584
1977–8	79,450	3769	83,219	94,070	3769	97,838
1978–9	78,261	3837	82,098	93,371	3837	97,208
1979–80	85,811	4745	90,556	101,805	4745	106,550
1980–1	95,794	5779	101,572	114,765	5779	120,544
1981–2	107,766	6281	114,047	130,514	6281	136,795
1982–3	115,552	6608	122,160	138,352	6608	144,960
1983–4	131,394	7106	138,500	160,514	7106	167,621
1984–5	139,946	7652	147,598	169,856	7652	177,508
1985–6	139,869	8162	148,032	171,549	8162	179,711
1986–7	154,926	8587	163,513	189,280	8587	197,867
1987–8	175,312	9233	184,544	214,053	9233	223,286
1988–9	185,843	10,025	195,868	230,932	10,025	240,956
1989–90	189,473	11,015	200,488	234,965	11,015	245,980
1990–1	215,514	11,895	227,410	270,885	11,895	282,780
1991–2	257,174	13,478	270,652	319,995	13,478	333,474
1992–3	277,769	15,178	292,947	349,456	15,178	364,634
1993–4	295,651	16,569	312,220	374,031	16,569	390,600
1994–5	342,438	18,460	360,897	435,359	18,460	453,818
1995–6	370,354	19,976	390,330	471,335	19,976	491,311
1996–7	401,057	20,589	421,645	513,919	20,589	534,507
1997–8	412,842	21,661	434,503	529,021	21,661	550,681
1998–9	462,509	22,600	485,109	592,664	22,600	615,264
1999–2000	467,606	23,422	491,028	599,195	23,422	622,617

Sources: Col. (1) from Appendix Table 4(p), Col. (7); Col. (2) from Appendix Table 4(q), Col. (5); Col. (3) = Col. (1) + Col. (2); Col. (4) from Appendix Table 4(p), Col. (12); Col. (5) = Col. (2); Col. (6) = Col. (4) + Col. (5).

GROSS CAPITAL STOCK PLUS LAND AT CURRENT PRICES FOR THE NON-RESIDENTIAL SECTOR

The total values of gross capital stock (structures + equipment + inventories) and land at current prices are presented in Table 4.12. Cols (7) to (10) show the percentage share of each component to the total. The share of structures increased from 27.2 per cent in 1950–1 to 53.0 per cent in 1999–2000 and that of equipment moved up from 14.9 per cent to 33.1 per cent during the same period. The share of inventories remained between 5 to 6 per cent and that of land declined from 52.9 per cent in 1950–1 to 8.8 per cent in 1999–2000. These relative shares will now be used to develop the weighting system for the capital input index and total input index.

DISTRIBUTION OF PROPERTY (NON-LABOUR) INCOME BY TYPE OF ASSET

The distribution of GDP originating in the non-residential sector by type of income, that is, labour income and non-labour income, has already been

Table 4.12: Gross Capital Stock Plus Land for Non-residential Sector at Current Prices, 1950–1 to 1999–2000

Year	Gross capital stock (Rs crore)				Land (Rs crore)	GCS + land (Rs crore)	% distribution of GCS plus land			
	Structures	Equipment	Inventory	Total			Structures	Equipment	Inventory	Land
	(1)	(2)	(3)	(4)	(5)	(6)	(7)	(8)	(9)	(10)
1950–1	11,054	6044	2034	19,132	21,462	40,594	27.23	14.89	5.01	52.87
1951–2	12,642	6898	2222	21,763	22,621	44,384	28.48	15.54	5.01	50.97
1952–3	12,848	7669	2352	22,869	18,889	41,758	30.77	18.37	5.63	45.23
1953–4	12,959	8320	2407	23,686	20,395	44,081	29.40	18.87	5.46	46.27
1954–5	12,968	9728	2457	25,153	18,444	43,597	29.74	22.31	5.64	42.31
1955–6	13,351	10,591	2571	26,513	17,467	43,980	30.36	24.08	5.85	39.72
1956–7	14,516	10,415	2800	27,731	20,851	48,582	29.88	21.44	5.76	42.92
1957–8	15,835	10,603	3101	29,538	21,238	50,776	31.19	20.88	6.11	41.83
1958–9	16,469	12,814	3352	32,634	23,059	55,693	29.57	23.01	6.02	41.40
1959–60	17,427	15,117	3576	36,119	23,683	59,802	29.14	25.28	5.98	39.60
1960–1	19,502	16,184	3881	39,566	25,138	64,704	30.14	25.01	6.00	38.85
1961–2	21,797	17,737	4227	43,761	25,273	69,034	31.57	25.69	6.12	36.61
1962–3	24,194	19,118	4579	47,890	25,922	73,812	32.78	25.90	6.20	35.12
1963–4	26,315	21,433	4927	52,675	27,515	80,190	32.82	26.73	6.14	34.31
1964–5	28,861	24,288	5375	58,524	33,325	91,849	31.42	26.44	5.85	36.28
1965–6	33,059	26,922	6039	66,021	35,682	101,703	32.51	26.47	5.94	35.08
1966–7	37,567	32,654	6824	77,045	42,413	119,458	31.45	27.34	5.71	35.50
1967–8	42,231	38,991	7605	88,827	49,064	137,891	30.63	28.28	5.51	35.58
1968–9	47,793	41,836	8341	97,970	46,464	144,434	33.09	28.97	5.77	32.17
1969–70	54,355	44,180	9193	107,728	48,174	155,902	34.86	28.34	5.90	30.90
1970–1	62,346	47,833	10,223	120,402	52,971	173,373	35.96	27.59	5.90	30.55
1971–2	71,845	51,596	11,364	134,805	53,524	188,329	38.15	27.40	6.03	28.42
1972–3	82,979	56,961	12,687	152,626	58,878	211,504	39.23	26.93	6.00	27.84
1973–4	98,449	65,297	14,703	178,449	75,393	253,842	38.78	25.72	5.79	29.70

(Contd.)

170

Table 4.12 Contd.

	(1)	(2)	(3)	(4)	(5)	(6)	(7)	(8)	(9)	(10)
1974–5	121,058	81,634	17,927	220,619	92,273	312,892	38.69	26.09	5.73	29.49
1975–6	143,839	101,424	21,153	266,416	87,398	353,814	40.65	28.67	5.98	24.70
1976–7	160,653	111,680	23,289	295,622	87,584	383,206	41.92	29.14	6.08	22.86
1977–8	176,117	116,051	25,075	317,244	97,838	415,082	42.43	27.96	6.04	23.57
1978–9	197,643	125,499	27,693	350,835	97,208	448,043	44.11	28.01	6.18	21.70
1979–80	233,111	147,926	32,257	413,294	106,550	519,844	44.84	28.46	6.21	20.50
1980–1	276,574	171,792	37,941	486,308	120,544	606,852	45.58	28.31	6.25	19.86
1981–2	333,448	198,779	45,127	577,353	136,795	714,148	46.69	27.83	6.32	19.15
1982–3	406,275	228,005	52,965	687,245	144,960	832,205	48.82	27.40	6.36	17.42
1983–4	477,066	255,782	59,237	792,084	167,621	959,705	49.71	26.65	6.17	17.47
1984–5	550,322	285,922	66,760	903,004	177,508	1,080,512	50.93	26.46	6.18	16.43
1985–6	636,307	323,536	77,796	1,037,639	179,711	1,217,350	52.27	26.58	6.39	14.76
1986–7	733,103	371,278	89,400	1,193,780	197,867	1,391,647	52.68	26.68	6.42	14.22
1987–8	833,175	414,388	99,118	1,346,681	223,286	1,569,967	53.07	26.39	6.31	14.22
1988–9	932,881	475,277	57,930	1,466,088	240,956	1,707,044	54.65	27.84	3.39	14.12
1989–90	1,041,642	563,136	77,219	1,681,997	245,980	1,927,977	54.03	29.21	4.01	12.76
1990–1	1,164,867	658,998	151,535	1,975,400	282,780	2,258,180	51.58	29.18	6.71	12.52
1991–2	1,339,096	790,523	169,142	2,298,761	333,474	2,632,235	50.87	30.03	6.43	12.67
1992–3	1,541,486	942,987	192,189	2,676,662	364,634	3,041,296	50.69	31.01	6.32	11.99
1993–4	1,733,109	1,058,781	214,765	3,006,655	390,600	3,397,255	51.01	31.17	6.32	11.50
1994–5	1,968,928	1,213,755	239,867	3,422,550	453,818	3,876,368	50.79	31.31	6.19	11.71
1995–6	2,339,984	1,452,504	279,536	4,072,024	491,311	4,563,335	51.28	31.83	6.13	10.77
1996–7	2,752,950	1,722,495	302,687	4,778,131	534,507	5,312,638	51.82	32.42	5.70	10.06
1997–8	3,105,965	1,967,450	317,938	5,391,353	550,681	5,942,034	52.27	33.11	5.35	9.27
1998–9	3,441,961	2,163,194	337,407	5,942,562	615,264	6,557,826	52.49	32.99	5.15	9.38
1999–2000	3,753,529	2,347,630	361,178	6,462,337	622,617	7,084,954	52.98	33.14	5.10	8.79

Sources: Cols (1) and (2) from Table 4.9, Cols (14) to (15); Col. (3) from Appendix Table 4(k), Col. (9); Col. (4) = Col. (1) + Col. (2) + Col. (3); Col. 5, Table 4.11, Col. (6); Col. (6) = Col. (4) + Col. (5); Cols. (7) to (10) derived.

obtained [see Table 2.2, Cols (7) and (8)]. Non-labour income is allocated to the different types of assets, that is, structures, equipment, inventory, and land, according to their relative shares at current prices in the total of gross capital stock and land. The results of the allocation are presented in Table 4.13.

DISTRIBUTION OF TOTAL FACTOR INCOMES BY SOURCES OF INCOME

Table 4.14 shows the distribution of GDP into labour income and non-labour (property) income by category of asset in Cols (1) to (5). The percentage income shares to total GDP shown in Cols (7) to (11) are adopted as the weights to combine the inputs.[36]

DERIVATION OF CAPITAL INPUT INDEX

From the indexes of structures, equipment, and inventories, total capital input indexes are computed as a chain index of the weighted averages of the annual percentage changes in the component series. The weights are based on the earning shares shown in Table 4.14. Two–year averages of the weights are used to obtain a smooth system of weights. The relative change over the previous year in the component index is multiplied by the two–year average of weights to obtain the weighted yearly change. Adding the weighted annual changes in the indexes of structures, equipment, and inventories gives the total of the weighted annual changes. The latter, when divided by the sum of the annual weights for the three components, gives the average of the weighted annual changes shown in Col. (16) of Table 4.15. These annual changes were then linked together to obtain the annual indexes. Taking the value of capital input for 1950–1 = 100, the values for the subsequent years are obtained by multiplying the index for the previous year with the weighted average annual change for the current year. Thus, index for 1951–2 = index for 1950–1 X annual change in 1951–2, and index for 1952–3 = index for 1951–2 X annual change in 1952–3, and so on. The indexes so calculated and given in Col. (17) are with base 1950–1 = 100. These are recalculated to base 1993–4 = 100 and shown in Col. 18. These are the relevant capital input indexes. The capital input index increased from 15.17 in 1950–1 to 148.65 in 1999–2000, a nearly tenfold increase, that is at the rate of 4.76 per cent per annum.

TOTAL FACTOR INPUT

The input indexes developed so far for labour, structures, equipment, inventories, combined capital input, and land are reproduced in Table 4.16. These indexes are developed for the non-residential sector.

The movement of the indexes of labour, structures, equipment, inventories, and land are shown in Fig. 4.1.

---

[36] Denison, *Accounting for United States Economic Growth, 1929–69*, p. 51.

Table 4.13: Distribution of Property Income by Type of Asset, Non-residential Sector at Current Prices, 1950–1 to 1999–2000

Year	Total property income (Rs crore)	% distribution of GCS plus land				Distribution of property income (Rs crore)			
		Structures	Equipment	Inventory	Land	Structures	Equipment	Inventory	Land
	(1)	(2)	(3)	(4)	(5)	(6)	(7)	(8)	(9)
1950–1	3735	27.23	14.89	5.01	52.87	1017	556	187	1975
1951–2	3985	28.48	15.54	5.01	50.97	1135	619	200	2031
1952–3	3833	30.77	18.37	5.63	45.23	1179	704	216	1734
1953–4	4369	29.40	18.87	5.46	46.27	1284	824	239	2021
1954–5	3905	29.74	22.31	5.64	42.31	1161	871	220	1652
1955–6	3887	30.36	24.08	5.85	39.72	1180	936	227	1544
1956–7	4905	29.88	21.44	5.76	42.92	1466	1052	283	2105
1957–8	4555	31.19	20.88	6.11	41.83	1421	951	278	1905
1958–9	5464	29.57	23.01	6.02	41.40	1616	1257	329	2262
1959–60	5542	29.14	25.28	5.98	39.60	1615	1401	331	2195
1960–1	6319	30.14	25.01	6.00	38.85	1904	1580	379	2455
1961–2	6893	31.57	25.69	6.12	36.61	2176	1771	422	2524
1962–3	7139	32.78	25.90	6.20	35.12	2340	1849	443	2507
1963–4	8411	32.82	26.73	6.14	34.31	2760	2248	516	2886
1964–5	9908	31.42	26.44	5.85	36.28	3113	2620	580	3595
1965–6	10,064	32.51	26.47	5.94	35.08	3272	2664	598	3531
1966–7	11,292	31.45	27.34	5.71	35.50	3551	3087	645	4009
1967–8	12,480	30.63	28.28	5.51	35.58	3823	3529	688	4441
1968–9	12,969	33.09	28.97	5.77	32.17	4291	3757	748	4172
1969–70	15,031	34.86	28.34	5.90	30.90	5240	4260	887	4645
1970–1	15,944	35.96	27.59	5.90	30.55	5734	4399	941	4871
1971–2	17,029	38.15	27.40	6.03	28.42	6497	4666	1027	4840
1972–3	18,436	39.23	26.93	6.00	27.84	7232	4965	1106	5133
1973–4	24,137	38.78	25.72	5.79	29.70	9360	6208	1398	7169

(Contd.)

173

Table 4.13 Contd.

	(1)	(2)	(3)	(4)	(5)	(6)	(7)	(8)	(9)
1974–5	29,711	38.69	26.09	5.73	29.49	11,495	7752	1702	8762
1975–6	30,173	40.65	28.67	5.98	24.70	12,265	8651	1804	7453
1976–7	33,654	41.92	29.14	6.08	22.86	14,108	9807	2046	7693
1977–8	37,109	42.43	27.96	6.04	23.57	15,745	10,376	2241	8747
1978–9	40,202	44.11	28.01	6.18	21.70	17,733	11,260	2484	8724
1979–80	45,140	44.84	28.46	6.21	20.50	20,241	12,847	2803	9254
1980–1	53,489	45.58	28.31	6.25	19.86	24,380	15,143	3343	10,623
1981–2	65,473	46.69	27.83	6.32	19.15	30,569	18,221	4138	12,538
1982–3	72,492	48.82	27.40	6.36	17.42	35,391	19,863	4611	12,628
1983–4	84,946	49.71	26.65	6.17	17.47	42,227	22,638	5241	14,840
1984–5	92,515	50.93	26.46	6.18	16.43	47,118	24,479	5717	15,200
1985–6	106,441	52.27	26.58	6.39	14.76	55,637	28,292	6802	15,711
1986–7	111,944	52.68	26.68	6.42	14.22	58,972	29,867	7187	15,918
1987–8	124,320	53.07	26.39	6.31	14.22	65,976	32,808	7845	17,678
1988–9	159,069	54.65	27.84	3.39	14.12	86,931	44,285	5392	22,461
1989–90	194,039	54.03	29.21	4.01	12.76	104,839	56,679	7781	24,759
1990–1	223,669	51.58	29.18	6.71	12.52	115,369	65,267	15,008	28,003
1991–2	256,846	50.87	30.03	6.43	12.67	130,658	77,131	16,515	32,542
1992–3	286,044	50.69	31.01	6.32	11.99	144,996	88,702	18,078	34,297
1993–4	375,798	51.01	31.17	6.32	11.50	191,695	117,136	23,750	43,217
1994–5	463,796	50.79	31.31	6.19	11.71	235,562	145,215	28,709	54,311
1995–6	523,407	51.28	31.83	6.13	10.77	268,403	166,600	32,085	56,371
1996–7	657,646	51.82	32.42	5.70	10.06	340,792	213,209	37,486	66,159
1997–8	702,556	52.27	33.11	5.35	9.27	367,226	232,616	37,587	65,127
1998–9	830,465	52.49	32.99	5.15	9.38	435,911	273,970	42,769	77,898
1999–2000	913,456	52.98	33.14	5.10	8.79	483,949	302,719	46,586	80,293

Sources: Col. (1) from Table 2.2, Col. (8); Cols (2) to (5), Table 4.12, Cols (7) to (10); Cols (6) to (9) derived (see text).

174

Table 4.14: Distribution of Factor Incomes, Non-residential Sector at
Current Prices, 1950-1 to 1999-2000

Year	Labour income (Rs crore)	Property income by category of asset (Rs crore)				Total GDP (Rs crore)
		Structures	Equipment	Inventories	Land	
	(1)	(2)	(3)	(4)	(5)	(6)
1950–1	4964	1017	556	187	1975	8699
1951–2	5187	1135	619	200	2031	9172
1952–3	5134	1179	704	216	1734	8967
1953–4	5409	1284	824	239	2021	9778
1954–5	5137	1161	871	220	1652	9042
1955–6	5241	1180	936	227	1544	9128
1956–7	6137	1466	1052	283	2105	11,042
1957–8	6672	1421	951	278	1905	11,227
1958–9	7161	1616	1257	329	2262	12,625
1959–60	7686	1615	1401	331	2195	13,228
1960–1	8199	1904	1580	379	2455	14,518
1961–2	8506	2176	1771	422	2524	15,398
1962–3	9205	2340	1849	443	2507	16,344
1963–4	10,394	2760	2248	516	2886	18,805
1964–5	12,257	3113	2620	580	3595	22,164
1965–6	13,094	3272	2664	598	3531	23,158
1966–7	15,242	3551	3087	645	4009	26,534
1967–8	18,924	3823	3529	688	4441	31,404
1968–9	20,113	4291	3757	748	4172	33,082
1969–70	21,456	5240	4260	887	4645	36,487
1970–1	22,851	5734	4399	941	4871	38,795
1971–2	24,191	6497	4666	1027	4840	41,220
1972–3	26,974	7232	4965	1106	5133	45,410
1973–4	32,081	9360	6208	1398	7169	56,216
1974–5	36,853	11,495	7752	1702	8762	66,564
1975–6	40,411	12,265	8651	1804	7453	70,584
1976–7	42,161	14,108	9807	2,046	7693	75,815
1977–8	49,745	15,745	10,376	2241	8747	86,854
1978–9	53,142	17,733	11,260	2484	8724	93,344
1979–80	56,789	20,241	12,847	2803	9254	101,934
1980–1	69,223	24,380	15,143	3343	10,623	122,712
1981–2	78,057	30,569	18,221	4138	12,538	143,523
1982–3	87,285	35,391	19,863	4611	12,628	159,777
1983–4	102,534	42,227	22,638	5241	14,840	187,480
1984–5	117,528	47,118	24,479	5717	15,200	210,043
1985–6	128,581	55,637	28,292	6802	15,711	235,022
1986–7	149,713	58,972	29,867	7187	15,918	261,657
1987–8	172,622	65,976	32,808	7845	17,678	296,930
1988–9	197,533	86,931	44,285	5392	22,461	356,602
1989–90	218,909	104,839	56,679	7781	24,759	412,967
1990–1	258,716	115,369	65,267	15,008	28,003	482,363
1991–2	299,456	130,658	77,131	16,515	32,542	556,302
1992–3	349,510	144,996	88,702	18,078	34,297	635,583
1993–4	362,277	191,695	117,136	23,750	43,217	738,075
1994–5	406,794	235,562	145,215	28,709	54,311	870,590
1995–6	499,339	268,403	166,600	32,085	56,371	1,022,798
1996–7	530,921	340,792	213,209	37,486	66,159	1,188,567
1997–8	628,211	367,226	232,616	37,587	65,127	1,330,767
1998–9	718,103	435,911	273,970	42,769	77,898	1,548,651
1999–2000	795,498	483,949	302,719	46,586	80,293	1,709,045

(Cols Contd.)

Table 4.14 Contd.: Distribution of Factor Incomes, Non-residential Sector at
Current Prices, 1950–1 to 1999–2000

Year	Weighting structure						Non-labour earnings as % of non-residential GDP
	Labour	Structures	Equipment	Inventories	Land	Total	
	(7)	(8)	(9)	(10)	(11)	(12)	(13)
1950–1	57.07	11.69	6.39	2.15	22.70	100.00	42.93
1951–2	56.55	12.37	6.75	2.18	22.15	100.00	43.45
1952–3	57.25	13.15	7.85	2.41	19.33	100.00	42.75
1953–4	55.32	13.14	8.43	2.44	20.67	100.00	44.68
1954–5	56.82	12.84	9.63	2.44	18.27	100.00	43.18
1955–6	57.41	12.93	10.25	2.49	16.91	100.00	42.59
1956–7	55.58	13.27	9.52	2.56	19.06	100.00	44.42
1957–8	59.42	12.65	8.47	2.48	16.97	100.00	40.58
1958–9	56.72	12.80	9.96	2.61	17.92	100.00	43.28
1959–60	58.10	12.21	10.59	2.51	16.59	100.00	41.90
1960–1	56.48	13.12	10.89	2.61	16.91	100.00	43.52
1961–2	55.24	14.13	11.50	2.74	16.39	100.00	44.76
1962–3	56.32	14.32	11.31	2.71	15.34	100.00	43.68
1963–4	55.27	14.68	11.96	2.75	15.35	100.00	44.73
1964–5	55.30	14.05	11.82	2.62	16.22	100.00	44.70
1965–6	56.54	14.13	11.50	2.58	15.25	100.00	43.46
1966–7	57.44	13.38	11.64	2.43	15.11	100.00	42.56
1967–8	60.26	12.17	11.24	2.19	14.14	100.00	39.74
1968–9	60.80	12.97	11.36	2.26	12.61	100.00	39.20
1969–70	58.80	14.36	11.67	2.43	12.73	100.00	41.20
1970–1	58.90	14.78	11.34	2.42	12.56	100.00	41.10
1971–2	58.69	15.76	11.32	2.49	11.74	100.00	41.31
1972–3	59.40	15.93	10.93	2.44	11.30	100.00	40.60
1973–4	57.07	16.65	11.04	2.49	12.75	100.00	42.93
1974–5	55.36	17.27	11.65	2.56	13.16	100.00	44.64
1975–6	57.25	17.38	12.26	2.56	10.56	100.00	42.75
1976–7	55.61	18.61	12.94	2.70	10.15	100.00	44.39
1977–8	57.27	18.13	11.95	2.58	10.07	100.00	42.73
1978–9	56.93	19.00	12.06	2.66	9.35	100.00	43.07
1979–80	55.71	19.86	12.60	2.75	9.08	100.00	44.29
1980–1	56.41	19.87	12.34	2.72	8.66	100.00	43.59
1981–2	54.39	21.30	12.70	2.88	8.74	100.00	45.61
1982–3	54.63	22.15	12.43	2.89	7.90	100.00	45.37
1983–4	54.69	22.52	12.07	2.80	7.92	100.00	45.31
1984–5	55.95	22.43	11.65	2.72	7.24	100.00	44.05
1985–6	54.71	23.67	12.04	2.89	6.68	100.00	45.29
1986–7	57.22	22.54	11.41	2.75	6.08	100.00	42.78
1987–8	58.14	22.22	11.05	2.64	5.95	100.00	41.86
1988–9	55.39	24.38	12.42	1.51	6.30	100.00	44.61
1989–90	53.01	25.39	13.72	1.88	6.00	100.00	46.99
1990–1	53.64	23.92	13.53	3.11	5.81	100.00	46.36
1991–2	53.83	23.49	13.86	2.97	5.85	100.00	46.17
1992–3	54.99	22.81	13.96	2.84	5.40	100.00	45.01
1993–4	49.08	25.97	15.87	3.22	5.86	100.00	50.92
1994–5	46.73	27.06	16.68	3.30	6.24	100.00	53.27
1995–6	48.82	26.24	16.29	3.14	5.51	100.00	51.18
1996–7	44.67	28.67	17.94	3.15	5.57	100.00	55.33
1997–8	47.21	27.60	17.48	2.82	4.89	100.00	52.79
1998–9	46.37	28.15	17.69	2.76	5.03	100.00	53.63
1999–2000	46.55	28.32	17.71	2.73	4.70	100.00	53.45

Sources: Col. (1) from Table 2.2, Col. (7); Cols (2) to (5) from Table 4.13, Col. (6) to (9); Col. (6) from Appendix Table 1(d), Col. (3); Cols (7) to (12), see the text; Col. (13) = Col. (12)–Col. (7).

Table 4.15: Capital Input Index Weighted by Relative Share of Factor Earnings, 1950–1 to 1999–2000

Year	Structures					Equipment				
	Capital stock structures index	Relative change over previous year	% share of earnings	Two-year average of weights	Weighted annual change	Capital stock equipment index	Relative annual change	% share of earnings	Two-year average of weights	Weighted annual change
	(1)	(2)	(3)	(4)	(5)	(6)	(7)	(8)	(9)	(10)
1950–1	14.36	1.0000	11.69	11.69	11.69	14.38	1.0000	6.39	6.39	6.39
1951–2	14.43	1.0048	12.37	12.03	12.09	14.79	1.0285	6.75	6.57	6.76
1952–3	14.49	1.0045	13.15	12.76	12.82	15.08	1.0196	7.85	7.30	7.44
1953–4	14.95	1.0314	13.14	13.15	13.56	15.23	1.0105	8.43	8.14	8.23
1954–5	15.66	1.0473	12.84	12.99	13.60	15.33	1.0064	9.63	9.03	9.09
1955–6	16.25	1.0377	12.93	12.89	13.37	15.82	1.0317	10.25	9.94	10.25
1956–7	16.65	1.0249	13.27	13.10	13.43	16.80	1.0619	9.52	9.89	10.50
1957–8	16.86	1.0123	12.65	12.96	13.12	18.33	1.0915	8.47	9.00	9.82
1958–9	17.39	1.0314	12.80	12.73	13.13	19.65	1.0715	9.96	9.22	9.87
1959–60	18.47	1.0623	12.21	12.51	13.28	20.22	1.0293	10.59	10.28	10.58
1960–1	19.76	1.0696	13.12	12.67	13.55	20.85	1.0310	10.89	10.74	11.07
1961–2	21.16	1.0710	14.13	13.63	14.59	21.56	1.0340	11.50	11.20	11.58
1962–3	22.56	1.0663	14.32	14.23	15.17	22.47	1.0423	11.31	11.41	11.89
1963–4	24.14	1.0701	14.68	14.50	15.52	23.55	1.0482	11.96	11.64	12.20
1964–5	25.74	1.0664	14.05	14.37	15.32	24.68	1.0477	11.82	11.89	12.46
1965–6	27.43	1.0653	14.13	14.09	15.01	25.86	1.0482	11.50	11.66	12.22
1966–7	29.45	1.0738	13.38	13.76	14.77	26.57	1.0273	11.64	11.57	11.89
1967–8	31.58	1.0725	12.17	12.78	13.70	26.78	1.0079	11.24	11.44	11.53
1968–9	33.49	1.0603	12.97	12.57	13.33	27.05	1.0099	11.36	11.30	11.41
1969–70	35.25	1.0527	14.36	13.67	14.39	27.41	1.0134	11.67	11.52	11.67
1970–1	37.27	1.0573	14.78	14.57	15.40	27.60	1.0072	11.34	11.51	11.59
1971–2	39.56	1.0613	15.76	15.27	16.21	27.64	1.0013	11.32	11.33	11.34
1972–3	42.18	1.0663	15.93	15.85	16.90	27.67	1.0009	10.93	11.13	11.14

(Contd.)

177

Table 4.15 Contd.

	(1)	(2)	(3)	(4)	(5)	(6)	(7)	(8)	(9)	(10)
1973–4	44.56	1.0565	16.65	16.29	17.21	28.36	1.0250	11.04	10.99	11.26
1974–5	46.43	1.0420	17.27	16.96	17.67	29.59	1.0435	11.65	11.35	11.84
1975–6	48.64	1.0475	17.38	17.33	18.15	30.62	1.0348	12.26	11.96	12.37
1976–7	51.09	1.0503	18.61	18.00	18.90	31.60	1.0320	12.94	12.60	13.00
1977–8	53.57	1.0487	18.13	18.37	19.26	32.52	1.0293	11.95	12.45	12.81
1978–9	56.38	1.0523	19.00	18.57	19.54	33.58	1.0324	12.06	12.01	12.39
1979–80	59.34	1.0526	19.86	19.43	20.45	34.81	1.0368	12.60	12.33	12.78
1980–1	62.27	1.0493	19.87	19.87	20.85	36.21	1.0401	12.34	12.47	12.97
1981–2	65.87	1.0578	21.30	20.59	21.77	38.55	1.0646	12.70	12.52	13.33
1982–3	69.61	1.0568	22.15	21.73	22.96	41.83	1.0853	12.43	12.57	13.64
1983–4	72.59	1.0428	22.52	22.34	23.29	45.37	1.0845	12.07	12.25	13.28
1984–5	75.23	1.0365	22.43	22.48	23.29	49.18	1.0840	11.65	11.86	12.86
1985–6	77.83	1.0346	23.67	23.05	23.85	53.38	1.0855	12.04	11.85	12.86
1986–7	80.73	1.0372	22.54	23.11	23.97	58.02	1.0868	11.41	11.73	12.74
1987–8	83.39	1.0329	22.22	22.38	23.12	63.16	1.0886	11.05	11.23	12.22
1988–9	85.64	1.0270	24.38	23.30	23.93	68.59	1.0860	12.42	11.74	12.74
1989–90	87.70	1.0240	25.39	24.89	25.48	74.39	1.0845	13.72	13.07	14.17
1990–1	89.74	1.0232	23.92	24.66	25.23	80.83	1.0866	13.53	13.63	14.81
1991–2	92.92	1.0354	23.49	23.71	24.54	87.28	1.0798	13.86	13.70	14.79
1992–3	96.60	1.0396	22.81	23.15	24.07	93.43	1.0705	13.96	13.91	14.89
1993–4	100.00	1.0352	25.97	24.39	25.25	100.00	1.0703	15.87	14.92	15.96
1994–5	104.67	1.0467	27.06	26.52	27.75	109.13	1.0913	16.68	16.28	17.76
1995–6	111.13	1.0618	26.24	26.65	28.30	122.87	1.1259	16.29	16.49	18.56
1996–7	117.93	1.0611	28.67	27.46	29.13	138.72	1.1290	17.94	17.12	19.32
1997–8	124.48	1.0556	27.60	28.14	29.70	152.73	1.1010	17.48	17.71	19.50
1998–9	130.47	1.0481	28.15	27.88	29.22	165.12	1.0811	17.69	17.59	19.01
1999–2000	135.68	1.0400	28.32	28.24	29.36	177.33	1.0740	17.71	17.70	19.01

(Cols Contd.)

Table 4.15 Contd.: Capital Input Index Weighted by Relative Share of Factor Earnings, 1950-1 to 1999-2000

Year	Inventories						Total capital input		
	Inventory stock index	Relative annual change	% share of earnings	Two-year average of weights	Weighted annual change	Weighted average annual changes	Weighted capital input index 1950-1 = 100	Weighted capital input index 1993-4 = 100	Total of weighted annual changes
	(11)	(12)	(13)	(14)	(15)	(16)	(17)	(18)	(19)
1950-1	16.65	1.0000	2.15	2.15	2.15	1.0000	100.00	15.17	20.23
1951-2	17.17	1.0310	2.18	2.17	2.23	1.0151	101.51	15.40	21.08
1952-3	17.63	1.0266	2.41	2.30	2.36	1.0117	102.69	15.58	22.62
1953-4	18.07	1.0254	2.44	2.43	2.49	1.0236	105.11	15.95	24.27
1954-5	18.59	1.0287	2.44	2.44	2.51	1.0304	108.30	16.43	25.20
1955-6	19.22	1.0341	2.49	2.47	2.55	1.0350	112.09	17.01	26.18
1956-7	20.00	1.0402	2.56	2.53	2.63	1.0408	116.66	17.70	26.55
1957-8	20.86	1.0430	2.48	2.52	2.63	1.0446	121.86	18.49	25.57
1958-9	21.68	1.0397	2.61	2.55	2.65	1.0474	127.64	19.36	25.65
1959-60	22.46	1.0357	2.51	2.56	2.65	1.0462	133.54	20.26	26.51
1960-1	23.33	1.0388	2.61	2.56	2.66	1.0506	140.30	21.28	27.28
1961-2	24.26	1.0400	2.74	2.68	2.78	1.0529	147.72	22.41	28.95
1962-3	25.26	1.0410	2.71	2.73	2.84	1.0542	155.73	23.63	29.89
1963-4	26.40	1.0452	2.75	2.73	2.85	1.0589	164.90	25.02	30.57
1964-5	27.62	1.0461	2.62	2.69	2.81	1.0569	174.28	26.44	30.59
1965-6	28.90	1.0466	2.58	2.60	2.72	1.0565	184.13	27.93	29.95
1966-7	30.17	1.0437	2.43	2.51	2.61	1.0517	193.66	29.38	29.27
1967-8	31.35	1.0391	2.19	2.31	2.40	1.0417	201.74	30.61	27.63
1968-9	32.44	1.0349	2.26	2.23	2.30	1.0363	209.07	31.72	27.04
1969-70	33.50	1.0328	2.43	2.35	2.42	1.0346	216.29	32.81	28.48
1970-1	34.61	1.0330	2.42	2.43	2.51	1.0350	223.86	33.96	29.50
1971-2	35.74	1.0327	2.49	2.46	2.54	1.0355	231.80	35.17	30.09
1972-3	37.02	1.0357	2.44	2.47	2.55	1.0390	240.85	36.54	30.58
1973-4	38.35	1.0359	2.49	2.47	2.55	1.0431	251.23	38.11	31.02

(Contd.)

Table 4.15 Contd.

	(11)	(12)	(13)	(14)	(15)	(16)	(17)	(18)	(19)
1974-5	39.55	1.0314	2.56	2.53	2.60	1.0417	261.71	39.70	32.12
1975-6	40.86	1.0330	2.56	2.56	2.64	1.0416	272.59	41.35	33.16
1976-7	42.35	1.0364	2.70	2.63	2.73	1.0422	284.11	43.10	34.63
1977-8	43.90	1.0368	2.58	2.64	2.74	1.0405	295.62	44.85	34.81
1978-9	45.64	1.0396	2.66	2.62	2.72	1.0441	308.66	46.83	34.65
1979-80	47.57	1.0422	2.75	2.71	2.82	1.0461	322.90	48.99	36.05
1980-1	48.79	1.0256	2.72	2.74	2.80	1.0442	337.17	51.15	36.62
1981-2	52.27	1.0714	2.88	2.80	3.00	1.0612	357.81	54.28	38.10
1982-3	57.94	1.1084	2.89	2.89	3.20	1.0704	383.02	58.11	39.79
1983-4	61.15	1.0554	2.80	2.85	3.00	1.0574	404.99	61.44	39.58
1984-5	64.16	1.0493	2.72	2.76	2.90	1.0526	426.30	64.67	39.05
1985-6	70.27	1.0953	2.89	2.81	3.07	1.0551	449.78	68.24	39.78
1986-7	76.98	1.0954	2.75	2.82	3.09	1.0570	475.44	72.13	39.80
1987-8	80.73	1.0488	2.64	2.70	2.83	1.0513	499.83	75.83	38.17
1988-9	84.69	1.0491	1.51	2.08	2.18	1.0469	523.28	79.39	38.85
1989-90	89.82	1.0605	1.88	1.70	1.80	1.0455	547.09	83.00	41.45
1990-1	93.87	1.0451	3.11	2.50	2.61	1.0458	572.13	86.80	42.64
1991-2	95.66	1.0190	2.97	3.04	3.10	1.0492	600.29	91.07	42.43
1992-3	97.94	1.0239	2.84	2.91	2.97	1.0492	629.83	95.55	41.93
1993-4	100.00	1.0210	3.22	3.03	3.09	1.0466	659.16	100.00	44.31
1994-5	102.58	1.0258	3.30	3.26	3.34	1.0609	699.33	106.09	48.86
1995-6	110.37	1.0760	3.14	3.22	3.46	1.0856	759.17	115.17	50.32
1996-7	113.37	1.0271	3.15	3.15	3.23	1.0832	822.37	124.76	51.69
1997-8	114.75	1.0122	2.82	2.99	3.02	1.0694	879.46	133.42	52.22
1998-9	117.81	1.0267	2.76	2.79	2.86	1.0589	931.24	141.28	51.09
1999-2000	122.17	1.0370	2.73	2.75	2.85	1.0522	979.83	148.65	51.22

Sources: Col. (1) from Table 4.8, Col. (16); Col. (2) derived from Col. (1); Col. (3) from Table 4.14, Col. (8); Col. (4) derived from Col. (3); Col. (5) = Col. (2) × Col. (4); Col. (6) from Table 4.8, Col. (6); Col. (7) derived from Col. (6); Col. (8) from Table 4.14, Col. (9); Col. (9) derived from Col. (8); Col. (10) = Col. (7) × Col. (9). Col. (11) from Appendix Table 4(k), Col. (8); Col. (12) derived from Col. (11); Col. (13), from Table 4.14, Col. (10); Col. (14) derived from Col. (10); Col. (15) = Col. (12) × Col. (14); Col. (16), Col. (17) and (18), see the text; Col. (19) = Col. (15) + Col. (10) + Col. (5).

180

Table 4.16: Non-residential Sector: Indexes of Sector Output, Inputs, and Output Per Unit of Total Factor Input, 1950-1 to 1999-2000 (1993-4 = 100)

| Year | GDP at 1993-4 prices | Labour | Structures | Equipment | Inventories | Reproducible capital | Land | Total factor input | Output per unit of input |
| | | | Index of inputs | | | | | | |
	(1)	(2)	(3)	(4)	(5)	(6)	(7)	(8)	(9)
1950-1	18.06	38.12	14.36	14.38	16.65	15.17	74.29	30.39	59.43
1951-2	18.49	38.86	14.43	14.79	17.17	15.40	76.02	30.98	59.68
1952-3	19.02	39.60	14.49	15.08	17.63	15.58	76.78	31.46	60.46
1953-4	20.21	40.37	14.95	15.23	18.07	15.95	78.44	32.11	62.94
1954-5	21.09	41.15	15.66	15.33	18.59	16.43	79.38	32.78	64.34
1955-6	21.64	41.94	16.25	15.82	19.22	17.00	80.47	33.50	64.60
1956-7	22.91	42.75	16.65	16.80	20.00	17.70	81.11	34.26	66.87
1957-8	22.59	43.58	16.86	18.33	20.86	18.49	80.38	34.96	64.62
1958-9	24.37	44.41	17.39	19.65	21.68	19.36	82.31	35.90	67.88
1959-60	24.90	45.27	18.47	20.22	22.46	20.26	82.67	36.75	67.76
1960-1	26.72	46.12	19.76	20.85	23.33	21.28	82.55	37.62	71.03
1961-2	27.56	46.95	21.16	21.56	24.26	22.41	83.55	38.63	71.34
1962-3	28.13	47.85	22.56	22.47	25.26	23.62	83.71	39.65	70.95
1963-4	29.59	48.76	24.14	23.55	26.40	25.02	83.85	40.75	72.61
1964-5	31.90	49.69	25.74	24.68	27.62	26.44	84.47	41.91	76.12
1965-6	31.88	50.65	27.43	25.86	28.90	27.93	83.59	42.97	74.19
1966-7	30.94	51.61	29.45	26.57	30.17	29.38	84.63	44.13	70.11
1967-8	33.53	52.60	31.58	26.78	31.35	30.60	86.70	45.27	74.07
1968-9	34.41	53.60	33.49	27.05	32.44	31.72	85.99	46.18	74.51
1969-70	36.71	54.63	35.25	27.41	33.50	32.81	86.61	47.19	77.79
1970-1	38.58	55.67	37.27	27.60	34.61	33.96	87.47	48.24	79.98
1971-2	38.91	56.74	39.56	27.64	35.74	35.17	87.80	49.31	78.91
1972-3	38.76	57.83	42.18	27.67	37.02	36.54	87.89	50.44	76.84
1973-4	40.55	59.30	44.56	28.36	38.35	38.11	89.41	51.94	78.07

(Contd.)

181

Table 4.16 Contd.

	(1)	(2)	(3)	(4)	(5)	(6)	(7)	(8)	(9)
1974–5	40.99	61.07	46.43	29.59	39.55	39.70	89.61	53.49	76.63
1975–6	44.79	62.91	48.64	30.62	40.86	41.35	91.30	55.23	81.10
1976–7	45.32	64.80	51.09	31.60	42.35	43.10	90.76	56.91	79.63
1977–8	48.79	66.62	53.57	32.52	43.90	44.85	92.18	58.68	83.15
1978–9	51.52	68.41	56.38	33.58	45.64	46.83	93.03	60.49	85.17
1979–80	48.68	70.23	59.34	34.81	47.57	48.98	92.51	62.33	78.10
1980–1	52.26	72.11	62.27	36.21	48.79	51.15	93.47	64.29	81.29
1981–2	55.32	74.05	65.87	38.55	52.27	54.28	94.56	66.72	82.91
1982–3	56.90	76.13	69.61	41.83	57.94	58.11	93.52	69.43	81.95
1983–4	61.27	77.95	72.59	45.37	61.15	61.44	95.88	71.97	85.13
1984–5	63.84	79.59	75.23	49.18	64.16	64.67	95.41	74.18	86.06
1985–6	66.59	81.33	77.83	53.38	70.27	68.23	96.41	76.67	86.85
1986–7	69.34	83.15	80.73	58.02	76.98	72.13	96.23	79.26	87.48
1987–8	71.81	85.06	83.39	63.16	80.73	75.83	96.12	81.78	87.81
1988–9	79.36	87.08	85.64	68.59	84.69	79.38	98.09	84.41	94.02
1989–90	84.67	89.51	87.70	74.39	89.82	83.00	97.82	87.19	97.11
1990–1	89.27	92.01	89.74	80.83	93.87	86.80	99.08	90.19	98.98
1991–2	90.10	94.60	92.92	87.28	95.66	91.07	98.15	93.30	96.57
1992–3	94.60	97.26	96.60	93.43	97.94	95.55	99.42	96.64	97.89
1993–4	100.00	100.00	100.00	100.00	100.00	100.00	100.00	100.00	100.00
1994–5	107.58	102.13	104.67	109.13	102.58	106.09	100.21	103.85	103.59
1995–6	115.69	103.52	111.13	122.87	110.37	115.17	100.23	108.65	106.48
1996–7	125.08	104.93	117.93	138.72	113.37	124.76	100.88	113.70	110.01
1997–8	131.16	106.35	124.48	152.73	114.75	133.42	100.88	118.26	110.91
1998–9	140.00	107.83	130.47	165.12	117.81	141.28	100.88	122.39	114.39
1999–2000	149.15	109.32	135.68	177.33	122.17	148.65	100.88	126.29	118.10

Sources: Col. (1) from Table 1.2, Col. (3); Col. (2) from Table 3.1, Col. (4); Cols (3) and (4) from Table 4.8, Cols (16) and (17); Col. (5), from Appendix Table 4(k), Col. (8); Col. (6) from Table 4.15, Col. (18); Col. (7) from Table 4.10; Col. (8) from Appendix Table 4(k), Col. (14); Col. (9) = Col. (1)/Col. (8).

182

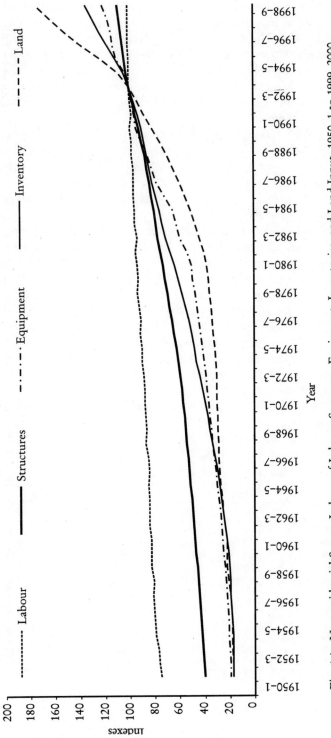

Fig. 4.1: Non-residential Sector: Indexes of Labour, Strucures, Equipment, Inventories, and Land Input, 1950–1 to 1999–2000

Source: Table 4.16.

183

These indexes are now combined following a procedure similar to the one used for the capital input index. Details of these calculations are shown in Appendix Table 4(u). The year to year percentage changes in labour input are multiplied by the two-year average of the relative share of labour earnings in total factor incomes to obtain the weighted annual change in labour input. A similar series is obtained for land input. The sum of the weighted annual changes in labour input, capital input, and land input gives the total weighted annual changes shown in Col. (12) of Appendix Table 4(u). These are then linked taking 1950–1 as equal to 100 to derive the total factor input index. These indexes with 1950–1 = 100 are then converted to base 1993–4 = 100 and shown in Col. (14) of Appendix Table 4(u) and Col. (8) of Table 4.16.

The output index of the non-residential sector, shown in Col. (1) of Table 4.16, divided by the total factor input index gives the series for output per unit of input [Col. (9) of Table 4.16].

For the period as a whole, labour input accounted for 55.2 per cent of the total input, capital 33.2 per cent, and land 11.6 per cent. This is in sharp contrast to the experience in the United States between 1929 and 1969 when, on the average, labour comprised nearly 80 per cent of the total input, capital 16 per cent and land 4 per cent.[37] For the UK, France, Germany, the Netherlands, and Japan, for the period 1973–82 the average share of labour income in GDP varied between 70 and 75 per cent and that of capital ranged between 25 and 30 per cent.[38] Maddison did not include land and inventories in the capital estimates due to lack of data. But the relative importance of the different categories of input varied over the period. The share of labour declined from 57 per cent in the decade 1950–1 to 1960–1 to 49.2 per cent in the period 1990–1 to 1999–2000. In the meanwhile, the share of capital input increased from 24.2 per cent to 45.3 per cent (see Table 4.17). Among the components of capital, the share of structures and equipment nearly doubled

Table 4.17: Relative Importance of Different Components of Input, 1950–1 to 1999–2000

Period	Labour	Structures	Equipment	Inventory	Land
	(1)	(2)	(3)	(4)	(5)
Long periods					
1950–1 to 1999–2000	55.23	18.53	12.07	2.62	11.56
1950–1 to 1964–5	56.59	13.16	9.69	2.51	18.05
1964–5 to 1980–1	57.52	16.13	11.41	2.52	12.08
1980–1 to 1999–2000	52.32	24.43	14.14	2.79	6.32
Shorter periods					
1950–1 to 1960–1	56.97	12.74	8.98	2.44	18.86
1960–1 to 1970–1	57.40	13.83	11.47	2.52	14.78
1970–1 to 1980–1	57.15	17.57	11.86	2.58	10.85
1980–1 to 1990–1	55.29	22.76	12.31	2.62	7.02
1990–1 to 1999–2000	49.19	26.22	16.10	3.00	5.48

Source: Table 4.14.

[37] Ibid., p. 59.
[38] Maddison, *Explaining the Economic Performance of Nations*, p. 80.

and that of inventories remained stagnant. The share of land in total input declined from 18.9 per cent in the first decade to 5.5 per cent in the last decade.

Corresponding to the eight-fold increase in sector output over the whole period, total factor input quadrupled and output per unit of input nearly doubled. Input of labour increased nearly three times and that of capital almost ten times. The growth rates of different inputs and total factor input are presented in Table 4.18.

Table 4.18: Non-residential Sector: Growth Rates of Factor Inputs and Employment, 1950–1 to 1999–2000

Period			Factor inputs					Number of persons engaged
	Labour	Structures	Equipment	Inventories	All reproducible capital	Land	Total factor input	
	(1)	(2)	(3)	(4)	(5)	(6)	(7)	(8)
Long periods								
1950–1 to 1999–2000	2.17	4.68	5.26	4.15	4.76	0.63	2.95	1.85
1950–1 to 1964–5	1.91	4.24	3.93	3.68	4.03	0.92	2.32	1.63
1964–5 to 1980–1	2.35	5.68	2.42	3.62	4.21	0.63	2.71	2.16
1980–1 to 1999–2000	2.21	4.18	8.72	4.95	5.78	0.40	3.62	1.74
Shorter periods								
1950–1 to 1960–1	1.92	3.21	3.80	3.43	3.42	1.06	2.16	1.58
1960–1 to 1970–1	1.90	6.55	2.81	4.02	4.79	0.58	2.52	1.79
1970–1 to 1980–1	2.62	5.27	2.75	3.49	4.18	0.67	2.91	2.37
1980–1 to 1990–1	2.47	3.72	8.36	6.76	5.43	0.58	3.44	2.02
1990–1 to 1999–2000	1.93	4.70	9.12	2.97	6.13	0.20	3.81	1.43

Source: Cols (1) to (6) from Table 4.7; Col. (7) from Table 3.1, Col. (1); Col. (10) from Appendix Table 3(b).

186

Appendix Table 4(a): GFCF at Current Prices, 1950–1 to 1999–2000

Year	Gross fixed capital formation (Rs crore)			% share in GFCF		GDP at market prices (Rs crore)	% to GDP at current market prices		
	Construction	M & E	Total	Construction	M & E		Construction	M & E	Total GFCF
	(1)	(2)	(3)	(4)	(5)	(6)	(7)	(8)	(9)
1950–1	639	245	884	72.29	27.71	9934	6.43	2.47	8.90
1951–2	681	295	976	69.77	30.23	10,566	6.45	2.79	9.24
1952–3	618	279	897	68.90	31.10	10,366	5.96	2.69	8.65
1953–4	632	272	904	69.91	30.09	11,282	5.60	2.41	8.01
1954–5	703	330	1033	68.05	31.95	10,678	6.58	3.09	9.67
1955–6	818	481	1299	62.97	37.03	10,873	7.52	4.42	11.95
1956–7	1036	605	1641	63.13	36.87	12,951	8.00	4.67	12.67
1957–8	987	726	1713	57.62	42.38	13,349	7.39	5.44	12.83
1958–9	1098	630	1728	63.54	36.46	14,874	7.38	4.24	11.62
1959–60	1199	695	1894	63.31	36.69	15,675	7.65	4.43	12.08
1960–1	1351	832	2183	61.89	38.11	17,167	7.87	4.85	12.72
1961–2	1473	967	2440	60.37	39.63	18,196	8.10	5.31	13.41
1962–3	1564	1134	2698	57.97	42.03	19,566	7.99	5.80	13.79
1963–4	1789	1400	3189	56.10	43.90	22,482	7.96	6.23	14.18
1964–5	2057	1649	3706	55.50	44.50	26,220	7.85	6.29	14.13
1965–6	2384	1801	4185	56.97	43.03	27,668	8.62	6.51	15.13
1966–7	2742	1917	4659	58.85	41.15	31,305	8.76	6.12	14.88
1967–8	3140	2007	5147	61.01	38.99	36,649	8.57	5.48	14.04
1968–9	3370	2073	5443	61.91	38.09	38,823	8.68	5.34	14.02
1969–70	3714	2257	5971	62.20	37.80	42,750	8.69	5.28	13.97
1970–1	4000	2383	6383	62.67	37.33	45,677	8.76	5.22	13.97
1971–2	4317	2856	7173	60.18	39.82	48,932	8.82	5.84	14.66
1972–3	4825	3408	8233	58.61	41.39	53,947	8.94	6.32	15.26
1973–4	5020	4166	9186	54.65	45.35	65,613	7.65	6.35	14.00

(Contd.)

187

Appendix Table 4(a) Contd.

	(1)	(2)	(3)	(4)	(5)	(6)	(7)	(8)	(9)
1974–5	5886	5260	11,146	52.81	47.19	77,479	7.60	6.79	14.39
1975–6	7414	6087	13,501	54.91	45.09	83,269	8.90	7.31	16.21
1976–7	8586	6913	15,499	55.40	44.60	89,739	9.57	7.70	17.27
1977–8	10,047	7390	17,437	57.62	42.38	101,597	9.89	7.27	17.16
1978–9	10,422	8697	19,119	54.51	45.49	110,133	9.46	7.90	17.36
1979–80	11,065	10,520	21,585	51.26	48.74	120,841	9.16	8.71	17.86
1980–1	13,787	12,831	26,618	51.80	48.20	143,764	9.59	8.93	18.52
1981–2	16,567	15,364	31,931	51.88	48.12	168,600	9.83	9.11	18.94
1982–3	18,497	17,741	36,238	51.04	48.96	188,262	9.83	9.42	19.25
1983–4	21,096	20,273	41,369	50.99	49.01	219,496	9.61	9.24	18.85
1984–5	24,491	23,641	48,132	50.88	49.12	245,515	9.98	9.63	19.60
1985–6	29,581	27,730	57,311	51.61	48.39	277,991	10.64	9.98	20.62
1986–7	33,002	32,537	65,539	50.35	49.65	311,177	10.61	10.46	21.06
1987–8	37,618	38,391	76,009	49.49	50.51	354,343	10.62	10.83	21.45
1988–9	44,747	46,514	91,261	49.03	50.97	421,567	10.61	11.03	21.65
1989–90	51,773	57,106	108,879	47.55	52.45	486,179	10.65	11.75	22.39
1990–1	62,722	67,949	130,671	48.00	52.00	568,674	11.03	11.95	22.98
1991–2	72,638	71,223	143,861	50.49	49.51	653,117	11.12	10.91	22.03
1992–3	81,919	86,054	167,973	48.77	51.23	748,367	10.95	11.50	22.45
1993–4	87,625	96,668	184,293	47.55	52.45	859,220	10.20	11.25	21.45
1994–5	100,369	121,867	222,236	45.16	54.84	1,012.770	9.91	12.03	21.94
1995–6	121,210	168,199	289,409	41.88	58.12	1,188,012	10.20	14.16	24.36
1996–7	132,792	179,074	311,866	42.58	57.42	1,368,208	9.71	13.09	22.79
1997–8	157,876	172,899	330,775	47.73	52.27	1,522,441	10.37	11.36	21.73
1998–9	180,132	193,076	373,208	48.27	51.73	1,758,276	10.24	10.98	21.23
1999–2000	203,351	212,749	416,100	48.87	51.13	1,956,997	10.39	10.87	21.26

Note: M & E denotes machinery and equipment.
Sources: Cols (1) to (3) from *NAS Back Series, 1950–1 to 1992–3*, pp. 50–3 and *NAS 2001*, p. 34; Cols (4) and (5) derived; Col. (6) from *NAS 2001*, pp. 196–201; Cols (7) to (9) derived.

188

Appendix Table 4(b): GFCF as Percentage of GDP at Constant (1993-4) Market Prices, 1950-1 to 1999-2000

Year	Gross fixed capital formation (Rs crore)			% share in GFCF		GDP at 1993-4 market prices (Rs crore)	% to GDP at current market prices		
	Construction	M & E	Total	Construction	M & E		GFCF in Construction	GFCF in M & E	GFCF in Total
	(1)	(2)	(3)	(4)	(5)	(6)	(7)	(8)	(9)
1950-1	15,913	6924	22,837	69.68	30.32	148,503	10.72	4.66	15.38
1951-2	16,452	7292	23,744	69.29	30.71	152,979	10.75	4.77	15.52
1952-3	14,849	6430	21,279	69.78	30.22	156,960	9.46	4.10	13.56
1953-4	15,458	5683	21,141	73.12	26.88	166,625	9.28	3.41	12.69
1954-5	17,603	5477	23,080	76.27	23.73	174,745	10.07	3.13	13.21
1955-6	19,769	8649	28,418	69.57	30.43	180,530	10.95	4.79	15.74
1956-7	23,271	11,581	34,852	66.77	33.23	190,578	12.21	6.08	18.29
1957-8	21,107	14,984	36,091	58.48	41.52	189,960	11.11	7.89	19.00
1958-9	22,683	9054	31,737	71.47	28.53	203,958	11.12	4.44	15.56
1959-60	24,028	10,100	34,128	70.41	29.59	209,408	11.47	4.82	16.30
1960-1	25,964	11,569	37,533	69.18	30.82	220,560	11.77	5.25	17.02
1961-2	26,923	12,707	39,630	67.94	32.06	228,921	11.76	5.55	17.31
1962-3	27,490	14,841	42,331	64.94	35.06	235,834	11.66	6.29	17.95
1963-4	30,925	16,056	46,981	65.82	34.18	250,208	12.36	6.42	18.78
1964-5	33,855	18,350	52,205	64.85	35.15	268,821	12.59	6.83	19.42
1965-6	36,480	19,079	55,559	65.66	34.34	262,029	13.92	7.28	21.20
1966-7	39,059	15,437	54,496	71.67	28.33	261,586	14.93	5.90	20.83
1967-8	42,389	14,914	57,303	73.97	26.03	281,971	15.03	5.29	20.32
1968-9	42,970	15,447	58,417	73.56	26.44	291,759	14.73	5.29	20.02
1969-70	43,971	16,171	60,142	73.11	26.89	310,847	14.15	5.20	19.35
1970-1	44,334	16,155	60,489	73.29	26.71	326,925	13.56	4.94	18.50
1971-2	44,647	18,713	63,360	70.47	29.53	332,516	13.43	5.63	19.05
1972-3	46,404	20,032	66,436	69.85	30.15	330,594	14.04	6.06	20.10

(Contd.)

189

Appendix Table 4(b) Contd.

	(1)	(2)	(3)	(4)	(5)	(6)	(7)	(8)	(9)
1973–4	41,880	22,428	64,308	65.12	34.88	341,050	12.28	6.58	18.86
1974–5	40,553	21,762	62,315	65.08	34.92	345,101	11.75	6.31	18.06
1975–6	47,022	22,232	69,254	67.90	32.10	376,731	12.48	5.90	18.38
1976–7	52,527	25,300	77,827	67.49	32.51	383,163	13.71	6.60	20.31
1977–8	58,887	26,878	85,765	68.66	31.34	410,873	14.33	6.54	20.87
1978–9	56,178	29,215	85,393	65.79	34.21	434,437	12.93	6.72	19.66
1979–80	52,013	29,990	82,003	63.43	36.57	411,663	12.63	7.29	19.92
1980–1	56,963	33,717	90,680	62.82	37.18	439,201	12.97	7.68	20.65
1981–2	60,551	36,979	97,530	62.08	37.92	467,139	12.96	7.92	20.88
1982–3	58,727	41,436	100,163	58.63	41.37	484,217	12.13	8.56	20.69
1983–4	60,569	44,437	105,006	57.68	42.32	518,491	11.68	8.57	20.25
1984–5	61,469	49,367	110,836	55.46	44.54	539,874	11.39	9.14	20.53
1985–6	65,164	52,420	117,584	55.42	44.58	570,267	11.43	9.19	20.62
1986–7	65,774	58,309	124,083	53.01	46.99	597,850	11.00	9.75	20.75
1987–8	68,199	67,230	135,429	50.36	49.64	623,371	10.94	10.78	21.73
1988–9	73,887	72,544	146,431	50.46	49.54	684,832	10.79	10.59	21.38
1989–90	76,858	79,991	156,849	49.00	51.00	728,952	10.54	10.97	21.52
1990–1	83,768	86,660	170,428	49.15	50.85	771,295	10.86	11.24	22.10
1991–2	87,287	80,243	167,530	52.10	47.90	778,289	11.22	10.31	21.53
1992–3	89,526	88,456	177,982	50.30	49.70	819,318	10.93	10.80	21.72
1993–4	87,625	96,668	184,293	47.55	52.45	859,220	10.20	11.25	21.45
1994–5	92,920	113,136	206,056	45.09	54.91	924,456	10.05	12.24	22.29
1995–6	98,023	147,745	245,768	39.88	60.12	995,450	9.85	14.84	24.69
1996–7	100,166	149,479	249,645	40.12	59.88	1,067,445	9.38	14.00	23.39
1997–8	113,019	142,109	255,128	44.30	55.70	1,114,919	10.14	12.75	22.88
1998–9	121,218	155,945	277,163	43.74	56.26	1,181,881	10.26	13.19	23.45
1999–2000	131,003	170,105	301,108	43.51	56.49	1,266,723	10.34	13.43	23.77

Sources: Cols (1) to (3) from *NAS Back Series, 1950–1 to 1992–3*, pp. 54–7 and *NAS 2001*, p. 35; Cols (4) and (5) derived; Col. (6) from *NAS 2001*, pp. 202–7; Cols (7) to (9) derived.

Appendix Table 4(c): Estimates of GFCF in Residential Construction at Current Prices, 1950-1 to 1999-2000

Year	GFCF not adjusted (Rs crore)		GFCF adjusted (Rs crore)				
	Total	Real estate, dwellings, and business services	Total	Real estate, dwellings, and business services	Dwellings (Rs crore)	Construction (Rs crore)	Dwellings as % of construction
	(1)	(2)	(3)	(4)	(5)	(6)	(7)
1950-1	779	163	884	185	176	639	27.50
1951-2	924	172	976	182	173	681	25.34
1952-3	882	179	897	182	173	618	27.98
1953-4	975	183	904	170	161	632	25.50
1954-5	1154	187	1033	167	159	703	22.62
1955-6	1362	195	1299	186	177	818	21.60
1956-7	1669	212	1641	208	198	1036	19.11
1957-8	1788	223	1713	214	203	987	20.56
1958-9	1860	242	1728	225	214	1098	19.45
1959-60	2007	262	1894	247	235	1199	19.59
1960-1	2464	277	2183	245	233	1351	17.26
1961-2	2478	299	2440	294	280	1473	18.99
1962-3	2930	313	2698	288	274	1564	17.51
1963-4	3317	326	3189	313	298	1789	16.64
1964-5	3716	353	3706	352	334	2057	16.26
1965-6	4337	366	4185	353	336	2384	14.07
1966-7	4812	395	4659	382	363	2742	13.25
1967-8	5068	443	5147	450	427	3140	13.61
1968-9	5129	481	5443	510	485	3370	14.39
1969-70	5751	541	5971	562	534	3714	14.37
1970-1	6462	537	6383	530	504	4000	12.60
1971-2	7121	599	7173	603	573	4317	13.28
1972-3	8290	680	8233	675	642	4825	13.30

(Contd.)

191

Appendix Table 4(c) Contd.

	(1)	(2)	(3)	(4)	(5)	(6)	(7)
1973–4	9576	834	9186	800	760	5020	15.14
1974–5	11,738	1073	11,146	1019	968	5886	16.44
1975–6	14,765	1227	13,501	1122	1066	7414	14.38
1976–7	15,312	1330	15,499	1346	1279	8586	14.90
1977–8	16,959	1467	17,437	1508	1433	10,047	14.26
1978–9	20,242	1673	19,119	1580	1501	10,422	14.40
1979–80	22,845	2048	21,585	1935	1838	11,065	16.61
1980–1	27,533	2762	26,618	2670	2537	13,787	18.40
1981–2	28,354	3462	31,931	3899	3704	16,567	22.36
1982–3	39,758	3596	36,238	3278	3114	18,497	16.83
1983–4	41,839	4161	41,369	4114	3909	21,096	18.53
1984–5	53,076	4951	48,132	4490	4265	24,491	17.42
1985–6	64,228	5904	57,311	5268	5005	29,581	16.92
1986–7	70,946	5746	65,539	5308	5043	33,002	15.28
1987–8	68,325	7437	76,009	8273	7860	37,618	20.89
1988–9	92,163	8919	91,261	8832	8390	44,747	18.75
1989–90	106,199	11,504	108,879	11,794	11,205	51,773	21.64
1990–1	119,922	13,880	130,671	15,124	14,368	62,722	22.91
1991–2	150,695	15,418	143,861	14,719	13,983	72,638	19.25
1992–3	157,929	17,681	167,973	18,805	17,865	81,919	21.81
1993–4	182,807	20,678	184,293	20,846	19,804	87,625	22.60
1994–5	234,192	23,514	222,236	22,314	21,198	100,369	21.12
1995–6	312,498	27,917	289,409	25,854	24,562	121,210	20.26
1996–7	326,979	31,927	311,866	30,451	28,929	132,792	21.79
1997–8	321,949	35,131	330,775	36,094	34,289	157,876	21.72
1998–9	327,707	38,168	373,208	43,467	41,294	180,132	22.92
1999–2000	347,557	41,905	416,100	50,169	47,661	203,351	23.44

Sources: Cols (1) and (2) from *NAS Back Series*, pp. 58–102 and *NAS 2001*, pp. 36, 38–48; Cols (3) and (6) from *NAS Back Series*, pp. 50–3 and *NAS 2001*, p. 34; Col. (4) = Col. (2) × Col. 3/Col. (1); Col. (5) = Col. (4) × 0.95; Col. (7) = Col. (5)/Col. (6).

192

Appendix Table 4(d): Estimates of GFCF in Residential Construction at 1993–4 Prices, 1950–1 to 1999–2000

Year	GFCF not adjusted (Rs crore)		GFCF adjusted (Rs crore)				
	Total	Real estate, dwellings, and business services	Total	Real estate, dwellings, and business services	Dwellings (Rs crore)	Construction (Rs crore)	Dwellings as % of construction
	(1)	(2)	(3)	(4)	(5)	(6)	(7)
1950–1	17,171	4134	22,837	5498	5223	15,913	32.82
1951–2	18,588	4227	23,744	5399	5130	16,452	31.18
1952–3	17,068	4341	21,279	5412	5141	14,849	34.62
1953–4	19,018	4545	21,141	5052	4800	15,458	31.05
1954–5	21,457	4634	23,080	4985	4735	17,603	26.90
1955–6	25,561	4807	28,418	5344	5077	19,769	25.68
1956–7	29,676	4993	34,852	5864	5571	23,271	23.94
1957–8	31,212	4990	36,091	5770	5482	21,107	25.97
1958–9	29,354	5273	31,737	5701	5416	22,683	23.88
1959–60	30,640	5552	34,128	6184	5875	24,028	24.45
1960–1	35,983	5625	37,533	5867	5574	25,964	21.47
1961–2	35,461	5725	39,630	6398	6078	26,923	22.58
1962–3	40,863	5787	42,331	5995	5695	27,490	20.72
1963–4	43,831	5949	46,981	6377	6058	30,925	19.59
1964–5	46,543	6194	52,205	6948	6600	33,855	19.50
1965–6	50,663	6015	55,559	6596	6266	36,480	17.18
1966–7	50,218	6060	54,496	6576	6247	39,059	15.99
1967–8	50,550	6384	57,303	7237	6875	42,389	16.22
1968–9	49,038	6515	58,417	7761	7373	42,970	17.16
1969–70	52,057	6695	60,142	7735	7348	43,971	16.71
1970–1	54,262	6315	60,489	7040	6688	44,334	15.08
1971–2	56,788	6639	63,360	7407	7037	44,647	15.76
1972–3	63,754	6988	66,436	7282	6918	46,404	14.91

(Contd.)

193

Appendix Table 4(d) Contd.

	(1)	(2)	(3)	(4)	(5)	(6)	(7)
1973–4	62,691	7278	64,308	7466	7092	41,880	16.94
1974–5	62,230	6456	62,315	6465	6142	40,553	15.14
1975–6	70,456	8020	69,254	7883	7489	47,022	15.93
1976–7	72,841	8579	77,827	9166	8708	52,527	16.58
1977–8	76,985	8934	85,765	9953	9455	58,887	16.06
1978–9	85,511	9393	85,393	9380	8911	56,178	15.86
1979–80	83,614	9945	82,003	9753	9266	52,013	17.81
1980–1	91,193	10,832	90,680	10,771	10,233	56,963	17.96
1981–2	111,034	11,233	97,530	9867	9373	60,551	15.48
1982–3	103,706	9997	100,163	9655	9173	58,727	15.62
1983–4	101,493	10,087	105,006	10,436	9914	60,569	16.37
1984–5	117,880	10,695	110,836	10,056	9553	61,469	15.54
1985–6	128,614	11,550	117,584	10,559	10,031	65,164	15.39
1986–7	131,006	9985	124,083	9457	8984	65,774	13.66
1987–8	118,002	11,818	135,429	13,563	12,885	68,199	18.89
1988–9	144,508	13,259	146,431	13,435	12,764	73,887	17.27
1989–90	150,398	16,098	156,849	16,788	15,949	76,858	20.75
1990–1	157,430	18,350	170,428	19,865	18,872	83,768	22.53
1991–2	173,527	17,936	167,530	17,316	16,450	87,287	18.85
1992–3	167,378	19,278	177,982	20,499	19,474	89,526	21.75
1993–4	182,807	20,678	184,293	20,846	19,804	87,625	22.60
1994–5	216,690	21,840	206,056	20,768	19,730	92,920	21.23
1995–6	263,002	21,925	245,768	20,488	19,464	98,023	19.86
1996–7	259,394	23,585	249,645	22,699	21,564	100,166	21.53
1997–8	247,064	24,799	255,128	25,608	24,328	113,019	21.53
1998–9	241,480	25,726	277,163	29,527	28,051	121,218	23.14
1999–2000	248,236	27,068	301,108	32,833	31,192	131,003	23.81

Sources: Cols (1) and (2) from *NAS Back Series*, pp. 58–102 and *NAS 2001*, pp. 36, 38–48; Cols (3) and (6) from *NAS Back Series*, pp. 50–3 and *NAS 2001*, p. 34; Col. (4) = Col. (2) × Col. (3)/Col. (1); Col. (5) = Col. (4) × 0.95; Col. (7) = Col. (5)/Col. (6).

194

Appendix Table 4(e): Estimates of GDP and GFCF at 1980–1 Prices, 1900–1 to 1949–50

Year	NDP (Rs crore)	Depreciation (Rs crore)	GDP (Rs crore)	Gross fixed capital formation (Rs crore)			% distribution of GFCF		GFCF as % of GDP
				Construction	M & E	Total GFCF	Construction	M & E	
	(1)	(2)	(3)	(4)	(5)	(6)	(7)	(8)	(9)
1900–1	18,385	363	18,748	638	485	1123	56.81	43.19	5.99
1901–2	18,978	375	19,353	419	362	781	53.65	46.35	4.04
1902–3	19,575	398	19,973	573	474	1047	54.73	45.27	5.24
1903–4	19,192	415	19,607	547	477	1024	53.42	46.58	5.22
1904–5	19,996	430	20,426	607	538	1145	53.01	46.99	5.61
1905–6	20,263	450	20,713	683	649	1332	51.28	48.72	6.43
1906–7	20,865	470	21,335	614	644	1258	48.81	51.19	5.90
1907–8	21,685	495	22,180	320	362	682	46.92	53.08	3.07
1908–9	22,785	500	23,285	602	840	1442	41.75	58.25	6.19
1909–10	23,693	523	24,216	468	456	924	50.65	49.35	3.82
1910–1	24,366	546	24,912	758	670	1428	53.08	46.92	5.73
1911–2	24,616	550	25,166	808	653	1461	55.30	44.70	5.81
1912–3	24,784	563	25,347	756	754	1510	50.07	49.93	5.96
1913–4	25,336	575	25,911	798	863	1661	48.04	51.96	6.41
1914–5	25,930	588	26,518	521	693	1214	42.92	57.08	4.58
1915–6	26,931	600	27,531	928	664	1592	58.29	41.71	5.78
1916–7	27,483	615	28,098	657	487	1144	57.43	42.57	4.07
1917–8	26,881	625	27,506	694	508	1202	57.74	42.26	4.37
1918–9	27,197	648	27,845	1148	913	2061	55.70	44.30	7.40
1919–20	26,528	650	27,178	209	177	386	54.15	45.85	1.42
1920–1	27,885	653	28,538	494	563	1057	46.74	53.26	3.70
1921–2	28,247	673	28,920	203	239	442	45.93	54.07	1.53
1922–3	29,086	675	29,761	652	860	1512	43.12	56.88	5.08
1923–4	29,146	685	29,831	1028	1178	2206	46.60	53.40	7.39

(Contd.)

195

Appendix Table 4(e) Contd.

	(1)	(2)	(3)	(4)	(5)	(6)	(7)	(8)	(9)
1924–5	28,897	690	29,587	905	717	1622	55.80	44.20	5.48
1925–6	29,265	700	29,965	1015	793	1808	56.14	43.86	6.03
1926–7	29,320	713	30,033	874	625	1499	58.31	41.69	4.99
1927–8	29,710	725	30,435	1348	1056	2404	56.07	43.93	7.90
1928–9	30,110	738	30,848	824	685	1509	54.61	45.39	4.89
1929–30	30,671	748	31,419	1042	820	1862	55.96	44.04	5.93
1930–1	31,049	750	31,799	1081	782	1863	58.02	41.98	5.86
1931–2	31,498	753	32,251	957	534	1491	64.19	35.81	4.62
1932–3	31,649	755	32,404	953	505	1458	65.36	34.64	4.50
1933–4	31,843	758	32,601	1359	839	2198	61.83	38.17	6.74
1934–5	31,693	763	32,456	1140	626	1766	64.55	35.45	5.44
1935–6	31,717	765	32,482	1540	865	2405	64.03	35.97	7.40
1936–7	31,449	765	32,214	1512	828	2340	64.62	35.38	7.26
1937–8	30,931	766	31,697	1596	995	2591	61.60	38.40	8.17
1938–9	30,850	768	31,618	1602	903	2505	63.95	36.05	7.92
1939–40	31,052	770	31,822	1444	709	2153	67.07	32.93	6.77
1940–1	31,416	774	32,190	1399	606	2005	69.78	30.22	6.23
1941–2	31,819	900	32,719	1938	888	2826	68.58	31.42	8.64
1942–3	32,342	1025	33,367	1275	504	1779	71.67	28.33	5.33
1943–4	33,177	1175	34,352	2077	595	2672	77.73	22.27	7.78
1944–5	33,461	1325	34,786	2271	970	3241	70.07	29.93	9.32
1945–6	33,951	1475	35,426	2402	1356	3758	63.92	36.08	10.61
1946–7	34,669	1625	36,294	2539	1711	4250	59.74	40.26	11.71
1947–8	35,551	1750	37,301	2305	1745	4050	56.91	43.09	10.86
1948–9	36,786	1925	38,711	2762	2201	4963	55.65	44.35	12.82
1949–50	38,391	2050	40,441	2404	2056	4460	53.90	46.10	11.03

Sources: Bina Roy, *An Analysis of Long-term Growth of National Income and Capital Formation in India, 1850–1 to 1950–1.* Col. (1) from Table 17, Col. (2), pp. 207–9; Col. (2), (4), and (5) from Table 39, pp. 303–5; Col. (3) = Col. (1) + Col. (2); Col. (6) = Col. (4) + Col. (5); Cols (7) to (9) derived.

Appendix Table 4(f): Preliminary Estimates of Fixed Capital Stock (1900–1 to 1999–2000)

Year	Bina Roy's GFCF estimates (Rs crore)		Index of Bina Roy's figures 1950–1 = 100		GFCF at 1993–4 prices (Rs crore)		50 years cumulative construction (Rs crore)
	Construction	Machinery and equipment	Construction	Machinery and equipment	Construction	Machinery and equipment	
	(1)	(2)	(3)	(4)	(5)	(6)	(7)
1900–1	638	485	16.73		2663		112,247
1901–2	419	362	10.99		1749		112,242
1902–3	573	474	15.03		2391		112,797
1903–4	547	477	14.35		2283		113,327
1904–5	607	538	15.92		2533		114,066
1905–6	683	649	17.91		2850		115,130
1906–7	614	644	16.10		2562		115,823
1907–8	320	362	8.39		1335		115,326
1908–9	602	840	15.79		2512		115,990
1909–10	468	456	12.27		1953		116,036
1910–1	758	670	19.88		3163		117,497
1911–2	808	653	21.19		3372		118,774
1912–3	756	754	19.83		3155		120,005
1913–4	798	863	20.93		3330		121,478
1914–5	521	693	13.66		2174		121,795
1915–6	928	664	24.34		3873		123,803
1916–7	657	487	17.23		2742		124,562
1917–8	694	508	18.20		2896		125,539
1918–9	1148	913	30.11		4791		128,406
1919–20	209	177	5.48	6.83	872	473	127,342
1920–1	494	563	12.96	21.71	2062	1503	127,079
1921–2	203	239	5.32	9.22	847	638	125,376
1922–3	652	860	17.10	33.17	2721	2296	126,194

(Contd.)

197

Appendix Table 4(f) Contd.

	(1)	(2)	(3)	(4)	(5)	(6)	(7)
1923-4	1028	1178	26.96	45.43	4290	3146	127,913
1924-5	905	717	23.73	27.65	3777	1915	129,111
1925-6	1015	793	26.62	30.58	4236	2118	130,772
1926-7	874	625	22.92	24.10	3648	1669	131,870
1927-8	1348	1056	35.35	40.73	5626	2820	134,891
1928-9	824	685	21.61	26.42	3439	1829	135,713
1929-30	1042	820	27.33	31.62	4349	2190	137,445
1930-1	1081	782	28.35	30.16	4511	2088	139,803
1931-2	957	534	25.10	20.59	3994	1426	141,548
1932-3	953	505	24.99	19.48	3977	1348	143,447
1933-4	1359	839	35.64	32.36	5672	2240	146,944
1934-5	1140	626	29.90	24.14	4758	1672	149,519
1935-6	1540	865	40.39	33.36	6427	2310	153,867
1936-7	1512	828	39.65	31.93	6310	2211	158,099
1937-8	1596	995	41.86	38.37	6661	2657	162,490
1938-9	1602	903	42.01	34.82	6686	2411	166,492
1939-40	1444	709	37.87	27.34	6026	1893	169,680
1940-1	1399	606	36.69	23.37	5839	1618	172,647
1941-2	1938	888	50.83	34.25	8088	2371	178,248
1942-3	1275	504	33.44	19.44	5321	1346	179,104
1943-4	2077	595	54.47	22.95	8668	1589	185,430
1944-5	2271	970	59.56	37.41	9478	2590	192,550
1945-6	2402	1356	63.00	52.29	10,024	3621	200,484
1946-7	2539	1711	66.59	65.99	10,596	4569	208,551
1947-8	2305	1745	60.45	67.30	9620	4660	215,871
1948-9	2762	2201	72.44	84.88	11,527	5877	225,015
1949-50	2404	2056	63.05	79.29	10,033	5490	232,410
1950-1	3813	2593	100.00	100.00	15,913	6924	245,660
1951-2					16,452	7292	260,364

(Contd.)

198

Appendix Table 4(f) Contd.

	(1)	(2)	(3)	(4)	(5)	(6)	(7)
1952-3					14,849	6430	272,821
1953-4					15,458	5683	285,997
1954-5					17,603	5477	301,066
1955-6					19,769	8649	317,985
1956-7					23,271	11,581	338,693
1957-8					21,107	14,984	358,465
1958-9					22,683	9054	378,636
1959-60					24,028	10,100	400,711
1960-1					25,964	11,569	423,511
1961-2					26,923	12,707	447,062
1962-3					27,490	14,841	471,397
1963-4					30,925	16,056	498,992
1964-5					33,855	18,350	530,672
1965-6					36,480	19,079	563,279
1966-7					39,059	15,437	599,597
1967-8					42,389	14,914	639,089
1968-9					42,970	15,447	677,268
1969-70					43,971	16,171	720,367
1970-1					44,334	16,155	762,639
1971-2					44,647	18,713	806,439
1972-3					46,404	20,032	850,122
1973-4					41,880	22,428	887,712
1974-5					40,553	21,762	924,488
1975-6					47,022	22,232	967,274
1976-7					52,527	25,300	1,016,154
1977-8					58,887	26,878	1,069,415
1978-9					56,178	29,215	1,122,154
1979-80					52,013	29,990	1,169,818
1980-1					56,963	33,717	1,222,270

(Contd.)

199

Appendix Table 4(f) Contd.

(1)	(2)	(3)	(4)	(5)	(6)	(7)
1981–2				60,551	36,979	1,278,827
1982–3				58,727	41,436	1,333,577
1983–4				60,569	44,437	1,388,474
1984–5				61,469	49,367	1,445,186
1985–6				65,164	52,420	1,503,923
1986–7				65,774	58,309	1,563,387
1987–8				68,199	67,230	1,624,925
1988–9				73,887	72,544	1,692,126
1989–90				76,858	79,991	1,762,958
1990–1				83,768	86,660	1,840,887
1991–2				87,287	80,243	1,920,086
1992–3				89,526	88,456	2,004,291
1993–4				87,625	96,668	2,083,248
1994–5				92,920	113,136	2,166,691
1995–6				98,023	147,745	2,254,689
1996–7				100,166	149,479	2,344,259
1997–8				113,019	142,109	2,447,659
1998–9				121,218	155,945	2,557,350
1999–2000				131,003	170,105	2,678,320

(Cols Contd.)

200

Appendix Table 4(f) Contd.: Preliminary Estimates of Fixed Capital Stock (1900–1 to 1999–2000)

Year	15 years cumulative Machinery and equipment (Rs crore)	GFCS total (Rs crore)	CFC (Rs crore) Construction	CFC (Rs crore) Machinery and equipment	50 years cumulative CFC construction (Rs crore)	15 years cumulative CFC Machinery and equipment (Rs crore)
	(8)	(9)	(10)	(11)	(12)	(13)
1900–1			2245			
1901–2			2245			
1902–3			2256			
1903–4			2267			
1904–5			2281			
1905–6			2303			
1906–7			2316			
1907–8			2307			
1908–9			2320			
1909–10			2321			
1910–1			2350			
1911–2			2375			
1912–3			2400			
1913–4			2430			
1914–5			2436			
1915–6			2476			
1916–7			2491			
1917–8			2511			
1918–9			2568			
1919–20			2547			
1920–1			2542			
1921–2			2508			
1922–3			2524			
1923–4			2558			

(Contd.)

Appendix Table 4(f) Contd.

	(8)	(9)	(10)	(11)	(12)	(13)
1924–5			2582			
1925–6			2615			
1926–7			2637			
1927–8			2698			
1928–9			2714			
1929–30			2749			
1930–1			2796			
1931–2			2831			
1932–3			2869			
1933–4	27,699		2939	1856		
1934–5	28,898		2990	1936		
1935–6	29,704		3077	1990		
1936–7	31,277		3162	2096		
1937–8	31,637		3250	2120		
1938–9	30,903		3330	2071		
1939–40	30,882		3394	2069		
1940–1	30,382		3453	2036		
1941–2	31,085		3565	2083		
1942–3	29,611		3582	1984		
1943–4	29,370		3709	1968		
1944–5	29,771		3851	1995		
1945–6	31,304		4010	2097		
1946–7	34,446		4171	2308		
1947–8	37,758		4317	2530		
1948–9	41,394		4500	2773	141,593	
1949–50	45,213	277,623	4648	3029	144,015	33,147
1950–1	49,827	295,487	4913	3338	146,683	34,496
1951–2	54,908	315,272	5207	3679	149,646	36,079
1952–3	58,681	331,503	5456	3932	152,846	37,891

(Contd.)

Appendix Table 4(f) Contd.

	(8)	(9)	(10)	(11)	(12)	(13)
1953-4	61,953	347,950	5720	4151	156,300	39,971
1954-5	65,537	366,603	6021	4391	160,040	42,293
1955-6	72,568	390,553	6360	4862	164,097	45,119
1956-7	81,777	420,471	6774	5479	168,554	48,516
1957-8	95,416	453,881	7169	6393	173,417	52,925
1958-9	102,881	481,516	7573	6893	178,670	57,850
1959-60	110,391	511,101	8014	7396	184,363	63,252
1960-1	118,339	541,850	8470	7929	190,483	69,083
1961-2	126,477	573,539	8941	8474	197,049	75,249
1962-3	136,658	608,055	9428	9156	204,077	81,875
1963-4	146,837	645,829	9980	9838	211,627	88,940
1964-5	159,697	690,369	10,613	10,700	219,805	96,610
1965-6	171,852	735,131	11,266	11,514	228,594	104,786
1966-7	179,997	779,594	11,992	12,060	238,095	113,167
1967-8	188,481	827,570	12,782	12,628	248,366	121,864
1968-9	198,245	875,513	13,545	13,282	259,343	130,995
1969-70	208,939	929,306	14,407	13,999	271,204	140,603
1970-1	216,445	979,084	15,253	14,502	283,915	150,243
1971-2	223,577	1,030,016	16,129	14,980	297,536	159,743
1972-3	228,625	1,078,747	17,002	15,318	312,015	168,669
1973-4	241,999	1,129,711	17,754	16,214	327,211	177,989
1974-5	253,661	1,178,149	18,490	16,995	343,118	187,589
1975-6	264,324	1,231,598	19,345	17,710	359,848	197,370
1976-7	276,917	1,293,071	20,323	18,553	377,534	207,449
1977-8	288,954	1,358,369	21,388	19,360	396,225	217,653
1978-9	302,113	1,424,267	22,443	20,242	415,953	228,056
1979-80	313,753	1,483,571	23,396	21,021	436,601	238,378
1980-1	328,391	1,550,661	24,445	22,002	458,250	248,866
1981-2	349,933	1,628,760	25,577	23,446	480,996	260,252

(Contd.)

Appendix Table 4(f) Contd.

	(8)	(9)	(10)	(11)	(12)	(13)
1982-3	376,455	1,710,032	26,672	25,222	504,798	272,846
1983-4	405,445	1,793,919	27,769	27,165	529,629	286,729
1984-5	438,641	1,883,827	28,904	29,389	555,542	302,119
1985-6	474,906	1,978,829	30,078	31,819	582,544	319,435
1986-7	514,502	2,077,889	31,268	34,472	610,649	338,927
1987-8	561,700	2,186,625	32,498	37,634	639,898	361,243
1988-9	611,816	2,303,942	33,843	40,992	670,411	386,021
1989-90	670,045	2,433,003	35,259	44,893	702,276	413,919
1990-1	734,473	2,575,360	36,818	49,210	735,641	445,419
1991-2	789,416	2,709,502	38,402	52,891	770,478	479,756
1992-3	850,994	2,855,285	40,086	57,017	806,982	517,413
1993-4	918,447	3,001,695	41,665	61,536	844,938	558,707
1994-5	1,001,593	3,168,284	43,334	67,107	884,421	604,793
1995-6	1,115,621	3,370,310	45,094	74,747	925,505	657,537
1996-7	1,228,121	3,572,380	46,885	82,284	968,219	716,376
1997-8	1,328,794	3,776,453	48,953	89,029	1,012,855	780,182
1998-9	1,440,302	3,997,652	51,147	96,500	1,059,501	849,518
1999-2000	1,561,040	4,239,360	53,566	104,590	1,108,420	924,719

(Cols Contd.)

Appendix Table 4(f) Contd.: Preliminary Estimates of Fixed Capital Stock (1900-1 to 1999-2000)

Year	Preliminary estimates at 1993–4 prices (Rs crore)			CSO estimate NFCS total 1993–4 prices (Rs crore)	Bina Roy's estimate of NFCS			
	NFCS structures	NFCS equipment	NFCS total		GFCS/NFCS (9)/(15)	Net/Gross ratio (15)/(9)	% distribution of NFCS	
							Structures	Equipment
	(14)	(15)	(16)	(17)	(18)	(19)	(20)	(21)
1949–50	88,395	12,066	100,461					
1950–1	98,977	15,332	114,309	377,924	2.585	0.387	86.59	13.41
1951–2	110,718	18,829	129,547	389,082	2.434	0.411	85.47	14.53
1952–3	119,975	20,790	140,766	398,306	2.355	0.425	85.23	14.77
1953–4	129,697	21,982	151,679	409,054	2.294	0.436	85.51	14.49
1954–5	141,027	23,244	164,271	421,445	2.232	0.448	85.85	14.15
1955–6	153,888	27,448	181,336	437,337	2.154	0.464	84.86	15.14
1956–7	170,139	33,262	203,401	455,972	2.067	0.484	83.65	16.35
1957–8	185,048	42,491	227,539	475,763	1.995	0.501	81.33	18.67
1958–9	199,966	45,031	244,997	492,967	1.965	0.509	81.62	18.38
1959–60	216,347	47,139	263,486	510,330	1.940	0.516	82.11	17.89
1960–1	233,028	49,256	282,283	531,928	1.920	0.521	82.55	17.45
1961–2	250,013	51,228	301,241	552,029	1.904	0.525	82.99	17.01
1962–3	267,320	54,783	322,103	576,356	1.888	0.530	82.99	17.01
1963–4	287,364	57,897	345,261	602,986	1.871	0.535	83.23	16.77
1964–5	310,867	63,087	373,954	630,773	1.846	0.542	83.13	16.87
1965–6	334,685	67,066	401,751	660,449	1.830	0.547	83.31	16.69
1966–7	361,501	66,830	428,331	687,194	1.820	0.549	84.40	15.60
1967–8	390,723	66,617	457,340	713,176	1.810	0.553	85.43	14.57
1968–9	417,925	67,250	485,175	736,025	1.805	0.554	86.14	13.86
1969–70	449,163	68,336	517,499	760,725	1.796	0.557	86.79	13.21
1970–1	478,724	66,202	544,926	785,429	1.797	0.557	87.85	12.15
1971–2	508,903	63,834	572,736	811,261	1.798	0.556	88.85	11.15

(Contd.)

Appendix Table 4(f) Contd.

	(14)	(15)	(16)	(17)	(18)	(19)	(20)	(21)
1972–3	538,107	59,956	598,064	842,408	1.804	0.554	89.97	10.03
1973–4	560,501	64,010	624,511	870,632	1.809	0.553	89.75	10.25
1974–5	581,370	66,072	647,442	896,281	1.820	0.550	89.79	10.21
1975–6	607,426	66,954	674,380	929,024	1.826	0.548	90.07	9.93
1976–7	638,619	69,468	708,087	962,718	1.826	0.548	90.19	9.81
1977–8	673,190	71,301	744,491	998,557	1.825	0.548	90.42	9.58
1978–9	706,201	74,057	780,257	1,040,403	1.825	0.548	90.51	9.49
1979–80	733,218	75,375	808,592	1,078,594	1.835	0.545	90.68	9.32
1980–1	764,020	79,525	843,545	1,121,610	1.838	0.544	90.57	9.43
1981–2	797,831	89,681	887,512	1,188,209	1.835	0.545	89.90	10.10
1982–3	828,778	103,609	932,387	1,244,576	1.834	0.545	88.89	11.11
1983–4	858,845	118,716	977,562	1,295,600	1.835	0.545	87.86	12.14
1984–5	889,643	136,522	1,026,166	1,347,822	1.836	0.545	86.70	13.30
1985–6	921,379	155,471	1,076,850	1,402,628	1.838	0.544	85.56	14.44
1986–7	952,737	175,575	1,128,312	1,462,759	1.842	0.543	84.44	15.56
1987–8	985,027	200,457	1,185,483	1,517,223	1.845	0.542	83.09	16.91
1988–9	1,021,716	225,795	1,247,510	1,575,554	1.847	0.541	81.90	18.10
1989–90	1,060,682	256,126	1,316,808	1,634,309	1.848	0.541	80.55	19.45
1990–1	1,105,246	289,054	1,394,300	1,704,760	1.847	0.541	79.27	20.73
1991–2	1,149,609	309,660	1,459,268	1,781,854	1.857	0.539	78.78	21.22
1992–3	1,197,310	333,581	1,530,891	1,853,469	1.865	0.536	78.21	21.79
1993–4	1,238,310	359,740	1,598,050	1,921,762	1.878	0.532	77.49	22.51
1994–5	1,282,270	396,800	1,679,070	2,048,289	1.887	0.530	76.37	23.63
1995–6	1,329,184	458,084	1,787,268	2,212,699	1.886	0.530	74.37	25.63
1996–7	1,376,040	511,745	1,887,785	2,365,943	1.892	0.528	72.89	27.11
1997–8	1,434,804	548,612	1,983,415	2,499,312	1.904	0.525	72.34	27.66
1998–9	1,497,848	590,784	2,088,632	2,620,206	1.914	0.522	71.71	28.29
1999–2000	1,569,900	636,321	2,206,222	2,739,223	1.922	0.520	71.16	28.84

(Cols Contd.)

206

Appendix Table 4(f) Contd.: Preliminary Estimates of Fixed Capital Stock (1900–1 to 1999–2000)

Year	Bina Roy's estimate of GFCS % share of		Based on CSO's estimates of NFCS (Rs crore)			Our estimate of GFCS (Rs crore)		
	Structures	Equipment	Structures $(16) \times (20)$	Equipment $(16) \times (21)$	Total	Total $(26) \times (18)$	Structures $(27) \times (22)$	Equipment $(27) \times (23)$
	(22)	(23)	(24)	(25)	(26)	(27)	(28)	(29)
1949–50								
1950–1	83.14	16.86	327,235	50,689	377,924	976,932	812,195	164,737
1951–2	82.58	17.42	332,530	56,552	389,082	946,886	781,975	164,911
1952–3	82.30	17.70	339,478	58,828	398,306	938,009	771,966	166,043
1953–4	82.19	17.81	349,772	59,282	409,054	938,365	771,288	167,078
1954–5	82.12	17.88	361,812	59,633	421,445	940,540	772,402	168,138
1955–6	81.42	18.58	371,139	66,198	437,337	941,913	766,898	175,014
1956–7	80.55	19.45	381,408	74,564	455,972	942,586	759,263	183,324
1957–8	78.98	21.02	386,919	88,844	475,763	949,022	749,517	199,505
1958–9	78.63	21.37	402,359	90,608	492,967	968,877	761,867	207,010
1959–60	78.40	21.60	419,029	91,301	510,330	989,919	776,111	213,809
1960–1	78.16	21.84	439,112	92,816	531,928	1,021,049	798,054	222,995
1961–2	77.95	22.05	458,153	93,876	552,029	1,051,020	819,249	231,771
1962–3	77.53	22.47	478,330	98,026	576,356	1,088,026	843,496	244,530
1963–4	77.26	22.74	501,871	101,115	602,986	1,127,916	871,470	256,445
1964–5	76.87	23.13	524,361	106,412	630,773	1,164,492	895,120	269,372
1965–6	76.62	23.38	550,198	110,251	660,449	1,208,502	925,990	282,512
1966–7	76.91	23.09	579,975	107,219	687,194	1,250,742	961,963	288,778
1967–8	77.22	22.78	609,293	103,883	713,176	1,290,512	996,595	293,917
1968–9	77.36	22.64	634,005	102,020	736,025	1,328,181	1,027,437	300,744
1969–70	77.52	22.48	660,271	100,454	760,725	1,366,083	1,058,942	307,141
1970–1	77.89	22.11	690,009	95,420	785,429	1,411,202	1,099,229	311,973
1971–2	78.29	21.71	720,843	90,418	811,261	1,458,982	1,142,293	316,689

(Contd.)

207

Appendix Table 4(f) Contd.

	(22)	(23)	(24)	(25)	(26)	(27)	(28)	(29)
1972–3	78.81	21.19	757,956	84,452	842,408	1,519,479	1,197,447	322,032
1973–4	78.58	21.42	781,396	89,236	870,632	1,574,933	1,237,562	337,371
1974–5	78.47	21.53	804,814	91,467	896,281	1,630,961	1,279,807	351,153
1975–6	78.54	21.46	836,788	92,236	929,024	1,696,646	1,332,514	364,132
1976–7	78.58	21.42	868,269	94,449	962,718	1,758,063	1,381,566	376,497
1977–8	78.73	21.27	902,924	95,633	998,557	1,821,927	1,434,364	387,563
1978–9	78.79	21.21	941,655	98,748	1,040,403	1,899,132	1,496,292	402,841
1979–80	78.85	21.15	978,050	100,544	1,078,594	1,978,959	1,560,439	418,520
1980–1	78.82	21.18	1,015,871	105,739	1,121,610	2,061,820	1,625,178	436,642
1981–2	78.52	21.48	1,068,143	120,066	1,188,209	2,180,598	1,712,105	468,493
1982–3	77.99	22.01	1,106,276	138,300	1,244,576	2,282,597	1,780,095	502,502
1983–4	77.40	22.60	1,138,261	157,339	1,295,600	2,377,550	1,840,198	537,352
1984–5	76.72	23.28	1,168,506	179,316	1,347,822	2,474,321	1,898,186	576,135
1985–6	76.00	24.00	1,200,123	202,505	1,402,628	2,577,482	1,958,903	618,579
1986–7	75.24	24.76	1,235,142	227,617	1,462,759	2,693,803	2,026,796	667,007
1987–8	74.31	25.69	1,260,672	256,551	1,517,223	2,798,519	2,079,635	718,883
1988–9	73.44	26.56	1,290,385	285,169	1,575,554	2,909,784	2,137,086	772,698
1989–90	72.46	27.54	1,316,427	317,882	1,634,309	3,019,635	2,188,032	831,602
1990–1	71.48	28.52	1,351,344	353,416	1,704,760	3,148,799	2,250,786	898,013
1991–2	70.86	29.14	1,403,741	378,113	1,781,854	3,308,465	2,344,541	963,924
1992–3	70.20	29.80	1,449,598	403,871	1,853,469	3,456,930	2,426,621	1,030,309
1993–4	69.40	30.60	1,489,151	432,611	1,921,762	3,609,739	2,505,245	1,104,494
1994–5	68.39	31.61	1,564,234	484,055	2,048,289	3,864,973	2,643,135	1,221,838
1995–6	66.90	33.10	1,645,576	567,123	2,212,699	4,172,559	2,791,382	1,381,177
1996–7	65.62	34.38	1,724,578	641,365	2,365,943	4,477,229	2,938,037	1,539,192
1997–8	64.81	35.19	1,808,004	691,308	2,499,312	4,758,727	3,084,307	1,674,420
1998–9	63.97	36.03	1,879,063	741,143	2,620,206	5,015,086	3,208,216	1,806,870
1999–2000	63.18	36.82	1,949,173	790,050	2,739,223	5,263,547	3,325,375	1,938,172

(Cols Contd.)

Appendix Table 4(f) Contd.: Preliminary Estimates of Fixed Capital Stock (1900–1 to 1999–2000)

Year	Net/Gross ratio			Gross/Net ratio			Corrected gross/net ratio	GFCS (Rs crore)		
	Structures (24)/(28)	Equipment (25)/(29)	Overall (26)/(27)	Structures (28)/(24)	Equipment (29)/(25)	FCS (27)/(26)		Total revised (26) × (36)	Structures revised	Equipment
	(30)	(31)	(32)	(33)	(34)	(35)	(36)	(37)	(38)	(39)
1949–50										
1950–1	0.403	0.308	0.387	2.482	3.250	2.585	2.355	890,011	739,931	150,080
1951–2	0.425	0.343	0.411	2.352	2.916	2.434	2.355	916,288	756,706	159,582
1952–3	0.440	0.354	0.425	2.274	2.823	2.355	2.355	938,009	771,966	166,043
1953–4	0.453	0.355	0.436	2.205	2.818	2.294	2.294	938,365	771,288	167,078
1954–5	0.468	0.355	0.448	2.135	2.820	2.232	2.232	940,540	772,402	168,138
1955–6	0.484	0.378	0.464	2.066	2.644	2.154	2.154	941,913	766,898	175,014
1956–7	0.502	0.407	0.484	1.991	2.459	2.067	2.067	942,586	759,263	183,324
1957–8	0.516	0.445	0.501	1.937	2.246	1.995	1.995	949,022	749,517	199,505
1958–9	0.528	0.438	0.509	1.894	2.285	1.965	1.965	968,877	761,867	207,010
1959–60	0.540	0.427	0.516	1.852	2.342	1.940	1.940	989,919	776,111	213,809
1960–1	0.550	0.416	0.521	1.817	2.403	1.920	1.920	1,021,049	798,054	222,995
1961–2	0.559	0.405	0.525	1.788	2.469	1.904	1.904	1,051,020	819,249	231,771
1962–3	0.567	0.401	0.530	1.763	2.495	1.888	1.888	1,088,026	843,496	244,530
1963–4	0.576	0.394	0.535	1.736	2.536	1.871	1.871	1,127,916	871,470	256,445
1964–5	0.586	0.395	0.542	1.707	2.531	1.846	1.846	1,164,492	895,120	269,372
1965–6	0.594	0.390	0.547	1.683	2.562	1.830	1.830	1,208,502	925,990	282,512
1966–7	0.603	0.371	0.549	1.659	2.693	1.820	1.820	1,250,742	961,963	288,778
1967–8	0.611	0.353	0.553	1.636	2.829	1.810	1.810	1,290,512	996,595	293,917
1968–9	0.617	0.339	0.554	1.621	2.948	1.805	1.805	1,328,181	1,027,437	300,744
1969–70	0.624	0.327	0.557	1.604	3.058	1.796	1.796	1,366,083	1,058,942	307,141
1970–1	0.628	0.306	0.557	1.593	3.269	1.797	1.797	1,411,202	1,099,229	311,973
1971–2	0.631	0.286	0.556	1.585	3.503	1.798	1.798	1,458,982	1,142,293	316,689
1972–3	0.633	0.262	0.554	1.580	3.813	1.804	1.804	1,519,479	1,197,447	322,032
1973–4	0.631	0.265	0.553	1.584	3.781	1.809	1.809	1,574,933	1,237,562	337,371

(Contd.)

Appendix Table 4(f) Contd.

	(30)	(31)	(32)	(33)	(34)	(35)	(36)	(37)	(38)	(39)
1974–5	0.629	0.260	0.550	1.590	3.839	1.820	1.820	1,630,961	1,279,807	351,153
1975–6	0.628	0.253	0.548	1.592	3.948	1.826	1.826	1,696,646	1,332,514	364,132
1976–7	0.628	0.251	0.548	1.591	3.986	1.826	1.826	1,758,063	1,381,566	376,497
1977–8	0.629	0.247	0.548	1.589	4.053	1.825	1.825	1,821,927	1,434,364	387,563
1978–9	0.629	0.245	0.548	1.589	4.079	1.825	1.825	1,899,132	1,496,292	402,841
1979–80	0.627	0.240	0.545	1.595	4.163	1.835	1.835	1,978,959	1,560,439	418,520
1980–1	0.625	0.242	0.544	1.600	4.129	1.838	1.838	2,061,820	1,625,178	436,642
1981–2	0.624	0.256	0.545	1.603	3.902	1.835	1.835	2,180,598	1,712,105	468,493
1982–3	0.621	0.275	0.545	1.609	3.633	1.834	1.834	2,282,597	1,780,095	502,502
1983–4	0.619	0.293	0.545	1.617	3.415	1.835	1.835	2,377,550	1,840,198	537,352
1984–5	0.616	0.311	0.544	1.624	3.213	1.836	1.836	2,474,321	1,898,186	576,135
1985–6	0.613	0.327	0.544	1.632	3.055	1.838	1.838	2,577,482	1,958,903	618,579
1986–7	0.609	0.341	0.543	1.641	2.930	1.842	1.842	2,693,803	2,026,796	667,007
1987–8	0.606	0.357	0.542	1.650	2.802	1.845	1.845	2,798,519	2,079,635	718,883
1988–9	0.604	0.369	0.541	1.656	2.710	1.847	1.847	2,909,784	2,137,086	772,698
1989–90	0.602	0.382	0.541	1.662	2.616	1.848	1.848	3,019,635	2,188,032	831,602
1990–1	0.600	0.394	0.541	1.666	2.541	1.847	1.847	3,148,799	2,250,786	898,013
1991–2	0.599	0.392	0.539	1.670	2.549	1.857	1.857	3,308,465	2,344,541	963,924
1992–3	0.597	0.392	0.536	1.674	2.551	1.865	1.865	3,456,930	2,426,621	1,030,309
1993–4	0.594	0.392	0.532	1.682	2.553	1.878	1.878	3,609,739	2,505,245	1,104,494
1994–5	0.592	0.396	0.530	1.690	2.524	1.887	1.887	3,864,973	2,643,135	1,221,838
1995–6	0.590	0.411	0.530	1.696	2.435	1.886	1.886	4,172,559	2,791,382	1,381,177
1996–7	0.587	0.417	0.528	1.704	2.400	1.892	1.892	4,477,229	2,938,037	1,539,192
1997–8	0.586	0.413	0.525	1.706	2.422	1.904	1.904	4,758,727	3,084,307	1,674,420
1998–9	0.586	0.410	0.522	1.707	2.438	1.914	1.914	5,015,086	3,208,216	1,806,870
1999–2000	0.586	0.408	0.520	1.706	2.453	1.922	1.922	5,263,547	3,325,375	1,938,172

Sources: Cols (1) and (2) from Bina Roy, *An Analysis of Long-term Growth of Income and Capital Formation in India*, pp. 302–5; Cols (3) and (4) computed from Cols (1) and (2); Cols (5) and (6) for 1950–1 to 1949–50 projected backwards using indicators indicators in Cols (3) and (4), and for 1950–1 to 1999–2000 from *NAS 1950–51 to 1992–93* and *NAS 2001* Cols (3) and (4); Cols (7) to (13) derived. Col. (14) = Col. (7) – Col. (12); Col. (15) = Col. (8) – Col. (13); Col. (16) = Col. (14) + Col. (15); Col. (17) from *NAS 1950–1 to 1992–3* and *NAS 2001*; Col. (18) to (26) derived. Cols (27) to (37) derived as indicated; Col. (38) = Col. (37) × Col. (22); Col. (39) = Col. (37) – Col. (38).

Appendix Table 4(g): Capital Stock of Dwellings at Constant (1993–4) Prices and Current Prices, 1950–1 to 1999–2000

Year	NFCS at 1993–4 prices (Rs crore)		NFCS at current prices (Rs crore)		Implicit deflator	Gross/Net ratio Construction at 1993–4 prices	GFCS Dwellings at 1993–4 prices (Rs crore)	Adjusted deflator for dwellings	GFCS Dwellings at current prices (Rs crore)
	Real estate, ownership of dwellings, and business services	Dwellings (1) × 0.95	Real estate, ownership of dwellings, and business services	Dwellings (3) × 0.95					
	(1)	(2)	(3)	(4)	(5)	(6)	(7)	(8)	(9)
1949–50	221,922	210,826	9276	8813	4.18	2.482	523,270	4.55	23,809
1950–1	224,051	212,848	9057	8604	4.04	2.482	528,288	4.40	23,238
1951–2	225,447	214,175	9442	8970	4.19	2.352	503,651	4.60	23,156
1952–3	226,951	215,603	9615	9134	4.24	2.274	490,278	4.58	22,452
1953–4	228,680	217,246	9605	9125	4.20	2.205	479,052	4.45	21,341
1954–5	230,462	218,939	9602	9122	4.17	2.135	467,394	4.24	19,794
1955–6	232,432	220,810	9859	9366	4.24	2.066	456,268	4.44	20,248
1956–7	234,576	222,847	10,470	9947	4.46	1.991	443,618	4.83	21,429
1957–8	236,703	224,868	11,162	10,604	4.72	1.937	435,601	5.23	22,787
1958–9	239,100	227,145	11,618	11,037	4.86	1.894	430,099	4.98	21,411
1959–60	241,818	229,727	12,133	11,526	5.02	1.852	425,492	5.23	22,253
1960–1	244,560	232,332	12,946	12,299	5.29	1.817	422,247	5.50	23,219
1961–2	247,402	235,032	13,855	13,162	5.60	1.788	420,274	5.75	24,152
1962–3	250,281	237,767	14,559	13,831	5.82	1.763	419,283	6.00	25,164
1963–4	253,339	240,672	14,974	14,225	5.91	1.736	417,913	5.99	25,035
1964–5	256,692	243,857	15,686	14,902	6.11	1.707	416,282	6.38	26,561
1965–6	259,799	246,809	16,912	16,066	6.51	1.683	415,383	6.97	28,933
1966–7	262,721	249,585	18,280	17,366	6.96	1.659	413,969	7.22	29,890
1967–8	265,991	252,691	19,543	18,566	7.35	1.636	413,317	7.70	31,813
1968–9	269,373	255,904	21,088	20,034	7.83	1.621	414,706	8.27	34,309
1969–70	272,917	259,271	23,188	22,029	8.50	1.604	415,819	9.02	37,512
1970–1	275,847	262,055	24,549	23,322	8.90	1.593	417,470	9.78	40,827
1971–2	279,092	265,137	26,432	25,110	9.47	1.585	420,153	10.66	44,809

(Contd.)

Appendix Table 4(g) Contd.

	(1)	(2)	(3)	(4)	(5)	(6)	(7)	(8)	(9)
1972–3	282,677	268,543	29,052	27,599	10.28	1.580	424,255	11.50	48,803
1973–4	286,512	272,186	34,186	32,477	11.93	1.584	431,084	13.39	57,706
1974–5	290,467	275,944	43,680	41,496	15.04	1.590	438,803	15.95	69,999
1975–6	295,171	280,412	48,151	45,743	16.31	1.592	446,533	17.33	77,373
1976–7	300,070	285,067	49,896	47,401	16.63	1.591	453,590	18.08	82,014
1977–8	305,239	289,977	52,482	49,858	17.19	1.589	460,651	18.94	87,259
1978–9	310,802	295,262	59,057	56,104	19.00	1.589	469,172	20.53	96,308
1979–80	316,864	301,021	71,053	67,500	22.42	1.595	480,266	23.64	113,549
1980–1	323,828	307,637	82,620	78,489	25.51	1.600	492,153	26.28	129,341
1981–2	330,109	313,604	101,755	96,667	30.82	1.603	502,669	30.52	153,419
1982–3	335,007	318,257	120,451	114,428	35.95	1.609	512,103	34.97	179,084
1983–4	339,852	322,859	139,968	132,970	41.18	1.617	521,959	38.74	202,217
1984–5	345,144	327,887	159,657	151,674	46.26	1.624	532,637	43.20	230,106
1985–6	351,119	333,563	179,212	170,251	51.04	1.632	544,459	48.26	262,783
1986–7	355,387	337,618	204,800	194,560	57.63	1.641	554,011	53.20	294,735
1987–8	361,314	343,248	227,712	216,326	63.02	1.650	566,231	58.33	330,303
1988–9	368,621	350,190	248,224	235,813	67.34	1.656	579,971	63.13	366,110
1989–90	378,630	359,699	270,707	257,172	71.50	1.662	597,854	69.20	413,694
1990–1	390,698	371,163	295,474	280,700	75.63	1.666	618,206	75.30	465,530
1991–2	402,173	382,064	345,790	328,501	85.98	1.670	638,127	84.90	541,792
1992–3	414,785	394,046	380,097	361,092	91.64	1.674	659,631	92.48	610,048
1993–4	421,218	400,157	421,218	400,157	100.00	1.682	673,197	100.00	673,197
1994–5	438,413	416,492	468,286	444,872	106.81	1.690	703,760	108.58	764,155
1995–6	448,211	425,800	574,178	545,469	128.10	1.696	722,283	124.41	898,591
1996–7	462,936	439,789	631,640	600,058	136.44	1.704	749,237	133.94	1,003,548
1997–8	478,476	454,552	685,643	651,361	143.30	1.706	775,429	142.07	1,101,642
1998–9	494,355	469,637	745,643	708,361	150.83	1.707	801,835	149.76	1,200,806
1999–2000	510,871	485,327	805,339	765,072	157.64	1.706	827,990	156.30	1,294,121

Sources: Col. (1) from *NAS 1950–1 to 1992–3*, pp. 157–67 and *NAS 2001*, p. 53, 55, 57; Col. (2) = Col. (1) × 0.95; Col. (3) from *NAS 1950–1 to 1992–3*, pp. 146–56 and *NAS 2001*, p. 52, 54, 56; Col. (4) = Col. (3) × 0.95; Col. (5) = Col. (3)/Col. (1) × 100; Col. (6) from Appendix Table 4(f), Col. (33); Col. (7) = Col. (2) × Col. (6); Col. (8) from Appendix Table 4(m), Col. (16); Col. (9) = Col. (7) × Col. (8)/100.

212

Appendix Table 4(h): Net Fixed Capital Stock at 1993-4 Prices, Whole Economy and Non-residential Sector, 1950-1 to 1999-2000

(Rs crore)

Year	NFCS of whole economy			NFCS of dwellings	NFCS of non-residential sector		
	Structures	Equipment	Total		Structures	Equipment	Total
	(1)	(2)	(3)	(4)	(5)	(6)	(7)
1949–50	319,218	46,816	366,034	210,826	108,392	46,816	155,208
1950–1	327,235	50,689	377,924	212,848	114,387	50,689	165,076
1951–2	332,530	56,552	389,082	214,175	118,355	56,552	174,907
1952–3	339,478	58,828	398,306	215,603	123,875	58,828	182,703
1953–4	349,772	59,282	409,054	217,246	132,526	59,282	191,808
1954–5	361,812	59,633	421,445	218,939	142,873	59,633	202,506
1955–6	371,139	66,198	437,337	220,810	150,329	66,198	216,527
1956–7	381,408	74,564	455,972	222,847	158,561	74,564	233,125
1957–8	386,919	88,844	475,763	224,868	162,051	88,844	250,895
1958–9	402,359	90,608	492,967	227,145	175,214	90,608	265,822
1959–60	419,029	91,301	510,330	229,727	189,302	91,301	280,603
1960–1	439,112	92,816	531,928	232,332	206,780	92,816	299,596
1961–2	458,153	93,876	552,029	235,032	223,121	93,876	316,997
1962–3	478,330	98,026	576,356	237,767	240,563	98,026	338,589
1963–4	501,871	101,115	602,986	240,672	261,199	101,115	362,314
1964–5	524,361	106,412	630,773	243,857	280,503	106,412	386,916
1965–6	550,198	110,251	660,449	246,809	303,389	110,251	413,640
1966–7	579,975	107,219	687,194	249,585	330,390	107,219	437,609
1967–8	609,293	103,883	713,176	252,691	356,602	103,883	460,485
1968–9	634,005	102,020	736,025	255,904	378,101	102,020	480,121
1969–70	660,271	100,454	760,725	259,271	401,000	100,454	501,454
1970–1	690,009	95,420	785,429	262,055	427,954	95,420	523,374
1971–2	720,843	90,418	811,261	265,137	455,706	90,418	546,124

(Contd.)

Appendix Table 4(h) Contd.

	(1)	(2)	(3)	(4)	(5)	(6)	(7)
1972–3	757,956	84,452	842,408	268,543	489,413	84,452	573,865
1973–4	781,396	89,236	870,632	272,186	509,210	89,236	598,446
1974–5	804,814	91,467	896,281	275,944	528,871	91,467	620,337
1975–6	836,788	92,236	929,024	280,412	556,375	92,236	648,612
1976–7	868,269	94,449	962,718	285,067	583,203	94,449	677,652
1977–8	902,924	95,633	998,557	289,977	612,947	95,633	708,580
1978–9	941,655	98,748	1,040,403	295,262	646,393	98,748	745,141
1979–80	978,050	100,544	1,078,594	301,021	677,029	100,544	777,573
1980–1	1,015,871	105,739	1,121,610	307,637	708,234	105,739	813,973
1981–2	1,068,143	120,066	1,188,209	313,604	754,540	120,066	874,605
1982–3	1,106,276	138,300	1,244,576	318,257	788,019	138,300	926,319
1983–4	1,138,261	157,339	1,295,600	322,859	815,401	157,339	972,741
1984–5	1,168,506	179,316	1,347,822	327,887	840,619	179,316	1,019,935
1985–6	1,200,123	202,505	1,402,628	333,563	866,560	202,505	1,069,065
1986–7	1,235,142	227,617	1,462,759	337,618	897,524	227,617	1,125,141
1987–8	1,260,672	256,551	1,517,223	343,248	917,423	256,551	1,173,975
1988–9	1,290,385	285,169	1,575,554	350,190	940,195	285,169	1,225,364
1989–90	1,316,427	317,882	1,634,309	359,699	956,729	317,882	1,274,611
1990–1	1,351,344	353,416	1,704,760	371,163	980,181	353,416	1,333,597
1991–2	1,403,741	378,113	1,781,854	382,064	1,021,677	378,113	1,399,790
1992–3	1,449,598	403,871	1,853,469	394,046	1,055,553	403,871	1,459,423
1993–4	1,489,151	432,611	1,921,762	400,157	1,088,994	432,611	1,521,605
1994–5	1,564,234	484,055	2,048,289	416,492	1,147,742	484,055	1,631,797
1995–6	1,645,576	567,123	2,212,699	425,800	1,219,775	567,123	1,786,899
1996–7	1,724,578	641,365	2,365,943	439,789	1,284,788	641,365	1,926,154
1997–8	1,808,004	691,308	2,499,312	454,552	1,353,452	691,308	2,044,760
1998–9	1,879,063	741,143	2,620,206	469,637	1,409,425	741,143	2,150,569
1999–2000	1,949,173	790,050	2,739,223	485,327	1,463,845	790,050	2,253,896

Sources: Cols (1) to (3) from Appendix Table 4(f), Cols (24) to (26); Col. (4) from Appendix Table 4(g), Col. (2); Col. (5) = Col. (1) − Col. (4); Col. (6) = Col. (2); Col. (7) = Col. (5) + Col. (6).

Appendix Table 4(i): Gross Fixed Capital Stock at 1993-4 Prices, Whole Economy and Non-residential Sector, 1950-1 to 1999-2000

(Rs crore)

Year	GFCS of whole economy			GFCS of dwellings	GFCS of non-residential sector		
	Structures	Equipment	Total		Structures (1) - (4)	Equipment =(2)	Total (5) + (6)
	(1)	(2)	(3)	(4)	(5)	(6)	(7)
1949–50	803,586	161,525	965,111	523,270	280,316	161,525	441,841
1950–1	812,195	164,737	976,932	528,288	283,907	164,737	448,644
1951–2	781,975	164,911	946,886	503,651	278,324	164,911	443,235
1952–3	771,966	166,043	938,009	490,278	281,688	166,043	447,731
1953–4	771,288	167,078	938,365	479,052	292,236	167,078	459,313
1954–5	772,402	168,138	940,540	467,394	305,008	168,138	473,146
1955–6	766,898	175,014	941,913	456,268	310,630	175,014	485,644
1956–7	759,263	183,324	942,586	443,618	315,645	183,324	498,968
1957–8	749,517	199,505	949,022	435,601	313,916	199,505	513,421
1958–9	761,867	207,010	968,877	430,099	331,768	207,010	538,778
1959–60	776,111	213,809	989,919	425,492	350,619	213,809	564,427
1960–1	798,054	222,995	1,021,049	422,247	375,807	222,995	598,802
1961–2	819,249	231,771	1,051,020	420,274	398,975	231,771	630,746
1962–3	843,496	244,530	1,088,026	419,283	424,213	244,530	668,743
1963–4	871,470	256,445	1,127,916	417,913	453,557	256,445	710,002
1964–5	895,120	269,372	1,164,492	416,282	478,839	269,372	748,210
1965–6	925,990	282,512	1,208,502	415,383	510,607	282,512	793,119
1966–7	961,963	288,778	1,250,742	413,969	547,995	288,778	836,773
1967–8	996,595	293,917	1,290,512	413,317	583,278	293,917	877,195
1968–9	1,027,437	300,744	1,328,181	414,706	612,731	300,744	913,475
1969–70	1,058,942	307,141	1,366,083	415,819	643,123	307,141	950,264
1970–1	1,099,229	311,973	1,411,202	417,470	681,759	311,973	993,732
1971–2	1,142,293	316,689	1,458,982	420,153	722,140	316,689	1,038,829

(Contd.)

215

Appendix Table 4(i) Contd.

	(1)	(2)	(3)	(4)	(5)	(6)	(7)
1972–3	1,197,447	322,032	1,519,479	424,255	773,193	322,032	1,095,224
1973–4	1,237,562	337,371	1,574,933	431,084	806,478	337,371	1,143,849
1974–5	1,279,807	351,153	1,630,961	438,803	841,005	351,153	1,192,158
1975–6	1,332,514	364,132	1,696,646	446,533	885,981	364,132	1,250,113
1976–7	1,381,566	376,497	1,758,063	453,590	927,976	376,497	1,304,473
1977–8	1,434,364	387,563	1,821,927	460,651	973,713	387,563	1,361,276
1978–9	1,496,292	402,841	1,899,132	469,172	1,027,120	402,841	1,429,961
1979–80	1,560,439	418,520	1,978,959	480,266	1,080,173	418,520	1,498,693
1980–1	1,625,178	436,642	2,061,820	492,153	1,133,025	436,642	1,569,666
1981–2	1,712,105	468,493	2,180,598	502,669	1,209,436	468,493	1,677,929
1982–3	1,780,095	502,502	2,282,597	512,103	1,267,992	502,502	1,770,495
1983–4	1,840,198	537,352	2,377,550	521,959	1,318,239	537,352	1,855,591
1984–5	1,898,186	576,135	2,474,321	532,637	1,365,548	576,135	1,941,683
1985–6	1,958,903	618,579	2,577,482	544,459	1,414,444	618,579	2,033,023
1986–7	2,026,796	667,007	2,693,803	554,011	1,472,785	667,007	2,139,792
1987–8	2,079,635	718,883	2,798,519	566,231	1,513,405	718,883	2,232,288
1988–9	2,137,086	772,698	2,909,784	579,971	1,557,114	772,698	2,329,813
1989–90	2,188,032	831,602	3,019,635	597,854	1,590,178	831,602	2,421,780
1990–1	2,250,786	898,013	3,148,799	618,206	1,632,580	898,013	2,530,593
1991–2	2,344,541	963,924	3,308,465	638,127	1,706,413	963,924	2,670,338
1992–3	2,426,621	1,030,309	3,456,930	659,631	1,766,990	1,030,309	2,797,300
1993–4	2,505,245	1,104,494	3,609,739	673,197	1,832,049	1,104,494	2,936,543
1994–5	2,643,135	1,221,838	3,864,973	703,760	1,939,375	1,221,838	3,161,213
1995–6	2,791,382	1,381,177	4,172,559	722,283	2,069,099	1,381,177	3,450,276
1996–7	2,938,037	1,539,192	4,477,229	749,237	2,188,800	1,539,192	3,727,992
1997–8	3,084,307	1,674,420	4,758,727	775,429	2,308,878	1,674,420	3,983,298
1998–9	32,8,216	1,806,870	5,015,086	801,835	2,406,381	1,806,870	4,213,251
1999–2000	3,325,375	1,938,172	5,263,547	827,990	2,497,385	1,938,172	4,435,557

Sources: Cols (1) to (3) **from Appendix** Table 4(f), Cols (28), (29), and (27); Col. (4) from Appendix Table 4(g), Col. (7); Col. (5) =
Col. (1) – Col. (4); Col. (6) = Col. (2); Col. (7) = Col. (5) + Col. (6).

216

Appendix Table 4(j): Non-residential Fixed Capital Stock at 1993–4 Prices Per Person Engaged, 1950–1 to 1999–2000

Year	Number in the workforce ('000)	Fixed capital Stock at 1993–4 prices		Fixed capital stock per person engaged		Index of FCS per person engaged 1993–4 = 100	
		Gross (Rs crore)	Net (Rs crore)	Gross (Rs)	Net (Rs)	Gross	Net
	(1)	(2)	(3)	(4)	(5)	(6)	(7)
1950-1	160,139	445,242	160,142	27,803	10,000	35.96	24.88
1951-2	162,661	445,939	169,991	27,415	10,451	35.45	26.00
1952-3	165,223	445,483	178,805	26,963	10,822	34.87	26.92
1953-4	167,825	453,522	187,255	27,024	11,158	34.95	27.75
1954-5	170,468	466,230	197,157	27,350	11,566	35.37	28.77
1955-6	173,153	479,395	209,516	27,686	12,100	35.80	30.10
1956-7	175,880	492,306	224,826	27,991	12,783	36.20	31.80
1957-8	178,651	506,195	242,010	28,334	13,547	36.64	33.70
1958-9	181,464	526,100	258,359	28,992	14,237	37.49	35.42
1959-60	184,322	551,603	273,212	29,926	14,823	38.70	36.87
1960-1	187,225	581,614	290,099	31,065	15,495	40.17	38.54
1961-2	190,389	614,774	308,297	32,290	16,193	41.76	40.28
1962-3	193,822	649,745	327,793	33,523	16,912	43.35	42.07
1963-4	197,317	689,373	350,452	34,937	17,761	45.18	44.18
1964-5	200,874	729,106	374,615	36,297	18,649	46.94	46.39
1965-6	204,496	770,665	400,278	37,686	19,574	48.74	48.69
1966-7	208,183	814,946	425,625	39,146	20,445	50.62	50.86
1967-8	211,937	856,984	449,047	40,436	21,188	52.29	52.70
1968-9	215,758	895,335	470,303	41,497	21,798	53.67	54.22
1969-70	219,648	931,869	490,787	42,426	22,344	54.87	55.58
1970-1	223,608	971,998	512,414	43,469	22,916	56.22	57.00
1971-2	227,640	1,016,280	534,749	44,644	23,491	57.74	58.43

(Contd.)

217

Appendix Table 4(j) Contd.

	(1)	(2)	(3)	(4)	(5)	(6)	(7)
1972–3	231,744	1,067,027	559,994	46,043	24,164	59.54	60.11
1973–4	237,021	1,119,537	586,155	47,234	24,730	61.08	61.52
1974–5	243,520	1,168,004	609,391	47,963	25,024	62.03	62.25
1975–6	250,198	1,221,135	634,474	48,807	25,359	63.12	63.08
1976–7	257,059	1,277,293	663,132	49,689	25,797	64.26	64.17
1977–8	263,614	1,332,874	693,116	50,562	26,293	65.39	65.40
1978–9	269,845	1,395,618	726,861	51,719	26,936	66.88	67.00
1979–80	276,222	1,464,327	761,357	53,013	27,563	68.56	68.56
1980–1	282,751	1,534,180	795,773	54,259	28,144	70.17	70.01
1981–2	289,434	1,623,798	844,289	56,103	29,170	72.55	72.56
1982–3	296,688	1,724,212	900,462	58,115	30,350	75.16	75.50
1983–4	302,957	1,813,043	949,530	59,845	31,342	77.39	77.96
1984–5	307,784	1,898,637	996,338	61,687	32,371	79.78	80.52
1985–6	312,688	1,987,353	1,044,500	63,557	33,404	82.19	83.09
1986–7	317,671	2,086,408	1,097,103	65,678	34,536	84.94	85.91
1987–8	322,732	2,186,040	1,149,558	67,735	35,620	87.60	88.60
1988–9	329,197	2,281,050	1,199,669	69,291	36,442	89.61	90.65
1989–90	337,119	2,375,797	1,249,987	70,474	37,079	91.14	92.23
1990–1	345,231	2,476,187	1,304,104	71,726	37,775	92.76	93.96
1991–2	353,539	2,600,465	1,366,693	73,555	38,657	95.12	96.16
1992–3	362,047	2,733,819	1,429,606	75,510	39,487	97.65	98.22
1993–4	370,759	2,866,921	1,490,514	77,326	40,202	100.00	100.00
1994–5	376,705	3,048,878	1,576,701	80,935	41,855	104.67	104.11
1995–6	379,793	3,305,744	1,709,348	87,041	45,007	112.56	111.95
1996–7	382,907	3,589,134	1,856,526	93,734	48,485	121.22	120.60
1997–8	386,047	3,855,645	1,985,457	99,875	51,430	129.16	127.93
1998–9	389,212	4,098,275	2,097,664	105,297	53,895	136.17	134.06
1999–2000	392,403	4,324,404	2,202,232	110,203	56,122	142.52	139.60

Sources: Col. (1) from Table 3(b), Col. (1); Col. (2) from Table 4.4, Col. (9); Col. (3) from Table 4.3, Col. (9); Col. (4) = Col. (2)/ Col. (1); Col. (5) = Col. (3)/Col. (1); Cols (6) and (7) derived.

218

Appendix Table 4(k): Inventory Stock in Relation to NFCS at Current and Constant Prices

Year	At 1993-4 prices			At current prices			At 1993-4 prices mid-year values (Rs crore)		At current prices mid-year values (Rs crore)
	NFCS (Rs crore)	Inventory (Rs crore)	Inventory as % of NFCS	NFCS (Rs crore)	Inventory (Rs crore)	Inventory as % of NFCS	Inventory	Index	
	(1)	(2)	(3)	(4)	(5)	(6)	(7)	(8)	(9)
1949-50	366,034	36,603		14,932	1941		37,198	16.65	2034
1950-1	377,924	37,792		16,359	2127		38,350	17.17	2222
1951-2	389,082	38,908		17,830	2318		39,369	17.63	2352
1952-3	398,306	39,831		18,355	2386		40,368	18.07	2407
1953-4	409,054	40,905		18,673	2427		41,525	18.59	2457
1954-5	421,445	42,145		19,133	2487		42,939	19.22	2571
1955-6	437,337	43,734		20,419	2654		44,665	20.00	2800
1956-7	455,972	45,597		22,651	2945		46,587	20.86	3101
1957-8	475,763	47,576		25,056	3257		48,437	21.68	3352
1958-9	492,967	49,297		26,514	3447		50,165	22.46	3576
1959-60	510,330	51,033		28,500	3705		52,113	23.33	3881
1960-1	531,928	53,193		31,201	4056		54,198	24.26	4227
1961-2	552,029	55,203		33,832	4398		56,419	25.26	4579
1962-3	576,356	57,636		36,609	4759		58,967	26.40	4927
1963-4	602,986	60,299		39,194	5095		61,688	27.62	5375
1964-5	630,773	63,077		43,499	5655		64,561	28.90	6039
1965-6	660,449	66,045		49,416	6424		67,382	30.17	6824
1966-7	687,194	68,719		55,571	7224		70,019	31.35	7605
1967-8	713,176	71,318		61,423	7985		72,460	32.44	8341
1968-9	736,025	73,603		66,894	8696		74,838	33.50	9193
1969-70	760,725	76,073		74,540	9690		77,308	34.61	10,223
1970-1	785,429	78,543		82,737	10,756		79,835	35.74	11,364
1971-2	811,261	81,126		92,098	11,973		82,683	37.02	12,687
1972-3	842,408	84,241		103,084	13,401				

(Contd.)

Appendix Table 4(k) Contd.

	(1)	(2)	(3)	(4)	(5)	(6)	(7)	(8)	(9)
1973–4	870,632	87,063		123,110	16,004		85,652	38.35	14,703
1974–5	896,281	89,628		152,685	19,849		88,346	39.55	17,927
1975–6	929,024	92,902		172,747	22,457		91,265	40.86	21,153
1976–7	962,718	96,272		185,540	24,120		94,587	42.35	23,289
1977–8	998,557	99,856		200,230	26,030		98,064	43.90	25,075
1978–9	1,040,403	104,040	10.000	225,822	29,357	13.000	101,948	45.64	27,693
1979–80	1,078,594	108,470	10.057	270,436	35,157	13.109	106,255	47.57	32,257
1980–1	1,121,610	109,475	9.761	310,669	40,726	12.977	108,973	48.79	37,941
1981–2	1,188,209	124,029	10.438	381,653	49,528	12.461	116,752	52.27	45,127
1982–3	1,244,576	134,790	10.830	452,612	56,402	11.918	129,410	57.94	52,965
1983–4	1,295,600	138,363	10.679	520,828	62,072	11.949	136,577	61.15	59,237
1984–5	1,347,822	148,261	11.000	597,918	71,448	12.139	143,312	64.16	66,760
1985–6	1,402,628	165,674	11.812	693,136	84,143	11.955	156,968	70.27	77,796
1986–7	1,462,759	178,201	12.183	791,770	94,656	11.634	171,938	76.98	89,400
1987–8	1,517,223	182,449	12.025	890,329	103,579	1.222	180,325	80.73	99,118
1988–9	1,575,554	195,905	12.434	1,005,150	12,281	12.426	189,177	84.69	57,930
1989–90	1,634,309	205,350	12.565	1,144,039	142,157	12.413	200,628	89.82	77,219
1990–1	1,704,760	214,001	12.553	1,296,299	160,913	11.561	209,676	93.87	151,535
1991–2	1,781,854	213,336	11.973	1,534,234	177,371	11.912	213,669	95.66	169,142
1992–3	1,853,469	224,206	12.097	1,737,747	207,007	11.579	218,771	97.94	192,189
1993–4	1,921,762	222,523	11.579	1,921,762	222,523	11.572	223,365	100.00	214,765
1994–5	2,048,289	235,710	11.508	2,222,611	257,211	11.193	229,117	102.58	239,867
1995–6	2,212,699	257,364	11.631	2,696,837	301,861	9.834	246,537	110.37	279,536
1996–7	2,365,943	249,080	10.528	3,086,238	303,512	9.707	253,222	113.37	302,687
1997–8	2,499,312	263,557	10.545	3,424,020	332,364	9.159	256,319	114.75	317,938
1998–9	2,620,206	262,749	10.028	3,738,780	342,449	9.400	263,153	117.81	337,407
1999–2000	2,739,223	283,041	10.333	4,041,414	379,907		272,895	122.17	361,178

Sources: Cols (1) and (4) from *NAS 1950–1 to 1992–3*, pp. 157–67 and *NAS 2001*, p. 51; Cols (2) and (5) for the years 1980–1 to 1992–3 from *NAS 1950–1 to 1992–3*, pp. 161–7 and *NAS 2001*, p. 51; for 1950–1 to 1980–1 derived at 10 per cent of NFCS at constant prices and at 13 per cent of NFCS at current prices; Cols (7) and (9) are averages of two consecutive years from Cols (2) and (5) respectively; Col. (8) derived.

Appendix Table 4(l): Implicit Deflators for GFCF, 1950–1 to 1999–2000

Year	Gross fixed capital formation at 1993-4 prices (Rs crore)			Gross fixed capital formation (Rs crore)			Implicit deflator			Net fixed capital stock (Rs crore)		
	Construction	M & E	GFCF	Construction	Total M & E	Total GFCF	Construction	M & E GFCF	GFCF	At current Prices	At constant prices	Implicit deflator
	(1)	(2)	(3)	(4)	(5)	(6)	(7)	(8)	(9)	(10)	(11)	(12)
1950–1	15,913	6924	22,837	639	245	884	4.02	3.54	3.87	16,359	377,924	4.33
1951–2	16,452	7292	23,744	681	295	976	4.14	4.05	4.11	17,830	389,082	4.58
1952–3	14,849	6430	21,279	618	279	897	4.16	4.34	4.22	18,355	398,306	4.61
1953–4	15,458	5683	21,141	632	272	904	4.09	4.79	4.28	18,673	409,054	4.56
1954–5	17,603	5477	23,080	703	330	1033	3.99	6.03	4.48	19,133	421,445	4.54
1955–6	19,769	8649	28,418	818	481	1299	4.14	5.56	4.57	20,419	437,337	4.67
1956–7	23,271	11,581	34,852	1036	605	1641	4.45	5.22	4.71	22,651	455,972	4.97
1957–8	21,107	14,984	36,091	987	726	1713	4.68	4.85	4.75	25,056	475,763	5.27
1958–9	22,683	9054	31,737	1098	630	1728	4.84	6.96	5.44	26,514	492,967	5.38
1959–60	24,028	10,100	34,128	1199	695	1894	4.99	6.88	5.55	28,500	510,330	5.58
1960–1	25,964	11,569	37,533	1351	832	2183	5.20	7.19	5.82	31,201	531,928	5.87
1961–2	26,923	12,707	39,630	1473	967	2440	5.47	7.61	6.16	33,832	552,029	6.13
1962–3	27,490	14,841	42,331	1564	1134	2698	5.69	7.64	6.37	36,609	576,356	6.35
1963–4	30,925	16,056	46,981	1789	1400	3189	5.78	8.72	6.79	39,194	602,986	6.50
1964–5	33,855	18,350	52,205	2057	1649	3706	6.08	8.99	7.10	43,499	630,773	6.90
1965–6	36,480	19,079	55,559	2384	1801	4185	6.54	9.44	7.53	49,416	660,449	7.48
1966–7	39,059	15,437	54,496	2742	1917	4659	7.02	12.42	8.55	55,571	687,914	8.08
1967–8	42,389	14,914	57,303	3140	2007	5147	7.41	13.46	8.98	61,423	713,176	8.61
1968–9	42,970	15,447	58,417	3370	2073	5443	7.84	13.42	9.32	66,894	736,025	9.09
1969–70	43,971	16,171	60,142	3714	2257	5971	8.45	13.96	9.93	74,540	760,725	9.80
1970–1	44,334	16,155	60,489	4000	2383	6383	9.02	14.75	10.55	82,737	785,429	10.53
1971–2	44,647	18,713	63,360	4317	2856	7173	9.67	15.26	11.32	92,098	811,261	11.35
1972–3	46,404	20,032	66,436	4825	3408	8233	10.40	17.01	12.39	103,084	842,408	12.24

(Contd.)

221

Appendix Table 4(I) Contd.

	(1)	(2)	(3)	(4)	(5)	(6)	(7)	(8)	(9)	(10)	(11)	(12)
1973-4	41,880	22,428	64,308	5020	4166	9186	11.99	18.57	14.28	123,110	870,632	14.14
1974-5	40,553	21,762	62,315	5886	5260	11,146	14.51	24.17	17.89	152,685	896,281	17.04
1975-6	47,022	22,232	69,254	7414	6087	13,501	15.77	27.38	19.49	172,747	929,024	18.59
1976-7	52,527	25,300	77,827	8586	6913	15,499	16.35	27.32	19.91	185,540	962,718	19.27
1977-8	58,887	26,878	85,765	10,047	7390	17,437	17.06	27.49	20.33	200,230	998,557	20.05
1978-9	56,178	29,215	85,393	10,422	8697	19,119	18.55	29.77	22.39	225,822	1,040,403	21.71
1979-80	52,013	29,990	82,003	11,065	10,520	21,585	21.27	35.08	26.32	270,436	1,078,594	25.07
1980-1	56,963	33,717	90,680	13,787	12,831	26,618	24.20	38.05	29.35	310,669	1,121,610	27.70
1981-2	60,551	36,979	97,530	16,567	15,364	31,931	27.36	41.55	32.74	381,653	1,188,209	32.12
1982-3	58,727	41,436	100,163	18,497	17,741	36,238	31.50	42.82	36.18	452,612	1,244,576	36.37
1983-4	60,569	44,437	105,006	21,096	20,273	41,369	34.83	45.62	39.40	520,828	1,295,600	40.20
1984-5	61,469	49,367	110,836	24,491	23,641	48,132	39.84	47.89	43.43	597,918	1,347,822	44.36
1985-6	65,164	52,420	117,584	29,581	27,730	57,311	45.39	52.90	48.74	693,136	1,402,628	49.42
1986-7	65,774	58,309	124,083	33,002	32,537	65,539	50.17	55.80	52.82	791,770	1,462,759	54.13
1987-8	68,199	67,230	135,429	37,618	38,391	76,009	55.16	57.10	56.12	890,329	1,517,223	58.68
1988-9	73,887	72,544	146,431	44,747	46,514	91,261	60.56	64.12	62.32	1,005,150	1,575,554	63.80
1989-90	76,858	79,991	156,849	51,773	57,106	108,879	67.36	71.39	69.42	1,144,039	1,634,039	70.01
1990-1	83,768	86,660	170,428	62,722	67,949	130,671	74.88	78.41	76.67	1,296,299	1,704,760	76.04
1991-2	87,287	80,243	167,530	72,638	71,223	143,861	83.22	88.76	85.87	1,534,234	1,781,854	86.10
1992-3	89,526	88,456	177,982	81,919	86,054	167,973	91.50	97.28	94.38	1,737,747	1,853,469	93.76
1993-4	87,625	96,668	184,293	87,625	96,668	184,293	100.00	100.00	100.00	1,921,762	1,921,762	100.00
1994-5	92,920	113,136	206,056	100,369	121,867	222,236	108.02	107.72	107.85	2,222,611	2,048,289	108.51
1995-6	98,023	147,745	245,768	121,210	168,199	289,409	123.65	113.84	117.76	2,696,837	2,212,699	121.88
1996-7	100,166	149,479	249,645	132,792	179,074	311,866	132.57	119.80	124.92	3,086,238	2,365,943	130.44
1997-8	113,019	142,109	255,128	157,876	172,899	330,775	139.69	121.67	129.65	3,424,020	2,499,312	137.00
1998-9	121,218	155,945	277,163	180,132	193,076	373,208	148.60	123.81	134.65	3,738,780	2,620,206	:42.69
1999-2000	131,003	170,105	301,108	203,351	212,749	416,100	155.23	125.07	138.19	4,041,414	2,739,223	147.54

Sources: Cols (1) to (6) and Cols (10) and (11) from *NAS 1950–1 to 1992–3* and *NAS 2001. Rest of the Cols derived.

222

Appendix Table 4(m): Net Fixed Capital Stock at Current Prices for the Whole Economy, 1949-50 to 1999-2000

As on 31 March	NFCS total at 1993-4 prices (Rs crore)			Implicit deflators		Estimated NFCS at current prices (Rs crore)			NFCS at current prices (Rs crore)	
	Structures	Equipment	Total	Structures	Equipment	Structures $(1) \times (4)/100$	Equipment $(2) \times (5)/100$	Total $(6) + (7)$	CSO'S total	Adjustment factor $(9)/(8)$
	(1)	(2)	(3)	(4)	(5)	(6)	(7)	(8)	(9)	(10)
1949-50	319,218	46,816	366,034	4.16	3.53	13,279	1653	14,932	16,359	1.0954
1950-1	327,235	50,689	377,924	4.02	3.54	13,140	1794	14,934	17,830	1.1107
1951-2	332,530	56,552	389,082	4.14	4.05	13,764	2288	16,052	18,355	1.1003
1952-3	339,478	58,828	398,306	4.16	4.34	14,129	2553	16,681	18,673	1.0896
1953-4	349,772	59,282	409,054	4.09	4.79	14,300	2837	17,138	19,133	1.0604
1954-5	361,812	59,633	421,445	3.99	6.03	14,449	3593	18,042	20,419	1.0725
1955-6	371,139	66,198	437,337	4.14	5.56	15,357	3681	19,038	22,651	1.0851
1956-7	381,408	74,564	455,972	4.45	5.22	16,980	3895	20,875	25,056	1.1187
1957-8	386,919	88,844	475,763	4.68	4.85	18,093	4305	22,398	26,514	1.0284
1958-9	402,359	90,608	492,967	4.84	6.96	19,477	6305	25,781	28,500	1.0481
1959-60	419,029	91,301	510,330	4.99	6.88	20,910	6283	27,192	31,201	1.0568
1960-1	439,112	92,816	531,928	5.20	7.19	22,849	6675	29,524	33,832	1.0503
1961-2	458,153	93,876	552,029	5.47	7.61	25,066	7144	32,210	36,609	1.0549
1962-3	478,330	98,026	576,356	5.69	7.64	27,214	7490	34,704	39,194	1.0355
1963-4	501,871	101,115	602,986	5.78	8.72	29,033	8817	37,850	43,499	1.0501
1964-5	524,361	106,412	630,773	6.08	8.99	31,860	9563	41,422	49,416	1.0658
1965-6	550,198	110,251	660,449	6.54	9.44	35,956	10,407	46,363	55,571	1.0285
1966-7	579,975	107,219	687,194	7.02	12.42	40,715	13,315	54,030	61,423	1.0391
1967-8	609,293	103,883	713,176	7.41	13.46	45,134	13,980	59,114	66,894	1.0549
1968-9	634,005	102,020	736,025	7.84	13.42	49,723	13,691	63,414	74,540	1.0681
1969-70	660,271	100,454	760,725	8.45	13.96	55,770	14,020	69,790	82,737	1.0839
1970-1	690,009	95,420	785,429	9.02	14.75	62,255	14,075	76,331	92,098	1.1030
1971-2	720,843	90,418	811,261	9.67	15.26	69,700	13,800	83,499		

(Contd.)

223

Appendix Table 4(m) Contd.

	(1)	(2)	(3)	(4)	(5)	(6)	(7)	(8)	(9)	(10)
1972-3	757,956	84,452	842,408	10.40	17.01	78,811	14,368	93,178	103,084	1.1063
1973-4	781,396	89,236	870,632	11.99	18.57	93,663	16,576	110,239	123,110	1.1168
1974-5	804,814	91,467	896,281	14.51	24.17	116,813	22,108	138,922	152,685	1.0991
1975-6	836,788	92,236	929,024	15.77	27.38	131,937	25,254	157,191	172,747	1.0990
1976-7	868,269	94,449	962,718	16.35	27.32	141,926	25,807	167,734	185,540	1.1062
1977-8	902,924	95,633	998,557	17.06	27.49	154,052	26,294	180,346	200,230	1.1103
1978-9	941,655	98,748	1,040,403	18.55	29.77	174,693	29,396	204,090	225,822	1.1065
1979-80	978,050	100,544	1,078,594	21.27	35.08	208,066	35,269	243,335	270,436	1.1114
1980-1	1,015,871	105,739	1,121,610	24.20	38.05	245,876	40,239	286,115	310,669	1.0858
1981-2	1,068,143	120,066	1,188,209	27.36	41.55	292,248	49,885	342,133	381,653	1.1155
1982-3	1,106,276	138,300	1,244,576	31.50	42.82	348,439	59,214	407,653	452,612	1.1103
1983-4	1,138,261	157,339	1,295,600	34.83	45.62	396,453	71,781	468,234	520,828	1.1123
1984-5	1,168,506	179,316	1,347,822	39.84	47.89	465,566	85,871	551,437	597,918	1.0843
1985-6	1,200,123	202,505	1,402,628	45.39	52.90	544,792	107,124	651,917	693,136	1.0632
1986-7	1,235,142	227,617	1,462,759	50.17	55.80	619,730	127,013	746,743	791,770	1.0603
1987-8	1,260,672	256,551	1,517,223	55.16	57.10	695,376	146,501	841,877	890,329	1.0576
1988-9	1,290,385	285,169	1,575,554	60.56	64.12	781,475	182,846	964,321	1,005,150	1.0423
1989-90	1,316,427	317,882	1,634,309	67.36	71.39	886,770	226,937	1,113,708	1,144,039	1.0272
1990-1	1,351,344	353,416	1,704,760	74.88	78.41	1,011,830	277,109	1,288,939	1,296,299	1.0057
1991-2	1,403,741	378,113	1,781,854	83.22	88.76	1,168,157	335,610	1,503,767	1,534,234	1.0203
1992-3	1,449,598	403,871	1,853,469	91.50	97.28	1,326,426	392,904	1,719,330	1,737,747	1.0107
1993-4	1,489,151	432,611	1,921,762	100.00	100.00	1,489,151	432,611	1,921,762	1,921,762	1.0000
1994-5	1,564,234	484,055	2,048,289	108.02	107.72	1,689,632	521,410	2,211,043	2,222,611	1.0052
1995-6	1,645,576	567,123	2,212,699	123.65	113.84	2,034,831	645,637	2,680,467	2,696,837	1.0061
1996-7	1,724,578	641,365	2,365,943	132.57	119.80	2,286,306	768,348	3,054,654	3,086,238	1.0103
1997-8	1,808,004	691,308	2,499,312	139.69	121.67	2,525,597	841,090	3,366,687	3,424,020	1.0170
1998-9	1,879,063	741,143	2,620,206	148.60	123.81	2,792,319	917,612	3,709,931	3,738,780	1.0078
1999-2000	1,949,173	790,050	2,739,223	155.23	125.07	3,025,627	988,110	4,013,737	4,041,414	1.0069

(Cols Contd.)

Appendix Table 4(m) Contd.: Net Fixed Capital Stock at Current Prices for the Whole Economy, 1949-50 to 1999-2000

As on 31 March	Adjusted NFCS at current prices (Rs crore)			% distribution of NFCS		Implicit deflators after adjustment		
	Structures	Equipment	NFCS	Structures	Equipment	Structures	Equipment	Total NFCS
	(11)	(12)	(13)	(14)	(15)	(16)	(17)	(18)
1949–50	13,279	1653	14,932	88.93	11.07	4.40	3.88	4.33
1950–1	14,394	1965	16,359	87.99	12.01	4.60	4.49	4.58
1951–2	15,289	2541	17,830	85.75	14.25	4.58	4.77	4.61
1952–3	15,546	2809	18,355	84.70	15.30	4.45	5.21	4.56
1953–4	15,581	3092	18,673	83.44	16.56	4.24	6.39	4.54
1954–5	15,323	3810	19,133	80.09	19.91	4.44	5.96	4.67
1955–6	16,471	3948	20,419	80.66	19.34	4.83	5.67	4.97
1956–7	18,424	4227	22,651	81.34	18.66	5.23	5.42	5.27
1957–8	20,240	4816	25,056	80.78	19.22	4.98	7.16	5.38
1958–9	20,030	6484	26,514	75.55	24.45	5.23	7.21	5.58
1959–60	21,915	6585	28,500	76.90	23.10	5.50	7.60	5.87
1960–1	24,147	7054	31,201	77.39	22.61	5.75	7.99	6.13
1961–2	26,328	7504	33,832	77.82	22.18	6.00	8.06	6.35
1962–3	28,708	7901	36,609	78.42	21.58	5.99	9.03	6.50
1963–4	30,064	9130	39,194	76.71	23.29	6.38	9.44	6.90
1964–5	33,457	10,042	43,499	76.91	23.09	6.97	10.06	7.48
1965–6	38,323	11,093	49,416	77.55	22.45	7.22	12.77	8.09
1966–7	41,877	13,694	55,571	75.36	24.64	7.70	13.98	8.61
1967–8	46,897	14,526	61,423	76.35	23.65	8.27	14.16	9.09
1968–9	52,452	14,442	66,894	78.41	21.59	9.02	14.91	9.80
1969–70	59,565	14,975	74,540	79.91	20.09	9.78	15.99	10.53
1970–1	67,480	15,257	82,737	81.56	18.44	10.66	16.83	11.35
1971–2	76,877	15,221	92,098	83.47	16.53	11.50	18.82	12.24
1972–3	87,189	15,895	103,084	84.58	15.42	13.39	20.74	14.14
1973–4	104,599	18,511	123,110	84.96	15.04	15.95	26.57	17.04
1974–5	128,387	24,298	152,685	84.09	15.91			

(Contd.)

225

Appendix Table 4(m) Contd.

	(11)	(12)	(13)	(14)	(15)	(16)	(17)	(18)
1975–6	144,994	27,753	172,747	83.93	16.07	17.33	30.09	18.59
1976–7	156,993	28,547	185,540	84.61	15.39	18.08	30.22	19.27
1977–8	171,037	29,193	200,230	85.42	14.58	18.94	30.53	20.05
1978–9	193,296	32,526	225,822	85.60	14.40	20.53	32.94	21.71
1979–80	231,239	39,197	270,436	85.51	14.49	23.64	38.99	25.07
1980–1	266,977	43,692	310,669	85.94	14.06	26.28	41.32	27.70
1981–2	326,006	55,647	381,653	85.42	14.58	30.52	46.35	32.12
1982–3	386,868	65,744	452,612	85.47	14.53	34.97	47.54	36.37
1983–4	440,984	79,844	520,828	84.67	15.33	38.74	50.75	40.20
1984–5	504,809	93,109	597,918	84.43	15.57	43.20	51.92	44.36
1985–6	579,238	113,898	693,136	83.57	16.43	48.26	56.24	49.42
1986–7	657,099	134,671	791,770	82.99	17.01	53.20	59.17	54.13
1987–8	735,397	154,932	890,329	82.60	17.40	58.33	60.39	58.68
1988–9	814,562	190,588	1,005,150	81.04	18.96	63.13	66.83	63.80
1989–90	910,921	233,118	1,144,039	79.62	20.38	69.20	73.33	70.00
1990–1	1,017,608	278,691	1,296,299	78.50	21.50	75.30	78.86	76.04
1991–2	1,191,825	342,409	1,534,234	77.68	22.32	84.90	90.56	86.10
1992–3	1,340,635	397,112	1,737,747	77.15	22.85	92.48	98.33	93.76
1993–4	1,489,151	432,611	1,921,762	77.49	22.51	100.00	100.00	100.00
1994–5	1,698,473	524,138	2,222,611	76.42	23.58	108.58	108.28	108.51
1995–6	2,047,257	649,580	2,696,837	75.91	24.09	124.41	114.54	121.88
1996–7	2,309,946	776,292	3,086,238	74.85	25.15	133.94	121.04	130.44
1997–8	2,568,606	855,414	3,424,020	75.02	24.98	142.07	123.74	137.00
1998–9	2,814,032	924,748	3,738,780	75.27	24.73	149.76	124.77	142.69
1999–2000	3,046,491	994,923	4,041,414	75.38	24.62	156.30	125.93	147.54

Sources: Cols (1), (2), and (3) from Appendix Table 4(h), Cols (1) to (3); Cols (4) and (5) from Appendix Table 4(e), Cols (7) and (8); Cols 6 and 7 derived as indicated; Col. (8) = Col. (6) + Col. (7); Col. (9) from *NAS 1950–1 to 1992–3*, pp. 46–56 and *NAS 2001*, p. 50; Col. (10) = Col. (9)/Col. (8). Col. (11) = Col. (6) × Col. (10); Col. (12) = Col. (7) × Col. (10); Col. (13) = Col. (11) + Col. (12); Cols (14) and (15) derived; Col. (16) = [Col. (11)/Col. (1)] × 100; Col. (17) = [Col. (12)/Col. (2)] × 100; Col. (18) = [Col. (13)/Col. (3)] × 100.

226

Appendix Table 4(n): Net Fixed Capital Stock at Current Prices for the Whole Economy and Non-residential Sector, 1950–1 to 1999–2000

As on 31 March	NFCS of whole economy (Rs crore)			NFCS of dwellings (Rs crore)	NFCS of non-residential sector (Rs crore)		
	Structures	Equipment	Total		Structures (1) – (4)	Equipment = (2)	Total (5) + (6)
	(1)	(2)	(3)	(4)	(5)	(6)	(7)
1949–50	13,279	1653	14,932	8813	4466	1653	6119
1950–1	14,394	1965	16,359	8604	5790	1965	7755
1951–2	15,289	2541	17,830	8970	6319	2541	8860
1952–3	15,546	2809	18,355	9134	6412	2809	9221
1953–4	15,581	3092	18,673	9125	6457	3092	9548
1954–5	15,323	3810	19,133	9122	6201	3810	10,011
1955–6	16,471	3948	20,419	9366	7105	3948	11,053
1956–7	18,424	4227	22,651	9947	8478	4227	12,705
1957–8	20,240	4816	25,056	10,604	9637	4816	14,452
1958–9	20,030	6484	26,514	11,037	8993	6484	15,477
1959–60	21,915	6585	28,500	11,526	10,389	6585	16,974
1960–1	24,147	7054	31,201	12,299	11,848	7054	18,902
1961–2	26,328	7504	33,832	13,162	13,166	7504	20,670
1962–3	28,708	7901	36,609	13,831	14,877	7901	22,778
1963–4	30,064	9130	39,194	14,225	15,839	9130	24,969
1964–5	33,457	10,042	43,499	14,902	18,555	10,042	28,597
1965–6	38,323	11,093	49,416	16,066	22,257	11,093	33,350
1966–7	41,877	13,694	55,571	17,366	24,511	13,694	38,205
1967–8	46,897	14,526	61,423	18,566	28,331	14,526	42,857
1968–9	52,452	14,442	66,894	20,034	32,418	14,442	46,860
1969–70	59,565	14,975	74,540	22,029	37,537	14,975	52,511
1970–1	67,480	15,257	82,737	23,322	44,159	15,257	59,415
1971–2	76,877	15,221	92,098	25,110	51,767	15,221	66,988

(Contd.)

227

Appendix Table 4(n) Contd.

	(1)	(2)	(3)	(4)	(5)	(6)	(7)
1972–3	87,189	15,895	103,084	27,599	59,590	15,895	75,485
1973–4	104,599	18,511	123,110	32,477	72,122	18,511	90,633
1974–5	128,387	24,298	152,685	41,496	86,891	24,298	111,189
1975–6	144,994	27,753	172,747	45,743	99,251	27,753	127,004
1976–7	156,993	28,547	185,540	47,401	109,592	28,547	138,139
1977–8	171,037	29,193	200,230	49,858	121,179	29,193	150,372
1978–9	193,296	32,526	225,822	56,104	137,191	32,526	169,718
1979–80	231,239	39,197	270,436	67,500	163,738	39,197	202,936
1980–1	266,977	43,692	310,669	78,489	188,488	43,692	232,180
1981–2	326,006	55,647	381,653	96,667	229,339	55,647	284,986
1982–3	386,868	65,744	452,612	114,428	272,439	65,744	338,184
1983–4	440,984	79,844	520,828	132,970	308,014	79,844	387,858
1984–5	504,809	93,109	597,918	151,674	353,134	93,109	446,244
1985–6	579,238	113,898	693,136	170,251	408,987	113,898	522,885
1986–7	657,099	134,671	791,770	194,560	462,539	134,671	597,210
1987–8	735,397	154,932	890,329	216,326	519,070	154,932	674,003
1988–9	814,562	190,588	1,005,150	235,813	578,750	190,588	769,337
1989–90	910,921	233,118	1,144,039	257,172	653,749	233,118	886,867
1990–1	1,017,608	278,691	1,296,299	280,700	736,908	278,691	1,015,599
1991–2	1,191,825	342,409	1,534,234	328,501	863,324	342,409	1,205,734
1992–3	1,340,635	397,112	1,737,747	361,092	979,542	397,112	1,376,655
1993–4	1,489,151	432,611	1,921,762	400,157	1,088,994	432,611	1,521,605
1994–5	1,698,473	524,138	2,222,611	444,872	1,253,601	524,138	1,777,739
1995–6	2,047,257	649,580	2,696,837	545,469	1,501,788	649,580	2,151,368
1996–7	2,309,946	776,292	3,086,238	600,058	1,709,888	776,292	2,486,180
1997–8	2,568,606	855,414	3,424,020	651,361	1,917,245	855,414	2,772,659
1998–9	2,814,032	924,748	3,738,780	708,361	2,105,672	924,748	3,030,419
1999–2000	3,046,491	994,923	4,041,414	765,072	2,281,419	994,923	3,276,342

(Cols Contd.)

Appendix Table 4(n) Contd.: Net Fixed Capital Stock at Current Prices for the Whole Economy and Non-residential Sector, 1950-1 to 1999-2000

Year	% distribution of NFCS non-residential sector		Mid-year values NFCS whole economy (Rs crore)			Mid-year values NFCS for non-residential sector (Rs crore)		
	Structures	Equipment	Structures	Equipment	Total	Structures	Equipment	Total
	(8)	(9)	(10)	(11)	(12)	(13)	(14)	(15)
1949-50	72.99	27.01						
1950-1	74.66	25.34	13,837	1809	15,646	5128	1809	6937
1951-2	71.32	28.68	14,842	2253	17,095	6055	2253	8307
1952-3	69.54	30.46	15,418	2675	18,093	6365	2675	9040
1953-4	67.62	32.38	15,564	2950	18,514	6434	2950	9385
1954-5	61.94	38.06	15,452	3451	18,903	6329	3451	9780
1955-6	64.28	35.72	15,897	3879	19,776	6653	3879	10,532
1956-7	66.73	33.27	17,447	4088	21,535	7791	4088	11,879
1957-8	66.68	33.32	19,332	4521	23,854	9057	4521	13,578
1958-9	58.11	41.89	20,135	5650	25,785	9315	5650	14,965
1959-60	61.21	38.79	20,973	6534	27,507	9691	6534	16,225
1960-1	62.68	37.32	23,031	6820	29,851	11,118	6820	17,938
1961-2	63.70	36.30	25,238	7279	32,517	12,507	7279	19,786
1962-3	65.31	34.69	27,518	7702	35,221	14,021	7702	21,724
1963-4	63.43	36.57	29,386	8516	37,902	15,358	8516	23,873
1964-5	64.88	35.12	31,761	9586	41,347	17,197	9586	26,783
1965-6	66.74	33.26	35,890	10,567	46,458	20,406	10,567	30,973
1966-7	64.16	35.84	40,100	12,394	52,494	23,384	12,394	35,777
1967-8	66.11	33.89	44,387	14,110	58,497	26,421	14,110	40,531
1968-9	69.18	30.82	49,674	14,484	64,159	30,375	14,484	44,859
1969-70	71.48	28.52	56,008	14,709	70,717	34,977	14,709	49,686
1970-1	74.32	25.68	63,523	15,116	78,639	40,848	15,116	55,963
1971-2	77.28	22.72	72,179	15,239	87,418	47,963	15,239	63,202
1972-3	78.94	21.06	82,033	15,558	97,591	55,678	15,558	71,236

(Contd.)

229

Appendix Table 4(n) Contd.

	(8)	(9)	(10)	(11)	(12)	(13)	(14)	(15)
1973-4	79.58	20.42	95,894	17,203	113,097	65,856	17,203	83,059
1974-5	78.15	21.85	116,493	21,405	137,898	79,506	21,405	100,911
1975-6	78.15	21.85	136,690	26,026	162,716	93,071	26,026	119,096
1976-7	79.33	20.67	150,994	28,150	179,144	104,421	28,150	132,571
1977-8	80.59	19.41	164,015	28,870	192,885	115,385	28,870	144,255
1978-9	80.83	19.17	182,166	30,860	213,026	129,185	30,860	160,045
1979-80	80.68	19.32	212,267	35,862	248,129	150,465	35,862	186,327
1980-1	81.18	18.82	249,108	41,445	290,553	176,113	41,445	217,558
1981-2	80.47	19.53	296,491	49,670	346,161	208,913	49,670	258,583
1982-3	80.56	19.44	356,437	60,696	417,133	250,889	60,696	311,585
1983-4	79.41	20.59	413,926	72,794	486,720	290,227	72,794	363,021
1984-5	79.13	20.87	472,896	86,477	559,373	330,574	86,477	417,051
1985-6	78.22	21.78	542,023	103,504	645,527	381,061	103,504	484,564
1986-7	77.45	22.55	618,169	124,284	742,453	435,763	124,284	560,047
1987-8	77.01	22.99	696,248	144,802	841,050	490,804	144,802	635,606
1988-9	75.23	24.77	774,980	172,760	947,740	548,910	172,760	721,670
1989-90	73.71	26.29	862,742	211,853	1,074,595	616,250	211,853	828,102
1990-1	72.56	27.44	964,264	255,905	1,220,169	695,329	255,905	951,233
1991-2	71.60	28.40	1,104,716	310,550	1,415,267	800,116	310,550	1,110,666
1992-3	71.15	28.85	1,266,230	369,761	1,635,991	921,433	369,761	1,291,194
1993-4	71.57	28.43	1,414,893	414,862	1,829,755	1,034,268	414,862	1,449,130
1994-5	70.52	29.48	1,593,812	478,375	2,072,187	1,171,297	478,375	1,649,672
1995-6	69.81	30.19	1,872,865	586,859	2,459,724	1,377,695	586,859	1,964,554
1996-7	68.78	31.22	2,178,602	712,936	2,891,538	1,605,838	712,936	2,318,774
1997-8	69.15	30.85	2,439,276	815,853	3,255,129	1,813,567	815,853	2,629,420
1998-9	69.48	30.52	2,691,319	890,081	3,581,400	2,011,459	890,081	2,901,539
1999-2000	69.63	30.37	2,930,262	959,835	3,890,097	2,193,545	959,835	3,153,381

Sources: Cols (1) to (3) from Appendix Table 4(m), Col. (6) to (8); Col. (4) from Appendix Table 4(g), Col. (4); Col. (5) = Col. (1) − (4); Col. (6); = Col. (6); = Col. (5) + Col. (6); Cols (8) and 9 derived. Cols (10) to (12) = average of two consecutive values of Cols (1) to (3) respectively; Cols (13) to (15) = average of two consecutive values of Cols (5) to (7) respectively.

230

Appendix Table 4(o): Gross Fixed Capital Stock at Current Prices, 1950–1 to 1999–2000

As on 31 March	GFCS whole economy at 1993–4 prices (Rs crore)			Adjusted implicit deflators			GFCS whole economy at current prices (Rs crore)			% distribution of GFCS at current prices	
	Structures	Equipment	Total	Structures	Equipment	Total GFCS	Structures	Equipment	Total	Structures	Equipment
	(1)	(2)	(3)	(4)	(5)	(6)	(7)	(8)	(9)	(10)	(11)
1949–50	803,586	161,525	965,111	4.16	3.53	4.05	33,429	5702	39,131	85.43	14.57
1950–1	812,195	164,737	976,932	4.40	3.88	4.33	35,726	6385	42,112	84.84	15.16
1951–2	781,975	164,911	946,886	4.60	4.49	4.58	35,953	7410	43,363	82.91	17.09
1952–3	771,966	166,043	938,009	4.58	4.77	4.61	35,352	7928	43,280	81.68	18.32
1953–4	771,288	167,078	938,365	4.45	5.21	4.56	34,359	8713	43,072	79.77	20.23
1954–5	772,402	168,138	940,540	4.24	6.39	4.54	32,711	10,743	43,454	75.28	24.72
1955–6	766,898	175,014	941,913	4.44	5.96	4.67	34,034	10,439	44,473	76.53	23.47
1956–7	759,263	183,324	942,586	4.83	5.67	4.97	36,677	10,392	47,069	77.92	22.08
1957–8	749,517	199,505	949,022	5.23	5.42	5.27	39,209	10,814	50,022	78.38	21.62
1958–9	761,867	207,010	968,877	4.98	7.16	5.38	37,927	14,814	52,741	71.91	28.09
1959–60	776,111	213,809	989,919	5.23	7.21	5.58	40,591	15,420	56,011	72.47	27.53
1960–1	798,054	222,995	1,021,049	5.50	7.60	5.87	43,885	16,948	60,833	72.14	27.86
1961–2	819,249	231,771	1,051,020	5.75	7.99	6.13	47,079	18,526	65,605	71.76	28.24
1962–3	843,496	244,530	1,088,026	6.00	8.06	6.35	50,624	19,710	70,334	71.98	28.02
1963–4	871,470	256,445	1,127,916	5.99	9.03	6.50	52,205	23,155	75,360	69.27	30.73
1964–5	895,120	269,372	1,164,492	6.38	9.44	6.90	57,113	25,420	82,534	69.20	30.80
1965–6	925,990	282,512	1,208,502	6.97	10.06	7.48	64,499	28,424	92,923	69.41	30.59
1966–7	961,963	288,778	1,250,742	7.22	12.77	8.09	69,458	36,884	106,342	65.32	34.68
1967–8	996,595	293,917	1,290,512	7.70	13.98	8.61	76,708	41,098	117,806	65.11	34.89
1968–9	1,027,437	300,744	1,328,181	8.27	14.16	9.09	85,000	42,575	127,575	66.63	33.37
1969–70	1,058,942	307,141	1,366,083	9.02	14.91	9.80	95,531	45,786	141,316	67.60	32.40
1970–1	1,099,229	311,973	1,411,202	9.78	15.99	10.53	107,501	49,881	157,382	68.31	31.69
1971–2	1,142,293	316,689	1,458,982	10.66	16.83	11.35	121,824	53,311	175,135	69.56	30.44
1972–3	1,197,447	322,032	1,519,479	11.50	18.82	12.24	137,744	60,611	198,355	69.44	30.56

(Contd.)

Appendix Table 4(o) Contd.

	(1)	(2)	(3)	(4)	(5)	(6)	(7)	(8)	(9)	(10)	(11)
1973–4	1,237,562	337,371	1,574,933	13.39	20.74	14.14	165,662	69,984	235,646	70.30	29.70
1974–5	1,279,807	351,153	1,630,961	15.95	26.57	17.04	204,159	93,285	297,444	68.64	31.36
1975–6	1,332,514	364,132	1,696,646	17.33	30.09	18.59	230,891	109,564	340,455	67.82	32.18
1976–7	1,381,566	376,497	1,758,063	18.08	30.22	19.27	249,803	113,796	363,599	68.70	31.30
1977–8	1,434,364	387,563	1,821,927	18.94	30.53	20.05	271,705	118,307	390,013	69.67	30.33
1978–9	1,496,292	402,841	1,899,132	20.53	32.94	21.71	307,147	132,691	439,838	69.83	30.17
1979–80	1,560,439	418,520	1,978,959	23.64	38.99	25.07	368,932	163,161	532,093	69.34	30.66
1980–1	1,625,178	436,642	2,061,820	26.28	41.32	27.70	427,106	180,424	607,530	70.30	29.70
1981–2	1,712,105	468,493	2,180,598	30.52	46.35	32.12	522,548	217,133	739,681	70.65	29.35
1982–3	1,780,095	502,502	2,282,597	34.97	47.54	36.37	622,504	238,877	861,381	72.27	27.73
1983–4	1,840,198	537,352	2,377,550	38.74	50.75	40.20	712,928	272,686	985,615	72.33	27.67
1984–5	1,898,186	576,135	2,474,321	43.20	51.92	44.36	820,039	299,157	1,119,196	73.27	26.73
1985–6	1,958,903	618,579	2,577,482	48.26	56.24	49.42	945,463	347,916	1,293,379	73.10	26.90
1986–7	2,026,796	667,007	2,693,803	53.20	59.17	54.13	1,078,261	394,639	1,472,900	73.21	26.79
1987–8	2,079,635	718,883	2,798,519	58.33	60.39	58.68	1,213,128	434,137	1,647,265	73.65	26.35
1988–9	2,137,086	772,698	2,909,784	63.13	66.83	63.80	1,349,047	516,418	1,865,465	72.32	27.68
1989–90	2,188,032	831,602	3,019,635	69.20	73.33	70.00	1,514,041	609,854	2,123,895	71.29	28.71
1990–1	2,250,786	898,013	3,148,799	75.30	78.86	76.04	1,694,918	708,141	2,403,059	70.53	29.47
1991–2	2,344,541	963,924	3,308,465	84.90	90.56	86.10	1,990,596	872,905	2,863,501	69.52	30.48
1992–3	2,426,621	1,030,309	3,456,930	92.48	98.33	93.76	2,244,216	1,013,068	3,257,285	68.90	31.10
1993–4	2,505,245	1,104,494	3,609,739	100.00	100.00	100.00	2,505,245	1,104,494	3,609,739	69.40	30.60
1994–5	2,643,135	1,221,838	3,864,973	108.58	108.28	108.51	2,869,961	1,323,017	4,192,978	68.45	31.55
1995–6	2,791,382	1,381,177	4,172,559	124.41	114.54	121.88	3,472,753	1,581,991	5,054,744	68.70	31.30
1996–7	2,938,037	1,539,192	4,477,229	133.94	121.04	130.44	3,935,286	1,862,999	5,798,285	67.87	32.13
1997–8	3,084,307	1,674,420	4,758,727	142.07	123.74	137.00	4,381,833	2,071,901	6,453,734	67.90	32.10
1998–9	3,208,216	1,806,870	5,015,086	149.76	124.77	142.69	4,804,535	2,254,488	7,059,023	68.06	31.94
1999–2000	3,325,375	1,938,172	5,263,547	156.30	125.93	147.54	5,197,449	2,440,772	7,638,220	68.05	31.95

(Cols Contd.)

Appendix Table 4(o) Contd.: Gross Fixed Capital Stock at Current Prices, 1950–1 to 1999–2000

As on 31 March	GFCS dwellings (Rs crore)	GFCS at current prices Non-residential sector (Rs crore)			Non-residential sector (Mid-year values) (Rs crore)			Whole economy (Mid-year values) (Rs crore)		
		Structures	Equipment	Total	Structures	Equipment	Total	Structures	Equipment	Total
	(12)	(13)	(14)	(15)	(16)	(17)	(18)	(19)	(20)	(21)
1949–50	23,809	9620	5702	15,322						
1950–1	23,238	12,488	6385	18,874	11,054	6044	17,098	34,578	6044	40,621
1951–2	23,156	12,797	7410	20,207	12,642	6898	19,540	35,840	6898	42,738
1952–3	22,452	12,900	7928	20,827	12,848	7669	20,517	35,653	7669	43,321
1953–4	21,341	13,018	8713	21,731	12,959	8320	21,279	34,855	8320	43,176
1954–5	19,794	12,917	10,743	23,660	12,968	9728	22,696	33,535	9728	43,263
1955–6	20,248	13,785	10,439	24,224	13,351	10,591	23,942	33,373	10,591	43,964
1956–7	21,429	15,248	10,392	25,639	14,516	10,415	24,932	35,355	10,415	45,771
1957–8	22,787	16,422	10,814	27,235	15,835	10,603	26,437	37,943	10,603	48,546
1958–9	21,411	16,516	14,814	31,330	16,469	12,814	29,282	38,568	12,814	51,381
1959–60	22,253	18,337	15,420	33,758	17,427	15,117	32,544	39,259	15,117	54,376
1960–1	23,219	20,666	16,948	37,614	19,502	16,184	35,686	42,238	16,184	58,422
1961–2	24,152	22,928	18,526	41,453	21,797	17,737	39,534	45,482	17,737	63,219
1962–3	25,164	25,460	19,710	45,170	24,194	19,118	43,312	48,851	19,118	67,969
1963–4	25,035	27,170	23,155	50,325	26,315	21,433	47,747	51,414	21,433	72,847
1964–5	26,561	30,552	25,420	55,973	28,861	24,288	53,149	54,659	24,288	78,947
1965–6	28,933	35,566	28,424	63,990	33,059	26,922	59,981	60,806	26,922	87,728
1966–7	29,890	39,567	36,884	76,451	37,567	32,654	70,221	66,978	32,654	99,632
1967–8	31,813	44,895	41,098	85,993	42,231	38,991	81,222	73,083	38,991	112,074
1968–9	34,309	50,692	42,575	93,266	47,793	41,836	89,630	80,854	41,836	122,690
1969–70	37,512	58,018	45,786	103,804	54,355	44,180	98,535	90,266	44,180	134,446
1970–1	40,827	66,674	49,881	116,554	62,346	47,833	110,179	101,516	47,833	149,349
1971–2	44,809	77,016	53,311	130,326	71,845	51,596	123,440	114,663	51,596	166,258
1972–3	48,803	88,942	60,611	149,552	82,979	56,961	139,939	129,784	56,961	186,745
1973–4	57,706	107,957	69,984	177,940	98,449	65,297	163,746	151,703	65,297	217,001

(Contd.)

233

Appendix Table 4(o) Contd.

	(12)	(13)	(14)	(15)	(16)	(17)	(18)	(19)	(20)	(21)
1974-5	69,999	134,160	93,285	227,445	121,058	81,634	202,692	184,911	81,634	266,545
1975-6	77,373	153,518	109,564	263,082	143,839	101,424	245,263	217,525	101,424	318,949
1976-7	82,014	167,789	113,796	281,584	160,653	111,680	272,333	240,347	111,680	352,027
1977-8	87,259	184,446	118,307	302,754	176,117	116,051	292,169	260,754	116,051	376,806
1978-9	96,308	210,839	132,691	343,530	197,643	125,499	323,142	289,426	125,499	414,925
1979-80	113,549	255,383	163,161	418,544	233,111	147,926	381,037	338,040	147,926	485,965
1980-1	129,341	297,765	180,424	478,189	276,574	171,792	448,367	398,019	171,792	569,812
1981-2	153,419	369,130	217,133	586,263	333,448	198,779	532,226	474,827	198,779	673,606
1982-3	179,084	443,420	238,877	682,297	406,275	228,005	634,280	572,526	228,005	800,531
1983-4	202,217	510,711	272,686	783,398	477,066	255,782	732,847	667,716	255,782	923,498
1984-5	230,106	589,933	299,157	889,090	550,322	285,922	836,244	766,484	285,922	1,052,405
1985-6	262,783	682,680	347,916	1,030,596	636,307	323,536	959,843	882,751	323,536	1,206,287
1986-7	294,735	783,526	394,639	1,178,165	733,103	371,278	1,104,381	1,011,862	371,278	1,383,139
1987-8	330,303	882,825	434,137	1,316,962	833,175	414,388	1,247,563	1,145,695	414,388	1,560,083
1988-9	366,110	982,937	516,418	1,499,355	932,881	475,277	1,408,158	1,281,088	475,277	1,756,365
1989-90	413,694	1,100,347	609,854	1,710,201	1,041,642	563,136	1,604,778	1,431,544	563,136	1,994,680
1990-1	465,530	1,229,388	708,141	1,937,529	1,164,867	658,998	1,823,865	1,604,479	658,998	2,263,477
1991-2	541,792	1,448,804	872,905	2,321,709	1,339,096	790,523	2,129,619	1,842,757	790,523	2,633,280
1992-3	610,048	1,634,169	1,013,068	2,647,237	1,541,486	942,987	2,484,473	2,117,406	942,987	3,060,393
1993-4	673,197	1,832,049	1,104,494	2,936,543	1,733,109	1,058,781	2,791,890	2,374,731	1,058,781	3,433,512
1994-5	764,155	2,105,806	1,323,017	3,428,823	1,968,928	1,213,755	3,182,683	2,687,603	1,213,755	3,901,358
1995-6	898,591	2,574,162	1,581,991	4,156,153	2,339,984	1,452,504	3,792,488	3,171,357	1,452,504	4,623,861
1996-7	1,003,548	2,931,738	1,862,999	4,794,737	2,752,950	1,722,495	4,475,445	3,704,019	1,722,495	5,426,514
1997-8	1,101,642	3,280,192	2,071,901	5,352,092	3,105,965	1,967,450	5,073,415	4,158,560	1,967,450	6,126,009
1998-9	1,200,806	3,603,730	2,254,488	5,858,218	3,441,961	2,163,194	5,605,155	4,593,184	2,163,194	6,756,379
1999-2000	1,294,121	3,903,328	2,440,772	6,344,100	3,753,529	2,347,630	6,101,159	5,000,992	2,347,630	7,348,622

Sources: Cols (1) to (3) from Appendix Table 4(i) Cols (1) to (3); Cols (4) to (6) from Appendix Table 4(m), Cols (16) to (18); Col. (7) = Col. (1) × Col. (4)/100; Col. (8) = Col. (2) × Col. (5)/100; Col. (9) = Col. (7) + Col. (8); Cols (10) and (11) derived. Col. (12) from Appendix Table 4(g), Col. (9); Col. (13) = Col. (7) – Col. (12); Col. (14) = Col. (8); Col. (15) = Col. (13) + Col. (14); Cols (16) to (18) are averages of two consecutive values of Col. (13) to (15) respectively; Col. (19) to (21) are averages of two consecutive values from Cols (7) to (9).

234

Appendix Table 4(p): Value of Agricultural Land at Current Prices, 1950–1 to 1999–2000

Year	Net area sown ('000 hectares)	Land under Agricultural Use—Definition I				
		Fallow lands ('000 hectares)	Total ('000 hectares)	Index (1960–1 = 100)	Land value at 1960–1 prices (Rs crore)	WPI of agricultural commodities (1960–1 = 100)
	(1)	(2)	(3)	(4)	(5)	(6)
1950–1	118,746	28,124	146,870	94.14	20,290	95.12
1951–2	119,400	28,962	148,362	95.09	20,496	98.04
1952–3	123,442	26,379	149,821	96.03	20,698	80.78
1953–4	126,806	24,775	151,581	97.16	20,941	85.46
1954–5	127,845	25,008	152,853	97.97	21,117	76.17
1955–6	129,516	24,127	153,643	98.48	21,226	71.08
1956–7	130,848	23,326	154,174	98.82	21,299	84.41
1957–8	129,080	25,320	154,400	98.96	21,330	86.75
1958–9	131,828	23,707	155,535	99.69	21,487	92.08
1959–60	132,939	23,001	155,940	99.95	21,543	94.10
1960–1	133,199	22,819	156,018	100.00	21,554	100.00
1961–2	135,399	21,613	157,012	100.64	21,691	99.27
1962–3	136,341	21,253	157,594	101.01	21,772	101.56
1963–4	136,483	21,288	157,771	101.12	21,796	107.61
1964–5	138,120	20,322	158,442	101.55	21,889	129.95
1965–6	136,198	22,446	158,644	101.68	21,917	140.67
1966–7	137,232	22,575	159,807	102.43	22,077	165.39
1967–8	139,876	20,724	160,600	102.94	22,187	186.83
1968–9	137,313	23,285	160,598	102.94	22,187	178.10
1969–70	138,772	21,806	160,578	102.92	22,184	183.46
1970–1	140,267	19,875	160,142	102.64	22,124	199.94
1971–2	139,721	20,981	160,702	103.00	22,201	200.74
1972–3	137,144	24,369	161,513	103.52	22,313	220.54

(Contd.)

Appendix Table 4(p) Contd.

	(1)	(2)	(3)	(4)	(5)	(6)
1973-4	132,416	19,947	152,363	97.66	21,049	278.32
1974-5	137,791	25,276	163,067	104.52	22,528	339.71
1975-6	141,652	21,775	163,427	104.75	22,578	314.51
1976-7	139,476	23,955	163,431	104.75	22,578	316.91
1977-8	141,953	22,595	164,548	105.47	22,732	349.50
1978-9	142,981	21,836	164,817	105.64	22,770	343.71
1979-80	138,903	25,724	164,627	105.52	22,743	377.30
1980-1	140,002	24,748	164,750	105.60	22,760	420.88
1981-2	141,928	23,035	164,963	105.73	22,790	472.87
1982-3	140,220	24,627	164,847	105.66	22,774	507.39
1983-4	142,841	22,837	165,678	106.19	22,889	574.06
1984-5	140,892	24,914	165,806	106.27	22,906	610.95
1985-6	140,901	24,945	165,846	106.30	22,912	610.47
1986-7	139,578	26,495	166,073	106.44	22,943	675.26
1987-8	134,085	31,774	165,859	106.31	22,914	765.10
1988-9	141,891	24,570	166,461	106.69	22,997	808.13
1989-90	142,339	23,967	166,306	106.59	22,975	824.68
1990-1	142,999	23,365	166,364	106.63	22,983	937.70
1991-2	141,632	24,613	166,245	106.56	22,967	1119.76
1992-3	142,717	23,830	166,547	106.75	23,009	1207.24
1993-4	142,419	24,212	166,631	106.80	23,020	1284.31
1994-5	142,960	23,219	166,179	106.51	22,958	1491.60
1995-6	142,197	23,847	166,044	106.43	22,939	1614.51
1996-7	142,819	23,215	166,034	106.42	22,938	1748.46
1997-8	142,819	23,215	166,034	106.42	22,938	1799.84
1998-9	142,819	23,215	166,034	106.42	22,938	2016.37
1999-2000	142,819	23,215	166,034	106.42	22,938	2038.59

(Cols Contd.)

Appendix Table 4(p) Contd.: Value of Agricultural Land at Current Prices, 1950–1 to 1999–2000

	Land value at current prices (Rs crore)	Total cropped area ('000 hectares)	Land under Agricultural Use—Definition II			
			Cropped area + fallow lands ('000 hectares)	Index (1960–1 = 100)	Land value at 1960–1 prices (Rs crore)	Land value at current prices (Rs crore)
	(7)	(8)	(9)	(10)	(11)	(12)
1950–1	19,300	131,893	160,017	91.13	22,106	21,028
1951–2	20,095	133,234	162,196	92.37	22,407	21,968
1952–3	16,720	137,675	164,054	93.43	22,664	18,308
1953–4	17,896	142,480	167,255	95.25	23,106	19,747
1954–5	16,085	144,087	169,095	96.30	23,361	17,794
1955–6	15,087	147,311	171,438	97.63	23,684	16,835
1956–7	17,979	149,492	172,818	98.42	23,875	20,153
1957–8	18,504	145,832	171,152	97.47	23,645	20,512
1958–9	19,785	151,629	175,336	99.85	24,223	22,304
1959–60	20,272	152,824	175,825	100.13	24,290	22,857
1960–1	21,554	152,772	175,591	100.00	24,258	24,258
1961–2	21,533	156,209	177,822	101.27	24,566	24,387
1962–3	22,111	156,760	178,013	101.38	24,593	24,976
1963–4	23,455	156,963	178,251	101.51	24,625	26,499
1964–5	28,445	159,229	179,551	102.26	24,805	32,234
1965–6	30,830	155,276	177,722	101.21	24,552	34,538
1966–7	36,514	157,355	179,930	102.47	24,857	41,112
1967–8	41,452	163,736	184,460	105.05	25,483	47,610
1968–9	39,515	159,529	182,814	104.11	25,256	44,981
1969–70	40,699	162,265	184,071	104.83	25,430	46,653
1970–1	44,234	165,791	185,666	105.74	25,650	51,284
1971–2	44,566	165,186	186,167	106.02	25,719	51,628
1972–3	49,209	162,150	186,519	106.22	25,768	56,828

(Contd.)

237

Appendix Table 4(p) Contd.

	(7)	(8)	(9)	(10)	(11)	(12)
1973–4	58,584	169,872	189,819	108.10	26,224	72,986
1974–5	76,529	164,191	189,467	107.90	26,175	88,919
1975–6	71,009	171,296	193,071	109.95	26,673	83,889
1976–7	71,552	167,334	191,289	108.94	26,427	83,749
1977–8	79,450	172,232	194,827	110.96	26,915	94,070
1978–9	78,261	174,802	196,638	111.99	27,166	93,371
1979–80	85,811	169,589	195,313	111.23	26,983	101,805
1980–1	95,794	172,630	197,378	112.41	27,268	114,765
1981–2	107,766	176,750	199,785	113.78	27,600	130,514
1982–3	115,552	172,748	197,375	112.41	27,267	138,352
1983–4	131,394	179,560	202,397	115.27	27,961	160,514
1984–5	139,946	176,330	201,244	114.61	27,802	169,856
1985–6	139,869	178,464	203,409	115.84	28,101	171,549
1986–7	154,926	176,405	202,900	115.55	28,031	189,280
1987–8	175,312	170,738	202,512	115.33	27,977	214,053
1988–9	185,843	182,277	206,847	117.80	28,576	230,932
1989–90	189,473	182,269	206,236	117.45	28,492	234,965
1990–1	215,514	185,742	209,107	119.09	28,888	270,885
1991–2	257,174	182,242	206,855	117.81	28,577	319,995
1992–3	277,769	185,700	209,530	119.33	28,947	349,456
1993–4	295,651	186,595	210,807	120.06	29,123	374,031
1994–5	342,438	188,053	211,272	120.32	29,187	435,359
1995–6	370,354	187,471	211,318	120.35	29,194	471,335
1996–7	401,057	189,543	212,758	121.17	29,393	513,919
1997–8	412,842	189,543	212,758	121.17	29,393	529,021
1998–9	462,509	189,543	212,758	121.17	29,393	592,664
2000	467,606	189,543	212,758	121.17	29,393	599,195

ols (1) and (2) from Appendix Table 4.10, Cols (6) and (5); Col. (3) = Col. (1) + Col. (2); Col. (4) derived; for Col.
Col. (6) calculated from Appendix Table 4(r) Col. (7); Col. (7) = Col. (5) × Col. (6); Col. (8) from Table 4.10,
= Col. (8) + Col. (2); Col. 10 derived; for Col. (11), see text; Col. (12) = Col. (11) × Col. 10.

238

Appendix Table 4(q): Value of Land under Non-agriculture Uses, 1950-1 to 1999-2000

Year	Area of land under non-agricultural use ('000 hectares)	Index 1960-1 = 100	Land value at 1960-1 prices (Rs crore)	WPI for non-agricultural items 1960-1 = 100	Value of land at current prices (Rs crore)
	(1)	(2)	(3)	(4)	(5)
1950-1	9357	63.05	555	78.35	435
1951-2	12,690	85.51	753	86.70	652
1952-3	12,321	83.03	731	79.49	581
1953-4	13,283	89.51	788	82.35	649
1954-5	13,784	92.88	817	79.57	650
1955-6	13,921	93.81	826	76.55	632
1956-7	13,981	94.21	829	84.26	699
1957-8	14,105	95.05	836	86.88	727
1958-9	14,300	96.36	848	89.03	755
1959-60	14,899	100.40	883	93.48	826
1960-1	14,840	100.00	880	100.00	880
1961-2	14,795	99.70	877	100.95	886
1962-3	15,111	101.83	896	105.49	945
1963-4	15,270	102.90	905	112.15	1016
1964-5	15,442	104.06	916	119.12	1091
1965-6	15,170	102.22	900	127.19	1144
1966-7	15,357	103.48	911	142.94	1302
1967-8	15,474	104.27	918	158.39	1453
1968-9	15,648	105.44	928	159.90	1484
1969-70	15,868	106.93	941	161.62	1521
1970-1	16,478	111.04	977	172.62	1687
1971-2	16,972	114.37	1006	188.33	1895
1972-3	16,658	112.25	988	207.49	2050
1973-4	16,799	113.20	996	241.67	2407
1974-5	18,377	123.83	1090	307.78	3354
1975-6	18,660	125.74	1107	317.10	3509
1976-7	19,834	133.65	1176	326.08	3835
1977-8	19,047	128.35	1129	333.67	3769
1978-9	19,201	129.39	1139	336.95	3837
1979-80	19,543	131.69	1159	409.45	4745
1980-1	19,656	132.45	1166	495.76	5779
1981-2	19,686	132.65	1167	538.05	6281
1982-3	19,914	134.19	1181	559.58	6608
1983-4	20,340	137.06	1206	589.17	7106
1984-5	20,551	138.48	1219	627.91	7652
1985-6	20,631	139.02	1223	667.19	8162
1986-7	20,879	140.69	1238	693.55	8587
1987-8	21,168	142.64	1255	735.52	9233
1988-9	21,229	143.05	1259	796.32	10,025
1989-90	21,258	143.25	1261	873.80	11,015
1990-1	21,087	142.10	1250	951.28	11,895
1991-2	21,465	144.64	1273	1058.89	13,478
1992-3	21,771	146.70	1291	1175.65	15,178
1993-4	21,771	146.70	1291	1283.42	16,569
1994-5	21,771	146.70	1291	1429.86	18,460
1995-6	21,771	146.70	1291	1547.29	19,976
1996-7	21,771	146.70	1291	1594.78	20,589
1997-8	21,771	146.70	1291	1677.81	21,661
1998-9	21,771	146.70	1291	1750.58	22,600
1999-2000	21,771	146.70	1291	1814.24	23,422

Sources: Col. (1) from Table 4.10 Col. (2); Col. (2) derived; for Col. (3), see text; Col. (4) calculated from Appendix Table 4(s), Col. (7), Col. (5) = Col. (3) × Col. (4).

Appendix Table 4(r): Wholesale Price Index for Agricultural Commodities, 1950–1 to 1999–2000

Year	Base 1939 = 100	Base 1952-3 As 100	Base 1961-2 As 100	Base 1970-1 As 100	Base 1982-3 As 100	Base 1993-4 As 100	Converted to base 1939 = 100	Converted to base 1980-1 = 100	Converted to base 1993-4 = 100
	(1)	(2)	(3)	(4)	(5)	(6)	(7)	(8)	(9)
1950-1	455.6						455.60	22.60	7.41
1951-2	469.6						469.60	23.29	7.63
1952-3	386.9	100.0					386.90	19.19	6.29
1953-4		105.8					409.34	20.30	6.65
1954-5		94.3					364.85	18.10	5.93
1955-6		88.0					340.47	16.89	5.53
1956-7		104.5					404.31	20.06	6.57
1957-8		107.4					415.53	20.61	6.75
1958-9		114.0					441.07	21.88	7.17
1959-60		116.5					450.74	22.36	7.33
1960-1		123.8					478.98	23.76	7.79
1961-2		122.9	100.0				475.50	23.59	7.73
1962-3			102.3				486.44	24.13	7.91
1963-4			108.4				515.44	25.57	8.38
1964-5			130.9				622.43	30.88	10.12
1965-6			141.7				673.78	33.42	10.95
1966-7			166.6				792.18	39.30	12.88
1967-8			188.2				894.89	44.39	14.55
1968-9			179.4				853.05	42.31	13.87
1969-70			184.8				878.72	43.59	14.28
1970-1			201.4	100.0			957.66	47.50	15.57
1971-2				100.4			961.53	47.70	15.63
1972-3				110.3			1056.34	52.40	17.17
1973-4				139.2			1333.12	66.13	21.67
1974-5				169.9			1627.13	80.71	26.45

(Contd.)

Appendix Table 4(r) Contd.

(1)	(2)	(3)	(4)	(5)	(6)	(7)	(8)	(9)
1975-6			157.3			1506.46	74.73	24.49
1976-7			158.5			1517.95	75.30	24.68
1977-8			174.8			1674.06	83.04	27.21
1978-9			171.9			1646.29	81.66	26.76
1979-80			188.7			1807.18	89.64	29.38
1980-1			210.5			2015.96	100.00	32.77
1981-2			236.5	100.0		2264.96	112.35	36.82
1982-3				107.3		2430.30	120.55	39.51
1983-4				121.4		2749.66	136.39	44.70
1984-5				129.2		2926.33	145.16	47.57
1985-6				129.1		2924.06	145.05	47.53
1986-7				142.8		3234.36	160.44	52.58
1987-8				161.8		3664.71	181.78	59.57
1988-9				170.9		3870.82	192.01	62.92
1989-90				174.4		3950.09	195.94	64.21
1990-1				198.3		4491.42	222.79	73.01
1991-2				236.8		5363.43	266.05	87.19
1992-3				255.3		5782.45	286.83	94.00
1993-4				271.6	100.0	6151.63	305.15	100.00
1994-5					116.1	7144.51	354.40	116.14
1995-6					125.7	7733.22	383.60	125.71
1996-7					136.1	8374.83	415.43	136.14
1997-8					140.1	8620.90	427.63	140.14
1998-9					157.0	9658.07	479.08	157.00
1999-2000					158.7	9764.49	484.36	158.73

Sources: Cols (1) to (5) from *Economic and Political Weekly*, September 18, 1993, p. 2022; Col. (6) from *Statistical Abstract of India*, 2000, Cols (7) to (9) derived.

Appendix Table 4(s): Wholesale Price Index for Non-Agricultural Commodities, 1950-1 to 1999-2000

Year	Base 1939 = 100	Base 1952-3 As 100	Base 1961-2 As 100	Base 1970-1 As 100	Base 1982-3 As 100	Base 1993-4 As 100	Converted to base 1939 = 100	Converted to base 1980-1 = 100	Converted to base 1993-4 = 100
	(1)	(2)	(3)	(4)	(5)	(6)	(7)	(8)	(9)
1950-1	370.8						370.80	15.80	6.10
1951-2	410.3						410.30	17.49	6.76
1952-3	376.2	100.0					376.20	16.03	6.19
1953-4		103.6					389.74	16.61	6.42
1954-5		100.1					376.58	16.05	6.20
1955-6		96.3					362.28	15.44	5.96
1956-7		106.0					398.77	17.00	6.57
1957-8		109.3					411.19	17.53	6.77
1958-9		112.0					421.34	17.96	6.94
1959-60		117.6					442.41	18.86	7.28
1960-1		125.8					473.26	20.17	7.79
1961-2		127.0	100.0				477.77	20.36	7.87
1962-3			104.5				499.24	21.28	8.22
1963-4			111.1				530.77	22.62	8.74
1964-5			118.0				563.73	24.03	9.28
1965-6			126.0				601.95	25.66	9.91
1966-7			141.6				676.48	28.83	11.14
1967-8			156.9				749.57	31.95	12.34
1968-9			158.4				756.74	32.25	12.46
1969-70			160.1				764.86	32.60	12.59
1970-1			171.0	100.0			816.94	34.82	13.45
1971-2				109.1			891.28	37.99	14.67
1972-3				120.2			981.96	41.85	16.17
1973-4				140.0			1143.71	48.75	18.83
1974-5				178.3			1456.60	62.08	23.98

(Contd.)

242

Appendix Table 4(s) Contd.

(1)	(2)	(3)	(4)	(5)	(6)	(7)	(8)	(9)
1975–6			183.7			1500.71	63.96	24.71
1976–7			188.9			1543.19	65.77	25.41
1977–8			193.3			1579.14	67.31	26.00
1978–9			195.2			1594.66	67.97	26.25
1979–80			237.2			1937.77	82.59	31.90
1980–1			287.2			2346.24	100.00	38.63
1981–2			311.7	100.00		2546.39	108.53	41.92
1982–3				104.00		2648.24	112.87	43.60
1983–4				109.50		2788.29	118.84	45.91
1984–5				116.70		2971.63	126.66	48.92
1985–6				124.00		3157.52	134.58	51.99
1986–7				128.90		3282.29	139.90	54.04
1987–8				136.70		3480.91	148.36	57.31
1988–9				148.00		3768.65	160.63	62.05
1989–90				162.40		4135.33	176.25	68.08
1990–1				176.80		4502.01	191.88	74.12
1991–2				196.80		5011.29	213.59	82.51
1992–3				218.50		5563.86	237.14	91.60
1993–4				238.53	100.00	6073.90	258.88	100.00
1994–5					111.41	6766.93	288.42	111.41
1995–6					120.56	7322.69	312.10	120.56
1996–7					124.26	7547.43	321.68	124.26
1997–8					130.73	7940.41	338.43	130.73
1998–9					136.40	8284.80	353.11	136.40
1999–2000					141.36	8586.06	365.95	141.36

Sources: Same as Appendix Table 4(r).

243

Appendix Table 4(t): Wholesale Price Index for All Commodities, 1950-1 to 1999-2000

Year	Base 1939 = 100	Base 1952-3 As 100	Base 1961-2 As 100	Base 1970-1 As 100	Base 1982-3 As 100	Base 1993-4 As 100	Converted to base 1939 = 100	Converted to base 1980-1 = 100	Converted to base 1993-4 = 100
	(1)	(2)	(3)	(4)	(5)	(6)	(7)	(8)	(9)
1950-1	409.7						409.70	18.55	6.82
1951-2	434.6						434.60	19.67	7.23
1952-3	380.6	100.0					380.60	17.23	6.33
1953-4		101.2					385.17	17.44	6.41
1954-5		89.6					341.02	15.44	5.67
1955-6		92.5					352.06	15.94	5.86
1956-7		105.3					400.77	18.14	6.67
1957-8		105.4					401.15	18.16	6.67
1958-9		112.9					429.70	19.45	7.15
1959-60		117.1					445.68	20.17	7.41
1960-1		124.9					475.37	21.52	7.91
1961-2		125.1	100.0				476.13	21.55	7.92
1962-3			103.8				494.22	22.37	8.22
1963-4			110.2				524.70	23.75	8.73
1964-5			122.3				582.31	26.36	9.69
1965-6			131.6				626.59	28.36	10.42
1966-7			149.9				713.72	32.31	11.87
1967-8			167.3				796.57	36.06	13.25
1968-9			165.4				787.52	35.65	13.10
1969-70			171.6				817.04	36.98	13.59
1970-1			181.1	100.0			862.27	39.03	14.35
1971-2				105.6			910.56	41.22	15.15
1972-3				116.2			1001.96	45.36	16.67
1973-4				139.7			1204.59	54.53	20.04
1974-5				174.9			1508.11	68.27	25.09

(Contd.)

Appendix Table 4(t) Contd.

(1)	(2)	(3)	(4)	(5)	(6)	(7)	(8)	(9)
1975–6			173.0			1491.73	67.53	24.82
1976–7			176.6			1522.77	68.93	25.33
1977–8			185.8			1602.10	72.52	26.65
1978–9			185.8			1602.10	72.52	26.65
1979–80			217.6			1876.30	84.93	31.22
1980–1			256.2			2209.14	100.00	36.75
1981–2			281.3	100.0		2425.57	109.80	40.36
1982–3				104.9		2544.43	115.18	42.33
1983–4				112.8		2736.05	123.85	45.52
1984–5				120.1		2913.11	131.87	48.47
1985–6				125.4		3041.67	137.69	50.61
1986–7				132.7		3218.74	145.70	53.55
1987–8				143.6		3483.12	157.67	57.95
1988–9				154.3		3742.66	169.42	62.27
1989–90				165.7		4019.17	181.93	66.87
1990–1				182.7		4431.52	200.60	73.73
1991–2				207.8		5040.34	228.16	83.86
1992–3				228.6		5544.86	251.00	92.25
1993–4				247.8	100.0	6010.57	272.08	100.00
1994–5				274.7	112.6	6767.90	306.36	112.60
1995–6				295.8	121.6	7308.85	330.85	121.60
1996–7				314.6	127.2	7645.45	346.08	127.20
1997–8				329.8	132.8	7982.04	361.32	132.80
1998–9				352.4	140.7	8456.87	382.81	140.70
1999–2000					145.3	8733.36	395.33	145.30

Sources: Same as Appendix Table 4(r).

245

Appendix Table 4(u): Total Factor Input: Non-Residential Sector, 1950-1 to 1999-2000

Year	Augumented labour input index	Relative annual change	% share of earnings of labour	Two-year average of % share	Weighted annual change in labour input	Weighted average annual change in capital input	Land input index	Relative annual change	% share of earnings of land	Two-year average of % share	Weighted annual change in land input	Total weighted annual changes	Total factor input index 1950-1 = 100	Total factor input index 1993-4 = 100
	(1)	(2)	(3)	(4)	(5)	(6)	(7)	(8)	(9)	(10)	(11)	(12)	(13)	(14)
1950-1	38.12	1.0000	57.07	57.07	57.07	20.23	77.86	1.0000	22.70	22.70	22.70	100.00	100.00	30.39
1951-2	38.86	1.0194	56.55	56.81	57.91	21.08	79.68	1.0234	22.15	22.43	22.95	101.94	101.93	30.98
1952-3	39.60	1.0190	57.25	56.90	57.98	22.62	80.47	1.0099	19.33	20.74	20.95	101.54	103.50	31.46
1953-4	40.37	1.0194	55.32	56.29	57.38	24.27	82.21	1.0216	20.67	20.00	20.43	102.08	105.66	32.11
1954-5	41.15	1.0193	56.82	56.07	57.15	25.20	83.20	1.0120	18.27	19.47	19.70	102.06	107.84	32.78
1955-6	41.94	1.0192	57.42	57.12	58.22	26.18	84.34	1.0137	16.91	17.59	17.83	102.22	110.23	33.50
1956-7	42.75	1.0193	55.58	56.50	57.59	26.55	85.01	1.0079	19.06	17.99	18.13	102.27	112.73	34.26
1957-8	43.58	1.0194	59.43	57.51	58.62	25.57	84.25	0.9911	16.97	18.02	17.85	102.04	115.04	34.96
1958-9	44.41	1.0190	56.72	58.08	59.18	25.65	86.27	1.0240	17.92	17.45	17.86	102.69	118.13	35.90
1959-60	45.27	1.0194	58.10	57.41	58.52	26.51	86.65	1.0044	16.59	17.26	17.33	102.36	120.92	36.75
1960-1	46.12	1.0188	56.48	57.29	58.37	27.28	86.52	0.9985	16.91	16.75	16.72	102.37	123.79	37.62
1961-2	46.95	1.0180	55.24	55.86	56.87	28.95	87.57	1.0121	16.39	16.65	16.85	102.67	127.09	38.63
1962-3	47.85	1.0192	56.32	55.78	56.85	29.89	87.73	1.0018	15.34	15.87	15.89	102.64	130.44	39.65
1963-4	48.76	1.0190	55.28	55.80	56.86	30.57	87.88	1.0017	15.35	15.35	15.37	102.80	134.09	40.75
1964-5	49.69	1.0191	55.30	55.29	56.34	30.59	88.54	1.0075	16.22	15.79	15.90	102.83	137.89	41.91
1965-6	50.65	1.0193	56.54	55.92	57.00	29.95	87.61	0.9895	15.25	15.74	15.57	102.52	141.37	42.97
1966-7	51.61	1.0190	57.44	56.99	58.07	29.27	88.70	1.0124	15.11	15.18	15.37	102.71	145.20	44.13
1967-8	52.60	1.0192	60.26	58.85	59.98	27.63	90.86	1.0244	14.14	14.63	14.98	102.59	148.96	45.27
1968-9	53.60	1.0190	60.80	60.53	61.68	27.04	90.13	0.9920	12.61	13.38	13.27	101.99	151.92	46.18
1969-70	54.63	1.0192	58.80	59.80	60.95	28.48	90.77	1.0071	12.73	12.67	12.76	102.19	155.24	47.19
1970-1	55.67	1.0190	58.90	58.85	59.97	29.50	91.67	1.0099	12.56	12.65	12.77	102.24	158.72	48.24
1971-2	56.74	1.0192	58.69	58.80	59.93	30.09	92.03	1.0039	11.74	12.15	12.20	102.21	162.22	49.31
1972-3	57.83	1.0192	59.40	59.05	60.18	30.58	92.12	1.0010	11.30	11.52	11.53	102.29	165.95	50.44

(Contd.)

Appendix Table 4(u) Contd.

	(1)	(2)	(3)	(4)	(5)	(6)	(7)	(8)	(9)	(10)	(11)	(12)	(13)	(14)
1973-4	59.30	1.0254	57.07	58.24	59.72	31.02	93.71	1.0173	12.75	12.03	12.23	102.97	170.88	51.94
1974-5	61.07	1.0298	55.36	56.22	57.89	32.12	93.92	1.0022	13.16	12.96	12.98	102.99	175.99	53.49
1975-6	62.91	1.0301	57.25	56.31	58.00	33.16	95.69	1.0188	10.56	11.86	12.08	103.25	181.71	55.23
1976-7	64.80	1.0300	55.61	56.43	58.13	34.63	95.12	0.9940	10.15	10.36	10.29	103.05	187.24	56.91
1977-8	66.62	1.0281	57.27	56.44	58.03	34.81	96.61	1.0157	10.07	10.11	10.27	103.10	193.06	58.68
1978-9	68.41	1.0269	56.93	57.10	58.63	34.65	97.50	1.0092	9.35	9.71	9.80	103.09	199.02	60.49
1979-80	70.23	1.0266	55.71	56.32	57.82	36.05	96.96	0.9945	9.08	9.22	9.16	103.04	205.06	62.33
1980-1	72.11	1.0268	56.41	56.06	57.56	36.62	97.96	1.0103	8.66	8.87	8.96	103.14	211.51	64.29
1981-2	74.05	1.0269	54.38	55.40	56.89	38.10	99.11	1.0117	8.74	8.70	8.80	103.79	219.52	66.72
1982-3	76.13	1.0281	54.63	54.51	56.04	39.79	98.02	0.9890	7.90	8.32	8.23	104.06	228.43	69.43
1983-4	77.95	1.0239	54.69	54.66	55.97	39.58	100.50	1.0253	7.92	7.91	8.11	103.65	236.78	71.97
1984-5	79.59	1.0210	55.96	55.33	56.49	39.05	100.00	0.9950	7.24	7.58	7.54	103.08	244.07	74.18
1985-6	81.33	1.0219	54.71	55.34	56.54	39.78	101.04	1.0104	6.68	6.96	7.03	103.35	252.25	76.67
1986-7	83.15	1.0224	57.22	55.97	57.22	39.80	100.86	0.9982	6.08	6.38	6.37	103.38	260.79	79.26
1987-8	85.06	1.0230	58.13	57.68	59.00	38.17	100.75	0.9989	5.95	6.02	6.01	103.18	269.07	81.78
1988-9	87.08	1.0237	55.39	56.76	58.11	38.85	102.81	1.0204	6.30	6.13	6.25	103.21	277.70	84.41
1989-90	89.51	1.0279	53.01	54.20	55.71	41.45	102.53	0.9973	6.00	6.15	6.13	103.30	286.87	87.19
1990-1	92.01	1.0279	53.64	53.33	54.81	42.64	103.84	1.0128	5.81	5.91	5.98	103.44	296.72	90.19
1991-2	94.60	1.0281	53.83	53.74	55.25	42.43	102.87	0.9907	5.85	5.83	5.78	103.45	306.97	93.30
1992-3	97.26	1.0281	55.00	54.42	55.95	41.93	104.21	1.0130	5.40	5.63	5.70	103.58	317.95	96.64
1993-4	100.00	1.0282	49.09	52.05	53.51	44.31	104.81	1.0058	5.86	5.63	5.66	103.48	329.01	100.00
1994-5	102.13	1.0213	46.73	47.91	48.93	48.86	105.03	1.0021	6.24	6.05	6.06	103.85	341.68	103.85
1995-6	103.52	1.0136	48.82	47.78	48.43	50.32	105.05	1.0002	5.51	5.88	5.88	104.62	357.47	108.65
1996-7	104.93	1.0136	44.67	46.75	47.38	51.69	105.73	1.0065	5.57	5.54	5.58	104.64	374.08	113.70
1997-8	106.35	1.0135	47.21	45.94	46.56	52.22	105.73	1.0000	4.89	5.23	5.23	104.01	389.08	118.26
1998-9	107.83	1.0139	46.37	46.79	47.44	51.09	105.73	1.0000	5.03	4.96	4.96	103.49	402.67	122.39
1999-2000	109.32	1.0138	46.55	46.46	47.10	51.22	105.73	1.0000	4.70	4.87	4.87	103.19	415.50	126.29

Sources: Col. (1) from Table 3.1, Col. (4); Col. (2) derived from Col. (1); Col. (3) from Table 2.2, Col. (9); Col. (4) derived from Col. (3); Col. (5) = Col. (2) × Col. (4); Col. (6) from Table 4.15, Col. (19); Col. (7) from Table 4.10, Col. (11); Col. (8) derived from Col. (7); Col. (9) from Table 4.11, Col. (11); Col. (10) derived from Col. (9); Col. (11) = Col. (8) × Col. (10); Col. (12) = Col. (5) + Col. (6) + Col. (11); for Cols (13) and (14), see text.

247

5

Output Per Unit of Input in the Non-residential Sector

The index of output per unit of input derived by dividing the index of output by the index of total factor input is shown in Col. (9) of Table 4.16. The factors influencing output per unit of output are not as easily identifiable and measurable as those of total factor input. An attempt to develop measures relating to some of the determinants of output per unit of input is presented in this chapter.

STRUCTURAL CHANGE

Productivity differs from sector to sector and varies over time. As economic growth takes place, resources are moved from sectors with low productivity to sectors with high productivity, leading to structural change. Structural changes had taken place only at a slow pace in India during the period. It is well known that agriculture is characterized by low productivity, and over time the gap in productivity between agriculture and non-agriculture has widened.[1] The relative shares of Sector A and Sector non-A in non-residential gross domestic product (GDP) at 1993–4 prices, employment and labour input, and the real product per person engaged in the two sectors during the period 1950–1 to 1999–2000 are shown in Table 5.1 and in Figs 5.1(a), (b), (c) and 5.2.

The share of Sector A in non-residential GDP declined gradually over the years from 60.8 per cent in 1950–1 to 26.4 per cent in 1999–2000. But the decline in the share of Sector A in total employment was not as pronounced as in the case of output. The share of Sector A in employment stayed at almost the same level with a slight tendency to move downward from 76.2 per cent to 74.2 per cent between 1950–1 and 1970–1. The drop in the share of Sector A in employment became somewhat more visible only after the mid 1970s. It declined from 74.2 per cent in 1970–1 to 60.4 in 1999–2000. The drop in the share of Sector A in total employment was only 15.8 percentage points for the whole period while the decline in the share of output of Sector A in real GDP was 34.4 points. The decline in the share of employment was less than half

---

[1] S. Sivasubramonian, *The National Income of India in the Twentieth Century*, New Delhi, 2000, pp. 482, 620.

Table 5.1: Percentage Share of Sector A and Sector Non-A in GDP, Employment, and Labour Input of the Non-residential Sector and GDP Per Person Engaged in Sector A and Sector Non-A, 1950-1 to 1999-2000

Year	% share of GDP at 1993-4 prices		% share in employment		% share in labour input		GDP per person engaged		
	Sector A	Sector non-A	Sector A	Sector non-A	Sector A	Sector non-A	Sector A (Rs)	Sector non-A (Rs)	Sector non-A/ Sector A
	(1)	(2)	(3)	(4)	(5)	(6)	(7)	(8)	(9)
1950-1	60.80	39.20	76.20	23.80	71.47	28.53	6644	13,711	2.06
1951-2	60.30	39.70	76.17	23.83	71.08	28.92	6641	13,974	2.10
1952-3	60.47	39.53	76.11	23.89	70.65	29.35	6750	14,057	2.08
1953-4	61.27	38.73	76.05	23.95	70.23	29.77	7162	14,376	2.01
1954-5	60.44	39.56	75.99	24.01	69.81	30.19	7264	15,046	2.07
1955-6	58.41	41.59	75.93	24.07	69.39	30.61	7095	15,933	2.25
1956-7	58.18	41.82	75.87	24.13	68.98	31.02	7371	16,659	2.26
1957-8	56.34	43.66	75.81	24.19	68.56	31.44	6936	16,844	2.43
1958-9	57.50	42.50	75.75	24.25	68.16	31.84	7522	17,370	2.31
1959-60	55.70	44.30	75.69	24.31	67.75	32.25	7337	18,168	2.48
1960-1	55.40	44.60	75.63	24.37	67.31	32.69	7716	19,275	2.50
1961-2	53.76	46.24	75.53	24.47	67.16	32.84	7604	20,187	2.65
1962-3	51.61	48.39	75.38	24.62	66.98	33.02	7335	21,061	2.87
1963-4	50.22	49.78	75.24	24.76	66.80	33.20	7388	22,253	3.01
1964-5	50.88	49.12	75.10	24.90	66.62	33.38	7941	23,118	2.91
1965-6	45.29	54.71	74.96	25.04	66.44	33.56	6952	25,136	3.62
1966-7	46.01	53.99	74.81	25.19	66.26	33.74	6745	23,515	3.49
1967-8	48.76	51.24	74.67	25.33	66.09	33.91	7625	23,625	3.10
1968-9	47.44	52.56	74.53	25.47	65.91	34.09	7492	24,288	3.24
1969-70	47.33	52.67	74.39	25.61	65.73	34.27	7848	25,365	3.23
1970-1	48.22	51.78	74.25	25.75	65.56	34.44	8271	25,604	3.10
1971-2	46.92	53.08	74.11	25.89	65.39	34.61	7987	25,865	3.24
1972-3	44.74	55.26	73.97	26.03	65.21	34.79	7466	26,207	3.51

(Contd.)

Table 5.1 Contd.

	(1)	(2)	(3)	(4)	(5)	(6)	(7)	(8)	(9)
1973-4	45.84	54.16	73.58	26.42	64.80	35.20	7866	25,890	3.29
1974-5	44.66	55.34	72.97	27.03	64.18	35.82	7604	25,433	3.34
1975-6	46.14	53.86	72.35	27.65	63.57	36.43	8425	25,740	3.06
1976-7	42.97	57.03	71.75	28.25	62.96	37.04	7792	26,264	3.37
1977-8	43.91	56.09	71.28	28.72	62.47	37.53	8416	26,672	3.17
1978-9	42.54	57.46	70.89	29.11	62.03	37.97	8457	27,809	3.29
1979-80	39.27	60.73	70.44	29.56	61.55	38.45	7252	26,723	3.69
1980-1	41.30	58.70	70.00	30.00	61.08	38.92	8048	26,695	3.32
1981-2	41.08	58.92	69.57	30.43	60.60	39.40	8330	27,312	3.28
1982-3	39.66	60.34	69.04	30.96	60.05	39.95	8133	27,586	3.39
1983-4	40.36	59.64	68.32	31.68	59.31	40.69	8817	28,101	3.19
1984-5	39.30	60.70	67.50	32.50	59.06	40.94	8913	28,593	3.21
1985-6	37.96	62.04	66.70	33.30	58.32	41.68	8945	29,284	3.27
1986-7	36.22	63.78	65.91	34.09	57.61	42.39	8853	30,142	3.40
1987-8	34.51	65.49	65.12	34.88	56.93	43.07	8702	30,837	3.54
1988-9	36.05	63.95	64.64	35.36	56.39	43.61	9924	32,177	3.24
1989-90	34.29	65.71	64.45	35.55	56.12	43.88	9864	34,264	3.47
1990-1	33.86	66.14	64.26	35.74	55.85	44.15	10,057	35,318	3.51
1991-2	33.03	66.97	64.07	35.93	55.58	44.42	9697	35,061	3.62
1992-3	33.28	66.72	63.88	36.12	55.31	44.69	10,048	35,626	3.55
1993-4	32.78	67.22	63.93	36.07	55.24	44.76	10,209	37,094	3.63
1994-5	32.00	68.00	63.72	36.28	54.97	45.03	10,585	39,508	3.73
1995-6	29.50	70.50	63.05	36.95	54.31	45.69	10,519	42,896	4.08
1996-7	29.91	70.09	62.38	37.62	53.64	46.36	11,558	44,922	3.89
1997-8	27.83	72.17	61.72	38.28	52.99	47.01	11,305	47,280	4.18
1998-9	27.91	72.09	61.07	38.93	52.34	47.66	12,133	49,163	4.05
1999-2000	26.37	73.63	60.43	39.57	51.70	48.30	12,245	52,192	4.26

Sources: Cols (1) and (2) from Appendix Table 1(e), Cols (6) and (7); Cols (3) and (4) from Appendix Table 3(b); Cols (10) and (11); Cols (5) and (6) from Table 3.27, Cols (4) and (5); Cols (7) and (8) derived from Appendix Tables 1(e) and 3(b); Col. (9) = Col (8)/Col (7).

250

Fig. 5.1(a): Percentage Share of **Sector A** and **Sector Non-A** in Employment

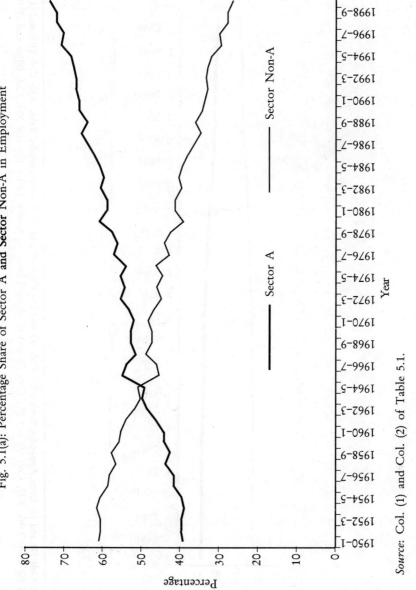

Source: Col. (1) and Col. (2) of Table 5.1.

251

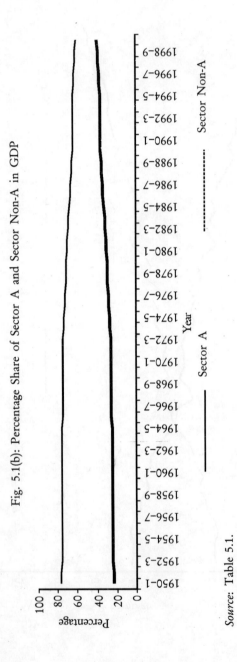

Fig. 5.1(b): Percentage Share of Sector A and Sector Non-A in GDP

Sector A ——— Sector Non-A --------

Source: Table 5.1.

252

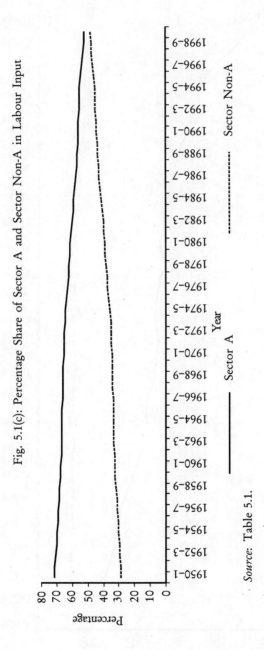

Fig. 5.1(c): Percentage Share of Sector A and Sector Non-A in Labour Input

Source: Table 5.1.

253

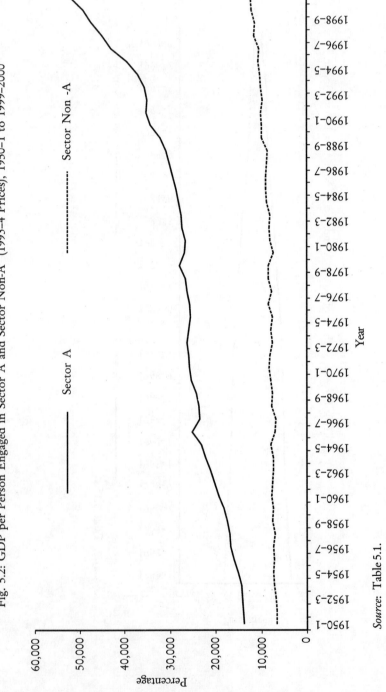

Fig. 5.2: GDP per Person Engaged in Sector A and Sector Non-A (1993–4 Prices), 1950–1 to 1999–2000

——— Sector A

-------- Sector Non -A

Percentage

Year

1950-1 1952-3 1954-5 1956-7 1958-9 1960-1 1962-3 1964-5 1966-7 1968-9 1970-1 1972-3 1974-5 1976-7 1978-9 1980-1 1982-3 1984-5 1986-7 1988-9 1990-1 1992-3 1994-5 1996-7 1998-9

0 10,000 20,000 30,000 40,000 50,000 60,000

Source: Table 5.1.

of the drop in the share of output of Sector A in the total. The picture becomes slightly better for the period as a whole, if instead of employment, labour input, that is, employment adjusted for changes in age–sex composition and education, is considered. The share of labour input, shown in Col. (5) of Table 5.1, dropped by twenty percentage points over the whole period compared to sixteen points in the share of employed. The difference between employment and labour input is more pronounced in the first two decades when the share of labour input declined by six percentage points compared to less than two per cent in the case of employment. During the last three decades, the drop in the share of labour input and employment was almost the same. Compared to this, the drop in the share of farm labour input in USA was much higher, almost 2.4 times that of the share of farm sector in total national income and far more dramatic from 22.7 per cent in 1929 to 5.1 per cent in 1969.[2] In the case of advanced capitalist countries studied by Maddison, the share of agriculture in employment declined from an average of 34 per cent in 1913 to 5.5 per cent in 1984.[3]

Productivity, that is GDP per person engaged in Sector A was just about half of the level in Sector non-A in the beginning in the period. While the productivity in Sector A doubled over the period, that of Sector non-A quadrupled, thus widening the gap between them. By the end of the period, productivity in Sector A was less than one-fourth of the productivity in Sector non-A.

The modest transfer of resources (labour) and the deepening gap in inter-sectoral productivity must have resulted in some gain to the output. Growth accountants have attempted to measure this gain in two parts: (i) corresponding to the increase in output per worker in Sector A due to the transfer of surplus labour and (ii) corresponding to the difference between Sector A and Sector non-A in output per person engaged. The former is called gain from reallocation of resources. Since the year-to-year variations in the percentage shares of employment of Sector A and Sector non-A, especially in the first two decades, are almost trivial, the gains from transfer of resources are calculated only for the selected long and shorter periods considered in this study.

The method adopted for estimating the gains from reallocation follows closely the one used by Denison in *Accounting for United States Economic Growth*.[4] It uses the shares of Sector A and Sector non-A in real GDP and in labour input given in Table 5.1. The calculations for the period 1950–1 to 1960–1 are shown below:

---

[2] Edward F. Denison, *Accounting for Economic Growth*, Washington, D.C., 1974, pp. 287–8.

[3] Angus Maddison, *Explaining the Economic Performance of Nations: Essays in Time and Space*, Cheltenham, England, 1995, p. 53.

[4] Denison, *Accounting for United States Economic Growth*, pp. 286–7.

	Year	Sector A	Sector Non-A	Total
1. Percentage of GDP at 1993–4 prices	1950–1	60.80	39.20	100
2. Percentage of labour input	1950–1	71.47	28.53	100
3. Percentage of labour input	1960–1	67.31	32.69	
4. Change: row 3 – row 2		–4.16	4.16	
5. Percentage change in 1950–1 labour input if distribution had been that of the end of the period [Row 4/ Row 2] × 100		–5.82	14.58	
6. Assumed ratio of percentage change in output to percentage change in labour input (see text)		0.1320	0.6277	
7. Percentage change in 1950–1 GDP Sector A/Sector Non-A with the end of period labour distribution (Row 5 × Row 6)		–0.77	9.15	
8. Percentage change in 1950–1 GDP in Sector (Row 1 × Row 7)		–0.47	3.59	3.12

Source: Table 5.1.

A calculation is made for the initial year of the percentage by which real GDP originating in the non-residential sector would have been raised if labour input has been distributed between Sector A and Sector non-A in the proportion that prevailed at the end of the period, that is in 1960–1. Two estimates are made: (i) the first estimate is made on the assumption that if labour input in Sector A falls by one per cent, output in Sector A will decline by one-fourth of the labour share in factor incomes in Sector A. The average share of labour income in GDP of Sector A was 52.8 per cent, during 1950–1 to 1960–1 (see Table 2.2). Accordingly, the output in Sector A is assumed to decline by one-fourth of 52.8 per cent, that is by 13.2 per cent. Similar percentages based on labour share of GDP are used for other periods. In their study on Japan, Denison and Chung assumed that if labour input used in farming in any year had been smaller by one per cent, agricultural output would have been smaller by 0.25 per cent. The selected ratio, one-fourth, is much below the labour share in agriculture (0.65 to 0.75) because labour could be withdrawn from many farms with little loss of output.[5] In his study on Japan, Dirk Pilat did not make any adjustments for age–sex effects or education on labour input and assumed that for every decline of one per cent in labour input, agricultural income would fall by half its labour share.[6] In his study on the United States, Denison estimated that the loss would be by 0.33 per cent and considered this to be generous.[7] Denison assumed that a one per cent reduction in farm employment would lead to a 0.25 per cent reduction in farm output in most

[5] E. F. Denison and William K. Chung, *How Japan's Economy Grew So Fast*, Washington, D.C., p. 226.

[6] 'Dirk Pilat, 'Explaining Japan's Post-war Economic Growth', in *Explaining Economic Growth: Essays in Honour of Angus Maddison*, Amsterdam, 1993, A. Szirmai, B. Van Ark, and D. Pilat (eds), p. 180.

[7] Denison, *Accounting for Growth*, p. 286.

of the north-west European countries except the United Kingdom and Denmark, for which a figure of 0.33 per cent was used, and Italy, for which a figure of zero was used with the implication that in Italy the reduction in farm labour had no adverse long-run effect on farm output.[8] Dholakia assumed this proportion to be only one-eighth in the case of India in view of the high volume of disguised unemployment and low marginal productivity of labour on a large number of small and fragmented farms.[9] In all the cases cited above, a constant fraction or percentage was assumed for the whole period. In this study the fraction is linked to the varying share of labour in GDP from Sector A during the period. The estimated percentage varies between 12.65 and 14.6 [see Appendix Table 5(a), line 6], quite close to the constant 12.5 per cent adopted by Dholakia. (ii) A second estimate is made of the rise in non-agricultural output corresponding to the increase in non-agricultural employment due to the inflow of former agricultural workers. Here, no underestimation is assumed.[10] If the share of labour input in the non-agricultural sector goes up by one per cent, non-agricultural GDP is assumed to increase by a fraction of one per cent equivalent to the labour share in Sector non-A.[11] For 1950–1 to 1960–1 this fraction is 0.6277, obtained as the average of the annual shares of that period. The detailed calculations for all the decades and long periods covered by this study are given in Appendix Table 5(a). The two estimates are added to give the percentage change in output due to structural change. No allowance is made for any change in output due to shifts, if any, in the distribution of capital and land. Similar calculations made on the basis of GDP at current prices are given in Appendix Table 5(b). Table 5.2 summarizes the percentage change in output over the period and the corresponding annual rates of changes.

The percentage changes in GDP according to 1993–4 prices and current prices are more or less same. The annual rates of change are also shown in Cols (2) and (4). The index of gain from reallocation of resources is worked out on the basis of interpolation of decennial growth rates and are shown in Table 5.3.

IRREGULAR FLUCTUATIONS IN OUTPUT PER UNIT OF INPUT CAUSED BY WEATHER

The effect on output per unit of input in the non-residential sector of irregular fluctuations in agricultural output is considered here. Irregular fluctuations in agricultural output mainly arise due to the vagaries of weather, destruction of crops by pests, and other natural conditions. A simple method developed

[8] Edward F. Denison, *Why Growth Rates Differ*, Washington, D.C. 1967, p. 214.
[9] Bapul H. Dholakia, *The Sources of Economic Growth in India*, Baroda, 1974, p. 220.
[10] Pilat, *Explaining Japan's Post-work Economic Growth*, p. 180.
[11] Denison and Chung, *How Japan's Economy Grew So Fast*, Washington, D.C. 1976, p. 227.

Table 5.2: Percentage Gains in Output due to Reallocation of
Resources from Sector A, 1950–1 to 1999–2000

| Period | At 1993–4 Prices | | At current prices | |
	% change over the period	Compound annual rate of growth	% change over the period	Compound annual rate of growth
	(1)	(2)	(3)	(4)
1950–1 to 1960–1	3.12	0.31	3.33	0.33
1960–1 to 1970–1	1.13	0.11	1.24	0.13
1970–1 to 1980–1	3.32	0.33	3.16	0.31
1980–1 to 1990–1	3.76	0.37	3.77	0.37
1990–1 to 1999–2000	2.70	0.30	2.74	0.30
1950–1 to 1999–2000	12.82	0.25	11.65	0.23
1950–1 to 1964–5	3.49	0.25	3.31	0.23
1964–5 to 1980–1	4.35	0.27	3.86	0.24
1980–1 to 1999–2000	6.41	0.33	6.42	0.33

Sources: Appendix Tables 5(a) and 5(b).

Table 5.3: Non-Residential Sector: Indexes of Gains from Reallocation of
Resources from Agriculture, 1950–1 to 1999–2000 (1993–4 = 100)

| Year | Reallocation index on the basis of decennial growth rate | |
	1950–1 = 100	1993–4 = 100
	(1)	(2)
1950–1	100.00	88.75
1951–2	100.31	89.03
1952–3	100.62	89.31
1953–4	100.93	89.58
1954–5	101.25	89.86
1955–6	101.56	90.14
1956–7	101.88	90.42
1957–8	102.19	90.70
1958–9	102.51	90.98
1959–60	102.83	91.27
1960–1	103.15	91.55
1961–2	103.27	91.65
1962–3	103.39	91.76
1963–4	103.51	91.87
1964–5	103.63	91.97
1965–6	103.75	92.08
1966–7	103.87	92.18
1967–8	103.99	92.29
1968–9	104.11	92.40
1969–70	104.23	92.50
1970–1	104.35	92.61
1971–2	104.69	92.92
1972–3	105.04	93.23
1973–4	105.40	93.54
1974–5	105.75	93.85
1975–6	106.10	94.17

(Contd.)

Table 5.3 Contd.

	(1)	(2)
1976–7	106.45	94.48
1977–8	106.81	94.80
1978–9	107.17	95.11
1979–80	107.52	95.43
1980–1	107.88	95.75
1981–2	108.29	96.11
1982–3	108.70	96.47
1983–4	109.11	96.84
1984–5	109.52	97.20
1985–6	109.93	97.57
1986–7	110.34	97.93
1987–8	110.76	98.30
1988–9	111.18	98.67
1989–90	111.60	99.05
1990–1	112.02	99.42
1991–2	112.35	99.71
1992–3	112.68	100.01
1993–4	113.02	100.30
1994–5	113.35	100.60
1995–6	113.69	100.90
1996–7	114.02	101.20
1997–8	114.36	101.50
1998–9	114.70	101.80
1999–2000	115.04	102.10

Sources: Table 5.2, Col. (2).

by Denison[12] is used to measure the effect of the irregular fluctuations on output. The effect upon non-residential GDP is taken to be equal to the excess of actual GDP of Sector A over an estimated 'normal' GDP of the sector.

Normal GDP of Sector A is estimated to be equal to a five-year moving average of the actual GDP of Sector A. The excess of actual over normal GDP of Sector A, calculated from the above figures, is shown in Appendix Table 5(c). The adjusted non-residential GDP obtained by subtracting the excess from actual non-residential GDP is shown in Table 5.4. The ratio of the actual to adjusted GDP indicates the deviations in output due to weather. The index of this ratio (1993–4 = 100) shown in Column (5) of Table 5.4 measures the effect of irregular fluctuations on output per unit of input. An index value above 100 means that conditions were favourable to agriculture than in the base year and that below 100 indicates unfavourable conditions. The low values for 1965–6, 1966–7, 1972–3, 1979–80, and 1987–8 correspond to years of near severe to severe drought affecting more than forty per cent of the area[13] in the country.

[12] Denison, *Accounting for Economic Growth*, p. 291.
[13] For a ranking of the severity of the droughts in India, Mumbai, 1994, Centre for Monitoring Indian Economy, *Basic Statistics, India, August 1994*, see, Table 1.16.

Table 5.4: Non-residential GDP at 1993–4 Prices, Actual and Adjusted for Influence of Weather, 1950–1 to 1999–2000

Year	Actual non-residential GDP (Rs crore)	Effect of weather (Rs crore)	Adjusted non-residential GDP (Rs crore)	Ratio of actual to adjusted GDP	Index of ratio with 1993–4 = 100
	(1)	(2)	(3)	(4)	(5)
1950–1	133,328	−832	134,160	0.9938	99.11
1951–2	136,448	−1993	138,441	0.9856	98.30
1952–3	140,364	−1872	142,236	0.9868	98.42
1953–4	149,196	2221	146,975	1.0151	101.24
1954–5	155,683	1693	153,990	1.0110	100.83
1955–6	159,695	−933	160,628	0.9942	99.15
1956–7	169,060	1740	167,320	1.0104	100.77
1957–8	166,734	−4331	171,065	0.9747	97.21
1958–9	179,840	1940	177,900	1.0109	100.82
1959–60	183,773	−1299	185,072	0.9930	99.03
1960–1	197,202	2948	194,254	1.0152	101.25
1961–2	203,400	1784	201,616	1.0088	100.62
1962–3	207,655	−3878	211,533	0.9817	97.91
1963–4	218,393	−833	219,226	0.9962	99.35
1964–5	235,429	10,143	225,286	1.0450	104.22
1965–6	235,296	−5786	241,082	0.9760	97.34
1966–7	228,343	−9463	237,806	0.9602	95.76
1967–8	247,489	4473	243,016	1.0184	101.57
1968–9	253,945	−1868	255,813	0.9927	99.00
1969–70	270,912	−63	270,975	0.9998	99.71
1970–1	284,755	7570	277,185	1.0273	102.46
1971–2	287,195	1649	285,546	1.0058	100.31
1972–3	286,083	−6489	292,572	0.9778	97.52
1973–4	299,302	−313	299,615	0.9990	99.63
1974–5	302,545	−4196	306,741	0.9863	98.37
1975–6	330,574	7189	323,385	1.0222	101.95
1976–7	334,463	−6540	341,003	0.9808	97.82
1977–8	360,087	6683	353,404	1.0189	101.62
1978–9	380,255	8970	371,285	1.0242	102.14
1979–80	359,282	−16,499	375,781	0.9561	95.35
1980–1	385,704	−2	385,706	1.0000	99.73
1981–2	408,299	4283	404,016	1.0106	100.79
1982–3	419,990	−5678	425,668	0.9867	98.40
1983–4	452,221	4787	447,434	1.0107	100.80
1984–5	471,155	3947	467,208	1.0084	100.58
1985–6	491,473	2067	489,406	1.0042	100.15
1986–7	511,807	−4877	516,684	0.9906	98.79
1987–8	529,997	−13,167	543,164	0.9758	97.32
1988–9	585,737	7809	577,928	1.0135	101.08
1989–90	624,960	4081	620,879	1.0066	100.39
1990–1	658,889	2982	655,907	1.0045	100.19
1991–2	665,018	−6628	671,646	0.9901	98.75
1992–3	698,241	−1857	700,098	0.9973	99.47
1993–4	738,075	1968	736,107	1.0027	100.00
1994–5	794,008	2805	791,203	1.0035	100.09
1995–6	853,893	−6793	860,686	0.9921	98.95
1996–7	923,148	8120	915,028	1.0089	100.62
1997–8	968,030	−5837	973,867	0.9940	99.14
1998–9	1,033,306	3541	1,029,765	1.0034	100.08
1999–2000	1,100,834	−2327	1,103,161	0.9979	99.52

Sources: Col. (1) from Appendix Table 1(e), Col. (3); Col. (2) from Appendix Table 5(c), Col. (3); Col. (3) = Col. (1) − Col. (2); Col. (4) = Col. (1)/Col. (3); Col. (5) = Col. (4) with 1993–4 value = 100.

FOREIGN TRADE EFFECT

The proportionate importance of foreign trade depends on the size of an economy. It is very much bigger in the Netherlands than in the United States.[14] Because of the large size of the Indian economy and the severe restrictions placed on foreign trade for most of the post-1950 period, foreign trade has had only relatively minor influence on output growth in India. The ratio of merchandise trade to GDP, defined as the average of the ratios of export and import values to GDP at current prices,[15] has been less than 7 per cent for the period as a whole. The annual ratios of foreign trade to GDP for the period 1950–1 to 1999–2000 are shown in Appendix Table 5(d) and that for selected periods in Table 5.5.

Table 5.5: Ratio of Merchandise Trade to Non-residential GDP at
Current Prices, 1950–1 to 1999–2000

Period	Imports as % of GDP	Exports as % of GDP	Average trade to GDP ratio
	(1)	(2)	(3)
1950–1 to 1960–1	7.82	5.84	6.83
1960–1 to 1970–1	6.27	4.03	5.15
1970–1 to 1980–1	6.58	5.30	5.94
1980–1 to 1990–1	8.57	5.54	7.05
1990–1 to 1999–2000	10.65	9.08	9.86
1950–1 to 1999–2000	7.95	5.96	6.95

Sources: Appendix Table 5(d).

The ratios varied between 5.15 and 9.86 over the decades. The trade to GDP ratio declined from 7 per cent in 1950–1 to 4.1 per cent in 1970–1. Between 1970–1 to 1980–1 it almost doubled to 7.9 per cent but declined again during most of the 1980s. Buoyancy in the ratios was discernible only since 1991–2 with the liberalization of foreign trade regimes and relaxation of controls.

The effect of foreign trade on output per unit of input has been estimated by Maddison as the product of a certain (assumed) percentage of economies of scale due to trade growth and the trade to GDP ratios.[16]

Maddison assumed that foreign trade produced 10 per cent economies of scale during 1913–50 and 1973–84 when foreign trade growth was slow in the case of the six capitalist countries studied by him and 20 per cent during 1950–73 when the foreign trade grew faster.[17] Growth in foreign trade volume has been calculated as the average on the basis of import and export growth.

---

[14] Angus Maddison, *Monitoring the World Economy, 1820–1992*, OECD Development Centre, Paris, 1995, p. 38.
[15] Maddison, *Explaining the Economic Performance of Nations*, p. 66, 82.
[16] Ibid., p. 66.
[17] Ibid., p. 57.

These are estimated on the basis of the quantum indexes of exports and imports. Such indexes are available from the *Economic Survey* for the period 1969–70 to 1998–9 with base 1978–9 = 100. For 1960–1 to 1968–9 the indexes with base 1958 = 100 are given in the *Basic Statistics Relating to Indian Economy, August 1994* by the Centre for Monitoring Indian Economy (CMIE). For 1950–1 to 1959–60, rough estimates of the quantum indexes have been prepared using the current value figures of imports and exports and the corresponding unit value indexes with base 1952–3 = 100. The volume indexes are presented in Appendix Table 5(e). While a continuous series is not available on a comparable basis for the entire period, nor could one be obtained by splicing due to the non-availability of overlapping values for the relevant years, decade-wise growth rates of foreign trade volume have been compiled and shown in Table 5.6.

Table 5.6: Relation between Growth of Trade Volume and GDP, 1950–1 to 1999–2000

Period	Growth of trade volume			Growth of GDP
	Imports	Exports	Average	
	(1)	(2)	(3)	(4)
1950–1 to 1960–1	3.57	1.89	2.73	3.99
1960–1 to 1970–1	2.09	4.48	3.28	3.74
1970–1 to 1980–1	7.45	6.24	6.84	3.08
1980–1 to 1990–1	5.56	6.03	5.79	5.50
1990–1 to 1999–2000	11.71	8.34	10.02	5.87
1970–1 to 1999–2000	8.11	6.82	7.46	4.77
1980–1 to 1999–2000	8.45	7.13	7.79	5.67

Sources: Col. (1) from Appendix Table 5(e), Col. (1)–Col. (3); Col. (2) from Appendix Table 5(e), Col. (4)–Col. (6); Col. (3) = average of Col. (1) × Col. (2).

Foreign trade effect has been estimated assuming the economies of scale due to trade growth to be 10 per cent. The relevant estimates are presented in Table 5.7.

Table 5.7: Estimated Effect of Foreign Trade, 1950–1 to 1999–2000

Period	Foreign trade volume growth	Trade to GDP ratio	Foreign trade effect %
	(1)	(2)	(3)
1950–1 to 1960–1	2.73	6.83	0.02
1960–1 to 1970–1	3.28	5.15	0.02
1970–1 to 1980–1	6.84	5.94	0.04
1980–1 to 1990–1	5.79	7.05	0.04
1990–1 to 1999–2000	10.02	9.86	0.10
1970–1 to 1999–2000	7.46	7.53	0.06
1980–1 to 1999–2000	7.79	8.25	0.07

Sources: Col. 1, Table 5.6, Col. (3): Col. (2) from Table 5.5, Col. (3); Col. (3) = Col. (2) × 0.01 × Col. (1)/100.

ENERGY EFFECT

The following observation by CMIE on energy consumption in India is quite relevant: 'India ranked sixth in the world in terms of total consumption of commercial energy during 1999. The consumption of energy during the year was 276.4 million tonnes of oil equivalent. This implies that the country's consumption was only 12.5 per cent of USA, the world's highest consumer, and just 37 per cent of China, the world's most populous country. The per capita energy use in India was 277 kilograms of oil equivalent which is quite low compared to the world average of 1428 kilograms. China consumed 602 kilograms of oil equivalent of commercial energy in the same year.'[18]

The overall availability of commercial energy in terms of million tonnes of oil equivalent (MTOE)[19] is available for the years 1970–1 to 1999–2000 from the publications by the CMIE.[20] For the years 1950–1, 1960–1 and 1964–5, oil equivalents have been worked out using the conversion factors provided by the CMIE for lignite, coal, natural gas, hydropower, and nuclear power. The series of commercial energy available by source are presented in Appendix Table 5(f).

The total energy available increased 17 times from 18.4 million tonnes oil equivalent in 1951 to 306 million tonnes by 1999–2000, that is, at the rate of 5.9 per cent a year. The rates of growth of energy available from different sources during the selected periods are given in Table 5.8.

Starting from low levels of energy consumption, the period 1950–1 to 1964–5 recorded the highest rate of growth of 7.2 per cent per annum. The growth rate of energy availability slipped to 4.5 per cent during the middle period when GDP also recorded the lowest rate of growth. The energy consumption picked up in the last period but the rate achieved was lower than that in the first period. Considering decade-wise, the last decade which included the post-reform period, recorded a lower growth at 5.4 per cent, compared to 6.9 per cent during 1980–1 to 1990–1. The consumption of energy by residential users are included in the above data. This accounted for 10 to 11 per cent of the net availability (gross availability – conversion losses) during the 1980s.[21] It might have been lower in the earlier years.

The composition of energy by source indicated that the share of coal declined from 86 per cent in 1950–1 to 51.2 per cent in 1999–2000. Over the same period the share of oil moved up from 12.8 per cent to 35.2 per cent, and that of natural gas from 2.1 per cent in 1970–1 to 7.5 per cent in 1999–2000.

---

[18] Centre for Monitoring Indian Economy (CMIE), Economic Intelligence Unit, *Energy, April 2001*, Mumbai, p. 1.

[19] MTOE is a conversion of energy data into oil equivalent by measuring the useful energy per unit of a particular fuel and then estimating the quantity of oil required to obtain the same amount of useful energy.

[20] CMIE, Economic Intelligence Unit, *Current Energy Scene in India, June 1994* and *Energy, April 2001*.

[21] CMIE, *Current Energy Scene in India, May 1993*, Mumbai, p. 10.

(per cent)

Table 5.8: Annual Growth Rate of Commercial Energy Available, 1950–1 to 1999–2000

Period	Lignite	Coal	Oil	Natural gas	Hydropower	Nuclear power	Total	Real GDP growth
	(1)	(2)	(3)	(4)	(5)	(6)	(7)	(8)
Long periods								
1950–1 to 1999–2000	..	4.79	8.11	..	7.32	..	5.91	4.39
1950–1 to 1964–5	..	5.05	13.59	..	12.72	..	7.16	4.06
1964–5 to 1980–1	4.38	3.65	5.68	9.16	7.26	..	4.50	3.12
1980–1 to 1999–2000	8.00	5.56	6.26	16.32	2.89	7.08	6.18	5.71
Shorter periods								
1950–1 to 1960–1	..	5.51	9.78	..	11.96	..	6.24	3.91
1960–1 to 1970–1	..	2.82	11.92	..	12.44	..	5.84	3.70
1970–1 to 1980–1	4.18	4.59	6.27	0.47	6.39	4.14	5.12	3.08
1980–1 to 1990–1	10.69	6.73	5.79	23.69	4.40	5.24	6.93	5.62
1990–1 to 1999–2000	5.10	4.29	6.78	8.70	1.23	9.16	5.35	5.81

Sources: Cols (1) to (7) based on Appendix Table 5(f); Col. (8) from Table 1.3, Col. (1); .. means nil.

264

The share of hydropower declined from 3.98 per cent to 2.13 per cent between 1980–1 and 1999–2000. Details are shown in Table 5.9.

Table 5.9: Availability of Commercial Energy by Source, 1950–1 to 1999–2000

(per cent)

Period	Lignite	Coal	Oil	Natural Gas	Hydropower	Nuclear power	Total
	(1)	(2)	(3)	(4)	(5)	(6)	(7)
1950–1	.	86.03	12.82	.	1.15	.	100.00
1960–1	..	80.27	17.80	..	1.93	..	100.00
1970–1	2.79	60.12	31.13	2.08	3.53	0.35	100.00
1980–1	2.55	57.14	34.69	1.33	3.98	0.31	100.00
1990–1	3.60	56.08	31.12	5.69	3.13	0.38	100.00
1999–2000	3.53	51.21	35.17	7.51	2.19	0.39	100.00

Sources: Table 5(f).

The value of energy consumed, evaluated using the price of crude oil effective from April 1993 (assumed applicable for 1993–4), that is, at Rs 3296 per tonne,[22] and the ratio of energy consumption to real GDP are shown in Appendix Table 5(g). The relation between energy consumption and real GDP is presented in Table 5.10.

For the period as a whole, the growth rate of energy consumption exceeded that of GDP by 1.5 percentage points. The difference between the two rates

Table 5.10: Growth Rates of Energy Consumption and GDP, 1950–1 to 1999–2000

(per cent)

Period	Growth rates			
	Energy consumption	GDP	Difference (1)–(2)	Energy input as % of GDP
	(1)	(2)	(3)	(4)
Long periods				
1950–1 to 1999–2000	5.91	4.40	1.51	7.60
1950–1 to 1964–5	7.16	4.15	3.01	5.67
1964–5 to 1980–1	4.50	3.13	1.37	7.26
1980–1 to 1999–2000	6.18	5.67	0.51	9.35
Shorter periods				
1950–1 to 1960–1	6.24	3.99	2.25	5.09
1960–1 to 1970–1	5.84	3.74	2.10	6.26
1970–1 to 1980–1	5.12	3.08	2.04	7.52
1980–1 to 1990–1	6.93	5.50	1.43	9.10
1990–1 to 1999–2000	5.35	5.87	−0.52	9.64

Sources: Col. (1) based on Appendix Table 5(g), Col. (2), from Table 1.3, Col. (5); Col. (3) = Col. (1)–Col. (2); Col. (4) from Appendix Table 5(g), Col. (4).

[22] CMIE, Economic Intelligence Service, *India's Energy Sector, July 1995*, Mumbai, pp. 131–2.

declined from 2.25 during the period 1950–1 to 1960–1 to 1.43 in the period 1980–1 to 1990–1 and became negative (–0.52 percentage points) only during the last decade, when GDP grew faster than energy consumption. It is noteworthy that all the six capitalist countries studied by Maddison had slower growth in energy consumption than GDP and hence negative differences in the three periods covered by him, i.e. 1913–50, 1950–73, and 1973–84 (except for the Netherlands in 1950–73).[23] Maddison attributes this negative difference to the energy economy achieved by them.[24] Viewed in this way, the declining positive difference between the growth rates of energy consumption and GDP in India can be considered as an indication of improvement in the utilization of energy over the period.

To measure the energy effect, Maddison compares actual growth of GDP grossed up by energy inputs with a hypothetical situation that would have occurred if it had been possible to maintain the relation between energy growth and GDP growth in the previous period.[25] Table 5.11 presents a comparison of the growth rates of actual and hypothetical growth of GDP plus energy consumption for the selected periods.

Table 5.11: Actual and Hypothetical Growth of GDP Plus Energy Consumption, 1950–1 to 1999–2000
(Average Annual Compound Growth Rate)

Period	Actual	Hypothetical	Actual minus hypothetical
	(1)	(2)	(3)
Long periods			
1950–1 to 1964–5	4.30	–	–
1964–5 to 1980–1	3.23	3.40	–0.17
1980–1 to 1999–2000	5.72	5.56	0.16
Shorter periods			
1950–1 to 1960–1	4.10	–	–
1960–1 to 1970–1	3.86	3.89	–0.03
1970–1 to 1980–1	3.22	3.27	–0.05
1980–1 to 1990–1	5.62	5.47	0.15
1990–1 to 1999–2000	5.82	5.96	–0.14

Sources: Table 5.10 and Appendix Table 5(g).

The difference between the actual and hypothetical growth of GDP plus energy consumption shown in Col. (3) above is taken to indicate the energy effect. The negative values show that the need for energy economy retarded growth in most of the period.

[23] Maddison, *Explaining the Economic Performance of Nations*, p. 58.
[24] Ibid., p. 58.
[25] Ibid., p. 59.

ECONOMIES OF SCALE

If the output increases by more than one per cent corresponding to a one per cent increase in inputs, then the economy is said to be operating under increasing returns to scale. This increasing returns to scale may be due to economies of scale, that is increase in the size of the markets, and may also be due to the effect of other determinants on output per unit of input such as gains from reallocation of resources, advances in knowledge etc. Denison observes that economies of scale are hard to estimate[26] and considers it a purely passive factor in growth that cannot be independently influenced. In his study *Why Growth Rates Differ*, he assumed the scale economies to be 9 per cent of growth.[27] In his later study *Accounting for United States Economic Growth*, he attempted to derive estimates of the gain from economies of scale by correlating the index of real national income with the effect of irregular factors removed with an index constructed as the product of the index of total factor input and the indexes from gains of reallocation of resources from farming and non-farm self-employment. He estimated that 13.4 per cent of long-term growth in the sector (non-residential sector) resulted from economies of scale.[28] According to Maddison, 'empirical evidence on economies of scale is scarce'. He further states that in time series it is difficult to disentangle scale economies from the effects of technical progress.[29] On the basis of data relating to 56 countries, Maddison concluded that there is no significant relationship between size and productivity performance.[30] He assumed the scale bonus at the national level to be 3 per cent of GDP growth for the six countries—France, Germany, Japan, the Netherlands, UK, and the US— studied by him.[31] In the case of India it may be noted that the unorganized sector accounted for a larger share of the net domestic product. During the years 1960–1 to 1964–5, 72.8 per cent of the NDP originated from the unorganized sector,[32] and during 1994–5 to 1998–9 the share had declined only to 61.2 per cent.[33] This means that only 40 per cent of the NDP originated from the organized sector towards the end of the period. In view of the fact that there is limited scope for economies of scale to be achieved in the unorganized sector and also because the organized sector includes public administration and defence, I have, following Maddison, allowed for only a limited role of economies of scale and assumed it to be 3 per cent of GDP

[26] Edward F. Denison, 'Classification of Sources of Growth', *The Review of Income and Wealth*, Series 18, No. 1, March 1972, p. 11.

[27] Denison, *Why Growth Rates Differ*, p. 226.

[28] Denison, *Accounting for Growth*, p. 75.

[29] Maddison, *Explaining the Economic Performance of Nations*, p. 58.

[30] Maddison, *Monitoring the World Economy, 1820–1992*, p. 39.

[31] Maddison, *Explaining the Economic Performance of Nations*, p. 58.

[32] Sivasubramonian, *The National Income of India in the Twentieth Century*, p. 607.

[33] CSO, *National Accounts Statistics, 2001*, New Delhi, July 2001, pp. 184–5.

growth. Dholakia in his study *The Sources of Economic Growth in India* assumed that the gain from economies of scale would be 12 per cent.[34]

OTHER DETERMINANTS OF OUTPUT

Denison has included the effect of work stoppages due to industrial disputes among the irregular fluctuations affecting output per unit of input. The number of workers involved in industrial disputes and the number of man-days lost are given in Cols (1) and (2) of Appendix 5(h). The number of man-days has been converted to man-year equivalent by assuming the effective number of working days in a year to be 270 after allowing for Sundays, declared holidays, and leave entitlements. The number reported to be in the workforce is taken as equal to the number of man-years available. The highest number of man-years lost due to work stoppages was in 1982 and even this was less than 0.1 per cent of the number of man-years available. It is, therefore, presumed that industrial disputes would have had little effect on output per unit of input in India.

Yet another aspect studied by Denison was the effect of intensity of demand on output per unit of input. For this, he chose as indicator the variations in the percentage of non-labour earnings in corporations to corporate national income and its correlation with the variations in adjusted output per unit of input (that is, output per unit of input with the irregular fluctuations due to gains from reallocation of resources from farming, non-farm self-employment, and effect of weather on farm output removed). He found that the two series are closely correlated in the case of the United States[35] and proceeded to evolve a measure of the effect of intensity of demand. A similar attempt using Indian data showed that there was no correlation between the changes in adjusted output per unit of input and variations in the percentage share of non-labour income. This may be due to the fact that under the rigid labour laws prevailing in India, labour share of national income is not subject to variations corresponding to fluctuations in demand.

ADVANCES IN KNOWLEDGE AND N.E.C.

The contribution of advances in knowledge to production growth cannot be measured directly.[36] It is, therefore, taken as a residual or what remains of the contribution of output per unit of input after deducting the separately estimated contributions of structural changes or gains from reallocation of resources, effect of fluctuations due to weather, foreign trade effect, energy effect, and economies of scale.

---

[34] Dholakia, *The Sources of Economic Growth in India*, p. 223.
[35] Denison, *Accounting for Growth*, p. 298.
[36] Ibid., p. 79.

Appendix Table 5(a): Non-residential Sector: Gains from Reallocation of Resources from Agriculture over Long and Short Periods at 1993–4 Prices, 1950–1 to 1999–2000

1950–1 to 1960–1:

	Year	Sector A	Sector non-A	Total
1. % of GDP in 1993–4 prices	1950–1	60.8	39.2	100
2. % of labour input	1950–1	71.47	28.53	100
3. % of labour input	1960–1	67.31	32.69	100
4. Change: Row 3 – Row 2		–4.16	4.16	
5. % change in current labour input if distribution had been that of the following year: Row 4/Row 2 × 100		–5.82	14.58	
6. Annual rate of % change in output to % change in labour input		0.132	0.6277	
7. % in current year GDP with the following year distribution: Row 5 × Row 6		–0.77	9.15	
8. % change in current year GDP in sector: Row 1 × Row 7		–0.47	3.59	3.12
Compound rate of growth 1950–1 to 1960–1				0.31

1960–1 to 1970–1:

	Year	Sector A	Sector non-A	Total
1. % of GDP in 1993–4 prices	1960–1	55.4	44.6	100
2. % of labour input	1960–1	67.31	32.69	100
3. % of labour input	1970–1	65.56	34.44	100
4. Change: Row 3 – Row 2		–1.75	1.75	
5. % change in current labour input if distribution had been that of the following year: Row 4/Row 2 × 100		–2.60	5.35	
6. Annual rate of % change in output to % change in labour input		0.146	0.5632	
7. % in current year GDP with the following year distribution: Row 5 × Row 6		–0.38	3.01	
8. % change in current year GDP in sector: Row 1 × Row 7		–0.21	1.34	1.13
Compound rate of growth 1960–1 to 1970–1				0.11

1970–1 to 1980–1:

	Year	Sector A	Sector non-A	Total
1. % of GDP in 1993–4 prices	1970–1	48.22	51.78	100
2. % of labour input	1970–1	65.56	34.44	100
3. % of labour input	1980–1	61.08	38.92	100
4. Change: Row 3 – Row 2		–4.48	4.48	
5. % change in current labour input if distribution had been that of the following year: Row 4/Row 2 × 100		–6.83	13.01	
6. Annual rate of % change in output to % change in labour input		0.1454	0.564	
7. % in current year GDP with the following year distribution: Row 5 × Row 6		–0.99	7.34	
8. % change in current year GDP in sector: Row 1 × Row 7		–0.48	3.80	3.32
Compound rate of growth 1970–1 to 1980–1				0.33

(Cols Contd.)

Appendix Table 5(a) Contd.

1980–1 to 1990–1:

	Year	Sector A	Sector non-A	Total
1. % of GDP in 1993–4 prices	1950–1	41.3	58.7	100
2. % of labour input	1950–1	61.08	38.92	100
3. % of labour input	1960–1	55.85	44.15	100
4. Change: Row 3 – Row 2		–5.23	5.23	
5. % change in current labour input if distribution had been that of the following year: Row 4/Row 2 × 100		–8.56	13.44	
6. Annual rate of % change in output to % change in labour input		0.1434	0.5411	
7. % in current year GDP with the following year distribution: Row 5 × Row 6		–1.23	7.27	
8. % change in current year GDP in sector: Row 1 × Row 7		–0.51	4.27	3.76
Compound rate of growth 1980–1 to 1990–1				0.37

1990–1 to 1999–2000:

	Year	Sector A	Sector non-A	Total
1. % of GDP in 1993–4 prices	1960–1	33.86	66.14	100
2. % of labour input	1960–1	55.85	44.15	100
3. % of labour input	1970–1	51.7	48.3	100
4. Change: Row 3 – Row 2		–4.15	4.15	
5. % change in current labour input if distribution had been that of the following year: Row 4/Row 2 × 100		–7.43	9.40	
6. Annual rate of % change in output to % change in labour input		0.1265	0.4852	
7. % in current year GDP with the following year distribution: Row 5 × Row 6		–0.94	4.56	
8. % change in current year GDP in sector: Row 1 × Row 7		–0.32	3.02	2.70
Compound rate of growth 1990–1 to 1999–2000				0.30

1950–1 to 1999–2000:

	Year	Sector A	Sector non-A	Total
1. % of GDP in 1993–4 prices	1970–1	60.8	39.2	100
2. % of labour input	1970–1	71.47	28.53	100
3. % of labour input	1980–1	51.7	48.3	100
4. Change: Row 3 – Row 2		–19.77	19.77	
5. % change in current labour input if distribution had been that of the following year: Row 4/Row 2 × 100		–27.66	69.30	
6. Annual rate of % change in output to % change in labour input		0.1385	0.5578	
7. % in current year GDP with the following year distribution: Row 5 × Row 6		–3.83	38.65	
8. % change in current year GDP in sector: Row 1 × Row 7		–2.33	15.15	12.82
Compound rate of growth 1950–1 to 1999–2000				0.25

(Cols Contd.)

Appendix Table 5(a) Contd.

1950–1 to 1964–5:

	Year	Sector A	Sector non-A	Total
1. % of GDP in 1993–4 prices	1950–1	60.8	39.2	100
2. % of labour input	1950–1	71.47	28.53	100
3. % of labour input	1960–1	66.62	33.38	100
4. Change: Row 3 – Row 2		–4.85	4.85	
5. % change in current labour input if distribution had been that of the following year: Row 4/Row 2 × 100		–6.79	17.00	
6. Annual rate of % change in output to % change in labour input		0.1341	0.6074	
7. % in current year GDP with the following year distribution: Row 5 × Row 6		–0.91	10.33	
8. % change in current year GDP in sector: Row 1 × Row 7		–0.55	4.05	3.49
Compound rate of growth 1950–1 to 1964–5				0.25

1964–5 to 1980–1:

	Year	Sector A	Sector non-A	Total
1. % of GDP in 1993–4 prices	1960–1	50.88	49.12	100
2. % of labour input	1960–1	66.62	33.38	100
3. % of labour input	1970–1	60.57	39.43	100
4. Change: Row 3 – Row 2		–6.05	6.05	
5. % change in current labour input if distribution had been that of the following year: Row 4/Row 2 × 100		–9.08	18.12	
6. Annual rate of % change in output to % change in labour input		0.1468	0.5643	
7. % in current year GDP with the following year distribution: Row 5 × Row 6		–1.33	10.23	
8. % change in current year GDP in sector: Row 1 × Row 7		–0.68	5.02	4.35
Compound rate of growth 1964–5 to 1980–1				0.27

1980–1 to 1999–2000:

	Year	Sector A	Sector non-A	Total
1. % of GDP in 1993–4 prices	1970–1	41.3	58.7	100
2. % of labour input	1970–1	61.08	38.92	100
3. % of labour input	1980–1	51.7	48.3	100
4. Change: Row 3 – Row 2		–9.38	9.38	
5. % change in current labour input if distribution had been that of the following year: Row 4/Row 2 × 100		–15.36	24.10	
6. Annual rate of % change in output to % change in labour input		0.1352	0.5137	
7. % in current year GDP with the following year distribution: Row 5 × Row 6		–2.08	12.38	
8. % change in current year GDP in sector: Row 1 × Row 7		–0.86	7.27	6.41
Compound rate of growth 1980–1 to 1999–2000				0.33

Appendix Table 5(b): Non-residential Sector: Gains from Reallocation of Resources from Agriculture over Long and Short Periods at Current Prices, 1950–1 to 1999–2000

1950–1 to 1960–1:

	Year	Sector A	Sector non-A	Total
1. % of GDP in 1993–4 prices	1950–1	62.44	37.56	100
2. % of labour input	1950–1	71.47	28.53	100
3. % of labour input	1960–1	66.79	33.21	100
4. Change: Row 3 – Row 2		–4.68	4.68	
5. % change in current labour input if distribution had been that of the following year: Row 4/Row 2 × 100		–6.55	16.40	
6. Annual rate of % change in output to % change in labour input		0.132	0.6277	
7. % in current year GDP with the following year distribution: Row 5 × Row 6		–0.86	10.30	
8. % change in current year GDP in sector: Row 1 × Row 7		–0.54	3.87	3.33
Compound rate of growth 1950–1 to 1960–1				0.33

1960–1 to 1970–1:

	Year	Sector A	Sector non-A	Total
1. % of GDP in 1993–4 prices	1960–1	52.22	47.78	100
2. % of labour input	1960–1	67.31	32.69	100
3. % of labour input	1970–1	65.56	34.44	100
4. Change: Row 3 – Row 2		–1.75	1.75	
5. % change in current labour input if distribution had been that of the following year: Row 4/Row 2 × 100		–2.60	5.35	
6. Annual rate of % change in output to % change in labour input		0.146	0.5632	
7. % in current year GDP with the following year distribution: Row 5 × Row 6		–0.38	3.01	
8. % change in current year GDP in sector: Row 1 × Row 7		–0.20	1.44	1.24
Compound rate of growth 1960–1 to 1970–1				0.13

1970–1 to 1980–1:

	Year	Sector A	Sector non-A	Total
1. % of GDP in 1993–4 prices	1970–1	50.14	49.86	100
2. % of labour input	1970–1	65.56	34.44	100
3. % of labour input	1980–1	61.08	38.92	100
4. Change: Row 3 – Row 2		–4.48	4.48	
5. % change in current labour input if distribution had been that of the following year: Row 4/Row 2 × 100		–6.83	13.01	
6. Annual rate of % change in output to % change in labour input		0.1454	0.564	
7. % in current year GDP with the following year distribution: Row 5 × Row 6		–0.99	7.34	
8. % change in current year GDP in sector: Row 1 × Row 7		–0.50	3.66	3.16
Compound rate of growth 1970–1 to 1980–1				0.31

(Cols Contd.)

Appendix Table 5(b) Contd.

1980–1 to 1990–1:

Year	Sector A	Sector non-A	Total
1950–1	41.23	58.77	100
1950–1	61.08	38.92	100
1960–1	55.85	44.15	100

1. % of GDP in 1993–4 prices
2. % of labour input
3. % of labour input
4. Change: Row 3 – Row 2 → –5.23 | 5.23
5. % change in current labour input if distribution had been that of the following year: Row 4/Row 2 × 100 → –8.56 | 13.44
6. Annual rate of % change in output to % change in labour input → 0.1434 | 0.5411
7. % in current year GDP with the following year distribution: Row 5 × Row 6 → –1.23 | 7.27
8. % change in current year GDP in sector: Row 1 × Row 7 → –0.51 | 4.27 | 3.77
   Compound rate of growth 1980–1 to 1990–1 → 0.37

1990–1 to 1999–2000:

Year	Sector A	Sector non-A	Total
1960–1	33.12	66.88	100
1960–1	55.85	44.15	100
1970–1	51.7	48.3	100

1. % of GDP in 1993–4 prices
2. % of labour input
3. % of labour input
4. Change: Row 3 – Row 2 → –4.15 | 4.15
5. % change in current labour input if distribution had been that of the following year: Row 4/Row 2 × 100 → –7.43 | 9.40
6. Annual rate of % change in output to % change in labour input → 0.1265 | 0.4852
7. % in current year GDP with the following year distribution: Row 5 × Row 6 → –0.94 | 4.56
8. % change in current year GDP in sector: Row 1 × Row 7 → –0.31 | 3.05 | 2.74
   Compound rate of growth 1990–1 to 1999–2000 → 0.27

1950–1 to 1999–2000:

Year	Sector A	Sector non-A	Total
1970–1	62.44	37.56	100
1970–1	71.47	28.92	100.39
1980–1	51.7	48.3	100

1. % of GDP in 1993–4 prices
2. % of labour input
3. % of labour input
4. Change: Row 3 – Row 2 → –19.77 | 19.38
5. % change in current labour input if distribution had been that of the following year: Row 4/Row 2 × 100 → –27.66 | 67.01
6. Annual rate of % change in output to % change in labour input → 0.1385 | 0.5578
7. % in current year GDP with the following year distribution: Row 5 × Row 6 → –3.83 | 37.38
8. % change in current year GDP in sector: Row 1 × Row 7 → –2.39 | 14.04 | 11.65
   Compound rate of growth 1950–1 to 1999–2000 → 0.25

(Cols Contd.)

Appendix Table 5(b) Contd.

1950–1 to 1964–5:

Year	Sector A	Sector non-A	Total

1. % of GDP in 1993–4 prices   1950–1   62.44   37.56   100

2. % of labour input   1950–1   71.47   28.53   100

3. % of labour input   1960–1   66.62   33.38   100

4. Change: Row 3 – Row 2   –4.85   4.85

5. % change in current labour input if distribution had been that of the following year: Row 4/Row 2 × 100   –6.79   17.00

6. Annual rate of % change in output to % change in labour input   0.1341   0.6074

7. % in current year GDP with the following year distribution: Row 5 × Row 6   –0.91   10.33

8. % change in current year GDP in sector: Row 1 × Row 7   –0.57   3.88   3.31

Compound rate of growth 1950–1 to 1964–5   0.24

1964–5 to 1980–1:

Year	Sector A	Sector non-A	Total

1. % of GDP in 1993–4 prices   1960–1   52.01   47.99   100

2. % of labour input   1960–1   66.62   33.38   100

3. % of labour input   1970–1   61.08   38.92   100

4. Change: Row 3 – Row 2   –5.54   5.54

5. % change in current labour input if distribution had been that of the following year: Row 4/Row 2 × 100   –8.32   16.60

6. Annual rate of % change in output to % change in labour input   0.1468   0.5643

7. % in current year GDP with the following year distribution: Row 5 × Row 6   –1.22   9.37

8. % change in current year GDP in sector: Row 1 × Row 7   –0.63   4.49   3.86

Compound rate of growth 1964–5 to 1980–1   0.24

1980–1 to 1999–2000:

Year	Sector A	Sector non-A	Total

1. % of GDP in 1993–4 prices   1970–1   41.23   58.77   100

2. % of labour input   1970–1   61.08   38.92   100

3. % of labour input   1980–1   51.7   48.3   100

4. Change: Row 3 – Row 2   –9.38   9.38

5. % change in current labour input if distribution had been that of the following year: Row 4/Row 2 × 100   –15.36   24.10

6. Annual rate of % change in output to % change in labour input   0.1352   0.5137

7. % in current year GDP with the following year distribution: Row 5 × Row 6   –2.08   12.38

8. % change in current year GDP in sector: Row 1 × Row 7   –0.86   7.28   6.42

Compound rate of growth 1980–1 to 1999–2000   0.33

Appendix Table 5(c): Moving Average of Sector A Output at
1993–4 Prices, 1950–1 to 1999–2000

(Rs crore)

Year	Actual sector A real GDP	Normal sector A GDP	Excess of actual over normal
	(1)	(2)	(3)
1948–9	79,561		
1949–50	81,726		
1950–1	81,069	81,901	−832
1951–2	82,278	84,271	−1993
1952–3	84,873	86,745	−1872
1953–4	91,409	89,188	2221
1954–5	94,096	92,403	1693
1955–6	93,283	94,216	−933
1956–7	98,354	96,614	1740
1957–8	93,936	98,267	−4331
1958–9	103,401	101,461	1940
1959–60	102,360	103,659	−1299
1960–1	109,254	106,306	2948
1961–2	109,346	107,562	1784
1962–3	107,171	111,049	−3878
1963–4	109,678	110,511	−833
1964–5	119,795	109,652	10,143
1965–6	106,567	112,353	−5786
1966–7	105,051	114,514	−9463
1967–8	120,673	116,200	4473
1968–9	120,482	122,350	−1868
1969–70	128,226	128,289	−63
1970–1	137,320	129,750	7570
1971–2	134,742	133,093	1649
1972–3	127,980	134,469	−6489
1973–4	137,197	137,510	−313
1974–5	135,107	139,303	−4196
1975–6	152,522	145,333	7189
1976–7	143,709	150,249	−6540
1977–8	158,132	151,449	6683
1978–9	161,773	152,803	8970
1979–80	141,107	157,606	−16,499
1980–1	159,293	159,295	−2
1981–2	167,723	163,440	4283
1982–3	166,577	172,255	−5678
1983–4	182,498	177,711	4787
1984–5	185,186	181,239	3947
1985–6	186,570	184,503	2067
1986–7	185,363	190,240	−4877
1987–8	182,899	196,066	−13,167
1988–9	211,184	203,375	7809
1989–90	214,315	210,234	4081
1990–1	223,114	220,132	2982
1991–2	219,660	226,288	−6628
1992–3	232,386	234,243	−1857
1993–4	241,967	239,999	1968
1994–5	254,090	251,285	2805

(Contd.)

Appendix Table 5(c) Contd.

	(1)	(2)	(3)
1995–6	251,892	258,685	–6793
1996–7	276,091	267,971	8120
1997–8	269,383	275,220	–5837
1998–9	288,401	284,860	3541
1999–2000	290,334	292,661	–2327
2000–1	300,089		
2001–2	315,099		

Sources: Col. (1) from Appendix Table 1(e), Col. (4) for 1950–1 to 1999–2000, for 1948–9, 1949–50, 2000–1, and 2001–2 estimated; Col. (2) shows five-year averages based on Col. (1); Col. (3) = Col. (1) – Col. (2).

Appendix Table 5(d): Ratio of Foreign Trade to GDP at Current Prices, 1950–1 to 1999–2000

Year	Imports (Rs crore)	Exports (Rs crore)	Non-residential GDP (Rs crore)	as % of GDP		
				Imports	Exports	Average
	(1)	(2)	(3)	(4)	(5)	(6)
1950–1	608	606	8699	6.99	6.97	6.98
1951–2	890	716	9172	9.70	7.81	8.75
1952–3	702	578	8967	7.83	6.45	7.14
1953–4	610	531	9778	6.24	5.43	5.83
1954–5	700	593	9042	7.74	6.56	7.15
1955–6	774	609	9128	8.48	6.67	7.58
1956–7	841	605	11,042	7.62	5.48	6.55
1957–8	1035	561	11,227	9.22	5.00	7.11
1958–9	906	581	12,625	7.18	4.60	5.89
1959–60	961	640	13,228	7.26	4.84	6.05
1960–1	1122	642	14,518	7.73	4.42	6.08
1961–2	1090	660	15,399	7.08	4.29	5.68
1962–3	1131	675	16,344	6.92	4.13	5.52
1963–4	1223	793	18,805	6.50	4.22	5.36
1964–5	1349	816	22,165	6.09	3.68	4.88
1965–6	1409	810	23,158	6.08	3.50	4.79
1966–7	2078	1157	26,534	7.83	4.36	6.10
1967–8	2008	1199	31,404	6.39	3.82	5.11
1968–9	1909	1358	33,082	5.77	4.10	4.94
1969–70	1582	1413	36,487	4.34	3.87	4.10
1970–1	1634	1535	38,795	4.21	3.96	4.08
1971–2	1825	1608	41,220	4.43	3.90	4.16
1972–3	1867	1971	45,410	4.11	4.34	4.23
1973–4	2955	2523	56,218	5.26	4.49	4.87
1974–5	4519	3329	66,564	6.79	5.00	5.90
1975–6	5265	4036	70,584	7.46	5.72	6.59
1976–7	5074	5142	75,815	6.69	6.78	6.74
1977–8	6020	5408	86,854	6.93	6.23	6.58
1978–9	6811	5726	93,344	7.30	6.13	6.72
1979–80	9143	6418	101,929	8.97	6.30	7.63

(Contd.)

Appendix Table 5(d) Contd.

	(1)	(2)	(3)	(4)	(5)	(6)
1980–1	12,549	6711	122,712	10.23	5.47	7.85
1981–2	13,608	7806	143,530	9.48	5.44	7.46
1982–3	14,293	8803	159,777	8.95	5.51	7.23
1983–4	15,831	9771	187,480	8.44	5.21	6.83
1984–5	17,134	11,744	210,043	8.16	5.59	6.87
1985–6	19,658	10,895	235,022	8.36	4.64	6.50
1986–7	20,096	12,452	261,657	7.68	4.76	6.22
1987–8	22,244	15,674	296,942	7.49	5.28	6.38
1988–9	28,235	20,232	356,602	7.92	5.67	6.80
1989–90	35,416	27,681	412,948	8.58	6.70	7.64
1990–1	43,193	32,553	482,385	8.95	6.75	7.85
1991–2	47,851	44,042	556,302	8.60	7.92	8.26
1992–3	63,375	53,688	635,554	9.97	8.45	9.21
1993–4	73,101	69,751	738,075	9.90	9.45	9.68
1994–5	89,971	82,674	870,590	10.33	9.50	9.92
1995–6	122,678	106,353	1,022,746	11.99	10.40	11.20
1996–7	138,920	118,817	1,188,567	11.69	10.00	10.84
1997–8	154,176	130,101	1,330,767	11.59	9.78	10.68
1998–9	178,332	139,753	1,548,568	11.52	9.02	10.27
1999–2000	204,583	162,925	1,708,954	11.97	9.53	10.75

Sources: Col. (1) and (2), 1950–1 to 1991–2 from *CMIE Basic Statistics Relating to Indian Economy, August 1997*, Table 10.1 for 1992–3 to 1999–2000 from Table 7.1(1) *Economic Survey 2000–2001*, p. S.81; Col. (3) from Appendix Table 1(d) Col. 3; Cols (4) and (5) derived; Col. (6) = Average of Cols (4) and (5).

Appendix Table 5(e): Foreign Trade Indexes, 1950–1 to 1999–2000

	Import volume index			Export volume index		
Year	1952–3 = 100	1958 = 100	1978–9 = 100	1952–3 = 100	1958 = 100	1978–9 = 100
	(1)	(2)	(3)	(4)	(5)	(6)
1950–1	110.97			102.77		
1951–2	128.06			84.78		
1952–3	100.00			100.00		
1953–4	103.42			101.04		
1954–5	109.54			102.60		
1955–6	126.78			117.13		
1956–7	122.22			111.42		
1957–8	153.56			104.33		
1958–9	141.88			110.38		
1959–60	152.14			121.30		
1960–1		128			100	
1961–2		121			105	
1962–3		131			112	
1963–4		135			126	
1964–5		146			132	
1965–6		154			124	
1966–7		149			119	
1967–8		166			122	
1968–9		151			142	
1969–70			64.9			55.7

(Contd.)

Appendix Table 5(e) Contd.

	(1)	(2)	(3)	(4)	(5)	(6)
1970–1			67.2			59.0
1971–2			80.6			59.2
1972–3			76.7			66.5
1973–4			87.2			69.5
1974–5			77.2			73.7
1975–6			76.0			81.7
1976–7			76.1			96.8
1977–8			100.0			93.2
1978–9			100.0			100.0
1979–80			116.4			106.2
1980–1			137.9			108.1
1981–2			150.6			110.1
1982–3			154.6			116.7
1983–4			185.4			113.0
1984–5			156.1			120.8
1985–6			182.3			111.3
1986–7			212.3			121.3
1987–8			204.8			140.0
1988–9			224.2			152.1
1989–90			227.8			174.9
1990–1			237.7			194.1
1991–2			228.0			208.6
1992–3			282.0			222.9
1993–4			329.1			257.5
1994–5			408.3			292.7
1995–6			514.8			384.3
1996–7			511.8			411.8
1997–8			562.1			386.0
1998–9			644.2			399.2

Sources: For 1969–70 and 1998–9 from *Economic Survey, 2000–1*, Table 7.6, p. S.97; for 1960–1 to 1968–9 from *CMIE Basic Statistics Relating to Indian Economy, August 1994*, Table 10.3; for 1950–1 to 1959–60, see the text.

Appendix Table 5(f): Supply of Commercial Energy, 1950–1 to 1999–2000
(in million tonnes oil equivalent)

Year	Lignite	Coal	Oil	Natural gas	Hydro-power	Nuclear power	Total
	(1)	(2)	(3)	(4)	(5)	(6)	(7)
1950–1	–	15.83	2.36	–	0.21	–	18.40
1960–1	–	27.06	6.00	–	0.65	–	33.71
1964–5	1.26	31.56	14.05	0.32	1.27	–	48.46
1970–1	1.66	35.75	18.51	1.24	2.10	0.20	59.46
1971–2	1.81	35.49	20.25	1.32	2.34	0.10	61.31
1972–3	1.52	37.84	19.41	1.34	2.27	0.09	62.47
1973–4	1.62	38.31	21.04	1.47	2.41	0.20	65.05
1974–5	1.47	43.36	21.70	1.75	2.32	0.18	70.78
1975–6	1.48	48.84	22.07	2.03	2.78	0.22	77.42
1976–7	1.97	49.51	22.95	2.08	2.90	0.27	79.68
1977–8	1.75	49.43	25.27	2.43	3.17	0.19	82.24

(Contd.)

Appendix Table 5(f) Contd.

	(1)	(2)	(3)	(4)	(5)	(6)	(7)
1978–9	1.62	49.96	26.29	2.41	3.93	0.23	84.44
1979–80	1.42	50.94	27.89	2.37	3.79	0.24	86.65
1980–1	2.50	56.00	34.00	1.30	3.90	0.30	98.00
1981–2	3.10	61.30	35.50	1.90	4.10	0.30	106.20
1982–3	3.40	64.40	37.70	2.50	4.00	0.20	112.20
1983–4	3.60	68.90	39.30	2.90	4.20	0.30	119.20
1984–5	3.80	72.50	41.20	3.50	4.50	0.30	125.80
1985–6	3.90	76.70	46.70	4.20	4.30	0.40	136.20
1986–7	4.70	82.30	46.50	6.10	4.50	0.40	144.50
1987–8	5.50	89.90	48.80	6.80	4.00	0.40	155.40
1988–9	6.20	98.20	54.10	7.90	4.80	0.50	171.70
1989–90	6.10	101.90	57.50	9.60	5.20	0.40	180.70
1990–1	6.90	107.40	59.70	10.90	6.00	0.50	191.40
1991–2	7.80	116.60	60.80	12.40	6.10	0.50	204.20
1992–3	8.10	121.60	63.80	13.80	5.80	0.60	213.70
1993–4	8.90	125.20	65.90	14.00	5.90	0.40	220.30
1994–5	9.50	131.20	72.20	14.90	6.90	0.50	220.30
1995–6	10.90	139.80	81.60	18.20	6.00	0.70	257.20
1996–7	11.10	148.00	85.80	18.40	5.70	0.80	269.80
1997–8	11.30	155.00	89.40	21.00	6.20	0.80	283.70
1998–9	11.50	152.60	95.70	22.00	6.90	1.00	289.70
1999–2000	10.80	156.80	107.70	23.00	6.70	1.10	306.10

Sources: For 1970–1 to 1979–80, CMIE *Current Energy Scene in India, June 1994*, p. vi; for 1980–1 to 1999–2000, CMIE *Energy April 2001*, p. 12; for 1950–1, 1960–1, and 1964–5 estimated on the basis of data available from *Statistical Abstracts* (various issues) issued by CSO for the relevant years.

Appendix Table 5(g): Energy Consumption in Relation to GDP, 1950–1 to 1999–2000

(Rs crore)

Year	Supply of commercial energy MTOE	Value of energy consumption at 1993–4 prices	Non-residential GDP at 1993–4 prices	Ratio of energy consumption to GDP	GDP plus energy consumption
	(1)	(2)	(3)	(4)	(5)
1950–1	18.40	6065	133,328	4.55	139,393
1960–1	33.71	11,111	197,202	5.63	208,313
1970–1	59.46	19,598	284,755	6.88	304,353
1971–2	61.30	20,204	287,195	7.04	307,399
1972–3	62.46	20,587	286,083	7.20	306,670
1973–4	65.05	21,440	299,302	7.16	320,742
1974–5	70.79	23,332	302,545	7.71	325,877
1975–6	77.42	25,518	330,574	7.72	356,092
1976–7	79.68	26,263	334,463	7.85	360,726
1977–8	82.24	27,106	360,087	7.53	387,193
1978–9	84.44	27,831	380,255	7.32	408,086
1979–80	86.64	28,557	359,282	7.95	387,839
1980–1	91.38	30,119	385,704	7.81	415,823

(Contd.)

Appendix Table 5(g)

	(1)	(2)	(3)	(4)	(5)
1981–2	102.48	33,777	408,299	8.27	442,076
1982–3	109.72	36,164	419,990	8.61	456,154
1983–4	117.51	38,731	452,221	8.56	490,952
1984–5	123.56	40,725	471,155	8.64	511,880
1985–6	137.12	45,195	491,473	9.20	536,668
1986–7	146.33	48,230	511,807	9.42	560,037
1987–8	157.38	51,872	529,997	9.79	581,869
1988–9	170.37	56,154	585,737	9.59	641,891
1989–90	180.61	59,529	624,960	9.53	684,489
1990–1	191.50	63,118	658,889	9.58	722,007
1991–2	204.20	67,304	665,018	10.12	732,322
1992–3	213.70	70,436	698,241	10.09	768,677
1993–4	220.30	72,611	738,075	9.84	810,686
1994–5	235.10	77,489	794,008	9.76	871,497
1995–6	257.10	84,740	853,893	9.92	938,633
1996–7	269.90	88,959	923,148	9.64	1,012,107
1997–8	283.70	93,508	968,030	9.66	1,061,538
1998–9	289.70	95,485	1,033,306	9.24	1,128,791
1999–2000	306.20	100,924	1,100,834	9.17	1,201,758

Note: MTOE = Million tonnes of oil equivalent.
Sources: Col. (1) from 1970–1 to 1989–90 from CMIE, *Current Energy, Scene in India, June 1994*, p. vi; from 1990–1 to 1999–2000 from CMIE, *Energy, April 2001*, p. 12; for 1950–1 and 1960–1 estimated on the basis of data available in *Economic Survey 1996–7*, p. S.33 and *Statistical Abstract 1961*; Col. (2) = Col. (1) × Rs 3296, i.e., crude oil price per tonne; from CMIE, *India's Energy Sector, July 1995*, p. 132; Col. (3) from Table 3.4, Col. (3); Col. (4) = Col. (2)/Col. (3) × 100; Col. (5) = Col. (2) + Col. (3).

Appendix Table 5(h): Industrial Disputes: Number of Workers Involved, Man-days and Man-years Lost, and their Effect of Output Per Unit of Input, 1951–2000

Year	Number of workers ('000)	Number of man-days lost ('000)	Number of man-years lost ('000)	Man-years worked ('000)	Man-years worked/ man-years lost ('000)	Man-years worked as a percentage of the sum of man-years worked and not worked due to industrial disputes	Estimated impact of labour disputes	Index of effect of work stoppages 1993–4 = 100
	(1)	(2)	(3)	(4)	(5)	(6)	(7)	(8)
1951	691	3819	14	160,139	160,153	99.9912	99.9974	100.0036
1952	809	3337	12	162,661	162,673	99.9924	99.9977	100.0040
1953	467	3383	13	165,223	165,236	99.9924	99.9977	100.0040
1954	477	3373	12	167,825	167,837	99.9926	99.9978	100.0041
1955	528	5098	19	170,468	170,487	99.9889	99.9967	100.0030
1956	715	6992	26	173,153	173,179	99.9850	99.9955	100.0018
1957	889	6429	24	175,880	175,904	99.9865	99.9959	100.0022
1958	929	7798	29	178,651	178,680	99.9838	99.9952	100.0014
1959	693	5633	21	181,464	181,485	99.9885	99.9966	100.0028
1960	986	6470	24	184,322	184,346	99.9870	99.9961	100.0024
1961	512	4919	18	187,225	187,243	99.9903	99.9971	100.0034
1962	705	6121	23	190,389	190,412	99.9881	99.9964	100.0027
1963	563	3269	12	193,822	193,834	99.9938	99.9981	100.0044
1964	1003	7725	29	197,317	197,346	99.9855	99.9957	100.0019
1965	991	6470	24	200,874	200,898	99.9881	99.9964	100.0027
1966	1410	13,846	51	204,496	204,547	99.9749	99.9925	99.9988
1967	1491	17,148	64	208,183	208,247	99.9695	99.9909	99.9971
1968	1669	17,244	64	211,937	212,001	99.9699	99.9910	99.9972
1969	1827	19,048	71	215,758	215,829	99.9673	99.9902	99.9965
1970	1828	20,563	76	219,648	219,724	99.9653	99.9896	99.9959
1971	1615	16,546	61	223,608	223,669	99.9726	99.9918	99.9981
1972	1737	20,544	76	227,640	227,716	99.9666	99.9900	99.9963
1973	2545	20,626	76	231,744	231,820	99.9670	99.9901	99.9964

(Contd.)

Appendix Table 5(h) Contd.

	(1)	(2)	(3)	(4)	(5)	(6)	(7)	(8)
1974	2855	40,262	149	237,021	237,170	99.9371	99.9811	99.9874
1975	1143	21,901	81	243,520	243,601	99.9667	99.9900	99.9963
1976	736	12,746	47	250,198	250,245	99.9811	99.9943	100.0006
1977	2193	25,320	94	257,059	257,153	99.9635	99.9891	99.9953
1978	1916	28,340	105	263,614	263,719	99.9602	99.9881	99.9943
1979	2873	43,854	162	269,845	270,007	99.9398	99.9820	99.9882
1980	1900	21,925	81	276,222	276,303	99.9706	99.9912	99.9975
1981	1588	36,583	135	282,751	282,886	99.9521	99.9856	99.9919
1982	1469	74,615	276	289,434	289,710	99.9046	99.9714	99.9777
1983	1461	46,858	174	296,688	296,862	99.9415	99.9825	99.9887
1984	1949	56,025	208	302,957	303,165	99.9316	99.9795	99.9858
1985	1079	29,240	108	307,784	307,892	99.9648	99.9894	99.9957
1986	1645	32,749	121	312,688	312,809	99.9612	99.9884	99.9947
1987	1770	35,358	131	317,671	317,802	99.9588	99.9876	99.9939
1988	1191	33,947	126	322,732	322,858	99.9611	99.9883	99.9946
1989	1364	32,663	121	329,197	329,318	99.9633	99.9890	99.9953
1990	1308	24,086	89	337,119	337,208	99.9735	99.9921	99.9984
1991	1342	26,428	98	345,231	345,329	99.9717	99.9915	99.9978
1992	1252	31,259	116	353,539	353,655	99.9673	99.9902	99.9965
1993	954	20,301	75	362,047	362,122	99.9792	99.9938	100.0001
1994	846	20,983	78	370,759	370,837	99.9790	99.9937	100.0000
1995	990	16,290	60	376,705	376,765	99.9840	99.9952	100.0015
1996	939	20,284	75	379,793	379,868	99.9802	99.9941	100.0004
1997	981	16,971	63	382,907	382,970	99.9836	99.9951	100.0014
1998	1289	22,062	82	386,047	386,129	99.9788	99.9937	99.9999
1999				389,212				
2000				392,403				

Sources: Cols (1) and (2) for 1951 to 1991 from *CMIE-Basic Statistics, August 1994*, Table 8.18; for 1992 to 1998 from *Statistical Abstract 2000*, p. 306; Col. (3) = Col. (2) × 1000/270 to obtain equivalent man-years lost. Man-years Col. (4) from Table C-1 from *CMIE-Basic Statistics*, Col. (4); Col. (5) = Col. (3)/Col. (4) × 100; Col. (6) = Col. (4)/Col. (5); for Col. (7) and (8), see the text.

6

Sources of Growth in the Non-residential Sector

The basic indicators required to analyse the sources of growth in the non-residential sector of the economy have been developed so far. The output indicator selected is gross domestic product (GDP) originating in the non-residential sector, that is, GDP excluding the services of dwellings. This accounted for 95 to 96 per cent of the total GDP during the period. Hence, sources of growth for the economy as a whole are not separately considered. The rationale for excluding GDP from services of dwellings has already been explained.

An attempt has been made in this chapter to identify the determinants that influence output, estimate the changes in them, and assess their contribution to the fluctuations in output. The size of the contribution of a determinant depends upon its importance, that is its weight measured by its share in total factor earnings and by the extent to which it has changed, that is its rate of growth between terminal years of the period considered. Nine periods are selected, four long-term and five short-term. The selection of long periods is based on the trend growth rates of GDP during the periods. Apart from the whole period spanning fifty years, the other long periods considered are: 1950–1 to 1964–5, 1964–5 to 1980–1, and 1980–1 to 1999–2000. The first period is characterized by the transformation of the Indian economy from a stagnant state under colonial rule with less than one per cent annual trend rate of growth during the first half of the century,[1] to one of moderate growth of 4.15 per cent immediately after the commencement of the era of planned economic development. The next sixteen years 1964–5 to 1980–1 is marked by a slowdown in the rate of growth of GDP to 3.13 per cent. During this period, the economy was affected by severe droughts, two armed conflicts, and the two oil price shocks of 1973 and 1979. The last period 1980–1 to 1999–2000 marked a significant break from 3 per cent growth, referred to as the 'Hindu rate of growth', to a path of rapid economic growth nearing 6 per cent, to become one of the fastest growing economies of the world, stimulated by the limited liberalization of the 1980s and the radical economic reforms of the

---

[1] S. Sivasubramonian, *The National Income of India in the Twentieth Century*, New Delhi, 2000, p. 563.

1990s.[2] India also moved up from being the sixth largest economy in the world in the early 1950s to the fourth largest economy by the close of the 1990s,[3] next only to USA, China, and Japan. The choice of short periods is limited to the decades covered. The basic indicators of growth performance are presented in Table 6.1.

ESTIMATES OF THE SOURCES OF GROWTH OF NON-RESIDENTIAL GDP

The procedure followed for estimating the sources of growth of non-residential GDP in each of the selected periods is as follows. The growth rate of GDP was allocated between total input and total output per unit of input in proportion to the growth rates of the two series. The growth rates in the two series as calculated from the indexes developed and as allocated proportionately to match with the observed growth rate of GDP are indicated in Table 6.2.

The contribution of total factor input was allocated among labour, non-residential structures, equipment, inventories, and land in proportion to the products of the growth rates of the input indexes and their average weight during the period. The calculations for the whole period 1950–1 to 1999–2000 are presented in Table 6.3.

The contribution of labour input was allocated among its components in proportion to the separate growth rates of the labour input indexes. The allocation for the period 1950–1 to 1999–2000 is presented in Table 6.4.

For other periods, the total factor input and labour input were allocated among the components in a similar manner. The resulting allocations are shown in Table 6.6.

CLASSIFICATION OF THE SOURCES OF GROWTH

The principal determinants of output are labour, capital, and land. Growth in output can be achieved by increasing the resources used for production, that is, labour, capital, and land, or by increasing the output realized from the same quantity of resources. These are measured respectively by the total factor input and output per unit of input, that is, total factor productivity (TFP), the components of which are described below.

Labour

Changes in labour input occur consequent to the increase in the numbers in the workforce and variations in their quality as indicated by the age–sex

[2] S. Sivasubramonian, 'Twentieth Century Economic Performance of India', in Angus Maddison, D. S. Prasada Rao, *The Asian Economies of the Twentieth Century*, and William Shepherd (eds), Cheltenham, 2002, pp. 102–42.

[3] Angus Maddison, *The World Economy: A Millennial Perspective*, OECD, Development Centre Studies, Paris, 2001, p. 261.

Table 6.1: Basic Indicators of Growth Performance of the Non-residential Sector, 1950–1 to 1999–2000

(per cent)

Indicator	Long periods				Shorter periods				
	1950–1 to 1999–2000	1950–1 to 1964–5	1964–5 to 1980–1	1980–1 to 1999–2000	1950–1 to 1960–1	1960–1 to 1970–1	1970–1 to 1980–1	1980–1 to 1990–1	1990–1 to 1999–2000
	(1)	(2)	(3)	(4)	(5)	(6)	(7)	(8)	(9)
1. Population	2.09	2.00	2.27	2.01	1.92	2.23	2.30	2.14	1.87
2. Non-residential GDP	4.40	4.15	3.13	5.67	3.99	3.74	3.08	5.50	5.87
3. Employment	1.85	1.63	2.16	1.74	1.57	1.79	2.37	2.02	1.43
4. Age–sex composition	0.05	0.03	-0.02	0.13	0.06	-0.03	-0.02	0.13	0.12
5. Education	0.27	0.24	0.22	0.34	0.29	0.12	0.26	0.31	0.37
6. Labour input	2.17	1.91	2.35	2.22	1.92	1.90	2.62	2.47	1.93
7. Non-residential structures	4.68	4.24	5.68	4.18	3.21	6.55	5.27	3.72	4.70
8. Equipment	5.26	3.93	2.42	8.72	3.80	2.81	2.75	8.36	9.12
9. Inventories	4.15	3.68	3.62	4.05	3.43	4.02	3.49	6.76	2.97
10. All reproducible capital	4.76	4.03	4.21	5.78	3.42	4.79	4.18	5.43	6.13
11. Land	0.63	0.92	0.63	0.40	1.06	0.58	0.67	0.58	0.20
12. Impact of structural change	0.25	0.25	0.27	0.33	0.31	0.11	0.33	0.37	0.30
13. Effect of weather	0.09	0.36	-0.27	-0.01	0.21	0.12	-0.27	0.05	0.07
14. Foreign trade volume	–	–	–	7.78	2.73	3.28	6.84	5.79	10.02
15. Energy consumption	5.91	7.16	4.50	6.18	6.24	5.84	5.12	6.93	5.35

Sources: Row (1) Table 1.1, Col. (4); Row (2) from Table 1.3, Col. (4); Row (3) from Table 3.5, Col. (1); Rows (4) to (6) from Table 3.22, Cols (2), (3), and (4); Rows (7)–(11) from Table 4.18 Cols (2) to (7); Row (12) from Appendix Table 5(a); Row (13) based on Table 5.3, Col. (5); Row (14) from Table 5.6, Col. (1); Row (15) from Table 5.7, Col (7).

285

Table 6.2: Growth Rates of Total Factor Input and Output Per Unit of Input as Calculated and as Allocated, 1950–1 to 1999–2000

(per cent)

Period	As Calculated			As allocated		
	Total factor input	Output per unit of input	GDP	Total factor input	Output per unit of input	GDP
	(1)	(2)	(3)	(4)	(5)	(6)
Long periods						
1950–1 to 1999–2000	2.95	1.41	4.36	2.98	1.42	4.40
1950–1 to 1964–5	2.32	1.78	4.10	2.35	1.80	4.15
1964–5 to 1980–1	2.71	0.41	3.12	2.72	0.41	3.13
1980–1 to 1999–2000	3.62	1.99	5.61	3.66	2.01	5.67
Shorter periods						
1950–1 to 1960–1	2.16	1.80	3.96	2.18	1.81	3.99
1960–1 to 1970–1	2.52	1.19	3.71	2.54	1.20	3.74
1970–1 to 1980–1	2.91	0.16	3.07	2.92	0.16	3.08
1980–1 to 1990–1	3.44	1.99	5.43	3.48	2.02	5.50
1990–1 to 1999–2000	3.81	1.98	5.79	3.86	2.01	5.87

Sources: Col. (1) from Table 4.8, Col. (7); Col. (2) from Table 4.16, Col. (9); Col. (3) = Col. (1) + Col. (2); for Cols (4) and (5), see the text; Col. (6) from Table 1.3, Col. (5).

Table 6.3: Allocation of Total Factor Input Among Components, 1950–1 to 1999–2000

Component	Growth rate	Weight	Growth rate × Weight	Allocated growth rate
	(1)	(2)	(3)	(4)
Labour	2.17	0.5523	1.1985	1.24
Structures	4.68	0.1853	0.8672	0.90
Equipment	5.26	0.1207	0.6349	0.66
Inventories	4.15	0.0262	0.1087	0.11
Land	0.63	0.1155	0.0728	0.07
Total factor input	–	1.0000	2.8821	2.98

Sources: Col. (1) from Table 6.1, Col. (1); Col. (2) calculated from Table 4.14, Cols (7) to (11); Col. (3) = Col. (1) × Col. (2); Col. (4) total from Table 6.2, Col. (4) others allocated proportionately.

Table 6.4: Allocation of Labour Input Among its Components 1950–1 to 1999–2000

Component	Observed growth rate	Allocated growth rate
	(1)	(2)
Employment	1.85	1.05
Age–Sex	0.05	0.03
Education	0.27	0.16
Labour input	2.17	1.24

Sources: Col. (2) from Table 6.1, Col. (1); Col. (2) total from Table 6.3, Col. (4), rest of the entries allocated proportionately.

composition and educational attainments. The numbers in the workforce, as already pointed out, increased 2.45 times during the period, that is at an annual rate of 1.85 per cent. As data relating to man-days or manhours worked are not available, the numbers in the workforce are taken as indicative of the changes in employment. As regards age–sex composition, it was possible to consider only three broad age-groups, 5–14, 15–59, and 60 plus. It was found that the percentage of workers in the age-group 5–14 years (that is child labour) gradually declined over the years and that in the age-group 15–59 years increased. The variation in the labour input of workers in different age–sex groups is measured in terms of the relative wage differentials [see Table 3.12, Col. (3)]. The effect of changes in the age–sex composition is measured as the weighted average of the products of the percentage distribution of workers in each age-group and the corresponding wage differentials.

In a similar manner, numbers in the workforce were classified according to their educational levels. Their relative inputs were measured in terms of the differences in their average earnings. Combining the two, that is the distribution of workers by educational levels and the earning differentials, the effect of education on labour input is measured. It may be noted that only quantitative aspects of formal education were taken into account. Education outside this sphere such as nursery and kindergarten, commercial and training institutes, on-the-job training, etc. were not considered. Also, those with higher education, especially in specialized fields, were not adequately recognized as they were all lumped into one category: graduates and above.

Capital and Land

Fixed capital is distinguished from inventories and the former is further divided into structures and equipment. To measure the input of fixed capital, a weighted average of the gross and net stock with weights in the proportion of 3:1 respectively is adopted.

Land reported to be utilized for agricultural and non-agricultural purposes form the basis of the corresponding input measure. The former is defined as the sum of cropped area and fallow lands and for the latter, half the reported area under non-agricultural uses is taken into account to allow for land used for residential purposes. Capital input plus land input is taken as the weighted average of the component series, structures, equipment, inventories, and land, the weights being their respective shares in the non-labour earnings.

Components of Output per Unit of Input

The components of output per unit of input specially identified and measured are (i) those due to structural changes, that is gains from reallocation of resources from agriculture, (ii) irregular fluctuations due to changes in weather, (iii) economies of scale, (iv) foreign trade effect, and (v) energy effect. The effect of industrial disputes was found to be negligible and that due to intensity of demand not very noticeable. The contribution of advances in knowledge and n.e.c. is taken as a residual. Denison has observed that 'the contribution of advances in knowledge relate to the gains in measured output that may be achieved that result from the incorporation in production of any knowledge of any type, regardless of the source of that knowledge, the way it is transmitted to those who can make use of it or the way it is incorporated into production'.[4] The 'n.e.c.' portion refers to the effect of a number of determinants that have not been quantified for want of adequate data and also to the possible errors arising from the assumptions made to estimate the effect of other determinants.

IMPACT OF SUCCESSIVE ROUNDS OF GROWTH ACCOUNTING

Growth accounting has been carried out in stages and at each stage more of growth has been accounted for. At the first stage, labour input, including both quantity and quality of labour, has been estimated. The difference between the growth rates of GDP and labour input explains how much growth is left unexplained. At the second stage, the inputs of capital and land are taken into consideration. The residual of the growth rates of GDP and the weighted average growth rate of capital and land inputs explains more of growth and indicates how much is still to be explained. At the third stage, the combined effects of labour, capital, and land inputs, termed total factor input, is considered. The residual at this stage explains more than what has hitherto been possible and is termed output per unit of input or TFP. The latter is influenced by a number of determinants, five of which have been quantified in this exercise. At the fourth stage, the residual obtained by deducting the sum of the growth rates of these determinants affecting TFP, that is structural change, influence of weather, foreign trade effect, energy effect, and economies of scale from the growth rate of output per unit of input indicates how much of growth is left 'unexplained'.[5] The impact of successive rounds of growth accounting is presented in Table 6.5.

It is seen that the simplest measure—labour productivity—measures the least.[6] Capital (including land) productivity explains more than labour as the residuals are smaller. It also seems to explain the slowdown and acceleration. The combined factor productivity explains much more as the residuals are even smaller than before. The residual after taking into account the identifiable components of output per unit of input helps isolate the influence of advances of knowledge and n.e.c. on the slowdown and acceleration of GDP growth. The share of this residual slips from 25.8 per cent to 15.6 per cent between the periods 1950-1 to 1964-5 and 1964-5 to 1980-1 corresponding to the deceleration in the GDP growth rate of 24.6 per cent. Similarly, the share of the residual moved up from 15.6 per cent to 22.9 per cent corresponding to an acceleration in the GDP growth rate from 3.13 per cent to 5.67 per cent

---

[4] Edward F. Denison, *Accounting for United States Economic Growth*, Washington, D.C., 1974, p. 108.

[5] Angus Maddison, *Explaining the Economic Performance of Nations: Essays in Time and Space*, Cheltenham, 1995, p. 62.

[6] Ibid., p. 62.

Table 6.5: Reducing the Residual: Impact of Successive Rounds of Growth Accounting, 1950–1 to 1999–2000 (Annual Average Compound Growth Rates)

	Long periods				Shorter periods					Deceleration	Acceleration
	1950–1 to 1999–2000	1950–1 to 1964–5	1964–5 to 1980–1	1980–1 to 1999–2000	1950–1 to 1960–1	1960–1 to 1970–1	1970–1 to 1980–1	1980–1 to 1990–1	1990–1 to 1999–2000	1964–5 to 1980–1 compared to 1950–1 to 1964–5	1980–1 to 1999–2000 compared to 1964–5 to 1980–1
	(1)	(2)	(3)	(4)	(5)	(6)	(7)	(8)	(9)	(10)	(11)
1. GDP growth	4.40	4.15	3.13	5.67	3.99	3.74	3.08	5.50	5.87	-1.02	2.54
2. GDP–Labour input	3.16	3.04	1.78	4.48	2.78	2.64	1.58	4.12	4.89	-1.26	2.70
3. GDP–Capital and land input	2.64	2.91	1.76	3.20	2.93	2.30	1.66	1.40	2.98	-1.15	1.50
4. GDP–Total factor input = TFP	1.42	1.80	0.41	2.01	1.81	1.20	0.16	2.02	2.01	-1.39	1.60
5. Residual = TFP – Other explained items	1.00	1.07	0.49	1.30	1.15	0.87	0.02	1.25	1.64	-0.58	0.81
6. Unexplained as % of GDP growth	22.73	25.78	15.65	22.93	28.82	23.26	0.65	22.73	44.97	–	–
7. Explained as % of GDP growth	77.27	74.22	84.35	77.07	71.18	76.74	99.35	77.27	55.03	–	–

Sources: Row (1) from Table 1.3, Col. (5) for rest, see the text.

between the periods 1964–5 to 1980–1 and 1980–1 to 1990–1 that is by 81.1 per cent.

The last row of Table 6.5 demonstrates the net explanatory power of the twelve growth components that were used in the analysis. For the period as a whole, the degree of explanation offered is around 77 per cent, which is considered to be quite high. But it varies between periods, with the level of explanation highest during slowdown and least during the period 1990–1 to 1999–2000 when GDP recorded the highest rate of growth of all periods. In his article 'Growth and Slowdown in Advanced Capitalist Economies: Techniques of Quantitative Assessment', Maddison showed that the average explained growth in the six advanced capitalist countries was between 75 to 76 per cent during the periods 1913–50, 1950–73, and 1973–4.[7]

SOURCES OF GROWTH DURING 1950–1 TO 1999–2000

For the period as a whole, real GDP increased at 4.4 per cent per annum. The growth rate varied during the sub-periods, being highest at 5.67 per cent in the period 1980–1 to 1999–2000 and lowest at 3.13 per cent during the middle period 1964–5 to 1980–1. During the initial period, the growth rate of GDP was 4.15 per cent, closer to the overall average. The fluctuations in the growth rates are caused by the changes in the determinants. The absolute and relative contributions of the various determinants to the growth of GDP are shown in Tables 6.6 and 6.7 and Figures 6.1 and 6.2.

Capital accumulation is seen to be the most important source of growth for the period as a whole. It was 1.67 percentage points or 38 per cent of the total growth rate. This compares well with the experience of the other countries. According to Kendrick, the average contribution to capital of the growth of real gross *business* product in eight Western countries (Belgium, Denmark, France, Germany, the Netherlands, Norway, United Kingdom, and Italy) during 1960–73 was 35.8 per cent, compared with 37.9 per cent in the United States.[8] Next in importance is total factor productivity with a growth rate of 1.42 per cent or 32.3 per cent of the total growth rate. Labour input seems to have had a relatively less important place, accounting for 28.2 per cent of the growth.

Considering labour input separately, the quantity of labour, that is numbers employed, contributed 84.6 per cent to the labour input, and education, the main component of quality of labour, accounted for only 13 per cent. The role of education has been rather unimpressive, being only 3.6 per cent of the GDP growth rate. This is in sharp contrast to the experience in the USA where 15 per cent of the growth rate in national income and nearly 50 per cent of the growth of labour input during 1929–69 were accounted for by education.[9]

[7] Ibid., p. 64.

[8] John W. Kendrick, 'How Much Does Capital Explain' in A. Szirmai, B. Van Ark, and D. Pilat (eds), *Explaining Economic Growth, Essays in Honour of Angus Maddison*, Amsterdam, 1993, pp. 140–1.

[9] Denison, *Accounting for Economic Growth*, p. 110.

Table 6.6: Sources of GDP Growth in the Non-residential Sector, Selected Periods, 1950–1 to 1999–2000
(Contributions to GDP Growth in Percentage Points)

| | 1950–1 to 1999–2000 | Long periods | | | Shorter periods | | | | | Deceleration 1964–5 to 1980–1 compared to 1950–1 to 1964–5 | Acceleration 1980–1 to 1999–2000 compared to 1964–5 to 1980–1 |
| | | 1950–1 to 1964–5 | 1964–5 to 1980–1 | 1980–1 to 1999–2000 | 1950–1 to 1960–1 | 1960–1 to 1970–1 | 1970–1 to 1980–1 | 1980–1 to 1990–1 | 1990–1 to 1999–2000 | | |
	(1)	(2)	(3)	(4)	(5)	(6)	(7)	(8)	(9)	(10)	(11)
Non-residential GDP	4.40	4.15	3.13	5.67	3.99	3.74	3.08	5.50	5.87	-1.02	2.54
Labour input	1.24	1.11	1.35	1.19	1.12	1.10	1.50	1.38	0.98	0.24	-0.16
Employment	1.05	0.96	1.23	0.94	0.92	1.05	1.37	1.13	0.74	0.27	-0.29
Age–sex composition	0.03	0.00	-0.01	0.06	0.03	-0.02	-0.01	0.07	0.05	-0.01	0.07
Education	0.16	0.15	0.13	0.19	0.17	0.07	0.14	0.18	0.14	-0.02	0.06
Capital input	1.67	1.06	1.29	2.44	0.85	1.35	1.35	2.06	2.88	0.23	1.15
Non-residential structures	0.90	0.58	0.92	1.04	0.42	0.92	0.93	0.85	1.27	0.34	0.12
Equipment	0.66	0.39	0.28	1.26	0.35	0.33	0.33	1.03	1.51	-0.11	0.98
Inventories	0.11	0.09	0.09	0.14	0.08	0.10	0.09	0.18	0.10	0.00	0.05
Land	0.07	0.18	0.08	0.03	0.21	0.09	0.07	0.04	0.01	-0.10	-0.05
Total factor input	2.98	2.35	2.72	3.66	2.18	2.54	2.92	3.48	3.86	0.37	0.94
Output per unit of input	1.42	1.80	0.41	2.01	1.81	1.20	0.16	2.02	2.01	-1.39	1.60
Structural change	0.25	0.25	0.27	0.33	0.31	0.11	0.33	0.37	0.30	0.02	0.06
Influence of weather	0.01	0.36	-0.27	-0.01	0.21	0.12	-0.27	0.05	-0.07	-0.63	0.26
Economies of scale	0.13	0.12	0.09	0.17	0.12	0.11	0.09	0.16	0.18	-0.03	0.08
Foreign trade effect	0.03	–	–	0.06	0.02	0.02	0.04	0.04	0.10		
Energy effect	–	–	-0.17	0.16	–	-0.03	-0.05	0.15	-0.14		0.33
Residual (advances in knowledge and n.e.c.)	1.00	1.07	0.49	1.30	1.15	0.87	0.06	1.25	1.64	-0.58	0.81

Sources: See the text.

291

Table 6.7: Relative Contribution to Growth Rate of GDP of the Non-residential Sector,
Selected Periods, 1950-1 to 1999-2000

	Long periods				Shorter periods				
	1950-1 to 1999-2000	1950-1 to 1964-5	1964-5 to 1980-1	1980-1 to 1999-2000	1950-1 to 1960-1	1960-1 to 1970-1	1970-1 to 1980-1	1980-1 to 1990-1	1990-1 to 1999-2000
	(1)	(2)	(3)	(4)	(5)	(6)	(7)	(8)	(9)
Labour input	28.18	26.75	43.13	20.99	28.07	29.41	48.70	25.09	16.70
Employment	23.86	23.13	39.30	16.58	23.06	28.07	44.48	20.55	12.61
Age-sex composition	0.63	0.01	-0.32	1.11	0.75	-0.46	-0.36	1.35	0.92
Education	3.64	3.61	4.04	3.35	4.14	2.00	4.67	3.22	2.39
Capital input	37.95	25.54	41.21	43.03	21.30	36.10	43.83	37.45	49.06
Non-residential structures	20.35	13.99	29.39	18.34	10.53	24.60	30.19	15.45	21.64
Equipment	14.92	9.40	8.95	22.29	8.87	8.82	10.71	18.73	25.72
Inventory	2.55	2.17	3.03	2.49	2.01	2.67	3.05	3.28	1.70
Land	1.59	4.34	2.56	0.53	5.26	2.41	2.27	0.73	0.17
Total factor input	67.73	56.63	86.90	64.55	54.64	67.91	94.81	63.27	65.93
Output per unit of input	32.27	43.37	13.10	35.45	45.36	32.09	5.19	36.73	34.07
Non-residential GDP	100.00	100.00	100.00	100.00	100.00	100.00	100.00	100.00	100.00

Source: Table 6.7.

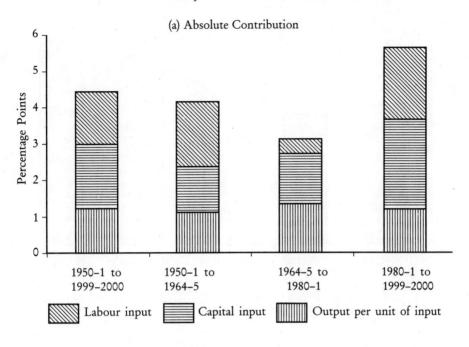

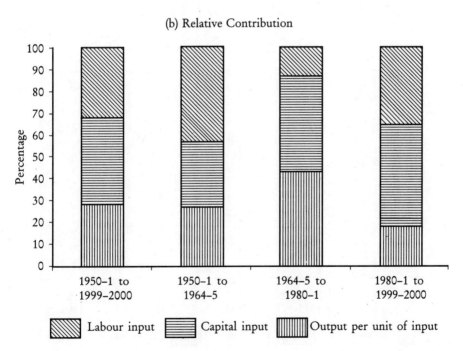

Fig. 6.1: Sources of Growth of GDP in the Non-residential Sector: Long
Periods, 1950–1 to 1999–2000

Source: Tables 6.6 and 6.7.

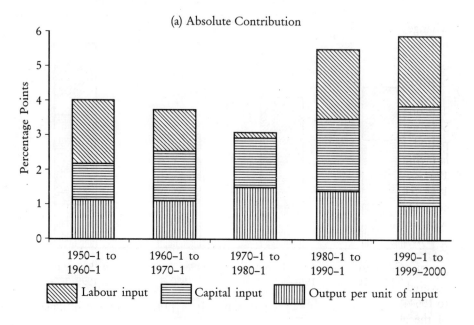

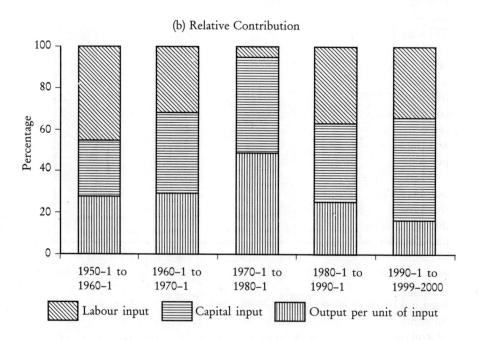

Fig. 6.2: Sources of Growth of GDP in the Non-residential Sector: Shorter
Periods, 1950–1 to 1999–2000

Changes in the age–sex composition of the workforce did not have any noticeable effect on the growth of labour input.

SOURCES OF GROWTH DURING SUB-PERIODS

The order of importance of the determinants changes during the sub-periods. Starting from the low rate of growth of GDP during the pre-independence period and stimulated by massive public investment consequent to the launching of the Five-Year Plans in 1951–2, the first phase, from 1950–1 to 1964–5, marked a period of moderate growth. During the next period, from 1964–5 to 1980–1, there was a slowdown in the growth rate of GDP to 3.13 per cent. During the last twenty years, the economy was on a high growth path with near 6 per cent annual growth of GDP; it was in an acceleration phase.

The first period witnessed the highest contribution of 43.4 per cent to the GDP growth rate, through TFP. Labour and capital contributed more or less equally, at around 26 to 27 per cent of the total rate of growth. Dholakia covered the period 1948–9 to 1968–9, which includes the first period 1950–1 to 1964–5 covered in this study. According to him, labour accounted for most of the growth, accounting for nearly 40 per cent of the real net national product (NNP) growth. Capital and TFP contributed more or less equally, at between 28 and 29 per cent, the rest being realized through land input.[10] During the deceleration phase from 1964–5 to 1980–1, TFP was relegated to the third place, its contribution to the growth rate being only 13.1 per cent. TFP staged a comeback in the acceleration phase and recorded its contribution at 35.5 per cent, lower than in the first period but close to the overall average of 32.3 per cent for the period as a whole. Labour was the most dominant source during the slowdown, with its share amounting to 43.1 per cent, closely followed by capital at 41.2 per cent. During the acceleration phase, capital contributed much more to the total growth rate than labour and TFP, their respective shares being 43.0, 21.0, and 35.5 per cent. The contribution of labour was the lowest during this phase. The role of land declined steadily from 4.3 per cent in the first period to 0.5 per cent in the third.

Most of the growth in labour input was realized through the growth of the numbers employed. Over 91 per cent of the growth in labour input during the slowdown phase was accounted for by the increase in the working force during that period, with the corresponding figure during the acceleration phase being 79 per cent. In the initial period, the share of employment growth in labour input growth was 86.4 per cent, quite close to the share in the period as a whole.

Despite the progress made in education, its contribution to growth has been minimal, at only between 3 to 4 per cent of GDP growth during the different periods. The estimate of the contribution of education to the growth of real NNP made by Dholakia for the period 1948–9 to 1968–9 differs

---

[10] Bapul H. Dholakia, *The Sources of Economic Growth in Indian*, Baroda, 1974, p. 210.

considerably, being 6.8 per cent[11] as against 3.6 per cent derived in this study. But the two estimates are not directly comparable due to the differences in source data for the distribution of workers by education and the weighting system. The contribution of age–sex composition was negligible during 1950–1 to 1964–5 and was negative during the next period 1964–5 to 1980–1. It amounted to 5 per cent of labour input during the acceleration phase.

Nearly 41 per cent of the growth in GDP was realized through the increase in non-residential structures and equipment during the acceleration phase. The contribution of fixed capital was the highest during the last twenty years as it was slightly lower at 38.3 per cent in the slowdown phase and much lower at 23.4 per cent in the initial period. The contribution of structures to the GDP growth rate exceeded that of equipment for the period as a whole, the respective shares being 20.3 per cent and 14.9 per cent. The same pattern continued during the first and second sub-periods, when structures accounted for 54.8 per cent and 71.1 per cent of the contribution of capital input respectively. Only during the period of acceleration did equipment play a more important role, accounting for 22.3 per cent of GDP growth as against 18.3 per cent by structures. It has been already pointed out that more resources were devoted to the creation of non-residential structures during the first two sub-periods, and machinery and equipment became a more important component of capital formation only from 1993–4 [see Appendix Table 4(b)]. The contribution of inventories remained more or less steady at between 2 and 3 per cent over the different sub-periods.

SOURCES OF GROWTH DURING SHORTER PERIODS

Analysing the sources of growth by shorter periods, it is seen that during the early stages of growth, that is the 1950s, 45.4 per cent of GDP growth was realized through TFP growth, followed by labour contributing 28.1 per cent and capital 21.3 per cent. During the next two decades, when GDP was decelerating, the contribution of TFP declined to 32.1 per cent in the 1960s and a mere 5.2 per cent in the 1970s and that of labour input increased to 29.4 per cent and 48.7 per cent. Capital input played a prominent role during the acceleration phase of the 1980s and 1990s. Its contribution was 37.5 per cent in the 1980s and 49.1 per cent in the 1990s. Over the same periods, the realization through labour input growth was 25.1 per cent and 16.7 per cent respectively. TFP contributed 36.7 per cent to GDP growth in the 1980s and 34.1 per cent in the 1990s.

ADVANCES IN KNOWLEDGE AND N.E.C.

The contribution of advances in knowledge and n.e.c. obtained as a residual from TFP after allowing for structural change, influence of weather, economies

---

[11] Ibid., p. 212.

of scale, foreign trade effect, and energy effect amounted to 23.4 per cent of the total GDP growth for the period as a whole, and was lowest during the deceleration phase and highest during the acceleration phase. The decline in the contribution of advances of knowledge and n.e.c. during deceleration and the increase during acceleration can be seen from Cols (10) and (11) of Table 6.6. The category of n.e.c. includes the influence of a number of determinants which could not be quantified, viz. government policies, scientific research and development, environmental degradation and pollution, regulation of crime, etc.

CONCLUSION

Summing up, it is seen that the importance of the three major determinants has varied over the periods. During the transition stage of the economy from a state of stagnation to moderate growth, TFP was the most important source of growth, with its contribution declining to a very low level during the deceleration phase. Labour input played a more important role than capital input during deceleration and the reverse was seen during acceleration of growth. The contributions of education, which reflects the possible improvement in the quality of labour input, and that of machinery and equipment, which reflects the adoption of modern technology, have not yet become as important as they should be in a rapidly growing economy.

7

Sources of Growth in Sector A and Sector Non-A

For the period as a whole, gross domestic product (GDP) at 1993–4 prices from Sector non-A (excluding dwellings) grew more than twice as fast as GDP from Sector A, their respective growth rates being 5.75 per cent and 2.64 per cent (see Fig. 7.1). The differentials between the growth rates of real GDP from these two sectors varied in a similar manner over the sub-periods and decades (see Table 1.3). This chapter examines the changes in the determinants that contribute to the variations in the growth rate of GDP originating in these two sectors.

LABOUR INPUT IN SECTOR A AND SECTOR NON-A

Indexes of labour input (adjusted for age–sex composition and education) in Sector A for the period 1950–1 to 1999–2000 are presented in Table 3.27. It may be noted that for deriving the labour input in Sector A corresponding to the workforce engaged in the sector, I have used the age–sex distribution and educational levels of the rural workforce. The index of labour input in Sector A is shown in Table 7.1. But a similar approach could not be adopted for Sector non-A because the age–sex composition and educational levels of the urban workforce could not be assumed to be applicable to it. Comparison of the labour input for Sector non-A, obtained by deducting the labour input for Sector A from the labour input of non-residential sector, with the workforce in Sector non-A revealed some distortions in the effects of age–sex composition and education. Hence, the labour input in Sector non-A estimated in Chapter 3 is not used. The labour input in Sector non-A has been taken as equal to the workforce, that is, unadjusted for quality change.

ESTIMATES OF CAPITAL INPUT IN SECTOR A AND SECTOR NON-A AT 1993–4 PRICES

Estimates of net fixed capital stock (NFCS) at 1993–4 prices in Sector A are available in the industry-wise distribution of NFCS in National Accounts Statistics (NAS) *Back Series* for 1950–1 to 1992–3 and *NAS 2001* for 1993–4 to

Table 7.1: Labour Input in Sector A, 1950–1 to 1999–2000

Year	Indexes 1993–4 = 100			
	Workforce in Sector A	Age–Sex composition	Education	Labour input
	(1)	(2)	(3)	(4)
1950–1	51.48	98.52	92.30	46.82
1951–2	52.27	98.60	92.56	47.71
1952–3	53.05	98.65	92.82	48.58
1953–4	53.85	98.71	93.09	49.48
1954–5	54.65	98.77	93.35	50.39
1955–6	55.47	98.84	93.62	51.32
1956–7	56.30	98.90	93.88	52.27
1957–8	57.14	98.96	94.15	53.24
1958–9	57.99	99.04	94.42	54.23
1959–60	58.86	99.10	94.68	55.23
1960–1	59.74	99.06	94.95	56.19
1961–2	60.67	99.01	95.01	57.08
1962–3	61.65	98.98	95.07	58.01
1963–4	62.64	98.94	95.14	58.96
1964–5	63.65	98.90	95.20	59.92
1965–6	64.67	98.86	95.26	60.90
1966–7	65.71	98.82	95.32	61.90
1967–8	66.77	98.80	95.38	62.92
1968–9	67.85	98.76	95.44	63.95
1969–70	68.94	98.72	95.51	65.00
1970–1	70.05	98.68	95.57	66.06
1971–2	71.18	98.66	95.63	67.15
1972–3	72.32	98.62	95.69	68.25
1973–4	73.58	98.60	95.86	69.54
1974–5	74.97	98.56	96.02	70.95
1975–6	76.38	98.53	96.18	72.38
1976–7	77.81	98.51	96.35	73.85
1977–8	79.28	98.47	96.51	75.34
1978–9	80.70	98.44	96.68	76.81
1979–80	82.10	98.42	96.85	78.26
1980–1	83.51	98.39	97.03	79.73
1981–2	84.95	98.37	97.20	81.23
1982–3	86.42	98.34	97.37	82.75
1983–4	87.32	98.24	97.54	83.68
1984–5	87.66	99.24	97.82	85.10
1985–6	88.00	99.46	98.10	85.85
1986–7	88.33	99.78	98.38	86.71
1987–8	88.67	100.18	98.65	87.64
1988–9	89.78	100.13	98.88	88.88
1989–90	91.67	100.09	99.10	90.93
1990–1	93.60	100.06	99.33	93.03
1991–2	95.57	100.04	99.55	95.18
1992–3	97.58	100.01	99.77	97.37
1993–4	100.00	100.00	100.00	100.00
1994–5	101.28	100.09	100.26	101.63
1995–6	101.03	100.20	100.52	101.76
1996–7	100.78	100.30	100.78	101.87
1997–8	100.53	100.43	101.04	102.01
1998–9	100.29	100.56	101.30	102.15
1999–2000	100.04	100.68	101.56	102.29

Sources: Col. (1) from Table 3.23, Col. (5); Col. (2) from Table 3.25, Col. (4); Col. (3) from Table 3.26, Col. (3); Col. (4) = [Col. (1) × Col. (2) × Col. (3)]/10000.

1999–2000. Corresponding gross fixed capital stock (GFCS) estimates are obtained by applying the gross/net ratio calculated earlier [Appendix Table 4(f), Col. (36)]. Estimates of fixed capital stock (FCS) are derived as the weighted average of GFCS and NFCS with weights 3 and 1 respectively. Mid-year values of FCS at 1993–4 prices are presented in Appendix Table 7(a). A major difference between the fixed capital stock estimates for non-residential sector presented in Chapter 3 and the estimates of NFCS for Sector A given here is that the latter does not contain any breakdown of structures and equipment separately.

Estimates of fixed capital stock in Sector non-A have been obtained as a residual from FCS of the non-residential sector. The relevant figures, the corresponding indexes, and the shares of Sector A and Sector non-A in total FCS are shown in Table 7.2.

Fixed capital stock at 1993–4 prices in Sector non-A grew almost three times as fast as the FCS in Sector A during the period, the respective growth rates being 6.23 per cent and 2.25 per cent respectively. Consequently, the share of Sector A in FCS declined from 55.2 per cent in 1950–1 to 14.7 per cent in 1999–2000 while that of Sector non-A moved up from 44.8 per cent to 85.3 per cent.

As regards inventories, *NAS* provides data only from 1980–1 onwards. For Sector A, for the years prior to 1980–1, stock of inventories has been estimated at 5 per cent of the NFCS. It may be noted that for the period 1980–1 to 1999–2000, inventories were found to vary from 5.3 per cent to 8.7 per cent of the NFCS. The derivation of the stock of inventories in Sector A is shown in Appendix Table 7(b) and the mid-year values of stock of inventories in Sector A and Sector non-A obtained as a residual along with corresponding indexes are shown in Table 7.3.

ESTIMATES OF CAPITAL STOCK AT CURRENT PRICES FOR SECTOR A AND SECTOR NON-A

Net fixed capital stock values at current prices and at 1993–4 prices in Sector A are available in *NAS*. The implicit price index worked out from these values are applied to GFCS at 1993–4 prices to get the corresponding estimates of GFCS at current prices, as is shown in Appendix Table 7(c). Gross fixed capital stock in current prices in Sector A and Sector non-A are shown in Appendix Table 7(d).

The stock of inventories in Sector A at current prices for the period 1950–1 to 1979–80 is estimated at 5 per cent of the NFCS at current prices. For the period 1980–1 to 1999–2000, the relevant values are directly taken from *NAS*. Inventories of Sector non-A are obtained as a residual and are shown in Appendix Table 7(e).

Estimates of gross capital stock plus land under agricultural use at current prices and the corresponding percentage distribution are presented in Table 7.4.

Table 7.2: Fixed Capital Stock Values at 1993–4 Prices for Non-residential Sector, Sector A and Sector Non-A, 1950–1 to 1999–2000

Year	Non-residential sector (Rs crore)			Fixed capital stock (Rs crore)		% distribution of FCS			Indexes of FCS	
	GFCS	NFCS	Weighted FCS	Sector A	Sector non-A	Sector A	Sector non-A	Sector A	Sector non-A
	(1)	(2)	(3)	(4)	(5)	(6)	(7)	(8)	(9)
1950–1	445,242	160,141	373,967	206,404	167,563	55.19	44.81	41.53	8.27
1951–2	445,939	169,991	376,952	213,317	163,635	56.59	43.41	42.92	8.08
1952–3	445,483	178,805	378,813	219,540	159,273	57.95	42.05	44.17	7.86
1953–4	453,522	187,255	386,955	222,906	164,049	57.61	42.39	44.85	8.10
1954–5	466,230	197,157	398,961	223,555	175,406	56.03	43.97	44.98	8.66
1955–6	479,395	209,516	411,925	223,021	188,904	54.14	45.86	44.87	9.33
1956–7	492,306	224,826	425,436	221,316	204,121	52.02	47.98	44.53	10.08
1957–8	506,195	242,010	440,149	219,244	220,905	49.81	50.19	44.11	10.90
1958–9	526,100	258,359	459,164	219,097	240,067	47.72	52.28	44.08	11.85
1959–60	551,603	273,212	482,005	220,089	261,916	45.66	54.34	44.28	12.93
1960–1	581,614	290,099	508,736	221,647	287,088	43.57	56.43	44.59	14.17
1961–2	614,774	308,297	538,155	224,541	313,613	41.72	58.28	45.17	15.48
1962–3	649,745	327,793	569,257	227,868	341,389	40.03	59.97	45.84	16.85
1963–4	689,373	350,452	604,642	231,658	372,984	38.31	61.69	46.61	18.41
1964–5	729,106	374,615	640,483	235,631	404,852	36.79	63.21	47.41	19.99
1965–6	770,665	400,278	678,068	240,035	438,033	35.40	64.60	48.29	21.62
1966–7	814,946	425,625	717,616	245,136	472,480	34.16	65.84	49.32	23.32
1967–8	856,984	449,047	755,000	250,968	504,032	33.24	66.76	50.49	24.88
1968–9	895,335	470,303	789,077	257,457	531,619	32.63	67.37	51.80	26.24
1969–70	931,869	490,787	821,599	264,270	557,329	32.17	67.83	53.17	27.51
1970–1	971,998	512,414	857,102	271,446	585,656	31.67	68.33	54.61	28.91
1971–2	1,016,280	534,749	895,897	278,976	616,921	31.14	68.86	56.13	30.45
1972–3	1,067,027	559,994	940,268	287,184	653,085	30.54	69.46	57.78	32.24
1973–4	1,119,537	586,155	986,191	295,535	690,656	29.97	70.03	59.46	34.09

(Contd.)

301

Table 7.2 Contd.

	(1)	(2)	(3)	(4)	(5)	(6)	(7)	(8)	(9)
1974-5	1,168,004	609,391	1,028,351	303,249	725,102	29.49	70.51	61.01	35.79
1975-6	1,221,135	634,474	1,074,470	310,865	763,605	28.93	71.07	62.54	37.69
1976-7	1,277,293	663,132	1,123,753	320,100	803,652	28.48	71.52	64.40	39.67
1977-8	1,332,874	693,116	1,172,935	330,589	842,346	28.18	71.82	66.51	41.58
1978-9	1,395,618	726,861	1,228,429	342,206	886,223	27.86	72.14	68.85	43.75
1979-80	1,464,327	761,357	1,288,584	355,918	932,667	27.62	72.38	71.61	46.04
1980-1	1,534,180	795,773	1,349,578	369,970	979,608	27.41	72.59	74.43	48.36
1981-2	1,623,798	844,289	1,428,921	380,835	1,048,085	26.65	73.35	76.62	51.74
1982-3	1,724,212	900,462	1,518,274	389,375	1,128,900	25.65	74.35	78.34	55.73
1983-4	1,813,043	949,530	1,597,165	398,492	1,198,672	24.95	75.05	80.17	59.17
1984-5	1,898,637	996,338	1,673,062	407,586	1,265,477	24.36	75.64	82.00	62.47
1985-6	1,987,353	1,044,500	1,751,640	415,881	1,335,758	23.74	76.26	83.67	65.94
1986-7	2,086,408	1,097,103	1,839,082	423,597	1,415,484	23.03	76.97	85.22	69.87
1987-8	2,186,040	1,149,558	1,926,920	431,681	1,495,238	22.40	77.60	86.85	73.81
1988-9	2,281,050	1,199,669	2,010,705	440,935	1,569,770	21.93	78.07	88.71	77.49
1989-90	2,375,797	1,249,987	2,094,344	449,342	1,645,002	21.46	78.54	90.40	81.20
1990-1	2,476,187	1,304,104	2,183,166	458,272	1,724,894	20.99	79.01	92.20	85.15
1991-2	2,600,465	1,366,693	2,292,022	469,212	1,822,810	20.47	79.53	94.40	89.98
1992-3	2,733,819	1,429,606	2,407,766	480,510	1,927,256	19.96	80.04	96.67	95.14
1993-4	2,866,921	1,490,514	2,522,819	497,050	2,025,769	19.70	80.30	100.00	100.00
1994-5	3,048,878	1,576,701	2,680,833	511,832	2,169,001	19.09	80.91	102.97	107.07
1995-6	3,305,744	1,709,348	2,906,645	519,481	2,387,164	17.87	82.13	104.51	117.84
1996-7	3,589,134	1,856,526	3,155,982	527,662	2,628,320	16.72	83.28	106.16	129.74
1997-8	3,855,645	1,985,457	3,388,098	537,290	2,850,808	15.86	84.14	108.10	140.73
1998-9	4,098,275	2,097,664	3,598,122	547,355	3,050,767	15.21	84.79	110.12	150.60
1999-2000	4,324,404	2,202,232	3,793,861	557,196	3,236,665	14.69	85.31	112.10	159.77

Sources: Col. (1) and (2) from Table 4.8, Cols (3) and (6); Col. (3) = [Col. (1) × 3 + Col. 2]/4; Col. (4) from Appendix Table 7(a), Col. (5); Col. (5) = Col. (3)-Col. (4); Cols (6) to (9) derived.

Table 7.3: Inventories in the Non-residential Sector, Sector A and Sector Non-A at 1993–4 Prices, 1950–1 to 1999–2000

Year	Non-residential sector (Rs crore)	Sector A (Rs crore)	Sector non-A (Rs crore)	% distribution of inventories		Indexes of inventories	
				Sector A	Sector non-A	Sector A	Sector non-A
	(1)	(2)	(3)	(4)	(5)	(6)	(7)
1950–1	37,198	5118	32,080	13.76	86.24	23.38	15.92
1951–2	38,350	5290	33,060	13.79	86.21	24.16	16.41
1952–3	39,369	5444	33,925	13.83	86.17	24.86	16.84
1953–4	40,368	5592	34,776	13.85	86.15	25.54	17.26
1954–5	41,525	5741	35,784	13.83	86.17	26.22	17.76
1955–6	42,939	5887	37,052	13.71	86.29	26.89	18.39
1956–7	44,665	6039	38,627	13.52	86.48	27.58	19.17
1957–8	46,587	6183	40,404	13.27	86.73	28.24	20.05
1958–9	48,437	6314	42,122	13.04	86.96	28.84	20.91
1959–60	50,165	6419	43,746	12.80	87.20	29.32	21.71
1960–1	52,113	6530	45,583	12.53	87.47	29.82	22.63
1961–2	54,198	6668	47,530	12.30	87.70	30.45	23.59
1962–3	56,419	6815	49,604	12.08	87.92	31.13	24.62
1963–4	58,967	6981	51,986	11.84	88.16	31.88	25.80
1964–5	61,688	7168	54,520	11.62	88.38	32.74	27.06
1965–6	64,561	7370	57,191	11.42	88.58	33.66	28.39
1966–7	67,382	7572	59,810	11.24	88.76	34.58	29.69
1967–8	70,019	7789	62,230	11.12	88.88	35.57	30.89
1968–9	72,460	8019	64,441	11.07	88.93	36.63	31.99
1969–70	74,838	8258	66,579	11.03	88.97	37.72	33.05
1970–1	77,308	8498	68,810	10.99	89.01	38.81	34.15
1971–2	79,835	8728	71,107	10.93	89.07	39.86	35.29
1972–3	82,683	8970	73,714	10.85	89.15	40.97	36.59
1973–4	85,652	9208	76,444	10.75	89.25	42.05	37.94

(Contd.)

303

Table 7.3 Contd.

	(1)	(2)	(3)	(4)	(5)	(6)	(7)
1974–5	88,346	9413	78,933	10.65	89.35	42.99	39.18
1975–6	91,265	9611	81,654	10.53	89.47	43.89	40.53
1976–7	94,587	9882	84,705	10.45	89.55	45.13	42.04
1977–8	98,064	10,210	87,854	10.41	89.59	46.63	43.61
1978–9	101,948	10,570	91,378	10.37	89.63	48.28	45.36
1979–80	106,255	10,967	95,288	10.32	89.68	50.09	47.30
1980–1	108,973	11,740	97,232	10.77	89.23	53.62	48.26
1981–2	116,752	12,649	104,103	10.83	89.17	57.77	51.67
1982–3	129,410	13,367	116,043	10.33	89.67	61.05	57.60
1983–4	136,577	14,148	122,429	10.36	89.64	64.61	60.77
1984–5	143,312	15,098	128,214	10.54	89.46	68.95	63.64
1985–6	156,968	16,185	140,783	10.31	89.69	73.92	69.88
1986–7	171,938	17,180	154,758	9.99	90.01	78.46	76.81
1987–8	180,325	18,099	162,227	10.04	89.96	82.66	80.52
1988–9	189,177	18,772	170,406	9.92	90.08	85.73	84.58
1989–90	200,628	19,333	181,295	9.64	90.36	88.30	89.99
1990–1	209,676	19,987	189,689	9.53	90.47	91.28	94.15
1991–2	213,669	20,502	193,167	9.60	90.40	93.63	95.88
1992–3	218,771	20,977	197,795	9.59	90.41	95.80	98.18
1993–4	223,365	21,896	201,469	9.80	90.20	100.00	100.00
1994–5	229,117	22,982	206,135	10.03	89.97	104.96	102.32
1995–6	246,537	24,074	222,464	9.76	90.24	109.95	110.42
1996–7	253,222	27,016	226,206	10.67	89.33	123.39	112.28
1997–8	256,319	27,646	228,673	10.79	89.21	126.26	113.50
1998–9	263,153	26,608	236,546	10.11	89.89	121.52	117.41
1999–2000	272,895	28,063	244,833	10.28	89.72	128.17	121.52

Sources: Col. (1) from Appendix Table 4(k), Col. (7); Col. (2) from Appendix Table 7(b), Col. (6); Col. (3) = Col. (1) – Col. (2); Cols (4) to (7) derived.

Table 7.4: Gross Capital Stock Plus Land for Sector A at Current Prices, 1950–1 to 1999–2000

Year	GFCS (Rs crore)	Inventories (Rs crore)	Gross capital stock (Rs crore)	Agricultural land (Rs crore)	Gross capital stock plus Agr. land (Rs crore)	% distribution of GCS + Land GFCS	% distribution of GCS + Land Inventories	% distribution of GCS + Land Agr. land
	(1)	(2)	(3)	(4)	(5)	(6)	(7)	(8)
1950–1	11,072	228	11,300	21,028	32,328	34.25	0.70	65.05
1951–2	12,238	252	12,489	21,968	34,457	35.52	0.73	63.75
1952–3	12,348	265	12,613	18,308	30,921	39.93	0.86	59.21
1953–4	12,213	266	12,479	19,747	32,226	37.90	0.83	61.28
1954–5	11,984	267	12,251	17,794	30,045	39.89	0.89	59.22
1955–6	12,490	278	12,768	16,835	29,603	42.19	0.94	56.87
1956–7	12,553	295	12,848	20,153	33,001	38.04	0.89	61.07
1957–8	12,977	312	13,290	20,512	33,802	38.39	0.92	60.68
1958–9	13,390	332	13,723	22,304	36,027	37.17	0.92	61.91
1959–60	14,011	351	14,362	22,857	37,219	37.64	0.94	61.41
1960–1	14,477	370	14,848	24,258	39,106	37.02	0.95	62.03
1961–2	15,319	392	15,711	24,387	40,098	38.20	0.98	60.82
1962–3	15,959	415	16,374	24,976	41,350	38.59	1.00	60.40
1963–4	16,573	436	17,009	26,499	43,508	38.09	1.00	60.91
1964–5	18,544	476	19,020	32,234	51,254	36.18	0.93	62.89
1965–6	21,051	543	21,594	34,538	56,132	37.50	0.97	61.53
1966–7	23,658	619	24,276	41,112	65,388	36.18	0.95	62.87
1967–8	25,915	691	26,606	47,610	74,216	34.92	0.93	64.15
1968–9	27,897	754	28,650	44,981	73,631	37.89	1.02	61.09
1969–70	31,094	830	31,924	46,653	78,577	39.57	1.06	59.37
1970–1	34,978	932	35,910	51,284	87,194	40.12	1.07	58.82
1971–2	38,843	1041	39,884	51,628	91,512	42.45	1.14	56.42
1972–3	42,028	1139	43,167	56,828	99,995	42.03	1.14	56.83
1973–4	51,167	1308	52,475	72,986	125,461	40.78	1.04	58.17

(Contd.)

305

Table 7.4 Contd.

	(1)	(2)	(3)	(4)	(5)	(6)	(7)	(8)
1974–5	59,868	1550	61,418	88,919	150,337	39.82	1.03	59.15
1975–6	65,814	1745	67,559	83,889	151,448	43.46	1.15	55.39
1976–7	72,403	1920	74,323	83,749	158,072	45.80	1.21	52.98
1977–8	79,391	2112	81,504	94,070	175,574	45.22	1.20	53.58
1978–9	86,394	2310	88,705	93,371	182,076	47.45	1.27	51.28
1979–80	100,746	2607	103,353	101,805	205,158	49.11	1.27	49.62
1980–1	115,510	3159	118,669	114,765	233,434	49.48	1.35	49.16
1981–2	133,354	3769	137,123	130,514	267,637	49.83	1.41	48.77
1982–3	148,315	4315	152,630	138,352	290,982	50.97	1.48	47.55
1983–4	157,681	5014	162,695	160,514	323,209	48.79	1.55	49.66
1984–5	187,685	5972	193,656	169,856	363,512	51.63	1.64	46.73
1985–6	215,932	7035	222,967	171,549	394,516	54.73	1.78	43.48
1986–7	239,611	8017	247,628	189,280	436,908	54.84	1.83	43.32
1987–8	271,487	8961	280,448	214,053	494,501	54.90	1.81	43.29
1988–9	299,683	10,639	310,321	230,932	541,253	55.37	1.97	42.67
1989–90	342,535	13,356	355,890	234,965	590,855	57.97	2.26	39.77
1990–1	398,294	15,543	413,837	270,885	684,722	58.17	2.27	39.56
1991–2	452,368	16,061	468,429	319,995	788,424	57.38	2.04	40.59
1992–3	508,256	17,465	525,720	349,456	875,176	58.07	2.00	39.93
1993–4	562,556	20,383	582,939	374,031	956,970	58.79	2.13	39.08
1994–5	641,897	20,448	662,344	435,359	1,097,703	58.48	1.86	39.66
1995–6	734,707	19,131	753,837	471,335	1,225,172	59.97	1.56	38.47
1996–7	825,747	21,772	847,519	513,919	1,361,438	60.65	1.60	37.75
1997–8	922,979	26,868	949,847	529,021	1,478,868	62.41	1.82	35.77
1998–9	997,007	29,961	1,026,968	592,664	1,619,632	61.56	1.85	36.59
1999–2000	1,074,266	32,458	1,106,724	599,195	1,705,919	62.97	1.90	35.12

Sources: Col. (1) from Appendix Table 7(a), Col. (5); Col. (2), Table 7(e), Col. (5); Col. (3) = Col. (1) + Col. (2); Col. (4) from Appendix Table 4(p), Col. (12); Col. (5) = Col. (3) + Col. (4); Cols (6) to (8) derived.

306

DISTRIBUTION OF PROPERTY INCOME AND FACTOR INCOME BY TYPE IN SECTOR A

Using the relative importance of GFCS, inventories, and agricultural land, the property income in Sector A has been distributed and is shown in Appendix Table 7(f). Property income so distributed among its components—GFCS, inventories, and agricultural land—along with labour income in Sector A give total factor incomes. The percentage distribution of these components provide the weighting structure for the computation of total factor input. The weighting structure is shown in Appendix Table 7(g).

CAPITAL INPUT INDEX AND TOTAL FACTOR INPUT FOR SECTOR A

Following exactly the same procedures as for the non-residential sector, capital input indexes and total factor input indexes have been derived for Sector A and are shown in Appendix Tables 7(h) and 7(i) respectively.

INDEXES OF INPUT, TOTAL FACTOR INPUT, AND OUTPUT PER UNIT OF INPUT IN SECTOR A

On the basis of the different indexes compiled so far, the indexes of output, input, and output per unit of input for Sector A are presented in Table 7.5.

SOURCES OF GROWTH OF GDP IN SECTOR A

The basic indicators of growth performance in Sector A are presented in Table 7.6

Based on these indicators and following the same procedure as adopted for the non-residential sector, the contribution of the different determinants to the growth of GDP has been worked out and presented in Tables 7.7 and 7.8. To avoid repetition, the methodology is not described in detail.

For the period as a whole, real GDP from Sector A increased at 2.64 per cent per annum. This is in sharp contrast to the stagnation experienced during the pre-independence period. Due to favourable weather conditions and stimulated by planned investment, GDP from Sector A grew at 2.83 per cent per year during the first sub-period 1950–1 to 1964–5. The middle period 1964–5 to 1980–1, characterized by severe droughts, witnessed a decline in growth rate of GDP to 1.80 per cent per year. Extension of irrigation facilities and the introduction of high yielding variety (HYV) seeds from the late 1970s resulted in a rapid increase in yield rates during the 1980s. During the period 1980–1 to 1999–2000, GDP from Sector A recorded a high growth rate of 3.2 per cent per year. Analysing by decades, the annual growth rate of GDP from Sector A was highest at 3.43 per cent during the period 1980–1 to 1990–1 and lowest at 1.5 per cent during the years 1970–1 to 1980–1. During the

Table 7.5: Indexes of Output, Labour Input, Capital Input, Land Input, Total Factor Input, and Output Per Unit of Input for Sector A, 1950–1 to 1999–2000

Year	Index of GDP from Sector A	Labour input				Capital input			Land input	Total factor input	Output per unit of input
		Working force	Age-Sex composition	Education	Labour input	Structures and equipment	Inventories	Capital input			
	(1)	(2)	(3)	(4)	(5)	(6)	(7)	(8)	(9)	(10)	(11)
1950–1	33.50	51.48	98.52	92.30	46.82	41.53	23.38	40.86	75.91	50.87	65.86
1951–2	34.00	52.27	98.60	92.56	47.71	42.92	24.16	42.23	76.94	51.87	65.55
1952–3	35.08	53.05	98.65	92.82	48.58	44.17	24.86	43.46	77.82	52.82	66.40
1953–4	37.78	53.85	98.71	93.09	49.48	44.85	25.54	44.14	79.34	53.79	70.24
1954–5	38.89	54.65	98.77	93.35	50.39	44.98	26.22	44.29	80.21	54.49	71.36
1955–6	38.55	55.47	98.84	93.62	51.32	44.87	26.89	44.21	81.32	55.20	69.84
1956–7	40.65	56.30	98.90	93.88	52.27	44.53	27.58	43.90	81.98	55.77	72.89
1957–8	38.82	57.14	98.96	94.15	53.24	44.11	28.24	43.53	81.19	56.07	69.23
1958–9	42.73	57.99	99.04	94.42	54.23	44.08	28.84	43.52	83.17	57.02	74.94
1959–60	42.30	58.86	99.10	94.68	55.23	44.28	29.32	43.73	83.41	57.68	73.34
1960–1	45.15	59.74	99.06	94.95	56.19	44.59	29.82	44.05	83.29	58.29	77.46
1961–2	45.19	60.67	99.01	95.01	57.08	45.17	30.45	44.63	84.35	59.14	76.41
1962–3	44.29	61.65	98.98	95.07	58.01	45.84	31.13	45.30	84.44	59.86	73.99
1963–4	45.33	62.64	98.94	95.14	58.96	46.61	31.88	46.07	84.56	60.60	74.79
1964–5	49.51	63.65	98.90	95.20	59.92	47.41	32.74	46.87	85.17	61.45	80.57
1965–6	44.04	64.67	98.86	95.26	60.90	48.29	33.66	47.76	84.31	62.05	70.98
1966–7	43.42	65.71	98.82	95.32	61.90	49.32	34.58	48.78	85.35	63.05	68.86
1967–8	49.87	66.77	98.80	95.38	62.92	50.49	35.57	49.94	87.50	64.30	77.56
1968–9	49.79	67.85	98.76	95.44	63.95	51.80	36.63	51.24	86.72	65.05	76.54
1969–70	52.99	68.94	98.72	95.51	65.00	53.17	37.72	52.60	87.32	66.08	80.20
1970–1	56.75	70.05	98.68	95.57	66.06	54.61	38.81	54.03	88.07	67.15	84.51
1971–2	55.69	71.18	98.66	95.63	67.15	56.13	39.86	55.53	88.31	68.17	81.68
1972–3	52.89	72.32	98.62	95.69	68.25	57.78	40.97	57.16	88.48	69.22	76.41

(Contd.)

308

Table 7.5 Contd.

	(1)	(2)	(3)	(4)	(5)	(6)	(7)	(8)	(9)	(10)	(11)
1973–4	56.70	73.58	98.60	95.86	69.54	59.46	42.05	58.82	90.04	70.63	80.28
1974–5	55.84	74.97	98.56	96.02	70.95	61.01	42.99	60.35	89.88	71.73	77.84
1975–6	63.03	76.38	98.53	96.18	72.38	62.54	43.89	61.86	91.59	73.22	86.09
1976–7	59.39	77.81	98.51	96.35	73.85	64.40	45.13	63.69	90.74	74.34	79.89
1977–8	65.35	79.28	98.47	96.51	75.34	66.51	46.63	65.78	92.42	76.00	85.99
1978–9	66.86	80.70	98.44	96.68	76.81	68.85	48.28	68.09	93.28	77.55	86.21
1979–80	58.32	82.10	98.42	96.85	78.26	71.61	50.09	70.82	92.65	78.94	73.88
1980–1	65.83	83.51	98.39	97.03	79.73	74.43	53.62	73.67	93.63	80.64	81.63
1981–2	69.32	84.95	98.37	97.20	81.23	76.62	57.77	75.93	94.77	82.26	84.27
1982–3	68.84	86.42	98.34	97.37	82.75	78.34	61.05	77.70	93.63	83.35	82.59
1983–4	75.42	87.32	98.24	97.54	83.68	80.17	64.61	79.60	96.01	84.78	88.96
1984–5	76.53	87.66	99.24	97.82	85.10	82.00	68.95	81.53	95.46	85.96	89.03
1985–6	77.11	88.00	99.46	98.10	85.85	83.67	73.92	83.32	96.49	87.02	88.61
1986–7	76.61	88.33	99.78	98.38	86.71	85.22	78.46	84.98	96.25	87.89	87.16
1987–8	75.59	88.67	100.18	98.65	87.64	86.85	82.66	86.70	96.07	88.83	85.09
1988–9	87.28	89.78	100.13	98.88	88.88	88.71	85.73	88.60	98.12	90.36	96.58
1989–90	88.57	91.67	100.09	99.10	90.93	90.40	88.30	90.32	97.83	91.94	96.34
1990–1	92.21	93.60	100.06	99.33	93.03	92.20	91.28	92.17	99.19	93.84	98.26
1991–2	90.78	95.57	100.04	99.55	95.18	94.40	93.63	94.37	98.13	95.47	95.09
1992–3	96.04	97.58	100.01	99.77	97.37	96.67	95.80	96.64	99.39	97.52	98.48
1993–4	100.00	100.00	100.00	100.00	100.00	100.00	100.00	100.00	100.00	100.00	100.00
1994–5	105.01	101.28	100.09	100.26	101.63	102.97	104.96	103.04	100.22	101.78	103.17
1995–6	104.10	101.03	100.20	100.52	101.76	104.51	109.95	104.67	100.24	102.34	101.72
1996–7	114.10	100.78	100.30	100.78	101.87	106.16	123.39	106.61	100.93	103.12	110.65
1997–8	111.33	100.53	100.43	101.04	102.01	108.10	126.26	108.57	100.93	103.83	107.22
1998–9	119.19	100.29	100.56	101.30	102.15	110.12	121.52	110.42	100.93	104.50	114.06
1999–2000	119.99	100.04	100.68	101.56	102.29	112.10	128.17	112.53	100.93	105.26	113.99

Sources: Col. (1) from Table 1.2, Col. (4); Cols (2) to (5) from Table 7.1, Cols (1) to (4); Col. (6) from Table 7.2, Col. (8); Col. (7) from Table 7.3, Col. (6); Col. (8) from Table 7(h), Col. (13); Col. (9) Appendix Table 7(i), Col. (7); for Col. (10), see text of Chapter 4; Col. 11 = Col. (1)/Col. (10).

Table 7.6: Basic Indicators of Growth Performance in Sector A, Selected Periods, 1950-1 to 1999-2000

(per cent)

	Long periods				Shorter periods				
	1950-1 to 1999-2000	1950-1 to 1964-5	1964-5 to 1980-1	1980-1 to 1999-2000	1950-1 to 1960-1	1960-1 to 1970-1	1970-1 to 1980-1	1980-1 to 1990-1	1990-1 to 1999-2000
	(1)	(2)	(3)	(4)	(5)	(6)	(7)	(8)	(9)
1. GDP	2.64	2.83	1.80	3.20	3.03	2.31	1.50	3.43	2.97
2. Employment	1.37	1.53	1.71	0.96	1.50	1.60	1.77	1.15	0.74
3. Age-sex composition	0.04	0.03	-0.03	0.12	0.05	-0.04	-0.03	0.17	0.07
4. Education	0.20	0.22	0.12	0.24	0.28	0.07	0.15	0.23	0.25
5. Labour Input	1.61	1.78	1.80	1.32	1.84	1.63	1.90	1.55	1.06
6. Non-residential structures and equipment	2.05	0.95	2.86	2.18	0.71	2.05	3.14	2.16	2.20
7. Inventories	3.53	2.43	3.13	4.69	2.46	2.67	3.29	5.46	3.84
8. All reproducible capital	2.09	0.99	2.87	2.25	0.75	2.06	3.15	2.27	2.24
9. Land for agricultural uses	0.58	0.83	0.59	0.40	0.93	0.56	0.61	0.58	0.19
10. Impact of structural change	-0.05	-0.04	-0.04	-0.05	-0.05	-0.02	-0.05	-0.05	-0.04
11. Effect of weather	-	0.71	-0.55	-0.04	0.38	0.29	-0.56	0.13	-0.24

Sources: Row (1) from Table 1.3, Col. (3); Rows (2) and (5) from Table 3.28, Cols (1) and (2); Rows (3) and (4) derived from Table 7.1, Cols (2) and (3); Rows (6) to (9) derived from Table 7.5, Cols (6) to (9); Rows (10) and (11), see the text.

Table 7.7: Sources of GDP Growth in Sector A, Selected Periods, 1950–1 to 1999–2000
(Contributions to GDP Growth in Percentage Points)

	Long periods				Shorter periods				
	1950–1 to 1999–2000	1950–1 to 1964–5	1964–5 to 1980–1	1980–1 to 1999–2000	1950–1 to 1960–1	1960–1 to 1970–1	1970–1 to 1980–1	1980–1 to 1990–1	1990–1 to 1999–2000
	(1)	(2)	(3)	(4)	(5)	(6)	(7)	(8)	(9)
GDP from sector A	2.64	2.83	1.80	3.20	3.03	2.31	1.50	3.43	2.97
Labour input	0.91	0.94	1.07	0.73	0.97	0.95	1.11	0.89	0.55
Employment	0.78	0.81	1.01	0.53	0.80	0.94	1.04	0.66	0.38
Age-sex composition	0.02	0.02	-0.02	0.07	0.03	-0.02	-0.02	0.10	0.04
Education	0.11	0.12	0.07	0.13	0.15	0.04	0.09	0.13	0.13
Capital input	0.46	0.18	0.51	0.62	0.14	0.34	0.60	0.54	0.70
Non-residential structures and equipment	0.44	0.17	0.50	0.58	0.13	0.32	0.58	0.49	0.67
Inventories	0.02	0.01	0.01	0.04	0.01	0.01	0.02	0.04	0.04
Land	0.14	0.24	0.14	0.08	0.27	0.14	0.14	0.11	0.04
Total factor input	1.51	1.36	1.72	1.43	1.38	1.43	1.85	1.54	1.29
Output per unit of input	1.13	1.47	0.08	1.77	1.65	0.88	-0.35	1.89	1.68
Structural change	-0.05	-0.04	-0.04	-0.05	-0.05	-0.02	-0.05	-0.05	-0.04
Effect of weather	–	0.71	-0.55	-0.04	0.38	0.29	-0.56	0.13	-0.24
Residual (advances of knowledge and n.e.c.)	1.18	0.80	0.67	1.86	1.32	0.61	0.26	1.81	1.96

Sources: See text of Chapter 6.

311

Table 7.8: Relative Contribution to Growth Rate of GDP in Sector A (%), Selected Periods, 1950–1 to 1999–2000

	Long periods				Shorter periods				
	1950–1 to 1999–2000	1950–1 to 1964–5	1964–5 to 1980–1	1980–1 to 1999–2000	1950–1 to 1960–1	1960–1 to 1970–1	1970–1 to 1980–1	1980–1 to 1990–1	1990–1 to 1999–2000
	(1)	(2)	(3)	(4)	(5)	(6)	(7)	(8)	(9)
Labour input	34.47	33.22	59.44	22.81	32.01	41.13	74.00	25.95	18.52
Employment	29.55	28.62	56.11	16.56	26.40	40.69	69.33	19.24	12.79
Age-sex composition	0.76	0.71	-1.11	2.19	0.99	-0.87	-1.33	2.92	1.35
Education	4.17	4.24	3.89	4.06	4.95	1.73	6.00	3.79	4.38
Capital input	17.42	6.36	28.33	19.38	4.62	14.72	40.00	15.74	23.57
Non-residential structures and equipment	16.67	6.01	27.78	18.13	4.29	13.85	38.67	14.29	22.56
Inventories	0.76	0.35	0.56	1.25	0.33	0.43	1.33	1.17	1.35
Land	5.30	8.48	7.78	2.50	8.91	6.06	9.33	3.21	1.35
Total factor input	57.20	48.06	95.56	44.69	45.54	61.90	123.33	44.90	43.43
Output per unit of input	42.80	51.94	4.44	55.31	54.46	38.10	-23.33	55.10	56.57
Structural change	-1.89	-1.41	-2.22	-1.56	-1.65	-0.87	-3.33	-1.46	-1.35
Effect of weather	–	25.09	-30.56	-1.25	12.54	12.55	-37.33	3.79	-8.08
Residual (advances of knowledge and n.e.c.)	39.40	28.27	37.22	58.13	43.56	26.41	17.33	52.77	65.99
GDP from sector A	100.00	100.00	100.00	100.00	100.00	100.00	100.00	100.00	100.00
Explained as % of GDP	60.60	71.73	62.78	41.88	56.44	73.59	82.67	47.23	34.01

Sources: Table 7.7.

post-reform period, the growth rate of GDP was slightly lower at 2.97 per cent. The absolute and relative contribution of the principal determinants to the fluctuations in the growth rate of GDP are presented in Figs 7.1 (a) and (b) for long periods and Figs 7.2 (a) and (b) for shorter periods.

Some interesting observations can be made from the above tables and Figs 7.1 and 7.2.

(i) For the period as a whole, output per unit of input, or TFP, is seen to be the most important source of growth in Sector A, accounting for 42.8 per cent of the GDP growth rate. This is followed by labour input (34.5 per cent), whose contribution is double that of capital (17.4 per cent). Land accounted for 5.3 per cent only. The contribution of TFP was even higher, exceeding 50 per cent during the periods 1950–1 to 1964–5 and 1980–1 to 1999–2000, when GDP growth was accelerating to 3 per cent and above. But during the middle period, when GDP growth slumped to 1.8 per cent, nearly 96 per cent of the growth was explained by total factor inputs and only 4 per cent by TFP.

(ii) Among the factor inputs, labour input contributed more than capital input during the period as a whole, in all the long sub-periods considered and during all decades except the post-reform decade. The numbers engaged or workforce accounted for 85.6 per cent of the labour input for the period as a whole. Education contributed 12.1 per cent to the labour input or 4.2 per cent of the growth rate of GDP for the period as a whole. The effect of the age–sex composition was minimal. The contribution of education and the age–sex composition should be treated with some caution in view of the assumption made to estimate them.

(iii) As far as capital input is concerned, non-residential structures and equipment accounted for most of the growth, with the share of inventories being nominal. For the period as a whole, capital input accounted for 17.4 per cent of the growth rate of GDP. While its contribution was only 6.4 per cent during the initial sub-period, it increased in the next sub-period to 28.3 per cent. The contribution of land was only 5.3 per cent for the period as a whole. During the first two sub-periods, its contribution was around 8 per cent but declined to 2.5 period in the last sub-period.

(iv) Among the irregular fluctuations, weather has a positive impact during the first sub-period and during the first two decades. The effect of structural change has been negative.

(v) The residual, that is advances of knowledge and n.e.c. measured by deducting the effect of structural change and weather from TFP, seems to have played a very important role in promoting the growth of GDP from Sector A. It accounted for 39.4 per cent of the growth rate for the period as a whole and 58.1 per cent during the years 1980–1 to 1999–2000. This is reflected by the achievement in Sector A through the phenomenal increase in yield rates during the period achieved through

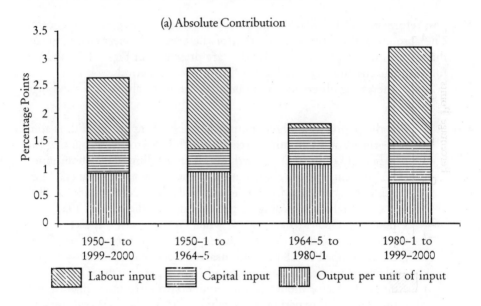

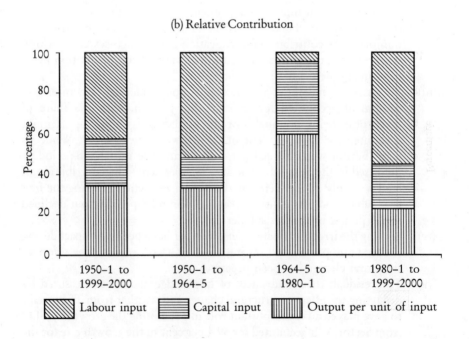

Fig. 7.1: Sources of Growth of GDP in Sector A, Long Periods,
1950–1 to 1999–2000

Source: Tables 7.7 and 7.8.

(a) Absolute Contribution

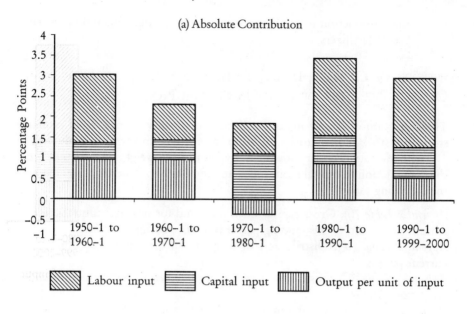

(b) Relative Contribution

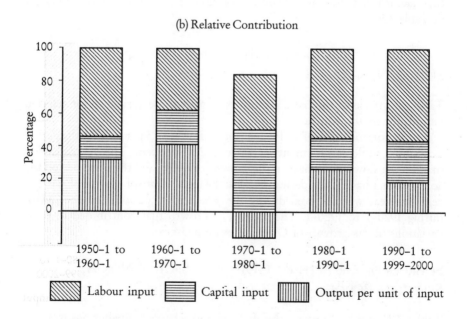

Fig. 7.2: Sources of Growth of GDP in Sector A, Shorter Periods,
1950–1 to 1999–2000

Source: Tables 7.7 and 7.8.

the introduction of HYV seeds, extension of irrigation, and increased use of fertilizers.

INDEXES OF OUTPUT, INPUT, TOTAL FACTOR INPUT, AND OUTPUT PER UNIT OF INPUT IN SECTOR NON-A

The derivation of labour input unadjusted for quality change, fixed capital stock, and stock of inventories for Sector non-A has already been dealt with.

The basic data necessary for the derivation of the weighting structure for the computation of capital input index and total factor input are presented in the following tables:

Appendix Table 7(j): Gross capital stock plus land for non-agricultural use at current prices and corresponding percentage distribution;
Appendix Table 7(k): Distribution of property income in Sector non-A at current prices;
Appendix Table 7(l): Distribution of factor incomes in Sector non-A and weighting structures;
Appendix Table 7(m): Capital input index for Sector non-A;
Appendix Table 7(n): Total factor input index for Sector non-A.

On the basis of the indexes developed so far, the index of output, input, total factor input, and output per unit of input in Sector non-A are presented in Table 7.9.

BASIC INDICATORS OF GROWTH PERFORMANCE IN SECTOR NON-A

Table 7.10 presents the basic indicators of growth performance for selected periods for Sector non-A.

For Sector non-A, GDP at 1993–4 prices grew at 5.75 per cent for the period as a whole while employment increased at 2.91 per cent. The middle period marked the slowdown phase in the growth of GDP, and the third period the acceleration phase. Considering decades, the highest rate of growth of 7.14 per cent per year was achieved during the post-reform period, and the lowest during 1970–1 to 1980–1. The sources of growth that contributed to these variations in the growth of GDP are examined next.

SOURCES OF GROWTH OF GDP FROM SECTOR NON-A, SELECTED PERIODS

Tables 7.11 and 7.12 present the absolute and relative contributions to GDP growth by the various determinants.

The contribution of the principal determinants of growth of GDP in Sector non-A are presented in Figs 7.3 and 7.4.

Table 7.9: Indexes of Output, Labour Input, Capital Input, Total Factor Input, and Output Per Unit of Input in Sector Non-A, 1950-1 to 1999–2000

Year	Index GDP from sector non-A	Labour input*	Capital input			Land input	Total factor input	Output per unit of input
			Structures and equipment	Inventories	Capital input			
	(1)	(2)	(3)	(4)	(5)	(6)	(7)	(8)
1950-1	10.53	28.50	8.27	15.92	8.94	42.98	17.45	60.33
1951-2	10.92	28.99	8.08	16.41	8.84	58.29	17.71	61.67
1952-3	11.19	29.52	7.86	16.84	8.70	56.59	17.80	62.85
1953-4	11.65	30.06	8.10	17.26	8.95	61.01	18.21	63.96
1954-5	12.41	30.61	8.66	17.76	9.50	63.31	18.82	65.95
1955-6	13.39	31.17	9.33	18.39	10.17	63.94	19.48	68.74
1956-7	14.25	31.73	10.08	19.17	10.92	64.22	20.20	70.54
1957-8	14.67	32.31	10.90	20.05	11.75	64.79	20.98	69.93
1958-9	15.41	32.90	11.85	20.91	12.69	65.68	21.81	70.64
1959-60	16.41	33.50	12.93	21.71	13.74	68.44	22.73	72.20
1960-1	17.73	34.12	14.17	22.63	14.95	68.16	23.78	74.56
1961-2	18.96	34.84	15.48	23.59	16.23	67.96	24.95	76.00
1962-3	20.25	35.67	16.85	24.62	17.57	69.41	26.20	77.30
1963-4	21.91	36.53	18.41	25.80	19.10	70.14	27.51	79.64
1964-5	23.31	37.40	19.99	27.06	20.64	70.93	28.83	80.86
1965-6	25.95	38.29	21.62	28.39	22.25	69.68	30.20	85.93
1966-7	24.85	39.20	23.32	29.69	23.91	70.54	31.58	78.68
1967-8	25.56	40.14	24.88	30.89	25.43	71.08	32.86	77.78
1968-9	26.90	41.09	26.24	31.99	26.77	71.88	34.02	79.08
1969-70	28.76	42.06	27.51	33.05	28.02	72.89	35.14	81.85
1970-1	29.72	43.05	28.91	34.15	29.39	75.69	36.34	81.79
1971-2	30.73	44.07	30.45	35.29	30.90	77.96	37.61	81.70
1972-3	31.87	45.11	32.24	36.59	32.64	76.51	38.99	81.73
1973-4	32.68	46.82	34.09	37.94	34.44	77.16	40.74	80.21

(Contd.)

317

Table 7.9 Contd.

	(1)	(2)	(3)	(4)	(5)	(6)	(7)	(8)
1974–5	33.75	49.22	35.79	39.18	36.10	84.41	42.79	78.87
1975–6	35.89	51.72	37.69	40.53	37.95	85.71	44.96	79.82
1976–7	38.45	54.31	39.67	42.04	39.88	91.10	47.23	81.40
1977–8	40.71	56.62	41.58	43.61	41.76	87.49	49.31	82.56
1978–9	44.04	58.74	43.75	45.36	43.89	88.20	51.43	85.62
1979–80	43.98	61.04	46.04	47.30	46.15	89.77	53.73	81.86
1980–1	45.64	63.42	48.36	48.26	48.34	90.29	56.01	81.48
1981–2	48.49	65.86	51.74	51.67	51.72	90.42	58.95	82.26
1982–3	51.08	68.69	55.73	57.60	55.89	91.47	62.49	81.74
1983–4	54.37	71.77	59.17	60.77	59.31	93.43	65.76	82.68
1984–5	57.64	74.78	62.47	63.64	62.57	94.40	68.90	83.66
1985–6	61.46	77.85	65.94	69.88	66.27	94.76	72.28	85.03
1986–7	65.80	80.98	69.87	76.81	70.46	95.90	75.93	86.66
1987–8	69.96	84.16	73.81	80.52	74.38	97.23	79.44	88.06
1988–9	75.50	87.04	77.49	84.58	78.09	97.51	82.70	91.29
1989–90	82.77	89.61	81.20	89.99	81.89	97.64	85.86	96.40
1990–1	87.84	92.26	85.15	94.15	85.85	96.86	89.15	98.53
1991–2	89.77	94.98	89.98	95.88	90.44	98.59	92.78	96.76
1992–3	93.90	97.77	95.14	98.18	95.38	100.00	96.59	97.21
1993–4	100.00	100.00	100.00	100.00	100.00	100.00	100.00	100.00
1994–5	108.83	102.18	107.07	102.32	106.69	100.00	104.54	104.11
1995–6	121.34	104.93	117.84	110.42	117.24	100.00	111.34	108.98
1996–7	130.43	107.70	129.74	112.28	128.35	100.00	118.37	110.19
1997–8	140.83	110.49	140.73	113.50	138.56	100.00	124.86	112.79
1998–9	150.15	113.29	150.60	117.41	147.96	100.00	130.83	114.77
1999–2000	163.37	116.11	159.77	121.52	156.74	100.00	136.46	119.72

Note: * Labour input unadjusted for quality changes.
Sources: Col. (1) from Table 1.2, Col. (6); Col. (2) from Appendix Table 7(n), Col. (1); Col. (3) from Table 7.2, Col. (9); Col. (4) from Table 7.2, Col. (7); Col. (5) from Appendix Table 7(m), Col. (13); Col. (6) based on Table 4.10, Col. (2); Col. (7), Table 7(n), Col. (14); Col. (8) = Col. (1)/Col. (7).

318

Table 7.10: Basic Indicators of Growth Performance in Sector Non-A, Selected Periods

(per cent)

	Long periods				Shorter periods				
	1950–1 to 1999–2000	1950–1 to 1964–5	1964–5 to 1980–1	1980–1 to 1999–2000	1950–1 to 1960–1	1960–1 to 1970–1	1970–1 to 1980–1	1980–1 to 1990–1	1990–1 to 1999–2000
	(1)	(2)	(3)	(4)	(5)	(6)	(7)	(8)	(9)
1. GDP	5.75	5.84	4.29	6.94	5.34	5.30	4.38	6.77	7.14
2. Employment	2.91	1.96	3.36	3.23	1.82	2.35	3.95	3.82	2.59
3. Non-residential structures and equipment	6.23	6.51	5.68	6.49	5.53	7.39	5.28	5.82	7.24
4. Inventories	4.24	3.86	3.68	4.98	3.58	4.20	3.52	6.91	2.88
5. All reproducible capital	6.02	6.16	5.46	6.39	5.28	6.99	5.10	5.91	6.92
6. Land for non-agricultural uses	1.74	3.64	1.52	0.54	4.72	1.05	1.78	0.70	0.36
7. Impact of Structural change	0.29	0.28	0.31	0.37	0.35	0.13	0.37	0.42	0.33

Sources: Row (1) from Table 1.3. Col. (4); Row (2) from Table 3.28, Col. (3); Rows (3) to (6) compiled from Table 7.9, Row (7); Row (7) from Appendix Table 5(a).

Table 7.11: Sources of GDP Growth in Sector Non-A, Selected Periods, 1950–1 to 1999–2000
(Contributions to GDP Growth in Percentage Points)

	Long periods				Shorter periods				
	1950–1 to 1999–2000	1950–1 to 1964–5	1964–5 to 1980–1	1980–1 to 1999–2000	1950–1 to 1960–1	1960–1 to 1970–1	1970–1 to 1980–1	1980–1 to 1990–1	1990–1 to 1999–2000
	(1)	(2)	(3)	(4)	(5)	(6)	(7)	(8)	(9)
GDP from sector non-A	5.75	5.84	4.29	6.94	5.34	5.30	4.38	6.77	7.14
Labour input	1.77	1.56	1.89	1.73	1.66	1.35	2.20	2.08	1.34
Capital input	2.84	2.99	2.33	3.20	2.68	3.05	2.16	2.71	3.76
Non-residential structures and equipment	2.62	2.68	2.16	3.01	2.35	2.82	2.01	2.45	3.65
Inventories	0.22	0.31	0.17	0.19	0.33	0.23	0.15	0.26	0.11
Land	0.02	0.08	0.01	0.00	0.12	0.01	0.01	0.00	0.00
Total factor input	4.62	4.63	4.22	4.93	4.46	4.41	4.37	4.79	5.10
Output per unit of input	1.13	1.21	0.07	2.01	0.88	0.89	0.01	1.98	2.04
Structural change	0.29	0.28	0.31	0.37	0.35	0.13	0.37	0.42	0.33
Residual (advances of knowledge and n.e.c.)	0.84	0.93	−0.24	1.64	0.53	0.77	−0.37	1.56	1.71

Source: Table 7.10.

320

Table 7.12: Relative Contribution to Growth Rate of GDP in Sector Non-A, Selected Periods, 1950-1 to 1999-2000

(per cent)

	Long periods				Shorter periods				
	1950-1 to 1999-2000	1950-1 to 1964-5	1964-5 to 1980-1	1980-1 to 1999-2000	1950-1 to 1960-1	1960-1 to 1970-1	1970-1 to 1980-1	1980-1 to 1990-1	1990-1 to 1999-2000
	(1)	(2)	(3)	(4)	(5)	(6)	(7)	(8)	(9)
Labour input	30.78	26.71	44.06	24.93	31.09	25.47	50.23	30.72	18.77
Employment	0.00	0.00	0.00	0.00	0.00	0.00	0.00	0.00	0.00
Age-sex and education	0.00	0.00	0.00	0.00	0.00	0.00	0.00	0.00	0.00
Capital input	49.39	51.20	54.31	46.11	50.19	57.55	49.32	40.03	52.66
Non-residential structures and equipment	45.57	45.89	50.35	43.37	44.01	53.21	45.89	36.19	51.12
Inventories	3.83	5.31	3.96	2.74	6.18	4.34	3.42	3.84	1.54
Land	0.35	1.37	0.23	0.00	2.25	0.19	0.23	0.00	0.00
Total factor input	80.52	79.28	98.60	71.04	83.52	83.21	100.00	70.75	71.43
Output per unit of input	19.48	20.72	1.40	28.96	16.48	16.79	0.22	29.25	28.57
Structural change	5.04	4.79	7.23	5.33	6.55	2.45	8.45	6.20	4.62
Residual (advances of knowledge and n.e.c.)	14.44	15.93	-5.83	23.63	9.93	14.34	-8.23	23.05	23.95
GDP from Sector non-A	100.00	100.00	100.00	100.00	100.00	100.00	100.00	100.00	100.00
Explained as % of GDP	85.56	84.08	105.83	76.37	90.07	85.11	108.23	76.96	76.05

Source: Table 7.11.

321

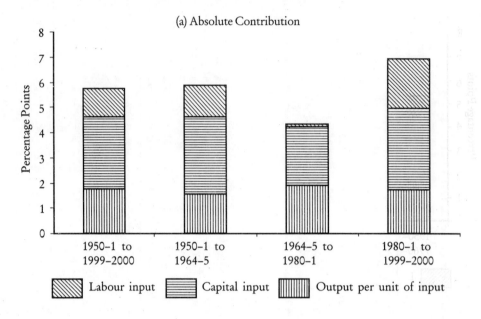

(a) Absolute Contribution

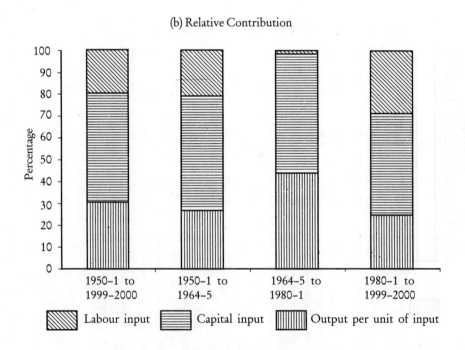

(b) Relative Contribution

Fig. 7.3: Sources of Growth of GDP in Sector Non-A, Long Periods,
1950–1 to 1999–2000

Source: **Tables 7.11 and 7.12.**

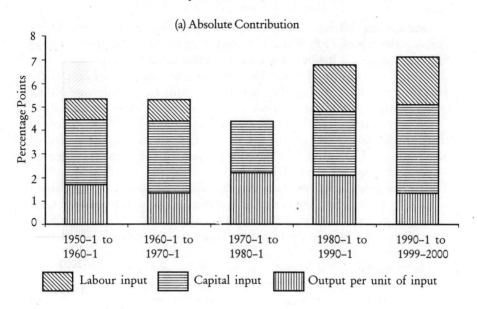

(a) Absolute Contribution

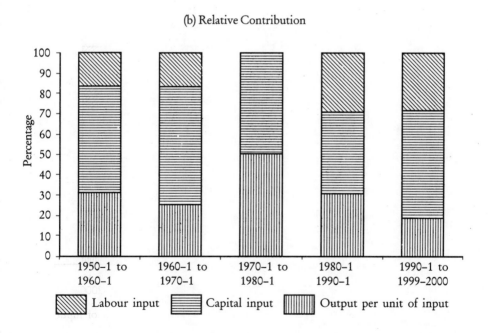

(b) Relative Contribution

Fig. 7.4: Sources of Growth of GDP in Sector Non-A, Shorter Periods,
1950–1 to 1999–2000

Source: Tables 7.11 and 7.12.

One striking difference in the sources of growth in Sector A and Sector non-A is the role of TFP. While TFP contributed most to the growth rate of GDP in Sector A, it has been the least important factor in Sector non-A. For the period as a whole, TFP accounted for only less than 20 per cent of the growth rate of GDP and total factor input contributed slightly over 80 per cent. During the middle sub-period when the economy experienced a slump in the growth rate of GDP, total factor input accounted for 98.6 per cent of the growth and TFP for only 1.4 per cent. Even during the period of acceleration of GDP growth in the last two decades TFP accounted for only 24 per cent of the growth of GDP.

Another noteworthy feature is that capital contributed more than labour to GDP growth during the period as a whole and in all sub-periods except during the period 1970–1 to 1980–1 in Sector non-A while the reverse was the case in Sector A. Capital input constituted mostly of non-residential structures and equipment.

The contribution of advances in knowledge and n.e.c., obtained as a residual from TFP after deducting the effects of structural change, was only 14.4 per cent in Sector non-A, as compared to 39.4 per cent in Sector A. In a sense, it is a reflection of the spectacular performance of Sector A during the period covered.

APPENDIX: 7

Appendix Table 7(a): Fixed Capital Stock in Sector A at 1993–4 Prices, 1950–1 to 1999–2000

(Rs crore)

Year as on 31 March	NFCS	Gross/ Net ratio	GFCS	Weighted FCS	Centred FCS
	(1)	(2)	(3)	(4)	(5)
1950	100,685	2.355	237,112	203,005	
1951	104,056	2.355	245,052	209,803	206,404
1952	107,542	2.355	253,261	216,832	213,317
1953	110,229	2.355	259,589	222,249	219,540
1954	113,456	2.294	260,267	223,564	222,906
1955	116,202	2.232	259,328	223,547	223,555
1956	119,281	2.154	256,901	222,496	223,021
1957	122,270	2.067	252,757	220,135	221,316
1958	125,055	1.995	249,452	218,353	219,244
1959	127,515	1.965	250,618	219,842	219,097
1960	129,243	1.940	250,701	220,336	220,089
1961	131,956	1.920	253,293	222,959	221,647
1962	134,763	1.904	256,578	226,124	224,541
1963	137,837	1.888	260,204	229,612	227,868
1964	141,389	1.871	264,475	233,704	231,658
1965	145,331	1.846	268,301	237,558	235,631
1966	149,480	1.830	273,521	242,511	240,035
1967	153,407	1.820	279,212	247,760	245,136
1968	158,153	1.810	286,182	254,175	250,968
1969	162,617	1.805	293,448	260,740	257,457
1970	167,708	1.796	301,164	267,800	264,270
1971	172,197	1.797	309,391	275,093	271,446
1972	176,919	1.798	318,173	282,860	278,976
1973	181,874	1.804	328,052	291,508	287,184
1974	186,444	1.809	337,269	299,562	295,535
1975	190,079	1.820	345,886	306,935	303,249
1976	194,354	1.826	354,942	314,795	310,865
1977	200,916	1.826	366,902	325,405	320,100
1978	207,469	1.825	378,540	335,772	330,589
1979	215,338	1.825	393,074	348,640	342,206
1980	223,358	1.835	409,808	363,195	355,918
1981	231,316	1.838	425,221	376,745	369,970
1982	236,674	1.835	434,343	384,926	380,835
1983	242,274	1.834	444,339	393,823	389,375
1984	247,898	1.835	454,917	403,162	398,492
1985	253,257	1.836	464,927	412,010	407,586
1986	257,801	1.838	473,737	419,753	415,881
1987	262,042	1.842	482,574	427,441	423,597
1988	266,884	1.845	492,268	435,922	431,681
1989	272,730	1.847	503,687	445,947	440,935
1990	276,778	1.848	511,390	452,737	449,342
1991	283,623	1.847	523,869	463,808	458,272
1992	288,948	1.857	536,505	474,616	469,212
1993	294,998	1.865	550,205	486,403	480,510
1994	306,070	1.878	574,906	507,697	497,050
1995	309,854	1.887	584,672	515,968	511,832
1996	314,243	1.886	592,578	522,994	519,481

(Contd.)

Appendix Table 7(a) Contd.

	(1)	(2)	(3)	(4)	(5)
1997	318,899	1.892	603,473	532,330	527,662
1998	323,151	1.904	615,284	542,251	537,290
1999	327,771	1.914	627,355	552,459	547,355
2000	332,276	1.922	638,484	561,932	557,196

Sources: Col. (1) for 1951 to 1993 from *NAS Back Series, 1950–1 to 1992–3*, pp. 157–67, and for 1994 to 2000 from *NAS 2001*, pp. 53–7; Col. (2) from Appendix Table 4(f), Col. (36); Col. (3) = [Col. (1) × Col. (2)]/100; Col. (4) = [Col. (1) + 3 × Col. (3)]/4; Col. (5) = Average of two consecutive values in Col. (4) starting from 1950.

Appendix Table 7(b): Inventories in Sector A at 1993–4 Prices, 1950–1 to 1999–2000

(Rs crore)

Year as on 31 March	NFCS	Inventories	Ratio of Inventories to NFCS	Estimated Inventories	Inventories	Centered values of Inventories
	(1)	(2)	(3)	(4)	(5)	(6)
1950	100,685			5034	5034	
1951	104,056			5203	5203	5118
1952	107,542			5377	5377	5290
1953	110,229			5511	5511	5444
1954	113,456			5673	5673	5592
1955	116,202			5810	5810	5741
1956	119,281			5964	5964	5887
1957	122,270			6114	6114	6039
1958	125,055			6253	6253	6183
1959	127,515			6376	6376	6314
1960	129,243			6462	6462	6419
1961	131,956			6598	6598	6530
1962	134,763			6738	6738	6668
1963	137,837			6892	6892	6815
1964	141,389			7069	7069	6981
1965	145,331			7267	7267	7168
1966	149,480			7474	7474	7370
1967	153,407			7670	7670	7572
1968	158,153			7908	7908	7789
1969	162,617			8131	8131	8019
1970	167,708			8385	8385	8258
1971	172,197			8610	8610	8498
1972	176,919			8846	8846	8728
1973	181,874			9094	9094	8970
1974	186,444			9322	9322	9208
1975	190,079			9504	9504	9413
1976	194,354			9718	9718	9611
1977	200,916			10,046	10,046	9882
1978	207,469			10,373	10,373	10,210
1979	215,338			10,767	10,767	10,570
1980	223,358			11,168	11,168	10,967
1981	231,316	12,313	5.32		12,313	11,740
1982	236,674	12,985	5.49		12,985	12,649
1983	242,274	13,748	5.67		13,748	13,367

(Contd.)

Appendix Table 7(b) Contd.

	(1)	(2)	(3)	(4)	(5)	(6)
1984	247,898	14,547	5.87		14,547	14,148
1985	253,257	15,649	6.18		15,649	15,098
1986	257,801	16,720	6.49		16,720	16,185
1987	262,042	17,639	6.73		17,639	17,180
1988	266,884	18,558	6.95		18,558	18,099
1989	272,730	18,985	6.96		18,985	18,772
1990	276,778	19,681	7.11		19,681	19,333
1991	283,623	20,292	7.15		20,292	19,987
1992	288,948	20,711	7.17		20,711	20,502
1993	294,998	21,242	7.20		21,242	20,977
1994	306,070	22,549	7.37		22,549	21,896
1995	309,854	23,415	7.56		23,415	22,982
1996	314,243	24,732	7.87		24,732	24,074
1997	318,899	29,300	9.19		29,300	27,016
1998	323,151	25,991	8.04		25,991	27,646
1999	327,771	27,224	8.31		27,224	26,608
2000	332,276	28,901	8.70		28,901	28,063

Sources: Col. (1) from Appendix Table 7(a) Col. (1); Col. (2) from *NAS Back Series*, pp. 161–7 and *NAS 2001*, pp 53–7; Col. (4) = Col. (1) × 0.05; Col. (5) from Col. (3) and Col. (4); Col. (6) average of two consecutive values in Col. (5).

Appendix Table 7(c): NFCS in Sector A at Current and Constant (1993–4) Prices, at 1993–4 prices, Implicit Deflator and GFCS at Current and Constant (1993–4) Prices, 1950 to 2000

Year as on 31 March	NFCS at current prices (Rs crore)	NFCS at 1993–4 prices (Rs crore)	Implicit deflator	Centred GFCS at 1993–4 prices (Rs crore)	Centred GFCS at current prices (Rs crore)
	(1)	(2)	(3)	(4)	(5)
1950					
1951	4779	104,056	4.5927	241,082	11,072
1952	5282	107,542	4.9116	249,157	12,238
1953	5308	110,229	4.8154	256,425	12,348
1954	5331	113,456	4.6987	259,928	12,213
1955	5360	116,202	4.6127	259,798	11,984
1956	5772	119,281	4.8390	258,115	12,490
1957	6023	122,270	4.9260	254,829	12,553
1958	6463	125,055	5.1681	251,104	12,977
1959	6829	127,515	5.3554	250,035	13,390
1960	7224	129,243	5.5895	250,659	14,011
1961	7581	131,956	5.7451	251,997	14,477
1962	8098	134,763	6.0091	254,935	15,319
1963	8513	137,837	6.1761	258,391	15,959
1964	8932	141,389	6.3173	262,340	16,573
1965	10,117	145,331	6.9614	266,388	18,544
1966	11,615	149,480	7.7703	270,911	21,051
1967	13,132	153,407	8.5602	276,366	23,658

(Contd.)

Appendix Table 7(c) Contd.

	(1)	(2)	(3)	(4)	(5)
1968	14,498	158,153	9.1671	282,697	25,915
1969	15,653	162,617	9.6257	289,815	27,897
1970	17,540	167,708	10.4587	297,306	31,094
1971	19,730	172,197	11.4578	305,278	34,978
1972	21,901	176,919	12.3791	313,782	38,843
1973	23,657	181,874	13.0074	323,113	42,028
1974	28,677	186,444	15.3810	332,660	51,167
1975	33,315	190,079	17.5269	341,578	59,868
1976	36,503	194,354	18.7817	350,414	65,814
1977	40,305	200,916	20.0606	360,922	72,403
1978	44,192	207,469	21.3005	372,721	79,391
1979	48,221	215,338	22.3932	385,807	86,394
1980	56,054	223,358	25.0960	401,441	100,746
1981	63,996	231,316	27.6660	417,514	115,510
1982	73,436	236,674	31.0283	429,782	133,354
1983	81,788	242,274	33.7585	439,341	148,315
1984	86,936	247,898	35.0693	449,628	157,681
1985	103,349	253,257	40.8080	459,922	187,685
1986	118,610	257,801	46.0084	469,332	215,932
1987	131,313	262,042	50.1114	478,156	239,611
1988	148,651	266,884	55.6987	487,421	271,487
1989	164,129	272,730	60.1800	497,977	299,683
1990	186,796	276,778	67.4895	507,538	342,535
1991	218,236	283,623	76.9458	517,630	398,294
1992	246,537	288,948	85.3223	530,187	452,368
1993	275,942	294,998	93.5403	543,355	508,256
1994	306,070	306,070	100.0000	562,556	562,556
1995	343,046	309,854	110.7121	579,789	641,897
1996	392,230	314,243	124.8174	588,625	734,707
1997	440,332	318,899	138.0788	598,026	825,747
1998	489,452	323,151	151.4623	609,379	922,979
1999	525,961	327,771	160.4660	621,320	997,007
2000	563,978	332,276	169.7318	632,920	1,074,266

Sources: Cols (1) and (2) from *NAS Back Series*, pp. 146–56; and *NAS 2001*, pp. 52–7; Col. (3) = Implicit deflation of Col. (2)/Col. (1); Col. (4) from Appendix Table 7(a), Col. (3); Col. (5) = Col. (4)/Col. (3).

Appendix Table 7(d): GFCS at Current Prices in Non-residential
Sector, Sector A and Sector Non-A, 1950–1 to 1999–2000

(Rs crore)

Year	Non-residential sector	Sector A	Sector non-A
	(1)	(2)	(3)
1950–1	17,098	11,072	6026
1951–2	19,540	12,238	7303
1952–3	20,517	12,348	8169
1953–4	21,279	12,213	9066
1954–5	22,696	11,984	10,712
1955–6	23,942	12,490	11,452

(Contd.)

Appendix Table 7(d) Contd.

	(1)	(2)	(3)
1956–7	24,932	12,553	12,379
1957–8	26,437	12,977	13,460
1958–9	29,282	13,390	15,892
1959–60	32,544	14,011	18,533
1960–1	35,686	14,477	21,208
1961–2	39,534	15,319	24,214
1962–3	43,312	15,959	27,353
1963–4	47,747	16,573	31,175
1964–5	53,149	18,544	34,605
1965–6	59,981	21,051	38,931
1966–7	70,221	23,658	46,563
1967–8	81,222	25,915	55,307
1968–9	89,630	27,897	61,733
1969–70	98,535	31,094	67,441
1970–1	110,179	34,978	75,201
1971–2	123,440	38,843	84,597
1972–3	139,939	42,028	97,911
1973–4	163,746	51,167	112,580
1974–5	202,692	59,868	142,824
1975–6	245,263	65,814	179,449
1976–7	272,333	72,403	199,930
1977–8	292,169	79,391	212,777
1978–9	323,142	86,394	236,748
1979–80	381,037	100,746	280,291
1980–1	448,367	115,510	332,857
1981–2	532,226	133,354	398,872
1982–3	634,280	148,315	485,965
1983–4	732,847	157,681	575,166
1984–5	836,244	187,685	648,559
1985–6	959,843	215,932	743,911
1986–7	1,104,381	239,611	864,770
1987–8	1,247,563	271,487	976,076
1988–9	1,408,158	299,683	1,108,476
1989–90	1,604,778	342,535	1,262,243
1990–1	1,823,865	398,294	1,425,571
1991–2	2,129,619	452,368	1,677,251
1992–3	2,484,473	508,256	1,976,217
1993–4	2,791,890	562,556	2,229,334
1994–5	3,182,683	641,897	2,540,786
1995–6	3,792,488	734,707	3,057,781
1996–7	4,475,445	825,747	3,649,698
1997–8	5,073,415	922,979	4,150,435
1998–9	5,605,155	997,007	4,608,148
1999–2000	6,101,159	1,074,266	5,026,893

Sources: Col. (1) from Appendix Table 4(o), Col. (18); Col. (2) from Appendix Table 7(c), Col. (5); Col. (3) = Col. (1) – Col. (2).

Appendix Table 7(e): Inventories in Sector A and Sector Non-A at
Current Prices, 1950 to 2000

Year as on 31 March	NFCS (Rs crore)	Inventories (Rs crore)	% of inventories to NFCS	Inventories (Rs crore)			
				Estimated inventories	Mid-year values Sector A	Non-residential sector	Sector non-A
	(1)	(2)	(3)	(4)	(5)	(6)	(7)
1950	4324			216			
1951	4779			239	228	2034	1806
1952	5282			264	252	2222	1971
1953	5308			265	265	2352	2087
1954	5331			267	266	2407	2141
1955	5360			268	267	2457	2190
1956	5772			289	278	2571	2293
1957	6023			301	295	2800	2505
1958	6463			323	312	3101	2789
1959	6829			341	332	3352	3020
1960	7224			361	351	3576	3225
1961	7581			379	370	3881	3510
1962	8098			405	392	4227	3835
1963	8513			426	415	4579	4163
1964	8932			447	436	4927	4491
1965	10,117			506	476	5375	4899
1966	11,615			581	543	6039	5496
1967	13,132			657	619	6824	6205
1968	14,498			725	691	7605	6914
1969	15,653			783	754	8341	7587
1970	17,540			877	830	9193	8363
1971	19,730			987	932	10,223	9291
1972	21,901			1095	1041	11,364	10,324
1973	23,657			1183	1139	12,687	11,548
1974	28,677			1434	1308	14,703	13,394
1975	33,315			1666	1550	17,927	16,377
1976	36,503			1825	1745	21,153	19,408
1977	40,305			2015	1920	23,289	21,368
1978	44,192			2210	2112	25,075	22,963
1979	48,221			2411	2310	27,693	25,383
1980	56,054			2803	2607	32,257	29,650
1981	63,996	3515	5.49	3515	3159	37,941	34,782
1982	73,436	4022	5.48	4022	3769	45,127	41,359
1983	81,788	4608	5.63	4608	4315	52,965	48,650
1984	86,936	5420	6.23	5420	5014	59,237	54,223
1985	103,349	6523	6.31	6523	5972	66,760	60,789
1986	118,610	7547	6.36	7547	7035	77,796	70,761
1987	131,313	8487	6.46	8487	8017	89,400	81,383
1988	148,651	9435	6.35	9435	8961	99,118	90,157
1989	164,129	11,842	7.22	11,842	10,639	57,930	47,292
1990	186,796	14,869	7.96	14,869	13,356	77,219	63,864
1991	218,236	16,217	7.43	16,217	15,543	151,535	135,992
1992	246,537	15,905	6.45	15,905	16,061	169,142	153,081
1993	275,942	19,024	6.89	19,024	17,465	192,189	174,725
1994	306,070	21,742	7.10	21,742	20,383	214,765	194,382
1995	343,046	19,153	5.58	19,153	20,448	239,867	219,420
1996	392,230	19,108	4.87	19,108	19,131	279,536	260,406

(Contd.)

Appendix Table 7(e) Contd.

	(1)	(2)	(3)	(4)	(5)	(6)	(7)
1997	440,332	24,435	5.55	24,435	21,772	302,687	280,915
1998	489,452	29,300	5.99	29,300	26,868	317,938	291,071
1999	525,961	30,622	5.82	30,622	29,961	337,407	307,446
2000	563,978	34,294	6.08	34,294	32,458	361,178	328,720

Sources: Col. (1) from *NAS Back Series*, pp. 146–56; and *NAS 2001*, pp. 52–7; Col. (4) from 1950 to 1980 estimated at 0.05 per cent of Col. (1); for 1981 to 2000 from *NAS Back Series*, pp. 150–6 and *NAS 2001*, pp. 52–7; Col. (5) average of two consecutive values of Col. (4); Col. (6) from Appendix Table 4(k), Col. (9); Col. (7) = Col. (6) – Col. (5).

Appendix Table 7(f): Distribution of Property Income by Type of Asset in Sector A at Current Prices, 1950–1 to 1999–2000

Year	Property income (Rs crore)	% distribution of GCS + land			Distribution of property income (Rs crore)		
		GFCS	Inventories	Agricultural land	GFCS	Inventories	Agricultural land
	(1)	(2)	(3)	(4)	(5)	(6)	(7)
1950–1	2513	34.25	0.70	65.05	861	18	1635
1951–2	2616	35.52	0.73	63.75	929	19	1668
1952–3	2594	39.93	0.86	59.21	1036	22	1536
1953–4	3041	37.90	0.83	61.28	1152	25	1863
1954–5	2565	39.89	0.89	59.22	1023	23	1519
1955–6	2423	42.19	0.94	56.87	1022	23	1378
1956–7	3161	38.04	0.89	61.07	1202	28	1930
1957–8	2714	38.39	0.92	60.68	1042	25	1647
1958–9	3429	37.17	0.92	61.91	1274	32	2123
1959–60	3250	37.64	0.94	61.41	1223	31	1996
1960–1	3196	37.02	0.95	62.03	1183	30	1983
1961–2	3392	38.20	0.98	60.82	1296	33	2063
1962–3	3331	38.59	1.00	60.40	1286	33	2012
1963–4	4617	38.09	1.00	60.91	1759	46	2812
1964–5	4940	36.18	0.93	62.89	1787	46	3107
1965–6	4768	37.50	0.97	61.53	1788	46	2934
1966–7	5480	36.18	0.95	62.87	1983	52	3445
1967–8	6434	34.92	0.93	64.15	2247	60	4127
1968–9	6486	37.89	1.02	61.09	2457	66	3962
1969–70	7535	39.57	1.06	59.37	2982	80	4474
1970–1	7845	40.12	1.07	58.82	3147	84	4614
1971–2	8039	42.45	1.14	56.42	3412	91	4535
1972–3	8622	42.03	1.14	56.83	3624	98	4900
1973–4	12,449	40.78	1.04	58.17	5077	130	7242
1974–5	14,360	39.82	1.03	59.15	5719	148	8493
1975–6	13,162	43.46	1.15	55.39	5720	152	7291
1976–7	13,738	45.80	1.21	52.98	6293	167	7279
1977–8	15,964	45.22	1.20	53.58	7219	192	8553
1978–9	15,712	47.45	1.27	51.28	7455	199	8057
1979–80	16,563	49.11	1.27	49.62	8134	210	8219
1980–1	21,455	49.48	1.35	49.16	10,617	290	10,548

(Contd.)

Appendix Table 7(f) Contd.

	(1)	(2)	(3)	(4)	(5)	(6)	(7)
1981–2	24,967	49.83	1.41	48.77	12,440	352	12,175
1982–3	26,258	50.97	1.48	47.55	13,384	389	12,485
1983–4	31,473	48.79	1.55	49.66	15,354	488	15,630
1984–5	32,459	51.63	1.64	46.73	16,759	533	15,167
1985–6	36,262	54.73	1.78	43.48	19,847	647	15,768
1986–7	35,595	54.84	1.83	43.32	19,521	653	15,421
1987–8	39,442	54.90	1.81	43.29	21,654	715	17,073
1988–9	52,820	55.37	1.97	42.67	29,246	1038	22,536
1989–90	62,915	57.97	2.26	39.77	36,474	1422	25,019
1990–1	71,501	58.17	2.27	39.56	41,591	1623	28,287
1991–2	80,608	57.38	2.04	40.59	46,250	1642	32,716
1992–3	86,302	58.07	2.00	39.93	50,120	1722	34,460
1993–4	119,930	58.79	2.13	39.08	70,501	2554	46,875
1994–5	144,222	58.48	1.86	39.66	84,336	2686	57,200
1995–6	142,631	59.97	1.56	38.47	85,532	2227	54,871
1996–7	199,184	60.65	1.60	37.75	120,810	3185	75,188
1997–8	201,128	62.41	1.82	35.77	125,526	3654	71,948
1998–9	251,132	61.56	1.85	36.59	154,591	4646	91,896
1999–2000	264,763	62.97	1.90	35.12	166,729	5038	92,997

Sources: Col. (1) from Table 2.2, Col. (13); Col. (2) to (4) from Table 7.4, Cols (5) to (8); Cols (5) to (7) derived.

Appendix Table 7(g): Distribution of Factor Incomes in Sector A at Current Prices, 1950-1 to 1999-2000

Year	Labour income (Rs crore)	Property income by type of asset (Rs crore)			Sector A GDP (Rs crore)	Weighting structure				
		GFCS	Inventories	Agricultural land		Labour	GFCS	Inventories	Land	Total
	(1)	(2)	(3)	(4)	(5)	(6)	(7)	(8)	(9)	(10)
1950–1	2919	861	18	1635	5432	53.74	15.84	0.33	30.09	100.00
1951–2	2993	929	19	1668	5609	53.36	16.56	0.34	29.73	100.00
1952–3	2870	1036	22	1536	5464	52.53	18.96	0.41	28.11	100.00
1953–4	2979	1152	25	1863	6020	49.49	19.14	0.42	30.95	100.00
1954–5	2556	1023	23	1519	5121	49.91	19.98	0.45	29.66	100.00
1955–6	2543	1022	23	1378	4966	51.21	20.59	0.46	27.75	100.00
1956–7	3148	1202	28	1930	6309	49.90	19.06	0.45	30.60	100.00
1957–8	3464	1042	25	1647	6178	56.07	16.87	0.41	26.66	100.00
1958–9	3739	1274	32	2123	7168	52.16	17.78	0.44	29.62	100.00
1959–60	3951	1223	31	1996	7201	54.87	16.99	0.43	27.72	100.00
1960–1	4385	1183	30	1983	7581	57.84	15.61	0.40	26.15	100.00
1961–2	4460	1296	33	2063	7852	56.80	16.50	0.42	26.27	100.00
1962–3	4686	1286	33	2012	8017	58.45	16.04	0.42	25.10	100.00
1963–4	4818	1759	46	2812	9435	51.07	18.64	0.49	29.80	100.00
1964–5	6588	1787	46	3107	11,528	57.15	15.50	0.40	26.95	100.00
1965–6	6728	1788	46	2934	11,496	58.52	15.55	0.40	25.52	100.00
1966–7	7893	1983	52	3445	13,373	59.02	14.83	0.39	25.76	100.00
1967–8	10,301	2247	60	4127	16,735	61.55	13.42	0.36	24.66	100.00
1968–9	10,764	2457	66	3962	17,250	62.40	14.25	0.38	22.97	100.00
1969–70	11,332	2982	80	4474	18,867	60.06	15.80	0.42	23.71	100.00
1970–1	11,608	3147	84	4614	19,453	59.67	16.18	0.43	23.72	100.00
1971–2	11,833	3412	91	4535	19,872	59.55	17.17	0.46	22.82	100.00
1972–3	13,235	3624	98	4900	21,857	60.55	16.58	0.45	22.42	100.00
1973–4	16,354	5077	130	7242	28,803	56.78	17.63	0.45	25.14	100.00

(Contd.)

Appendix Table 7(g) Contd.

	(1)	(2)	(3)	(4)	(5)	(6)	(7)	(8)	(9)	(10)
1974–5	17,195	5719	148	8493	31,555	54.49	18.12	0.47	26.92	100.00
1975–6	18,114	5720	152	7291	31,276	57.92	18.29	0.49	23.31	100.00
1976–7	18,215	6293	167	7279	31,953	57.01	19.69	0.52	22.78	100.00
1977–8	21,868	7219	192	8553	37,832	57.80	19.08	0.51	22.61	100.00
1978–9	23,169	7455	199	8057	38,881	59.59	19.17	0.51	20.72	100.00
1979–80	23,660	8134	210	8219	40,223	58.82	20.22	0.52	20.43	100.00
1980–1	29,137	10,617	290	10,548	50,592	57.59	20.98	0.57	20.85	100.00
1981–2	31,916	12,440	352	12,175	56,883	56.11	21.87	0.62	21.40	100.00
1982–3	34,623	13,384	389	12,485	60,881	56.87	21.98	0.64	20.51	100.00
1983–4	41,256	15,354	488	15,630	72,729	56.73	21.11	0.67	21.49	100.00
1984–5	45,829	16,759	533	15,167	78,288	58.54	21.41	0.68	19.37	100.00
1985–6	47,890	19,847	647	15,768	84,152	56.91	23.59	0.77	18.74	100.00
1986–7	54,946	19,521	653	15,421	90,541	60.69	21.56	0.72	17.03	100.00
1987–8	61,317	21,654	715	17,073	100,759	60.86	21.49	0.71	16.94	100.00
1988–9	71,081	29,246	1038	22,536	123,901	57.37	23.60	0.84	18.19	100.00
1989–90	73,976	36,474	1422	25,019	136,891	54.04	26.64	1.04	18.28	100.00
1990–1	88,259	41,591	1623	28,287	159,760	55.24	26.03	1.02	17.71	100.00
1991–2	105,104	46,250	1642	32,716	185,712	56.60	24.90	0.88	17.62	100.00
1992–3	121,963	50,120	1722	34,460	208,265	58.56	24.07	0.83	16.55	100.00
1993–4	122,037	70,501	2554	46,875	241,967	50.44	29.14	1.06	19.37	100.00
1994–5	134,551	84,336	2686	57,200	278,773	48.27	30.25	0.96	20.52	100.00
1995–6	160,471	85,532	2227	54,871	303,102	52.94	28.22	0.73	18.10	100.00
1996–7	163,421	120,810	3185	75,188	362,605	45.07	33.32	0.88	20.74	100.00
1997–8	185,880	125,526	3654	71,948	387,008	48.03	32.44	0.94	18.59	100.00
1998–9	208,768	154,591	4646	91,896	459,900	45.39	33.61	1.01	19.98	100.00
1999–2000	219,458	166,729	5038	92,997	484,221	45.32	34.43	1.04	19.21	100.00

Sources: Col. (1) from Table 2.2, Col. (12); Cols (2) to (4) from Appendix Table 7(f), Cols (5) to (7); Cols (5) to (9) derived.

334

Appendix Table 7(h): Capital Input Index for Sector A Weighted by Relative Share of Factor Earnings, 1950–1 to 1999–2000

Year	Index	Fixed capital stock				Inventories	
		Relative change over previous year	% share of earnings	Two-year average of weights	Weighted yearly change	Index	Relative change over previous year
	(1)	(2)	(3)	(4)	(5)	(6)	(7)
1950–1	41.53	1.0000	15.84	15.84	15.84	23.38	1.00
1951–2	42.92	1.0335	16.56	16.20	16.75	24.16	1.03
1952–3	44.17	1.0292	18.96	17.76	18.28	24.86	1.03
1953–4	44.85	1.0153	19.14	19.05	19.34	25.54	1.03
1954–5	44.98	1.0029	19.98	19.56	19.62	26.22	1.03
1955–6	44.87	0.9976	20.59	20.28	20.23	26.89	1.03
1956–7	44.53	0.9924	19.06	19.82	19.67	27.58	1.03
1957–8	44.11	0.9906	16.87	17.96	17.79	28.24	1.02
1958–9	44.08	0.9993	17.78	17.32	17.31	28.84	1.02
1959–60	44.28	1.0045	16.99	17.38	17.46	29.32	1.02
1960–1	44.59	1.0071	15.61	16.30	16.41	29.82	1.02
1961–2	45.17	1.0131	16.50	16.06	16.27	30.45	1.02
1962–3	45.84	1.0148	16.04	16.27	16.51	31.13	1.02
1963–4	46.61	1.0166	18.64	17.34	17.63	31.88	1.02
1964–5	47.41	1.0171	15.50	17.07	17.36	32.74	1.03
1965–6	48.29	1.0187	15.55	15.53	15.82	33.66	1.03
1966–7	49.32	1.0213	14.83	15.19	15.51	34.58	1.03
1967–8	50.49	1.0238	13.42	14.13	14.46	35.57	1.03
1968–9	51.80	1.0259	14.25	13.84	14.19	36.63	1.03
1969–70	53.17	1.0265	15.80	15.02	15.42	37.72	1.03
1970–1	54.61	1.0272	16.18	15.99	16.43	38.81	1.03
1971–2	56.13	1.0277	17.17	16.67	17.14	39.86	1.03
1972–3	57.78	1.0294	16.58	16.88	17.37	40.97	1.03
1973–4	59.46	1.0291	17.63	17.10	17.60	42.05	1.03
1974–5	61.01	1.0261	18.12	17.87	18.34	42.99	1.02
1975–6	62.54	1.0251	18.29	18.21	18.66	43.89	1.02
1976–7	64.40	1.0297	19.69	18.99	19.55	45.13	1.03
1977–8	66.51	1.0328	19.08	19.39	20.02	46.63	1.03
1978–9	68.85	1.0351	19.17	19.13	19.80	48.28	1.04
1979–80	71.61	1.0401	20.22	19.70	20.49	50.09	1.04
1980–1	74.43	1.0395	20.98	20.60	21.42	53.62	1.07
1981–2	76.62	1.0294	21.87	21.43	22.06	57.77	1.08
1982–3	78.34	1.0224	21.98	21.93	22.42	61.05	1.06
1983–4	80.17	1.0234	21.11	21.55	22.05	64.61	1.06
1984–5	82.00	1.0228	21.41	21.26	21.74	68.95	1.07
1985–6	83.67	1.0204	23.59	22.50	22.95	73.92	1.07
1986–7	85.22	1.0186	21.56	22.57	22.99	78.46	1.06
1987–8	86.85	1.0191	21.49	21.53	21.94	82.66	1.05
1988–9	88.71	1.0214	23.60	22.55	23.03	85.73	1.04
1989–90	90.40	1.0191	26.64	25.12	25.60	88.30	1.03
1990–1	92.20	1.0199	26.03	26.34	26.86	91.28	1.03
1991–2	94.40	1.0239	24.90	25.47	26.08	93.63	1.03
1992–3	96.67	1.0241	24.07	24.48	25.07	95.80	1.02
1993–4	100.00	1.0344	29.14	26.60	27.52	100.00	1.04

(Contd.)

Appendix Table 7(h) Contd.

	(1)	(2)	(3)	(4)	(5)	(6)	(7)
1994–5	102.97	1.0297	30.25	29.69	30.58	104.96	1.05
1995–6	104.51	1.0149	28.22	29.24	29.67	109.95	1.05
1996–7	106.16	1.0157	33.32	30.77	31.25	123.39	1.12
1997–8	108.10	1.0182	32.44	32.88	33.48	126.26	1.02
1998–9	110.12	1.0187	33.61	33.02	33.64	121.52	0.96
1999–2000	112.10	1.0180	34.43	34.02	34.63	128.17	1.05

(Cols Contd.)

Appendix Table 7(h) Contd.: Capital Input Index for Sector A Weighted by Relative Share of Factor Earnings, 1950–1 to 1999–2000

Year	Inventories			Total capital input			
	% share of earnings	Two year average of weights	Weighted yearly change	Total weighted average annual change	Weighted capital input index 1950–1 = 100	Weighted capital input index 1993–4 = 100	Total weighted annual changes
	(8)	(9)	(10)	(11)	(12)	(13)	(14)
1950–1	0.33	0.33	0.33	1.00	100.00	40.86	16.17
1951–2	0.34	0.33	0.34	1.03	103.35	42.23	17.09
1952–3	0.41	0.37	0.38	1.03	106.36	43.46	18.66
1953–4	0.42	0.41	0.42	1.02	108.02	44.14	19.77
1954–5	0.45	0.43	0.44	1.00	108.39	44.29	20.06
1955–6	0.46	0.45	0.46	1.00	108.20	44.21	20.70
1956–7	0.45	0.45	0.46	0.99	107.45	43.90	20.14
1957–8	0.41	0.43	0.44	0.99	106.53	43.53	18.23
1958–9	0.44	0.42	0.43	1.00	106.51	43.52	17.74
1959–60	0.43	0.43	0.44	1.00	107.03	43.73	17.90
1960–1	0.40	0.41	0.42	1.01	107.81	44.05	16.83
1961–2	0.42	0.41	0.42	1.01	109.24	44.63	16.68
1962–3	0.42	0.42	0.43	1.01	110.88	45.30	16.94
1963–4	0.49	0.45	0.46	1.02	112.74	46.07	18.09
1964–5	0.40	0.44	0.46	1.02	114.71	46.87	17.82
1965–6	0.40	0.40	0.41	1.02	116.88	47.76	16.23
1966–7	0.39	0.39	0.41	1.02	119.38	48.78	15.92
1967–8	0.36	0.37	0.38	1.02	122.23	49.94	14.84
1968–9	0.38	0.37	0.38	1.03	125.41	51.24	14.58
1969–70	0.42	0.40	0.42	1.03	128.74	52.60	15.84
1970–1	0.43	0.43	0.44	1.03	132.24	54.03	16.86
1971–2	0.46	0.45	0.46	1.03	135.90	55.53	17.59
1972–3	0.45	0.45	0.47	1.03	139.90	57.16	17.84
1973–4	0.45	0.45	0.46	1.03	143.96	58.82	18.06
1974–5	0.47	0.46	0.47	1.03	147.70	60.35	18.81
1975–6	0.49	0.48	0.49	1.03	151.39	61.86	19.15
1976–7	0.52	0.50	0.52	1.03	155.89	63.69	20.07
1977–8	0.51	0.51	0.53	1.03	160.99	65.78	20.55
1978–9	0.51	0.51	0.53	1.04	166.65	68.09	20.33
1979–80	0.52	0.52	0.54	1.04	173.32	70.82	21.02

(Contd.)

Appendix Table 7(h) Contd.

	(8)	(9)	(10)	(11)	(12)	(13)	(14)
1980–1	0.57	0.55	0.59	1.04	180.30	73.67	22.00
1981–2	0.62	0.60	0.64	1.03	185.83	75.93	22.70
1982–3	0.64	0.63	0.66	1.02	190.18	77.70	23.08
1983–4	0.67	0.66	0.69	1.02	194.83	79.60	22.75
1984–5	0.68	0.68	0.72	1.02	199.54	81.53	22.47
1985–6	0.77	0.72	0.78	1.02	203.92	83.32	23.73
1986–7	0.72	0.74	0.79	1.02	207.98	84.98	23.78
1987–8	0.71	0.72	0.75	1.02	212.18	86.70	22.69
1988–9	0.84	0.77	0.80	1.02	216.84	88.60	23.83
1989–90	1.04	0.94	0.97	1.02	221.06	90.32	26.57
1990–1	1.02	1.03	1.06	1.02	225.57	92.17	27.92
1991–2	0.88	0.95	0.97	1.02	230.97	94.37	27.05
1992–3	0.83	0.86	0.88	1.02	236.52	96.64	25.95
1993–4	1.06	0.94	0.98	1.03	244.74	100.00	28.50
1994–5	0.96	1.01	1.06	1.03	252.18	103.04	31.64
1995–6	0.73	0.85	0.89	1.02	256.18	104.67	30.56
1996–7	0.88	0.81	0.91	1.02	260.91	106.61	32.16
1997–8	0.94	0.91	0.93	1.02	265.71	108.57	34.41
1998–9	1.01	0.98	0.94	1.02	270.26	110.42	34.58
1999–2000	1.04	1.03	1.08	1.02	275.41	112.53	35.72

Sources: Col. (1) from Table 7.2, Col. (6); Col. (2) based on Col. (1); Col. (3) from Appendix Table 7(g), Col. (6); Col. (4) based on Col. (3); Col. (5) = Col. (2) × Col. (4); Col. (6) from Table 7.3, Col. (6); Col. (7) based on Col. (6); Col. (8) from Table 7(g), Col. (7); Col. (9) based on Col. (8); Col. (10) = Col. (7) × Col. (9). For Cols (11) to (14), see text of Chapter 4.

Appendix Table 7(i): Total Factor Input Index for Sector A, 1950–1 to 1999–2000

Year	Labour input index	Relative annual change	% share of earnings of labour = wt.	Two-year average of weight	Weighted annual change	Weighted annual change in capital input	Agricultral land input index
	(1)	(2)	(3)	(4)	(5)	(6)	(7)
1950–1	46.82	1.0000	53.74	53.74	53.74	16.17	75.91
1951–2	47.71	1.0190	53.36	53.55	54.57	17.09	76.94
1952–3	48.58	1.0182	52.53	52.94	53.91	18.66	77.82
1953–4	49.48	1.0185	49.49	51.01	51.95	19.77	79.34
1954–5	50.39	1.0184	49.91	49.70	50.61	20.06	80.21
1955–6	51.32	1.0185	51.21	50.56	51.49	20.70	81.32
1956–7	52.27	1.0185	49.90	50.55	51.49	20.14	81.98
1957–8	53.24	1.0186	56.07	52.98	53.97	18.23	81.19
1958–9	54.23	1.0186	52.16	54.12	55.12	17.74	83.17
1959–60	55.23	1.0184	54.87	53.51	54.50	17.90	83.41
1960–1	56.19	1.0174	57.84	56.35	57.33	16.83	83.29
1961–2	57.08	1.0158	56.80	57.32	58.23	16.68	84.35
1962–3	58.01	1.0163	58.45	57.63	58.56	16.94	84.44
1963–4	58.96	1.0164	51.07	54.76	55.65	18.09	84.56
1964–5	59.92	1.0163	57.15	54.11	54.99	17.82	85.17
1965–6	60.90	1.0164	58.52	57.84	58.78	16.23	84.31
1966–7	61.90	1.0164	59.02	58.77	59.74	15.92	85.35
1967–8	62.92	1.0165	61.55	60.29	61.28	14.84	87.50
1968–9	63.95	1.0164	62.40	61.98	62.99	14.58	86.72
1969–70	65.00	1.0164	60.06	61.23	62.24	15.84	87.32
1970–1	66.06	1.0163	59.67	59.87	60.84	16.86	88.07
1971–2	67.15	1.0165	59.55	59.61	60.59	17.59	88.31
1972–3	68.25	1.0164	60.55	60.05	61.03	17.84	88.48
1973–4	69.54	1.0189	56.78	58.67	59.77	18.06	90.04

(Contd.)

Appendix Table 7(i) Contd.

	(1)	(2)	(3)	(4)	(5)	(6)	(7)
1974–5	70.95	1.0203	54.49	55.64	56.76	18.81	89.88
1975–6	72.38	1.0202	57.92	56.20	57.34	19.15	91.59
1976–7	73.85	1.0203	57.01	57.46	58.63	20.07	90.74
1977–8	75.34	1.0202	57.80	57.40	58.56	20.55	92.42
1978–9	76.81	1.0195	59.59	58.70	59.84	20.33	93.28
1979–80	78.26	1.0189	58.82	59.21	60.32	21.02	92.65
1980–1	79.73	1.0188	57.59	58.21	59.30	22.00	93.63
1981–2	81.23	1.0188	56.11	56.85	57.92	22.70	94.77
1982–3	82.75	1.0187	56.87	56.49	57.55	23.08	93.63
1983–4	83.68	1.0112	56.73	56.80	57.44	22.75	96.01
1984–5	85.10	1.0170	58.54	57.63	58.61	22.47	95.46
1985–6	85.85	1.0088	56.91	57.72	58.23	23.73	96.49
1986–7	86.71	1.0100	60.69	58.80	59.39	23.78	96.25
1987–8	87.64	1.0107	60.86	60.77	61.42	22.69	96.07
1988–9	88.88	1.0141	57.37	59.11	59.95	23.83	98.12
1989–90	90.93	1.0231	54.04	55.70	56.99	26.57	97.83
1990–1	93.03	1.0231	55.24	54.64	55.90	27.92	99.19
1991–2	95.18	1.0231	56.60	55.92	57.21	27.05	98.13
1992–3	97.37	1.0230	58.56	57.58	58.90	25.95	99.39
1993–4	100.00	1.0270	50.44	54.50	55.97	28.50	100.00
1994–5	101.63	1.0163	48.27	49.35	50.15	31.64	100.22
1995–6	101.76	1.0013	52.94	50.60	50.67	30.56	100.24
1996–7	101.87	1.0011	45.07	49.01	49.06	32.16	100.93
1997–8	102.01	1.0014	48.03	46.55	46.61	34.41	100.93
1998–9	102.15	1.0014	45.39	46.71	46.78	34.58	100.93
1999–2000	102.29	1.0014	45.32	45.36	45.42	35.72	100.93

(Cols Contd.)

339

Appendix Table 7(i) Contd.: Total Factor Input Index for Sector A, 1950-1 to 1999-2000

Year	Relative annual change (8)	% share of earnings of land = wt. (9)	Two year average of weight (10)	Weighted annual change in land input (11)	Total weighted annual changes (12)	Total factor input index 1950-1 = 100 (13)	Total factor input index 1993-4 = 100 (14)
1950-1	1.0000	30.09	30.09	30.09	100.00	100.00	50.87
1951-2	1.0136	29.73	29.91	30.32	101.98	101.98	51.87
1952-3	1.0114	28.11	28.92	29.25	101.83	103.84	52.82
1953-4	1.0195	30.95	29.53	30.11	101.83	105.73	53.79
1954-5	1.0110	29.66	30.31	30.64	101.31	107.12	54.49
1955-6	1.0138	27.75	28.71	29.10	101.29	108.51	55.20
1956-7	1.0081	30.60	29.17	29.41	101.03	109.63	55.77
1957-8	0.9904	26.66	28.63	28.35	100.55	110.23	56.07
1958-9	1.0244	29.62	28.14	28.82	101.69	112.10	57.02
1959-60	1.0029	27.72	28.67	28.75	101.16	113.39	57.68
1960-1	0.9986	26.15	26.93	26.90	101.06	114.60	58.29
1961-2	1.0127	26.27	26.21	26.55	101.46	116.27	59.14
1962-3	1.0011	25.10	25.68	25.71	101.22	117.68	59.86
1963-4	1.0014	29.80	27.45	27.49	101.24	119.14	60.60
1964-5	1.0072	26.95	28.38	28.58	101.39	120.79	61.45
1965-6	0.9899	25.52	26.23	25.97	100.98	121.98	62.05
1966-7	1.0123	25.76	25.64	25.96	101.62	123.95	63.05
1967-8	1.0252	24.66	25.21	25.85	101.98	126.40	64.30
1968-9	0.9911	22.97	23.82	23.60	101.17	127.88	65.05
1969-70	1.0069	23.71	23.34	23.50	101.58	129.90	66.08
1970-1	1.0086	23.72	23.72	23.92	101.63	132.01	67.15
1971-2	1.0027	22.82	23.27	23.33	101.52	134.02	68.17
1972-3	1.0019	22.42	22.62	22.66	101.54	136.08	69.22
1973-4	1.0176	25.14	23.78	24.20	102.04	138.85	70.63
1974-5	0.9982	26.92	26.03	25.98	101.56	141.01	71.73

(Contd.)

340

Appendix Table 7(i) Contd.

	(8)	(9)	(10)	(11)	(12)	(13)	(14)
1975–6	1.0190	23.31	25.11	25.59	102.08	143.94	73.22
1976–7	0.9907	22.78	23.04	22.83	101.53	146.15	74.34
1977–8	1.0185	22.61	22.69	23.11	102.23	149.41	76.00
1978–9	1.0093	20.72	21.67	21.87	102.04	152.45	77.55
1979–80	0.9932	20.43	20.58	20.44	101.79	155.18	78.94
1980–1	1.0106	20.85	20.64	20.86	102.16	158.53	80.64
1981–2	1.0122	21.40	21.13	21.38	102.00	161.71	82.26
1982–3	0.9880	20.51	20.96	20.70	101.33	163.86	83.35
1983–4	1.0254	21.49	21.00	21.53	101.71	166.67	84.78
1984–5	0.9943	19.37	20.43	20.32	101.39	168.99	85.96
1985–6	1.0108	18.74	19.06	19.26	101.22	171.06	87.02
1986–7	0.9975	17.03	17.88	17.84	101.01	172.79	87.89
1987–8	0.9981	16.94	16.99	16.96	101.07	174.63	88.83
1988–9	1.0213	18.19	17.57	17.94	101.72	177.64	90.36
1989–90	0.9970	18.28	18.23	18.18	101.74	180.73	91.94
1990–1	1.0139	17.71	17.99	18.24	102.07	184.47	93.84
1991–2	0.9893	17.62	17.66	17.47	101.74	187.67	95.47
1992–3	1.0128	16.55	17.08	17.30	102.15	191.72	97.52
1993–4	1.0061	19.37	17.96	18.07	102.54	196.58	100.00
1994–5	1.0002	20.52	19.95	19.99	101.78	200.09	101.78
1995–6	1.0002	18.10	19.31	19.31	100.55	201.18	102.34
1996–7	1.0069	20.74	19.42	19.55	100.77	202.73	103.12
1997–8	1.0000	18.59	19.66	19.66	100.69	204.12	103.83
1998–9	1.0000	19.98	19.29	19.29	100.65	205.43	104.50
1999–2000	1.0000	19.21	19.59	19.59	100.73	206.93	105.26

Sources: Col. (1) from Table 7.1, Col. (4); Col. (2) from Col. (1); Col. (3) from Appendix Table 7(g), Col. (5); Col. (4) derived from Col. (3); Col. (5) = Col. (2) × Col. (4); Col. (6) from Appendix Table 7(h), Col. (14), Col. (7) based on Col. (7) and Col. (5) of Table 4.10; Col. (8) based on Col. (7); Col. (9) from Appendix Table 7(g), Col. (8); Col. (10) based on Col. (9); Col. (11) = Col. (8) × Col. (10); for Col. (12) to (14), see text in Chapter 4.

Appendix 7(j): Gross Capital Stock Plus Land for Sector Non-A at Current Prices, 1950–1 to 1999–2000

Year	GFCS (Rs crore)	Inventories (Rs crore)	Gross capital stock (Rs crore)	Non-agricultural land (Rs crore)	Gross capital stock plus non-agricultural land (Rs crore)	% distribution of GCS + land			
						GFCS	Inventories	Non-agricultural land	Total
	(1)	(2)	(3)	(4)	(5)	(6)	(7)	(8)	(9)
1950–1	6026	1806	7832	435	8267	72.89	21.85	5.26	100.00
1951–2	7303	1971	9274	652	9926	73.58	19.86	6.57	100.00
1952–3	8169	2087	10,256	581	10,837	75.38	19.26	5.36	100.00
1953–4	9066	2141	11,207	649	11,856	76.47	18.06	5.47	100.00
1954–5	10,712	2190	12,902	650	13,552	79.04	16.16	4.80	100.00
1955–6	11,452	2293	13,745	632	14,377	79.66	15.95	4.40	100.00
1956–7	12,379	2505	14,884	699	15,583	79.44	16.07	4.49	100.00
1957–8	13,460	2789	16,249	727	16,976	79.29	16.43	4.28	100.00
1958–9	15,892	3020	18,912	755	19,667	80.81	15.35	3.84	100.00
1959–60	18,533	3225	21,758	826	22,584	82.06	14.28	3.66	100.00
1960–1	21,208	3510	24,719	880	25,599	82.85	13.71	3.44	100.00
1961–2	24,214	3835	28,050	886	28,936	83.68	13.25	3.06	100.00
1962–3	27,353	4163	31,516	945	32,461	84.26	12.83	2.91	100.00
1963–4	31,175	4491	35,666	1016	36,682	84.99	12.24	2.77	100.00
1964–5	34,605	4899	39,503	1091	40,594	85.24	12.07	2.69	100.00
1965–6	38,931	5496	44,427	1144	45,571	85.43	12.06	2.51	100.00
1966–7	46,563	6205	52,769	1302	54,071	86.12	11.48	2.41	100.00
1967–8	55,307	6914	62,221	1453	63,674	86.86	10.86	2.28	100.00
1968–9	61,733	7587	69,320	1484	70,804	87.19	10.72	2.10	100.00
1969–70	67,441	8363	75,804	1521	77,325	87.22	10.82	1.97	100.00
1970–1	75,201	9291	84,492	1687	86,179	87.26	10.78	1.96	100.00
1971–2	84,597	10,324	94,920	1895	96,815	87.38	10.66	1.96	100.00
1972–3	97,911	11,548	109,459	2050	111,509	87.81	10.36	1.84	100.00
1973–4	112,580	13,394	125,974	2407	128,381	87.69	10.43	1.87	100.00

(Contd.)

Appendix 7(j) Contd.

	(1)	(2)	(3)	(4)	(5)	(6)	(7)	(8)	(9)
1974–5	142,824	16,377	159,201	3354	162,555	87.86	10.07	2.06	100.00
1975–6	179,449	19,408	198,857	3509	202,366	88.68	9.59	1.73	100.00
1976–7	199,930	21,368	221,298	3835	225,133	88.81	9.49	1.70	100.00
1977–8	212,777	22,963	235,740	3769	239,509	88.84	9.59	1.57	100.00
1978–9	236,748	25,383	262,131	3837	265,968	89.01	9.54	1.44	100.00
1979–80	280,291	29,650	309,941	4745	314,686	89.07	9.42	1.51	100.00
1980–1	332,857	34,782	367,640	5779	373,419	89.14	9.31	1.55	100.00
1981–2	398,872	41,359	440,230	6281	446,511	89.33	9.26	1.41	100.00
1982–3	485,965	48,650	534,615	6608	541,223	89.79	8.99	1.22	100.00
1983–4	575,166	54,223	629,389	7106	636,495	90.36	8.52	1.12	100.00
1984–5	648,559	60,789	709,348	7652	717,000	90.45	8.48	1.07	100.00
1985–6	743,911	70,761	814,671	8162	822,833	90.41	8.60	0.99	100.00
1986–7	864,770	81,383	946,152	8587	954,739	90.58	8.52	0.90	100.00
1987–8	976,076	90,157	1,066,233	9233	1,075,466	90.76	8.38	0.86	100.00
1988–9	1,108,476	47,292	1,155,767	10,025	1,165,792	95.08	4.06	0.86	100.00
1989–90	1,262,243	63,864	1,326,107	11,015	1,337,122	94.40	4.78	0.82	100.00
1990–1	1,425,571	135,992	1,561,563	11,895	1,573,458	90.60	8.64	0.76	100.00
1991–2	1,677,251	153,081	1,830,332	13,478	1,843,810	90.97	8.30	0.73	100.00
1992–3	1,976,217	174,725	2,150,942	15,178	2,166,120	91.23	8.07	0.70	100.00
1993–4	2,229,334	194,382	2,423,716	16,569	2,440,285	91.36	7.97	0.68	100.00
1994–5	2,540,786	219,420	2,760,205	18,460	2,778,665	91.44	7.90	0.66	100.00
1995–6	3,057,781	260,406	3,318,187	19,976	3,338,163	91.60	7.80	0.60	100.00
1996–7	3,649,698	280,915	3,930,613	20,589	3,951,202	92.37	7.11	0.52	100.00
1997–8	4,150,435	291,071	4,441,506	21,661	4,463,167	92.99	6.52	0.49	100.00
1998–9	4,608,148	307,446	4,915,594	22,600	4,938,194	93.32	6.23	0.46	100.00
1999–2000	5,026,893	328,720	5,355,613	23,422	5,379,035	93.45	6.11	0.44	100.00

Sources: Col. (1) from Appendix Table 7(d), Col. (3); Col. (2) from Appendix Table 7(e), Col. (7); Col. (3) = Col. (1) + Col. (2); Col. (4) from Appendix Table 4(g); Col. (5) = Col. (3) + Col. (4); Col. (6) to (9) derived.

Appendix Table 7(k): Distribution of Property Income by Type of Asset in Sector Non-A at Current Prices, 1950–1 to 1999–2000

Year	Property income (Rs crore)	% distribution of GCS + Land			Distribution of property income (Rs crore)		
		GFCS	Inventories	Non-agricultural land	GFCS	Inventories	Non-agricultural land
	(1)	(2)	(3)	(4)	(5)	(6)	(7)
1950–1	1222	72.89	21.85	5.26	891	267	64
1951–2	1368	73.58	19.86	6.57	1007	272	90
1952–3	1239	75.38	19.26	5.36	934	239	66
1953–4	1328	76.47	18.06	5.47	1016	240	73
1954–5	1340	79.04	16.16	4.80	1059	217	64
1955–6	1464	79.66	15.95	4.40	1166	233	64
1956–7	1744	79.44	16.07	4.49	1385	280	78
1957–8	1841	79.29	16.43	4.28	1460	302	79
1958–9	2035	80.81	15.35	3.84	1644	312	78
1959–60	2292	82.06	14.28	3.66	1881	327	84
1960–1	3123	82.85	13.71	3.44	2587	428	107
1961–2	3501	83.68	13.25	3.06	2930	464	107
1962–3	3808	84.26	12.83	2.91	3209	488	111
1963–4	3794	84.99	12.24	2.77	3224	465	105
1964–5	4968	85.24	12.07	2.69	4235	600	134
1965–6	5297	85.43	12.06	2.51	4525	639	133
1966–7	5812	86.12	11.48	2.41	5005	667	140
1967–8	6046	86.86	10.86	2.28	5252	656	138
1968–9	6483	87.19	10.72	2.10	5652	695	136
1969–70	7497	87.22	10.82	1.97	6539	811	147
1970–1	8099	87.26	10.78	1.96	7067	873	159
1971–2	8990	87.38	10.66	1.96	7855	959	176
1972–3	9814	87.81	10.36	1.84	8617	1016	180
1973–4	11,688	87.69	10.43	1.87	10,249	1219	219
1974–5	15,352	87.86	10.07	2.06	13,489	1547	317
1975–6	17,012	88.68	9.59	1.73	15,086	1632	295
1976–7	19,917	88.81	9.49	1.70	17,687	1890	339
1977–8	21,145	88.84	9.59	1.57	18,785	2027	333
1978–9	24,490	89.01	9.54	1.44	21,799	2337	353
1979–80	28,577	89.07	9.42	1.51	25,454	2693	431
1980–1	32,034	89.14	9.31	1.55	28,554	2984	496
1981–2	40,506	89.33	9.26	1.41	36,184	3752	570
1982–3	46,235	89.79	8.99	1.22	41,514	4156	565
1983–4	53,473	90.36	8.52	1.12	48,321	4555	597
1984–5	60,056	90.45	8.48	1.07	54,323	5092	641
1985–6	70,180	90.41	8.60	0.99	63,449	6035	696
1986–7	76,348	90.58	8.52	0.90	69,153	6508	687
1987–8	84,877	90.76	8.38	0.86	77,033	7115	729
1988–9	106,249	95.08	4.06	0.86	101,025	4310	914
1989–90	131,124	94.40	4.78	0.82	123,781	6263	1080
1990–1	152,169	90.60	8.64	0.76	137,867	13,152	1150
1991–2	176,238	90.97	8.30	0.73	160,318	14,632	1288
1992–3	199,741	91.23	8.07	0.70	182,230	16,112	1400
1993–4	255,868	91.36	7.97	0.68	233,749	20,381	1737
1994–5	319,574	91.44	7.90	0.66	292,216	25,235	2123
1995–6	380,776	91.60	7.80	0.60	348,794	29,704	2279
1996–7	458,462	92.37	7.11	0.52	423,478	32,595	2389
1997–8	501,429	92.99	6.52	0.49	466,294	32,701	2434
1998–9	579,333	93.32	6.23	0.46	540,613	36,069	2651
1999–2000	648,693	93.45	6.11	0.44	606,226	39,642	2825

Sources: Col. (1) from Table 2.2, Col. (18); Col. (2) to (4) from Appendix Table 7(j), Cols (6) to (8); Cols (5) to (7) derived.

Appendix Table 7(l): Distribution of Factor Incomes in Sector Non-A at Current Prices, 1950-1 to 1999-2000

Year	Labour income (Rs crore)	Property income by type of asset (Rs crore)			Sector non-A GDP (Rs crore)	Weighting structure				
		GFCS	Inventories	Non-agricultural land		Labour	GFCS	Inventories	Land	Total
	(1)	(2)	(3)	(4)	(5)	(6)	(7)	(8)	(9)	(10)
1950–1	2045	891	267	64	3267	62.60	27.26	8.17	1.97	100.00
1951–2	2195	1007	272	90	3563	61.61	28.25	7.62	2.52	100.00
1952–3	2264	934	239	66	3503	64.63	26.66	6.81	1.90	100.00
1953–4	2430	1016	240	73	3758	64.66	27.02	6.38	1.93	100.00
1954–5	2581	1059	217	64	3921	65.83	27.01	5.52	1.64	100.00
1955–6	2698	1166	233	64	4162	64.82	28.02	5.61	1.55	100.00
1956–7	2989	1385	280	78	4733	63.15	29.27	5.92	1.65	100.00
1957–8	3208	1460	302	79	5049	63.54	28.91	5.99	1.56	100.00
1958–9	3422	1644	312	78	5457	62.71	30.13	5.73	1.43	100.00
1959–60	3735	1881	327	84	6027	61.97	31.21	5.43	1.39	100.00
1960–1	3814	2587	428	107	6937	54.98	37.30	6.17	1.55	100.00
1961–2	4046	2930	464	107	7547	53.61	38.82	6.15	1.42	100.00
1962–3	4519	3209	488	111	8327	54.27	38.53	5.87	1.33	100.00
1963–4	5576	3224	465	105	9370	59.51	34.41	4.96	1.12	100.00
1964–5	5669	4235	600	134	10,637	53.30	39.81	5.64	1.26	100.00
1965–6	6365	4525	639	133	11,662	54.58	38.80	5.48	1.14	100.00
1966–7	7349	5005	667	140	13,161	55.84	38.03	5.07	1.06	100.00
1967–8	8623	5252	656	138	14,669	58.78	35.80	4.48	0.94	100.00
1968–9	9349	5652	695	136	15,832	59.05	35.70	4.39	0.86	100.00
1969–70	10,123	6539	811	147	17,620	57.45	37.11	4.60	0.84	100.00
1970–1	11,243	7067	873	159	19,342	58.13	36.54	4.51	0.82	100.00
1971–2	12,358	7855	959	176	21,348	57.89	36.80	4.49	0.82	100.00
1972–3	13,739	8617	1016	180	23,553	58.33	36.59	4.32	0.77	100.00

(Contd.)

Appendix Table 7(l) Contd.

	(1)	(2)	(3)	(4)	(5)	(6)	(7)	(8)	(9)	(10)
1973-4	15,727	10,249	1219	219	27,415	57.37	37.39	4.45	0.80	100.00
1974-5	19,657	13,489	1547	317	35,009	56.15	38.53	4.42	0.90	100.00
1975-6	22,296	15,086	1632	295	39,308	56.72	38.38	4.15	0.75	100.00
1976-7	23,945	17,687	1890	339	43,862	54.59	40.32	4.31	0.77	100.00
1977-8	27,877	18,785	2027	333	49,022	56.87	38.32	4.14	0.68	100.00
1978-9	29,973	21,799	2337	353	54,463	55.03	40.03	4.29	0.65	100.00
1979-80	33,129	25,454	2693	431	61,706	53.69	41.25	4.36	0.70	100.00
1980-1	40,086	28,554	2984	496	72,120	55.58	39.59	4.14	0.69	100.00
1981-2	46,141	36,184	3752	570	86,647	53.25	41.76	4.33	0.66	100.00
1982-3	52,661	41,514	4156	565	98,896	53.25	41.98	4.20	0.57	100.00
1983-4	61,278	48,321	4555	597	114,751	53.40	42.11	3.97	0.52	100.00
1984-5	71,699	54,323	5092	641	131,755	54.42	41.23	3.86	0.49	100.00
1985-6	80,690	63,449	6035	696	150,870	53.48	42.06	4.00	0.46	100.00
1986-7	94,768	69,153	6508	687	171,116	55.38	40.41	3.80	0.40	100.00
1987-8	111,306	77,033	7115	729	196,183	56.74	39.27	3.63	0.37	100.00
1988-9	126,452	101,025	4310	914	232,701	54.34	43.41	1.85	0.39	100.00
1989-90	144,933	123,781	6263	1080	276,057	52.50	44.84	2.27	0.39	100.00
1990-1	170,456	137,867	13,152	1150	322,625	52.83	42.73	4.08	0.36	100.00
1991-2	194,352	160,318	14,632	1288	370,590	52.44	43.26	3.95	0.35	100.00
1992-3	227,548	182,230	16,112	1400	427,289	53.25	42.65	3.77	0.33	100.00
1993-4	240,240	233,749	20,381	1737	496,108	48.42	47.12	4.11	0.35	100.00
1994-5	272,243	292,216	25,235	2123	591,817	46.00	49.38	4.26	0.36	100.00
1995-6	338,868	348,794	29,704	2279	719,644	47.09	48.47	4.13	0.32	100.00
1996-7	367,500	423,478	32,595	2389	825,962	44.49	51.27	3.95	0.29	100.00
1997-8	442,330	466,294	32,701	2434	943,759	46.87	49.41	3.47	0.26	100.00
1998-9	509,335	540,613	36,069	2651	1,088,668	46.79	49.66	3.31	0.24	100.00
1999-2000	576,040	606,226	39,642	2825	1,224,733	47.03	49.50	3.24	0.23	100.00

Sources: Col. (1) from Table 2.2, Col. (17); Cols (2) to (4) from Appendix Table 7(k), Cols (5) to (7); Col. (5) from Appendix Table 1(d), Col. (5); Cols (6) to (10) derived.

346

Appendix Table 7(m): Capital Input Index for Sector Non-A, 1950–1 to 1999–2000

Year	Fixed capital stock					Inventories	
	Index	Relative change over previous year	% share of earnings	Two-year average of weights	Weighted yearly change	Index	Relative change over previous year
	(1)	(2)	(3)	(4)	(5)	(6)	(7)
1950–1	8.27	1.00	27.26	27.26	27.26	15.92	1.00
1951–2	8.08	0.98	28.25	27.76	27.11	16.41	1.03
1952–3	7.86	0.97	26.66	27.46	26.72	16.84	1.03
1953–4	8.10	1.03	27.02	26.84	27.65	17.26	1.03
1954–5	8.66	1.07	27.01	27.02	28.89	17.76	1.03
1955–6	9.33	1.08	28.02	27.52	29.63	18.39	1.04
1956–7	10.08	1.08	29.27	28.65	30.95	19.17	1.04
1957–8	10.90	1.08	28.91	29.09	31.48	20.05	1.05
1958–9	11.85	1.09	30.13	29.52	32.08	20.91	1.04
1959–60	12.93	1.09	31.21	30.67	33.46	21.71	1.04
1960–1	14.17	1.10	37.30	34.25	37.55	22.63	1.04
1961–2	15.48	1.09	38.82	38.06	41.58	23.59	1.04
1962–3	16.85	1.09	38.53	38.68	42.10	24.62	1.04
1963–4	18.41	1.09	34.41	36.47	39.85	25.80	1.05
1964–5	19.99	1.09	39.81	37.11	40.28	27.06	1.05
1965–6	21.62	1.08	38.80	39.31	42.53	28.39	1.05
1966–7	23.32	1.08	38.03	38.42	41.44	29.69	1.05
1967–8	24.88	1.07	35.80	36.91	39.38	30.89	1.04
1968–9	26.24	1.05	35.70	35.75	37.71	31.99	1.04
1969–70	27.51	1.05	37.11	36.41	38.17	33.05	1.03
1970–1	28.91	1.05	36.54	36.82	38.70	34.15	1.03
1971–2	30.45	1.05	36.80	36.67	38.63	35.29	1.03

(Contd.)

347

Appendix Table 7(m)' Contd.

	(1)	(2)	(3)	(4)	(5)	(6)	(7)
1972–3	32.24	1.06	36.59	36.69	38.84	36.59	1.04
1973–4	34.09	1.06	37.39	36.99	39.11	37.94	1.04
1974–5	35.79	1.05	38.53	37.96	39.85	39.18	1.03
1975–6	37.69	1.05	38.38	38.45	40.50	40.53	1.03
1976–7	39.67	1.05	40.32	39.35	41.42	42.04	1.04
1977–8	41.58	1.05	38.32	39.32	41.22	43.61	1.04
1978–9	43.75	1.05	40.03	39.17	41.21	45.36	1.04
1979–80	46.04	1.05	41.25	40.64	42.77	47.30	1.04
1980–1	48.36	1.05	39.59	40.42	42.46	48.26	1.02
1981–2	51.74	1.07	41.76	40.68	43.52	51.67	1.07
1982–3	55.73	1.08	41.98	41.87	45.10	57.60	1.11
1983–4	59.17	1.06	42.11	42.04	44.64	60.77	1.06
1984–5	62.47	1.06	41.23	41.67	43.99	63.64	1.05
1985–6	65.94	1.06	42.06	41.64	43.96	69.88	1.10
1986–7	69.87	1.06	40.41	41.23	43.70	76.81	1.10
1987–8	73.81	1.06	39.27	39.84	42.08	80.52	1.05
1988–9	77.49	1.05	43.41	41.34	43.40	84.58	1.05
1989–90	81.20	1.05	44.84	44.13	46.24	89.99	1.06
1990–1	85.15	1.05	42.73	43.79	45.91	94.15	1.05
1991–2	89.98	1.06	43.26	43.00	45.44	95.88	1.02
1992–3	95.14	1.06	42.65	42.95	45.42	98.18	1.02
1993–4	100.00	1.05	47.12	44.88	47.18	100.00	1.02
1994–5	107.07	1.07	49.38	48.25	51.66	102.32	1.02
1995–6	117.84	1.10	48.47	48.92	53.84	110.42	1.08
1996–7	129.74	1.10	51.27	49.87	54.91	112.28	1.02
1997–8	140.73	1.08	49.41	50.34	54.60	113.50	1.01
1998–9	150.60	1.07	49.66	49.53	53.01	117.41	1.03
1999–2000	159.77	1.06	49.50	49.58	52.60	121.52	1.04

(Cols Contd.)

348

Appendix Table 7(m) Contd.: Capital Input Index for Sector Non-A, 1950–1 to 1999–2000

Year	Inventories				Total capital input		
	% share of earnings	Two-year average of weights	Weighted yearly change	Total weighted average annual change	Weighted capital input index 1950–1 = 100	Weighted capital input index 1993–4 = 100	Total weighted annual change
	(8)	(9)	(10)	(11)	(12)	(13)	(14)
1950–1	8.17	8.17	8.17	1.00	100.00	8.94	35.44
1951–2	7.62	7.90	8.14	0.99	98.86	8.84	35.25
1952–3	6.81	7.22	7.41	0.98	97.31	8.70	34.13
1953–4	6.38	6.60	6.76	1.03	100.13	8.95	34.41
1954–5	5.52	5.95	6.12	1.06	106.34	9.50	35.01
1955–6	5.61	5.57	5.76	1.07	113.78	10.17	35.40
1956–7	5.92	5.77	6.01	1.07	122.22	10.92	36.96
1957–8	5.99	5.96	6.23	1.08	131.51	11.75	37.71
1958–9	5.73	5.86	6.11	1.08	141.96	12.69	38.19
1959–60	5.43	5.58	5.79	1.08	153.73	13.74	39.26
1960–1	6.17	5.80	6.05	1.09	167.30	14.95	43.59
1961–2	6.15	6.16	6.42	1.09	181.60	16.23	48.00
1962–3	5.87	6.01	6.27	1.08	196.59	17.57	48.37
1963–4	4.96	5.41	5.67	1.09	213.65	19.10	45.52
1964–5	5.64	5.30	5.55	1.08	230.93	20.64	45.84
1965–6	5.48	5.56	5.83	1.08	248.91	22.25	48.36
1966–7	5.07	5.27	5.51	1.07	267.50	23.91	46.95
1967–8	4.48	4.77	4.96	1.06	284.56	25.43	44.34
1968–9	4.39	4.43	4.59	1.05	299.53	26.77	42.30
1969–70	4.60	4.49	4.64	1.05	313.51	28.02	42.81
1970–1	4.51	4.56	4.71	1.05	328.85	29.39	43.41
1971–2	4.49	4.50	4.65	1.05	345.69	30.90	43.28
1972–3	4.32	4.40	4.56	1.06	365.14	32.64	43.41

(Contd.)

349

Appendix Table 7(m) Contd.

	(8)	(9)	(10)	(11)	(12)	(13)	(14)
1973-4	4.45	4.38	4.54	1.06	385.35	34.44	43.66
1974-5	4.42	4.43	4.58	1.05	403.87	36.10	44.43
1975-6	4.15	4.28	4.43	1.05	424.56	37.95	44.93
1976-7	4.31	4.23	4.39	1.05	446.21	39.88	45.80
1977-8	4.14	4.22	4.38	1.05	467.22	41.76	45.60
1978-9	4.29	4.21	4.38	1.05	491.01	43.89	45.60
1979-80	4.36	4.33	4.51	1.05	516.29	46.15	47.28
1980-1	4.14	4.25	4.34	1.05	540.80	48.34	46.79
1981-2	4.33	4.23	4.53	1.07	578.65	51.72	48.05
1982-3	4.20	4.27	4.76	1.08	625.27	55.89	49.85
1983-4	3.97	4.09	4.31	1.06	663.54	59.31	48.95
1984-5	3.86	3.92	4.10	1.06	700.04	62.57	48.09
1985-6	4.00	3.93	4.32	1.06	741.49	66.27	48.27
1986-7	3.80	3.90	4.29	1.06	788.28	70.46	47.98
1987-8	3.63	3.72	3.89	1.06	832.15	74.38	45.98
1988-9	1.85	2.74	2.88	1.05	873.66	78.09	46.28
1989-90	2.27	2.06	2.19	1.05	916.15	81.89	48.43
1990-1	4.08	3.17	3.32	1.05	960.51	85.85	49.23
1991-2	3.95	4.01	4.09	1.05	1011.88	90.44	49.52
1992-3	3.77	3.86	3.95	1.05	1067.08	95.38	49.37
1993-4	4.11	3.94	4.01	1.05	1118.82	100.00	51.19
1994-5	4.26	4.19	4.28	1.07	1193.68	106.69	55.94
1995-6	4.13	4.20	4.53	1.10	1311.73	117.24	58.37
1996-7	3.95	4.04	4.10	1.09	1435.97	128.35	59.01
1997-8	3.47	3.71	3.75	1.08	1550.27	138.56	58.35
1998-9	3.31	3.39	3.51	1.07	1655.46	147.96	56.51
1999-2000	3.24	3.27	3.39	1.06	1753.68	156.74	55.99

Note: Labour input = Workforce

Sources: Col. (1) from Table 7.2, Col. (9); Col. (2) based on Col. (1); Col. (3) from Appendix Table 7(l), Col. (7); Col. (4) based on Col. (3); Col. (5) = Col. (2) × Col. (4); Col. (6) from Table 7.3, Col. (7); Col. (7) based on Col. (6); Col. (8) from Appendix Table 7(l), Col. (9); based on Col. (8); Col. (10) = Col. (7) × Col. (9). For Cols (11) to (14), see text of Chapter 4.

Appendix Table 7(n): Total Factor Input Index for Sector Non-A,
1950–1 to 1999–2000

Year	Labour input index	Relative annual change	% share of earnings of labour = wt.	Two-year average of weight	Weighted annual change	Weighted annual change in capital input	Non-agricultural land input index
	(1)	(2)	(3)	(4)	(5)	(6)	(7)
1950–1	28.50	1.00	62.60	62.60	62.60	35.44	42.98
1951–2	28.99	1.02	61.61	62.10	63.17	35.25	58.29
1952–3	29.52	1.02	64.63	63.12	64.27	34.13	56.59
1953–4	30.06	1.02	64.66	64.65	65.83	34.41	61.01
1954–5	30.61	1.02	65.83	65.24	66.44	35.01	63.31
1955–6	31.17	1.02	64.82	65.32	66.52	35.40	63.94
1956–7	31.73	1.02	63.15	63.99	65.14	36.96	64.22
1957–8	32.31	1.02	63.54	63.34	64.50	37.71	64.79
1958–9	32.90	1.02	62.71	63.12	64.28	38.19	65.68
1959–60	33.50	1.02	61.97	62.34	63.48	39.26	68.44
1960–1	34.12	1.02	54.98	58.48	59.56	43.59	68.16
1961–2	34.84	1.02	53.61	54.30	55.44	48.00	67.96
1962–3	35.67	1.02	54.27	53.94	55.22	48.37	69.41
1963–4	36.53	1.02	59.51	56.89	58.26	45.52	70.14
1964–5	37.40	1.02	53.30	56.40	57.75	45.84	70.93
1965–6	38.29	1.02	54.58	53.94	55.22	48.36	69.68
1966–7	39.20	1.02	55.84	55.21	56.52	46.95	70.54
1967–8	40.14	1.02	58.78	57.31	58.69	44.34	71.08
1968–9	41.09	1.02	59.05	58.92	60.31	42.30	71.88
1969–70	42.06	1.02	57.45	58.25	59.63	42.81	72.89
1970–1	43.05	1.02	58.13	57.79	59.15	43.41	75.69
1971–2	44.07	1.02	57.89	58.01	59.38	43.28	77.96
1972–3	45.11	1.02	58.33	58.11	59.48	43.41	76.51
1973–4	46.82	1.04	57.37	57.85	60.04	43.66	77.16
1974–5	49.22	1.05	56.15	56.76	59.67	44.43	84.41
1975–6	51.72	1.05	56.72	56.43	59.30	44.93	85.71
1976–7	54.31	1.05	54.59	55.66	58.44	45.80	91.10
1977–8	56.62	1.04	56.87	55.73	58.10	45.60	87.49
1978–9	58.74	1.04	55.03	55.95	58.04	45.60	88.20
1979–80	61.04	1.04	53.69	54.36	56.49	47.28	89.77
1980–1	63.42	1.04	55.58	54.64	56.77	46.79	90.29
1981–2	65.86	1.04	53.25	54.42	56.51	48.05	90.42
1982–3	68.69	1.04	53.25	53.25	55.54	49.85	91.47
1983–4	71.77	1.04	53.40	53.32	55.72	48.95	93.43
1984–5	74.78	1.04	54.42	53.91	56.17	48.09	94.40
1985–6	77.85	1.04	53.48	53.95	56.17	48.27	94.76
1986–7	80.98	1.04	55.38	54.43	56.62	47.98	95.90
1987–8	84.16	1.04	56.74	56.06	58.26	45.98	97.23
1988–9	87.04	1.03	54.34	55.54	57.44	46.28	97.51
1989–90	89.61	1.03	52.50	53.42	55.00	48.43	97.64
1990–1	92.26	1.03	52.83	52.67	54.23	49.23	96.86
1991–2	94.98	1.03	52.44	52.64	54.19	49.52	98.59
1992–3	97.77	1.03	53.25	52.85	54.40	49.37	100.00
1993–4	100.00	1.02	48.42	50.84	52.00	51.19	100.00
1994–5	102.18	1.02	46.00	47.21	48.24	55.94	100.00
1995–6	104.93	1.03	47.09	46.54	47.80	58.37	100.00

(Contd.)

Appendix Table 7(n) Contd.

	(1)	(2)	(3)	(4)	(5)	(6)	(7)
1996–7	107.70	1.03	44.49	45.79	47.00	59.01	100.00
1997–8	110.49	1.03	46.87	45.68	46.86	58.35	100.00
1998–9	113.29	1.03	46.79	46.83	48.01	56.51	100.00
1999–2000	116.11	1.02	47.03	46.91	48.08	55.99	100.00

(Cols Contd.)

Appendix Table 7(n) Contd.: Total Factor Input Index for Sector Non-A, 1950–1 to 1999–2000

Year	Relative annual change	% share of earnings labour = wt	Two year average weight	Weighted annual change in land input	Total weighted annual changes	Total factor input index 1950–1 = 100	Total factor input index 1993–4 = 100
	(8)	(9)	(10)	(11)	(12)	(13)	(14)
1950–1	1.00	1.97	1.97	1.97	100.00	100.00	17.45
1951–2	1.36	2.52	2.25	3.04	101.46	101.46	17.71
1952–3	0.97	1.90	2.21	2.14	100.55	102.01	17.80
1953–4	1.08	1.93	1.92	2.06	102.30	104.36	18.21
1954–5	1.04	1.64	1.79	1.85	103.30	107.81	18.82
1955–6	1.01	1.55	1.59	1.61	103.53	111.61	19.48
1956–7	1.00	1.65	1.60	1.61	103.71	115.75	20.20
1957–8	1.01	1.56	1.61	1.62	103.84	120.20	20.98
1958–9	1.01	1.43	1.50	1.52	103.98	124.98	21.81
1959–60	1.04	1.39	1.41	1.47	104.20	130.24	22.73
1960–1	1.00	1.55	1.47	1.46	104.61	136.24	23.78
1961–2	1.00	1.42	1.48	1.48	104.92	142.95	24.95
1962–3	1.02	1.33	1.38	1.41	105.00	150.10	26.20
1963–4	1.01	1.12	1.23	1.24	105.02	157.63	27.51
1964–5	1.01	1.26	1.19	1.20	104.79	165.17	28.83
1965–6	0.98	1.14	1.20	1.18	104.76	173.03	30.20
1966–7	1.01	1.06	1.10	1.12	104.59	180.97	31.58
1967–8	1.01	0.94	1.00	1.01	104.04	188.28	32.86
1968–9	1.01	0.86	0.90	0.91	103.52	194.91	34.02
1969–70	1.01	0.84	0.85	0.86	103.30	201.33	35.14
1970–1	1.04	0.82	0.83	0.86	103.42	208.21	36.34
1971–2	1.03	0.82	0.82	0.85	103.51	215.51	37.61
1972–3	0.98	0.77	0.80	0.78	103.67	223.42	38.99
1973–4	1.01	0.80	0.78	0.79	104.49	233.45	40.74
1974–5	1.09	0.90	0.85	0.93	105.03	245.19	42.79
1975–6	1.02	0.75	0.83	0.84	105.07	257.61	44.96
1976–7	1.06	0.77	0.76	0.81	105.06	270.64	47.23
1977–8	0.96	0.68	0.73	0.70	104.39	282.53	49.31
1978–9	1.01	0.65	0.66	0.67	104.31	294.70	51.43
1979–80	1.02	0.70	0.67	0.69	104.46	307.83	53.73
1980–1	1.01	0.69	0.69	0.70	104.26	320.93	56.01
1981–2	1.00	0.66	0.67	0.67	105.24	337.74	58.95
1982–3	1.01	0.57	0.61	0.62	106.01	358.05	62.49
1983–4	1.02	0.52	0.55	0.56	105.23	376.76	65.76
1984–5	1.01	0.49	0.50	0.51	104.77	394.75	68.90

(Contd.)

Appendix Table 7(n) Contd.

	(8)	(9)	(10)	(11)	(12)	(13)	(14)
1985–6	1.00	0.46	0.47	0.48	104.91	414.15	72.28
1986–7	1.01	0.40	0.43	0.44	105.04	435.03	75.93
1987–8	1.01	0.37	0.39	0.39	104.63	455.17	79.44
1988–9	1.00	0.39	0.38	0.38	104.10	473.84	82.70
1989–90	1.00	0.39	0.39	0.39	103.82	491.96	85.86
1990–1	0.99	0.36	0.37	0.37	103.83	510.79	89.15
1991–2	1.02	0.35	0.35	0.36	104.07	531.59	92.78
1992–3	1.01	0.33	0.34	0.34	104.11	553.45	96.59
1993–4	1.00	0.35	0.34	0.34	103.53	572.97	100.00
1994–5	1.00	0.36	0.35	0.35	104.54	598.96	104.54
1995–6	1.00	0.32	0.34	0.34	106.51	637.93	111.34
1996–7	1.00	0.29	0.30	0.30	106.31	678.21	118.37
1997–8	1.00	0.26	0.27	0.27	105.49	715.41	124.86
1998–9	1.00	0.24	0.25	0.25	104.78	749.59	130.83
1999–2000	1.00	0.23	0.24	0.24	104.30	781.85	136.46

Note: Labour input = Workforce
Sources: Col. (1) derived from Appendix Table 3(b), Col. (7); Col. (2) based on Col. (1); Col. (3) from Appendix Table 7(l), Col. (6); Col. (4) based on Col. (3); Col. (5) = Col. (2) × Col. (4); Col. (6) from Appendix Table 7(m), Col. (14); Col. (7) based on Table 4.10, Col. (2); Col. (8) based on Col. (7); Col. (9) from Appendix Table 7(l), Col. (9); Col. (10) based on Col. (9); Col. (11) = Col. (8) × Col. (10); Col. (12) to (14), see text of Chapter 4.